Criminal Law

SIXTH EDITION

JOHN M. SCHEB, J.D., LL.M.
Judge, Florida Court of Appeal, Second District (Ret.)
Distinguished Professorial Lecturer, Emeritus
Stetson University College of Law

JOHN M. SCHEB II, Ph.D.
Professor and Head
Department of Political Science
University of Tennessee, Knoxville

 WADSWORTH
CENGAGE Learning™

Australia • Brazil • Japan • Korea • Mexico • Singapore • Spain • United Kingdom • United States

WADSWORTH
CENGAGE Learning

Criminal Law, Sixth Edition
John M. Scheb and John M. Scheb II

Publisher/Executive Editor: Linda Schreiber-Ganster

Acquisitions Editor: Carolyn Henderson Meier

Development Editor: Erin Abney

Editorial Assistant: Virginette Acacio

Associate Media Editor: Andy Yap

Marketing Manager: Michelle Williams

Marketing Assistant/Associate: Sean Foy

Marketing Communications Manager: Heather Baxley

Art Director: Maria Epes

Content Project Management: PreMediaGlobal

Rights Acquisitions Specialist: Dean Dauphinais

Rights Acquisitions Director: Bob Kauser

Manufacturing Buyer: Linda Hsu

Manufacturing Manager: Marcia Locke

Cover Designer: Riezebos Holzbaur/ Tae Hatayama

Cover Image: Copyright 2009 photolibrary.com

Photographer: John Knill

Compositor: PreMediaGlobal

For product information and technology assistance, contact us at
Cengage Learning Customer & Sales Support, 1-800-354-9706

For permission to use material from this text or product, submit all requests online at **cengage.com/permissions**
Further permissions questions can be emailed to
permissionrequest@cengage.com

Library of Congress Control Number: 2011923970

ISBN-13: 978-1-111-34695-9

ISBN-10: 1-111-34695-X

Wadsworth
20 Davis Drive
Belmont, CA 94002-3098
USA

Cengage Learning is a leading provider of customized learning solutions with office locations around the globe, including Singapore, the United Kingdom, Australia, Mexico, Brazil, and Japan. Locate your local office at: **international.cengage.com/region**

Cengage Learning products are represented in Canada by Nelson Education, Ltd.

For your course and learning solutions, visit **www.cengage.com**

Purchase any of our products at your local college store or at our preferred online store **www.cengagebrain.com**

Instructors: Please visit **login.cengage.com** and log in to access instructor-specific resources.

Printed in the United States of America
1 2 3 4 5 6 7 15 14 13 12 11

DISCLAIMER

In this textbook the authors have attempted to present the general principles of substantive and procedural criminal law. However, because of the variance in statutes and court decisions from state to state, it is recommended that students and officers conduct their own research or consult with their legal advisors and not assume that principles of law applicable in other states apply in their state

DEDICATION

This book is dedicated to Judge John M. Scheb, who passed away on November 17, 2010. He will be sorely missed by his family, his many friends, and by the judiciary and legal profession in the state of Florida.

About the Authors

JOHN M. SCHEB was born in Orlando, Florida in 1926. He practiced law in Sarasota, Florida from 1950 until 1974, serving as Associate Municipal Judge from 1957–1959 and as City Attorney from 1959–1970. In 1975, he was appointed to Florida's Second District Court of Appeal where he served until 1992. During the 1990s Judge Scheb served as Distinguished Professorial Lecturer at Stetson University College of Law. He was a member of the American Bar Association, the American Judicature Society, the Florida Bar, and the Sarasota County Bar Association. He was also Master Emeritus of the Judge John M. Scheb American Inn of Court in Sarasota. Judge Scheb held the B.A. from Florida Southern College, the J.D. from the University of Florida, and the LL.M. from the University of Virginia. He published articles in a number of law reviews and was co-author of *An Introduction to the American Legal System* (West/Thomson Learning 2002) and *Law and the Administrative Process* (Thomson/Wadsworth 2005). Judge Scheb passed away on November 17, 2010.

JOHN M. SCHEB II was born in Sarasota, Florida in 1955. He attended the University of Florida from 1974 to 1982, receiving the B.A., M.A., and Ph.D. in political science. He is now Professor and Head of Political Science at the University of Tennessee, Knoxville, where he specializes in public law and the judicial process. Professor Scheb has authored numerous articles in professional journals and is coauthor of several other textbooks, including *An Introduction to the American Legal System* (West/Thomson Learning 2002); *Law and the Administrative Process* (Thomson/ Wadsworth 2005); and *American Constitutional Law*, 4th ed. (Thomson/Wadsworth 2008).

Brief Contents

Table of Contents

Preface to the Sixth Edition

We are pleased to present to students in criminology, criminal justice, pre-law, political science, legal studies, and paralegal studies the sixth edition of a concise yet comprehensive introduction to American criminal law. We believe this text is also an appropriate reference for the criminal justice professional who seeks a better understanding of the functioning of the criminal justice system in the United States. Of course, laws vary substantially across jurisdictions, and this text is not intended to be a substitute for independent legal research or competent legal advice.

Criminal law is among the most dynamic fields of American law. In preparing the sixth edition, we have endeavored to capture the most significant recent developments in the criminal law, including state and federal statutes, appellate court decisions, and trials. And yet we recognize that what students need to know most are the basic concepts of criminal law and procedure—concepts rooted in the English common law, the United States Constitution, and the fifty state constitutions. Thus we continue to emphasize the common-law background and constitutional foundations of criminal law.

An Overview of the Text

Part I furnishes an overview of the criminal law. Chapter 1 introduces the reader to basic concepts, such as the legal definition of a crime, the development of the criminal law, the distinction between substantive and procedural criminal law, and the stages of the criminal process. Chapter 2 examines the organization of the criminal justice system, with emphasis on the roles of legislatures, courts, and other governmental actors in developing the criminal law.

Part II surveys the substantive criminal law from its common-law sources to its modern statutory development. In Chapter 3 we have attempted to give the reader an insight into the relevance of the U.S. Constitution and the state constitutions to the enactment and enforcement of criminal prohibitions. Chapter 4 discusses elements of crimes and parties to crimes. Chapter 5 explains the inchoate offenses of attempt, solicitation, and conspiracy. Chapters 6 and 7, respectively, examine homicidal crimes and other crimes against persons. Chapter 8 looks at basic property offenses, while Chapter 9 deals specifically with white-collar crime and organized crime. Chapter 10 discusses the crimes of vice, including alcohol and drug offenses. Chapter 11 explains offenses against public health and the natural environment. Chapter 12 deals with offenses against public order, safety, and national security, including terrorism. Chapter 13 looks at offenses against the administration of justice and against public administration generally. Finally, Chapter 14 provides an easy-to-follow classification of criminal defenses and includes some innovative defenses.

Features

- Chapter opening Learning Objectives highlight the chapter's key topics and themes.
- To enhance student comprehension, each chapter contains an outline delineating the major topics covered in the chapter.
- All chapters open with vignettes featuring high-profile criminal cases and controversies, which are designed to engage the student's interest and show the real-world relevance of the material in the chapter.
- Beginning with Chapter 3, each chapter includes boxes labeled "Case in Point." These concise summaries of cases illustrate key concepts and have proven to be popular with students.
- Key terms are identified in boldface type throughout each chapter and listed at the end of the chapter. The end-of-chapter key term list now includes definitions.
- To make the book more accessible and useful to students, summaries at the end of each chapter are now keyed to the learning objectives listed at the outset of the chapter.
- A set of discussion questions and one or more problems for discussion and solution to test understanding and stimulate classroom discussion are included.
- At the end of the book a comprehensive glossary includes definitions of all key terms.
- Edited versions of important court decisions are available to students and instructors on the companion website. Notations throughout the book indicate which cases are available online for further study.

What's New In The Sixth Edition?

Chapter 1, Fundamentals of Criminal Law and Procedure

A new section on criminal law, morality, and justice encourages students to examine what role the state should play in issues of public morality. The chapter also contains a new section on references to statutes and judicial decisions, which explains how federal and state court decisions are cited and gives both federal and state examples.

Chapter 2, Organization of the Criminal Justice System

A lengthy section has been added that discusses the immigration law enacted in Arizona and the subsequent suit filed against the state of Arizona and Arizona's governor in response.

Chapter 3, Constitutional Limitations on the Prohibition of Criminal Conduct

A newly expanded section on the right to keep and bear arms has been updated to include the recent Supreme Court decision in *District of Columbia v. Heller* (2008).

Also, a new opening vignette has been added that discusses that decision as well as the 2010 Supreme Court decision in *McDonald v. City of Chicago*.

Chapter 4, Elements of Crimes and Parties to Crimes

A new opening section has been added on the landmark Supreme Court decision in *Robinson v. California* (1961). Some new information has also been included in the section on the Model Penal Code approach to intent.

Chapter 5, Inchoate Offenses

A new opening section takes a fresh look at the Enron case and includes the recent Supreme Court decision in *United States vs. Skilling* (2010).

Chapter 6, Homicidal Offenses

This chapter has been focused solely on homicidal offenses and expanded to examine these offenses in greater depth. A new table depicts the different levels of criminal homicide in Tennessee. A new section on laws criminalizing acts other than abortion that result in the death of a fetus has been added. A new chapter-specific conclusion was written to encompass the new material.

Chapter 7, Other Offenses against Persons

New information has been added to the section on judicial reforms that have occurred in the law of rape. The section on hate crimes has been retooled and reorganized. A new chapter opening vignette has been added that discusses the case of the *United States v. Lanier* (1997).

Chapter 8, Property Crimes

The chapter contains a more in-depth analysis of statutory revisions of burglary. Newly updated Questions for Thought and Discussion encourage students to think critically about the chapter material, and can be used for in-class discourse or take-home exercises. The discussion on extortion has been updated and now includes the recent example of the David Letterman extortion case.

Chapter 9, White-Collar and Organized Crime

The chapter contains a much more detailed outline, necessary to encompass the large amount of new material that is included to cover the breadth of topics related to white-collar and organized crime. Two new Case-in-Points have been added, detailing cases related to federal computer crimes and identity theft. In addition, new sections have been added on anti-spam laws and state laws that proscribe computer offenses. The section on organized crime has also been expanded to include information on racketeering.

Chapter 10, Vice Crimes

The new title reflects the merging of two chapters from the previous edition, combining the material on offenses against public morality with that on alcohol and drug offenses. The sections on medicinal marijuana and exotic dancing have been updated. The freshly structured chapter includes a new introduction that defines the term "vice crime," as well as a new conclusion.

Chapter 11, Offenses against Public Health and the Environment

The chapter opens with a look at the recent BP oil spill and the criminal investigation that followed. The discussion on the Clean Water Act has been updated with new supporting court case information, and additional information has also been added on the Rivers and Harbors Act. There is a new Sidebar that presents Tennessee's littering statute. A new section on the future of smoking bans has been added as well.

Chapter 12, Offenses against Public Order, Safety, and National Security

The chapter opens with a discussion on the attempted bombing of Times Square in 2010. This chapter also contains recent changes to the laws regarding cell phone usage in moving motor vehicles, addressing both phone calls and text messages. The discussion on gun control has been expanded, specifically the sections on interpreting the meaning of the Second Amendment. A section on marine piracy has been added to address recent events.

Chapter 13, Offenses against Justice and Public Administration

A new opening vignette examines the recent scandal and subsequent trial of Rod Blagojevich, and additional information on the federal statute that prohibits making false statements to government agencies has been added. There is updated material throughout the sections on bribery. The chapter also contains new information on modern developments in what constitutes obstruction of justice.

Chapter 14, Criminal Responsibility and Defenses

The chapter opens with a new discussion of John W. Hinckley, Jr.'s attempted assassination of Ronald Reagan and his plea of not guilty by reason of insanity. The discussion of self-defense has been updated to reflect new developments with respect to "stand your ground" laws.

Ancillaries

A number of supplements are provided by Wadsworth to help instructors use Criminal Law, Sixth Edition, in their courses and to aid students in preparing for exams. Supplements are available to qualified adopters. Please consult your local sales representative for details.

For the Instructor

Online Instructor's Resource Manual with Test Bank

An improved and completely updated *Instructor's Resource Manual with Test Bank* has been developed by John M. Scheb II. The manual includes learning objectives, chapter outlines, key terms, and a list of relevant cases for that chapter. Each chapter's test bank contains questions in multiple-choice, true–false, fill-in-the-blank, and essay formats, with a full answer key. The test bank is coded to the chapter objectives that appear in the main text and includes the page numbers in the main text where the answers can be found.

Criminal Justice Media Library

Cengage Learning's Criminal Justice Media Library includes nearly 300 media assets on the topics you cover in your courses. Available to stream from any Web-enabled computer, the Criminal Justice Media Library's assets include such valuable resources as

- Career Profile Videos featuring interviews with criminal justice professionals from a range of roles and locations
- simulations that allow students to step into various roles and practice their decision-making skills
- video clips on current topics from ABC® and other sources,
- animations that illustrate key concepts
- interactive learning modules that help students check their knowledge of important topics and
- Reality Check exercises that compare expectations and preconceived notions against the real-life thoughts and experiences of criminal justice professionals.

The Criminal Justice Media Library can be uploaded and used within many popular learning management systems. You can also customize it with your own course material. You can also purchase an institutional site license. Please contact your Cengage Learning representative for ordering and pricing information.

Careers in Criminal Justice Website

Available bundled with this text at no additional charge. Featuring plenty of self-exploration and profiling activities, the interactive Careers in Criminal Justice Website helps students investigate and focus on the criminal justice career choices that are right for them. Includes interest assessment, video testimonials from career professionals, resume and interview tips, and links for reference.

Book Companion Website

The instructor area of the book's companion website at www.cengage.com/criminaljustice/scheb offers access to password-protected resources such as electronic versions of the instructor manual and test bank.

For the Student

Online Cases

For the student or instructor who wishes to go above and beyond the content of the text, the companion website contains more than 200 court decisions edited by the authors. Throughout the book are pointers indicating where one or more of these cases are relevant to the material.

CLeBook

CLeBook allows students to access Cengage Learning textbooks in an easy-to-use online format. Highlight, take notes, bookmark, search your text, and, in some titles, link directly into multimedia: CLeBook combines the best aspects of paper books and e-books in one package.

Acknowledgments

We wish to acknowledge the assistance of Kristin Wagers, a law student at the University of Tennessee. Kristin's legal research and proofreading skills were invaluable in the completion of this edition. We also want to thank the team at Cengage—in particular, Carolyn Henderson-Meier and Erin Abney—for their help and support throughout this project. We also need to thank the reviewers of this and previous editions for their excellent guidance. We must also acknowledge the many emails we have received over the years from students and instructors who have used our book. Their questions, comments, and suggestions have been extremely useful. Finally, we thank our wives, Mary Burns Scheb and Sherilyn Claytor Scheb, for their patience and support, without which the project could not have been undertaken, much less completed.

As always, we assume full responsibility for any errors contained herein. We welcome comments and suggestions from our readers.

John M. Scheb
[deceased]

John M. Scheb II
scheb@utk.edu
December 15, 2010

Reviewers

We would like to thank the reviewers of the fifth edition for their helpful comments as we prepared this sixth edition:

David Aylor
Trident Technical College

William Bower
Park University

Frank Butler
La Salle University

Earl G. Penrod
Oakland City University

Larry Rosintoski
Trident Technical College

Vincent M. Russo
Richard J. Daley College

Marcia Scott
Hilbert College

William Stielow
Troy University

Jonah Triebwasser
Marist College

Jason Wall
Tyler Junior College

PART ONE

Legal Foundations of Criminal Justice

CHAPTER 1

Fundamentals of Criminal Law and Procedure

LEARNING OBJECTIVES

After reading this chapter, you should be able to explain . . .

1. the essential elements of a crime and how crimes differ from other legal wrongs
2. the difference between substantive and procedural law
3. how American criminal law has developed from its medieval English origins
4. how various crimes protect different societal interests
5. the relevance of the U.S. Constitution, Bill of Rights, and the constitutions of the fifty states to the criminal justice system
6. the different roles of legislatures and courts of law in developing the criminal law and procedure
7. how to read citations to statutes and cases and how to "brief" a case
8. basic procedural steps associated with criminal prosecutions
9. the variety of sanctions imposed on people convicted of crimes

CHAPTER OUTLINE

In what many in the media called the "trial of the century," former football and movie star O.J. Simpson was accused of murdering his ex-wife, Nicole Brown Simpson, and her companion, Ron Goldman. The trial began on January 24, 1995. The prosecution's case again Simpson appeared to be strong. But on October 3, 1995, the jury delivered a stunning verdict, declaring Simpson not guilty. A year later the families of the decedents initiated a civil suit against Simpson, alleging that he was liable for wrongful death. On February 4, 1997, a different jury in the civil trial found Simpson liable for the wrongful death of Nicole Brown Simpson and Ron Goldman and awarded the plaintiffs $8.5 million in damages.

The Simpson case illustrates dramatically how a defendant can be accused of a crime and a civil wrong based on the same alleged act. Many observers have wondered how the two cases could have come out differently. One answer is that they were independent legal actions resulting in separate trials before entirely different juries. Moreover, the standards of proof were different. In the criminal trial, the jury had to find Simpson guilty of murder beyond a reasonable doubt. In the civil case, the standard of proof was less demanding: the jury had only to find Simpson liable by a preponderance of the evidence. Why do we have these parallel systems of justice? How are crimes distinguished from civil wrongs? These are among the questions addressed in this chapter.

Introduction

A fundamental problem facing every society is how to achieve social control—protecting people's lives and property and establishing socially desirable levels of order, harmony, safety, and decency. Societies have developed several informal means of achieving this control, including family structures, social norms, and religious precepts. In contrast, law is a formal means of social control. Law can be defined as a body of rules prescribed and enforced by government for the regulation and protection of society. Criminal law is that branch of the law prohibiting certain forms of conduct and imposing penalties on those who engage in prohibited behavior.

All modern societies have developed systems for administering criminal justice. What distinguishes democratic societies from authoritarian ones is a commitment to the **rule of law**. In democratic societies such as ours, a person cannot be convicted of a crime unless he or she has committed a specific offense against a law that provides for a penalty. This principle is expressed in the maxim ***nullen crimen, nulla poena, sine lege***, a Latin phrase meaning, "there is no crime, there is no punishment, without law." In the United States, formal law governs every aspect of criminal justice, from the enactment of criminal prohibitions to the imposition of punishment upon those who violate these prohibitions.

Our criminal law prescribes both substantive and procedural rules governing the everyday operation of the criminal justice system. **Substantive criminal law** prohibits certain forms of conduct by defining crimes and establishing the parameters of penalties. **Procedural criminal law** regulates the enforcement of the substantive law, the determination of guilt, and the punishment of those found guilty of crimes. For example, although substantive law makes the possession of heroin a crime, the procedural law regulates the police search and seizure that produce the incriminating evidence. The substantive law makes premeditated murder a crime and sets the penalty to be imposed for those convicted of the offense; the procedural law determines the procedures to be observed at trial and, if a conviction ensues, at sentencing.

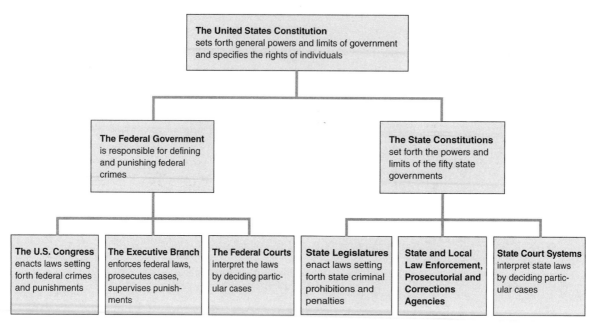

FIGURE 1.1 Overview of the American system of criminal law and procedure.

Figure 1.1 provides an overview of the system of criminal law and procedure that exists in this country. The figure suggests three fundamental principles at work:

- **Constitutional supremacy.** In keeping with the ideal of the rule of law, the entire system of criminal law and procedure is subordinate to the principles and provisions of the U.S. Constitution. The Constitution sets forth the powers of government, the limits of those powers, and the rights of individuals. The Constitution thus limits government's power to make and enforce criminal sanctions in several important ways. These limitations are enforced by **judicial review**, which is the power of courts of law to invalidate substantive laws and procedures that are determined to be contrary to the Constitution.

- **Federalism.** There is a fundamental division of authority between the national government in Washington, D.C., and the fifty state governments. Although both levels of government have authority and responsibility in the realm of criminal justice, most of the day-to-day peacekeeping function is exercised by the states and their political subdivisions (primarily counties and cities). Each of the states has its own machinery of government as well as its own constitution that empowers and limits that government. Each state constitution imposes limits on the criminal justice system within that state. Of course, the provisions of the state constitutions, as well as the statutes adopted by the state legislatures, are subordinate to the provisions of the U.S. Constitution and the laws adopted by Congress.

- **Separation of powers.** The national government and each of the fifty state governments are constructed on the principle that legislative, executive, and judicial powers must be separated into independent branches of government. Thus, the federal government and the states have their own legislative branches, their own executive branches, and their own systems of courts. The legislative branch is responsible for enacting laws that specify crimes and punishments. The executive branch is responsible for enforcing those prohibitions and for carrying out the punishments imposed by the judicial branch, but it is the judicial branch that interprets the laws and ensures that persons charged with crimes receive fair treatment by the criminal justice system.

What Is a Crime?

Every crime involves a wrongful act (***actus reus***) specifically prohibited by the criminal law. For example, in the crime of battery, the *actus reus* is the striking or offensive touching of another person. Even the failure to take action can be considered a wrongful act if the law imposes a duty to take action in a certain situation. For example, a person who fails to file a federal income tax return may be guilty of a federal offense.

In most cases, the law requires that the wrongful act be accompanied by criminal intent (***mens rea***). Criminal intent does not refer to a person's motive or reason for acting, but merely refers to having formed a mental purpose to act. To convict a person of a crime, it is not necessary to know why that person committed the crime. It is only necessary to show that the individual intentionally committed a prohibited act. An unintentional act is usually not a crime, although, as we will discover, there are exceptions to this principle. Moreover, in certain instances, one may be held criminally responsible irrespective of intent. Crimes of this latter nature are classified as **strict liability offenses.** A good example of a strict liability offense is selling liquor to a minor. (Strict liability offenses and general elements of crimes are discussed in Chapter 4.)

Felonies and Misdemeanors

Criminal law distinguishes between serious crimes, known as **felonies**, and less serious offenses, called **misdemeanors**. Generally speaking, felonies are offenses for which the offender can be imprisoned for more than one year; misdemeanors carry jail terms of less than one year. Common examples of felonies include murder, rape, robbery, burglary, aggravated assault, aggravated battery, and grand theft. Typical misdemeanors include petit theft, simple assault and battery, disorderly conduct, prostitution, and driving while intoxicated.

Societal Interests Served by the Criminal Law

We can distinguish among types of crimes by the underlying societal interests that give rise to criminal prohibitions. Obviously, government has a duty to protect the lives and property of citizens—this is the essence of the social contract on which democratic government is based. Society also has an interest in protecting the public peace, order, and safety. Today, the protection of the national security from terrorism has become an important concern of the criminal law. Over the last several decades, the protection of the public health and the preservation of the natural environment have also come to be seen as interests that should be furthered by the criminal law. And, of course, society has an interest in efficient and honest public administration and, in particular, the administration of justice.

Table 1.1 lists the societal interests served by the criminal law and shows some particular crimes that relate to each interest. The table also indicates the chapters in this book that deal with the different types of crimes. Note that some of the crimes relate to more than one societal interest.

TABLE 1.1 An Overview of Types of Crimes and the Societal Interests Involved

Societal Interest Served	Examples of Crimes	Discussed in Chapter(s)
Protection of Persons against Violence	Assault and Battery, Rape and Sexual Battery, Murder, Manslaughter, Spousal and Child Abuse, Kidnapping, Stalking	Chapter 6, Homicidal Offenses; Chapter 7, Other Offenses against Persons
Protection of Property and Economic Interests	Vandalism, Theft, Burglary, Arson, Robbery, Extortion, Forgery, Larceny, Embezzlement, Securities Fraud, Insider Trading, Mail Fraud	Chapter 8, Property Crimes; Chapter 9, White-Collar and Organized Crime
Maintenance of Standards of Decency	Prostitution, Obscenity, Bigamy, Indecent Exposure, Gambling, Alcohol and Drug Offenses	Chapter 10, Vice Crimes
Public Health and the Natural Environment	Fishing and Hunting Violations, Smoking Violations, Illegal Toxic Waste Disposal, Illegal Air Pollution	Chapter 11, Offenses against Public Health and the Environment
Public Peace, Order, and Safety	Disorderly Conduct, Incitement to Riot, Motor Vehicle Offenses, Loitering, Weapons Violations, Terrorism	Chapter 12, Offenses against Public Order, Safety, and Security
National Security	Treason, Espionage, Sabotage, Sedition, Terrorism	Chapter 12, Offenses against Public Order, Safety, and Security
Honest and Efficient Administration of Government and the Justice System	Resisting Arrest, Bribery, Perjury, Obstruction of Justice, Contempt, Escape	Chapter 13, Offenses against Justice and Public Administration

Criminal Law, Morality, and Justice

Traditionally, the preservation of public morality has been regarded as an important function of the criminal law. Today this assumption is often questioned by those who believe that morality, like religion, is a personal matter. They argue that the state should be neutral in matters of morality, much as it is constitutionally required to be with respect to religion. Others, stressing the practical aspect of the problem, invoke the aphorism "you can't legislate morality." Over the last several decades, arguments over law and morality have focused on criminal prohibitions of consensual sexual conduct. Offenses such as adultery, fornication, and sodomy, which were inherited from the English common law, have become obsolete in modern America. In some cases, legislatures have abolished these offenses as they have modernized their criminal codes. In other instances, courts have declared unconstitutional the laws defining these crimes. See, e.g., *Lawrence v. Texas*, 539 U.S. 558, 123 S.Ct. 2472, 156 L.Ed.2d 508 (2003) (invalidating laws proscribing sodomy between consenting adults). However, students must realize that the moral basis of the law extends far beyond ancient prohibitions of sexual conduct. Many proscriptions of the criminal law, from animal cruelty to insider stock trading, are based on collective societal judgments about what is right and what is wrong.

In order to maintain its legitimacy, the criminal law must reflect the prevailing morality of the people. In a democratic society, laws that do not reflect broadly shared values will be challenged and eventually likely be changed. Of course, there is considerable inertia in the law, and someone has to lead the effort for change. Sometimes interest groups lead the way by lobbying elected officials and even filing lawsuits in the courts. In some instances, such as the civil rights movement of the 1950s and 60s, grassroots social movements have resulted in profound changes in the law. In extreme situations, courageous people have resorted to **civil disobedience** in order to dramatize the injustice of a particular law. Such was the case when Dr. Martin Luther King, Jr. went to jail in Birmingham, Alabama rather than abide by racial segregation laws that he and many others deemed to be unjust. Today students read about the defunct Jim Crow laws in history books. It is hard for students today to understand that such laws once were supported by political majorities in many states and communities. Ultimately, after many years of struggle, most Americans came to believe that the laws requiring racial segregation were unjust and needed to be done away with, a concept reflected in the Supreme Court's decision in *Brown v. Board of Education*, 347 U.S. 483, 74 S.Ct. 686, 98 L.Ed.873 (1954). The idea that the law should not discriminate among people based on their race is a moral principle that has now become firmly established in our legal system. That is not to say that there is no racial discrimination in the criminal justice system. But the well-established principle of "equal protection of the laws" provides a moral and constitutional basis upon which to challenge any such discrimination.

Crime: An Injury against Society

As suggested by the previous discussion of societal interests served by the criminal law, our legal system regards crimes not merely as wrongs against particular victims but as offenses against the entire society. Indeed, there does not have to be an individual victim in order for there to be a crime. For example, it is a crime to possess cocaine, even though it is unlikely that a particular individual will claim to have been victimized by another person's use of the drug. This is a crime because society, through its governing institutions, has made a collective judgment that cocaine use is inimical to the public welfare. Similarly, certain consensual sexual acts (for example, incest) remain crimes in many jurisdictions because communities continue to regard such actions as contrary to public decency. Of course, as society evolves and its standards change, behaviors that were once defined as crimes (for example, blasphemy) are no longer subject to criminal sanction. Over time, the particular prohibitions of the criminal law more or less reflect an evolving social consensus about both what is right and wrong and what is public and private. When a particular criminal prohibition (for example, adultery) is no longer supported by societal consensus, it is apt to be unenforced or be stricken from the laws.

Because crime is an injury against society, the government, as society's legal representative, brings charges against persons accused of committing crimes. In the United States, we have a federal system—that is, a division of power and responsibility between the national and state governments. Both the national government and the states enact their own criminal laws. Thus, both the national government and the state governments may prosecute persons accused of crimes. The national government initiates a prosecution when a federal (national) law has been violated; a state brings charges against someone who is believed to have violated one of its laws.

Criminal Responsibility

The criminal law—indeed, our entire legal system—rests on the idea that individuals are responsible for their actions and must be held accountable for them. This is the essential justification and rationale for imposing punishments on persons convicted of crimes. On the other hand, society recognizes that certain individuals (for example, young children) lack the capacity to appreciate the wrongfulness of their conduct.

Similarly, factors beyond individuals' control can lead them to commit criminal acts. In such instances the law exempts individuals from responsibility. Moreover, there are situations in which acts that would otherwise be crimes might be justified. The best example of this is committing a homicide in self-defense. Individuals can invoke a host of defenses beyond a simple denial of guilt. Indeed, a substantial body of law is devoted to the topic of criminal responsibility and defenses. We examine this topic in some detail in Chapter 14.

The Role of the Crime Victim

Because the government prosecutes criminals on behalf of society, the **victim** of a crime is not a party to the criminal prosecution. By filing a complaint with a law enforcement agency, a victim initiates the process that leads to prosecution, but once the prosecution begins, the victim's participation is primarily that of being a witness. Quite often, victims feel lost in the shuffle of the criminal process. They sometimes feel that the system is insensitive or even hostile to their interests in seeing justice done. Some states are now taking steps to address victims' concerns. Despite some measures being proposed and others that have been adopted, crime victims remain secondary players in the criminal justice system. The principal parties in a criminal case are the prosecution (that is, the government) and the defendant (that is, the accused person). In some situations, however, the victim might have another remedy: a civil suit to recover damages for losses or injuries suffered.

Criminal Law Distinguished from Civil Law

The criminal law is not the only body of law that regulates the conduct of persons. The civil law provides remedies for essentially private wrongs, offenses in which the state has a less direct interest. Most civil wrongs are classified as **breaches of contract** or **torts.** A breach of contract occurs when a party to a contract violates the terms of the agreement. A tort, on the other hand, is a wrongful act that does not violate any enforceable agreement but nevertheless violates a legal right of the injured party. Common examples of torts include wrongful death, intentional or negligent infliction of personal injury, wrongful destruction of property, trespass, and defamation of character. A crime normally entails intentional conduct; thus, a driver whose car accidentally hits and kills another person would not necessarily be guilty of a crime, depending on the circumstances (see discussions of manslaughter and vehicular homicide in Chapter 6). If the accident resulted from the driver's negligence, the driver would have committed the tort of wrongful death and would be subject to a civil suit for damages.

The criminal law and the civil law often overlap. Conduct that constitutes a crime can also involve a tort. For example, suppose Randy Wrecker intentionally damages a house belonging to Harvey Homeowner. Wrecker's act might well result in both criminal and civil actions being brought against him. Wrecker may be prosecuted by the state for the crime of willful destruction of property and may also be sued by Homeowner for the tort of wrongful destruction of property. The state would be seeking to punish Wrecker for his antisocial conduct, whereas Homeowner would be seeking compensation for the damage to his property. The criminal case would be designated *State v. Wrecker (or People v. Wrecker, or even Commonwealth v. Wrecker,* depending on the state); the civil suit would be styled *Homeowner v. Wrecker.*

Origins and Sources of the Criminal Law

Many antisocial acts classified as crimes have their origin in the norms of primitive societies. Humanity has universally condemned certain types of behavior since ancient times. Acts such as murder, rape, robbery, and arson are considered ***mala in se***, or inherent wrongs. Many other acts that the modern law regards as criminal are merely ***mala prohibita***; they are offenses only because they are so defined by the law. Many so-called victimless crimes, such as gambling or possession of marijuana, are generally not regarded as offensive to universal principles of morality. Rather, they are wrong simply because the law declares them wrong. In the case of *mala prohibita* offenses, society has made a collective judgment that certain conduct, although not contrary to universal moral principles, is nevertheless incompatible with the public good.

Development of Law in the Western World

The general consensus is that law developed in Western civilization as leaders began formalizing and enforcing customs that had evolved among their peoples. Eventually, informal norms and customs came to be formalized as codes of law. The Code of Hammurabi regulated conduct in ancient Babylonia some two thousand years before Christ. In the seventh century B.C., Draco developed a strict code of laws for the Athenian city-states. Even today, one hears strict rules or penalties characterized as being "Draconian." These laws influenced the Romans in their development of the Twelve Tables in the fifth century B.C. And, of course, long before the time of Jesus, the Hebrews had developed elaborate substantive and procedural laws.

In the sixth century A.D., the Emperor Justinian presided over a codification of the Roman law that would prove to be very influential in the evolution of law on the European continent. The Napoleonic Code, promulgated under Napoleon Bonaparte in 1804 as a codification of all the civil and criminal laws of France, was based largely on the Code of Justinian. The Napoleonic Code became a model for a uniform system of law for Western European nations. This is why the legal systems of Western Europe are often said to be "Roman law" systems. Roman law systems are based on the primacy of statutes enacted by the legislature. These statutes are integrated into a comprehensive code designed to be applied by the courts with a minimum of judicial interpretation.

Development of the English Common Law

American criminal law is derived largely from the **English common law**, which dates from the eleventh century. Before the Norman Conquest of 1066, English law was a patchwork of laws and customs applied by local courts. The new Norman kings appointed royal judges to settle disputes based on the customs of the people. By 1300, the decisions of the royal judges were being recorded to serve as precedents to guide judges in future similar cases. Eventually a common body of law emerged throughout the entire kingdom, hence the term *common law*. As the centuries passed, coherent principles of law and definitions of crimes emerged from the judges' decisions. Thus, in contrast with Roman law systems, which are based on legal codes, the common law developed primarily through judicial decisions. The common-law doctrine of following precedent, known as ***stare decisis***, remains an important component of both the English and American legal systems today.

By 1600, the common-law judges had defined as felonies the crimes of murder, manslaughter, mayhem, robbery, burglary, arson, larceny, rape, suicide, and sodomy. They had also begun to define a number of lesser offenses as misdemeanors. In contrast with the criminal law that was developing on the continent, England developed trial by jury and trained barristers to argue cases on an adversarial basis. A barrister is a lawyer permitted to cross the "bar" in the courtroom that separates the bench from the spectators. Thus, in England, a barrister is a trial lawyer. Although we do not use the term "barrister" in the United States, we do refer to licensed attorneys as having been "admitted to the bar."

As representative government emerged in England in the seventeenth century, the dominance of the common-law courts diminished. Parliament came to play a significant role in the formation of the criminal law by adopting **statutes** that revised and supplemented the common law. The adversarial system of justice continued, however, and most of the common-law felonies remain part of our criminal law today.

Reception of the Common Law in America

Our criminal laws are rooted in the common law as it existed when America proclaimed its independence from England in 1776. After independence, the new American states adopted the English common law to the extent that it did not conflict with the new state and federal constitutions. However, the federal government did not adopt the common law of crimes. From the outset, statutes passed by Congress defined federal crimes. Of the fifty states, Louisiana is the only one whose legal system is not based on the common law; rather, it is based primarily on the Napoleonic Code.

The new American judges and lawyers were greatly aided by Blackstone's *Commentaries on the Laws of England,* published in 1769, in which Sir William Blackstone, a professor at Oxford, codified the principles of the common law. Blackstone's seminal effort was a noble undertaking, but it demystified English law. Consequently, Blackstone's encyclopedic treatment of the law was less than popular among English barristers, who by this time had developed a close fraternity and took great pride in offering their services to "discover the law." In America, however, **Blackstone's Commentaries** became something of a "legal bible."

State and Local Authority to Enact Criminal Prohibitions

At the time of the American Revolution, the English common law constituted the criminal law of the new United States. As new states entered the Union, their legislatures usually enacted "reception statutes," adopting the common law to the extent that it did not conflict with the federal or their respective state constitutions. Eventually, most common-law definitions of crimes were superseded by legislatively defined offenses in the form of statutes adopted by the state legislatures. Today, the state legislatures are the principal actors in defining crimes and punishments. Persons who violate state criminal statutes are prosecuted in the state courts (see Chapter 2).

For the most part, modern state statutes retain the *mala in se* offenses defined by the common law, but many of the old common-law crime definitions have been modified to account for social and economic changes. For example, the offense of rape originated under English common law, but the offense is defined much differently under modern state statutes. Today, under most state laws, the offender and victim may be of either sex, and the offense encompasses anal and oral as well as vaginal penetrations by a sex organ or by another object. Indeed, the broader modern offense of sexual battery embraces all types of nonconsensual sexual impositions (see Chapter 7). As we shall see in subsequent chapters, modern criminal statutes often go far beyond the common law in prohibiting offenses that are *mala prohibita*. Drug and alcohol offenses, environmental crimes, offenses against public health, and traffic violations fall into this category.

When authorized by state constitutions or acts of state legislatures, cities and counties may adopt ordinances that define certain criminal violations. Local **ordinances** typically deal with traffic offenses, animal control, land use, building codes, licensing of businesses, and so forth. Usually these offenses are prosecuted in courts of limited jurisdiction, such as municipal or county courts (see Chapter 2).

Federal Authority to Define Crimes

As we have seen, the common law of crimes was more or less adopted by the various state legislatures. The U.S. Congress never adopted the common law, as there was no need for it to do so. The national government's responsibility in the criminal justice area has always been more limited than that of the states. Unlike the state legislatures, Congress does not possess **police power**, which is the broad authority to enact prohibitions to protect public order, safety, decency, and welfare. Yet Congress does possess authority to enact criminal statutes that relate to Congress's particular legislative powers and responsibilities. Thus, there are federal criminal laws that relate to military service, immigration and naturalization, use of the mail, civil rights, and so forth. In particular, Congress has used its broad power to regulate interstate commerce to criminalize a wide range of offenses, including carjacking, loan sharking, kidnapping, illicit drug dealing, wire fraud, and a variety of environmental crimes (see Chapter 3). Of course, persons who commit federal crimes are subject to prosecution in the federal courts.

The Model Penal Code

The American Law Institute (ALI) is an organization of distinguished judges, lawyers, and academics that have a strong professional interest in drafting model codes of laws. In 1962, after a decade of work that produced several tentative drafts, the ALI published its Proposed Official Draft of the **Model Penal Code** (MPC). The MPC consists of general provisions concerning criminal liability, definitions of specific crimes, defenses, and sentences. The MPC is not law; rather, it is designed as a model code of criminal law for all states. It has had a significant impact on legislative drafting of criminal statutes, particularly during the 1970s, when the majority of the states accomplished substantial reforms in their criminal codes. In addition, the MPC has been influential in judicial interpretation of criminal statutes and doctrines, thereby making a contribution to the continuing development of the decisional law. In this text, we illustrate many principles of law by selected statutes from federal and state jurisdictions; however, in some instances where the MPC is particularly influential, the reader will find references to specific provisions of the MPC.

Sources of Procedural Law

As we noted earlier, the criminal law has both substantive and procedural dimensions. The procedural criminal law is defined by legislative bodies through enactment of statutes and is promulgated by the courts through judicial decisions and the development of rules of court procedure. The U.S. Supreme Court prescribes **rules of procedure** for the federal courts. Generally, the highest court of each state, usually called the state supreme court, is empowered to promulgate rules of procedure for all the courts of that state.

Constitutional Limitations

Substantive and procedural criminal laws are subject to limitations contained in the federal and state constitutions. For example, the U.S. Constitution defines the crime of **treason** in Art. III, Sec. 3. In enacting the federal statute prohibiting treason against the United States, Congress must follow this constitutional definition. The Constitution (Art. I, Secs. 9 and 10) also prohibits Congress and the state legislatures from enacting ***ex post facto* laws** and **bills of attainder**. The prohibition of *ex post facto* laws means that an act cannot be made a crime retroactively. To be criminal, an act must be illegal at the time it was committed. A bill of attainder is a legislative act declaring someone guilty of a crime. The U.S. Constitution prohibits Congress and the state legislatures from doing this; only courts of law can convict people of criminal wrongdoing. (See Chapter 3 for more discussion of treason, *ex post facto* laws, and bills of attainder.)

The Bill of Rights

Many of the most important constitutional provisions relative to criminal justice are found in the **Bill of Rights** (the first ten amendments to the Constitution, adopted by Congress in 1789 and ratified by the states in 1791). Among other things, the First Amendment to the U.S. Constitution prohibits government from using the civil or criminal law to abridge freedom of speech. The courts have said, for example, that people cannot be prosecuted merely for advocating violence; there must be "imminent lawless action" to justify a criminal sanction on public expression. *Brandenburg v. Ohio*, 395 U.S. 444; 89 S.Ct. 1827; 23 L.Ed. 2d 430 (1969).

Go to the companion website for an edited version of the Supreme Court's decision in *Brandenburg v. Ohio*.

In addition to limitations on the enactment of criminal laws, the Bill of Rights has much to say about the enforcement of these laws. These provisions, which constitute much of the basis of criminal procedure, include the Fourth Amendment prohibition of unreasonable searches and seizures, the Fifth Amendment injunction against compulsory self-incrimination, and the Sixth Amendment right to trial by jury. Finally, the Eighth Amendment prohibition of "cruel and unusual punishments" protects citizens against criminal penalties that are barbaric or excessive.

Go to the companion website for an edited version of *Duncan v. Louisiana*.

Virtually all the provisions of the Bill of Rights have been held to apply with equal force to the states and to the national government. *Duncan v. Louisiana*, 391 U.S. 145, 88 S.Ct. 1444, 20 L.Ed.2d 491 (1968). Thus, the Bill of Rights limits the adoption of criminal laws, whether by Congress, the state legislatures, or the myriad city and county legislative bodies. The Bill of Rights also limits the actions of police, prosecutors, judges, and corrections officers at the local, state, and national levels.

State legislatures, courts, and law enforcement agencies must also be aware of the limitations contained in their own state constitutions. Although state constitutional provisions are subordinate to provisions of the federal constitution, state constitutions often go beyond the federal constitution in protecting citizens from governmental authorities. For example, in the area of search and seizure, a number of state courts have interpreted their respective state constitutions more stringently than the federal courts have interpreted the Fourth Amendment to the U.S. Constitution.

The Role of Courts in Developing the Criminal Law

Courts of law play a crucial role in the development of both the substantive and the procedural criminal law. **Trial courts** exist primarily to make factual determinations, apply settled law to established facts, and impose sanctions. In so doing, trial courts are bound, as are all courts of law, by relevant constitutional provisions and principles. In reviewing the decisions of trial courts, **appellate courts** must interpret the federal and state constitutions and statutes. The federal and state constitutions are replete with majestic phrases, such as "equal protection of the laws" and "privileges and immunities," that require interpretation. That is, courts must define exactly what these grand phrases mean within the context of particular legal disputes. Likewise, federal and state statutes often use vague language like "affecting commerce" or "reasonable likelihood." Courts must assign meaning to these and a multitude of other terms. Although most states have abolished all, or nearly all, common-law crimes and replaced them with statutorily defined offenses, the common law remains a valuable source of statutory interpretation. This is because legislatures frequently use terms known to the common law without defining such terms. For example, in proscribing burglary, the legislature might use the term "curtilage" without defining it. In such an instance, a court would look to the common law, which defined the term to mean "an enclosed space surrounding a dwelling."

In rendering interpretations of the law, appellate courts generally follow precedent, in keeping with the common-law doctrine of *stare decisis.* In our rapidly changing society, however, courts often encounter situations to which precedent arguably does not or should not apply. In such situations, courts will sometimes deviate from or even overturn precedent. Moreover, there are situations in which there is no applicable precedent. When this occurs, the appellate courts will have the opportunity to "make new law." Thus, appellate courts perform an important **lawmaking function** as well as an **error correction function**. Therefore, any serious student of criminal law must follow developments in the **decisional law**—that is, law as developed by courts in deciding cases.

Legal Reasoning in Judicial Decisions

The English common-law judges originally arrived at decisions by applying community norms—the common customs of the English people. They then judged subsequent cases by analogizing issues to their previous decisions. In the United States we have written federal and state constitutions, but the process of reasoning by analogy continues, albeit on a more sophisticated basis. Students are prone to look upon these basic instruments of legal policy as a body of established rules that are applied by judges to determined facts. But the framers of our federal and state constitutions painted with a broad brush, leaving the courts to mold such concepts as "due process of law" to a dynamic society. Moreover, legislative rules are usually drafted with particular situations in mind and frequently are unclear when applied to situations the lawmakers did not contemplate or could not have contemplated. Legal reasoning develops rules to resolve ambiguities based on the presumed intent of the legislators, where necessary, "to fill in gaps," always subject to constitutional mandates. Thus, the use of analogy becomes an indispensable tool as lawyers and judges look for similarities to previously adjudicated cases. Finally, although reasoning by analogy preserves the experience of the past, increasingly it also requires a consideration of contemporary social, cultural, and economic norms when considering the importance given to the facts that resulted in decisions in analogous cases.

References to Statutes and Judicial Decisions

Throughout this text the reader will find references to federal and state statutes and decisions of federal and state courts. Appendix A, "Access to the Law through Legal Research," explains how to find the law in statutes, court decisions, and

---

SIDEBAR "Briefing Cases"

As noted earlier in the chapter, edited cases relevant to this book have been placed on a companion website. Reading these decisions can be useful to anyone seeking to understand the criminal law, and instructors may also ask their students to "brief" some or all of these cases. A case brief is simply a summary of a court decision, usually in outline format. Typically, a case brief contains the following elements:

- The name of the case and the date of the decision
- The essential facts of the case
- The key issue(s) of law involved (or those applicable to a point of law being considered)
- The holding of the court
- A brief summary of the court's opinion, especially as it relates to key issue(s) in the case
- Summaries of concurring and dissenting opinions, if any
- A statement commenting on the significance of the decision

Here is a sample case brief:

Brandenburg v. Ohio
U.S. SUPREME COURT
95 U.S. 444; 89 S.Ct. 1827; 23 L.Ed. 2d 430 (1969)

FACTS: Brandenburg, a member of the Ku Klux Klan, was convicted under Ohio law of "advocate[ing] . . . the duty, necessity, or propriety of crime, sabotage, violence, or unlawful methods of terrorism as a means of accomplishing industrial or political reform" and for "voluntarily assembling with any society, group, or assemblage of persons formed to teach or advocate the doctrines of criminal syndicalism." He was fined $1,000 and sentenced to 1–10 years in prison. His appeal was dismissed by the Ohio Supreme Court, and the U.S. Supreme Court granted review.

ISSUE: Does the First Amendment to the U.S. Constitution permit a state to criminalize the mere advocacy of violence?

DECISION: Conviction overturned; Ohio statute declared unconstitutional.

OPINIONS: Speaking through a *per curiam* opinion, the Court unanimously held that "the constitutional guarantees of free speech and free press do not permit a State to forbid or proscribe advocacy of the use of force or of law violation except where such advocacy is directed to inciting or producing imminent lawless action and is likely to incite or produce such action." Justices Black and Douglas wrote concurring opinions.

COMMENT: The Court narrowed the long-standing "clear and present danger" test to limit it to instances of expression involving "imminent lawless action." While recognizing that the protections of the First Amendment are not absolute, the Supreme Court in this decision afforded broad constitutional protection to speech, even that which is hateful, bigoted, or regarded by many in the community as dangerous.

other publications. But at this point we simply mention that statutes enacted by Congress are usually cited to the *United States Code Annotated* (U.S.C.A.), published by the West Group, while state criminal codes are cited to books published by state or commercial publishers. For example, a citation to 18 U.S.C.A. Sec. 2101(a) defines "riot"; a citation to Ariz. Rev. Stat. Sec. 13-2002 refers to a section of the Arizona Criminal Code that defines forgery. Court decisions cited in the text are almost always decisions of federal or state appellate courts. For example, *Brandenburg v. Ohio* indicates the name of the defendant petitioning for review and the state that prosecuted the defendant. Data under the name of the case indicates the name of the court and date of its decision, followed by numbers indicating the volume and page number of the Reporter, a compendium of judicial decisions, where the decision is found. To illustrate, in *Brandenburg v. Ohio*, the decision was made in 1969 by the U.S. Supreme Court and is found at 95 U.S. 444; 89 S.Ct. 1827; 23 L.Ed. 2d 430 (1969). The U.S. citation refers to the volume and page number of an official set of reports; the remainder of the citation refers to commercial publications, the Supreme Court Reporter (S.Ct.) and Lawyers Edition (L.Ed.2d). *Whitner v. State*, 482 S.E.2d 777 (S.C. 1997) illustrates a state court decision—in this instance a 1997 decision of the Supreme Court of South Carolina—found in volume 482, page 777 of the second series of Reporters for the region encompassing South Carolina.

The Criminal Process

By far the broadest and most important constitutional principle relating to criminal justice is found in the Due Process Clauses of the Fifth and Fourteenth Amendments to the Constitution. The same principle can be found in similar provisions of every state constitution. Reflecting a legacy that can be traced to the Magna Carta (1215), such provisions forbid the government from taking a person's life, liberty, or property, whether as punishment for a crime or any other reason, without **due process of law**. Due process refers to those procedural safeguards necessary to ensure the fundamental fairness of a legal proceeding. Daniel Webster defined due process to mean "a law which hears before it condemns, which proceeds on inquiry and renders judgment only after trial."

Most fundamentally, due process requires **fair notice** and a **fair hearing**. That is, persons accused of crimes must have ample opportunity to learn of the charges and evidence being brought against them as well as the opportunity to contest those charges and that evidence in open court.

One of the most basic tenets of due process in criminal cases is the **presumption of innocence.** Unless the defendant pleads guilty, the prosecution must establish the defendant's guilt by evidence produced in court. Everyone accused of a nonpetty offense has the right to a trial by jury (although, we shall see, trials are actually conducted in only a small minority of cases). In a criminal trial, the standard of proof is "beyond a reasonable doubt." The **reasonable doubt standard** differs markedly from the "preponderance of evidence" standard that applies to civil cases. In a civil trial, the judge or jury must find only that the weight of the evidence favors the plaintiff or the defendant. In a criminal case, the fact finder must achieve the "moral certainty" that arises from eliminating "reasonable doubt" as to the defendant's guilt. Of course, it is difficult to define with precision the term "reasonable." Ultimately, this is a judgment call left to the individual judge or juror.

Basic Procedural Steps

Certain basic procedural steps are common to all criminal prosecutions, although specific procedures vary greatly among jurisdictions. (Figure 1.2 illustrates the major components of the criminal process.) In every jurisdiction law enforcement agencies make arrests, interrogate persons in custody, and conduct searches and seizures. All of these functions are regulated by the procedural law. In every jurisdiction there are procedures through which persons accused of crimes are formally notified of the charges against them and given an opportunity to answer these charges in court. There is a formal charging process which, depending on the jurisdiction, involves an **indictment** by a **grand jury** or an **information** filed by a prosecutor. In every jurisdiction there is a procedure known as an **arraignment**, in which the defendant enters a plea of guilty or not guilty, or in some instances a plea of *nolo contendere* (no contest). Only a plea of not guilty necessitates a **criminal trial.** The trial is the crown jewel of criminal procedure—an elaborate, highly formal process, governed by **rules of procedure** and **rules of evidence,** for determining guilt or innocence and imposing punishment on those found guilty.

The decisions of trial courts, with respect to pretrial matters as well as the conduct of criminal trials, are subject to review by appellate courts. All court procedures, from the initial appearance of an accused before a magistrate to the decision of an appellate court upholding a criminal conviction and/or sentence, are governed by an elaborate framework of laws, rules, and judicial decisions.

The Sieve Effect

As cases move through the criminal justice system from arrest through adjudication and, in many instances, toward the imposition of punishment, there is considerable attrition. Of any one hundred felony arrests, perhaps as few as twenty-five will result in convictions. This "sieve effect" occurs for many reasons, including insufficient evidence, police misconduct, procedural errors, and the transfer of young offenders to juvenile courts.

Nationwide, less than 5 percent of criminal cases go to trial. Some cases are dropped by the prosecutor for lack of evidence or because of obvious police misconduct. Others are dismissed by judges at preliminary hearings, usually for similar reasons. In those cases that are not dismissed, defendants usually enter pleas of guilty, very frequently in exchange for concessions from the prosecution. To avoid trial, which is characterized by both delay and uncertainty, the prosecutor may attempt to persuade the defendant to plead guilty, either by reducing the number or severity of charges or by promising not to seek the maximum penalty allowed by law.

The U.S. Supreme Court has upheld the practice of **plea bargaining** against claims that it violates the Due Process Clauses of the Fifth and Fourteenth Amendments. *Brady v. United States,* 397 U.S. 742, 90 S.Ct. 1463, 25 L.Ed.2d 747 (1970); *North Carolina v. Alford,* 400 U.S. 25, 91 S.Ct. 160, 27 L.Ed.2d 162 (1970). However, because there is always a danger of coerced guilty pleas, especially when defendants are ignorant of the law, it is the judge's responsibility to ascertain whether the defendant's guilty plea is voluntarily and knowingly entered and that there is some factual basis for the offense charged. *Boykin v. Alabama,* 395 U.S. 238, 89 S.Ct. 1709, 23 L.Ed.2d 274 (1969).

Go to the companion website for an edited version of *Boykin v. Alabama.*

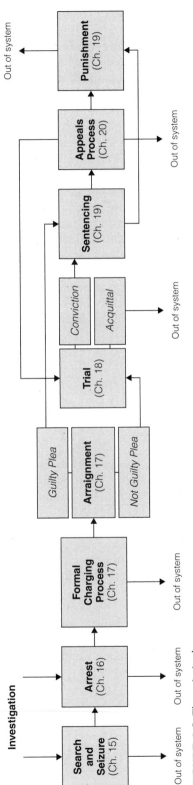

FIGURE 1.2 The criminal process.

| Criminal Sanctions

Courts have at their disposal a variety of sanctions to impose on persons convicted of crimes. During the colonial period of American history, and indeed well into the nineteenth century, the **death penalty** was often inflicted for a variety of felonies, including rape, arson, and horse theft. Today, the death penalty is reserved for only the most aggravated forms of murder and is infrequently carried out. **Incarceration** is the conventional mode of punishment prescribed for persons convicted of felonies, while **monetary fines** are by far the most common punishment for those convicted of misdemeanors. For first-time offenders, especially those convicted of nonviolent crimes, **probation** is a common alternative to incarceration, although probation usually entails a number of restrictions on the offender's freedom.

As society becomes more cognizant of the rights of crime victims, courts are increasingly likely to require that persons convicted of crimes pay sums of money to their victims by way of **restitution**. Requiring offenders to make restitution and perform community service are common conditions of release on probation. Community service is often imposed as a condition as part of a **pretrial diversion** program in which first-time nonviolent offenders are offered the opportunity to avoid prosecution by completing a program of counseling or service. Increasingly, courts are requiring drug offenders to undergo **treatment programs** as conditions of probation.

Conclusion

The American system of criminal justice is deeply rooted in the English common law, but the specifics of criminal law and procedure have evolved substantially from their medieval English origins. Today, American criminal law is largely codified in statutes adopted by Congress and the state legislatures, as interpreted by the courts in specific cases.

One of the more tragic aspects of the crime problem is that many Americans are losing faith in the ability of their government to protect them from criminals. Indeed, in some areas of the country, victims are unlikely even to report crimes to the police. Some victims are unwilling to endure the ordeal of being a witness. Others simply believe that the perpetrator will not be apprehended or, if so, will not be punished. It also must be recognized that in many of the nation's inner cities, many people do not trust the police. Moreover, in certain communities cooperation with the police can be dangerous, as criminal gangs will often retaliate against those who cooperate with the authorities.

Our state and federal governments are severely constrained by both law and economic reality in their efforts to fight crime. Not only is the specter of "a cop on every corner" distasteful to most Americans, but it is also impossible to achieve, given the fiscal constraints on government. Local governments in particular often find it very difficult to provide adequate support to their law enforcement agencies.

Even though the nation's prison system is filled beyond capacity, the public is demanding that more convicted criminals be incarcerated and for longer periods of time. Yet the public appears unwilling to provide the revenues needed to build the additional prisons necessary to house these inmates. Increasingly courts are turning to alternatives to incarceration, especially for first-time and nonviolent offenders.

Finally, society must confront the problem of the constitutional limitations on crime definition and law enforcement. Judges do have considerable discretion in interpreting the state and federal constitutions. But if these documents are to be viable protections of our cherished liberties, we must accept that they place significant constraints on our efforts to control crime. For instance, to what degree is the public willing to allow erosion of the constitutional protection against unreasonable searches and seizures? To what degree are we willing to sacrifice our constitutionally protected privacy and liberty to aid the ferreting out of crime? Today the question is amplified by the threat of terrorism and the belief of many that government needs greater powers to address the terrorist threat. These are the fundamental questions of criminal law and procedure in a society that prides itself on preserving the rights of the individual.

Chapter Summary

- **LO1** Elements of crimes include a wrongful act (*actus reus*) and criminal intent (*mens rea*), yet certain offenses are strict liability crimes, which do not require criminal intent. Some conduct historically was classified as *mala in se* or *mala prohibita* and this has given rise to classification of felonies and misdemeanors based on the seriousness of offenses. Crimes are punished by the state, whereas civil disputes such as torts and breaches of contract often are formally resolved in litigation between the disputants.
- **LO2** Substantive criminal law prohibits certain forms of conduct by defining crimes and establishing the parameters of penalties. Procedural criminal law regulates the enforcement of the substantive law, the determination of guilt, and the punishment of those found guilty of crimes.
- **LO3** We inherited our legal system from the common law of England, where after 1066 judges began to record their decisions and adjudicate controversies based on rules developed in analogous situations. This led to development of the doctrine of *stare decisis*, largely followed by American courts. Later, as English Parliaments began defining crimes, a new America instituted legislative bodies that defined criminal conduct largely based on the English common law. In 1776 Professor Blackstone attempted to demystify the law in his famous treatise; today a proposed Model Penal Code (MPC) advocates uniformity in crime definitions.
- **LO4** The criminal law serves a number of important societal interests. Obviously, government has a duty to protect the lives and property of citizens. Society also has an interest in protecting the public peace, order, and safety. Today, the protection of the national security from terrorism has become an important concern of the criminal law. Over the last several decades, the protection of the public health and the preservation of the natural environment have also come to be seen as interests that should be furthered by the criminal law. And, of course, society has an interest in efficient and honest public administration and the administration of justice.
- **LO5** The federal and state constitutions impose substantive and procedural limits on the criminal justice system. Congress and the state legislatures are not free to enact any and all criminal prohibitions; they must respect constituitional limits on their powers and the constitutional rights of individuals. Law enforcement agencies and courts must respect the procedural rules that flow from the basic constitutional principle of due process of law.
- **LO6** Legislatures enact criminal prohibitions in the form of statutes. Courts interpret these statutes on a case-by-case basis and thus play an important role in developing the criminal law. Rules of criminal procedure are developed primarily by the courts in furtherance of due process and the various constitutitonal protections of persons suspected or accused of crimes.

- **LO7** Statutes enacted by Congress are usually cited to the *United States Code Annotated* (U.S.C.A.), while state criminal codes are cited to books published by state or commercial publishers. Court decisions cited in the text are almost always decisions of federal or state appellate courts. Data under the name of the case indicates the name of the court and date of its decision, followed by numbers indicating the volume and page number of the Reporter, a compendium of judicial decisions, where the decision is found. A case brief is simply a summary of a court decision, usually in outline format. Typically, a brief includes a summary of the facts and procedural history of the case, a statement of issue before the court, a statement of the court's decision, and summaries of any opinions produced by the court.
- **LO8** Before a person can be adjudicated guilty of a crime, the authorities prosecuting a defendant must follow strict guidelines set out in the in the federal and state constitutions and the substantive and procedural law. There is a certain "sieve effect" in the criminal justice system as cases proceed from arrest through pretrial procedures, trial, and sentencing. Cases that do not merit prosecution are strained out. Others are dismissed after courts exclude key evidence. Negotiated guilty pleas remove the need for many criminal trials.
- **LO9** Criminal sanctions include the death penalty, incarceration, monetary fines, and probation. Requiring offenders to make restitution and perform community service are common conditions of release on probation. Increasingly, courts are requiring drug offenders to undergo treatment programs as conditions of probation.

Key Terms

rule of law The idea that law, not the discretion of officials, should govern public affairs.

nullen crimen, nulla poena, sine lege "There is no crime, there is no punishment, without law." Refers to the doctrine that one cannot be found guilty of a crime unless there is a violation of an existing provision of law defining the applicable criminal conduct.

substantive criminal law That branch of the criminal law that defines criminal offenses and defenses and specifies criminal punishments.

procedural criminal law The branch of the criminal law that deals with the processes by which crimes are investigated, prosecuted, and punished.

constitutional supremacy The doctrine that the Constitution is the supreme law of the land and that all actions and policies of government must be consistent with it.

judicial review The power of courts of law to review governmental acts and declare them null and void if they are found to be unconstitutional.

federalism The constitutional distribution of government power and responsibility between the national government and the states.

separation of powers Constitutional assignment of legislative, executive, and judicial powers to different branches of government.

actus reus A "wrongful act" which, combined with other necessary elements of crime, constitutes criminal liability.

mens rea "Guilty mind"; criminal intent.

strict liability offenses Offenses that do not require proof of the defendant's intent.

felonies Serious crimes for which a person may be imprisoned for more than one year.

misdemeanors Minor offenses, usually punishable by fine or imprisonment for less than one year.

civil disobedience Deliberate violation of a criminal law considered to be unjust or unconstitutional in order to dramatize one's objection to the law.

victim A person who is the object of a crime or tort.

breaches of contract Violations of provisions of legally enforceable agreements that give the damaged party the right to recourse in a court of law.

torts Noncriminal wrongs or injuries, other than breaches of contract, for which the remedy is a civil suit for damages.

mala in se "Evils in themselves." Refers to crimes such as murder, rape, arson, robbery, etc., which are universally condemned.

mala prohibita "Prohibited evils." Refers to crimes that are wrong primarily because the law declares them to be wrong.

English common law The body of decisional law based largely on custom as declared by English judges after the Norman Conquest of 1066.

stare decisis The doctrine of deciding cases based on precedent.

statutes Generally applicable laws enacted by a legislature.

Blackstone's *Commentaries* A massive treatise on the English common law published 1765–1769 by Sir William Blackstone, a professor at Oxford University.

ordinance Laws enacted by local governing bodies such as city councils and county commissions.

police power The power of government to legislate to protect public health, safety, welfare, and morality.

Model Penal Code (MPC) Published by the American Law Institute (ALI), the MPC consists of general provisions concerning criminal liability, sentences, defenses, and definitions of specific crimes. The MPC is not law; rather, it is designed to serve as a model code of criminal law for all states.

rules of procedure Rules promulgated by courts of law under constitutional or statutory authority governing procedures for trials and other judicial proceedings.

treason The crime of making war against one's own government or giving aid and comfort to its enemies.

ex post facto **laws** Retroactive laws that criminalize actions that were legal at the time they were performed or increase punishment for a criminal act after it was committed.

bills of attainder Legislative acts (prohibited by the U.S. Constitution) imposing punishment without trial upon persons deemed guilty of treason or felonies.

Bill of Rights A written enumeration of basic rights, usually part of a written constitution—for example, the first ten amendments to the U.S. Constitution.

trial courts Judicial tribunals, usually presided over by one judge, which conduct proceedings and trials in civil and criminal cases with or without a jury.

appellate courts Judicial tribunals that review decisions from lower tribunals.

lawmaking function One of the principal functions of an appellate court; often referred to as the law development function.

error correction function The function of appellate courts in reviewing routine appeals and correcting the errors of trial courts.

decisional law Law declared by appellate courts in their written decisions and opinions.

due process of law Procedural and substantive rights of citizens against government actions that threaten the denial of life, liberty, or property.

fair notice The requirement, stemming from due process, that government provide adequate notice to a person before it deprives that person of life, liberty, or property.

fair hearing A hearing in which both parties have a reasonable opportunity to be heard—to present evidence and make arguments to an impartial decision maker

presumption of innocence In a criminal prosecution, a person accused of a crime is presumed innocent until proven guilty beyond a reasonable doubt.

reasonable doubt standard The standard of proof used by a judge or jury to determine whether criminal charges against a defendant have been proven. The term "beyond a reasonable doubt" is often defined as "moral certainty."

indictment A formal document handed down by a grand jury accusing one or more persons of the commission of a crime or crimes.

grand jury A group of citizens convened either to conduct an investigation or to determine whether there is sufficient evidence to warrant the prosecution of an accused.

information A document filed by a prosecutor under oath charging one or more persons with commission of a crime.

arraignment An appearance before a court of law for the purpose of pleading to a criminal charge.

criminal trial A trial in a court of law to determine the guilt or innocence of a person charged with a crime.

rules of procedure Rules promulgated by courts of law under constitutional or statutory authority governing procedures for trials and other judicial proceedings.

rules of evidence Legal rules governing the admissibility of evidence at trial.

plea bargaining Negotiations between a defendant and a prosecutor whereby the defendant agrees to plead guilty in exchange for some concession (such as a reduction in the number of charges brought).

death penalty Capital punishment; a sentence to death for the commission of a crime.

incarceration Another term for imprisonment.

monetary fines Sums of money that offenders are required to pay as punishment for the commission of crimes.

probation Conditional release of a convicted criminal in lieu of incarceration.

restitution The act of compensating someone for losses suffered.

pretrial diversion A program in which a first-time offender is afforded the opportunity to avoid criminal prosecution by participating in some specified treatment, counseling, or community service.

treatment programs Programs designed to rehabilitate offenders. The term is most commonly used in connection with alcohol or drug abuse rehabilitation.

Questions for Thought and Discussion

1. Should morality, in and of itself, be considered a sufficient basis for defining particular conduct as criminal? Give reasons to support your view.
2. What are the chief distinctions between the civil law and the criminal law? Why do criminal and civil law sometimes overlap?
3. To what extent is the English common law significant in contemporary American criminal law?
4. What is the essential difference between substantive criminal law and procedural criminal law? Give examples of each.
5. What means of punishment for criminal offenses exist in your state? Is capital punishment available for persons convicted of first-degree murder? Which punishments, if any, do you think are most effective in controlling crime?

CHAPTER 2

Organization of the Criminal Justice System

LEARNING OBJECTIVES

After reading this chapter, you should be able to explain . . .

1. why federalism is such an important concept in understanding the American system of criminal justice
2. why there are variations in criminal justice systems across the states
3. the different roles played by legislatures, courts, and law enforcement agencies at the federal, state, and local levels of government
4. the differences and similarities between Congress and the state legislatures with respect to their legislative powers
5. how and why courts interpret criminal laws enacted by legislatures
6. how modern American policing has evolved from its medieval English origins
7. the roles of prosecutor and defense counsel
8. how grand juries differ from trial juries
9. how the federal and state judicial systems are structured
10. how military tribunals differ from civilian criminal courts
11. how the juvenile justice system differs from the criminal justice system for adults
12. how the system of corrections is structured and how criminal punishment has evolved

CHAPTER OUTLINE

Introduction
Legislatures
Law Enforcement Agencies
Prosecutorial Agencies
Counsel for the Defense
Juries
The Courts

One of the most important principles of the American system of criminal justice is *federalism*—the constitutional division of power and responsibility between the national government and the fifty states. Our federal system sometimes produces uncertainty and even conflict over what powers reside exclusively in the federal government, what powers are reserved to the states, and what powers may be exercised concurrently. The issue of illegal immigration provides a good example. Frustrated at what it perceived to be an inadequate effort by the federal government to control illegal immigration across the nation's southern border, the state of Arizona enacted a law allowing the state to enforce the federal law prohibiting unauthorized entry into the country. Senate Bill 1070 required state and local law enforcement agents who have made a lawful stop, detention, or arrest to verify a person's immigration status if they have "reasonable suspicion" that the person is in the United States illegally. The law set off a firestorm of criticism from immigrants' rights and civil rights groups, who expressed fear that the law would lead to racial profiling. President Obama called the Arizona law "ill-conceived" and said that it was an affront to civil rights to require people to produce proof of citizenship or lawful status based only on the suspicion of a police officer.

On July 6, 2010, the U.S. Department of Justice filed suit in federal court against the state of Arizona and Arizona's governor, claiming that S.B. 1070 was a usurpation of federal authority. The complaint in *United States v. Arizona* asserted that "the federal government has preeminent authority to regulate immigration matters" and that "a state may not establish its own immigration policy or enforce state laws in a manner that interferes with the federal immigration laws." Legal commentators expressed mixed views on the merits of the lawsuit. In *De Canas v. Bica*, 424 U.S. 351, 96 *S.Ct.* 933, 47 *L.Ed.2d* 43 (1976), the U.S. Supreme Court unanimously upheld a California law that forbade employers from knowingly employing illegal immigrants. And in *Plyler v. Doe*, 457 U.S. 202, 225, 102 S.Ct. 2382, 2399, 72 L.Ed. 2d 786, 805 (1982), the Court said that "the States do have some authority to act with respect to illegal aliens, at least where such action mirrors federal objectives and furthers a legitimate state goal." In late July a federal district judge issued an injunction against enforcement of key provisions of the law. In the wake of that ruling, most commentators agreed that this question of *federalism* would end up in the U.S. Supreme Court. Nevertheless, other states have considered legislation modeled after Arizona's controversial statute.

Introduction

In every modern country, criminal justice is a complex process involving a plethora of agencies and officials. In the United States, criminal justice is particularly complex, largely because of **federalism,** the constitutional division of authority between the national and state governments. Under our federal scheme the national government operates one criminal justice system to enforce federal criminal laws; additionally, each

TABLE 2.1	Criminal Justice Agencies and Their Functions
Type of Agency	**Functions**
Legislatures	Enacting Criminal Prohibitions
Law Enforcement Agencies	Enforcing Criminal Prohibitions Maintaining Public Order and Security Conducting Investigations of Crimes Performing Searches and Seizures Making Arrests of Persons Suspected of Crimes Interrogating Suspects
Prosecutorial Agencies	Enforcing Criminal Prohibitions Conducting Investigations Gathering Evidence Initiating Criminal Prosecutions Representing the Government in Court
Public Defenders	Representing Indigent Persons Accused of Crimes
Grand Juries	Reviewing Evidence Obtained by Prosecutors Indicting Persons Accused of Crimes Granting Immunity to Witnesses
Courts of Law	Issuing Search Warrants Issuing Arrest Warrants Conducting Summary Trials in Minor Cases Conducting Initial Appearances Conducting Preliminary Hearings Conducting Arraignments Holding Hearings on Pretrial Motions Conducting Trials Sentencing Persons Convicted of Crimes Conducting Posttrial Hearings Hearing Appeals from Lower Court Rulings
Corrections Agencies	Incarceration of Persons Convicted of Crimes Supervision of Persons on Probation or Parole Carrying out Executions of Persons Sentenced to Death

state has a justice system to apply its own criminal laws. As a result of this structural complexity, it is difficult to provide a coherent overview of criminal justice in America. Each system is to some extent different in both substantive and procedural law.

Despite the differences that exist between federal and state criminal justice systems, there are certain similarities. Like the federal system, all fifty states have legislative bodies, law enforcement agencies, prosecutors, defense attorneys, courts of law, and corrections agencies (see Table 2.1). All follow certain general procedures beginning with arrest and, in some cases, ending in punishment. Finally, all systems are subject to the limitations of the United States Constitution, as interpreted by the courts. In this chapter we present an overview of the roles played by the institutions that make up the criminal justice system in the United States.

Legislatures

The governmental institution with primary responsibility for enacting laws is the **legislature.** Because the United States is organized on the principle of federalism, there are fifty-one legislatures in this country—the **United States Congress** and the fifty state legislatures. Each of these bodies has the power to enact **statutes** that apply within its respective jurisdiction. The U.S. Congress adopts statutes that apply throughout the United States and its territories, whereas the Illinois General Assembly, for example, adopts laws that apply only within the state of Illinois. For the most part, federal and state statutes complement one another. When there is a conflict, the federal statute prevails.

Legislative Powers of Congress

Congress's legislative authority may be divided into two broad categories: **enumerated powers** and **implied powers.** Enumerated powers are those that are mentioned specifically in Article I, Section 8 of the Constitution, such as the power to tax and the power to borrow money on the credit of the United States. Among the constitutionally enumerated powers of Congress, there are only two direct references to criminal justice. Congress is explicitly authorized to "provide for the Punishment of counterfeiting the Securities and current Coin of the United States" and to "define and punish Piracies and Felonies committed on the high Seas, and Offenses against the Law of Nations." Of course, Congress's power to define federal crimes is much more extensive than these two clauses suggest.

The enumerated power to "regulate commerce among the states" has provided Congress with a vast reservoir of legislative power. Many of the criminal statutes enacted by Congress in recent decades have been justified on the basis of the Commerce Clause of Article I, Section 8 (see Chapter 3).

Congress's implied powers are those that are deemed to be "necessary and proper for carrying into Execution the foregoing Powers, and all other Powers vested . . . in the Government of the United States, or in any Department or Officer thereof." As long as Congress's policy goal is permissible, any legislative means that are "plainly adapted" to that goal are likewise permissible. *McCulloch v. Maryland,* 17 U.S. (4 Wheat.) 316, 4 L.Ed. 579 (1819). Under the doctrine of implied powers, scarcely any area exists over which Congress is absolutely barred from legislating, because most social and economic problems have a conceivable relationship to the broad powers and objectives contained in the Constitution.

As the nation expanded and evolved, Congress became more active in passing social and economic legislation. In the twentieth century, and especially the last several decades, Congress established a host of federal crimes. There is now an elaborate body of federal criminal law. Of course, Congress may not enact laws that violate constitutional limitations such as those found in the Bill of Rights (see Chapter 3).

Publication of Federal Statutes

Federal statutes are published in *United States Statutes at Large,* an annual publication dating from 1789 in which federal statutes are arranged in order of their adoption. Statutes are not arranged by subject matter, nor is there any indication of how they affect existing laws. Because the body of federal statutes is quite voluminous, and because new statutes often repeal or amend their predecessors, it is essential that new statutes be merged into legal codes that systematically arrange the statutes by subject. To find federal law as it currently stands, arranged by subject matter, one must consult the latest edition of the *Official Code of the Laws of the United States,* generally known as the **U.S. Code**. The U.S. Code is broken down into fifty subjects, called "titles." Title 18, "Crimes and Criminal Procedure," contains many of the federal crimes established by Congress.

The most popular compilation of the federal law, used by lawyers, judges, and criminal justice professionals, is the ***United States Code Annotated*** (**U.S.C.A.**). Published by West Group, the U.S.C.A. contains the entire current U.S. Code, but each section of statutory law in U.S.C.A. is followed by a series of annotations consisting of court decisions interpreting the particular statute along with historical notes, cross-references, and other editorial features (for more discussion, see Appendix A).

State Legislatures

Under the U.S. Constitution, each state must have a democratically elected **legislature** because that is the most fundamental element of a "republican form of government." State legislatures for the most part resemble the U.S. Congress. Each is composed of representatives chosen by the citizens of their respective states. All of them are bicameral (i.e., two-house) institutions, with the exception of Nebraska, which has a unicameral legislature. In adopting statutes, they all follow the same basic procedures. When state legislatures adopt statutes, they are published in volumes known as **session laws.** Then statutes are integrated into state codes. Lawyers make frequent use of annotated versions of state codes. These are available at law school libraries, and often at local law libraries, to those who wish to see how state statutes have been interpreted and applied by the state courts.

As we noted in Chapter 1, after the American Revolution, states adopted the English common law as their own state law to the extent that it did not conflict with their new state constitutions. (Congress, on the other hand, never did.) Eventually, however, state legislatures codified much of the common law by enacting statutes, which in turn have been developed into comprehensive state codes. Periodically, states revise portions of their codes to make sure they remain relevant to a constantly changing society. For example, in 1989 the Tennessee General Assembly undertook a modernization of its criminal code. Old offenses that were no longer being enforced were repealed, other offenses were redefined, and sentencing laws were completely overhauled.

Statutory Interpretation

Statutes are necessarily written in general language, so legislation often requires judicial interpretation. Because legislative bodies have enacted vast numbers of laws defining offenses that are *mala prohibita,* such interpretation assumes an importance largely unknown to the English common law. Courts have responded by developing certain techniques to apply when a statute appears unclear as related to a specific factual scenario. These techniques are generally referred to as **rules of statutory interpretation** and over the years have given rise to reference to legislative history and various maxims that courts apply in attempting to determine the legislature's intention in enacting a statute.

Courts recognize that it is the legislative bodies and not the courts that exercise the power to define crimes and penalties. It follows that the most frequent maxim applied by courts in determining legislative intention is the **plain meaning rule.** As the U.S. Supreme Court observed early in the twentieth century, "Where the language [of a statutory law] is plain and admits of no more than one meaning the duty of interpretation does not arise. . . . ." *Caminetti v. United States,* 242 U.S. 470, 37 S.Ct. 192, 61 L.Ed. 442 (1917). The Court's dictum seems self-evident, yet even learned judges often disagree as to whether the language of a given statute is plain. This gives rise to certain **canons of construction** applied by courts to determine the **legislative intent** behind a statutory definition of a crime.

A primary canon of construction is that criminal statutes must be strictly construed. The rule originated at common law, when death was the penalty for committing a felony, but the rule has remained. However, it is now based on the rationale that every criminal statute should be sufficiently precise to give fair warning of its meaning. Today we see the rule applied most frequently in a constitutional context when courts determine a criminal statute to be **void for vagueness.** We address this aspect in more detail in the following chapter. Another canon of construction provides for an **implied exception** to a statute. For example, courts have ruled that there is an implied exception to a law imposing speed limits on the highway in instances where police or other emergency vehicles violate the literal text of the law. Would a court apply a statute that makes it an offense for any person to sleep in a bus terminal and thereby find a ticketed passenger guilty who fell asleep while waiting for a bus that was overdue? The implied exception doctrine seems to reflect a commonsense approach to determining the meaning of a statute.

Often a statute uses a term that has a definite meaning at common law. In general, courts interpret such terms according to their common-law meaning. Recall that in Chapter 1 we observed that in defining the crime of burglary a legislature might use the term "curtilage" without defining it. In such an instance, we noted that a court would ordinarily look to the common law, which defined the term to mean "an enclosed space surrounding a dwelling."

But this rule does not always apply when dealing with modern statutes, particularly at the federal level, where there is generally considerable legislative history in the form of committee reports and floor debates recorded in the *Congressional Record* that can aid in determining the true intent of a statute. Thus, in *Perrin v. United States,* 444 U.S. 37, 100 S.Ct. 311, 62 L.Ed.2d 199 (1979), the Supreme Court determined that the word "bribery" in a federal statute was not limited to its common-law definition because the legislative history revealed an intent to deal with bribery in organized crime beyond its common-law definition. In general, there is considerably less legislative history available at the state legislative level. However, at times state courts seek to determine legislative intent based on available resources.

Law Enforcement Agencies

Law enforcement agencies are charged with enforcing the criminal law. They have the power to investigate suspected criminal activity, to arrest suspected criminals, and to detain arrested persons until their cases come before the appropriate courts of law. Society expects law enforcement agencies not only to arrest those suspected of crimes but also to take steps to prevent crimes from occurring.

Historical Development

Before the Norman Conquest in 1066, there were no organized police in England, but by the thirteenth century constables and justices of the peace came to symbolize enforcement of the rule of law in England. Large communities, somewhat similar to counties in America, were called "shires." The king would send a royal officer called a "reeve" to each shire to keep order and to exercise broad powers within the shire. The onset of the Industrial Revolution led to the development of large cities. Industrialists and merchants began to establish patrols to protect their goods and buildings. But the need for more effective policing became evident. In 1829, Sir Robert Peel, the British Home Secretary, organized a uniformed but unarmed police force for

London. The name "Bobbies" is still applied to police officers in England in honor of Peel. In later years, Parliament required counties and boroughs to establish police departments modeled along the lines of the London force.

Colonial America basically followed the English system, with local constables and county sheriffs following the English concept of constables and shire reeves. These early law officers were often aided by local vigilante groups of citizens known as "posses." Once America became a nation, states and local communities began to follow the Peel model, and by the mid-1800s, Boston, New York, and Philadelphia had developed professional police departments. By the twentieth century, police were aided by technological developments, and by the 1930s, many departments were equipped with motorcycles and patrol cars. Detectives were soon added to the force, police became equipped with modern communications equipment, and police were trained in ballistics and the scientific analysis of blood samples and handwriting.

Policing in Modern America

In the United States nearly 20,000 federal, state, and local agencies are involved in law enforcement and crime prevention. Collectively, these agencies employ nearly 800,000 **sworn officers.** Increasingly, law enforcement officers are trained professionals who must acquire a good working knowledge of the criminal law. At the local level, the typical police recruit now completes about 1,000 hours of training before being sworn in. Modern police forces are highly mobile and, except in the smallest communities, are equipped with computers, sophisticated communications technology, and scientific crime detection equipment.

Policing at the National Level

At the national level, the **Federal Bureau of Investigation** (FBI) is the primary agency empowered to investigate violations of federal criminal laws. Located in the **Department of Justice,** the FBI is by far the most powerful of the federal law enforcement agencies, with broad powers to enforce the many criminal laws adopted by the Congress. On September 30, 2008, the FBI employed 12,851 **special agents** and 18,393 support professionals, such as intelligence analysts, language specialists, forensic scientists, information technology specialists, and other professionals. Its personnel are spread out over fifty-six field offices in major cities in the United States and more than sixty international offices in embassies worldwide. The FBI uses the most sophisticated methods in crime prevention and investigation. Its crime laboratory figures prominently in the investigation and prosecution of numerous state and federal crimes. In fiscal year 2008, the FBI's total budget was approximately $6.8 billion, including $410 million in program enhancements for intelligence, counterterrorism, laboratory, information technology, and cybersecurity (see http://www.fbi.gov/quickfacts.htm).

The **United States Marshals Service** is the oldest unit of federal law enforcement, dating back to 1790. The Marshals execute orders of federal courts and serve as custodians for the transfer of prisoners. U.S. Marshals played a prominent role in the crises in school integration during the civil rights struggles of the 1950s and early 1960s.

Nearly fifty other federal agencies have law enforcement authority in specific areas. Among them are the Bureau of Alcohol, Tobacco, and Firearms; the Internal

Revenue Service; the Bureau of Indian Affairs; the Drug Enforcement Administration; the Bureau of Postal Inspection; the Tennessee Valley Authority; the National Park Service; the Forest Service; the U.S. Capitol Police; the U.S. Mint; the Secret Service; and the Bureau of Citizenship and Immigration Services within the Department of Homeland Security.

State and Local Policing

All states have law enforcement agencies that patrol the highways, investigate crimes, and furnish skilled technical support to local law enforcement agencies. Similarly, every state has a number of state agencies responsible for enforcing specific areas of the law, ranging from agricultural importation to food processing and from casino gambling to dispensing alcoholic beverages. Probably among the best known to all citizens are the state highway patrol and the fish and game warden. Generally, cases developed by state officers are processed through local law enforcement and prosecution agencies.

At the local level, we find both county and municipal law enforcement agencies. Nearly every county in America (more than three thousand of them) has a **sheriff.** In most states, sheriffs are elected to office and exercise broad powers as the chief law enforcement officers of their respective counties. They are usually dependent on funding provided by a local governing body, generally the county commission. In some areas, particularly the urban Northeast, many powers traditionally exercised by sheriffs have been assumed by state or metropolitan police forces. In the rest of the country, however, especially in the rural areas, sheriffs (and their deputies) are the principal law enforcement agents at the county level.

Nearly 15,000 cities and towns have their own **police departments.** Local police are charged with enforcing the criminal laws of their states, as well as of their municipalities. Although the county sheriff usually has jurisdiction within the municipalities of the county, he or she generally concentrates enforcement efforts on those areas outside municipal boundaries.

In addition to city and county law enforcement agencies, there are numerous special districts and authorities that have their own police forces. Most state universities have their own police departments, as do many airports and seaports.

Besides providing law enforcement in the strictest sense of the term, local law enforcement agencies initiate the criminal justice process and assist prosecutors in preparation of cases. Sheriffs in many larger counties and many metropolitan police departments have developed SWAT (special weapons and tactics) teams to assist in the rescue of victims of catastrophes and persons taken hostage. They are also heavily involved in **order maintenance** or "keeping the peace," hence the term "peace officers." Often, keeping the peace involves more of a process of judgment and discretion rather than merely applying the criminal law.

Some of the newer and more innovative policing responsibilities include community relations departments that seek to foster better relations among groups of citizens, especially minorities and juveniles, and to assist social agencies in efforts to rehabilitate drug and alcohol abusers. Finally, the public looks to the police to prevent crime through their presence in the community and through education of the public on crime prevention measures. Under the rubric of **community policing,** police agencies are making an effort to become actively involved in their communities in order to earn the trust and confidence of the citizens they serve. Most police departments in cities of 50,000 people or more now have specialized community policing divisions.

Prosecutorial Agencies

Although law enforcement agencies are the "gatekeepers" of the criminal justice system, prosecutors are central to the administration of criminal justice. It is the **prosecutor** who determines whether to bring charges against suspected criminals. Prosecutors have enormous discretion, not only in determining whether to prosecute but also in determining what charges to file. Moreover, prosecutors frequently set the tone for **plea bargaining** and have a powerful voice in determining the severity of sanctions imposed on persons convicted of crimes. Accordingly, prosecutors play a crucial role in the criminal justice system.

Historical Background

The early English common law considered many crimes to be private matters between individuals; however, the role of the public prosecutor evolved as early as the thirteenth century, when the king's counsel would pursue crimes considered to be offenses against the Crown and, in some instances, when injured victims declined to prosecute. Today in England, a public prosecutor prosecutes crimes that have great significance to the government, but the majority of offenses are handled by police agencies that hire barristers to prosecute charges. Unlike American prosecutors, the English barrister may represent the police in one case and in the next case represent the defendant.

The office of public prosecutor in England became the prototype for the office of attorney general in this country at the national and state levels. In colonial days, an attorney general's assistants handled local prosecutions. However, as states became independent, the practice ceased. The state attorneys general assumed the role of chief legal officers, and local governments began electing their own prosecuting attorneys.

Federal Prosecutors

In the United States, the chief prosecutor at the federal level is the **Attorney General,** who is the head of the Department of Justice. Below the Attorney General are the **United States Attorneys,** each responsible for prosecuting crimes within a particular federal district. The United States Attorneys, in turn, have a number of assistants who handle most of the day-to-day criminal cases brought by the federal government. The president, subject to the consent of the Senate, appoints the Attorney General and the U.S. Attorneys. Assistant U.S. Attorneys are federal civil service employees.

In addition to the regular federal prosecutors, Congress has provided for the appointment of **independent counsel** (special prosecutors) in cases involving alleged misconduct by high government officials. By far, the most infamous such case was "Watergate," which resulted in the convictions of several high-ranking officials and led to the resignation of President Nixon in 1974. But there have been numerous cases where, under congressional direction, a special prosecutor has been appointed. A more recent example of this was Kenneth Starr's appointment to investigate the Whitewater scandal, which involved close associates of President Bill Clinton and First Lady Hillary Rodham Clinton. This investigation eventually culminated in President Clinton's impeachment and his subsequent acquittal by the U.S. Senate in February 1999.

State and Local Prosecutors

Each state likewise has its own attorney general, who acts as the state's chief legal officer, and a number of assistant attorneys general, plus a number of district or **state's attorneys** at the local level. Generally speaking, local prosecutors are elected for set terms of office and have the responsibility for the prosecution of crimes within the jurisdiction for which they are elected. In most states, local prosecutors act autonomously and possess broad discretionary powers. Many local prosecutors function on a part-time basis, but in the larger offices the trend is for the prosecutor and assistant prosecutors to serve on a full-time basis. Larger offices are establishing educational programs and developing specially trained assistants or units to handle specific categories of crime—for example, white-collar crime and governmental corruption, narcotics offenses, and consumer fraud.

Cities and counties also have their own attorneys. These attorneys, generally appointed by the governing bodies they represent, sometimes prosecute violations of city and county ordinances, but increasingly their function is limited to representing their cities or counties in civil suits and giving legal advice to local councils and officials.

The Prosecutor's Broad Discretion

Federal and state prosecutors (whether known as district attorneys, state attorneys, or county prosecutors) play a vital role in the criminal justice system in the United States. As mentioned, a politically appointed U.S. Attorney supervises prosecutors at the federal level, whereas state and local prosecutors generally come into office by election in partisan contests. Thus, prosecutors become sensitive to community norms while exercising the broad discretion that the law vests in prosecutorial decision making.

Prosecutors not only determine the level of offense to be charged; in exercise of their very broad discretion they also exercise the power of ***nolle prosequi,*** usually called *nol pros,* which allows a prosecutor not to proceed in a given case, irrespective of the factual basis for prosecution. Prosecutors sometimes *nol pros* cases to secure cooperation of a defendant in furthering other prosecutions; in other instances, a prosecutor may allow a defendant to participate in some diversionary program of rehabilitation. In recent years, completion of a prescribed program in a drug court has often resulted in a case being *nol prossed* by a prosecutor. (See the discussion of drug courts in Chapter 10.)

Counsel for the Defense

In American criminal law, individuals accused of any crime, no matter how minor the offense, have the right to employ counsel for their defense. U.S. Const. Amend. VI. Indeed, the U.S. Supreme Court has held that a defendant has the right to be represented by an attorney at all criminal proceedings that may substantially affect the rights of the accused. *Mempa v. Rhay,* 389 U.S. 128, 88 S.Ct. 254, 19 L.Ed.2d 336 (1967).

In this country, many lawyers specialize in criminal defense work. Of course, defendants are free to employ an attorney of their choice at their own expense. Some well-known attorneys specialize in representing defendants in high-profile trials. However, most criminal defendants are not wealthy, and few people accused of crimes can afford to hire legal "dream teams" to represent them.

Many attorneys are highly skilled in handling criminal cases and are available for employment in federal and state criminal proceedings. In fact, it is not uncommon for attorneys who start their careers as prosecutors eventually to enter private practice in criminal matters. Today some state bar associations grant special recognition to lawyers who qualify by virtue of experience and examination as "certified criminal defense attorneys."

Go to the companion website for an edited version of the Supreme Court's decision in *Gideon v. Wainwright.*

Representation of Indigent Defendants

Beginning in the 1960s, the United States Supreme Court greatly expanded the right to counsel by requiring states to provide attorneys to **indigent defendants.** *Gideon v. Wainwright,* 372 U.S. 335, 83 S.Ct. 792, 9 L.Ed.2d 799 (1963); *Argersinger v. Hamlin,* 407 U.S. 25, 92 S.Ct. 2006, 32 L.Ed.2d 530 (1972). In some states, courts appoint attorneys from the private bar to represent indigent defendants. However, most states have chosen to handle the problem of indigent defense by establishing the office of public defender. Like public prosecutors, **public defenders** are generally elected to set terms of office. Because of their constant contact with criminal cases, public defenders acquire considerable expertise in representing defendants. Moreover, because they are public officials who, like prosecutors, are provided with budgets, public defenders are often able to hire investigators to aid their staff of assistant public defenders in their representation of indigent defendants.

The Role of Defense Attorneys

The role of the **defense attorney** is perhaps the most misunderstood in the criminal justice system. First and foremost, a defense attorney is charged with zealously representing his or her client and ensuring that the defendant's constitutional rights are fully protected. To anyone who has watched *Law and Order* or a similar television program, the defense attorney's most visible role is that of vigorously cross-examining prosecution witnesses and passionately pleading for a client before a jury. However, the defense attorney's role is far greater than being a courtroom advocate. As a counselor, a defense attorney must evaluate the alternative courses of action that may be available to a defendant. The great majority of criminal cases are disposed of through plea bargaining. As part of this process, defense counsel must attempt to gauge the strength of the prosecution's case, advise the client on the feasibility of entering a plea of guilty, and attempt to negotiate a fair and constructive sentence. In instances where a defendant elects to plead not guilty, defense attorneys challenge the police and prosecution. Many observers point out that these efforts by defense attorneys "keep the system honest" by causing police and prosecuting authorities to be scrupulous in their adherence to constitutional standards.

Perhaps the most frequently voiced reservation concerning defense attorneys relates to representation of a defendant who, from all facts available, is believed to be guilty. Defense attorneys are quick to point out that it is not their function to make a judgment of the defendant's guilt or innocence; there are other functionaries in the system charged with that responsibility. The answer does not easily satisfy critics. Nevertheless, in our system of adversarial justice the defense attorney is required to represent a defendant with fidelity, to protect the defendant's constitutional rights, to assert all defenses available under the law of the land, and to make sure before a defendant is found guilty that the prosecution has sustained its burden of proving the defendant guilty beyond a reasonable doubt. A defense attorney must make sufficient objections and other tactical moves to preserve any contention of error for review by a higher court. If the defendant is convicted, the defense attorney's duty continues. He or she must seek a fair sentence, advise as to the right to appeal to a higher court, and, in some instances, seek postconviction relief if an appeal fails.

Juries

The **jury** is one of the great contributions of the English common law. By the twelfth century, juries had begun to function in England, but not as we know juries today. Rather, these early juries comprised men who had knowledge of the disputes they were to decide. However, eventually juries began to hear evidence and make their verdicts accordingly. By the eighteenth century, juries occupied a prominent role in the English common-law system and served as a buffer between the Crown and the citizenry. The colonists brought the concept to the New World. Today, juries composed of both men and women represent an important component of the American system of criminal justice.

There are two types of juries: the **grand jury** and the **petit (trial) jury.** The juries derive their names from the number of persons who serve, with the grand jury consisting of a larger number than the petit jury.

Grand Juries

Grand juries essentially serve to consider whether there is sufficient evidence to bring charges against a person; petit or trial juries sit to hear evidence at a trial and render a verdict accordingly. The Fifth Amendment to the U.S. Constitution stipulates that "[n]o person shall be held to answer for a capital, or otherwise infamous crime, unless on a presentment or indictment of a grand jury." The constitutional requirement binds all federal courts; however, the Supreme Court has held that states are not bound to abide by the grand jury requirement. *Hurtado v. California,* 110 U.S. 516, 4 S.Ct. 111, 28 L.Ed.232 (1884).

Sixteen to twenty-three persons serve on a federal grand jury. The number varies according to each state but usually consists of between twelve and twenty-three citizens. Grand jurors serve for a limited time to hear evidence and to determine whether to hand down an indictment, sometimes referred to as a **true bill,** or to refuse to indict when the jury determines there is insufficient evidence of a crime by returning a **no bill.** Twelve jurors must vote to return an indictment in federal court, and states usually require at least a majority of grand jurors to return an indictment. Courts have broad authority to call a grand jury into session, and grand juries are authorized to make wide-ranging inquiries and investigations into public matters. Grand juries may make accusations, called *presentments,* independently of a prosecutor.

Although the English common law system gave birth to the grand jury, England abolished grand juries in the 1930s, having found that the return of **indictments** was almost automatic and that the use of grand juries tended to delay the criminal process. Today, critics argue that grand juries are so dominated by the prosecutors who appear before them that they have ceased to serve as an independent body to evaluate evidence. Indeed, many states have eliminated the requirement that a grand jury hand down indictments and have substituted a **prosecutor's information,** an accusatorial document charging a crime. Yet many reformers would retain the grand jury as an institution for investigation of corruption in government.

Go to the companion website for an edited version of *Hurtado v. California.*

Trial Juries

Go to the companion website for an edited version of the Supreme Court's decision in *Duncan v. Louisiana.*

Article III, Section 2 of the U.S. Constitution establishes the right to trial by jury in criminal cases. The Sixth Amendment guarantees "the right to a **speedy and public trial** by an impartial jury." The Seventh Amendment grants a right to a trial by jury in civil suits at common law. All state constitutions confer the right of trial by jury in criminal cases; however, the federal constitutional right to a jury trial applies to the states, thereby guaranteeing a defendant a right to a jury trial in a state criminal prosecution if such a right would exist in a federal prosecution. *Duncan v. Louisiana,* 391 U.S. 145, 88 S.Ct. 1444, 20 L.Ed.2d 491 (1968). However, as we note below, the right to trial by jury does not extend to juvenile delinquency proceedings.

Go to the companion website for an edited version of the Supreme Court's decision in *Williams v. Florida.*

A common-law trial jury consisted of "twelve men good and true." Today, twelve persons are required in federal juries; however, the number varies in states, although all states require twelve-person juries in capital cases. The Supreme Court has approved the use of six-person juries in noncapital felony prosecutions. *Williams v. Florida,* 399 U.S. 78, 90 S.Ct. 1893, 26 L.Ed. 2d 446 (1970).

The Courts

Courts of law are the centerpieces of the federal and state criminal justice systems. Courts of law are responsible for determining both the factual basis and legal sufficiency of criminal charges and for ensuring that criminal defendants are provided due process of law. Essentially, the federal courts adjudicate criminal cases where defendants are charged with violating federal criminal laws; state courts adjudicate alleged violations of state laws.

Basically, there are two kinds of courts: trial and appellate courts. **Trial courts** conduct criminal trials and various pretrial and posttrial proceedings. **Appellate courts** hear appeals from the decisions of the trial courts. Trial courts are primarily concerned with ascertaining facts, determining guilt or innocence, and imposing punishments, whereas appellate courts are primarily concerned with matters of law. Appellate courts correct legal errors made by trial courts and develop law when new legal questions arise. In some instances appellate courts must determine whether there is legally sufficient evidence to uphold a conviction.

The first question facing a court in any criminal prosecution is that of **jurisdiction,** the legal authority to hear and decide the case. A court must have jurisdiction over both the subject matter of a case and the parties to a case before it may proceed to adjudicate that controversy. The jurisdiction of the federal courts is determined by both the language of Article III of the Constitution and the statutes enacted by Congress. The respective state constitutions and statutes determine the jurisdiction of the state courts.

The Federal Court System

Article III of the U.S. Constitution provides that "[t]he judicial Power of the United States shall be vested in one supreme Court, and in such inferior Courts as the Congress may from time to time ordain and establish." Under this authority Congress enacted the Judiciary Act of 1789, creating the federal court system. After Congress passed the Judiciary Act of 1801, the Supreme Court justices were required to "ride circuit," a practice that had its roots in English legal history. The circuit courts then consisted of district court judges who heard appeals alongside "circuit-riding"

Supreme Court justices. In 1891 Congress created separate appellate courts, and since then Supreme Court justices have remained as reviewing justices.

United States District Courts handle prosecutions for violations of federal statutes. In addition, federal courts sometimes review convictions from state courts when defendants raise issues arising under the U.S. Constitution. Appeals are heard by United States Courts of Appeals, and, of course, the Supreme Court is at the apex of the judicial system.

United States District Courts

The principal trial court in the federal system is the United States District Court. There are district courts in ninety-four federal judicial districts around the country. A criminal trial in the district court is presided over by a judge appointed for life by the president with the consent of the Senate. Federal magistrate judges, who are appointed by federal district judges, often handle pretrial proceedings in the district courts and trials of misdemeanors.

In 2007 there were 68,413 criminal cases filed in U.S. District Courts (see Administrative Office of the United States Courts, *2007 Annual Report of the Director*, Washington, DC: USGPO, p. 26). In 2008 the number of criminal cases rose to 70,896, due largely to an increase in prosecution for immigration violations. (Chief Justice's 2008 Year-End Report on the Federal Judiciary, December 31, 2008, p. 13.)

Congress created the district courts by the Judiciary Act of 1789. Since then, Congress has created specialized courts to handle specific kinds of cases (for example, the United States Court of International Trade and the United States Claims Court).

The United States Courts of Appeals

The **intermediate appellate courts** in the federal system are the **United States Courts of Appeals** (also known as circuit courts). Twelve geographical circuits (and one "federal circuit") cover the United States and its possessions. Figure 2.1 indicates the geographical distribution of the circuit courts. The circuit courts hear criminal and civil appeals from the district courts and from quasi-judicial tribunals in the independent regulatory agencies. In 2007, 58,410 appeals were commenced in the federal circuit courts (Administrative Office of the United States Courts, *2007 Annual Report of the Director*, Washington, DC: USGPO, p. 19).

SIDEBAR

Jurisdiction over Crimes Committed by Native Americans on Reservations

Article I, Section 8 of the U.S. Constitution mentions Indian tribes as being subject to Congressional legislation. Congress has provided that federal courts have jurisdiction over specified offenses committed by Native Americans on Indian reservations. 18 U.S.C.A. § 1153. At the same time, Congress has permitted certain states to exercise jurisdiction over such offenses. 18 U.S.C.A. § 1162. Furthermore, offenses committed by one Native American against another on a reservation are generally subject to the jurisdiction of tribal courts, unless the crime charged has been expressly made subject to federal jurisdiction. *Keeble v. United States,* 412 U.S. 205, 93 S.Ct. 1993, 36 L.Ed.2d 844 (1973).

Courts of the state where a Native American reservation is located have jurisdiction over crimes on the reservation when the offense is perpetrated by a non-Indian against a non-Indian, but non-Indian defendants charged with committing a crime on a reservation are subject to federal jurisdiction if the victim is a member of the tribe. *United States v. Antelope,* 430 U.S. 641, 97 S.Ct. 1395, 51 L.Ed.2d 701 (1977).

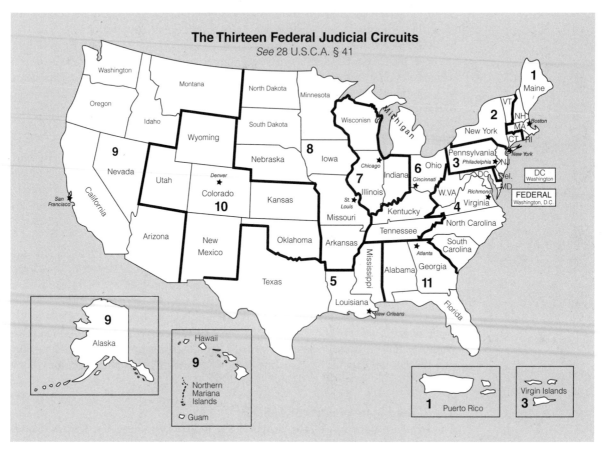

FIGURE 2.1 The Federal Judicial Circuits. Source: *Federal Reporter,* 2nd series (West Publishing Company).

Generally, decisions of the courts of appeals are rendered by panels of three judges who vote to affirm, reverse, or modify the lower-court decisions under review. There is a procedure by which the circuit courts provide an ***en banc* hearing,** where all judges assigned to the court (or a substantial number of them) participate in a decision. Like their counterparts in the district courts, federal appeals court judges are appointed to life terms by the president with the consent of the Senate.

The United States Supreme Court

The highest appellate court in the federal judicial system is the **United States Supreme Court.** The Supreme Court has jurisdiction to review, either on appeal or by **writ of certiorari** (discretionary review), all the decisions of the lower federal courts and many decisions of the highest state courts. The Supreme Court comprises nine justices who, like district and circuit judges, are appointed for life by the president with the consent of the Senate. These nine individuals have the final word in determining what the U.S. Constitution requires, permits, and prohibits in the areas of law enforcement, prosecution, adjudication, and punishment. The Supreme Court also promulgates **rules of procedure** for the lower federal courts to follow in both criminal and civil cases.

As of October 1, 2010, John Roberts was the chief justice of the Supreme Court, and the associate justices were Antonin Scalia, Anthony Kennedy, Clarence Thomas,

Ruth Bader Ginsburg, Stephen Breyer, Samuel Alito, Sonia Sotomayor, and Elena Kagan. During the October 2008 Term (which ended in June 2009), 7,738 cases were filed with the Court. The Court granted review in only 87 of these cases, which is just over 1 percent. During its 2008 Term, the Court issued only seventy-four signed opinions (Chief Justice's 2009 Year-End Report on the Federal Judiciary, December 31, 2009, p. 2). Of course, even a small number of Supreme Court opinions can have a major impact on the law, because they settle conflicts among lower courts and resolve salient issues of law and public policy.

Military Tribunals

Crimes committed by persons in military service are ordinarily prosecuted in proceedings before **courts-martial**. Article 1, Section 8 of the U.S. Constitution grants Congress the authority to regulate the armed forces. Under this authority, Congress has enacted the **Uniform Code of Military Justice** (UCMJ), 10 U.S.C.A. §§ 801–940. The UCMJ gives courts-martial jurisdiction to try all offenses under the code committed by military personnel. Notwithstanding this grant of authority, the United States Supreme Court held in 1969 that military jurisdiction was limited to offenses that were service connected. *O'Callahan v. Parker*, 395 U.S. 258, 89 S.Ct. 1683, 23 L.Ed.2d 291 (1969). The *O'Callahan* decision greatly narrowed military jurisdiction over offenses committed by servicepersons. In 1987 the Court, in a 5–4 decision, overruled *O'Callahan* and said that military jurisdiction depends solely on whether an accused is a military member. *Solorio v. United States*, 483 U.S. 435, 107 S.Ct. 2924, 97 L.Ed.2d 364 (1987). Thus, courts-martial may now try all offenses committed by servicepersons in violation of the UCMJ.

Go to the companion website for an edited version of the Supreme Court's decision in *Solorio v. United States*.

Commanders of various military units convene court-martial proceedings and appoint those who sit similar to a civilian jury. These commanders are called the convening authorities and are assisted by military lawyers designated as staff judge advocates. Military trial procedures and rules of evidence are similar to the rules applied in federal district courts.

There are three classes of court-martial: summary, special, and general. The summary court-martial is composed of one military officer with jurisdiction to impose minor punishments over enlisted personnel. It is somewhat analogous to trial by a civilian magistrate, whereas special and general court-martial proceedings are formal military tribunals more analogous to civilian criminal courts of record.

A special court-martial must be composed of three or more members with or without a military judge, or a military judge alone, if requested by the accused. It can impose more serious punishments on both officers and enlisted personnel. A general court-martial tries the most serious offenses and must consist of five or more members and a military judge (or a military judge alone, if requested by the accused). A general court-martial may try any offense made punishable by the UCMJ and may impose any punishment authorized by law against officers and enlisted personnel, including death for a capital offense. Trial by a military judge alone is not permitted in capital cases.

A military judge presides at special and general courts-martial. A trial counsel serves as prosecutor, and a defendant is furnished legal counsel by the government unless the accused chooses to employ private defense counsel. The extent of punishment that may be imposed varies according to the offense and the authority of the type of court-martial convened.

Decisions of courts-martial are reviewed by military courts of review in each branch of the armed forces. In specified instances, appeals are heard by the United States **Court of Appeals for the Armed Forces.** This court is staffed by civilian judges who are appointed to fifteen-year terms by the president with the consent of the Senate.

Only under conditions of martial law do military tribunals have the authority to try American citizens in civilian life who are not connected with the military or naval services. *Ex parte Milligan,* 71 U.S. (4 Wall.) 2, 18 L.Ed. 281 (1866). Historically, the Supreme Court has permitted "enemy aliens" captured during wartime to be tried by military tribunals. See *Ex parte Quirin*, 317 U.S. 1, 63 S. Ct. 2, 87 L.Ed. 7 (1942). Under an executive order issued by President George W. Bush on November 13, 2001, the military established special tribunals to try foreign nationals accused of terrorism against the United States. Several accused terrorists detained at the U.S. Naval Base at Guantanamo Bay, Cuba were brought to trial, but the proceedings were interrupted by a dramatic decision from the nation's highest court. In *Hamdan v. Rumsfeld*, 548 U.S. 547, 126 S.Ct. 2749, 165 L.Ed.2d 723 (2006), the U.S. Supreme Court ruled that the military tribunals were neither authorized by federal law nor required by military necessity. Moreover, the Court held that they ran afoul of the Geneva Conventions governing the treatment of prisoners of war.

Go to the companion website for edited versions of the Supreme Court's decisions in *Ex parte Milligan, Ex parte Quirin*, and *Hamdan v. Rumsfeld*.

In passing the Military Commissions Act of 2006, Pub. L. No. 109-366, 120 Stat. 2600 (Oct. 17, 2006), Congress provided for "the use of military commissions to try alien unlawful enemy combatants engaged in hostilities against the United States for violations of the law of war and other offenses triable by military commission." Immediately after his inauguration in January 2009, President Obama issued executive orders closing the Guantanamo Bay detention facility and suspending trials underway there. President Obama's orders created new uncertainties as to the future role of military tribunals in the war on terrorism.

State Court Systems

Each state has its own independent judicial system. These courts handle more than 90 percent of criminal prosecutions in the United States. State judicial systems are characterized by variations in structure, jurisdiction, and procedure but have certain commonalities. Every state has one or more levels of trial courts and at least one appellate court. Most states have **courts of general jurisdiction,** which conduct trials in felony and major misdemeanor cases, and **courts of limited jurisdiction,** which handle pretrial matters and conduct trials in minor misdemeanor cases. Most states also have some form of intermediate appellate courts that relieve the **state supreme court** (known as the Court of Appeals in New York and Maryland) from hearing routine appeals. Many states also have separate **juvenile courts,** which operate in ways that differ significantly from the criminal courts for adults.

Some states, like North Carolina, have adopted tidy, streamlined court systems (see Figure 2.2). Other states' court systems are extremely complex, as is the case in Texas (see Figure 2.3). In structural complexity, most states' systems fall somewhere between the two extremes.

Contrasting Judicial Functions and Environments

As we noted in Chapter 1, trial courts primarily make factual determinations, often assisted by juries; apply settled law to established facts; and impose sanctions. Appellate courts, on the other hand, interpret the federal and state constitutions and statutes, correct errors in law made by trial courts, and develop the law by "filling in the gaps" that often become apparent in the application of statutory laws.

The difference in the roles of trial and appellate courts is also evident in the environment where trial and appellate judges perform their functions. A trial court usually sits in a county courthouse or other county judicial building. Trial judges preside over courtrooms where there is considerable daily activity with the impaneling of juries, testimony of witnesses, and attorneys making objections and pleas for their clients. At other times the judges are busy hearing arguments in their chambers. In short, the trial scene is one of high visibility and is often attended by numerous

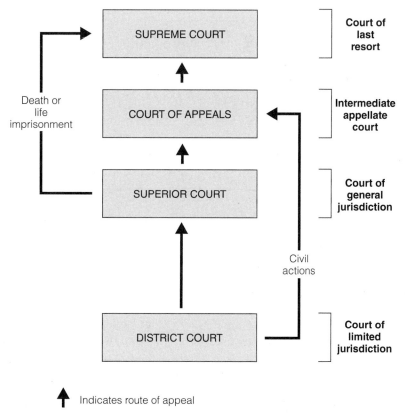

FIGURE 2.2 The North Carolina court system. Source: U.S. Department of Justice/ National Center for State Courts.

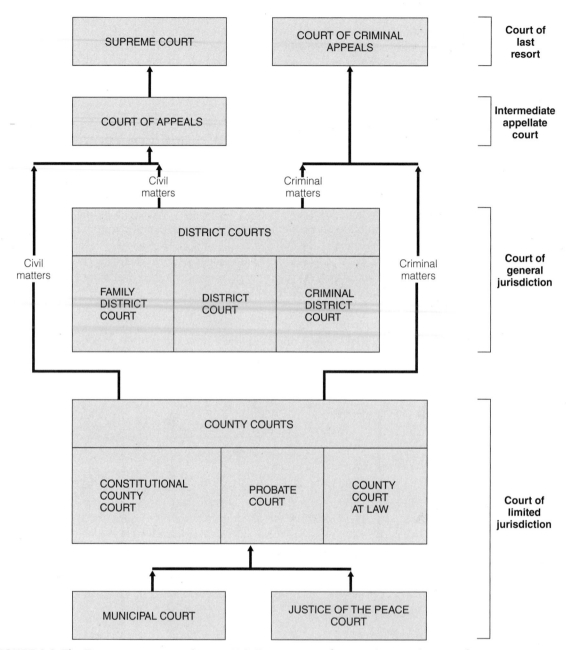

FIGURE 2.3 The Texas court system. Source: U.S. Department of Justice/National Center for State Courts.

spectators and, where a high-profile case is being tried, by members of the print and television media. In short, the trial court setting is a venue of daily interaction between court personnel and the citizens of the community.

In contrast, appellate courts are often described as "invisible courts" because their public proceedings are generally limited to hearing legal arguments by attorneys on prescribed oral argument days. Few clients and even fewer spectators are generally in attendance. Media representatives usually attend only when some high-profile appeal is being argued. Many of the documents are delivered by mail to a staff of clerks. Proceedings are resolved primarily by review of records from the lower court or administrative agency, by study of the law briefs submitted by counsel, and by discussion among the panel of judges assigned a particular case, often supplemented by independent research by judges and their staff attorneys.

Unlike a trial court, which is normally surrounded by a busy atmosphere, an appellate court often sits in the state capitol building or in its own facility, usually with a complete law library. The décor in the buildings that house appellate courts is usually quite formal, and often features portraits of former judges regarded as oracles of the law. When a panel of judges sits to hear oral arguments, they normally emerge from behind a velvet curtain on a precise schedule and to the cry of the court's marshal. When not hearing oral arguments, appellate judges usually occupy a suite of offices with their secretaries and law clerks. It is in these individual chambers that appellate judges study and write their opinions on cases assigned to them.

The United States Supreme Court occupies a majestic building in Washington, D.C., with spacious office suites and impressive corridors and library facilities. With enhancements and attributes similar to those of appellate courts, the elegance and dignity of the facilities comport with the significant role of the Court as final arbiter in the nation's judicial system. There is a sparse crowd at most state and intermediate federal appellate courts; at the Supreme Court, by contrast, parties interested in the decisions that will result from arguments, a coterie of media persons, and many spectators fill the courtroom to hear arguments in cases that often significantly affect the economic, social, and political life of the nation. Photography is not allowed, and the arguments and dialogue between the counsel and the justices are observed silently and respectfully by those who attend. There is sometimes a contrasting scene outside the Supreme Court building, where demonstrators gather to give visibility to the causes they represent.

The Juvenile Justice System

The juvenile justice system includes specialized courts, law enforcement agencies, social services agencies, and corrections facilities designed to address problems of **juvenile delinquency** as well as child neglect and abuse. "Delinquency" refers to conduct that would be criminal if committed by an adult. In addition to being charged with delinquency, young people may be subjected to the jurisdiction of a juvenile court for engaging in conduct that is prohibited only for minors. Such behaviors, which include truancy (chronic absence from school) and incorrigibility, are often called **status offenses,** because they are peculiar to the status of children.

Historical Basis

The common law treated all persons above the age of fourteen as adults for purposes of criminal responsibility (see Chapter 14). Because the American legal system was based on English common law, American courts followed the common-law rules for the treatment of juveniles. Young teenagers were treated essentially as adults for the purposes of criminal justice. During the colonial period of American history, it was not uncommon for teenagers to be hanged, flogged, or placed in the public pillory as punishment for their crimes. Later, as state penitentiaries were established, it was not unusual for 20 percent of prison populations to be juveniles.

In the late nineteenth century, public outcry against treating juveniles like adults led to the establishment of a separate juvenile justice system in the United States.

Reformers were convinced that the existing system of criminal justice was inappropriate for young offenders who were more in need of guidance than punishment. Reformers proposed specialized courts to deal with young offenders not as hardened criminals, but as misguided youth in need of special care. This special treatment was justified legally by the concept of **parens patriae,** the power of the state to act to protect the interests of those who cannot protect themselves.

The first state to act in this area was Illinois in 1899. By the 1920s, many states had followed suit, and by 1945, juvenile court legislation had been enacted by Congress and all state legislatures. The newly created juvenile courts were usually separate from the regular tribunals. Often, the judges or referees presiding over these courts did not have formal legal training. The proceedings were generally nonadversarial, and there was little in the way of procedural regularity or even the opportunity for the juvenile offender to confront his or her accusers. In fact, juvenile delinquency proceedings were conceived as civil, as opposed to criminal, proceedings. Dispositions of cases were usually nonpunitive in character; therefore, accused juvenile offenders were not afforded most of the rights of criminal defendants.

Because the juvenile justice system emphasized rehabilitation (rather than retribution, incapacitation, or deterrence), juveniles who were found delinquent were often placed in reformatories for indeterminate periods, sometimes until they reached the age of majority. Juvenile courts often suffered from lack of trained staff and adequate facilities, and by the 1960s, a system that was conceived by reformers was itself under attack by a new generation of reformers.

The Constitutional Reform of Juvenile Justice

Go to the companion website for an edited version of the Supreme Court's decision in *In re Gault.*

The abuses that came to be associated with juvenile courts were addressed by the Supreme Court in the landmark case of *In re Gault,* 387 U.S. 1, 87 S.Ct. 1428, 18 L.Ed.2d 527 (1967). In *Gault,* the Court essentially required that juvenile courts adhere to standards of due process, applying most of the basic procedural safeguards enjoyed by adults accused of crimes. Moreover, *Gault* held that juvenile courts must respect the right to counsel, the freedom from compulsory self-incrimination, and the right to confront (cross-examine) hostile witnesses. Writing for a nearly unanimous bench, Justice Fortas observed that "under our Constitution, the condition of being a boy does not justify a kangaroo court." 387 U.S. at 28, 87 S.Ct. at 1444, 18 L.Ed.2d at 546.

Four years later in *McKeiver v. Pennsylvania,* 403 U.S. 528, 91 S.Ct. 1976, 29 L.Ed.2d 647 (1971), the Court refused to extend the right to trial by jury to juvenile proceedings. In *Schall v. Martin,* 467 U.S. 253, 104 S.Ct. 2403, 81 L.Ed.2d 207 (1984), the Court upheld a pretrial detention program for juveniles that might well have been found violative of due process had it applied to adults. Writing for the Court, Justice Rehnquist stressed that "the Constitution does not mandate elimination of all differences in the treatment of juveniles." 467 U.S. at 263, 104 S.Ct. at 2409, 81 L.Ed.2d at 216.

In the wake of *Gault,* a number of states revised their juvenile codes to reflect the requirements of those decisions and to increase the qualifications of persons serving as juvenile judges and to transform juvenile courts into courts of record. Today it is common for the juvenile court to be simply a division of a court of general jurisdiction, such as a circuit or a superior court. Nevertheless, juvenile courts retain their distinctive character. For example, juvenile court proceedings are not subject to the constitutional "public trial" requirement. The Federal Juvenile Delinquency Act, 18 U.S.C.A. §§ 5031–5042, gives the court discretion on the issue of whether to close proceedings involving a child and whether to grant public access to the records of the proceedings. State laws vary, often allowing the presiding judge to exercise discretion in these matters. Despite reforms enacted after *Gault*, there remain significant differences in the adjudication of juvenile cases and adult criminal proceedings as well as the punishments imposed.

The Corrections System

The **corrections system** is designed to fulfill the criminal justice system's objective of providing punishment and rehabilitation of offenders. As with the court system, corrections facilities are operated at the federal and state levels. The system includes prisons and jails as well as a variety of programs such as probation, parole, and supervised community service.

Historical Background

Punishments inflicted under the English common law were quite severe—the death penalty was prescribed for most felonies, and those convicted of misdemeanors were generally subjected to such corporal punishment as flogging in the public square. The new American colonies generally followed common-law practice; by the time of the American Revolution, the death penalty was in wide use for a variety of felonies, and corporal punishment, primarily flogging, was widely used for a variety of crimes.

The American **Bill of Rights** (the first ten amendments to the Constitution, ratified in 1791) prohibited the imposition of "cruel and unusual punishments" (Eighth Amendment). The Framers sought to prevent the use of torture, which had been common in Europe as late as the eighteenth century; however, they did not intend to outlaw the death penalty or abolish all forms of corporal punishment.

During the nineteenth century, reformers introduced the concept of the **penitentiary**—literally, "a place to do penance." The idea was that criminals could be reformed through isolation, Bible study, and hard labor. This gave rise to the notion of *rehabilitation*—the idea that the criminal justice system could reform criminals and reintegrate them into society. Many of the educational, occupational training, and psychological programs found in modern prisons are based on this theory.

Contemporary Developments in Criminal Punishment

By the twentieth century, incarceration largely replaced corporal punishment as the states, as well as the federal government, constructed prisons to house persons convicted of felonies. Even cities and counties constructed jails for the confinement of persons convicted of misdemeanors. The **death penalty,** an intensely controversial penalty, remains in effect today for certain federal offenses and in more than half the states for the most aggravated cases of murder. Today, the focus of criminal punishment is on the goal of incapacitation to prevent commission of further crimes.

There are procedural as well as substantive issues in the area of sentencing and punishment. Sharp disagreements exist regarding the roles that legislatures, judges, and corrections officials should play in determining punishments. Specifically, criminal punishment is limited by the Eighth Amendment prohibition of **cruel and unusual punishments,** the Due Process Clauses of the Fifth and Fourteenth

Amendments, and by similar provisions in all fifty state constitutions. Today the criminal law provides for a variety of criminal punishments, including **monetary fines, incarceration, probation, community service,** and, of course, the death penalty.

As with courts, there is a federal corrections system and fifty separate state corrections systems. Each of these systems is responsible for supervising those persons sentenced to prison by courts of law. Originally, prisons were conceived as places for criminals to reflect on their misdeeds and repent; hence the term "penitentiary." In the twentieth century, the emphasis shifted to rehabilitation through psychological and sociopsychological methods. Unfortunately, these efforts were less than successful. Ironically, prisons appear to "criminalize" individuals more than they rehabilitate them. Inmates are exposed to an insular society with norms of conduct antithetical to those of civil society. As essentially totalitarian institutions, prisons do not encourage individuals to behave responsibly; furthermore, prisons provide an excellent venue for the spreading of criminal techniques. It is probably unrealistic to expect rehabilitation programs to succeed in such an environment. Today, prisons are generally regarded as little more than a way to punish and isolate those persons deemed unfit to live in civil society.

The Burgeoning Prison Population

At midyear 2007, there were nearly 2.4 million inmates in the United States. About 1.6 million prisoners were incarcerated in the federal or state prison systems; nearly 800,000 more were held in local jails, juvenile facilities, territorial prisons, military prisons, detention facilities operated by federal immigration authorities, or jails located on Indian reservations (U.S. Department of Justice, Office of Justice Programs, Bureau of Justice Statistics Bulletin, "Prison and Jail Inmates at Midyear 2007," June 6, 2008, NCJ-221944). In 2007, more than 7.3 million people were in jail or prison or on probation or parole, which is slightly more than 3 percent of all adult residents in the United States. Incarceration rates vary greatly by gender and race. At the end of 2005, 92 percent of inmates in state and federal prisons and local jails were male (U.S. Department of Justice, Office of Justice Programs, Bureau of Justice Statistics Bulletin, "Census of State and Federal Correctional Facilities, 2005," October 2008, NCJ 222182). At midyear 2007, black males comprised 36 percent of all inmates held in custody in the nation's prisons and jails. Nearly 5 percent of all black males in the general population were in prison or jail, compared to roughly 2 percent of Hispanic males and less than 1 percent of white males (U.S. Department of Justice, Office of Justice Programs, Bureau of Justice Statistics Bulletin, "Prison and Jail Inmates at Midyear 2007," June 6, 2008, NCJ-221944).

After two decades of very rapid growth, the last few years have seen slower growth rates in state and federal prison populations (see "Slower Growth in the Nation's Prison and Jail Populations," Bureau of Justice Statistics, June 6, 2008). Despite a boom in prison construction in recent decades, most prisons are operating beyond design capacity and some prisons are seriously overcrowded. Responding to lawsuits based on the Eighth Amendment's Cruel and Unusual Punishments Clause, federal courts have imposed limits on some prison populations. In 2005, about one in eight state prisons were under federal court orders to reduce prison populations (U.S. Department of Justice, Office of Justice Programs, Bureau of Justice Statistics Bulletin, "Census of State and Federal Correctional Facilities, 2005," October 2008, NCJ 222182).

The Future Outlook

The public continues to demand harsh sentences for convicted felons, but legislators (and taxpayers) are often unwilling to pay the price of constructing more prisons. Moreover, local residents often object to prisons being built in their "backyards." Even those states that have been aggressive in prison construction have found that demand for cell space continues to exceed supply. In many instances, federal courts have ordered prison officials to reduce overcrowding to comply with the U.S. Constitution's prohibition against "cruel and unusual punishments."

In many state prisons, cells originally designed for one or two inmates now house three or four prisoners. Increasingly, state prison systems must rely on local jails to house inmates, a situation that presents its own set of problems relating both to security and to conditions of confinement. Aside from the threat of federal judicial intervention, overcrowded prisons are more likely to produce inmate violence and even riots.

In addition to prisons, corrections systems include agencies that supervise probation, parole, community service, and other forms of alternative sentences. With burgeoning prison populations, these alternatives to incarceration are assuming more importance and consuming more resources, especially at the state level.

Conclusion

The American system of criminal justice is extremely complicated. The primary reason for this complexity is the principle of federalism, which refers to the division of political and legal authority in this country between one national government and fifty state governments. The United States Congress on behalf of the national government and each state legislature on behalf of its respective state enact their own criminal laws. The national government and all fifty state governments have their own law enforcement agencies, prosecutors, courts, and prison systems. No two systems are exactly alike. Indeed, there is tremendous variation from one jurisdiction to the next, both in the substantive criminal law and in the practices and procedures used by the various components of the criminal process. Yet, despite their substantive and procedural differences, all jurisdictions share two basic goals: to protect society from crime and, at the same time, to protect the rights of the individuals suspected of having committed offenses. Much of the conflict and inefficiency inherent in our criminal justice system stems from the need to balance these two competing objectives.

Chapter Summary

- **LO1** Under our system of federalism, the national government and each of the fifty states operates its own system of criminal justice. Each has its own legislature, law enforcement and corrections agencies, and courts of law.
- **LO2** Because the federal government and the government of each state enacts its own criminal laws and has its own system of courts to interpret those laws, there are significant variations across the states and between the state and federal systems.
- **LO3** The U.S. Congress enacts laws defining federal crimes and setting punishments for those crimes. State legislatures define offenses and set punishments for their states and authorize local governing bodies to enact ordinances defining minor offenses and setting penalties. Federal courts interpret and apply acts of

Congress; state courts do likewise with regard to their respective states' laws. Federal law enforcement agencies enforce federal laws; state and local agencies enforce state criminal prohibitions.

- **LO4** State legislatures have inherently broad powers to enact laws to further the public safety, order, health, and welfare. Congress's legislative powers are restricted to constitutionally enumerated and implied powers, although in the modern era these powers have been exercised and interpreted quite broadly.

- **LO5** Criminal laws are written in general terms and sometimes the meaning of criminal prohibitions is unclear. Courts must interpret statutes to determine their meaning as applied to particular cases. American courts basically follow the doctrine of following precedent (*stare decisis*). This provides predictability and stability in the law. Where legislative bodies use certain terms that are not defined, judges look to the common law for definitions and follow certain canons of construction for interpreting statutes that are unclear.

- **LO6** Numerous federal and state agencies are responsible for enforcement of the criminal law. They investigate suspected criminal activity, arrest suspected criminals, and detain arrested persons until their cases come before the appropriate courts. Unlike their medieval forebears, modern law enforcement agencies are highly constrained by law and emphasize professionalism.

- **LO7** The U.S. Attorney General heads the Department of Justice. United States. Attorneys and their assistants prosecute federal offenses. At the state level a state or district attorney is the prosecutor. The prosecutor serves a vital function in the criminal justice system and is vested with broad discretion in determining whether to bring charges and if so, the level of those charges. Defense counsel are guardians of the defendant's constitutional rights and the legality of the system. Defense attorneys serve as counselors to assist defendants in determining their best course of action and represent a defendant at trial when he or she elects to plead not guilty. Indigent defendants are entitled to government-furnished counsel, usually a public defender.

- **LO8** At the federal level and in many states grand juries review evidence of criminal activity and determine whether to hand down an indictment or presentment. In other states a prosecutor files a sworn accusatorial document (an "information") and a court empanels a trial jury is to hear evidence against a defendant who pleads not guilty and requests a trial by jury.

- **LO9** The judicial branch operates through trial and appellate courts at both the national and state levels. At the national level U.S. District Courts are staffed by judges and U.S. Attorneys who prosecute federal offenses. The United States Courts of Appeal hear appeals from decisions of these courts. At the state levels, where most criminal trials occur, trial courts conduct trials, sentence defendants found guilty and deal with post-trial functions. Appellate courts correct errors made at the trial level and, where it becomes necessary, fill in the gaps of the statutory law by exercising a lawmaking function. At the apex of the system is the U.S. Supreme Court, where nine justices who serve for life become the final arbiters of whether federal and state laws pass constitutional muster. The Supreme Court has jurisdiction to review, either on appeal or by writ of certiorari (discretionary review), all the decisions of the lower federal courts and many decisions of the highest state courts.

- **LO10** Military tribunals have both similarities to and differences from civilian courts. A military commander convenes a court-martial composed of military officers and, in some instances, enlisted personnel. These tribunals are empowered to try any offense by military personnel under the Uniform Code of Military

Justice. A trial counsel serves as prosecutor and defendants are furnished military lawyers unless they choose to employ civilian attorneys. Court-martial jurisdiction and level of authorized punishment depends on whether the court-martial is summary, special, or general. A military judge presides at special and general courts-martial. Military courts basically follow federal court procedures and rules of evidence. The military has an appellate system consisting of courts of review and the U.S. Court of Appeals for the Armed Forces.

- **LO11** Juvenile justice is administered differently from regular courts and is beyond the purview of this book. It should be noted that the system has evolved from one that focused on rehabilitation to an adversarial system due process model. Today the juvenile justice system includes specialized courts, law enforcement agencies, social services agencies, and corrections facilities that address juvenile delinquency and child neglect and abuse. In addition to statutory offenses, juveniles are subject to punishment for certain status offenses. Juveniles are entitled to most constitutional rights afforded adults but they are not entitled to jury trials.

- **LO12** Federal and state corrections facilities include prisons and jails as well as probation, parole, and supervised community service. The corrections process includes the death penalty for certain federal offenses and for murder under the laws of many states. Additional corrective procedures include incarceration, monetary fines, probation, and parole. Today, the focus of criminal punishment is on the goal of incapacitation to prevent commission of further crimes. Increasingly, the public demands that those who commit the most serious felonies be sentenced to lengthy prison terms. As a result, prisons are overflowing, and in many instances federal courts have ordered prison officials to reduce overcrowding to comply with the U.S. Constitution's prohibition against "cruel and unusual punishments."

Key Terms

federalism The constitutional distribution of government power and responsibility between the national government and the states.

legislature An elected lawmaking body such as the Congress of the United States or a state assembly.

United States Congress The national legislature of the United States, consisting of the Senate and the House of Representatives.

statute A generally applicable law enacted by a legislature.

enumerated powers Powers explicitly granted to governments by their constitutions.

implied powers Powers not expressly granted to government by a constitution but fairly implied by the document.

U.S. Code The comprehensive and systematic collection of federal laws currently in effect.

United States Code Annotated (U.S.C.A.) An annotated version of the United States Code. The annotations include references to court decisions and other legal authorities.

session laws Collection of laws enacted during a particular legislative session.

mala prohibita "Prohibited evil." *Mala prohibita* offenses are those that are wrong primarily because the law declares them to be wrong, as distinct from *mala in se* offenses, which are deemed to be inherently evil.

rules of statutory interpretation Rules developed by courts to determine the meaning of legislative acts.

plain meaning rule The judicial doctrine holding that if the meaning of a text is plain, a court may not interpret it but must simply apply it as written.

canons of construction Rules governing the judicial interpretation of constitutions, statutes, and other written instruments.

legislative intent The purpose the legislature sought to achieve in enacting a particular provision of law.

void for vagueness Doctrine of constitutional law holding unconstitutional (as a violation of due process) legislation that fails to clearly inform the person of what is required or proscribed.

implied exception An exclusion that can reasonably be inferred or assumed based on the purpose and intent of an ordinance, statute, or contract.

sworn officers Law enforcement officers sworn to uphold the Constitution and laws of the United States and of their own states.

Federal Bureau of Investigation (FBI) The primary federal agency charged with investigating violations of federal criminal laws.

Department of Justice (DOJ) The department within the executive branch of the federal government that is headed by the Attorney General and staffed by U.S. Attorneys.

special agents Officers of the FBI with the power to make arrests and use force in the enforcement of federal law.

United States Marshals Service Law enforcement officers of the U.S. Department of Justice who are responsible for enforcing federal laws, enforcing federal court decisions, and effecting the transfer of federal prisoners.

sheriff The chief law enforcement officer of a county.

police departments Agencies, established by municipalities and sometimes states, whose function is to enforce the criminal laws within their respective jurisdictions

order maintenance The police officer's function of keeping the peace, as distinct from enforcement of the law.

community policing Style of police work that stresses development of close ties between police officers and the communities they serve.

prosecutor A public official empowered to initiate criminal charges and conduct prosecutions.

plea bargaining Negotiations between defense lawyers and prosecutors, often leading to agreements under which defendants agree to plead guilty in exchange for concessions (such as a reduction in the number or severity of charges brought).

Attorney General The highest legal officer of a state or of the United States.

United States Attorneys Lawyers appointed by the president with consent of the U.S. Senate to prosecute federal crimes in federal judicial districts.

independent counsel A special prosecutor appointed to investigate and, if warranted, prosecute official misconduct.

state's attorneys State prosecutors.

nolle prosequi A formal entry by a prosecutor who declines to proceed further in the prosecution of an offense; commonly called a *nol pros.*

indigent defendants Persons accused of crimes who cannot afford to retain private legal counsel and are therefore entitled to be represented by a public defender or a court-appointed lawyer.

public defender An attorney responsible for defending indigent persons charged with crimes.

defense attorney A lawyer who represents defendants in criminal cases.

jury A group of citizens convened for the purpose of deciding factual questions relevant to a civil or criminal case.

grand jury A group of citizens convened either to conduct an investigation or to determine whether there is sufficient evidence to warrant the prosecution of an accused.

petit (trial) jury A trial jury, usually composed of either six or twelve persons.

true bill An indictment handed down by a grand jury in a criminal case.

no bill Decision of a grand jury not to return an indictment.

indictment A formal document handed down by a grand jury accusing one or more persons of the commission of a crime or crimes.

prosecutor's information An accusatorial document filed under oath by a prosecutor charging a person with one or more violations of the criminal law; similar to an indictment issued by a grand jury.

speedy and public trial An open and public criminal trial held without unreasonable delay as required by the Sixth Amendment to the U.S. Constitution.

trial courts Judicial tribunals usually presided over by one judge who conducts proceedings and trials in civil and criminal cases with or without a jury.

appellate courts Judicial tribunals that review decisions from lower tribunals.

jurisdiction The authority of a court to hear and decide certain categories of legal disputes. Jurisdiction relates to the authority of a court over the person, subject matter, and geographical area.

United States District Courts The principal trial courts in the federal system, which sit in ninety-four districts. Usually, one judge hears proceedings and trials in civil and criminal cases.

intermediate appellate courts Judicial tribunals consisting of three or more judges that review decisions of trial courts but that are subordinate to the final appellate tribunals.

United States Courts of Appeals The twelve intermediate appellate courts of appeals in the federal system that sit in specified geographical areas of the United States and in which panels of appellate judges hear appeals in civil and criminal cases, primarily from the U.S. District Courts.

***en banc* hearing** A hearing in an appellate court in which all or a substantial number of the judges assigned to that court participate.

United States Supreme Court The highest court in the United States, consisting of nine justices, that has jurisdiction to review, by appeal or writ of certiorari, the decisions of lower federal courts and many decisions of the highest courts of each state.

writ of certiorari Order issued by an appellate court to grant discretionary review of a case decided by a lower court.

rules of procedure Rules promulgated by courts of law under constitutional or statutory authority governing procedures for trials and other judicial proceedings.

court-martial A military tribunal convened by a commander of a military unit to try a person subject to the Uniform Code of Military Justice who is accused of violating a provision of that code.

Uniform Code of Military Justice (UCMJ) A code of laws enacted by Congress that governs military service personnel and defines the procedural and evidentiary requirements in military law and the substantive criminal offenses and punishments.

Court of Appeals for the Armed Forces The court (formerly known as the Court of Military Appeals), consisting of five civilian judges, which reviews sentences affecting a general or flag officer or imposing the death penalty and cases certified for review by the judge advocate general of a branch of service. May grant review of convictions and sentences on petitions by service members.

courts of general jurisdiction Courts that conduct trials in felony and major misdemeanor cases. Also refers to courts that have jurisdiction to hear civil as well as criminal cases.

courts of limited jurisdiction Courts that handle pretrial matters and conduct trials in minor misdemeanor cases.

state supreme court The highest appellate court of a state.

juvenile court A judicial tribunal having jurisdiction over minors defined as juveniles who are alleged to be status offenders or to have committed acts of delinquency.

juvenile delinquency Actions of a juvenile in violation of the criminal law.

status offenses Noncriminal conduct on the part of juveniles that may subject them to the authority of a juvenile court.

parens patriae "The parent of the country." Refers to the role of the state as the guardian of minors, mentally ill individuals, and other legally disabled persons.

corrections system The system of prisons, jails, and other penal and correctional institutions.

Bill of Rights A written enumeration of basic rights, usually part of a written constitution—for example, the first ten amendments to the U.S. Constitution.

penitentiary Prison. Literally, a place for doing penance.

death penalty Capital punishment; a sentence to death for the commission of a crime.

cruel and unusual punishments Criminal penalties that shock the moral conscience of the community—for example, torture and other extreme forms of corporal punishment. Prohibited by the Eighth Amendment to the U.S. Constitution.

monetary fines Sums of money that offenders are required to pay as punishment for the commission of crimes.

incarceration Imprisonment.

probation Conditional release of a convicted criminal in lieu of incarceration.

parole Conditional release from jail or prison of a person who has served part of his or her sentence.

community service A sentence or condition of probation requiring that the criminal perform some specific service to the community for some specified period of time.

Questions for Thought and Discussion

1. How does the concept of federalism complicate the administration of criminal justice in the United States?
2. Describe the functions of federal and state law enforcement agencies.
3. Compare and contrast the functions of trial and appellate courts. How are they similar? How are they different?
4. What function does a grand jury serve? Does replacement of the indictment function of grand juries at the state level with prosecutors authorized to charge crimes by filing a sworn information impair the rights of citizens charged with crimes?
5. Is there a justification for the broad discretion vested in a prosecutor?
6. To what extent does the United States Constitution protect the right to trial by jury in a criminal case?
7. What are the arguments for and against allowing trial judges broad discretion in criminal sentencing?
8. What factors do you think a prosecutor should take into consideration in determining whether to prosecute an individual the police have arrested for possession of illegal drugs?
9. What chief characteristics distinguish the military justice system under the Uniform Code of Military Justice from civilian criminal prosecutions?
10. What factors should a judge consider in determining whether to sentence a convicted felon to prison?

PART TWO

The Substantive Criminal Law

CHAPTER **3**

Constitutional Limitations on the Prohibition of Criminal Conduct

LEARNING OBJECTIVES

After reading this chapter, you should be able to explain . . .

1. what judicial review is and why it is important to the criminal law
2. how and why the U.S. Congress has created a body of federal criminal law
3. how the federal constitution defines the crime of treason
4. bills of attainder and *ex post facto* laws and why they are constitutionally prohibited
5. how and why the Bill of Rights impacts the criminal law at both the federal and state levels
6. how the freedoms of speech, religion, and assembly enshrined in the First Amendment limit the enactment and enforcement of certain criminal prohibitions such as obscenity laws
7. the different interpretations of the Second Amendment right to keep and bear arms and the implications of these different interpretations for the criminal law
8. how and why the U.S. Constitution prohibits criminal laws that are overbroad and/or excessively vague
9. how the freedom from compulsory self-incrimination limits laws that require parties to report certain types of information to the government
10. how and why the Eighth Amendment's prohibition against cruel and unusual punishments makes it unconstitutional for government to criminalize "status"
11. how the constitutional right of privacy has evolved to protect people from criminal prohibitions of consensual sexual conduct
12. how and why courts have recognized a "right to die"
13. why the provision of the Fourteenth Amendment regarding equal protection of the laws is important in limiting the enforcement of criminal prohibitions
14. the standards that courts employ when reviewing statutes challenged as being unconstitutional
15. why the state constitutions also provide significant constraints on the enactment and enforcement of statutes

CHAPTER OUTLINE

The Second Amendment provides, "A well regulated Militia, being necessary to the security of a free State, the right of the people to keep and bear Arms, shall not be infringed." Over the years this language has been the source of considerable scholarly commentary and political controversy. In recent decades governments at all levels have enacted laws regulating, and in some instances, prohibiting the possession and use of firearms. Many of these prohibitions are criminal in nature. Are such gun control laws consistent with the Second Amendment? Until recently the Supreme Court, stressing the "well regulated Militia" language of the Amendment, seemed to have little problem with gun control laws. However, in *District of Columbia v. Heller*, 554 U.S. ___, 128 S.Ct. 2783, 171 L.Ed.2d 637 (2008), the Court held that the Second Amendment protects an individual's right to possess a firearm in the home for personal protection. In so holding, the Court struck down a Washington, D.C. ordinance that effectively banned possession of handguns in the District, even in the home.

The *Heller* decision left open the question of whether this personal right to bear arms limits state and local governments from enforcing similar prohibitions. After all, the Second Amendment, like the other amendments found in the Bill of Rights, was adopted as a limitation on the national government. Because Washington, D.C. is a federal enclave, there was never any question that the Second Amendment applied to it. Immediately after the *Heller* decision, gun rights activists sought to challenge handgun bans in cities across America. In 2010 one of these challenges resulted in a decision by the Supreme Court.

In *McDonald v. Chicago*, 561 U.S. ___, 130 S.Ct. 3020, 177 L. Ed. 2d 894 (2010), the Supreme Court held that the Second Amendment applies to state and local governments via the Fourteenth Amendment, which prohibits states from depriving persons of liberty without due process of law. The Court basically held that the right to keep and bear arms is an essential aspect of liberty. Furthermore, the Court reaffirmed what it said in *Heller*—that the right to keep and bear arms is a personal right irrespective of any service in a militia.

Both *Heller* and *McDonald* were 5–4 decisions. Both produced strongly worded dissenting opinions from justices in the minority. Both show the ongoing relevance of the U.S. Constitution to the criminal law. Congress, the state legislatures, and city and county lawmaking bodies cannot enact just any criminal prohibition that they deem to be in keeping with the public interest. Criminal laws must be consistent with the federal and state constitutions. This chapter examines the most important constitutional limitations on the enactment and enforcement of criminal laws.

Introduction

In most democratic countries, legislative bodies are supreme in enacting statutes defining crimes and providing penalties. The only overarching authority is the will of the people, as manifested through the ballot box. Being very familiar with the English monarchy and its parliamentary system, the framers of the U.S. Constitution understood that unbridled power to make and enforce criminal prohibitions constitutes a serious threat to liberty. Thus, they framed a Constitution that limits the power of Congress and state legislatures to enact criminal statutes. Although federal and state legislative bodies have authority to enact statutes defining crimes and setting penalties, various provisions of the U.S. Constitution and state constitutions limit that power.

Our goal in this chapter is to provide an overview of the various constitutional provisions that limit legislative authority to define conduct as criminal and prescribe penalties for violations or offenses. We discuss the effect of judicial interpretations of criminal statutes and the power of courts to declare void laws that violate the constitutional principles.

The Importance of Judicial Review

Constitutional limits on the enactment and enforcement of criminal statutes do not depend for their vitality only on the voluntary compliance of legislators, prosecutors, and police officers. Under the doctrine of judicial review, courts are empowered to declare null and void laws that violate constitutional principles. In a landmark decision in 1803, the Supreme Court first asserted the power to invalidate legislation that is in conflict with the Constitution. *Marbury v. Madison*, 5 U.S. (1 Cranch) 137, 2 L.Ed. 60 (1803). Speaking for the Court in *Marbury*, Chief Justice John Marshall said, "It is emphatically the province and duty of the judicial department to say what the law is." 5 U.S. (1 Cranch) at 177, 2 L.Ed. at 175. Although the power of judicial review is generally associated with the Supreme Court, all courts of record, whether state or federal, can exercise the power to strike down unconstitutional legislation. It is doubtful whether constitutional limitations on governmental power would be meaningful in the absence of judicial review.

Throughout this textbook, we will be discussing constitutional limitations on the criminal justice system. Many of these principles are procedural in nature, imposing restrictions and obligations on law enforcement, prosecution, adjudication, and sentencing. In this chapter we are concerned only with those constitutional provisions that place limits on the substantive criminal law, both in the types of laws that legislatures are barred from enacting and the situations in which police and prosecutors are barred from enforcing existing statutes.

Unconstitutional Per Se and Unconstitutional as Applied

In addressing constitutional assaults on criminal statutes, courts are sometimes asked to declare that a statute is unconstitutional under any circumstances, whereas in other instances a court might simply be asked to rule that the statute cannot constitutionally apply to certain conduct. A statute may be declared **unconstitutional per se** in that it inherently trenches on some constitutionally protected liberty or exceeds the constitutional powers of government. For example, a law that would restrict citizens' freedom to profess their religious beliefs would be inherently unconstitutional. Alternatively, a law that is facially valid, such as an ordinance prohibiting disorderly conduct, may be declared **unconstitutional as applied** if it is enforced in a way that impermissibly restricts or punishes the exercise of constitutional rights.

The Power to Enact Criminal Laws

Because our nation is committed to the rule of law, "there is no crime, there is no punishment, without law." As we saw in Chapter 1, no one can be guilty of a crime in the absence of a law that prohibits a particular type of wrongful conduct. As Chapter 2 pointed out, it is the role of legislatures to enact statutes that define crimes and provide for punishments.

Police Powers of State Legislatures

The police power of government is the authority to enact legislation to protect the public health, safety, order, welfare, and morality. Under our system of federalism, the police power of government is vested primarily in the state legislatures. State legislatures have comprehensive power to adopt statutes regulating the activities of individuals and corporations as long as these statutes do not violate limitations contained in the state and federal constitutions. State legislatures, in turn, may delegate some of this power to local governments, which enact ordinances defining criminal offenses within their jurisdictions.

The Federal Lawmaking Power

Unlike the state legislatures, the U.S. Congress does not possess plenary legislative authority (except over the District of Columbia and federal territories). As James Madison observed in 1788,

> The powers delegated by the proposed Constitution to the federal government are few and defined. Those which are to remain in the State governments are numerous and indefinite. *The Federalist* No. 45, pp. 292–293 (C. Rossiter, ed., 1961).

Article I, Section 8 of the U.S. Constitution enumerates Congress's legislative powers. Several of these enumerated powers allow Congress to enact criminal laws in certain areas. These include the power to establish rules governing immigration and naturalization, to "define and punish piracies and felonies committed on the high seas," and to "provide for the punishment of counterfeiting the securities and current coin of the United States."

Congress also possesses a reservoir of implied powers, which are justified by the Necessary and Proper Clause of Article I, Section 8. The doctrine of implied powers was established by the Supreme Court in *McCulloch v. Maryland,* 17 U.S. (4 Wheat.) 316, 4 L.Ed. 579 (1819). Writing for the Court, Chief Justice Marshall articulated the doctrine as follows:

> Let the end be legitimate, let it be within the scope of the Constitution, and all means which are plainly adapted to that end, which are not prohibited, but consist with the letter and spirit of the Constitution, are constitutional. 17 U.S. (4 Wheat.) at 421, 4 L.Ed. at 605.

The doctrine of implied powers expands the legislative capabilities of Congress but by no means confers on Congress the plenary legislative authority possessed by state legislatures. To qualify as a valid expression of implied powers, federal legislation must be "plainly adapted" to the goal of furthering one or more of Congress's enumerated powers.

The Commerce Clause

In terms of the criminal law, by far the most significant of Congress's enumerated powers is the power to regulate **interstate commerce**. For example, Congress is not empowered to prohibit prostitution per se, but Congress may make it a crime to transport persons across state lines for "immoral purposes" by drawing on its broad power to regulate interstate commerce. *Hoke v. United States,* 227 U.S. 308, 33 S.Ct. 281, 57 L.Ed. 523 (1913). Congress has relied on the Commerce Clause to enact a wide variety of criminal laws, including prohibitions against the following:

- interstate transportation of kidnapped persons (see 18 U.S.C.A. § 1201)
- interstate transportation of stolen automobiles (see 18 U.S.C.A. § 2312)
- manufacture, sale, distribution, and possession of controlled substances (see 21 U.S.C.A. § 801 *et seq.*)
- carjacking (see 18 U.S.C.A. § 2119)
- fraudulent schemes that use interstate television, radio, or wire communications (see 18 U.S.C.A. § 1343)
- conspiracies to restrain trade (see 15 U.S.C.A. § 1 *et seq.*)
- loan sharking (see 18 U.S.C.A. § 891 *et seq.*)
- computer crimes (see 18 U.S.C.A. § 1030)
- racketeering and organized crime (see 18 U.S.C.A. §§ 1961–1963)
- air pollution (see 42 U.S.C.A. §§ 7401–7642)
- water pollution (see 33 U.S.C.A. §§ 1251–1376)
- violations of regulations protecting endangered species (see 16 U.S.C.A. §§ 1531–1544)

In the modern era, Congress has stretched the concept of interstate commerce to justify broader authority to enact criminal statutes. For the most part, the courts have been willing to accommodate this expansion of federal legislative power. See, for example, *Perez v. United States,* 402 U.S. 146, 91 S.Ct. 1357, 28 L.Ed.2d 686 (1971). However, in recent years the Supreme Court has circumscribed this authority somewhat. In *United States v. Lopez,* 514 U.S. 549, 115 S.Ct. 1624, 131 L.Ed.2d 626 (1995), the Court struck down the Gun-Free School Zones Act of 1990, which made it a federal crime for any person to knowingly possess a firearm while close to a school. Writing for the Court, Chief Justice William Rehnquist observed that "the challenged statute has nothing to do with 'commerce' or any sort of economic enterprise, however broadly one might define those terms." 514 U.S. at 560, 115 S.Ct. at 1631, 131 L.Ed.2d at 639.

The Court's *Lopez* decision was reinforced by its decision in *United States v. Morrison,* 529 U.S. 598, 120 S.Ct. 1740, 146 L.Ed.2d 658 (2000), where the Court struck down a provision of the Violence Against Women Act of 1994 that provided a federal civil remedy to victims of gender-motivated violence. Together, *Lopez* and *Morrison* called into question a number of the criminal statutes enacted by Congress under the Commerce Clause. One of these was the federal Controlled Substances Act, 21 U.S.C.A. § 801, *et seq.,* which defines federal drug crimes (see Chapter 10). In 1996 the U.S. Court of Appeals for the Second Circuit rejected a *Lopez*-based challenge to 21 U.S.C.A. § 841, which makes it a crime "for any person knowingly or intentionally to manufacture, distribute, or dispense, or possess with intent to manufacture, distribute, or dispense, a controlled substance." The statute criminalizes the mere possession of even small quantities of controlled substances and does not require proof that a particular defendant's conduct affected interstate commerce. The circuit court distinguished 21 U.S.C.A. § 841 from the statute struck down in *Lopez,* observing that

Go to the companion website for edited versions of the Supreme Court's decisions in *Perez v. United States, United States v. Lopez,* and *United States v. Morrison.*

> the *Lopez* Court did not purport to overrule those cases that have upheld application of the Commerce Clause power to wholly intrastate activities, and we find no basis for extending the *Lopez* holding to the case before us. The Controlled Substances Act concerns an obviously economic activity. In addition, Congress has made specific findings that local narcotics activity has a substantial effect on interstate commerce. In contrast, the conduct that was criminalized in *Lopez* did not obviously concern economic activity, as the Court recognized. *United States v. Genao,* 79 F.3d 1333, 1337 (2nd Cir. 1996).

A more interesting problem was presented in *Gonzales v. Raich,* 545 U.S. 1, 125 S.Ct. 2195, 162 L.Ed.2d 1 (2005). The case involved two women who used marijuana for medical reasons based on the recommendation of their doctor as authorized by California's Compassionate Use Act of 1996. Under the federal Controlled Substances Act (CSA), the possession or use of marijuana is a crime and there is no exception for medicinal use (see *United States v. Oakland Cannabis Buyers' Cooperative,* 532 U.S. 483, 121 S.Ct. 1711, 149 L.Ed.2d 722 (2001)). When agents of the federal Drug Enforcement Administration learned that one of the women was cultivating marijuana in her home, they obtained a search warrant and seized and destroyed the plants. Subsequently, the women brought suit in federal court, claiming that Congress had no authority under the Commerce Clause to prohibit the possession and use of marijuana that is not intended for interstate distribution. Although the District Court rejected the claim, the U.S. Court of Appeals for the Ninth Circuit reversed on the basis of *Lopez* and *Morrison.* The Supreme Court reversed the Ninth Circuit, however, holding that Congress may criminalize the possession and medicinal use of marijuana. Writing for the Court in *Gonzales v. Raich,* Justice John Paul Stevens stressed the commercial aspects of the marijuana prohibition:

One need not have a degree in economics to understand why a nationwide exemption for the vast quantity of marijuana (or other drugs) locally cultivated for personal use (which presumably would include use by friends, neighbors, and family members) may have a substantial impact on the interstate market for this extraordinarily popular substance. The congressional judgment that an exemption for such a significant segment of the total market would undermine the orderly enforcement of the entire regulatory scheme is entitled to a strong presumption of validity. 545 U.S. at 28, 125 S.Ct. at 2212, 162 L.Ed.2d at 26.

Go to the companion website for an edited version of the Supreme Court's decision in *Gonzales v. Raich.*

In a dissenting opinion joined by Chief Justice Rehnquist and Associate Justice Clarence Thomas, Justice Sandra Day O'Connor suggested that the Court had backtracked from the commitment to principles of federalism expressed in decisions like *Lopez* and *Morrison. Gonzales v. Raich* suggests that despite the decisions in *Lopez* and *Morrison,* Congress retains broad authority under the Commerce Clause to deal with social problems of national scope.

Delimiting the Crime of Treason

Treason involves betrayal of one's country, either by making war against it or by giving aid and comfort to its enemies. At common law, treason was the most heinous crime a person could commit. It was in a category by itself, considered far worse than any felony. Because all felonies were punishable by death, the common law provided a special punishment for the crime of treason:

> 1. That the offender be drawn to the gallows, and not be carried or walk . . . 2. That he be hanged by the neck, and cut down alive. 3. That his entrails be taken out and burned, while he is yet alive. 4. That his head be cut off. 5. That his body be divided into four parts. 6. That his head and quarters be at the king's disposal. These refinements in cruelty . . . were, in former times, literally and studiously executed; and indicate at once a savage and ferocious spirit, and a degrading subserviency to royal resentments, real or supposed. 3 J. Story, *Commentaries on the Constitution* § 1293.

English kings had used the crime of treason to punish and deter political opposition. For example, in 1683 one Algernon Sidney was executed for treason based primarily on published writings deemed to be subversive of the Crown. Being aware of these abuses of the criminal law, the framers of the U.S. Constitution sought to prohibit the federal government from using the offense of treason to punish political dissenters. Thus, they specifically defined treason against the United States in Article III, Section 3, paragraph 1, saying it "shall consist only in levying War against them, or in adhering to their Enemies, giving them Aid and Comfort." To make it more difficult for the government to prosecute people for treason, the same paragraph included the following injunction: "No Person shall be convicted of Treason unless on the Testimony of two Witnesses to the same overt Act, or on Confession in open Court." Thus, no one may be convicted of treason against the United States based solely on circumstantial evidence.

Levying War against the United States

As the constitutional language indicates, there are two types of treason—"levying war against" the United States and giving "aid and comfort" to its enemies. In *Ex Parte Bollman,* 8 U.S. (4 Cranch) 75 (U.S. Dist. Col. 1807), Chief Justice Marshall observed,

As there is no crime which can more excite and agitate the passions of men than treason, no charge demands more from the tribunal before which it is made, a deliberate and temperate inquiry. Whether this inquiry be directed to the fact or to the law, none can be more solemn, none more important to the citizen or to the government; none can more affect the safety of both. . . . It is therefore more safe as well as more consonant to the principles of our constitution, that the crime of treason should not be extended by construction to doubtful cases; and that crimes not clearly within the constitutional definition, should receive such punishment as the legislature in its wisdom may provide. *Ex parte Bollman*, 8 U.S. (4 Cranch) at 125, 127.

Presiding over the trial of Aaron Burr in 1807, Chief Justice Marshall produced a lengthy opinion on the law of treason and its application to the Burr case. Marshall read the entire opinion aloud as a means of instructing the jury. The opinion made it clear that in Marshall's view, Burr could not be convicted of treason based on evidence that could lawfully be considered by the court. Consequently, in the most infamous treason trial in American history, the jury returned a verdict of not guilty. *United States v. Burr*, 25 F. Cas. 55 (Circuit Court of the District of Virginia, August 31, 1807). The upshot of *Ex Parte Bollman* and the acquittal of Aaron Burr was that it became extremely difficult to convict a person of treason by virtue of levying war against the United States.

> John Marshall's classic opinion in *United States v. Burr* is reproduced on the companion website.

Giving Aid and Comfort to the Enemies of the United States

In *Cramer v. United States*, 325 U.S. 1, 65 S.Ct 918, 89 L.Ed. 1441 (1945), the Supreme Court reversed the treason conviction of Anthony Cramer, a German immigrant accused of giving aid and comfort to two Nazi saboteurs who infiltrated the United States in 1942. Writing for the Court, Justice Robert Jackson pointed out that to be guilty of this form of treason, a defendant must both adhere to the enemy and provide them aid and comfort:

> A citizen intellectually or emotionally may favor the enemy and harbor sympathies or convictions disloyal to this country's policy or interest, but so long as he commits no act of aid and comfort to the enemy, there is no treason. On the other hand, a citizen may take actions, which do aid and comfort the enemy—making a speech critical of the government or opposing its measures, profiteering, striking in defense plants or essential work, and the hundred other things which impair our cohesion and diminish our strength—but if there is no adherence to the enemy in this, if there is no intent to betray, there is no treason. 325 U.S. at 29, 65 S.Ct. at 932, 89 L.Ed. at 1458.

Two years later, the Court upheld the conviction of a man who sheltered one of the Nazi saboteurs. *Haupt v. United States*, 330 U.S. 631, 67 S.Ct. 874, 91 L.Ed. 1145 (1947). Writing for the Court, Justice Jackson observed that "[t]he law of treason makes and properly makes conviction difficult but not impossible." 330 U.S. at 644, 67 S.Ct. at 880, 91 L.Ed. at 1155.

Bills of Attainder and *Ex Post Facto* Laws

Two historic abuses of the English Parliament that the framers of the Constitution sought to correct were bills of attainder and *ex post facto* laws. Article I, Section 9 of the Constitution prohibits Congress from adopting bills of attainder and *ex post facto* laws. Article I, Section 10 extends these same prohibitions to the state legislatures.

Bills of Attainder

A **bill of attainder** is a legislative act inflicting punishment on an individual or on a group of easily identifiable individuals. Laws of this character are antithetical to the basic principle that a person accused of wrongdoing is entitled to a fair trial in a court of law. Writing for the Supreme Court in *United States v. Lovett*, 328 U.S. 303, 66 S.Ct. 1073, 90 L. Ed. 1252 (1946), Justice Hugo Black reflected on the constitutional prohibition against bills of attainder:

Go to the companion website for an edited version of the Supreme Court's decision in *United States v. Brown*.

> When our Constitution and Bill of Rights were written, our ancestors had ample reason to know that legislative trials and punishments were too dangerous to liberty to exist in the nation of free men they envisioned. And so they proscribed bills of attainder. 328 U.S. at 318, 66 S.Ct. at 1080, 90 L. Ed. at 1261.

In *United States v. Brown*, 381 U.S. 437, 85 S.Ct. 1707, 14 L.Ed.2d 484 (1965), the Supreme Court struck down a law barring Communist Party members from holding positions as officers of labor unions. The Court found the prohibition to constitute a bill of attainder in that it punished easily identifiable members of a class by imposing upon them the sanction of a mandatory forfeiture of a position to which they would otherwise be entitled. Subsequently, in *Nixon v. Administrator of General Services*, 433 U.S. 425, 97 S.Ct. 2777, 53 L.Ed.2d 867 (1977), the Supreme Court said that in reviewing a law challenged as a bill of attainder, a court must consider (1) whether the statute falls within the historic meaning of legislative punishment; (2) whether the statute, viewed in terms of the type and severity of the burdens imposed, reasonably can be said to further nonpunitive legislative purposes; and (3) whether the legislative record evinces a legislative intent to punish. A statute that fails any of the prongs of the test may be declared unconstitutional.

Ex Post Facto Laws

Sir William Blackstone, the great commentator on the English common law, wrote that an ***ex post facto* law** exists "when after an action (indifferent in itself) is committed, the legislator then for the first time declares it to have been a crime, and inflicts a punishment upon the person who has committed it." 1 W. Blackstone, *Commentaries* 46. Because the essence of the *ex post facto* law is retroactivity, it is flatly inconsistent with the **principle of legality**, which holds that individuals are entitled to know in advance if particular contemplated conduct is illegal. The framers of the U.S. Constitution viewed *ex post facto* laws as one of the "favorite and most formidable instruments of tyranny." *The Federalist* No. 84, p. 512 (C. Rossiter ed. 1961) (A. Hamilton). In his *Commentaries on the Constitution of the United States*, Justice Joseph Story expressed strong support for the prohibition of *ex post facto* laws:

> If the laws in being do not punish an offender, let him go unpunished; let the legislature, admonished of the defect of the laws, provide against the commission of future crimes of the same sort. The escape of one delinquent can never produce so much harm to the community, as may arise from the infraction of a rule, upon which the purity of public justice, and the existence of civil liberty, essentially depend. 3 J. Story, *Commentaries on the Constitution* § 1338, at 211, n. 2.

Although the phrase "*ex post facto* law" literally includes any law passed "after the fact," the Supreme Court has long recognized that the constitutional prohibition applies only to criminal statutes. Writing for the Supreme Court in *Calder v. Bull*,

3 U.S. (3 Dall.) 386, 1 L.Ed. 648 (1798), Justice Samuel Chase identified four types of laws that fall within the prohibition of the *ex post facto* laws:

> 1st. Every law that makes an action done before the passing of the law, and which was innocent when done, criminal, and punishes such action. 2d. Every law that aggravates a crime, or makes it greater than it was when committed. 3d. Every law that changes the punishment, and inflicts a greater punishment, than the law annexed to the crime when committed. 4th. Every law that alters the legal rules of evidence and receives less or different testimony than the law required at the time of the commission of the offense in order to convict the offender. 3 U.S. (3 Dall.) at 390, 1 L. Ed. at 651.

Although modern statutes are seldom invalidated as *ex post facto* laws, the courts continue to recognize Justice Chase's formulation. For example, in *Miller v. Florida,* 482 U.S. 423, 107 S.Ct. 2446, 96 L.Ed.2d 351 (1987), the Supreme Court held that Florida's sentencing guidelines, as revised by the state legislature in 1984, violated the *Ex Post Facto* Clause of the federal constitution insofar as their application caused an increase in punishment to persons whose crimes occurred before the effective date of the 1984 act.

A more interesting example is provided by *Carmell v. Texas,* 529 U.S. 513, 120 S.Ct. 1620, 146 L.Ed.2d 577 (2000). In 1997 Scott Leslie Carmell was convicted in a Texas court of sexual assault, aggravated sexual assault, and indecency with a child. Evidence showed that between 1991 and 1995, Carmell committed various sex acts with his stepdaughter, starting when she was only twelve years old. Carmell was sentenced to life in prison on two convictions for aggravated sexual assault and twenty years in prison on thirteen other counts. The U.S. Supreme Court reversed four of Carmell's convictions by a vote of 5–4. These convictions were for sexual assaults that were alleged to have occurred in 1991 and 1992, when Texas law provided that a defendant could not be convicted merely on the testimony of the victim unless she was under fourteen. At the time of the alleged assaults in question, the victim was fourteen or fifteen. The law was later amended to extend the "child victim exception" to victims under eighteen years old. Carmell was convicted under the amended law, which the Supreme Court held to be an unconstitutional *ex post facto* law as defined by *Calder v. Bull,* 3 U.S. (3 Dall.) 386, 1 L.Ed. 648 (1798).

Similarly, in *Stogner v. California,* 539 U.S. 607, 123 S.Ct. 2446, 156 L.Ed.2d 544 (2003), the Supreme Court broadened the prohibition against *ex post facto* laws. In 1994, California enacted a law lifting the statute of limitations in child molestation cases where the victim remembers the abuse after the statute of limitations runs out. In 2001, seventy-two-year-old Marion Stogner was charged with molesting his daughters nearly fifty years earlier. Before the enactment of the new law, the state's statute of limitations would have barred Stogner's prosecution, as it prohibited prosecution more than three years after the crime had occurred. In a 5–4 decision, the Supreme Court held that California's new law extending the statute of limitations could not be constitutionally applied to allow prosecution of cases in which prosecution would have been foreclosed by the statute of limitations prior to the enactment of the new law.

The Bill of Rights

Although the original Constitution contained few express limitations on legislative power, the Bill of Rights added several important constraints on Congress. Ratified in 1791, the Bill of Rights consists of the first ten amendments to the Constitution.

Go to the companion website for an edited version of the Supreme Court's decision in *Carmell v. Texas.*

Go to the companion website for an edited version of the Supreme Court's decision in *Stogner v. California.*

From the standpoint of the substantive criminal law the most significant of these are the **First Amendment** freedoms of expression, religion, and assembly; the Second Amendment protection of "the right to keep and bear arms"; the Fifth Amendment Due Process Clause; the Eighth Amendment Cruel and Unusual Punishments Clause; and the Ninth Amendment guarantee of "rights retained by the people."

The First Amendment begins with the injunction that *"Congress* shall make no law . . ."* [emphasis added]. Unlike certain provisions in the original, unamended Constitution, the Bill of Rights makes no mention of limitations on the state and local governments. Throughout much of the nineteenth century, the Bill of Rights was viewed as imposing limitations only on Congress, having no effect on state legislatures or local governing bodies. The Supreme Court officially adopted this view in *Barron v. Baltimore,* 32 U.S. (7 Pet.) 243, 8 L.Ed. 672 (1833). Under this interpretation of the Bill of Rights, citizens had to look to their state constitutions and state courts for protection against state and local actions that infringed on their rights and liberties.

Application of the Bill of Rights to State and Local Laws

The ratification of the **Fourteenth Amendment** in 1868 provided a justification for extending the scope of the Bill of Rights to apply against the states. Section 1 of the Fourteenth Amendment enjoins the states from depriving "any person of life, liberty, or property, without due process of law." It also prohibits states from adopting laws that "abridge the privileges and immunities of citizens of the United States."

In a series of decisions, the Supreme Court has held that the **Due Process Clause** of the Fourteenth Amendment makes enforceable against the states those provisions of the Bill of Rights that are "implicit in the concept of ordered liberty." *Palko v. Connecticut*, 302 U.S. 319, 58 S.Ct. 149, 82 L.Ed. 288 (1937). This doctrine of incorporation has been employed by the Court to enforce the procedural guarantees of the Bill of Rights in state criminal prosecutions. For example, in *Wolf v. Colorado*, 338 U.S. 25, 69 S.Ct. 1359, 93 L.Ed. 1782 (1949), the Court said that the Fourth Amendment protection against unreasonable searches and seizures is applicable to state and local, as well as federal, law enforcement authorities. Similarly, in *Duncan v. Louisiana*, 391 U.S. 145, 88 S.Ct. 1444, 20 L.Ed.2d 491 (1968), the Court held that the Fourteenth Amendment requires states to observe the jury trial requirement of the Sixth Amendment.

In addition to incorporating the procedural protections of the Bill of Rights into the Fourteenth Amendment, the Court has extended the substantive limitations of the Bill of Rights to the states. In 1925 the Supreme Court recognized that the First Amendment protections of free speech and free press apply to state as well as federal laws. *Gitlow v. New York*, 268 U.S. 652, 45 S.Ct. 625, 69 L.Ed. 1138 (1925). Likewise, in 1934 the Court said that the First Amendment guarantee of free exercise of religion is enforceable against state and local governments. *Hamilton v. Regents of the University of California*, 293 U.S. 245, 55 S.Ct. 197, 79 L.Ed. 343 (1934).

The Supreme Court has incorporated virtually all the provisions of the Bill of Rights into the Fourteenth Amendment, making them applicable to state and local governments. The U.S. Constitution, and in particular the Bill of Rights, now stands as a barrier to unreasonable or oppressive criminal laws, whether they are enacted by Congress, a state legislature, or a local governing body.

Go to the companion website for edited versions of the Supreme Court's decisions in *Palko v. Connecticut* and *Duncan v. Louisiana.*

The First Amendment Freedom of Expression

Perhaps the most treasured of our liberties, and the rights most essential to maintaining a democratic polity, are the First Amendment freedoms of speech and press. Often, freedom of speech and freedom of the press are referred to jointly as "freedom of expression." Although the concept of free expression is fundamental to our democratic society, the Supreme Court has said that the First Amendment has "never been thought to give absolute protection to every individual to speak whenever or wherever he pleases, or to use any form of address in any circumstances that he chooses." *Cohen v. California*, 403 U.S. 15, 19, 91 S.Ct. 1780, 1785, 29 L.Ed.2d 284, 290 (1971). The task of the courts, of course, is to strike a reasonable balance between the right of expression and the legitimate interests of society in maintaining security, order, peace, safety, and decency. In what has become a classic phrase, Justice Oliver Wendell Holmes Jr. observed that the "most stringent protection of free speech would not protect a man in falsely shouting fire in a theater, and causing a panic." *Schenck v. United States*, 249 U.S. 47, 51, 39 S.Ct. 247, 249, 63 L.Ed. 470, 473 (1919). Moreover, the Supreme Court has said that certain types of speech are so inherently lacking in value as not to merit any First Amendment protection:

> There are certain well-defined and narrowly limited classes of speech, the prevention and punishment of which have never been thought to raise any constitutional problem. These include the lewd and obscene, the profane, the libelous, and the insulting or "fighting" words—those which by their very utterance inflict injury or tend to incite an immediate breach of the peace. It has been well observed that such utterances are no essential part of any exposition of ideas, and are of such slight social value as a step to truth that any benefit that may be derived from them is clearly outweighed by the social interest in order and morality. *Chaplinsky v. New Hampshire*, 315 U.S. 568, 571, 62 S.Ct. 766, 769, 86 L.Ed. 1031, 1035 (1942).

Advocacy of Unlawful Conduct

Go to the companion website for an edited version of the Supreme Court's decision in *Schenck v. United States*.

One of the most basic problems posed by the First Amendment is whether speech advocating unlawful conduct might itself be made unlawful. The Supreme Court first encountered this problem in *Schenck v. United States,* supra, where an official of the Socialist Party appealed a conviction under the Espionage Act of 1917, 40 Stat. at L. 217, 219. Charles T. Schenck had been convicted of participating in a conspiracy to cause insubordination in the military services and to obstruct military recruitment at a time when the United States was at war. The "conspiracy" consisted of activities surrounding the mailing of a leaflet to draftees urging them to resist induction into the military. The Supreme Court upheld Schenck's conviction, saying that

> the question in every case is whether the words used are used in such circumstances and are of such a nature as to create clear and present danger that they will bring about the substantive evils that Congress has a right to prevent. . . . When a nation is at war many things that might be said in time of peace are such a hindrance to its effort that their utterance will not be endured so long as men fight, and that no court could regard them as protected by any constitutional right. 249 U.S. at 52, 39 S.Ct. at 249, 63 L.Ed. at 473.

The Supreme Court first invoked the **clear and present danger doctrine** to reverse a criminal conviction in a case involving a Georgia man who had been prosecuted under a state law prohibiting "any attempt, by persuasion or otherwise" to incite insurrection. *Herndon v. Lowry,* 301 U.S. 242, 57 S.Ct. 732, 81 L.Ed. 1066 (1937). Since then, the doctrine has been used by state and federal courts to reverse numerous convictions where persons have been prosecuted for merely advocating illegal acts.

The modern Supreme Court has refined the clear and present danger doctrine so that public advocacy may be prohibited only in situations when there is **imminent lawless action.** *Brandenburg v. Ohio,* 395 U.S. 444, 89 S.Ct. 1827, 23 L.Ed.2d 430 (1969). Today, it is questionable whether the courts would uphold a conviction in circumstances similar to those in the *Schenck* case. The courts might find that mailing a leaflet or standing on a street corner urging resistance to the draft—activities that were fairly common during the Vietnam War—are not fraught with imminent lawless action and therefore do not constitute a clear and present danger.

Go to the companion website for an edited version of the Supreme Court's decision in Brandenburg v. Ohio.

Symbolic Speech and Expressive Conduct

Freedom of expression is a broad concept embracing speech, publication, performances, and demonstrations. Even wearing symbols is considered to be constitutionally protected **symbolic speech**. *Tinker v. Des Moines Independent Community School District,* 393 U.S. 503, 89 S.Ct. 733, 21 L.Ed.2d 731 (1969). The Supreme Court has recognized a wide variety of conduct as possessing "sufficient communicative elements to bring the First Amendment to play." *Texas v. Johnson,* 491 U.S. 397, 404, 109 S.Ct. 2533, 2539, 105 L.Ed.2d 342, 353 (1989). The Court has accorded First Amendment protection to, among other things, "sit-ins" to protest racial segregation, *Brown v. Louisiana,* 383 U.S. 131, 86 S.Ct. 719, 15 L.Ed.2d 637 (1966); civilians wearing American military uniforms to protest the Vietnam War, *Schacht v. United States,* 398 U.S. 58, 90 S.Ct. 1555, 26 L.Ed.2d 44 (1970); and "picketing" over a variety of issues, *Amalgamated Food Employees Union v. Logan Valley Plaza, Inc.,* 391 U.S. 308, 88 S.Ct. 1601, 20 L.Ed.2d 603 (1968).

Go to the companion website for an edited version of the Supreme Court's decision in Texas v. Johnson.

Flag Burning

Without question, the most controversial applications of the concept of expressive conduct have been the Supreme Court's decisions holding that the public burning of the American flag is protected by the First Amendment. In *Texas v. Johnson, supra,* the Court invalidated a Texas statute banning flag desecration. Gregory Johnson had been arrested after he publicly burned an American flag outside the Republican National Convention in Dallas in 1984. The Supreme Court's decision to reverse Johnson's conviction and strike down the Texas law resulted in a firestorm of public criticism of the Court as well as the enactment of a new federal statute. The Flag Protection Act of 1989, amending 18 U.S.C.A. § 700, imposed criminal penalties on anyone who knowingly "mutilates, defaces, physically defiles, burns, maintains upon the floor or ground, or tramples upon" the American flag. In *United States v. Eichman,* 496 U.S. 310, 110 S.Ct. 2404, 110 L.Ed.2d 287 (1990), the Supreme Court invalidated this federal statute as well, saying that "punishing desecration of the flag dilutes the very freedom that makes this emblem so revered, and worth revering." 496 U.S. at 319, 110 S.Ct. at 2410, 110 L.Ed.2d at 296. On several occasions, Congress has attempted to pass a constitutional amendment to overturn the Supreme Court's flag burning decisions, but in every instance the measure has failed to receive the necessary two-thirds vote in the Senate.

Free Expression versus Maintenance of the Public Order

One type of expression that sometimes transgresses the criminal law is public speech that threatens the public peace and order. Numerous state and local laws prohibit incitement to riot and disturbing the peace. The Supreme Court has said, "[w]hen clear and present danger of riot, disorder, interference with traffic upon the public streets, or other immediate threat to public safety, peace, or order appears, the power of the State to prevent and punish is obvious." *Cantwell v. Connecticut*, 310 U.S. 296, 308, 60 S.Ct. 900, 905, 84 L.Ed. 1213, 1220 (1940). Moreover, the Court has held that so-called **fighting words** are unprotected by the Constitution. *Chaplinsky v. New Hampshire*, supra. Fighting words are "those personally abusive epithets which, when addressed to the ordinary citizen, are, as a matter of common knowledge, inherently likely to provoke violent reaction." *Cohen v. California*, 403 U.S. at 20, 91 S.Ct. at 1785, 29 L.Ed.2d at 291.

Although government must have the authority to maintain order, it may not, under the guise of preserving public peace, unduly suppress free communication of views. Again, the challenge for courts is to strike a reasonable balance between legitimate competing interests in the context of the particular facts in the case at hand.

Hate Speech

In recent years, legislatures and courts have become concerned with the problem of **hate speech.** Hate speech refers to any instance of hateful expression, whether verbal, written, or symbolic, that is based on racial, ethnic, or religious prejudice or some other similar animus. Because it constitutes expression, hate speech is generally protected by the Constitution unless it falls within one of the recognized exceptions to the First Amendment. Would a public cross burning by the Ku Klux Klan in a black neighborhood qualify as fighting words, or would it be considered expressive conduct protected by the First Amendment? What about the display of swastikas by Nazis parading through the streets of a predominantly Jewish city? Would police be justified in these instances to make arrests for incitement to riot? These questions became more real than hypothetical during the 1980s, when the country witnessed a resurgence of racist organizations, and cities and states countered with laws proscribing hate speech. One such law, the St. Paul, Minnesota, Bias-Motivated Crime Ordinance, provided,

> Whoever places on public or private property a symbol, object, appellation, characterization or graffiti, including, but not limited to, a burning cross or Nazi swastika, which one knows or has reasonable grounds to know arouses anger, alarm or resentment in others on the basis of race, color, creed, religion or gender commits disorderly conduct and shall be guilty of a misdemeanor. St. Paul, Minn. Legis. Code 292.02 (1990).

In *R.A.V. v. City of St. Paul*, 505 U.S. 377, 112 S.Ct. 2538, 120 L.Ed.2d 305 (1992), the Supreme Court declared this ordinance unconstitutional in the context of a criminal prosecution of a white teenager who burned a cross on the front lawn of a black family's home. Lest the public be tempted to conclude that the Supreme Court condoned racially motivated cross burnings, the Court stated the following:

> Let there be no mistake about our belief that burning a cross in someone's front yard is reprehensible. But St. Paul has sufficient means at its disposal to prevent such

behavior without adding the First Amendment to the fire. 505 U.S. at 396, 112 S.Ct. at 2550, 120 L.Ed.2d at 326.

Go to the companion website for an edited version of the Supreme Court's decision in *Virginia v. Black.*

Notwithstanding its earlier decision in *R.A.V. v. City of St. Paul*, the Supreme Court in 2003 upheld a Virginia law banning cross burning with "an intent to intimidate a person or group of persons." Va. Code Ann. § 18.2-423 (1996). Writing for the Court, Justice O'Connor concluded that the "First Amendment permits Virginia to outlaw cross burnings done with the intent to intimidate because burning a cross is a particularly virulent form of intimidation." *Virginia v. Black*, 535 U.S. 343, 363, 123 S.Ct. 1536, 1549, 155 L.Ed.2d 535, 554 (2003).

Obscenity

Traditionally, state and local governments have proscribed speech, pictures, films, and performances regarded as obscene, generally classifying these as misdemeanor offenses. Despite challenges to the constitutionality of such obscenity laws, the Supreme Court has held that **obscenity** is beyond the pale of the First Amendment and thus subject to criminal prosecution. *Roth v. United States*, 354 U.S. 476, 77 S.Ct. 1304, 1 L.Ed.2d 1498 (1957).

Go to the companion website for edited versions of *Miller v. California* and *Jenkins v. Georgia.*

The problem for the legislatures, police, prosecutors, and courts is to determine what is obscene and therefore unprotected by the First Amendment. The Supreme Court has held that for expression to be obscene, it must (1) appeal to a prurient interest in sex; (2) depict sexual conduct in a patently offensive way; and (3) lack serious literary, artistic, political, or scientific value. *Miller v. California*, 413 U.S. 15, 93 S.Ct. 2607, 37 L.Ed.2d 419 (1973). Despite this test, the concept of obscenity remains somewhat vague. Nevertheless, the Supreme Court has made it clear that obscenity refers only to "hard-core" pornography. *Jenkins v. Georgia*, 418 U.S. 153, 94 S.Ct. 2750, 41 L.Ed.2d 642 (1974). Today, with the easy availability of pornography on the Internet, police and prosecutors have shifted their focus away from the enforcement of traditional obscenity laws and toward enforcement of more recent statutes criminalizing child pornography. (Obscenity and pornography are examined more fully in Chapter 10.)

CASE-IN-POINT

Obscenity

Billy Jenkins managed a movie theater in Albany, Georgia, in which the film *Carnal Knowledge* was being shown. The film, which starred Jack Nicholson, Candice Bergen, Art Garfunkel, and Ann-Margret, appeared on many critics' "Ten Best" lists for 1971. The film contained scenes in which sexual conduct, including "ultimate sexual acts," was understood to be taking place, but the camera did not focus on the bodies of the actors at such times. On January 13, 1972, local law enforcement officers entered the theater, pursuant to a warrant, and seized the film. Jenkins was later convicted of distributing obscene material and was fined $750 and sentenced to twelve months' probation. By a divided vote, the Georgia Supreme Court affirmed the conviction. On appeal, the U.S. Supreme Court reversed Jenkins's conviction, holding that *Carnal Knowledge* was not hard-core pornography and was thus protected under the First Amendment standards delineated in *Miller v. California.*

Jenkins v. Georgia, 418 U.S. 153, 94 S.Ct. 2750, 41 L.Ed.2d 642 (1974).

Profanity

Go to the companion website for an edited version of the Supreme Court's decision in *Cohen v. California.*

Although in *Chaplinsky v. New Hampshire,* supra, the Supreme Court specifically enumerated profanity as being among those categories of speech so lacking in value as not to merit First Amendment protection, this view no longer prevails. In *Cohen v. California,* supra, the Supreme Court invalidated the "offensive conduct" conviction of a man who entered a courthouse wearing a jacket emblazoned with the slogan "Fuck the Draft." Writing for the Court, Justice John Marshall Harlan opined that

> while the particular four-letter-word being litigated here is perhaps more distasteful than others of its genre, it is nevertheless often true that one man's vulgarity is another's lyric. Indeed, we think it is largely because government officials cannot make principled distinctions in this area that the Constitution leaves matters of taste and style so largely to the individual. 403 U.S. at 25, 91 S.Ct. at 1788, 29 L.Ed.2d at 294.

Despite the Supreme Court's decision in *Cohen v. California,* most states and many cities retain laws proscribing profanity. These laws are seldom enforced and rarely challenged in court. One notable exception is the case of the "cussing canoeist" that made national news in 1998. When Timothy Boomer fell from his canoe into Michigan's Rifle River, he unleashed a tirade of profanities in a very loud voice. He was convicted of violating a nineteenth-century state law that prohibited the utterance of profanity in the presence of children. Boomer was fined $75 and ordered to perform four days of community service. With the assistance of the American Civil Liberties Union, Boomer appealed his conviction to the Michigan Court of Appeals, which reversed the conviction and struck down the statute on which it was based. Writing for the court, Judge William B. Murphy observed that the law, "as drafted, reaches constitutionally protected speech, and it operates to inhibit the exercise of First Amendment rights." *People v. Boomer,* 655 N.W.2d 255, 259 (Mich. App. 2002).

Freedom of Assembly

Go to the companion website for an edited version of the Supreme Court's decision in *Adderley v. Florida.*

Go to the companion website for an edited version of *Edwards v. South Carolina.*

The First Amendment specifically protects the "right of the people peaceably to assemble." Yet, as we have seen, one of the most important purposes of the criminal law is to maintain public peace and order. Sometimes these values conflict, as in the civil rights struggle of the 1960s, when public demonstrations became an important part of a powerful political movement. See, for example, *Cox v. Louisiana,* 379 U.S. 559, 85 S.Ct. 476, 13 L.Ed.2d 487 (1965); *Adderley v. Florida,* 385 U.S. 39, 87 S.Ct. 242, 17 L.Ed.2d 149 (1966); *Walker v. City of Birmingham,* 388 U.S. 307, 87 S.Ct. 1824, 18 L.Ed.2d 1210 (1967).

In one of the most memorable cases from the civil rights era, the Supreme Court reversed the breach-of-the-peace convictions of 187 students who participated in a peaceful demonstration on the grounds of the South Carolina statehouse. *Edwards v. South Carolina,* 372 U.S. 229; 83 S.Ct. 680; 9 L.Ed.2d 697 (1963). The Court characterized the students' conduct not as a breach of the peace but as "an exercise of . . . basic constitutional rights in their most pristine and classic form."

Governments may not ban assemblies in the **public forum** as long as they are peaceful and do not impede the operations of government or the activities of other citizens. Yet, to promote the interests of safety, order, and peace, governments may impose reasonable **time, place, and manner regulations** on public assemblies. The character of a given place and the pattern of its normal activities determine the type of time, place, and manner regulations that the courts consider reasonable. *Grayned v. City of Rockford*, 408 U.S. 104, 92 S.Ct. 2294, 33 L.Ed.2d 222 (1972). For example, a restriction against the use of sound amplifiers near a courthouse or library might well be judged reasonable, whereas a ban on "picketing" on the steps of the same buildings would not. In imposing time, place, and manner regulations, governments must be careful not to deprive demonstrations or protests of their essential content by imposing excessive or unnecessarily burdensome regulations. *United States v. Grace*, 461 U.S. 171, 103 S.Ct. 1702, 75 L.Ed.2d 736 (1983).

Go to the companion website for an edited version of the Supreme Court's decision in *United States v. Grace*.

Free Exercise of Religion

The value of **freedom of religion** is so deeply rooted in American culture that rarely have legislatures sought to impinge directly on that right. Yet from time to time lawmakers have sought to prevent certain unpopular religious groups from proselytizing. The Supreme Court has been quick to invalidate such efforts. In one leading case, the Court struck down a state statute that made it a misdemeanor for any person to solicit door to door for religious or philanthropic reasons without prior approval from local officials, who were authorized to make determinations as to whether solicitors represented *bona fide* religions. The law was successfully challenged by a member of the Jehovah's Witnesses sect who had been prosecuted for engaging in door-to-door proselytizing without a permit. *Cantwell v. Connecticut*, supra.

Unusual Religious Practices

Much more problematic are government attempts to enforce criminal statutes designed to protect the public health, safety, and welfare against religious practices deemed inimical to these interests. Does the right to exercise one's religion freely permit a person to violate an otherwise valid criminal statute? In 1878 the Supreme Court answered this question in the negative by upholding the prosecution of a polygamist. *Reynolds v. United States*, 98 U.S. (8 Otto) 145, 25 L.Ed. 244 (1878). More recently, however, the Supreme Court granted to members of the Old Order Amish sect an exemption to the Wisconsin compulsory education law. The Court found that the law significantly interfered with the Amish way of life and thus violated their right to freely exercise their religion. *Wisconsin v. Yoder*, 406 U.S. 205, 92 S.Ct. 1526, 32 L.Ed.2d 15 (1972).

Go to the companion website for edited versions of *Reynolds v. United States* and *Wisconsin v. Yoder*.

Several state courts have decided cases arising from unusual forms of worship. The Tennessee Supreme Court upheld the validity of a statute making it a crime to handle poisonous snakes in religious ceremonies against the claim that the law violated the right to free exercise of religion guaranteed by the state constitution. *Harden v. State*, 216 S.W.2d 708 (Tenn. 1949).

In a decision that cuts the other way, the California Supreme Court reversed the convictions of several members of the Native American Church for possession of peyote, which contains an illegal hallucinogen. *People v. Woody*, 394 P.2d 813 (Cal. 1964). In the court's view, the sacramental use of peyote was central to the worship by members of the Native American Church and thus protected by the First Amendment. In 1990, however, the U.S. Supreme Court held that the sacramental use of peyote by members of the Native American Church was

Go to the companion website for an edited version of the Supreme Court's decision in *Employment Division v. Smith*.

not protected by the Free Exercise Clause of the First Amendment. *Employment Division v. Smith,* 494 U.S. 872, 110 S.Ct. 1595, 108 L.Ed.2d 876 (1990). This decision by the nation's highest court means that state courts that have granted such protection might want to reconsider their positions. In our federal system, however, state courts are free to provide greater levels of protection to individual rights under the terms of their state constitutions than those provided by the federal constitution.

The principle that underlies *Employment Division v. Smith* is that the Free Exercise Clause does not provide the basis for an exemption to a generally applicable criminal statute. A law aimed specifically at the practices of one religious group is another matter, as the Supreme Court made clear in striking down a Hialeah, Florida, ordinance prohibiting animal sacrifices. After receiving a number of complaints about the practice of animal sacrifice associated with the Santeria religion, the city of Hialeah adopted an ordinance making it an offense to "unnecessarily kill, torment, torture, or mutilate an animal in a public or private ritual or ceremony not for the primary purpose of food consumption." Practitioners of Santeria sued to challenge the constitutionality of the ordinance. In a unanimous decision, the Supreme Court declared the ordinance unconstitutional. Writing for the Court, Justice Anthony Kennedy observed that "the laws in question were enacted by officials who did not understand, failed to perceive, or chose to ignore the fact that their official actions violated the Nation's essential commitment to religious freedom." *Church of the Lukumi Babalu Aye, Inc. v. City of Hialeah,* 508 U.S. 520, 524, 113 S.Ct. 2217, 2222, 124 L.Ed.2d 472, 477 (1993).

Go to the companion website for an edited version of the Supreme Court's decision in *Church of the Lukumi Babalu Aye, Inc. v. City of Hialeah*.

Refusal of Medical Treatment

One of the more troubling and tragic situations in which the Free Exercise Clause potentially conflicts with the criminal law involves the refusal of medical treatment. Certain religious groups, such as the Christian Scientists, believe that physical healing is to be achieved through spiritual power. Thus, when faced with an illness or injury, they are likely to refuse medical treatment. Other groups—for example, the Jehovah's Witnesses—believe that blood transfusions are specifically enjoined by scripture.

The courts have recognized the right of a competent adult to refuse medical treatment on religious grounds, even if the refusal results in death. See, for example, *In re Estate of Brooks,* 205 N.E.2d 435 (Ill. 1965); *In re Milton,* 505 N.E.2d 255 (Ohio 1987). It is another matter entirely when parents refuse to allow medical treatment for their children. The Supreme Court has recognized that

> parents may be free to become martyrs themselves. But it does not follow that they are free in identical circumstances to make martyrs of their children before they have reached the age of full legal discretion when they can make that choice for themselves. *Prince v. Massachusetts,* 321 U.S. 158, 170, 64 S.Ct. 438, 444, 88 L.Ed. 645, 654 (1944).

Accordingly, courts seldom allow freedom of religion as a defense to a criminal charge stemming from a situation in which parents refused to seek or allow medical treatment for their children. In one recent case, a member of the Christian Scientist faith was prosecuted for involuntary manslaughter after failing to seek medical treatment of her daughter's meningitis, which turned out to be fatal. The California

Supreme Court rejected the defendant's free-exercise-of-religion defense, saying that "parents have no right to free exercise of religion at the price of a child's life." *Walker v. Superior Court,* 763 P.2d 852 (Cal. 1988).

The Right to Keep and Bear Arms

There are numerous criminal prohibitions—at the federal, state, and local levels—against the sale, possession, and use of certain types of firearms. "Gun control" laws are seen by many as antithetical to the **right to keep and bear arms**. The Second Amendment to the U.S. Constitution provides, "A well regulated Militia, being necessary to the security of a free state, the right of the people to keep and bear arms, shall not be infringed."

In *United States v. Miller,* 307 U.S. 174, 59 S.Ct. 816, 83 L.Ed. 1206 (1939), the Supreme Court upheld a federal law criminalizing the interstate shipment of sawed-off shotguns, saying that "the right to keep and bear arms" had to be interpreted in relation to the "well regulated militia." The Court concluded that possession of sawed-off shotguns had no reasonable relationship to serving in the militia. In reaffirming *Miller,* the Court said that "the Second Amendment guarantees no right to keep and bear a firearm that does not have some reasonable relationship to the preservation or efficiency of a well regulated militia." *Lewis v. United States,* 445 U.S. 55, 65 n.8, 100 S.Ct. 915, 921 n.8, 63 L.Ed.2d 198, 209 n.8 (1980). However, in *District of Columbia v. Heller,* 554 U.S. ___, 128 S.Ct. 2783, 171 L.Ed.2d 637 (2008), the Court declared the right to keep and bear arms to be a personal right irrespective of actual or potential service in any militia. In *Heller,* the Court struck down a District of Columbia ordinance that effectively created a complete ban on handguns within the District. The Court did not define the scope of the right to keep and bear arms, nor did it indicate whether the right is secured against state action by the Fourteenth Amendment. It did indicate, though, that the right is subject to reasonable government regulations.

> Go to the companion website for an edited version of the Supreme Court's decision in *District of Columbia v. Heller.*

Like the federal constitution, many state constitutions contain language dealing with the right to keep and bear arms. Yet state courts tend to give wide latitude to state and local gun control laws. Conservatives and libertarians tend to criticize the courts for failing, in their view, to protect adequately the constitutional right to keep and bear arms. Members of the law enforcement community, however, are typically more supportive of legislative efforts to control the dissemination and use of firearms.

CASE-IN-POINT

The Right to Keep and Bear Arms

Article I, Section 2-a of the New Hampshire Constitution provides, "All persons have the right to keep and bear arms in defense of themselves, their families, their property and the state." At the same time, a New Hampshire statute proscribes possession of firearms by convicted felons. RSA 159:3. Scott Smith, who was convicted in the Rockingham Superior Court of being a felon in possession of a firearm, challenged the constitutionality of the statute. The New Hampshire Supreme Court affirmed the conviction and sustained the validity of the statute, saying, "the State constitutional right to keep and bear arms is not absolute and may be subject to restriction and regulation. . . . The governmental interest served by the statute, protection of human life and property, is patently significant."

State v. Smith, 571 A.2d 279, 281 (N.H. 1990).

The Doctrines of Vagueness and Overbreadth

The Fifth Amendment to the U.S. Constitution provides that "no person . . . shall be deprived of life, liberty or property without due process of law." The two fundamental aspects of due process are fair notice and fair hearing. The principle of fair notice implies that a person has a right to know whether particular contemplated conduct is illegal. Indeed, the Supreme Court has emphatically stated that "[n]o one may be required at peril of life, liberty or property to speculate as to the meaning of penal statutes." *Lanzetta v. New Jersey*, 306 U.S. 451, 453, 59 S.Ct. 618, 619, 83 L.Ed. 888, 890 (1939).

A criminal law that is excessively vague in its proscriptions offends this principle and is thus invalid under the Due Process Clause of the Fifth or Fourteenth Amendments (depending on whether it is a federal or state statute). However, we must realize that the **vagueness doctrine** is "designed more to limit the discretion of police and prosecutors than to ensure that statutes are intelligible to persons pondering criminal activity." *United States v. White*, 882 F.2d 250, 252 (7th Cir. 1989). Accordingly, the Supreme Court has held that the requisite specificity of criminal statutes may be achieved through judicial interpretation. *Rose v. Locke*, 423 U.S. 48, 96 S.Ct. 243, 46 L.Ed.2d 185 (1975). As interpreted by the Seventh Circuit Court of Appeals in *United States v. White*, "provided that conduct is of a sort widely known among the lay public to be criminal . . . , a person is not entitled to clear notice that the conduct violates a particular criminal statute." *United States v. White*, supra at 252.

Go to the companion website for an edited version of the Supreme Court's decision in *Papachristou v. City of Jacksonville.*

In a landmark decision, the Supreme Court struck down a Jacksonville, Florida, ordinance that prohibited various forms of vagrancy, including loitering and "prowling by auto." *Papachristou v. City of Jacksonville*, 405 U.S. 156, 92 S.Ct. 839, 31 L.Ed.2d 110 (1972). Writing for the Court in *Papachristou,* Justice William O. Douglas objected to the "unfettered discretion" the ordinance placed in the hands of the police, allowing for "arbitrary and discriminatory enforcement of the law." (For further discussion of the vagueness doctrine as it relates to the crimes of vagrancy and loitering, see Chapter 12.)

Closely related to the concept of vagueness, the **doctrine of overbreadth** was developed exclusively in the context of the First Amendment and concerns criminal laws that are written so broadly that they potentially infringe First Amendment freedoms. The evil of overbreadth of a law is that it may permit police to make arrests for constitutionally protected conduct, such as political speech, as well as for unprotected activity, such as inciting people to violence through the use of fighting words.

Go to the companion website for an edited version of the Supreme Court's decision in *Coates v. Cincinnati.*

Coates v. City of Cincinnati, 402 U.S. 611, 91 S.Ct. 1686, 29 L.Ed.2d 214 (1971), illustrates both the vagueness doctrine and the doctrine of overbreadth. In *Coates* the Supreme Court struck down a Cincinnati ordinance that made it unlawful for "three or more persons to assemble . . . on any sidewalks and there conduct themselves in a manner annoying to persons passing by." The Court found the ordinance to be excessively vague in that "men of common intelligence must necessarily guess at its meaning." The Court also found that the ordinance was so broad that it criminalized speech and assembly protected by the First Amendment.

Ordinarily a person can contest only a law that has been directed against him or her. However, the doctrine of overbreadth enables a person to contest a law imposing restrictions on First Amendment freedoms even when that person has not been charged with violating the law. This doctrine was designed to bring to the courts' attention laws that have a "chilling effect" on the exercise of First Amendment rights.

Go to the companion website for an edited version of the Supreme Court's decision in *New York v. Ferber.*

In the 1980s, the Supreme Court appeared to be retreating somewhat from the overbreadth doctrine. In *New York v. Ferber*, 458 U.S. 747, 102 S.Ct. 3348,

73 L.Ed.2d 1113 (1982), for example, the Court rejected an overbreadth challenge to a child pornography statute that criminalized child pornography well beyond the legal test of obscenity delineated in *Miller v. California*, supra. Although expressing concern that the statute might possibly be applied to punish constitutionally protected artistic expression, the Court concluded that the law was not "substantially overbroad" and that impermissible applications of the statute should be addressed on a case-by-case basis. According to the *Ferber* Court, a statute should not be invalidated for overbreadth if its legitimate reach "dwarfs its arguably impermissible applications." 458 U.S. at 773, 102 S.Ct. at 3363, 73 L.Ed.2d at 1133.

The overbreadth doctrine was given new life by the Supreme Court in 1997, when the Court struck down provisions of the Communications Decency Act (CDA) of 1996, 47 U.S.C.A. §§ 223(a), 223(d) (Supp. 1997). Under the CDA, Congress had attempted to ban "indecent" as well as "obscene" speech from the Internet. Criminal penalties were provided for persons who transmitted such messages in a fashion that they could be received by children. The Court found that the law swept within its ambit constitutionally protected speech as well as obscenity. *Reno v. American Civil Liberties Union*, 521 U.S. 844, 117 S.Ct. 2329, 138 L.Ed.2d 874 (1997).

Go to the companion website for an edited version of the Supreme Court's decision in *Reno v. ACLU*.

Freedom from Compulsory Self-Incrimination

The Fifth Amendment to the U.S. Constitution provides that no person "shall be compelled in any criminal case to be a witness against himself." We normally think of the prohibition against compulsory self-incrimination in terms of a defendant's right not to testify in a criminal trial or a suspect's right to remain silent in the face of police interrogation. However, the courts have held that this clause also limits the degree to which legislatures can write statutes that require parties to report information to the government that can place them in jeopardy of criminal prosecution. Consider the following Supreme Court decisions from the late 1960s:

- In *Marchetti v. United States*, 390 U.S. 39, 88 S.Ct. 697, 19 L.Ed.2d 889 (1968), the defendant was convicted for conspiring to evade payment of an occupational tax relating to illegal wagers as required by 26 U.S.C.A. § 4411. The Supreme Court ruled that the requirements relative to registration and payment of the tax would have had the "direct and unmistakable consequence of incriminating" the defendant and were thus unconstitutional under the Self-Incrimination Clause.

- In *Haynes v. United States*, 390 U.S. 85, 88 S.Ct. 722, 19 L.Ed.2d 923 (1968), the Court held that the privilege against self-incrimination provided a defense to prosecution either for failure to register a firearm under 26 U.S.C.A. § 5841 or for possession of an unregistered firearm under 26 U.S.C.A. § 5851.

- In *Leary v. United States*, 395 U.S. 6, 89 S.Ct. 1532, 23 L.Ed.2d 57 (1969), the Court held that the privilege against self-incrimination is a complete defense to a prosecution under 26 U.S.C.A. § 4744(a), the provision of the Marihuana Tax Act of 1937 that required payment of a tax when a person purchased marijuana (which was illegal under state laws at the time the statute was passed).

Go to the companion website for an edited version of the Supreme Court's decision in *Leary v. United States*.

The Supreme Court's decisions in this area indicate that a statutory reporting requirement violates the freedom from compulsory self-incrimination if it (1) applies to an area of activity that is "permeated with criminal statutes," (2) is directed at a "highly selective" group of persons that is "inherently suspect of criminal activities," and (3) poses a "substantial hazard" or "direct likelihood" of self-incrimination.

The Prohibition Against Cruel and Unusual Punishments

Go to the companion website for an edited version of the Supreme Court's decision in Furman v. Georgia.

The Eighth Amendment prohibits the imposition of **cruel and unusual punishments**. This principle applies both to the procedures by which criminal sentences are imposed, *Furman v. Georgia,* 408 U.S. 238, 92 S.Ct. 2726, 33 L.Ed.2d 346 (1972), and to the substantive laws that define punishments. For example, in *Coker v. Georgia,* 433 U.S. 584, 97 S.Ct. 2861, 53 L.Ed.2d 982 (1977), the Supreme Court invalidated a provision of a state death penalty law that allowed capital punishment in cases of rape. Writing for the plurality, Justice Byron White concluded that "the death penalty, which is 'unique in its severity and its irrevocability,' is an excessive penalty for the rapist who, as such, does not take human life." 433 U.S. at 598, 97 S.Ct. at 2869, 53 L.Ed.2d at 993.

Generally, however, in Eighth Amendment cases the Supreme Court does not rule on the validity of a statute but rather confines its inquiry to the constitutionality of a particular sentence. For example, in *Ewing v. California,* 538 U.S 11, 123 S.Ct. 1179, 155 L.Ed.2d 116 (2003), the Court upheld a sentence imposed under California's "three strikes and you're out" law. The defendant, who had been previously convicted of four felonies and was out on parole, was convicted of grand larceny and was sentenced to twenty-five years to life in prison. Writing for the Court, Justice O'Connor observed the following: "Ewing's sentence is a long one. But it reflects a rational legislative judgment, entitled to deference, that offenders who have committed serious or violent felonies and who continue to commit felonies must be incapacitated." 538 U.S. at 30, 123 S.Ct. 1179 at 1190, 155 L.Ed.2d at 123. In dissent, Justice Stephen Breyer pointed out that "Ewing's sentence is, at a minimum, two to three times the length of sentences that other jurisdictions would impose in similar circumstances." 538 U.S at 52, 123 S.Ct. at 1202, 155 L.Ed.2d at 137.

CASE-IN-POINT

A Constitutional Challenge to Reporting Requirements of the Federal Gun Control Act

Virgilio Patricio Flores was convicted under the Federal Gun Control Act, 18 U.S.C.A. § 922(e), for failing to provide written notice to a carrier before shipping firearms. On appeal, citing the Supreme Court decisions in *Marchetti, Haynes,* and *Leary,* Flores argued that the reporting requirement violated his Fifth Amendment privilege against self-incrimination. The Ninth Circuit Court of Appeals rejected his arguments. The court noted that the cited decisions are distinguishable because in each the Supreme Court invalidated a notice requirement in an area of activity permeated with criminal statutes or directed at a group of persons inherently suspect of criminal activities. The court found that in those cases, compliance with the reporting requirements produced an immediate or real and appreciable hazard of self-incrimination. In contrast, the Court determined that the Gun Control Act is a general regulatory statute. It is not directed at catching illegal firearm exporters, but rather at helping the states regulate firearm distribution for the safety of their citizens by shutting off the flow of weapons across their borders. A divided Court affirmed Flores's conviction; however, dissenting judges argued that the Gun Control Act has penal aspects that go beyond mere regulation and is a law designed to facilitate the discovery of criminal activity.

United States v. Flores, 753 F.2d. 1499 (9th Cir. 1985).

Go to the companion website for an edited version of the Supreme Court's decision in *Robinson v. California.*

On occasion, the Eighth Amendment has even been employed to limit the definition of crimes. In *Robinson v. California,* 370 U.S. 660, 82 S.Ct. 1417, 8 L.Ed.2d 758 (1962), the Supreme Court, relying on the Cruel and Unusual Punishments Clause, struck down a state law that made it a crime for a person to be "addicted to the use of narcotics." The Court found it unacceptable that an individual could be punished merely for a "status" without regard to any specific criminal conduct. In effect, the Court "constitutionalized" the traditional requirement that a crime involve a specific *actus reus.*

The Constitutional Right of Privacy

Go to the companion website for an edited version of the Supreme Court's decision in *Griswold v. Connecticut.*

Although there is no mention of "privacy" in the text of the Constitution, the Supreme Court has held that a sphere of intimate personal conduct is immune from legislative interference. In its first explicit recognition of this **constitutional right of privacy**, *Griswold v. Connecticut,* 381 U.S. 479, 85 S.Ct. 1678, 14 L.Ed.2d 510 (1965), the Court relied in part on the Ninth Amendment, which provides that "[t]he enumeration in the Constitution, of certain rights, shall not be construed to deny or disparage others retained by the people."

Go to the companion website for an edited version of the Supreme Court's decision in *Eisenstadt v. Baird.*

In the *Griswold* case, the Supreme Court invalidated a state law proscribing the use of birth control devices as it applied to married couples. In *Eisenstadt v. Baird,* 405 U.S. 438, 92 S.Ct. 1029, 31 L.Ed.2d 349 (1972), the Court extended the principle to protect single individuals from a similar anti-contraception statute. Writing for the Court in *Eisenstadt,* Justice William J. Brennan stated that the right of privacy is "the right of the individual, married or single, to be free from unwarranted governmental intrusion into matters so fundamentally affecting a person as the decision whether or not to beget a child." 405 U.S. at 453, 92 S.Ct. at 1038, 31 L. Ed.2d at 362.

Go to the companion website for an edited version of the Supreme Court's decision in *Roe v. Wade.*

Abortion

The Supreme Court's *Griswold* and *Eisenstadt* decisions paved the way for its landmark decision in *Roe v. Wade,* 410 U.S. 113, 93 S.Ct. 705, 35 L.Ed.2d 147 (1973). In *Roe,* the Court held that the right of privacy was broad enough to include a woman's decision to terminate her pregnancy. This 7–2 decision invalidated the Texas anti-abortion statute and rendered unenforceable similar laws in most states.

The essential holding in *Roe v. Wade* has been reaffirmed by the Supreme Court on several occasions, most notably in 2000 when it struck down a Nebraska law banning a procedure commonly described as "partial-birth abortion." *Stenberg v. Carhart,* 530 U.S. 914, 120 S.Ct. 2597, 147 L.Ed.2d 743 (2000). In April 2007, the Court upheld a similar federal enactment, but in so doing restated *Roe's* essential holding that, before fetal viability, the government may not prohibit a woman from exercising her right to terminate a pregnancy. *Gonzales v. Carhart,* 550 U.S. 124, 127 S.Ct. 1610, 167 L.Ed.2d 480 (2007).

Go to the companion website for an edited version of the Supreme Court's decision in *Stenberg v. Carhart.*

The continuing "pro-life" and "pro-choice" demonstrations around the country attest to the extremely controversial nature of legal abortion. (The abortion issue is discussed more thoroughly in Chapter 6**.)** Few questions today have greater philosophical, religious, ethical, medical, and political saliency than the issue of abortion. Seemingly irreconcilable views on the subject of abortion exist, and the issue continues to spawn legislative and judicial attention. The continuing clashes with demonstrators, resulting in injuries and even death, have caused some states to respond by restricting the proximity of demonstrators to clinics. In *Madsen v. Women's Health*

Center, 512 U.S. 753, 114 S.Ct. 2516, 129 L.Ed.2d 593 (1994), the U.S. Supreme Court attempted to balance the constitutional rights of those seeking access to abortion clinics against the First Amendment rights of the protesters. In a 6–3 decision, the Court upheld the basic provisions of a state court injunction intended to keep disruptive protesters from blocking access to the clinics.

On May 26, 1994, President Clinton signed the Freedom of Access to Clinic Entrances (FACE) Act, 18 U.S.C.A. § 248. This federal law was prompted by the 1993 killing outside a Pensacola, Florida, clinic of a doctor who performed abortions, as well as by numerous episodes around the country in which persons working at or seeking access to abortion clinics had been harassed and threatened by anti-abortion activists. The new act provides civil and criminal remedies against whomever

> by force or threat of force or by physical obstruction, intentionally injures, intimidates or interferes with or attempts to injure, intimidate or interfere with any person because that person is or has been, or in order to intimidate such person or any other person or any class of persons from, obtaining or providing reproductive health services. 18 U.S.C.A. § 248(a)(1).

The Fourth Circuit held the FACE Act does not violate the First Amendment's free speech or free exercise of religion clauses and is neither overbroad nor vague. *American Life League, Inc. v. Reno,* 47 F.3d 642 (4th Cir. 1995).

Privacy and Sexual Conduct

Prior to the 1960s, it was generally assumed that government had the authority to enforce traditional sexual mores through the criminal law. Even though laws against adultery, fornication, and sodomy were seldom enforced and had in fact been abolished in many states, few questioned the right of state and local governments to enact and enforce such prohibitions. Beginning in the 1960s, commentators began to question this assumption. The constitutional right of privacy recognized in *Griswold v. Connecticut* (1965), *Roe v. Wade* (1973), and similar decisions came to be viewed by many commentators as a shield against governmental interference with private, consensual sexual conduct between adults. Beginning in the 1970s, activists in the gay rights movement sought to use the right of privacy to attack laws criminalizing homosexual conduct.

Go to the companion website for an edited version of *Bowers v. Hardwick, Powell v. State,* and *Campbell v. Sundquist.*

In 1986 the Supreme Court declined to extend the right of privacy to protect homosexual conduct between consenting adults. In *Bowers v. Hardwick,* 478 U.S. 186, 106 S.Ct. 2841, 92 L.Ed.2d 140 (1986), the Court upheld a Georgia sodomy law as applied to homosexual conduct. After the decision in *Bowers v. Hardwick,* however, a number of state courts invalidated sodomy laws on state constitutional grounds. See, for example, *Powell v. State,* 510 S.E.2d 18 (Ga. 1998); *Campbell v. Sundquist,* 926 S.W.2d 250 (Tenn. App. 1996).

Go to the companion website for an edited version of the Supreme Court's decision in *Lawrence v. Texas.*

In 2003, the Supreme Court revisited and overturned its decision in *Bowers v. Hardwick. Lawrence v. Texas,* 539 U.S. 558, 123 S.Ct. 2472, 156 L.Ed.2d 508 (2003). Writing for the Court, Justice Kennedy asserted that a Texas law criminalizing private, consensual homosexual conduct intruded upon personal liberty and autonomy without a sufficient justification. Dissenting, Justice Antonin Scalia argued that the Court had undercut the foundations of other long-standing criminal prohibitions such as those against incest, bestiality, and bigamy. Whether Justice Scalia was correct as a matter of legal reasoning, it was clear that by 2003 public attitudes about homosexuality had changed to the point that most Americans did not believe that the state should concern itself with such conduct. On the other hand, society continues

The Virginia Supreme Court Strikes Down the State's Fornication Law

As recently as 2005, Virginia Code § 18.2-344 provided, "Any person, not being married, who voluntarily shall have sexual intercourse with any other person, shall be guilty of fornication, punishable as a Class 4 misdemeanor." Although the law had not been enforced against consenting adults for more than a century, the constitutionality of the statute was raised in a civil suit brought by a woman who accused a man of infecting her with a sexually transmitted disease. The defendant in the suit argued that the plaintiff could not recover damages inasmuch as she voluntarily participated in an unlawful act, to wit, the consensual sexual intercourse with him that resulted in her infection. The plaintiff then challenged the constitutionality of the fornication law, but the trial court upheld the statute as a rational means of protecting the public health. On appeal, the Virginia Supreme Court invalidated the prohibition as applied to consenting adults. Invoking the U.S. Supreme Court's decision in *Lawrence v. Texas* (2003), the state high court observed, "Because Code § 18.2-344, like the Texas statute at issue in *Lawrence*, is an attempt by the state to control the liberty interest which is exercised in making these personal decisions, it violates the Due Process Clause of the Fourteenth Amendment."

Martin v. Ziherl, 607 S.E.2d 367, 370 (Va. 2005).

to condemn bigamy, incest, and bestiality, and it is unlikely that courts will interpret constitutional principles so as to prevent government from expressing this condemnation through the criminal law.

The Right to Die

Since the mid-1970s, the right of privacy has been successfully asserted in state courts as a basis for refusing medical treatment. It is now settled law that a competent adult with a terminal illness has the **right to refuse medical treatment** that would unnaturally prolong his or her life. See, for example, *Satz v. Perlmutter*, 379 So.2d 359 (Fla. 1980). Under certain circumstances courts have allowed the family of a comatose individual to direct removal of extraordinary means of life support. See, for example, *In re Quinlan*, 355 A.2d 647 (N.J. 1976), featured in the Case-in-Point that follows. This manifestation of rights of privacy and personal autonomy came to be known as the **right to die**.

The right to die, if extended beyond the right of a terminally ill person to refuse artificial means of life support, runs headlong into criminal prohibitions against suicide and, potentially, homicide (see Chapter 6). As yet, courts have been unwilling to extend the right of privacy this far. For example, in *Gilbert v. State*, 487 So.2d 1185 (Fla. App. 1986), a Florida appeals court rejected Roswell Gilbert's "euthanasia" defense to the charge that he committed premeditated murder against his wife, who suffered from osteoporosis and Alzheimer's disease. More recently, the U.S. Supreme Court upheld state laws criminalizing doctor-assisted suicide. *Washington v. Glucksberg*, 521 U.S. 702, 117 S.Ct. 2258, 138 L.Ed.2d 772 (1997). Writing for the Court, Chief Justice Rehnquist observed,

Go to the companion website for an edited version of the Supreme Court's decision in *Washington v. Glucksberg*.

> Throughout the Nation, Americans are engaged in an earnest and profound debate about the morality, legality, and practicality of physician-assisted suicide. Our holding permits this debate to continue, as it should in a democratic society. 521 U.S. at 735, 117 S.Ct. at 2275, 138 L.Ed.2d at 797.

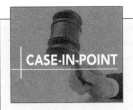

CASE-IN-POINT

The Landmark Karen Quinlan Case

Karen Quinlan was a healthy young woman who became permanently comatose after she ingested large quantities of drugs and alcohol. In this condition, she was unable to maintain normal breathing without a ventilator. After it became clear that Karen Quinlan would not regain consciousness, her parents asked her physicians to remove the respirator. The physicians refused, no doubt concerned about possible criminal prosecution or civil liability. The Quinlans went to court and obtained an order allowing removal of the life-support machine. According to the New Jersey Supreme Court, the right of privacy was "broad enough to encompass [Karen Quinlan's] decision to decline medical treatment under certain circumstances, in much the same way as it is broad enough to encompass a woman's decision to terminate pregnancy. . . ." Of course, Karen Quinlan, lying comatose in the hospital, was unable to communicate her intentions to exercise this aspect of the right of privacy. According to the Court's opinion, the "only practical way to prevent destruction of [Karen Quinlan's] right is to permit the guardian and family . . . to render their best judgment as to whether she would exercise [the right to decline treatment] in these circumstances." After Karen Quinlan was taken off the breathing machine, she lived for nine years in a coma, taking food and water through a nasogastric tube. Her parents never asked that this feeding be discontinued.
In re Quinlan, 355 A.2d 647 (N.J. 1976).

Equal Protection of the Laws

Go to the companion website for an edited version of the Supreme Court's decision in *Loving v. Virginia.*

The Fourteenth Amendment of the U.S. Constitution forbids states from denying persons **equal protection of the laws**. The Due Process Clause of the Fifth Amendment has been interpreted to impose a similar prohibition on the federal government. *Boling v. Sharpe,* 347 U.S. 497, 74 S.Ct. 693, 98 L.Ed. 884 (1954). Most state constitutions contain similar requirements. On occasion, the concept of equal protection has been used to challenge the validity of criminal statutes. For example, in *Loving v. Virginia,* 388 U.S. 1, 87 S.Ct. 1817, 18 L.Ed.2d 1010 (1967), the Supreme Court relied on the Equal Protection Clause of the Fourteenth Amendment in striking down a state statute that criminalized interracial marriage. The effect of *Loving* was that any law that criminalized conduct solely on the basis of the race of the parties was rendered null and void.

In *Eisenstadt v. Baird,* supra, the Court invoked the Equal Protection Clause in striking down a Massachusetts law that criminalized the use of birth control devices by single persons but not by married couples. And in *Craig v. Boren,* 429 U.S. 190, 97 S.Ct. 451, 50 L.Ed.2d 397 (1976), the Court invalidated an Oklahoma law that forbade the sale of beer containing 3.2 percent alcohol to females under the age of eighteen and males under the age of twenty-one. The Court concluded that the state lacked a sufficient justification for discriminating between the sexes regarding the legal availability of the contested beverage.

Go to the companion website for an edited version of *State v. Vogt.*

In recent years, women have challenged the constitutionality of laws that permit men but not women to go topless in public. For the most part these challenges have failed. For example, in *State v. Vogt,* 775 A.2d 551 (N.J. App. 2001), a New Jersey appellate court upheld an ordinance that prohibited "indecent or unnecessary exposure" of the human body in public. The law was challenged by Arlene Vogt, who was arrested for going topless on a public beach. Vogt argued that application of the law to topless women but not men "creates an invidious discrimination on the basis of gender in violation of both the federal and state constitutional guarantees of equal protection." 775 A.2d at 557. The appellate court rejected her challenge, observing, "Restrictions on exposure of the female breast are supported by the important governmental interest in safeguarding the public's moral sensibilities, and this ordinance is substantially related to that interest." 775 A.2d at 557. As the public's "moral sensibilities" change, it is likely that such restrictions will continue to be challenged.

Standards of Judicial Review

At a minimum, a criminal law prohibition that touches on a constitutionally protected interest must be "rationally related to furthering a legitimate government interest." *Massachusetts Board of Retirement v. Murgia,* 427 U.S. 307, 96 S.Ct. 2562, 49 L.Ed.2d 520 (1976). For example, a state law that makes it a crime for a person to perform surgery without a license is obviously a rational means of advancing the state's legitimate interests in public health and safety. Thus, even though the law deprives laypersons of their right to make contracts freely and discriminates against those unable to obtain a license, there is little doubt it would withstand judicial review under the **rational basis test**.

Criminal laws that infringe **fundamental rights** such as the First Amendment freedoms of speech and press are judged by a more stringent standard of review. Such laws are subject to **strict judicial scrutiny**, which means, in effect, that they are presumed to be unconstitutional. To survive judicial review, government must show that the challenged law furthers a **compelling government interest** and is narrowly tailored to that purpose. *Shapiro v. Thompson,* 394 U.S. 618, 89 S.Ct. 1322, 22 L.Ed.2d 600 (1969). This is a heavy burden for the government to carry. Consequently, most laws subjected to strict judicial scrutiny are declared unconstitutional. However, the application of strict scrutiny is not necessarily equivalent to a declaration of unconstitutionality. For example, in *New York v. Ferber,* supra, the Supreme Court upheld a child pornography law that impinged on the First Amendment freedom of expression because, in the view of the Court, the law served a compelling interest in protecting children from the abuse typically associated with the pornography industry.

The Importance of State Constitutions

Under our federal system of government, the highest court of each state possesses the authority to interpret with finality its state constitution and statutes. A decision by a state court is not subject to review by the U.S. Supreme Court, except insofar as the state law on which it is based is being challenged as a violation of the federal constitution or statutes. Because every state constitution contains language protecting individual rights and liberties, many state court decisions implicate both state and federal constitutional provisions. Under the relevant language of their constitutions and statutes, state courts are free to recognize greater (but not lesser) protections of individual rights than are provided by the U.S. Constitution as interpreted by the federal courts. As a result of the increased conservatism of the federal judiciary, and in particular the Supreme Court, over the last two decades, there has been a resurgence of interest in state constitutional law as it relates to civil rights and liberties.

In *Michigan v. Long,* 463 U.S. 1032, 1040, 103 S.Ct. 3469, 3476, 77 L.Ed.2d 1201, 1214 (1983), the U.S. Supreme Court said that "when a state court decision fairly appears to rest primarily on federal law, or to be interwoven with the federal law, and when the adequacy and independence of any possible state law ground is not clear from the face of the opinion, we will accept as the most reasonable expla-nation that the state court decided the case the way it did because it believed that federal law required it to do so." However, the Court also indicated that "if the state court decision indicates clearly and expressly that it is alternatively based on *bona fide* separate, adequate, and independent grounds, we, of course, will not undertake to review the decision." 463 U.S. at 1041, 103 S.Ct. at 3476, 77 L.Ed.2d at 1214 (1983).

Michigan v. Long effectively invited the state courts to consider the parallel pro-visions of their state constitutions independently. Some state courts have accepted the invitation. For example, 1989 the Florida Supreme Court struck down as a viola-tion of the right of privacy a statute that required parental consent in cases where minors sought abortions. The Florida court made it clear that it was basing its deci-sion on an amendment to the Florida Constitution that (unlike the federal constitu-tion) explicitly protects the right of privacy. These decisions, and many others like them, mean that a person interested in constitutional limitations on the prohibition of criminal conduct must not ignore the provisions of state constitutions that parallel the U.S. Constitution.

Conclusion

Enacting laws defining crimes and specifying punishments is a legislative function carried out by Congress and by state legislatures. The power to exercise that function is subject to the limitations in various provisions of the U.S. Constitution and state constitutions. Criminal laws must be rationally related to a legitimate public interest and must be specific to avoid being declared void for vagueness. Moreover, laws that restrict fundamental rights such as First Amendment freedoms are subject to strict judicial scrutiny. Courts address not only definitions of crimes but also the application of those definitions to specific conduct. These serious constraints on the definition of criminal conduct and the enforcement of the criminal law are sustained through the well-established power of judicial review. This protects the constitutional rights of the individual and ensures that the rule of law will prevail in the nation.

Chapter Summary

- **LO1** In *Marbury v. Madison* (1803) the U.S. Supreme Court ruled that courts have the power of judicial review, which allows them to strike down criminal laws that violate the U.S. Constitution. Without this power of judicial review, legislative compliance with the Constitution would be ineffective. Both federal and state courts exercise this power. Some statutes inherently trench on a consti-tutionally protected liberty or exceed the constitutional powers of government. Courts can declare them unconstitutional per se. Other laws may be facially valid, such as an ordinance prohibiting disorderly conduct, but may be declared unconstitutional as applied if enforced in a way that impermissibly restricts or punishes the exercise of constitutional rights.
- **LO2** Congress has used its enumerated powers, most notably the power to regu-late interstate commerce, as well as its implied powers to create a substantial body of federal criminal law. At times Supreme Court decisions have questioned the extent of Congress's legislative authority to criminalize certain conduct. In recent years, however, the Court has been inclined to view Congress as having broad authority to enact statutes to define crimes in order to deal with social problems of national scope.

- **LO3** The framers of the U.S. Constitution recognized serious abuses that occurred in England during the development of the common law. Thus, to prohibit the federal government from using the offense of treason to punish political dissenters, they narrowly defined treason to consist only of levying war against the nation or giving aid or comfort to its enemies. They then specified that "No Person shall be convicted of Treason unless on the Testimony of two Witnesses to the same overt Act, or on Confession in open Court."

- **LO4** The framers also sought to correct two other abuses by the English Parliament by constitutionally prohibiting federal and state governments from enacting bills of attainder and *ex post facto* laws. Bills of attainder are legislative acts imposing punishment without trial upon persons deemed guilty of crimes. *Ex post facto* laws are those that criminalize actions that were legal at the time they were performed or increase punishment for a criminal acts after they have been committed.

- **LO5** The Bill of Rights to the U.S. Constitution was ratified in 1791 to afford protection against the federal government. Over the years the Supreme Court has incorporated virtually all its provisions into the Fourteenth Amendment, thereby making these protections applicable to state and local governments.

- **LO6** The First Amendment, which protects freedom of speech, has been broadened in its application by the U.S. Supreme Court to protect publication, performances, demonstrations, and even expression such as wearing symbols. The Court has clearly stated that obscenity is not entitled to constitutional protection, yet the definition of "obscenity" remains somewhat vague. Probably the greatest reaction to the Court's First Amendment jurisprudence has been to its decisions allowing flag burning. In other areas the Court has struggled with whether laws against profanity and hate speech offend the First Amendment. In addition to the libelous and obscene, the genre of First Amendment protections allows government to criminalize the utterance of "fighting" words—words that tend to incite an immediate breach of the peace and create a "clear and present danger." The Court has refined the clear and present danger doctrine so that public advocacy may be prohibited only when there is imminent lawless action. Government may impose reasonable time, place, and manner regulations on public assemblies but may not otherwise ban peaceful assemblies that do not disrupt its government activities in the public forum. The First Amendment "free exercise" clause also protects religious liberty. The Supreme Court has been liberal in its approach to the right to worship in unusual ways and has invalidated ordinances prohibiting door-to-door solicitation for religious or philanthropic reasons. But it has upheld laws proscribing dangerous practices such as snake handling in religious ceremonies. While competent adults may refuse medical treatments, courts seldom allow freedom of religion as a defense to criminal charges stemming from parental refusal to seek medical treatment for their children.

- **LO7** The Second Amendment protects the right "to keep and bear arms." A long controversy over whether this protection is limited to the militia or whether it confers a personal right culminated in 2008, when the Supreme Court declared the right to keep and bear arms to be a personal right irrespective of actual or potential service in any militia. In 2010 the Court extended coverage of the Second Amendment to the states via the Fourteenth Amendment.

- **LO8** The Fifth Amendment provides that "no person . . . shall be deprived of life, liberty or property without due process of law." Similar language in the Fourteenth Amendment requires states to observe due process as well. The two fundamental aspects of due process are fair notice and fair hearing. Courts have developed a void-for-vagueness doctrine that requires that statutes define criminal offenses with sufficient definiteness so that people can understand what conduct is prohibited. An excessively vague criminal statute offends this principle and is thus invalid under the Due Process Clause of the Fifth or Fourteenth Amendments (depending on whether it is a federal or state statute). A similar doctrine known as overbreadth is used to scrutinize broad criminal laws that have the potential to intrude on freedoms protected by the First Amendment.

- **LO9** The Fifth Amendment provides that no person "shall be compelled in any criminal case to be a witness against himself." This protects a defendant's right not to testify in a criminal trial and a suspect's right to remain silent in the face of police interrogation. It also limits the degree to which legislatures can write statutes that require parties to report information to the government that can place them in jeopardy of criminal prosecution.

- **LO10** The Eighth Amendment prohibits cruel and unusual punishments and applies to sentencing procedures as well as to the substantive laws that define punishments. The Supreme Court gave it even a broader application when, in 1962, it struck down a state law that made it a crime for a person to be "addicted to the use of narcotics."

- **LO11** Prior to the 1960s it was generally assumed that government had the authority to enforce traditional sexual mores through the criminal law. The Constitution does not mention "privacy," but in 1965 the Court explicitly recognized a constitutional "right of privacy" when it invalidated a Connecticut law proscribing the use of birth control devices. This paved the way for the Court's landmark 1973 decision, which held that the right of privacy was broad enough to include a woman's decision to terminate her pregnancy. Subsequently, the Court in 2005 invalidated a Texas statute criminalizing private, consensual homosexual conduct on the ground that it intruded upon personal liberty without a sufficient justification.

- **LO12** Courts have considered the right of privacy as sufficiently broad to encompass decisions to decline medical treatment under certain circumstances. But as yet the right to die, if extended beyond the right of a terminally ill person to refuse artificial means of life support, runs into criminal prohibitions against suicide and, potentially, homicide. Courts have been unwilling to extend the right of privacy that far.

- **LO13** The Fourteenth Amendment expressly forbids states from denying equal protection of the laws to persons in their jurisdictions. The Due Process Clause of the Fifth Amendment has been interpreted to apply the same injunction to the federal government. In ruling on challenges based on equal protection of the law, courts closely scrutinize laws that make racial distinctions or treat men and women differently.

- **LO14** At a minimum, a criminal law prohibition that touches on a constitutionally protected interest must be "rationally related to furthering a legitimate government interest." Criminal laws that infringe fundamental rights such as the First Amendment freedoms of speech and press are judged by a more stringent standard of review. Such laws are subject to strict judicial scrutiny, which means, in effect, that they are presumed to be unconstitutional. To survive judicial review, government must show that the challenged law furthers a compelling government interest and is narrowly tailored to that purpose.

- **LO15** State courts can declare state laws invalid under both the federal constitution and their own state constitutions. The Supreme Court has said that if the state court decision indicates clearly and expressly that it is alternatively based on separate, adequate, and independent grounds, it will not undertake to review the decision. Thus it does not undertake to review decisions on state laws that are based on state constitutional authority that grants greater constitutional liberties than does the U.S. Constitution.

Key Terms

unconstitutional per se Refers to a law that is unconstitutional on its face, meaning that it is invalid under any given circumstances.

unconstitutional as applied Refers to a declaration by a court of law that a statute is invalid insofar as it is enforced in some particular context.

interstate commerce Economic activity between or among states or affecting more than one state.

treason The crime of making war against one's own government or giving aid and comfort to its enemies.

bill of attainder A legislative act imposing punishment without trial upon persons deemed guilty of treason or felonies. Bills of attainder are prohibited by the U.S. Constitution.

ex post facto **law** A retroactive law that criminalizes an action that was legal at the time it was performed or increases punishment for a criminal act after it was committed.

principle of legality The principle that there can be no crime or punishment in the absence of law.

First Amendment Article I of the Bill of Rights, which recognizes the freedoms of religion, speech, press, and assembly as well as the right to petition government for a redress of grievances.

Fourteenth Amendment Amendment to the U.S. Constitution ratified after the Civil War in 1868. Prohibits states from denying due process and equal protection of law to persons within their jurisdictions and provides Congress legislative power to enforce these prohibitions.

Due Process Clause The clause of the Fifth Amendment to the U.S. Constitution that prohibits the federal government from depriving persons within its jurisdiction of life, liberty, or property without due process of law. A similar provision in the Fourteenth Amendment imposes the same prohibition on state governments.

clear and present danger doctrine In constitutional law, the doctrine that the First Amendment does not protect those forms of expression that pose a "clear and present danger" of bringing about some substantive evil that government has a right to prevent.

imminent lawless action Unlawful conduct that is about to take place and that is inevitable unless there is intervention by the authorities.

freedom of expression The right of the individual to express thoughts and feelings through speech, writing, and other media of expression; protected by the First Amendment to the U.S. Constitution.

symbolic speech Expression by displaying symbols, making gestures, and so forth.

fighting words Utterances that are inherently likely to provoke a violent response from an individual or group to which they are directed.

hate speech Offensive speech directed at members of racial, religious, sexual, or ethnic minorities.

obscenity Explicit sexual material that is patently offensive, appeals to a prurient or unnatural interest in sex, and lacks serious scientific, artistic, or literary content.

public forum A public space generally acknowledged as appropriate for public assemblies or expressions of views.

time, place, and manner regulations Government limitations on the time, place, and manner of expressive activities in the public forum.

freedom of religion The First Amendment right to the free exercise of one's religion without undue interference by government.

right to keep and bear arms Right to possess certain weapons; protected against governmental infringement by the Second Amendment to the U.S. Constitution.

vagueness doctrine Doctrine of constitutional law holding unconstitutional (as a violation of due process) legislation that fails to clearly inform the person of what is required or proscribed.

doctrine of overbreadth Doctrine enabling a person to make a facial challenge to a law on the ground that the law might be applied in the future against activities protected by the First Amendment.

cruel and unusual punishments Criminal penalties that shock the moral conscience of the community—for example, torture and other extreme forms of corporal punishment. Prohibited by the Eighth Amendment to the U.S. Constitution.

constitutional right of privacy Implied constitutional right allowing individuals to be free of government interference in intimate activities, especially those involving sex and reproduction.

right to refuse medical treatment The right of a patient—or a patient's surrogate in some instances—to refuse to allow doctors to administer medical treatment.

right to die The asserted right to terminate one's own life under certain circumstances; also refers to termination of extraordinary means of life support.

equal protection of the laws Constitutional requirement, made explicit in the Fourteenth Amendment, that the government afford the same legal protection to all persons.

rational basis test The judicial requirement that legislation must be rationally related to a legitimate government objective in order to survive constitutional challenge.

fundamental rights Those constitutional rights that have been declared to be fundamental by the courts. Include First Amendment freedoms, the right to vote, and the right to privacy.

strict judicial scrutiny Judicial review of government action or policy in which the ordinary presumption of constitutionality is reversed.

compelling government interest A government interest sufficiently strong that it overrides the fundamental rights of persons adversely affected by government action or policy.

Questions for Thought and Discussion

Can you think of an example of an *ex post facto* law?

1. Is it possible for the criminal law to define the crime of obscenity precisely enough to avoid the "vice of vagueness" or the problem of overbreadth?

2. Can a municipality enforce an ordinance totally banning religious organizations from canvassing neighborhoods in search of new members? What about an ordinance that prohibits such canvassing between the hours of 8 P.M. and 8 A.M.?

3. Should the constitutional right of privacy invalidate criminal statutes that require a minor to obtain parental consent to obtain an abortion?

4. Would the constitutional right of privacy provide a defense to a charge of possession of obscene materials where videotapes were viewed only by the defendant in the privacy of his or her home?

5. Could a father who, without judicial approval, unplugs the respirator sustaining the breathing of his comatose, terminally ill child be prosecuted for murder?

6. Would a law making it an offense for a person to carry prescription medicine in other than the original, labeled container meet the test of being rationally related to a legitimate government interest?

7. How does the doctrine of judicial review affect the power of a state legislature to define criminal conduct? Would the constitutional limitations on legislative power be effective without the power of courts to declare laws unconstitutional?

8. Give an example of a law that would be constitutional per se, and point out how such a law might be unconstitutional in its application to a specific conduct.

9. Give an example of a law defining a crime that, although held to be constitutional by the U.S. Supreme Court, has been declared unconstitutional by some state courts. Why can such a result occur in our federal system?

Problems for Discussion and Solution

1. A federal statute enacted in 1999 makes it a crime for anyone to publish depictions of animal cruelty for commercial gain. A company operates a website that streams live videos of cockfights. The company claims that the cockfights take place in Puerto Rico, where cockfighting is not prohibited. The company is challenging the constitutionality of the federal statute on basis of the First Amendment, although it has not yet been prosecuted or even threatened with prosecution under the law. What are the company's chances of prevailing in its lawsuit?

2. Amelia Eyeland has been arrested for trespass, disorderly conduct, and resisting arrest. The charges stem from an incident in which Amelia and other members of the Green Warriors staged a raucous protest in a privately owned shopping mall during regular business hours. The protest was aimed at the decision of the mall's owners to expand the mall's parking lot into a wetlands area known to be a habitat for a number of animals. Amelia's attorney is considering a defense based on the First Amendment freedoms of speech and assembly. What chance does the attorney have at being successful with this defense?

3. John Masters, a licensed psychotherapist, has been charged with violating a new state statute making it a crime for "any licensed psychologist, psychiatrist, or psychotherapist to have sexual intercourse with a patient during the existence of the professional relationship." Masters is challenging the constitutionality of the

statute on two principal grounds: (a) that it intrudes on his right of privacy, and (b) that it violates the Equal Protection Clause of the Fourteenth Amendment in that it fails to apply the same prohibition to other health care professionals. Do you think Masters is likely to prevail in his challenge to the statute? If you were a judge faced with these constitutional questions, how would you be inclined to rule? What additional information would you need to render your decision?

CHAPTER **4**

Elements of Crimes and Parties to Crimes

LEARNING OBJECTIVES

After reading this chapter, you should be able to explain . . .

1. why a prohibited act is the one indispensable element of a crime
2. the circumstances under which the failure to act can be considered a criminal act
3. how possession can be considered a criminal act and the difference between actual and constructive possession
4. why one's status cannot be the basis for criminal prosecution
5. why criminal intent historically has been an important element of common-law crimes
6. the difference between general-intent and specific-intent crimes
7. why proving causation is important in prosecuting specific-intent crimes
8. how the Model Penal Code recognizes "culpable mental states"
9. why many modern *mala prohibita* crimes are considered strict liability offenses and why strict liability offenses do not require proof of criminal intent
10. how "principals" differ from "accessories" and how "accessories before the fact" differ from "accessories after the fact"
11. how and why the modern criminal law has largely abolished the distinction between principals and accessories before the fact

CHAPTER OUTLINE

Introduction
The *Actus Reus* (The Act Requirement)
The *Mens Rea* (The Criminal Intent Requirement)
Strict Liability Offenses
The Causation Requirement
Parties to a Crime
Conclusion

Chapter Summary

Key Terms

Questions for Thought and Discussion

Problems for Discussion and Solution

Police stopped Lawrence Robinson on a Los Angeles street and noticed scarring and discoloration on his arms. Upon questioning, Robinson admitted to occasional intravenous drug use. Robinson was arrested, tried, and convicted under a California statute that made it a misdemeanor for a person to "be addicted to the use of narcotics." The Appellate Department of the Los Angeles County Superior Court affirmed the conviction without opinion. After unsuccessful attempts to obtain further appellate review in the California courts, Robinson appealed to the U.S. Supreme Court. In *Robinson v. California*, 370 U.S. 660, 82 S.Ct. 1417, 8 L.Ed.2d 758 (1962), the high court overturned the conviction and declared unconstitutional the statute under which Robinson had been prosecuted. Speaking for the Court, Justice Potter Stewart noted that the law "makes the 'status' of narcotic addiction a criminal offense, for which the offender may be prosecuted 'at any time before he reforms.'" 370 U.S. at 663, 82 S.Ct. at 1418, 8 L.Ed.2d at 761. In what was at that time a novel interpretation of the Eighth Amendment, the Court held that "a state law which imprisons a person thus afflicted as a criminal, even though he has never touched any narcotic drug within the State or been guilty of any irregular behavior there, inflicts a cruel and unusual punishment. . . ." 370 U.S. at 667, 82 S.Ct. at 1421, 8 L.Ed.2d at 763.

The *Robinson* case has come to stand for the proposition that one's status cannot be the basis for criminal liability. Criminal liability can exist only where there is a wrongful act that is specifically prohibited by the law. Thus, although theft is a crime, the status of *being a thief* is not. Normally, but not always, this wrongful act must be accompanied by some culpable mental state. These are the basic elements of criminal liability that we have inherited from the English common law. These elements, along with the classification of parties to crimes, are the subjects of this chapter.

Introduction

As we noted in the opening vignette, the traditional elements of a crime are a wrongful act, often referred to as the *actus reus*, and the culpable state of mind or criminal intent, frequently called the *mens rea*. To establish that a defendant is guilty of a crime, the prosecution must prove the defendant committed some legally proscribed act or failed to act when the law required certain action. In most instances the prosecution must also prove that such act or failure to act occurred with a concurrent criminal intent. It would be contrary to our common-law heritage to punish someone who accidentally or unwittingly committed a wrongful act without any intent to commit a crime, but there are some exceptions to this common-law principle. Likewise, a person cannot be punished for a mere intention, however wrongful that intention may be.

Certain offenses, primarily regulatory and public-welfare–type offenses, are classified as strict liability crimes and are exceptions to the common-law concept of requiring proof of a defendant's criminal intent. They came into prominence in America during the Industrial Revolution, and today they form a significant part of the substantive criminal law, particularly the so-called "public welfare offenses" such as food and drug laws and traffic offenses.

In addition to the basic requirement of establishing a physical act and intent, in some instances the prosecution must establish that certain circumstances existed at the time the act was committed. For example, in some sexual battery offenses the prosecution must establish that the defendant's acts occurred without the victim's consent. Moreover, in other situations the prosecution must establish that a defendant's acts caused specific results. For instance, in homicide cases the prosecution must prove a causal relationship between the defendant's act and the victim's death.

The English common law classified crimes as *felonies* and *misdemeanors*. Felonies were very serious crimes; misdemeanors were lesser offenses. Early English common law imposed the death penalty on felons but developed categories of offenders to lessen the punishment meted out to those who assisted in the commission of felonies. At common law, parties to crimes were classified as **principals** in the first and second degree, **accessories before the fact**, and **accessories after the fact**. Crimes were classified as felonies and misdemeanors. An awareness of the history of these terms leads to a better understanding of their function in contemporary American criminal law and the procedure of federal and state court systems. In this chapter we first explain the elements of a crime; then we discuss parties to crimes.

The *Actus Reus* (The Act Requirement)

The term *actus reus* means "the act of a criminal." But simply committing a wrongful act does not mean that one has committed a crime. To fulfill the requirements of the criminal law, the actor must willfully commit a proscribed physical act or intentionally fail to act where the law requires a person to act. The rationale for the *actus reus* requirement is to prevent a person from being guilty of an offense based on thoughts or intent alone. Common-law crimes required commission of an act or omission and not merely possession of an evil state of mind. Of course, in the United States, a law that made it a criminal offense simply to entertain an evil thought would be patently unconstitutional.

What Is an Act?

Probably the most complete definition of an "act" as contemplated by the criminal law is found in the Model Penal Code (MPC), which we introduced in Chapter 1. In section 1.13(2) the MPC defines "act" as a "bodily movement whether voluntary or involuntary"; however, section 2.01(1) states that "a person is not guilty of an offense unless his liability is based on conduct that includes a voluntary act or the omission to perform an act of which he is capable." Indeed, courts have generally held that some outward manifestation of voluntary conduct must occur to constitute the physical act necessary in criminal law. The rationale for the requirement of a voluntary act is simple: Only those persons whose acts result from free choice should be criminally punished. Most acts are voluntary. For example, when you raise your hand, it is considered a voluntary act, but when your hand moves as a result of a muscle spasm, it is not a voluntary act. Likewise, movements committed by a person who is unconscious, or acts by someone having an epileptic seizure or sleepwalking, are not regarded as voluntary acts. On the other hand, a driver who takes sleeping pills before beginning to operate an automobile and then falls asleep at the wheel would generally be held criminally responsible for a traffic accident because the driver voluntarily committed the act of taking the pills. Consider the following examples:

- John enters Tom's house or strikes Tom. John has quite obviously committed an "act."
- John picks up a pistol and fires it in the direction of Tom. John, by pulling the trigger of the gun, has committed an "act."
- John hands Tom a glass of liquid to be given to Bob. Unknown to Tom, John added poison to the glass of liquid before handing it to Tom. Tom gives the liquid to Bob, who drinks it and dies. Here John has acted through Tom, an innocent agent; thus, John has committed the "act."
- While riding as a passenger on a bus, John suffers an unexpected attack of epilepsy. As a consequence, John violently kicks his leg, inflicting an injury on Tom, a fellow passenger. John would not be criminally responsible for the injury to Tom.

When Does Failure to Act Constitute an Act?

The requirement for an act is usually fulfilled by an affirmative act. But even a person's failure to act—that is, an **act of omission**—can satisfy the requirements of a physical act in the criminal law. To be guilty of a crime for failure to act, there must have been a legal duty to act in the first place. Such a duty can arise in one of three ways: (1) by relationship of the actor to the victim, for example, parent–child or husband–wife; (2) by a statutory duty; or (3) by contract between the actor and the victim. Consider these examples:

- Mark, an expert swimmer, is lying on the beach and sees a young girl, unrelated to him, struggling to stay afloat and crying for help. Mark disregards her cries, and she drowns. Is Mark criminally liable? The answer is no, for although we might agree that Mark had a strong moral obligation to attempt to save the child, there was no legal obligation to do so. If, on the other hand, Mark were the child's parent or guardian, or a lifeguard on duty, then Mark's failure to act would most likely qualify as a criminal act.

CASE-IN-POINT

The *Actus Reus* Requirement

Law officers found two whiskey stills and all the paraphernalia for making liquor on the defendant's land. Seeing no activity, they drove away. As they did, they met a car driven by the defendant heading toward the property. The car contained a quantity of sugar and other indicators of the illegal activity the officers suspected. The defendant committed no act of making liquor in the presence of the officers, but on the basis of what they observed, they arrested the defendant, and he was convicted of making liquor unlawfully.

On appeal, the South Carolina Supreme Court reversed the conviction, observing that "the evidence overwhelmingly tends to show an intention to manufacture liquor. . . . But intent alone, not coupled with some overt act . . . is not cognizable by the court. [T]he act must always amount to more than mere preparation, and move directly toward the commission of the crime." Citing respectable textbook authority, the court explained that the law does not concern itself with mere guilty intention unconnected with any overt act.

State v. Quick, 19 S.E.2d 101 (S.C. 1942).

- Jennifer receives an annual income of $50,000 from the operation of her business. She fails to file a federal income tax return as required by the laws of the United States. Is Jennifer's omission a criminal act? Clearly it is, for she has violated a statutory obligation, the breach of which is punishable by law.
- Dr. Gore, a surgeon, undertakes to perform an operation on a patient for a fee. Before completing the operation, Dr. Gore decides to cease his efforts. As a result of such inattention, the patient dies. Would Dr. Gore's failure to complete what he undertook professionally qualify as an act within the meaning of the criminal law? Yes, because Dr. Gore had a contractual relationship with his patient.

In some instances, failure to perform an **administrative-type act** required by law might not be a crime. In *Lambert v. California,* 355 U.S. 225, 78 S.Ct. 240, 2 L.Ed.2d 228 (1957), the U.S. Supreme Court reviewed a case where the defendant, a convicted felon, was charged with failing to register with authorities as required by a Los Angeles city ordinance. The Court held that as applied to one who has no actual knowledge of a duty to register and where no showing is made of the probability of such knowledge, the ordinance violates the Due Process Clause of the Fourteenth Amendment to the U.S. Constitution. In contrasting the ordinance requiring felon registration with various public welfare offenses it had upheld, the Court noted that public welfare offenses punish failure to act only in "circumstances that should alert the doer to the consequences of his deed." *Lambert v. California,* 355 U.S. at 228, 78 S.Ct. at 243, 2 L.Ed.2d at 231. However, *Lambert's* reach has been limited. In *Texaco, Inc. v. Short,* 454 U.S. 516, 537–38 n. 33, 102 S.Ct. 781, 70 L.Ed.2d 738 (1982), the Supreme Court noted that its application has been so circumscribed that it gives "some credence to Justice Frankfurter's colorful prediction in dissent [in *Lambert*] that the case would stand as 'an isolated deviation from the strong current of precedents—a derelict on the waters of the law'" (quoting *Lambert,* 355 U.S. at 232, 78 S.Ct. at 245 [Frankfurter, J., dissenting]).

Possession as a Criminal Act

In certain crimes, **possession** alone is considered to be the wrongful act. For example, in the offense of carrying a concealed weapon, the possession of the weapon concealed from ordinary observation is the wrongful act. Likewise, possession of contraband such as illegal drugs or untaxed liquors constitutes the wrongful act element of certain offenses. Possession is not usually defined in criminal statutes; however, courts generally define possession as the power to control something. The law recognizes two classes of possession: actual and constructive. **Actual possession** exists when a person has something under his or her direct physical control. An example of actual possession would be when an item is on your person, within your reach, or located in a place where you alone have access. **Constructive possession**, on the other hand, is a more difficult concept because it is based on a legal fiction. A person who has the power and intention to control something either directly or through another person is said to be in constructive possession. The exact meaning of these terms is usually determined by the context of the situation. The difficulty is exacerbated when two or more persons are in joint possession of the premises or vehicle where an object is found. Consider the following examples:

- Sarah and Tiffany rent and share an apartment. A police search yields contraband: Drugs are found on the coffee table in the living room, which is used by both Sarah and Tiffany. Can both be charged with possession of the contraband?

They probably can. Possession by both Sarah and Tiffany can be inferred because the drugs are in plain view and located in a place to which both have access.

- Under the same circumstances of a shared apartment, drugs are found in a privately owned, closed container in a dresser drawer where only Sarah keeps clothing and valuables. Because Tiffany has no access to this area, the law does not infer that Tiffany has constructive possession of the contents of the drawer. Of course, there might be circumstances under which the prosecution could prove that Tiffany actually had rights to the drugs, knowledge of their whereabouts, and/or access to them. Then the prosecution could establish that Tiffany was in constructive possession of the contraband.

People v. Valot, a Michigan appellate court decision illustrating divergent views of constructive possession, is reproduced on the companion website.

Status as a Criminal Act

Go to the companion website for an edited version of *Robinson v. California.*

Status refers to a person's state of being, and ordinarily the state cannot criminalize a person's status. For example, a person's race or gender represents a status. But is addiction to narcotics a status that cannot be criminalized? In *Robinson v. California,* 370 U.S. 660, 82 S.Ct. 1417, 8 L.Ed.2d 758 (1962), the U.S. Supreme Court declared unconstitutional a California statute that made it an offense for a person "to be addicted to the use of narcotics." The Court observed that

> we deal with a statute which makes the "status" of narcotic addiction a criminal offense, for which the offender may be prosecuted "at any time before he reforms.. . ." We hold that a state law which imprisons a person thus afflicted as a criminal, even though he has never touched any narcotic drug within the State or been guilty of any irregular behavior there, inflicts a cruel and unusual punishment in violation of the Fourteenth Amendment. 370 U.S. at 666–667, 82 S.Ct. at 1420–1421, 8 L.Ed.2d at 762–763.

Go to the companion website for an edited version of *Powell v. Texas.*

The issue of when a criminal statute proscribes status, as opposed to conduct, can be very close. This is illustrated by the Supreme Court's decision in *Powell v. Texas,* 392 U.S. 514, 88 S.Ct. 2145, 20 L.Ed.2d 1254 (1968). Powell was a chronic alcoholic who was convicted of public intoxication. Four justices held that Powell had been punished for being in a public place on a particular occasion while intoxicated rather than for his status as a chronic alcoholic. A fifth justice concurred in affirming Powell's conviction. But the four dissenting justices thought the case was indistinguishable from *Robinson v. California,* supra. In their view, both cases involved defendants who were prosecuted for being in a condition that they had no capacity to alter or avoid.

The *Mens Rea* (The Criminal Intent Requirement)

The common law developed the doctrine that there should be no crime without a *mens rea,* or "guilty mind." This element is customarily referred to as the criminal intent. To constitute a crime, there must be a concurrence of the *actus reus* with a person's criminal intent. Strict liability offenses, discussed later, are an exception to this principle.

Criminal intent must be distinguished from **motive**. To obtain a conviction, a prosecutor must establish the defendant's criminal intent but not necessarily the defendant's motive for committing a crime. A person's motive often equates with an impulse, an incentive, or a reason for certain behavior, and proof of one's motive can assist in establishing criminal intent. To illustrate, if the prosecution relies on circumstantial evidence to establish the defendant's guilt in a homicide case, the fact that the defendant had vowed "to get even" with the victim might be a relevant factor in the proof. Yet the failure to establish a defendant's motive is not fatal to proving guilt. On the other hand, good motives do not exonerate a person from a crime. Thus, one who steals food to feed a poor, hungry family might have a noble motive. Nevertheless, such a person would be guilty of a crime because of his or her act and intent.

The basic reason that the law requires proof of a criminal intent as well as an act or omission is to distinguish those acts or omissions that occur accidentally from those committed by a person with a "guilty mind." As the California Supreme Court observed in *In re Hayes*, 442 P.2d 366, 369 (Cal. 1968), "an essential element of every orthodox crime is a wrongful or blameworthy mental state of some kind."

Concurrence of Act and Intent

To constitute a crime, there must be a concurrence of the *mens rea* and the *actus reus*. Many years ago, the Massachusetts Supreme Court articulated this traditional common-law standard when it observed, "An evil intention and an unlawful action must concur in order to constitute a crime." *Commonwealth v. Mixer*, 93 N.E. 249 (Mass. 1910). In 1872, California stipulated in Section 20 of the California Penal Code that "the defendant's wrongful intent and his physical act must concur in the sense that the act must be motivated by the intent." See *People v. Green*, 609 P.2d 468, 500 (Cal. 1980). Concurrence of the act and intent usually, but not always, occurs simultaneously. For example, suppose an owner accidentally starts a fire in his or her building without any intention to defraud. The owner then takes no steps to extinguish the fire or notify the fire department. The owner's omission to act concurs with the owner's intent to defraud the insurer of the premises. See *Commonwealth v. Cali*, 141 N.E.510 (Mass. 1923). On the other hand, suppose Andrew forms an intent to kill his enemy, Bryan, but after completely abandoning the idea, Andrew later inadvertently kills Bryan in a traffic accident. There would be no concurrence of the original intent with the subsequent act.

General and Specific Intent

At common law, crimes were classified as requiring either general intent or specific intent. *United States v. Bailey*, 444 U.S. 394, 403, 100 S.Ct. 624, 631, 62 L.Ed.2d 575 (1980). American courts followed that tradition. **General intent** is the intent to do an act but not necessarily to cause the results that occur from that act.

Where a crime requires only proof of a general intent, the fact finder (that is, the judge or jury) may infer the defendant's intent from the defendant's acts and the circumstances surrounding those acts. Thus, the prosecution does not have to prove that the defendant had any specific intent to cause a particular result when the act was committed: "General intent exists when from the circumstances the prohibited result may reasonably be expected to follow from the offender's voluntary act, irrespective of a subjective desire to have accomplished such result." *Myers v. State*, 422 N.E.2d 745, 750 (Ind. App. 1981).

Historically, many trial judges instructed juries that "the law presumes that a person intends the ordinary consequences of his voluntary acts." In 1979, in *Sandstrom v. Montana*, 442 U.S. 510, 99 S.Ct. 2450, 61 L.Ed.2d 39, the Supreme

Court ruled that it is unconstitutional for a judge so to instruct the jury. The Court held that such a presumption conflicts with the presumption of innocence of the accused and violates the Due Process Clause of the Fourteenth Amendment, which requires that the state prove every element of a criminal offense beyond a reasonable doubt.

Most criminal statutes that prohibit particular voluntary acts are classified as **general-intent statutes**. "General intent means the intent to do that which the law prohibits; an individual need not have intended the precise harm or precise result which eventuated." *State v. Poss,* 298 N.W.2d 80, 83 (S.D. 1980). Statutory words such as "willfully" or "intentionally" generally indicate that the offender must have only intended to do the act and not to accomplish any particular result. Thus, a statute making it the crime of arson "willfully and unlawfully" to set fire to a building is generally viewed as defining a general-intent crime. *Linehan v. State,* 476 So.2d 1262 (Fla. 1985). On the other hand, **specific intent** refers to an actor's mental purpose to accomplish a particular result beyond the act itself. Again, in the context of the crime of arson, suppose the statute read that it was an offense for any person "to willfully and with the intent to injure or defraud an insurance company set fire to any building." In this instance the prosecution would be required to prove that the defendant had the specific intent to injure or defraud an insurance company when the proscribed act was perpetrated. Specific intent is the intent to accomplish the precise act that the law prohibits. *State v. Poss,* 298 N.W.2d 80, 83 (S.D.1980). Again, a statute defining murder that includes the language "premeditated killing of a human being" requires the prosecution to prove the defendant's specific intent. Courts have consistently said that a **specific-intent statute** designates "a special mental element which is required above and beyond any mental state required with respect to the *actus reus* of the crime." See, for example, *State v. Bridgeforth,* 750 P.2d 3, 5 (Ariz. 1988).

Assume that State X charged a defendant with burglary of a dwelling under a specific-intent statute that defines the offense as "the unauthorized entry of a dwelling by a person with the intent to commit theft therein." Three basic elements must be established to convict the defendant. First, the state must prove the defendant made an unauthorized entry. Second, it must prove that the entry was made into a dwelling. Finally, it must establish that the defendant made such unauthorized entry with the intent to commit a theft. Intent, of course, is a state of mind, but it can be (and almost always is) inferred from the defendant's actions and surrounding circumstances. Therefore, if some of the dwelling owner's property had been moved and other items left in disarray, the inference would be that the defendant who made the unauthorized entry intended to commit theft from the dwelling. Moreover, this would be true whether the defendant did in fact commit a theft within the dwelling.

The Michigan Supreme Court summed up the difference between specific and general intent in 2000 when it observed that its decisions have held that "the distinction between specific intent and general intent crimes is that the former involve a particular criminal intent beyond the act done, while the latter involve merely the intent to do the physical act." *People v. Nowack,* 614 N.W.2d 78, 84 (Mich. 2000).

In a situation where the defendant might not have had a specific intent to cause a particular result but there was a substantial likelihood of the result occurring, and the act was done with conscious disregard or indifference for the consequences, some courts have developed the concept of **constructive intent** as a substitute for the defendant's specific intent.

The Model Penal Code Approach to Intent

Over the years, the common-law classifications of general and specific intent have become subject to many variations in court decisions in the various jurisdictions. In the chapters of this text that discuss substantive offenses, the reader will find a variety of terms that legislatures and courts have used to describe the *mens rea* requirements of various crimes. Such terms include *unlawfully, feloniously, willfully, maliciously, wrongfully, deliberately, recklessly, negligently, with premeditated intent, with culpable negligence, with gross negligence,* and numerous others. In some instances courts have even disagreed on whether these *mens rea* requirements apply to every material element of an offense.

The wide variety of terms used to describe the mental element of crimes and the dichotomy between general and specific intent have led to considerable difficulty in determining intent requirements in statutory crimes. In 1980 the Supreme Court recognized the common-law classification of crimes as requiring either "general intent" or "specific intent" but observed how difficult it is to determine the proper *mens rea* in the definitions of crimes. Nevertheless, the Court pointed out that this distinction has been a continuing source of confusion. Congress has not adopted the Model Penal Code, although in 1980 the Supreme Court alluded to the merits of the MPC classification (referring to the 1962 tentative draft of the MPC) that replaces the term "intent" with a hierarchy of culpable states, ranked in descending order as purpose, knowledge, recklessness, and negligence. *United States v. Bailey*, 444 U.S. 394, 100 S.Ct. 624, 62 L.Ed.2d 575 (1980). However, courts must deal with the intent requirement that legislative bodies include when defining statutory crimes. Thus, in its decision in *Holloway v. United States*, 526 U.S. 1, 119 S.Ct. 966, 143 L.Ed.2d 1 (1999), the Court referred to a federal statute in 18 U.S.C.A. § 2119, which defined carjacking as "tak[ing] a motor vehicle . . . from . . . another by force and violence or by intimidation . . . with the intent to cause death or serious bodily harm," as a law including a specific-intent element.

Today, almost all crimes are statutory, and in 1985 the American Law Institute published the official draft of the MPC, with some revisions of the earlier tentative draft published in 1962. The MPC rejects the common-law terms for intent. Instead, it simplifies the terms describing culpability and proposes four states of mind: purposely, knowingly, recklessly, and negligently. M.P.C. § 2.02(2). Section 2.02(4) states that the prescribed culpability requirement applies to all material elements of an offense. (The term "purposely" seems to correspond roughly to the common-law specific-intent requirement, while other MPC categories seem to fall within the general-intent category.)

Several legislative revisions of state criminal codes have followed the MPC in setting standards of culpability. For example, in 1977 Alabama adopted section 13A-2-2 of its Criminal Code. The commentary following the new section notes that it attempts "to identify, define and reasonably delimit the main culpable mental states involved in the criminal law." It provides that the following definitions of culpability apply:

1. Intentionally. A person acts intentionally with respect to a result or to conduct described by a statute defining an offense, when his purpose is to cause that result or to engage in that conduct.
2. Knowingly. A person acts knowingly with respect to conduct or to a circumstance described by a statute defining an offense when he is aware that his conduct is of that nature or that the circumstance exists.

3. Recklessly. A person acts recklessly with respect to a result or to a circumstance described by a statute defining an offense when he is aware of and consciously disregards a substantial and unjustifiable risk that the result will occur or that the circumstance exists. The risk must be of such nature and degree that disregard thereof constitutes a gross deviation from the standard of conduct that a reasonable person would observe in the situation. A person who creates a risk but is unaware thereof solely by reason of voluntary intoxication, as defined in subdivision (e)(2) of Section 13A-3-2, acts recklessly with respect thereto.

4. Criminal negligence. A person acts with criminal negligence with respect to a result or to a circumstance that is defined by statute as an offense when he fails to perceive a substantial and unjustifiable risk that the result will occur or that the circumstance exists. The risk must be of such nature and degree that the failure to perceive it constitutes a gross deviation from the standard of care that a reasonable person would observe in the situation. A court or jury may consider statutes or ordinances regulating the defendant's conduct as bearing upon the question of criminal negligence.

Commentary following section 13A-2-2 further notes that this section "is derived principally from Michigan Revised Criminal Code § 305, which followed New York Penal Law § 15.05, which in turn is based on the Model Penal Code § 2.02." Some other states have essentially adopted the MPC proposals, and, like Alabama, several have opted to use the term "intentionally" instead of the MPC term "purposely" in the first category of culpability. This difference appears to be only one of terminology.

Section 13A-6-3 of Alabama's Criminal Code now begins defining "manslaughter" by stating, in part, that "[a] person commits the crime of manslaughter if (1) He recklessly causes the death of another person ...," whereas a state that has not adopted the MPC classifications might define manslaughter in terms of "an unlawful killing of a person by culpable negligence" or "a killing of a human being without malice aforethought."

In addition to understanding traditional concepts of general and specific intent, a student should become acquainted with previously quoted sections of the MPC that define "act" and relate to levels of culpability. While these are among the most widely relied-on provisions of the MPC, in later chapters dealing with substantive

---

CASE-IN-POINT

The *Mens Rea* Requirement

The defendant was convicted under a statute that made it an offense to fondle or caress the body of a child less than sixteen years old "with the intent to gratify the sexual desires or appetites of the offending person or . . . to frighten or excite such child." On appeal, the Indiana Supreme Court noted that the strongest evidence in favor of the prosecution was that both the defendant's daughters admitted that during playfulness the father touched and came in contact with the breasts of one of his daughters. However, there was no evidence that this was done with the intent to gratify the sexual desires of the defendant or to frighten the child.

In reversing the defendant's conviction, the court observed that "[a] crime has two components—an evil intent coupled with an overt act. The act alone does not constitute the crime unless it is done with a specific intent declared unlawful by the statute in this state. . . . There must also be proved beyond a reasonable doubt, the specific intent at the time of touching to gratify sexual desires or to frighten the child as stated in the statute."

Markiton v. State, 139 N.E.2d 440, 441 (Ind. 1957).

crimes we refer to instances where the MPC has been influential in the revision of criminal statutes.

In 1978 Arizona adopted the four MPC culpable mental states of intention, knowledge, recklessness, and criminal negligence, as defined in A.R.S. § 13-105; M.P.C. § 2.02(2). These replaced all previous mental states used in Arizona's criminal laws. See *State v. Robles*, 623 P.2d 1245, 1246 (Ariz. App.1981).

The Doctrine of Transferred Intent

The **doctrine of transferred intent** transfers an actor's original intent against an intended victim to an unintended victim who suffers the consequences. An English court invoked the doctrine in 1575 in the classic case *Regina v. Sounders & Archer*, 75 Eng. Rep. 706, where Saunders gave his wife a poisoned apple. After tasting it but suffering no consequences, the wife gave the apple to her daughter, who died from the poison. The court found that Saunders caused his daughter's death despite the fact he intended no harm to her. American courts apply the doctrine primarily in assaultive and homicide cases, often referred to as the "missed aim" cases, but it can apply to other crimes such as, for example, arson. Because the doctrine supplies an intent to commit a crime against a person where no such intent existed, it is often referred to as a "legal fiction." It is designed to avoid an otherwise unjust result by obviating the need for the prosecution to establish that it was predictable an accused's actions would have caused harm to an unintended victim. Instead of following the doctrine of transferred intent, the MPC deals with such a situation on the basis of causation. M.P.C. Sec. 2.02(2)(a).

In *State v. Gardner*, 203 A.2d 77 (Del. 1964), the Delaware Supreme Court ruled that where a defendant whose express malice aforethought was directed toward an intended victim but not in fact toward the actual victim who was killed, a defendant can nevertheless be convicted of first-degree murder. The court noted that courts in the great majority of other states consider the defendant guilty of the same crime as if the defendant had accomplished the original purpose. As more recently explained by the North Carolina Supreme Court,

> [U]nder the doctrine of transferred intent, it is immaterial whether the defendant intended injury to the person actually harmed; if he in fact acted with the required or elemental intent toward someone, that intent suffices as the intent element of the crime charged as a matter of substantive law. *State v. Locklear*, 415 S.E.2d 726, 730 (N.C. 1992).

Most transferred intent cases involve homicides. As the doctrine developed, some courts expressed disagreement as to whether a defendant's specific intent to kill an individual is transferred to an unintended victim. But even if the actor's *specific intent* is not transferred, the killing of an unintended victim can be prosecuted as a homicidal crime or other offense not requiring proof of the defendant's specific intent. Because the doctrine is designed to punish an offender who "misses aim" and kills or injures an unintended victim, jurisdictions have split on whether it also applies when the accused kills or injures both the intended and the unintended victims. Some courts reason that it is unnecessary to apply the doctrine in such cases. But in *Poe v. State*, 671 A.2d 501 (Md. 1996), Maryland's highest court held that the doctrine of transferred intent applied where the defendant, intending to kill a woman, fired a shot that wounded the woman who was targeted, passed through her, and killed a child standing nearby.

California Court Reaffirms the Doctrine of Transferred Intent

CASE-IN-POINT

On May 28, 2000, Lori Gonzalez, age 20, was sitting in the driver's seat of a Chevrolet Caprice that was stopped in the drive-through lane at a Popeye's Chicken and Biscuits restaurant in Los Angeles. Defendant Samuel Shabazz, a gang member, walked up to the passenger side and fired several shots at Gonzalez's passenger, Ernest Gray, a member of a rival gang. Gray ducked when he saw the firearm and the shots hit and killed Gonzalez. A jury found the defendant guilty of first-degree murder carried out by the defendant while he was an active participant in a street gang.

On appeal the defendant contended that the gang-murder statute that requires special circumstances was inapplicable to him because it requires that the defendant intentionally kill the victim, and that he had intended to kill Ernest Gray, not Lori Gonzalez. In rejecting his contention that the doctrine of transferred intent was inapplicable, the California Supreme Court held that the gang-murder special circumstances statute is directed against murderers who kill as part of any gang-related activity, and not simply against those who kill their intended targets. The court observed: "Under the classic formulation of California's common law doctrine of transferred intent, a defendant who shoots with the intent to kill a certain person and hits a bystander instead is subject to the same criminal liability that would have been imposed had the fatal blow reached the person for whom intended."

People v. Shabazz, 130 P.3d 519, 523 (Cal.2006).

The Importance of Determining the Intent Required

There are two reasons why it is essential to determine whether a particular offense is a general-intent or a specific-intent crime or, in some recent statutory revisions, whether it meets the MPC culpability requirements. First, the intent requirement in a criminal statute determines the extent of proof that must be offered by the prosecution. Second, as we will explain in later chapters, in certain crimes the intent required to be proven determines whether particular defenses are available to the defendant.

Strict Liability Offenses

As we previously noted, common-law crimes consist of a criminal act or omission known as the *actus reus* and the mental element known as the *mens rea.* However, legislative bodies have the power to dispense with the necessity for the mental element and authorize punishment of particular acts without regard to the actor's intent (see Figure 4.1). Such crimes are known as strict liability offenses.

As we pointed out in Chapter 1, *mala in se* offenses are inherent wrongs, whereas *mala prohibita* offenses are considered wrongs because they are so defined by the law. In such common-law felonies as murder, rape, robbery, and larceny, the proscribed conduct is considered *mala in se,* and the intent is deemed inherent in the offense. This holds true today even if the statute proscribing such conduct fails to specify intent as an element of the offense.

Many of the *mala prohibita* crimes are defined as strict liability offenses. For the most part, these include "regulatory" or "public welfare" types of offenses, which often are tailored to address public safety, environmental, and public health concerns. We see some of the earliest examples of strict liability in cases involving the sale of liquor and adulterated milk. Examples of strict liability laws today include mostly traffic regulations, food and drug laws, and laws prohibiting the sale of liquor and cigarettes to minors. Strict liability offenses now constitute a substantial part of the criminal law.

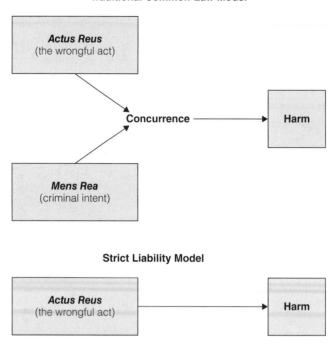

FIGURE 4.1 Elements of a Crime: Traditional and Strict Liability Models.

Go to the companion website for an edited version of *Morissette v. United States*.

The fact that a statute is silent on the matter of criminal intent does not necessarily mean that it defines a strict liability offense. If the prohibited conduct falls within a traditional common-law crime category, courts will likely interpret such statutes to contain a *mens rea* requirement. For example, in *Morissette v. United States*, 342 U.S. 246, 72 S.Ct. 240, 96 L.Ed. 288 (1952), the defendant had been convicted of violating federal law by taking some old bomb casings from a government bombing range. At trial, the district court refused to instruct the jury on the issue of intent, in effect holding that the government was required to prove only the defendant's act, not his intent, because the statute required proof of only the prohibited act. The Supreme Court reversed Morissette's conviction. The Court held that the crime for which he was prosecuted was a variant of the common-law offense of larceny and that failure to include the intent requirement in the statute did not eliminate the element of intent.

In *United States v. United States Gypsum Co.*, 438 U.S. 422, 98 S.Ct. 2864, 57 L.Ed.2d 854 (1978), the Supreme Court was called on to decide whether a criminal violation of the Sherman Act required proof of criminal intent or whether intent may be presumed conclusively from the anticompetitive effect of the defendants' actions. Despite the fact that the Sherman Act does not use the words "willfully" or "knowingly," the Court held that intent is an essential element of a criminal antitrust offense and must be established not only by proof of anticompetitive effects but by proof that the defendants had knowledge that the proscribed effects were probable.

Critics of strict liability offenses argue that they run counter to the standards of criminal culpability. Others argue that it is desirable to classify these offenses as regulatory or administrative, thereby removing the "criminal" stigma. Still others counter that to remove the criminal aspect from these offenses would remove their deterrent factor. One thing seems certain: If the prohibited conduct falls within a traditional

Court Implies a *Mens Rea* Requirement as an Element of a Federal Election Offense

CASE-IN-POINT

Ricardo Knight, an alien resident of the United States, was convicted of improperly voting in the 2000 presidential election, in violation of 18 U.S.C.A. § 611(a). On appeal he contended that Congress's failure to have incorporated a *mens rea* requirement into the law rendered the statute unconstitutional, and that the court was precluded from reading an implied intent into the statute.

In rejecting Knight's contention the court of appeals observed, "The existence of a *mens rea* is the rule of, rather than the exception to, the principles of Anglo-American criminal jurisprudence." Further, the court pointed out that the U.S. Supreme Court has held some congressional intent is required to dispense with *mens rea* as an element of a federal crime. Despite Congress's failure to incorporate a *mens rea* requirement into the statute prohibiting aliens from voting in federal elections, the statute includes an implied general intent and is not unconstitutional because the government must prove that a defendant knowingly engaged in the conduct prohibited by 18 U.S.C.A. § 611.

United States v. Knight, 490 F.3d 1268 (11th Cir. 2007).

common-law crime category, courts will likely interpret such statutes to contain a *mens rea* requirement. In the chapters that follow, note that as penalties for statutory offenses become heavier, courts are more reluctant to dispense with proof of intent. This is true in environmental crimes (see Chapter 11) and in some serious motor vehicle violations. For example, many state courts have addressed the issue of whether proof of a criminal intent is necessary to convict someone of the statutory crime of driving with a revoked or suspended license. In *Jeffcoat v. State*, 639 P.2d 308 (Alaska App. 1982), the Alaska Court of Appeals held that even though the statute is silent, the element of *mens rea* must be read into it by implication. In *State v. Keihn*, 530 N.E.2d 747 (Ind. 1989), the Indiana Supreme Court agreed that in a prosecution for driving with a suspended license, the State was required to prove the defendant's knowledge of the suspension. However, in 1998 the Connecticut Supreme Court disagreed with the Indiana Supreme Court's decision in *State v. Keihn* and held that actual knowledge of a license suspension is not an essential element of the crime of operating a motor vehicle with a suspended license as long as there was proof of a bulk certified mailing of the suspension notice. *State v. Swain*, 718 A.2d 1 (Conn. 1998).

The Causation Requirement

When an offense is defined in a manner that a specific result must occur, the concept of **causation** becomes important. This is most commonly associated with homicide offenses. For example, the various degrees of homicide require that to be guilty of murder or manslaughter, the accused's conduct must have resulted in the death of a human being. Sometimes lawyers refer to legal causation as **proximate cause**, defined as "a cause that in a natural, continuous sequence, unbroken by any intervening causes, produces the consequences that occur." Proximate cause is satisfied if the result that occurs was foreseeable. Sometimes the "but-for" test is employed here, meaning that "but for" the accused's actions, the harm would not have occurred. This can be illustrated by an instance where, but for the accused's firing a pistol, the victim would not have been killed. But suppose the victim was only slightly injured by the accused's having fired a pistol and was later taken to a hospital, where through the negligence of health care providers the victim died? If the victim's death occurred from such an intervening cause, it would likely result in the perpetrator's being charged with a lesser offense such as assault with a dangerous weapon.

Although causation is important in many crimes to link the elements of the accused's act and intent, in Chapter 5 we will study the incomplete offenses of attempt, solicitation, and conspiracy, which are classified as inchoate (incomplete) offenses. These offenses, among others that we will later study, do not require that specified results occur.

Parties to a Crime

Historically, the common law classified parties to crimes as either principals or accessories. Principals were persons whose conduct involved direct participation in a crime; accessories were **accomplices** or those who gave aid and comfort to principals. The common law classified crimes other than treason as felonies and misdemeanors. Felonies were very serious; in fact, at times, a person found guilty of a felony could be deprived of all worldly possessions and suffer either death or lengthy imprisonment. Because of the serious nature of felonious conduct and because all persons involved might not be equally guilty, the common law developed several technical distinctions among the various participants.

Common-Law Distinctions among Participants in Crime

To comprehend present criminal law regarding participants in a crime, a basic knowledge of the common-law scheme is essential. At common law, a person directly involved in committing a felony was classified as a principal; a person whose conduct did not involve direct participation was classified as an accessory. Principals were further classified by the degree of their participation. A person who directly or through the acts of an innocent agent actually committed the crime was a principal in the first degree. A principal in the second degree was a person not directly involved, but actually or constructively present at the commission of the crime, who aided and abetted the perpetrator. To be constructively present, one had to be sufficiently close to render assistance to the perpetrator. For example, suppose a man led a woman's escort away from her so that another man could sexually attack the woman. The man who led the escort away would probably be constructively present and would be classified as a principal in the second degree because he was **aiding and abetting** a crime. Aiding and abetting another in the commission of a crime means assenting to an act or lending countenance or approval, either by active participation in it or by encouraging it in some other manner.

An accessory at common law was classified as either an accessory before or after the fact. An accessory before the fact was one who procured or counseled another to commit a felony but who was not actually or constructively present at the commission of the offense. An accessory after the fact was one who, with knowledge of the other's guilt, rendered assistance to a felon in an effort to hinder the felon's arrest or punishment.

Because misdemeanors were far less serious than felonies, the common law found it unnecessary to distinguish between participants in misdemeanor offenses. As with treason, all participants in misdemeanors were regarded as principals.

Accessories to felonies were not regarded as being as culpable as the principals, so they were punished less severely at common law. Moreover, under the common law there were some procedural distinctions applicable to principals and accessories; for example, a party had to be charged either as a principal or as an accessory. The principal had to be tried first, and if the principal were found not guilty, the accessory could not be tried for the offense.

The Modern American Approach

The American approach has been to abolish both the substantive and procedural distinctions between principals and accessories before the fact. Federal law stipulates that "[w]hoever commits an offense against the United States or aids, abets, counsels, commands, induces, or procures its commission, is punishable as a principal. . . ." 18 U.S.C.A. § 2(a). The federal statute reflects the law of most of the states insofar as it abolishes the distinction between principals and accessories before the fact. As early as 1872, California enacted a statute defining principals as "all persons concerned in the commission of a crime, whether it be felony or misdemeanor, and whether they directly commit the act constituting the offense, or aid and abet in its commission, or, not being present, have advised and encouraged its commission." West's Ann. Cal. Penal Code § 31. As explained by the Supreme Court of Appeals of West Virginia in *State v. Fortner*, 387 S.E.2d 812, 822 (W.Va. 1989),

> Being an accessory before the fact or a principal in the second degree is not, of itself, a separate crime, but is a basis for finding liability for the underlying crime. . . . In essence, evidence of such complicity simply establishes an alternative theory of criminal liability, i.e., another way of committing the underlying crime.

The common-law distinction between principals and accessories before the fact has been largely abolished, but the concept of accessory after the fact as a separate offense has been retained by many jurisdictions. Modern statutes view an accessory after the fact as less culpable than someone who plans, assists, or commits a crime. Thus, statutes generally define being an accessory after the fact as a separate offense and provide for a less severe punishment. See, for example, West's Ann. Cal. Penal Code § 33. In most states, a lawful conviction as an accessory after the fact requires proof that a person knew that the person he or she aided or assisted had committed a felony. The gist of being an accessory after the fact lies essentially in obstructing justice, and a person is guilty who knows that an offense has been committed and receives, relieves, comforts, or assists the offender to hinder his or her apprehension, trial, or punishment. *United States v. Brown*, 33 F.3d 1002 (8th Cir. 1994). However, federal law does not distinguish whether the person assisted has committed a felony or a misdemeanor. 18 U.S.C.A. § 3.

The common-law rule that a woman who gave comfort and aid to her husband was exempt from being an accessory after the fact no longer prevails, yet some state statutes exempt spouses and other classes of relatives from penalty for being accessories after the fact. For example, Florida law has long prevented the prosecution as an accessory after the fact of any person standing in the relation of husband or wife, parent or grandparent, child or grandchild, or brother or sister, either by blood or marriage. West's Fla. Stat. Ann. § 777.03(1)(a). In 1999 the legislature amended the statute to add that, regardless of relation to the offender, a person who maintains or assists a principal or accessory before the fact knowing the offender has committed child abuse or a related offense is subject to prosecution as an accessory after the fact unless the court finds that such person is a victim of domestic violence. West's Fla. Stat. Ann. § 777.03(1)(b).

CASE-IN-POINT

Defendant with Intent to Commit Felony Convicted as an Accomplice Irrespective of Active Participation in Killing a Victim

Defendant Vernell Dixon appealed his conviction of capital felony murder that occurred during the course of an aggravated robbery. He argued that his conviction should not stand because the evidence showed that he did not take an active part in the killing of the victim.

In rejecting Dixon's argument the Arkansas Supreme Court observed,

> A defendant must only have the requisite intent for the underlying felony. Substantial evidence established defendant as an accomplice to the underlying aggravated robbery, and it was committed under circumstances manifesting extreme indifference

to the value of human life. Under the capital murder statute, Ark. Code Ann. § 5-10-101(a)(1) (Repl.1993), it is not necessary that the State show that the defendant took an active part in the killing so long as he assisted in the commission of the underlying crime. . . . A defendant must only have the requisite intent for the underlying felony. . . . The proof showed that [the defendant] was an accomplice and had the requisite intent for the aggravated robbery, supplied the .25 caliber pistol used in the robbery, and was present when the victim was killed in the course of the robbery. Such proof is sufficient to sustain the conviction for capital felony murder.

Dixon v. State, 891 S.W.2d 59 (Ark. 1995).

Conclusion

The concepts discussed in this chapter, though technical, are basic to an understanding of the criminal law in the United States. At this stage, concepts like *actus reus* and *mens rea* may seem abstract, but they will become more concrete in later chapters as we relate them to specific offenses.

Common-law crimes were considered *mala in se*, or wrongs in themselves, and required proof of a general or specific intent. The classification of intent as general or specific remains viable; however, in some criminal code revisions today, these traditional categories of intent are being replaced by categories of culpability recommended by the Model Penal Code. In contrast, many modern statutory offenses are classified as *mala prohibita*—that is, they are offenses simply because a legislative body has classified them as wrongs, and they are considered strict liability crimes. Yet even where a statute describes a strict liability crime, courts will imply an intent requirement if the crime is basically of common-law origin or imposes a heavy punishment.

The elements of crimes discussed in this chapter will be relevant throughout the text. In contrast, except for the offense of being an accessory after the fact, the common-law designation of parties to crimes is largely of historical importance. This is because modern criminal law at the federal and state levels treats parties who are complicit in crimes as principals, whether perpetrators or accomplices. Some jurisdictions make an exception for accessories after the fact where a close family relationship is involved. Society has found this approach necessary, and this principle has become firmly ingrained in modern criminal law.

Chapter Summary

- **LO1** The traditional elements of a crime are a person's wrongful act (*actus reus*) and criminal intent or guilty state of mind (*mens rea*). To be found guilty of a crime a person must commit a voluntary act, and in most instances, such act must be committed with a criminal intent. But an act is an indispensable element in all crimes, the rationale is to prevent a person from being guilty of an offense based on solely on intent.

- **LO2** The requirement for an act can be fulfilled by a person's failure to act where there is a family relationship or statutory or contractual duty to act.

- **LO3** In some instances possession can be a criminal act; examples include possession of concealed weapons and contraband. The law recognizes two classes: actual possession, where a person has something under direct physical control; and constructive possession, where a person has the power and intention to control something either directly or through another person.

- **LO4** The law recognizes that person's status cannot be criminalized, but there has been sharp disagreement on the Supreme Court as to what constitutes a status in certain instances.

- **LO5** Criminal intent is the conscious mental purpose to do a prohibited act. In most instances a prosecutor must establish the defendant's criminal intent as well as the commission of a prohibited act. This is because, unlike the civil law, the criminal law generally does not punish people for unintentional wrongs. Of course, laws allowing criminal liability irrespective of intent or in cases where there is culpable negligence are exceptions to this rule.

- **LO6** At common law, crimes were classified as requiring either general intent or specific intent. General intent is the intent to do an act but not necessarily to cause the results that occur from that act, while specific intent refers to an actor's mental purpose to accomplish a particular result beyond the act itself. There are two reasons that why it is essential to determine whether a particular offense is a general-intent or a specific-intent crime. First, the intent requirement in a criminal statute determines the extent of proof that must be offered by the prosecution; second, in certain crimes the intent that must be proven determines whether particular defenses are available to the defendant.

- **LO7** When an offense is defined in a manner that requires that a specific result must occur, the concept of causation becomes important. This is most commonly associated with homicide offenses, where various degrees of homicide require that to be guilty of murder or manslaughter, the accused's conduct must have resulted in the death of a human being. This legal causation or proximate cause is defined as "a cause that in a natural, continuous sequence, unbroken by any intervening causes, produces the consequences that occur." Proximate cause is satisfied if the result that occurs was foreseeable.

- **LO8** The Model Penal Code (MPC), which has influenced the criminal laws of some states, rejects the common-law terms for intent. Instead, the MPC recognizes four states of mind—purposely, knowingly, recklessly, and negligently—and states that the prescribed culpability requirement applies to all material elements of an offense.

- **LO9** Certain offenses are classified as strict liability crimes and are exceptions to the common-law concept of requiring proof of a defendant's criminal intent. Many *mala prohibita* crimes, usually "regulatory" or "public welfare" types of offenses, are strict liability offenses and do not require proof of intent. The fact that a statute is silent on the matter of criminal intent does not necessarily mean that it defines a strict liability offense. If the prohibited conduct falls within a traditional common-law crime category, courts will likely interpret such statutes to contain a *mens rea* requirement.

- **LO10** At common law, parties to felonies were denominated as principals in the first and second degree, and accessories before and after the fact. A person directly involved in committing a felony was a principal; a person whose conduct did not involve direct participation was an accessory. An accessory before the fact was one who procured or counseled another to commit a felony but who was not actually or constructively present at the commission of the offense. An accessory after the fact was one who, with knowledge of the other's guilt, rendered assistance to a felon in an effort to hinder the felon's arrest or punishment.

- **LO11** The American approach has been to abolish both the substantive and procedural distinctions between principals and accessories before the fact. Federal law stipulates that "[w]hoever commits an offense against the United States or aids, abets, counsels, commands, induces, or procures its commission, is punishable as a principal. . . ." This reflects the statutory law of most of the states insofar as it abolishes the common-law distinction between principal and accessories before the fact. In many states, the concept of an accessory after the fact remains as a separate offense.

Key Terms

principals Parties whose conduct involves direct participation in a crime.

accessories before the fact Persons who aid or assist others in commission of an offense.

accessories after the fact Persons who, with knowledge that a crime has been committed, conceal or protect the offender.

act of omission The failure to perform an act required by law

administrative-type act A ministerial act performed by executive officers in carrying out a duty assigned by law.

possession The actual or constructive control or occupancy of real or personal property.

actual possession Possession of something with the possessor having immediate control.

constructive possession Being in the position effectively to control something, even if it is not actually in one's possession.

status One's condition or situation.

motive A person's conscious reason for acting; what someone seeks to accomplish by engaging in particular conduct.

general intent The state of mind to do something prohibited by law without necessarily intending to accomplish the harm that results from the illegal act.

general-intent statutes Statutes defining crimes that require only general intent, as distinct from specific intent, on the part of the violator.

specific intent The mental purpose to accomplish a particular thing prohibited by law, such as the death of another person.

specific-intent statute A statute defining criminal conduct in which the offender must harbor a specific intent to accomplish a prohibited result.

constructive intent Criminal intent inferred by law as a result of circumstances surrounding a party's actions.

doctrine of transferred intent Doctrine originating in common law under which an actor's criminal intent associated with an act against an intended victim is transferred to an unintended victim who suffers the consequences of the defendant's act.

causation The linkage between cause and effect. "X" can be said to cause "Y" if X precedes Y and Y could not have occurred in the absence of X.

proximate cause The cause that is nearest a given effect in a causal relationship.

accomplices Persons who voluntarily unite with others in commission of an offense.

aiding and abetting Assisting in or otherwise facilitating the commission of a crime.

Questions for Thought and Discussion

1. Distinguish between the concepts of motive and intent in the criminal law. Can you cite an instance where, despite good motives, a person would be guilty of a crime?
2. What justifies the criminal law making mere possession of contraband articles illegal? Do you think this rationale extends to criminalizing the mere possession of such innocent items as a screwdriver, a pair of pliers, or an ice pick, which could be used to commit burglary?
3. Given the fact that the common-law requirement of intent is not an element of strict liability crimes, what rationale supports legislative enactment of such offenses? Name some examples of offenses that are classified as strict liability.
4. Should the criminal law punish a person whose mere carelessness, as opposed to willfulness, causes harm to another? Give reasons for your answer.
5. Is there a justification for the criminal law not punishing a person for failing to act when there is a clear moral duty to act?
6. Has the moral integrity of the criminal law been jeopardized by the increasing number of offenses for which a person can be convicted without proof of any criminal intent?
7. Why has the common-law doctrine distinguishing between principals and accessories before the fact diminished in importance in contemporary criminal law?
8. Contrast an offense that requires proof of causation with one that does not.
9. Is it fair to assess the same degree of fault and impose the same punishment on an accomplice as on a perpetrator? What rationale supports your conclusion?
10. Is there a valid reason to exempt close family relatives from punishment as accessories after the fact to felonious conduct?

Problems for Discussion and Solution

1. Arthur and Bob were friends and co-workers in an auto assembly plant. Arthur became enraged at Bob because he believed that Bob had sex with Charlotte, his girlfriend. Arthur had made statements that he hated Bob and wanted to see him dead. A few months later, after neither Arthur nor Bob were dating Charlotte, they resumed their friendship. While Arthur and Bob were hunting together, Arthur accidentally shot and killed Bob. Knowing of Arthur's previously expressed hate for Bob, Bob's family sought to have Arthur prosecuted for murder. What result would likely occur? Why?
2. Fred, experienced in rowing and canoeing, was hired by a boys' camp to supervise campers in their rowing and canoeing. During a teaching exercise, a boy who was not a good swimmer fell from a canoe. Fred took no action and the boy drowned. Does Fred have any criminal liability? What principle is applicable here?
3. A municipality enacts an ordinance making it an offense for a person who is addicted to narcotics to appear in public. Richard, who is addicted to heroin, is arrested for violating the ordinance when he is leaving the grocery store with his

purchases. He argues that the ordinance is unconstitutional because he has not committed any crime. What result should occur?

4. Nancy was charged with exceeding the posted speed limit by driving 50 m.p.h. in a 30-m.p.h. zone. She explains to the traffic court judge that she was distracted by thoughts of the unfortunate death of her younger sister, which had occurred a few days before. She contends that she had no intent to violate the speed limit. Evaluate her contention.

5. A state statute reads, "Any person, who with intent to defraud, files a claim for disability benefits under an insurance policy shall, upon conviction, be fined $500." What category of *mens rea* does this statute illustrate?

6. Sol Toolmaker visited his long-time friend, I. N. Mate, a prisoner in a state institution. Mate had previously told Toolmaker how much he wanted to escape from the prison. So, on this occasion, Toolmaker brought Mate two small saws. Mate hid the saws in a place where he thought the prison guards would not find them, but the guards promptly discovered and confiscated the saws. The warden turned this evidence over to the prison's legal counsel with a request that charges be prepared against Mate for attempting to escape from prison. Assuming Mate intended to escape from prison, did his conduct constitute a criminal act?

7. Alice Alpha had a long-standing grievance against Benjamin Beta and had threatened to kill him. When Alpha saw Beta standing on a street corner amidst a crowd of people, Alpha pulled out a gun and fired a shot. The bullet grazed Beta's arm, injuring him slightly. But it struck and killed Gerry Gamma, who was unknown to Alpha. Considering the concepts discussed in this chapter, what crime or crimes has Alpha committed?

CHAPTER 5

Inchoate Offenses

LEARNING OBJECTIVES

After reading this chapter, you should be able to explain . . .

1. why the law criminalizes inchoate offenses
2. why an attempt often requires a substantial step toward the commission of a crime
3. why an attempt usually merges into the target offense when the latter is committed
4. how solicitation differs from attempt
5. why courts differ on whether solicitation is more heinous than attempt
6. how conspiracy differs from solicitation
7. what are the most common types of conspiracy cases
8. why the federal government and some states require proof of an overt act in furtherance of a conspiracy
9. how Wharton's Rule prevents prosecution for conspiracy with respect to certain target crimes
10. why, under the *Pinkerton* Rule, a member of a conspiracy is vicariously liable for offenses committed by others in furtherance of the conspiracy
11. the defenses available in cases of attempt, solicitation and conspiracy

CHAPTER OUTLINE

Introduction

Attempt

Solicitation

Conspiracy

Conclusion

Chapter Summary

Key Terms

Questions for Thought and Discussion

Problems for Discussion and Solution

By the end of the 1990s, Enron Corporation was one of the most successful companies in the United States and a world leader in the field of energy. But after revelations of widespread accounting fraud, the company collapsed into bankruptcy in 2001. Some 20,000 employees lost their jobs and investors lost billions of dollars.

In one of the most dramatic white-collar crime cases ever prosecuted in the United States, Enron founder Kenneth Lay and former chief executive Jeffrey Skilling were convicted in federal court in May of 2006 of conspiracy to commit securities fraud and wire fraud. The government charged that Lay and Skilling entered into a conspiracy to defraud investors and employees by giving them false information about the giant energy company's financial health. In her closing argument to the jury, prosecutor Kathryn Ruemmler insisted that Lay and Skilling committed their crimes "through accounting tricks, fiction, hocus-pocus, trickery, misleading statements, half-truths, omissions and outright lies. . . ." Prosecution witnesses included eight former Enron employees who had pleaded guilty to other charges stemming from the scandal or entered into immunity agreements with the government. The jury deliberated for six days before returning guilty verdicts against Lay and Skilling. In July 2006, before sentences were imposed, Lay died of a heart attack. Because he died before he had an opportunity to challenge his conviction on appeal, the court dismissed the case against Lay.

In October 2006, Skilling, who was convicted of conspiracy, securities fraud, making false representations to auditors, and insider trading, was sentenced to twenty-four years and four months in prison, three years' supervised release, and $45 million in restitution. After the Fifth Circuit Court of Appeals affirmed his convictions, *United States v. Skilling*, 554 F.3d 529 (2009), Skilling petitioned the Supreme Court to review the case. On June 24, 2010, the Court ruled that one of the statutes Skilling was found guilty of conspiring to violate, 18 U.S.C.A. §1346, had been improperly interpreted by the lower courts. The Supreme Court remanded the case to the Fifth Circuit for reconsideration, giving Skilling hope that his conspiracy conviction ultimately would be overturned. The Skilling case shows the complexity of the contemporary criminal law, especially in the area of white-collar crime. It also shows that the offense of conspiracy is a powerful tool for prosecutors.

Introduction

The word "inchoate" means "underdeveloped" or "unripened." Thus, an **inchoate offense** is one involving activity or steps directed toward the completion of a crime. There are three such offenses: attempt, solicitation, and conspiracy. These are not crimes in themselves; rather there must be an attempt to commit a crime—for example, attempted murder—the solicitation of someone to commit a crime, or a conspiracy to commit an offense—for example, to sell contraband. Although preparatory to the commission of other offenses, they are separate and distinct crimes. During the 1800s, too late to become a part of the common law under the reception statutes adopted by most new American states, each was recognized as a misdemeanor at English common law. Most American jurisdictions now define these offenses by statute, frequently classifying them as felonies.

The development of the law in this area has been primarily through the courts. Courts have often found it difficult to determine when mere noncriminal activity has reached the stage of criminal conduct. Yet, by recognizing an actor's design toward commission of an offense, the law permits police to apprehend dangerous persons who have not yet accomplished their criminal objectives, thereby affording them an opportunity to terminate such conduct at an early stage.

Attempt

In *Bucklew v. State*, reproduced on the companion website, the Mississippi Supreme Court interprets a statute that defines attempt as an endeavor to commit a crime, coupled with the commission of an overt act.

Attempt is the most frequently charged of the inchoate crimes. Attempt, of course, means an effort to accomplish a particular purpose. As the Tennessee Supreme Court has explained, "An attempt, by nature, is a failure to accomplish what one intended to do." *State v. Kimbrough,* 924 S.W.2d 888 (Tenn. 1996). State penal codes often specifically provide for attempts to commit the most serious crimes, such as murder. The remaining offenses are then covered by a general attempt statute. A typical statute that covers all attempts provides that "[w]hoever attempts to commit an offense prohibited by law and in such attempt does any act toward the commission of such an offense, but fails in the perpetration or is intercepted or prevented in the execution of the same, commits the offense of criminal attempt." West's Fla. Stat. Ann. § 777.04(1). The "act" requirement contemplates an **overt act** that constitutes a **substantial step** toward the commission of an offense. Although the quoted statute makes no distinction between felony and misdemeanor offenses, statutes in some states limit the crime of attempt to attempts to commit felonies or certain specified crimes.

No specific federal statute proscribes or defines attempts generally; rather, various statutes focus on attempts to commit specific offenses. For example, Title 18 U.S.C.A. § 1113 proscribes attempts to commit murder or manslaughter. In general, federal courts have recognized the requisite elements of attempt as (1) an intent to engage in criminal conduct and (2) the performance of an act that constitutes a substantial step toward the completion of the substantive offense. See *United States v. Manley,* 632 F.2d 978 (2d Cir. 1980). This follows the Model Penal Code Section 5.01 view that the requisite elements of attempt are intent to engage in criminal conduct and the performance of acts, which constitute a "substantial step" toward the commission of the substantive offense. *United States v. Jackson,* 560 F.2d 112 (2d Cir. 1977).

The Act Requirement

As we have noted, the "act" element in the crime of attempt requires an act that constitutes a substantial step toward the commission of an offense; that is, it must be conduct beyond mere preparation. The Model Penal Code distinguishes **preparatory conduct** from an attempt. It allows conviction for the crime of attempt, where the actor engages in "an act or omission constituting a substantial step in a course of conduct planned to culminate in the commission of the crime." M.P.C. § 501 (1)(c).

CASE-IN-POINT

What Constitutes an Overt Act beyond the Preparation Stage?

A defendant was found guilty of attempting to escape from prison. He appealed, contending the state failed to prove beyond a reasonable doubt, as required by law, that he had committed an overt act. He characterized his actions as preparatory steps indicative only of an intention to attempt an escape. The Supreme Judicial Court of Maine recognized that the State must prove more than mere preparation; it must prove "a positive action . . . directed towards the execution of the crime." Yet the court rejected his contention and affirmed his conviction, stating, "[T]here was undisputed evidence that a dummy was found in defendant's cell; that defendant was in an unauthorized area attempting to conceal his presence; and that a rope ladder was found in a paper bag close to where he was concealed. [Defendant] had gone far beyond the preparation stage."

State v. Charbonneau, 374 A.2d 321, 322 (Me. 1977).

Federal courts apply this test. In *United States v. Mandujano,* 499 F.2d 370, 376 (5th Cir. 1974), the court observed, "A substantial step must be conduct strongly corroborative of the firmness of the defendant's criminal intent." Where multiple intentions underlie an act, one act may establish several different criminal attempts. For example, in *State v. Walters,* 804 P.2d 1164 (Or. 1991), the court held that the defendant's conduct established an intention to engage in conduct that constituted a substantial step toward commission of kidnapping, rape, and sodomy.

Many state statutes also include the term "substantial step" in defining the act requirement. Where they do not, courts usually imply that the act must constitute a substantial step toward the commission of a substantive offense. In either instance, it becomes necessary to distinguish between mere preparatory acts of planning or arranging means to commit a crime and those acts that constitute a direct movement toward the commission of an offense. Appellate courts have taken various approaches as to how close that act must be to accomplishment of the intended crime. This issue frequently turns on the specific factual situation involved. An early, and demanding, test held that an actor must have engaged in the "last proximate act necessary to accomplish the intended crime," but most courts have now rejected that test and apply a more realistic test that the actor's conduct must be "within dangerous proximity to success." An Illinois decision is illustrative. Two men armed with guns were found hiding behind a service station. One had a black nylon stocking in his pocket. The Illinois Supreme Court affirmed their convictions for attempted armed robbery because it found their act of "lying in wait . . . reconnoitering the place contemplated for the commission of the crime [while in] possession of materials to be employed in the commission of the crime" to be conduct sufficient to constitute a substantial step toward the commission of armed robbery. *People v. Terrell,* 459 N.E.2d 1337 (Ill. 1984).

New York courts have summed it up in a practical manner, opining simply that an accused's conduct must be "very near" to the completion of the intended crime. *People v. Mahboubian,* 543 N.E.2d 34 (N.Y. 1989).

The Requisite Criminal Intent

To find a defendant guilty of the crime of attempt, most courts require the prosecution to prove that the defendant had a specific intent to commit the intended offense, frequently referred to as the **target crime**. See, for example, *Thacker v. Commonwealth,* 114 S.E. 504 (Va. 1922); *State v. Earp,* 571 A.2d 1227 (Md. 1990). The rationale for this view is that it is logically impossible to attempt an unintended result.

The specific intent requirement raises an issue on which courts disagree: Can a person intend to commit a crime by unintentionally causing a result? Because specific intent is not an element of certain offenses, for example, manslaughter, some courts hold that a defendant cannot be convicted of an attempt to commit such a crime. See, for example, *State v. Zupetz,* 322 N.W.2d 730 (Minn. 1982). Other courts hold that if the prosecution is not required to show a defendant's specific intent in order to prosecute the completed crime successfully, it is not required to establish specific intent in order to prosecute an attempt to commit such a crime. In *Gentry v. State,* 437 So.2d 1097 (Fla.1983), the Florida Supreme Court held, "If the state is not required to show specific intent to successfully prosecute the completed crime, it will not be required to show specific intent to successfully prosecute an attempt to commit that crime." In any event, courts require at least the level of intent that must be established in proof of the target crime.

Attempts in Relation to Substantive Crimes

When a criminal attempt completes a substantive crime, the attempt usually merges into the target offense. The actor is then guilty of the substantive crime, rather than merely an attempt to commit it. Thus, a person who is successful in an attempt to commit murder is guilty of murder. However, there can be no attempt to commit certain crimes because some substantive offenses by definition embrace an attempt. To illustrate, consider the statutory crime of uttering a forged instrument. Statutes usually define the crime as including an attempt to pass a forged instrument to someone to obtain something of value. Therefore, one who makes such an attempt would be guilty of uttering a forged instrument, not merely an attempt to do so. In effect, the attempt is subsumed in the very definition of the substantive crime. Needless to say, it would be redundant to charge someone with attempting to attempt to commit a given crime.

Defenses to the Crime of Attempt

The Model Penal Code proposes that an accused who "purposely engages in conduct that would constitute the crime if the attendant circumstances were as he believed them to be" is guilty of an attempt. M.P.C. § 5.01(1)(a). Although many state statutes track this Model Penal Code language, it raises the issue of whether the law should pursue a conviction for an attempt to commit a crime that is impossible to commit.

The rule developed in most jurisdictions is that **legal impossibility** is a defense to the crime of attempt but **factual impossibility** is not. The distinction can be very close. For example, attempted rape requires a human victim. Therefore, a man who assaults a mannequin dressed as a woman would not be guilty of attempted rape because it would be legally impossible to commit that offense. Yet this example must be distinguished from the classic illustration in *State v. Mitchell*, 71 S.W. 175 (Mo. 1902). There, a man was held responsible for attempted murder when he shot into the room in which his target usually slept. Fortuitously, that person was sleeping elsewhere in the house at the time of the shooting. Although the bullet struck the target's customary pillow, attainment of the criminal objective was factually impossible. Likewise, a person who picks another's pocket intending to steal money may be found guilty of attempted theft even if the victim's pocket is empty. In these instances courts have said that although it was factually impossible to commit the crime, it was legally possible to do so.

New York law now provides that it is no defense to a prosecution that the crime charged to have been attempted was either factually or legally impossible to commit if it could have been committed had the circumstances been what the defendant believed them to be. McKinney's N.Y. Penal Law § 110.10; *People v. Davis*, 526 N.E.2d 20 (N.Y. 1988). The trend is toward finding an attempt to commit a crime in instances where the actor's intent has been frustrated merely because of some factor unknown at the time. Thus, if the accused believed a victim was alive when the accused shot at the victim, it follows that such an attempt to kill a dead person would constitute an attempt under New York law. *People v. Dlugash*, 363 N.E.2d 1155 (N.Y. 1977).

Some jurisdictions have laws providing that it is a defense to the crime of attempt if the defendant abandons an attempt to commit an offense or otherwise prevents its consummation. See, for example, Vernon's Tex. Ann. Penal Code § 15.04(a). Where recognized as a defense, abandonment must be wholly voluntary. It cannot be the result of any outside cause such as the appearance of the police on the scene. See, for example, *People v. Walker*, 191 P.2d 10 (Cal. 1948).

Solicitation

By the 1800s, the English common law specified that a person who counseled, incited, or solicited another to commit either a felony or a misdemeanor involving breach of the peace committed the offense of **solicitation**. A person who solicited another to commit a crime was guilty of solicitation even if the crime counseled, incited, or solicited was not committed. The offense of solicitation is now defined by statute in most American jurisdictions. Numerous federal statutes define solicitation as a crime in various contexts. See, for example, Title 18 U.S.C.A. § 373, which proscribes solicitation to commit a crime of violence.

Conviction under federal law requires the solicitation to be of a federal offense. *United States v. Korab*, 893 F.2d 212 (9th Cir. 1989). In explaining why its penal code makes solicitation an offense, a California appellate court offered two reasons: first, to protect individuals from being exposed to inducement to commit or join in the commission of crime, and second, to prevent solicitation from resulting in the commission of the crime solicited. *People v. Cook*, 199 Cal. Rptr. 269 (Cal. App. 1984).

The Act Requirement

The request, command, or enticement constitutes the *actus reus* required for solicitation. The statutory definition of solicitation in Illinois is typical: "A person commits solicitation when, with intent that an offense be committed, other than first-degree murder, he commands, encourages, or requests another to commit the offense." 720 I.L.C.S. 5/8-1.1, Ill. Stat. Ch. 720 § 5/8-1.1. (A separate statute defines solicitation for first-degree murder.) The gist of the offense is the solicitation itself, so the offender may be found guilty irrespective of whether the solicited crime is ever committed.

Commission of the crime of solicitation does not require direct solicitation of another; it may be perpetrated through an intermediary. Thus, if Abel solicits Barnes to solicit Cummings to commit a crime, Abel would be liable even though he did not directly contact Cummings, because Abel's solicitation of Barnes itself involves the commission of the offense.

Recall that in Chapter 3 we discussed the fact that the "void for vagueness doctrine" requires a penal statute to define an offense with sufficient definitiveness that ordinary people can understand what conduct is prohibited. In the next Case-in-Point, the court rejected a challenge that a child solicitation statute was unconstitutionally vague and explains that child solicitation is complete upon urging a child to perform a sexual act.

In *State v. Keen*, reproduced on the companion website, the North Carolina Court of Appeals explains that the crime of solicitation to commit a felony is complete with the solicitation and does not require acquiescence in the scheme by the one solicited.

Is an Uncommunicated Solicitation an Offense?

The Model Penal Code states, "It is immaterial . . . that the actor fails to communicate with the person he solicits to commit a crime if his conduct was designed to effect such communication." M.P.C. § 5.02(2). Nevertheless, courts have been reluctant to uphold a conviction of solicitation where there has been no communication of the solicitation to the intended solicitee. For example, in *State v. Cotton*, 790 P.2d 1050 (N.M. App. 1990), the New Mexico Court of Appeals explained that the language of its criminal code describes the offense of criminal solicitation in a manner that differs in several material respects from the Model Penal Code by specifically omitting that portion of the Model Penal Code subsection that declares an uncommunicated solicitation to commit a crime may constitute the offense of criminal solicitation. Thus,

Child Solicitation Is Complete upon Urging the Performance of a Sexual Act

In July 2002, Detective Mike Widner of the Noblesville, Indiana Police Department logged on to an Internet chat room and impersonated a thirteen-year-old girl. Allegedly, after two sessions with Michael LaRose, which included sexually explicit remarks, LaRose agreed to meet at a Wal-Mart parking lot. Upon arrival he was arrested and charged with felony child solicitation under Indiana Code section 35-42-4-6, which makes it an offense for a person eighteen years of age or older to knowingly or intentionally solicit a child under fourteen years of age, or an individual the person believes to be a child under fourteen years of age, to engage in sex acts. LaRose moved to dismiss the charges, arguing there was no allegation that he solicited an individual to engage in an act "at

some immediate time." Additionally, he contended the statute was unconstitutionally vague. The trial court denied LaRose's motion and the Court of Appeals accepted jurisdiction.

Noting that the crime of child solicitation is complete upon urging a child to perform a sexual act and rather than upon performance of the urged act, the Court of Appeals rejected LaRose's argument. Additionally, the court rejected LaRose's challenge that the statute was unconstitutionally vague, noting that it unequivocally informs individuals they may not use a computer to sexually solicit a child under the age of fourteen. The court affirmed the trial court's denial of LaRose's motion to dismiss.

LaRose v. State, 820 N.E.2d 727 (Ind. App. 2005).

the court concluded that the legislative intent was to require some form of actual communication from the defendant to either an intermediary or the intended solicitee. In *People v. Saephanh*, 94 Cal.Rptr.2d 910 (Cal. App. 2000), a corrections officer intercepted the defendant's letter of solicitation to commit murder. In a case of first impression, a California appellate court held that solicitation of murder requires receipt of solicitation by the intended recipient. The court, however, held that the defendant could be convicted of attempted solicitation of murder.

The Requisite Criminal Intent

The statutory language making solicitation a crime might not seem to require the prosecution to establish the defendant's specific intent. However, most courts hold that to commit solicitation, the solicitor must have specifically intended to induce or entice the person solicited to commit the target offense. See, for example, *Kimbrough v. State*, 544 So.2d 177 (Ala. Crim. App. 1989). If the particular jurisdiction does not require proof of the defendant's specific intent, the prosecution must at least establish that the actor who solicits someone to commit a crime had the requisite intent for the crime solicited.

Solicitation Distinguished from Other Inchoate Crimes

The offenses of solicitation and attempt are different crimes, analytically distinct in their elements. Although each is an inchoate offense, solicitation is complete when the request or enticement to complete the intended offense is made, and it is immaterial whether the solicitee agrees, the offense is carried out, or any steps are taken toward consummation of the offense. In contrast, mere solicitation is generally not sufficient to constitute an attempt, because attempt requires proof of an overt act to commit the intended criminal act. This principle was succinctly explained by the

Idaho Supreme Court: "The solicitation of another, assuming neither the solicitor nor solicitee proximately acts toward the crime's commission, cannot be held for an attempt." *State v. Otto,* 629 P.2d 646, 650 (Idaho 1981).

Is solicitation more serious than attempt? The Tennessee Supreme Court has suggested that it is not, stating, "There is not the same degree of heinousness in solicitation as in attempts, nor is solicitation as likely to result in a completed crime, there not being the same dangerous proximity to success as found in attempts." *Gervin v. State,* 371 S.W.2d 449, 451 (Tenn. 1963). The Connecticut Supreme Court has taken the contrary point of view, observing, "The solicitation to another to [commit] a crime is as a rule far more dangerous to society than the attempt to commit the same crime. For the solicitation has behind it an evil purpose, coupled with the pressure of a stronger intellect upon the weak and criminally inclined." *State v. Schleifer,* 121 A. 805, 809 (Conn. 1923).

If the crime solicited is committed or attempted by the solicitee, then the offense of solicitation ordinarily merges into the target crime. For example, if Andrew solicits Bob to murder Carl and Bob then murders or attempts to murder Carl, then Andrew would become an accessory before the fact to murder or attempted murder. As discussed in Chapter 4, this complicity would make Andrew a principal to the crime of murder or attempted murder. If, however, Bob refuses Andrew's solicitation, Andrew would still be guilty of solicitation.

Solicitation is distinguished from conspiracy because although solicitation requires an enticement, conspiracy, as we explain later, requires an agreement. Sometimes a solicitation results in a conspiracy, and some courts have regarded the offense of solicitation as "an offer to enter into a conspiracy." See, for example, *Commonwealth v. Carey,* 439 A.2d 151, 155 (Pa. Super. 1981).

Defenses to the Crime of Solicitation

Generally, the fact that the solicitor countermands the solicitation is not a defense to the crime of solicitation. Nor is it a defense that it was impossible for the person solicited to commit the crime. The Model Penal Code provides that a complete and

---

CASE-IN-POINT

When Is the Crime of Solicitation Committed?

Defendant Roger Gardner, an alleged contract killer, subcontracted the killing of Alvin Blum to a man named Tim McDonald for a fee of $10,000. Gardner met with McDonald and gave him some expense money, a gun, and ammunition. In talking with McDonald, Gardner said that he (Gardner) would first kill a man named Hollander, and if this did not create the desired result, then McDonald would be directed to kill Blum. Gardner's attempts were foiled when he was arrested and charged with solicitation to murder. It turned out that McDonald was a police informant whose assistance led to Gardner's arrest.

On appeal, Gardner argued that he did not commit the crime of solicitation because he did not actually direct McDonald to proceed with the murder of Blum or pay him all of the money he had promised. In affirming Gardner's conviction, the Maryland Court of Appeals said, "the crime of solicitation was committed when he asked McDonald to commit the murder." The Court explained that "[n]either a final direction to proceed nor fulfillment of conditions precedent (paying of the money) was required." In holding that the crime of solicitation was committed, the court observed that "[t]he gist of the offense is incitement."

Gardner v. State, 408 A.2d 1317, 1322 (Md. 1979).

voluntary renunciation of the accused's criminal purpose is a defense to a charge of solicitation. M.P.C. § 5.02(3). Some states have adopted this position. Kentucky law agrees; however, Section 506.060 of the Kentucky Statutes stipulates,

> A renunciation is not "voluntary and complete" . . . when it is motivated in whole or in part by: (a) A belief that circumstances exist which pose a particular threat of apprehension or detection of the accused or another participant in the criminal enterprise or which render more difficult the accomplishment of the criminal purpose; or (b) A decision to postpone the criminal conduct until another time or to transfer the criminal effort to another victim or another but similar object.

Conspiracy

Under English common law, **conspiracy** consisted of an agreement by two or more persons to accomplish a criminal act or to use unlawful means to accomplish a non-criminal objective. The gist of the offense was the unlawful agreement between the parties, and no overt act was required.

The common law regarded a husband and wife as one person for most purposes; therefore, a husband and wife could not be guilty of conspiring with each other. In recent years courts have recognized the separate identities of spouses, and there is no valid reason to continue the common-law approach. See, for example, *People v. Pierce*, 395 P.2d 893 (Cal. 1964). Thus, a husband and wife who conspire only between themselves ordinarily cannot claim immunity from prosecution for conspiracy on the basis of their marital status.

Today the offense of conspiracy is defined by statute in all jurisdictions. Most state laws define the elements of the offense along the lines of the common law. Thus, the agreement becomes the *acts reus* of the offense. Typically, as the Florida law states, "A person who agrees, conspires, combines, or confederates with another person or persons to commit any offense commits the offense of criminal conspiracy." West's Fla. Stat. Ann. § 777.04(3). Thus, under Florida law, both an agreement and an intention to commit an offense are necessary elements to support a conviction for conspiracy. *Webster v. State*, 646 So.2d 752 (Fla. App. 1994).

Several states, however, require proof of an overt act to convict someone for conspiracy. Where an overt act is required, courts simply require that the act be one taken in furtherance of the conspiracy without the qualifications required of an act required in an attempt to commit a crime. For example, Texas law provides that "[a] person commits criminal conspiracy if, with intent that a felony be committed, (1) he agrees with one or more persons that they or one or more of them engage in conduct that would constitute the offense, and (2) he or one or more of them performs an overt act in pursuance of the agreement." Vernon's Tex. Penal Code Ann. § 15.02 (a). Note that the Texas statute also requires an intent that a felony be committed, whereas in many states it is necessary only to prove an intent to commit a criminal offense.

Federal law (with some exceptions) requires proof of an overt act by one or more persons to effect the object of a conspiracy to commit an offense or to defraud the United States. 18 U.S.C.A. § 371. In *United States v. Jobe*, 101 F.3d 1046, 1063 (5th Cir. 1996), the court stated, "In order to establish a conspiracy under 18 U.S.C.A. § 371, the government must prove beyond a reasonable doubt the existence of an agreement between two or more people to violate a law of the United States and that any one of the conspirators committed an overt act in furtherance of that agreement."

Because of the variations encountered in statutory language, in reviewing any statute defining conspiracy it is necessary to determine at the outset (1) the type of the offense or unlawful activity the statute proscribes and (2) whether it requires proof of an overt act in furtherance of the parties' agreement.

Justification for Making Conspiracy a Crime

Go to the companion website for an edited version of *Callanan v. United States*.

Why is conspiracy considered an offense distinct from the substantive offense the conspirators agree to commit? The late U.S. Supreme Court Justice Felix Frankfurter articulated one of the most cogent responses to this question. In *Callanan v. United States*, 364 U.S. 587, 593–594, 81 S.Ct. 321, 325, 5 L.Ed.2d 312, 317 (1961), Frankfurter observed,

> Concerted action both increases the likelihood that the criminal object will be successfully attained and decreases the probability that the individuals involved will depart from their path of criminality. Group association for criminal purposes often, if not normally, makes possible the attainment of ends more complex than those which one criminal could accomplish. . . . Combination in crime makes more likely the commission of crimes unrelated to the original purpose for which the group was formed. In sum, the danger that a conspiracy generates is not confined to the substantive offense that is the immediate aim of the enterprise.

The Range of Conspiracies in Society

The range of conspiracies cuts across socioeconomic classes in society. Traditionally, state prosecutions for conspiracy have been directed at criminal offenses such as homicide, arson, perjury, kidnapping, and various offenses against property. In recent years an increasing number of both state and federal conspiracy prosecutions have been related to illicit drug trafficking. In addition to the numerous narcotics violations, federal prosecutions include a variety of conspiracies not found under state laws. Among these are customs violations, counterfeiting of currency, copyright violations, mail fraud, lotteries, and violations of antitrust laws, laws governing interstate commerce, and other areas of federal regulation. On September 15, 2008 a federal appellate court affirmed a defendant's conviction for violation of 18 U.S.C.A. § 371 for conspiracy to commit wire fraud in connection with a scheme to defraud mortgage lenders in mobile home financing. *United States v. Price*, 532 F.3d 617 (8th Cir. 2008). Recently, several federal prosecutions have involved conspiracies to deprive persons of civil rights secured by the Constitution or laws of the United States. See 18 U.S.C.A. § 241. Lower federal courts have held that this section, which prohibits conspiracy against rights of citizens, does not require proof of an overt act. See, for example, *United States v. Morado*, 454 F.2d 167 (5th Cir. 1972).

The Act Element in Conspiracy

In general, the *actus reus* of the crime of conspiracy is the unlawful agreement. But the agreement need not be formal or written. A simple understanding is sufficient. Where an overt act is required, such act need not be a substantial movement toward the target offense. For example, in California, where the law requires an overt act, the courts have said that an overt act tending to effect a conspiracy may merely be a part of preliminary arrangements for the commission of the ultimate crime. *People v.*

Buono, 12 Cal. Rptr. 604 (Cal. App. 1961). In *Bannon v. United States*, 156 U.S. 464, 15 S.Ct. 467, 39 L.Ed. 494 (1895), the U.S. Supreme Court held that an act committed by any one of the conspirators applies to all present members of the conspiracy. In fact, a single act, such as a telephone conversation arranging a meeting, has been held to be sufficient proof of an overt act. *United States v. Civella,* 648 F.2d 1167 (8th Cir. 1981).

In *State v. Dent*, 869 P.2d 392 (Wash. 1994), the Supreme Court of Washington articulated the difference between the *actus reus* requirements in the crimes of attempt and conspiracy. The court observed that the two crimes differ in the nature of the conduct sought to be prohibited and in the significance of the "substantial step" requirement (known as the "overt act" requirement in some jurisdictions) in each context. "A substantial step," the court noted, "is required in the context of attempt to prevent the imposition of punishment based on intent alone." But the court explained that the purpose of the substantial step or overt act requirement is different in the context of conspiracy: "The purpose of the 'substantial step' requirement is, therefore, to manifest that the conspiracy is at work, and is neither a project still resting solely in the minds of the conspirators nor a fully completed operation no longer in existence." 869 P.2d at 397.

Contrary to some popular views, the participants in a conspiracy need not even know or see one another as long as they otherwise participate in common deeds. The essence of the offense is the mutual agreement of the parties to the conspiracy, not the acts done to accomplish its objective. Moreover, the agreement need not be explicit. In fact, it seldom is. In most instances, the agreement is implied from the acts of the parties and the circumstances surrounding their activities. Furthermore, the conspirators do not all have to join the conspiracy at the same time.

The Requisite Criminal Intent

Statutes frequently fail to encompass the intent requirement in the offense of conspiracy. This difficulty is compounded by failure of the courts to define clearly the intent required for a conviction. In general, the prosecution must prove that a defendant intended to further the unlawful object of the conspiracy, and such intent must exist in the minds of at least two of the parties to the alleged conspiracy. *People v. Cohn,* 193 N.E. 150 (Ill. 1934). Many courts refer to the crime as requiring a specific intent. See, for example, *People v. Marsh,* 376 P.2d 300 (Cal. 1962). As previously noted relative to attempts, such intent may be inferable from the conduct of the parties and the surrounding circumstances. Although many federal court decisions have not required proof of a specific intent, the U.S. Supreme Court has said that in federal prosecutions there must be proof of at least the criminal intent necessary for the requirements of the substantive offense. *United States v. Feola,* 420 U.S. 671, 95 S.Ct. 1255, 43 L.Ed.2d 541 (1975).

Conspiracy Distinguished from Aiding and Abetting and Attempt

As we noted in Chapter 4, aiding and abetting someone in the commission of a crime makes a person either a principal or an accessory before the fact. Conspiracy is a separate offense and must be distinguished from aiding and abetting. Conspiracy involves proof of an agreement between two or more persons, an element often present in, but not essential to, proving that a defendant aided and abetted a crime. On the other hand, aiding and abetting requires some actual participation. Conspiracy differs from the crime of attempt in that it focuses on intent, whereas attempt places more emphasis on the defendant's actions.

The *Pinkerton* Rule

Go to the companion website for an edited version of *Pinkerton v. United States*.

In *Pinkerton v. United States*, 328 U.S. 640, 66 S.Ct. 1180, 90 L.Ed. 1489 (1946), Pinkerton was charged with conspiring with his brother to commit tax evasion, including some offenses allegedly committed by his brother during times that Pinkerton was incarcerated. The trial court instructed the jury that it could find Pinkerton guilty if it found he was a party to a conspiracy and that the offenses were in furtherance of the conspiracy. Pinkerton was convicted, and on review the U.S. Supreme Court upheld his conviction, stating that a member of a conspiracy is liable for all offenses committed in furtherance of the conspiracy. The Court did indicate that a different result may occur if the offenses were not reasonably foreseeable as a natural consequence of the unlawful agreement of the conspirators. This has come to be known as the **Pinkerton Rule**. It is based on the theory that conspirators are agents of one another, and just as principals are bound by the acts of their agents within the scope of the agency relationship, so too conspirators are bound by the acts of their co-conspirators. See *United States v. Troop*, 890 F.2d 1393 (7th Cir. 1989).

The *Pinkerton* doctrine has broad implications, and not all courts have accepted it. For example, in *People v. McGee*, 399 N.E.2d 1177 (N.Y. 1979), the court rejected the *Pinkerton* doctrine and observed,

> It is not offensive to permit a conviction of conspiracy to stand on the overt act committed by another, for the act merely provides corroboration of the existence of the agreement and indicates that the agreement has reached a point where it poses a sufficient threat to society to impose sanctions. . . . But it is repugnant to our system of jurisprudence, where guilt is generally personal to the defendant . . . to impose punishment, not for the socially harmful agreement to which the defendant is a party, but for substantive offenses in which he did not participate. 399 N.E.2d 1182.

Some Unique Aspects of the Offense of Conspiracy

Because the courts view each conspirator as an agent of the others, it follows that each will be held responsible for the acts of the others within the context of their common design. *Commonwealth v. Thomas*, 189 A.2d 255 (Pa. 1963). This principle permits an exception to the rule of evidence that ordinarily excludes hearsay statements from being used in a trial over the defendant's objection. Thus, statements made "in furtherance of" the conspiracy may be admitted into evidence. These include statements to inform other conspirators of the activities or status of the conspiracy and those identifying other conspirators. Federal courts have upheld the use of statements to establish the source or purchaser of controlled substances. Before receiving this type of evidence, a court must receive independent evidence that a conspiracy exists. In some instances, courts receive the hearsay evidence subject to its being tied into the offense by independent evidence of the conspiracy. Court procedures in this area are very technical because the court must determine the scope of the conspiracy and the inception of the conspirator's participation.

In *Territory v. Goto*, 27 Hawaii 65 (1923), the Supreme Court of Hawaii properly characterized the judicial approach to conspiracy: "In the eyes of the law conspirators are one man, they breathe one breath, they speak one voice, they wield one arm, and the law says that the acts, words, and declarations of each, while in the pursuit of the common design, are the words and declarations of all."

Courts have held that once formed, a conspiracy continues to exist until consummated, abandoned, or otherwise terminated by some affirmative act. *Cline v. State*, 319 S.W.2d 227 (Tenn. 1958). Consequently, upon joining a conspiracy and not withdrawing, a conspirator is not insulated from the actions of his or her co-conspirators.

These unique aspects are significant. They assist the prosecution in proof of cases that might be otherwise unprovable. Perhaps the law has established these exceptions in recognition of the difficulties of prosecuting persons involved in conspiracies, which are generally formed in secret.

Conspiracy is among the most commonly charged federal offenses. A law review article explains why this is the case:

> Conspiracy, the prosecutor's "darling," is one of the most commonly charged federal crimes. The offense of conspiracy is construed broadly by courts and is therefore applied by prosecutors to a variety of situations. . . . A conspiracy charge gives the prosecution certain unique advantages and . . . one who must defend against such a charge bears a particularly heavy burden. Raphael Prober and Jill Randall, *Federal Criminal Conspiracy*, 39 Am. Crim. L. Rev. 571 (Spring 2002).

Conspiracy Does Not Merge into the Target Crime

Conspiracy is regarded as a separate and distinct crime; therefore, it does not merge into the target offense. See *People v. Carter*, 330 N.W.2d 314 (Mich. 1982). A pragmatic consideration is that by not merging conspiracy into the target offense, the law can more effectively deal with organized crime, criminal street gangs, and other dangerous collective efforts to commit crimes.

The Wharton's Rule Exception

Wharton's Rule, named after Francis Wharton, a well-known commentator on criminal law, provides an exception to the principle that conspiracy does not merge into the target crime. Wharton's Rule holds, "An agreement by two persons to commit a particular crime cannot be prosecuted as a conspiracy when the crime is of such a nature as to necessarily require the participation of two persons for its commission." 1 R. Anderson, Wharton's Criminal Law and Procedure 89, p. 191 (1957). Thus, Wharton's Rule holds that two people cannot conspire to commit a crime such as adultery, incest, or bigamy because these offenses require only two participants.

The rationale behind Wharton's Rule is that, unlike the usual conspiracy (often viewed as a wheel with many spokes or as a chain of circumstances), the offenses named do not endanger the public generally. Wharton's Rule has been applied in many state and federal courts, but it has its limitations. In holding Wharton's Rule inapplicable to various federal gambling offenses under the Organized Crime Control Act of 1970, the Supreme Court pointed out that the rule itself is simply an aid to the determination of legislative intent and must defer to a discernible legislative judgment. *Iannelli v. United States*, 420 U.S. 770, 786, 95 S.Ct. 1284, 1294, 43 L. Ed.2d 616, 628 (1975).

Criticism of the Conspiracy Laws

There has been an increased tendency in recent years to prosecute defendants for conspiracies as well as target crimes. The offense of conspiracy is a potent weapon for prosecutors, particularly as they try to cope with the problem of organized crime. Because the intent requirement and the form of agreement required are somewhat

Conspiracy to Deliver Controlled Substances

CASE-IN-POINT

Cook, an undercover police officer, agreed to purchase fifty doses of LSD from Erickson at a park in Snohomish, Washington. Erickson asked Smith for a ride there, ostensibly to meet Hensler (who owed Smith $600). When Smith and Erickson arrived in Smith's vehicle, Cook approached the car and asked Erickson if he had the LSD. When Erickson produced a bag of LSD, Cook asked Smith if he had tried it. Smith replied that "he was going to college . . . and couldn't afford to get messed up, but that his wife had taken some of it, and . . . 'it really [messed] her up.'" At that point Cook agreed to purchase the LSD, handed the money to Erickson, and arrested both Smith and Erickson. Smith was found guilty of conspiracy to deliver LSD.

On appeal, Smith argued that there was no proof beyond a reasonable doubt (1) that he agreed to engage in delivery of LSD and (2) that he intended that it be delivered. The appellate court rejected both contentions and affirmed Smith's conviction. The court first pointed out that "a formal agreement is not necessary to the formation of a conspiracy." Then the court observed that although Smith's primary purpose in giving Erickson a ride to the park was to meet Hensler, his secondary purpose was to assist in delivering LSD. In finding the evidence sufficient to show that Smith intended to assist Erickson, the court opined that "there was evidence not only of knowledge of Erickson's unlawful purpose, but an agreement to assist with the plan by providing the necessary transportation. . . . Here there were two overt acts: first, that Smith drove Erickson to Snohomish knowing, according to Cook, Erickson's purpose for the trip; and second, that Smith provided encouragement for the sale by assuring the officer of the potency of the drug."

State v. Smith, 828 P.2d 654, 656, 657 (Wash. App. 1992).

imprecise, a conspiracy is easier to prove than specific substantive crimes. On this basis, some critics argue that prosecutors, judges, and juries are given too much latitude in finding a defendant guilty.

Critics also argue that prosecution for conspiracy can chill a person's exercise of freedom of speech to the First Amendment, especially in matters involving political dissent. Courts, however, have ruled that conduct is not protected by the First Amendment merely because it involves the use of language. This became an issue in the 1968 prosecution of the late Dr. Benjamin M. Spock, the renowned pediatrician and author. Dr. Spock and three alleged co-conspirators were convicted of violating the Universal Military Training and Service Act, § 12(a) as amended, 50 U.S.C.A. App. § 462(a), for conspiring to urge men to evade the military draft. The U.S. Court of Appeals found that the evidence at Spock's trial was insufficient and set aside his conviction. *United States v. Spock*, 416 F.2d 165 (1st Cir. 1969). The court explained in dicta that the First Amendment did not, per se, require acquittal on the charge of conspiracy to counsel men to resist the draft.

Defenses to the Charge of Conspiracy

In some states, statutes specifically provide for a defense of withdrawal from and renunciation of a conspiracy. As an illustration, Missouri law specifies that "[n]o one shall be convicted of conspiracy if, after conspiring to commit the offense, he prevented the accomplishment of the objectives of the conspiracy under circumstances manifesting a renunciation of his criminal purpose." Vernon's Mo. Ann. Stat. § 564.016(5)(1). In the absence of statutory authority, courts have been reluctant to approve a person's withdrawal as a defense. One difficulty in approving withdrawal as a defense is that even though a conspirator withdraws, the criminal objective of the conspiracy may proceed. Therefore, it seems reasonable to require that a person who would rely on such defense not only renounce any criminal purpose but also take the necessary steps to thwart the objective of the conspiracy. To accomplish this result, the conspirator would probably have to notify law enforcement authorities of the pertinent details of the conspiracy. In any event, if an accused is allowed to offer such a defense, the defendant has the burden of establishing his or her withdrawal from the conspiracy.

Entrapment, a defense to be examined in Chapter 14, may be a defense to conspiracy under some circumstances. For example, in *Stripling v. State*, 349 So.2d 187 (Fla. App. 1977), the court found reversible error in the trial judge's having instructed the jury that the defense of entrapment was not available to a defendant if the officer acted in good faith and merely furnished an opportunity for commission of a crime by one who already had the intent to commit the crime. As the appellate court said, "A defendant could deny being a party to a conspiracy and yet raise the issue that any overt acts done by him or her were done because of entrapment; that rationale being that inconsistencies in defenses in criminal cases are allowable so long as the proof of one does not necessarily disprove the other." *Id.* at 191.

In *Gomez v. People*, reproduced on the companion website, the Colorado Supreme Court details the evidence it found to be sufficient to support a conviction for conspiracy.

Conclusion

By criminalizing attempt, solicitation, and conspiracy, the law endeavors to prevent the occurrence of criminal acts that pose prospective harm to persons. These inchoate offenses often pose substantial problems for law enforcement agencies, courts, and legislative bodies.

Police and courts experience difficulty determining the stage at which an act tends toward commission of a crime such that it qualifies as criminal attempt. Moreover, there are difficulties in distinguishing between what is legally impossible and what is factually impossible.

Solicitation poses a major problem because the solicitor often exerts power by manipulating the solicitee to commit a crime. There remains controversy over whether legislatures should make it a criminal offense to solicit another person to commit a misdemeanor.

In conspiracy, group action can accomplish criminal purposes not otherwise likely from individual efforts. The offense of conspiracy affords prosecutors considerable leeway in proving offenses sometimes remote from a conspirator's intention. Yet, as will become apparent in later chapters, the offense of conspiracy has become a vital tool in coping with racketeering, drug trafficking, and white-collar crime. It is also an essential weapon in the ongoing war on terrorism.

Despite the problems associated with inchoate offenses, there is strong public support for criminalizing conduct directed toward future injuries to society. Most American jurisdictions have statutes making it an offense to attempt to commit a crime; some are directed at attempts to commit specific crimes. Not all jurisdictions make solicitation a crime, and those that do sometimes limit solicitation to certain classes of felonies. Conspiracy has been made a crime by statute in all jurisdictions. Criminalizing such incomplete and preparatory conduct permits timely intervention of law enforcement agencies to restrain dangerous persons and prevent intended crimes.

Chapter Summary

- **LO1** The law criminalizes inchoate conduct that involves steps taken toward completion of a crime—attempt, solicitation, and conspiracy—to allow police to apprehend dangerous persons before they accomplish their criminal objectives. To be a criminal offense there must be an attempt to commit a crime, solicitation of someone to commit a crime, or a conspiracy of persons to commit a criminal offense. Most American jurisdictions define these offenses by statute, frequently classifying them as felonies, but their development has been primarily through the courts.

- **LO2** With respect to criminal attempt, to prevent a person from being punished simply based on intent, laws often require an overt act that constitutes a substantial step toward the commission of an offense. Most courts require proof that the defendant has a specific intent to commit the target crime; if not, they require at least the level of intent required for proof of the target crime.

- **LO3** An attempt that completes a substantive crime merges into the target offense, making the actor guilty of the substantive crime. But there can be no attempt to commit a crime which, by definition, embraces an attempt. For example, an attempt to pass a forged instrument to someone to obtain something of value is itself a substantive crime.

- **LO4** Statutes generally provide that whoever commands, encourages, or requests another to commit an offense is guilty of solicitation. Solicitation of another is not an attempt, assuming neither the solicitor nor solicitee proximately acts toward the crime's commission. If the crime solicited is committed or attempted by the solicitee, then the offense of solicitation ordinarily merges into the target crime.

- **LO5** Numerous federal statutes define solicitation in various contexts. Some jurisdictions specifically define the crime of solicitation to murder. Irrespective of the statutory language courts often require the prosecution to establish the defendant's specific intent, but in any event the prosecution must establish that the solicitor had the requisite intent for the crime solicited.

- **LO6** Federal and state statutes define the offense of conspiracy as involving an agreement by one or more persons to commit any offense. In general, the *actus reus* of conspiracy is the unlawful agreement, which need not be formal or written. A simple understanding is sufficient. Some statutes require proof of an overt act; some state statutes require proof of intent to commit a felony. Conspiracy is a separate and distinct crime. The danger it generates is usually not confined to the immediate aim of the conspiracy, therefore, conspiracy does not merge into the target offense.

- **LO7** Federal conspiracy prosecutions often relate to illicit drug trafficking and conspiracies not found under state laws, for example, customs violations, counterfeiting of currency, copyright violations, mail fraud, wire fraud, lotteries, and antitrust violation; state prosecutions are commonly directed at criminal homicide, arson, perjury, kidnapping, and property offenses as well as illicit drug trafficking.

- **LO8** The purpose of some statutes requiring an overt act is to manifest that a conspiracy is at work. Because the intent requirement and form of agreement required are somewhat imprecise, a conspiracy is easier to prove than specific substantive crimes, leading critics to argue that conspiracy covers too broad a sphere and can chill exercise of First Amendment freedom of speech.

- **LO9** Wharton's Rule holds that two people cannot conspire to commit a crime such as adultery, incest, or bigamy because these offenses require only two participants.

- **LO10** The *Pinkerton* Rule holds that conspirators are agents of one another bound by the acts of their co-conspirators, so each conspirator is responsible for the acts of the others within the context of their common design. Thus, statements made in furtherance of the conspiracy may be admitted into evidence, an exception to the rule that ordinarily excludes admission of hearsay statements at trial over the defendant's objection.

- **LO11** In many jurisdictions it is a defense to a charge of committing an attempt if it would be legally impossible to commit the crime. But if it is simply factually impossible to commit a crime, it is no defense. Some jurisdictions allow a defense of abandonment of an attempt or a showing that the defendant prevents the consummation of the offense. Neither the fact that the solicitor countermanded the solicitation nor a showing that it was impossible for the person solicited to commit the crime is recognized as a defense, but the Model Penal Code provides that the accused's complete and voluntary renunciation of his or her criminal purpose is a defense to a charge of solicitation, and some states have adopted this position. In some states, statutes specifically provide for a defense of withdrawal from and renunciation of a conspiracy. To accomplish this result, the conspirator would probably have to notify law enforcement authorities of the pertinent details of the conspiracy. Entrapment, which we examine in a later chapter, may be a possible defense to a conspiracy charge.

Key Terms

inchoate offense An offense preparatory to committing another crime. Inchoate offenses include attempt, conspiracy, and solicitation.

attempt An intent to commit a crime coupled with an act taken toward committing the offense.

overt act A visible act by an individual.

substantial step A significant movement toward completion of an intended result.

preparatory conduct Actions taken in preparation to commit a crime.

target crime A crime that is the object of an attempt, solicitation, or conspiracy.

legal impossibility A defense allowed in some jurisdictions when, although the defendant intended to commit a crime, it was impossible to do so because the completed act is not a crime.

factual impossibility That which is in fact impossible to achieve. Unlike legal impossibility, this is not a defense to a charge of attempt.

solicitation The inchoate offense of requesting or encouraging someone to engage in illegal conduct.

conspiracy The inchoate offense of two or more persons agreeing or planning to commit a target crime.

***Pinkerton* Rule** Rule enunciated by the Supreme Court in *Pinkerton v. United States* (1946) holding that a member of a conspiracy is liable for all offenses committed in furtherance of the conspiracy.

Wharton's Rule Named after Francis Wharton, a well-known commentator on criminal law, this rule holds that two people cannot conspire to commit a crime such as adultery, incest, or bigamy inasmuch as these offenses involve only two participants.

Questions for Thought and Discussion

1. What justifies criminalizing attempt, solicitation, and conspiracy?
2. How does the criminal law distinguish between mere preparatory conduct and the overt act required for a criminal attempt? Can you think of a situation in which preparatory conduct might have the appearance of prospective criminal conduct but would not constitute a criminal attempt?

3. Should it be a defense to a charge of attempt that the accused voluntarily abandoned the attempt?
4. What is the rationale for making solicitation a crime even where a solicitor's requests are completely unheeded?
5. Which do you think poses a more serious threat to society: an attempt or a solicitation to commit murder? Why?
6. Should statutes defining conspiracy require proof of an overt act in furtherance of the conspirators' agreement? Why or why not?
7. Given the First Amendment protections of freedom of expression and association, under what circumstances can members of a revolutionary political organization be prosecuted for conspiring to overthrow the government of the United States?
8. Name some instances where the offense of conspiracy provides a means to protect the public from dangers incident to group activities.
9. What distinguishes the offense of conspiracy from the crime of aiding and abetting, discussed in Chapter 4?
10. What are the arguments for and against making the statute proscribing conspiracy require an overt act in furtherance of the conspiracy?

Problems for Discussion and Solution

1. To prove attempted rape, the prosecution must prove the defendant took a substantial step toward commission of the crime of rape. If a male physically forced a female into a bedroom and onto the bed, tried to force his hand under her clothing, and attempted to kiss her, do you think this would establish the substantial step required for attempted rape? What, if any, other crime might the male have committed?
2. Two adults, Alice and Joe, committed adultery in a public place in violation of an old state statute. Each was charged with conspiracy to violate the statute as well as with the violation itself. Would their actions constitute a conspiracy? Why or why not?
3. In an exchange of e-mails, Alex and Peter agreed to sell illicit drugs in a state where the law defining conspiracy requires an unlawful agreement and an overt act. Alex called a third party whom he believed could supply the drugs. Would Alex's actions be sufficient as an overt act or would the law require that there be a more substantial movement toward arranging to sell drugs?
4. Jill's friend, Bob, works at an electronics store at the mall. Jill urges Bob to steal a new laptop computer for her to use at college. Is Jill guilty of solicitation?
5. Leo Lothario was having an affair with Lucy Slarom, a woman separated from her husband, Joe. One night while Lothario and Lucy were playing tennis in her backyard, Joe appeared on the scene. Lothario demanded that Joe leave, but he declined and sat in one of the yard chairs. Lothario went to the garage, picked up a rifle, pointed it at Joe, and from a distance of approximately seventy-five feet, fired a shot in the direction of Joe. The bullet missed Joe by about eighteen inches. Lothario explained to the police that he was simply trying to scare Lucy's estranged husband so he would not bother her. On the strength of these facts, do you think there is a basis to charge Lothario with attempted murder?
6. John and Jane were running a student loan scam. They were convicted of soliciting several students to make false applications in exchange for a portion of the loan proceeds, and also for aiding and abetting those same students in making

false applications for loans. On appeal, they argue that the solicitation charges merged into their convictions for aiding and abetting the making of the false applications. The state responds that John and Jane were guilty of both crimes because the solicitation offenses were completed before John and Jane assisted the students in making the false applications. How should the appellate court rule on this appeal? Why?

7. A state statute makes it a criminal offense for "three or more persons to conduct, direct, or own a gambling business." Several defendants were convicted of "conspiring to violate the statute." In addition, each was convicted of the substantive offense of gambling. On appeal, each defendant argues that the conspiracy offense merged into the substantive offense of gambling because the offense of gambling required participation of a number of persons. The state counters that the harm attendant upon commission of the offense of gambling is not limited to the parties to the conspiracy. Moreover, it points out that those prosecuted for the conspiracy would not necessarily be identical to those who are prosecuted for the substantive offense of gambling. How do you think an appellate court should rule in this instance? Why?

CHAPTER 6

Homicidal Offenses

In 2001, Diane Whipple was attacked outside her San Francisco apartment by two dogs owned by her neighbors, Marjorie Noller and her husband Robert Noel. Another neighbor, who witnessed part of the attack, called 911. Shortly after arriving at the hospital, Whipple died from massive loss of blood due to more than seventy-five lacerations from dog bites. The attack made national news and attracted considerable media attention. Appearing on *Good Morning America*, Noller and Noel denied any responsibility for the attack. Nevertheless, Noller was charged with second-degree murder; her husband, who was not home during the attack, was charged with involuntary manslaughter. After a jury trial, which was moved to Los Angeles, both defendants were convicted of their respective homicide charges. However, the trial judge granted Noller's motion for a new trial on the charge of second-degree murder on the ground that her culpability did not rise to the level required for second-degree murder. Ultimately, in August 2010, a California appellate court ruled that the trial judge had erred in granting a new trial. In its unpublished opinion the appellate court held that Noller had been properly convicted of second-degree murder based on "implied malice." This case suggests the complexity of modern criminal law with respect to homicide. While the English common law divided criminal homicide into murder and manslaughter, modern American statutes provide for gradations of criminal homicide based on degrees of culpability. The modern law of homicide is sufficiently complex that we have decided to devote an entire chapter to it.

Introduction

The word **homicide** means the taking of the life of one human being by another. The English common law recognized both criminal and noncriminal homicides. The killing of a human being was the common factor in all classes of homicide; however, the perpetrator's state of mind was significant in determining whether an offense had been committed and, if so, the category of that offense. At common law, criminal homicide embraced the crimes of **murder** and **manslaughter**; noncriminal homicide included those killings of humans deemed either justifiable or excusable. Homicide was justifiable if performed by the command or permission of the law; it could be excusable if it occurred accidentally or when committed in self-defense.

Under English common law, murder was the unlawful killing of one person by another with **malice aforethought**. The required malice could be either express or implied. There were no degrees of murder. Manslaughter was the unlawful killing of one human being by another when no malice was involved. There were two categories: voluntary and involuntary. Voluntary manslaughter consisted of an intentional, unlawful killing that occurred in the **heat of passion** as a result of some adequate provocation. Involuntary manslaughter was the unintentional killing of another by the accused's gross or wanton negligence. Simply stated, the difference between the two was that the former was intentional whereas the latter was unintentional.

English common law viewed **suicide** as a serious offense against the Crown, inasmuch as the decedent had deprived the monarch of one of his or her subjects. It was also regarded as a serious moral offense by ecclesiastical authorities and by the English people. Suicide was punished by forfeiture of the decedent's personal property to the Crown and denial of a proper burial. William Blackstone observed that "the law has . . . ranked [suicide] among the highest crimes" but admitted that the punishment for it "border[s] a little upon severity." 4 W. Blackstone, *Commentaries* at 189–90.

At common law, abortion was not considered murder or manslaughter, as the law required the victim of a criminal homicide to have been born alive. Abortion was recognized as a misdemeanor, but only after the "quickening" of the fetus.

With respect to homicide, modern American criminal law has evolved considerably from its common-law origins. Yet certain basic terms and concepts remain viable. The criminal law still addresses murder, manslaughter, suicide, and abortion, but the law today is considerably more complex and nuanced.

The Modern Approach to Homicide

With some variations, the basic scheme of common-law homicide has been carried over into the statutory law of American jurisdictions. However, under modern statutes, homicide has been classified based on the degree of the offender's culpability (see, for example, the overview of Tennessee's homicide offenses contained in Table 6.1).

Most jurisdictions now classify murder as either first or second degree. First-degree murder is usually defined as requiring either malice aforethought or **premeditation**. Second-degree murder commonly requires proof that the accused

TABLE 6.1	Levels of Criminal Homicide in Tennessee
Level of Criminal Homicide	**Statutory Definition**
First-degree murder	"the premeditated and intentional killing of another" or the "killing of another committed in the perpetration of or attempt to perpetrate any first-degree murder, arson, rape, robbery, burglary, theft, kidnapping, aggravated child abuse, aggravated child neglect or aircraft piracy" or the "killing of another committed as the result of the unlawful throwing, placing or discharging of a destructive device or bomb"
Second-degree murder	"the knowing killing of another" or the "killing of another which results from the unlawful distribution of any Schedule I or Schedule II drug when such drug is the proximate cause of the death of the user"
Voluntary manslaughter	"the intentional or knowing killing of another in a state of passion produced by adequate provocation sufficient to lead a reasonable person to act in an irrational manner"
Vehicular homicide	"the reckless killing of another by the operation of an automobile, airplane, motorboat or other motor vehicle: (1) As the proximate result of conduct creating a substantial risk of death or serious bodily injury to a person; or (2) As the proximate result of the driver's intoxication. . . ."
Reckless homicide	"the reckless killing of another"
Criminally negligent homicide	"criminally negligent conduct which results in death"

Source: Tennessee Code Annotated § 39-13-201 *et seq.*

was guilty of imminently dangerous or outrageous conduct, albeit not malicious conduct in the common-law sense of malice aforethought.

All states make manslaughter a crime, although some statutes have abolished the distinction between **voluntary manslaughter** and **involuntary manslaughter**. Additionally, modern statutes extend the offense of manslaughter to embrace a person's responsibility for a person's death resulting from an omission to act in instances where the law imposes a duty to act.

Modern criminal codes generally provide that it is **justifiable homicide** for one to take another's life by authority of the law (for example, an executioner performing a duty). It is usually considered **excusable homicide** if death results from the inadvertent taking of another's life when the actor is not guilty of criminal negligence (for example, death occurring from an unavoidable traffic accident).

The overwhelming majority of homicide prosecutions are brought under state laws. However, federal statutes provide jurisdiction over the killing of certain officers and employees of the United States engaged in performance of their official duties, 18 U.S.C.A. § 1114, as well as certain foreign officials, 18 U.S.C.A. § 1116. Federal statutes classify criminal homicide as murder in the first degree, felony murder, and manslaughter (voluntary and involuntary). 18 U.S.C.A. § 1111–1112.F.

Suicide statutes are now designed primarily to punish those who assist others in committing suicide. Such laws, especially those prohibiting **doctor-assisted suicide**, have become problematic, as courts have recognized a **right to die** in certain instances.

First-Degree Murder

The California Penal Code illustrates a modern statutory approach to homicide. It defines murder as the "unlawful killing of a human being, or a fetus, with malice aforethought," but stipulates that the death of a fetus is not murder when an abortion is performed by a physician when the mother's life is endangered or with the mother's consent. West's Ann. Cal. Penal Code § 187. The malice required by the code may be either express or implied. When a deliberate intention is manifested to take a person's life unlawfully, the malice is considered express. Intent may be implied when no considerable **provocation** appears or under other circumstances indicating malice. West's Ann. Cal. Penal Code § 188. In defining degrees of murder, the California code states that

> all murder which is perpetrated by means of a destructive device or explosive, knowing use of ammunition designed primarily to penetrate metal or armor, poison, lying in wait, torture, or by any other kind of willful, deliberate, and premeditated killing, or which is committed in the perpetration of, or attempt to perpetrate, arson, rape, carjacking, robbery, burglary, mayhem, kidnapping . . . is murder of the first degree; and all other kinds of murder are of the second degree. West's Ann. Cal. Penal Code § 189.

The penalties in California and other jurisdictions for **first-degree murder** are the most severe, with decreasing penalties provided for second-degree murder and manslaughter.

First-degree murder is the highest classification of homicide. It contemplates a true "intent to kill" and, as noted, usually requires proof of either malice aforethought or premeditation. Thus, to obtain a conviction, the prosecution must establish the defendant's specific intent to take another's life.

The California Supreme Court has said that "when a defendant with a wanton disregard for human life, does an act that involves a high degree of probability that it will result in death, he acts with malice aforethought." Moreover, the court has opined that "willful, deliberate, and premeditated," as used in the statute, indicates the legislature's intent to require as an essential element of first-degree murder substantially more reflection "than the mere amount of thought necessary to form the intention to kill." *People v. Cruz*, 605 P.2d 830, 834 (Cal. 1980). The Pennsylvania Supreme Court has defined malice aforethought more elaborately, saying it is "not only a particular ill will, but a hardness of heart, cruelty, recklessness of consequences, and a mind regardless of social duty." *Commonwealth v. Buzard*, 76 A.2d 394, 396 (Pa. 1950). Such malice may be expressed or may be implied from the circumstances under which a homicidal act is performed. However, that court has noted that a single punch to a victim's face was insufficient to support a finding of malice. *Commonwealth v. Thomas*, 594 A.2d 300 (Pa. 1991).

Many jurisdictions define first-degree murder based on the "premeditated intent" of the offender. For example, Florida classifies a homicide as a first-degree murder if the unlawful killing of a human being is "perpetrated from a premeditated design to effect the death of the person killed or any human being." West's Fla. Stat. Ann. § 782.04. Initially, one might be inclined to think of a premeditated act as requiring a lengthy period of deliberation. Indeed, dictionaries commonly define "premeditation" as a conscious and deliberate preplanning over a period of time. However, judicial decisions defining premeditation emphasize that although it requires thought beforehand, no particular length of time is required. The length of time necessary to deliberate, or to form a specific intent to kill, need only be time enough to form the required intent before the killing. It matters not how short that time may be, as long as the process of premeditation occurs at any point before the killing. See, for example, *State v. Corn*, 278 S.E.2d 221 (N.C. 1981). (On the issue of premeditation, courts consider defendants' acts and comments before and after killing, use of grossly excessive force or infliction of lethal blows after the deceased has been felled, and history of altercations or ill will between the parties.)

The prosecution usually attempts to establish either malice aforethought or premeditation by introducing a variety of evidentiary facts and circumstances bearing on the defendant's motive and state of mind. These include the defendant's previous relationship with the victim, encompassing threats, quarrels, and expressions of ill will as well as conversations of the defendant at the time of and before and after the act of killing. Prosecutors also point to the nature of the wound inflicted, prior attacks on the victim, the defendant's actions before and after the crime, and the circumstances of the killing itself, including the weapon used and the nature and location of wounds inflicted.

State v. Corder, reproduced on the companion website, illustrates the factors a court considers in determining whether the evidence is sufficient to establish a defendant's premeditated design to effect death of a victim.

CASE-IN-POINT

First-Degree Murder: Evidence of Premeditation

Defendant Phillip Lee Young suggested to his two companions that they rob and kill John Cooke in order to obtain money to buy liquor. After the three men used a ruse to gain entry to Cooke's house, Young stabbed Cooke twice in the chest, and one of the companions stabbed the victim several times in the back. Cooke died as a result of the injuries. A jury found Young guilty of first-degree murder, and he appealed. After explaining that first-degree murder is the unlawful killing of a person with malice and with premeditation and deliberation, the North Carolina Supreme Court rejected Young's contention that the evidence was insufficient to support a conviction.

State v. Young, 325 S.E.2d 181 (N.C. 1985).

Felony Murder

The common law developed a doctrine that where an accused was engaged in the commission of a felony and a homicide occurred, the felonious act was regarded as a substitute for the proof of malice aforethought required to find the defendant guilty of murder. Thus, it became **felony murder** when an accused unintentionally killed a human being while committing, or attempting to commit, such common-law felonies as burglary, arson, rape, or robbery. The theory was that if a killing resulted, even though unintentional or accidental, the required malice was carried over from the original felony. Consequently, the felon would be found guilty of murder.

The felony murder doctrine has been incorporated into most criminal codes in the United States. See *People v. Aaron*, 299 N.W.2d 304 (Mich. 1980). With the proliferation of crimes classified as felonies, legislatures have generally limited the applicability of felony murder to felonies involving violence or posing great threat to life or limb (for example, rape, robbery, kidnapping, arson, and burglary). See, for example, West's Ann. Cal. Penal Code § 189, quoted above. Some state legislatures have sought to equate certain felonious drug offenses with violent felonies. Some statutes provide for degrees of felony murder depending on the seriousness of the felony attempted or perpetrated by the accused, whether the killing occurred by a person other than the person perpetrating or attempting to perpetrate the felony, and whether the accused was present at the scene when the killing occurred. See, for example, West's Fla. Stat. Ann. § 782.04. Felony murder statutes have produced much litigation in the criminal courts. Some of the pertinent questions raised include the following:

- Can a felon who perpetrates an offense be guilty of felony murder where the victim of the intended offense kills a co-felon?
- Should a felon committing a crime such as robbery be guilty of felony murder if a police officer mistakenly kills the felon's intended victim?
- Can a felon be guilty of felony murder when a co-felon accidentally kills a bystander or a police officer?

Most courts have held that the doctrine of felony murder does not extend to a killing stemming from the commission of the felony if it is directly attributable to the act of someone other than the defendant or those actively participating with the defendant in the unlawful enterprise. Nevertheless, courts have arrived at different solutions to these and other problems arising under felony murder laws.

Perhaps questions such as these led the Michigan Supreme Court in 1980 to abrogate the felony murder doctrine. After commenting on how its prior decisions had already significantly restricted the doctrine, the court concluded that the rule that substitutes the intent to commit the underlying felony for the malice element of murder had to be abolished. Its abrogation of the doctrine does not make irrelevant the fact that a death occurred in the course of a felony. Rather, the court noted that a jury could properly infer malice from evidence that a defendant intentionally set in motion a force likely to cause death or great bodily harm. However, Michigan juries are no longer instructed to find malice if they are satisfied from all the evidence that it does not exist. *People v. Aaron*, supra.

A cogent argument can be made that the felony murder rule violates the basic requirement of moral culpability in the criminal law. Moreover, critics point out that under the early common law, conviction of a felony was punishable by death. Consequently, they note, when a death occurred in the commission of a felony and the accused was guilty of felony murder, no additional consequences resulted. With the exception of certain federal offenses recently classified as capital crimes, no felony except murder committed under aggravating circumstances is punishable by death. Nevertheless, the felony murder doctrine is well established in most jurisdictions. With legislatures perceiving the need to take a "hard line" on crime, it is doubtful that many states will be motivated to repeal felony murder statutes. Therefore, courts have become increasingly conscious of the need to interpret such statutes strictly. Observing that it is the commission of a specified felony that supplants the requirement of premeditation for first-degree murder, the Florida Supreme Court declared that for the felon to be guilty of felony murder there must be some causal connection between the homicide and the underlying felony. *Bryant v. State*, 412 So.2d 347 (Fla. 1982). The State must prove that there was no break in the chain of circumstances beginning with the felony and ending with the murder. *Santiago v. State*, 874 So.2d 617 (Fla. App. 2004).

Second-Degree Murder

In many jurisdictions, **second-degree murder** is a residual classification applied to unlawful homicides not evidenced by malice aforethought or premeditation, not occurring in conjunction with other felonies, and not falling within the statutory definition of manslaughter. More commonly, second-degree murder is defined as an unlawful killing of a human being by a person having a **depraved mind or heart**. For example, in South Dakota second-degree murder is defined as follows:

> Homicide is murder in the second degree when perpetrated by any act imminently dangerous to others and evincing a depraved mind, regardless of human life, although without any premeditated design to effect the death of any particular individual, including an unborn child. S.D. St. § 22-16-7.

The South Dakota Supreme Court has held that the statutory language "although without any premeditated design" distinguishes premeditated murder from second-degree murder. *State v. Satter*, 543 N.W.2d 249 (S.D. 1996). Two years later that court held that a trial court properly defined the phrase "evincing a depraved mind" as conduct demonstrating an indifference to the life of others, that is, not only disregard for the safety of another but also a lack of regard for the life of another. *State v. Hart*, 584 N.W.2d 863 (S.D. 1998).

Shooting a firearm into a crowd or into an occupied house or automobile is a classic example of a depraved-heart-or-mind murder. But courts have also found such conduct as a parent spanking and shaking a young child so hard as to cause death, a driver running a police roadblock at a high rate of speed, a golfer swinging a golf club with great force against a victim, and a person tossing heavy stones from a building onto a busy street below to be conduct evincing a depraved heart or depraved mind.

We began the chapter by referring to a case where Diane Whipple was killed by dogs belonging to neighbors. In that case, a conviction for second-degree murder was sustained under a California statute that allows for conviction of second-degree murder based on "implied malice." The statute provides that malice "is implied, when no considerable provocation appears, or when the circumstances attending the killing show an abandoned and malignant heart." Cal. Pen. Code § 188. In *People v. Phillips*, 414 P.2d 353, 587 (1966), the California Supreme Court held that malice can be implied when the death of another results from "an act, the natural consequences of which are dangerous to life, which act was deliberately performed by a person who knows that his conduct endangers the life of another and who acts with conscious disregard for life."

Second-Degree Murder: Evidence of Depraved Indifference

CASE-IN-POINT

The state of New York charged a fifteen-and-a-half-year-old boy with murder in the second degree under N.Y. Penal Law §125.25 (2), which provides as follows: "A person is guilty of murder in the second degree when: . . . (2) Under circumstances evincing a depraved indifference to human life, he recklessly engages in conduct which creates a grave risk of death to another person, and thereby causes the death of another person." The evidence at trial revealed the defendant loaded a mix of "live" and "dummy" shells at random into the magazine of a 12-gauge shotgun and then pumped a shell into the firing chamber, not knowing whether it was a dummy or live round. He next raised the gun to his shoulder and, pointing it directly at the victim, exclaimed, "Let's play Polish roulette," and asked, "Who is first?" Then the defendant pulled the trigger, discharging a live round into the thirteen-year-old victim's chest, resulting in the eventual death of the victim.

On appeal, the defendant challenged the sufficiency of the evidence to support his conviction. In its review the court first distinguished the crime of second-degree murder by depraved indifference from manslaughter by saying that it must be shown that the actor's reckless conduct is imminently dangerous and presents a grave risk of death, whereas in manslaughter the conduct need only present the lesser "substantial risk" of death. Then, pointing out that the defendant had an intense interest in and a detailed knowledge of weapons and analogizing the incident to a macabre game of chance, the New York Court of Appeals held the evidence was legally sufficient to support the defendant's conviction of second-degree murder.

People v. Roe, 542 N.E.2d 610 (N.Y. 1989).

Manslaughter

As we have noted, there were two classes of manslaughter at common law: voluntary and involuntary. California, like many states, preserves that distinction and defines manslaughter as the "unlawful killing of a human being without malice." California law enumerates three categories: voluntary, involuntary, and vehicular. Voluntary manslaughter refers to instances where death of the victim occurs in a sudden quarrel or in the heat of passion. Involuntary manslaughter occurs where a death results from the commission of a lawful act that might produce death in an unlawful manner, or without due caution and circumspection. The third category, vehicular homicide, involves death resulting from the perpetrator's driving a vehicle while in the commission of an unlawful act not amounting to a felony and not with gross negligence, or driving a vehicle in the commission of a lawful act that might produce death in an unlawful manner, and with gross negligence. West's Ann. Cal. Penal Code § 192.

Many other states define manslaughter without categorizing it as voluntary or involuntary. Still other state legislatures have defined manslaughter by degrees. For example, New York law provides that a person who recklessly causes the death of another person, commits an unlawful abortion on a female that causes her death, or intentionally causes or aids another to commit suicide commits manslaughter in the second degree. McKinney's N.Y. Penal Law § 125.15. However, a person who inflicts certain intentional serious injuries that cause the death of another under circumstances that do not constitute murder may be guilty of the more serious offense of manslaughter in the first degree if he or she (1) acts under the influence of extreme emotional disturbance or (2) commits an unlawful abortional act that causes the death of a female pregnant for more than twenty-four weeks, unless it is an abortional act deemed justifiable by statutory exceptions. McKinney's N.Y. Penal Law

§ 125.20. Irrespective of whether a statute classifies manslaughter as voluntary, involuntary, or by degree, certain situations generally fall within the definition of the offense. Common examples include death resulting from mutual combat and killing someone by use of excessive force while defending oneself or a family member or acting in defense of property.

The intent the prosecution must establish to obtain a conviction of manslaughter may depend on the nature of the charge and whether the particular statute defines voluntary or involuntary manslaughter. To establish voluntary manslaughter, the prosecution may have to establish the defendant's specific intent. On the other hand, in a prosecution for involuntary manslaughter, the prosecution need only establish the defendant's general intent, and that may be inferred from the defendant's act and surrounding circumstances.

Often a charge of involuntary manslaughter is based on allegations of criminal negligence. A highly publicized example of this arose from a tragic accident in the film industry. In 1982, a movie crew shooting a scene for the movie *The Twilight Zone* used a helicopter that crashed on the set, decapitating an actor and a child and crushing another child. The state prosecuted the director and four of his associates for involuntary manslaughter, claiming they were guilty of criminal negligence. The defendants argued that the tragic deaths resulted from an unforeseeable accident. In May 1987, after a dramatic five-month trial, a jury found them all not guilty.

Provocation is frequently a factor in manslaughter trials. Provocation that would cause a reasonable person to lose control may be sufficient to convert an otherwise intentional killing of another to manslaughter. Mere words, however gross or insulting, are not sufficient to constitute provocation. Rather, to reduce a homicide from murder to manslaughter, it must generally be shown that there was sufficient provocation to excite in the defendant's mind such anger, rage, or terror as would obscure an ordinary person's reasoning and render the person incapable of cool reflection. A classic example is discovering one's spouse in an act of adultery with significant sexual contact taking place. The Maryland Special Court of Special Appeals has observed that

> if one spouse discovers another in an unexpected act of adultery, a killing of a spouse or paramour in hot-blooded fury may lower the blameworthiness from the murder level to the manslaughter level. The blood, however, must indeed be hot and, generally speaking, only the hot-blooded killer can attest to that. By an objective standard, moreover, the time frame must be close enough so that an average and reasonable man would not have had an adequate 'cooling period' for the first fury to abate. *Bartram v. State*, 364 A.2d 1119, 1153 (Md. App. 1976).

The Indiana Supreme Court has noted that

> all that is required to reduce a homicide from murder to voluntary manslaughter is sufficient provocation to excite in the mind of the defendant such emotions as either anger, rage, sudden resentment, or terror as may be sufficient to obscure the reason of an ordinary man, and to prevent deliberation and premeditation, to exclude malice, and to render the defendant incapable of cool reflection. *Hardin v. State*, 404 N.E.2d 1354, 1357 (Ind. 1980).

Modern statutes often provide that negligent performance of a legal duty or the doing of a lawful act in an unlawful manner constitutes manslaughter. In addition to the more common instances, courts have upheld manslaughter convictions under such statutes for death occurring because of criminal negligence of medical

In *Manuel v. State*, reproduced on the companion website, a Florida appellate court distinguishes second-degree murder from the offense of manslaughter.

Manslaughter by Culpable Negligence

CASE-IN-POINT

William Burge and Juanita Calloway became involved in an argument over an alleged sexual indiscretion. When Calloway displayed a knife, Burge pulled a gun that he carried to kill snakes that lurked in the walls of his house. Burge pointed the gun at Calloway and cocked it. Burge then pushed Calloway in an attempt to get her into his car. When he did, Calloway's hand hit the gun and it went off, severely wounding Calloway. While driving her to the hospital, Burge ran out of gas and called an ambulance. Calloway died en route to the hospital. Despite his plea of self-defense, a jury found Burge guilty of manslaughter by culpable negligence. In affirming the conviction, the Mississippi Supreme Court rejected the defendant's contentions of self-defense and excusable and justifiable homicide. The court observed that the jury could reasonably have determined that although the victim was holding a knife, the defendant was not in danger of great personal injury.

Burge v. State, 472 So.2d 392 (Miss. 1985).

practitioners or because of parental failure to provide medical attention or adequate nourishment for their children. See, for example, *People v. Ogg*, 182 N.W.2d 570 (Mich. App. 1970) (the mother of a young child who left the home while her child was locked in a bedroom and the child was killed in a fire of undetermined origin was guilty of manslaughter). The California Supreme Court held that a parent of a seriously ill child who only provides for treatment of the child by prayer may be guilty of such criminal negligence that the parent can be found guilty of involuntary manslaughter or child endangerment. *Walker v. Superior Court*, 763 P.2d 852 (Cal. 1988). Other courts have rejected the First Amendment right to free exercise of religion as a defense in such situations.

In a high-profile case, in October 1997 a Massachusetts jury found Louise Woodward, a young British *au pair* serving an American family, guilty of second-degree murder in the death of an eight-month-old child under her care. The child died a few days after receiving a severe head trauma while in Woodward's care. There was no evidence the defendant had ever abused or injured the child prior to the fatal injury. Fearing a compromise verdict, Woodward's counsel requested that the court not instruct the jury on the offense of manslaughter. After the jury returned a verdict of second-degree murder, the trial judge found the defendant's actions "were characterized by confusion, inexperience, frustration, immaturity and some anger, but not malice" and reduced the defendant's conviction to manslaughter. The prosecution challenged the trial judge's action; however, the Massachusetts Supreme Judicial Court concluded that the trial judge did not abuse his discretion. *Commonwealth v. Woodward*, 694 N.E.2d 1277 (Mass. 1998).

Vehicular Homicide

The carnage on American highways has prompted many states to enact statutes making **vehicular homicide** a specific felony rather than opting to rely on prosecutors to charge a defendant with manslaughter for causing a traffic death. Such statutes were originally directed at operators of motor vehicles but now frequently apply to operators of boats and airplanes as well.

In Kansas the legislature has provided that vehicular homicide is a class A misdemeanor and defines the offense as follows:

Vehicular Homicide: Criminal Liability for Second Accident

On the evening of February 14, 1987, Gary Dawson was a passenger in a car driven by Richard Peaslee, Jr., on a snow-packed, icy road in Maine. As a result of Peaslee's intentional "fish-tailing," the car went out of control and overturned, throwing Dawson onto the road. Dawson, unable to move, lay on the road, where he was run over by another vehicle several minutes later. Dawson died before help arrived on the scene. A jury found Peaslee guilty of vehicular manslaughter, and he appealed. In affirming Peaslee's conviction, the Maine Supreme Court rejected his contention that he was not criminally responsible for the second accident. "The separate accidents were not independent of each other," said the court, "because Dawson would not have been lying immobile on the road in the path of the other car were it not for Peaslee's conduct." Moreover, the court concluded that "[w]hether Dawson was killed by the first or second impact makes no difference."

State v. Peaslee, 571 A.2d 825 (Me. 1990).

Vehicular homicide is the unintentional killing of a human being committed by the operation of an automobile, airplane, motor boat or other motor vehicle in a manner which creates an unreasonable risk of injury to the person or property of another and which constitutes a material deviation from the standard of care which a reasonable person would observe under the same circumstances. K.S.A. § 21-3405.

Many states have opted to classify vehicular homicide as a felony. See, for example, West's Fla. Stat. Ann. § 782.071. ("Vehicular homicide" is the killing of a human being, or the killing of a viable fetus by any injury to the mother, caused by the operation of a motor vehicle by another in a reckless manner likely to cause the death of, or great bodily harm to, another.) The Florida Supreme Court has said that in enacting its vehicular homicide statute, the legislature created a separate offense with a lesser standard of proof than is required for conviction under the state's manslaughter statute. Thus, the statute enables the prosecution to secure a conviction where the state is unable to meet the level of proof otherwise required in establishing manslaughter. The court said the state could charge a defendant with manslaughter for operating a motor vehicle in a culpably negligent manner that causes the death of a human being or could proceed under vehicular homicide, a lesser included offense. *State v. Young*, 371 So.2d 1029 (Fla. 1979).

Justifiable and Excusable Homicide

As do most jurisdictions, California classifies nonculpable homicide as excusable or justifiable. It is excusable "when committed by accident or misfortune or in doing any other lawful act by lawful means, with usual and ordinary caution, and without any unlawful intent." It may also be excusable "when committed in the heat of passion, or on sudden and sufficient provocation, or on sudden combat where no undue advantage is taken nor any dangerous weapon is used and the killing is not done in a cruel or unusual manner." West's Ann. Cal. Penal Code § 195. Examples of excusable homicide include killing someone while resisting a murder attempt; when in defense of a person's home under certain circumstances; or in some instances of self-defense where there is a reasonable ground to apprehend imminent danger of great bodily harm to a person's self, spouse, parent, or child. See West's Ann. Cal. Penal Code § 196; *People v. Collins*, 11 Cal. Rptr. 504 (Cal. App. 1961).

Under California law, homicide is justifiable when committed by public officers and those acting by their command in their aid and assistance,

1. In obedience to any judgment of a competent Court; or,
2. When necessarily committed in overcoming actual resistance to the execution of some legal process, or in the discharge of any other legal duty; or,
3. When necessarily committed in retaking felons who have been rescued or have escaped, or when necessarily committed in arresting persons charged with felony, and who are fleeing from justice or resisting such arrest. West's Ann. Cal. Penal Code § 196; *People v. Young*, 29 Cal. Rptr. 595 (Cal. App. 1963).

Removal of Life-Support Systems

Another area of contemporary concern has resulted from technological advances in medicine that have enabled physicians to use sophisticated life-support systems to prolong life for indefinite periods. In a landmark case involving Karen Quinlan, the New Jersey Supreme Court in 1976 reviewed the request of Karen's parents to remove the life-support systems sustaining the life of their daughter, who lay in a comatose state with no reasonable medical probability of regaining a sapient existence. The court ruled that withdrawal of such life-support systems, under the circumstances, would not constitute a criminal homicide. *In re Quinlan*, 355 A.2d 647 (N.J. 1976).

A significant body of decisional law has now developed on the issue of when life-sustaining measures should be initiated and when they may be removed. Generally, a competent adult who is terminally ill may decide to forgo such extraordinary measures or may order such measures discontinued. *McKay v. Bergstedt*, 801 P.2d 617 (Nev. 1990). Moreover, the Florida Supreme Court has held that terminally ill

CASE-IN-POINT

The Terri Schiavo Case

Problems can result in acrimonious litigation when a patient has no living will or other written instructions on the issue of removal of life support and close family members disagree. This was dramatized in litigation involving the late Terri Schiavo. In 1990, Schiavo, age twenty-six, suffered cardiac arrest and remained in a coma for several weeks. She was then diagnosed as being in a persistent vegetative state. In 1998, Michael, her husband and guardian, petitioned a Florida court to remove her feeding tube. She had no living will. Over the strong objections of her parents, the court found the evidence revealed that Schiavo did not wish to be kept alive and ordered her feeding tube removed. The court's decision engendered numerous unsuccessful appeals in state courts. The Florida legislature became involved in the controversy, and even the U.S. Congress passed a law granting federal court jurisdiction over this particular case, an action that raised critical constitutional issues. The U.S. Supreme Court denied review of court decisions, denying the parents relief. Subsequently even Florida governor Jeb Bush was unsuccessful in an attempt to prohibit removal of the feeding tube. Finally, Schiavo's feeding tube was removed for the third time. Throughout the controversy, the media kept the public advised of the progress of the legal proceedings, Schiavo died on March 31, 2005, at the age of forty-one.

The Schiavo case did not develop any new legal principles or procedures. But it did focus national attention on the need for individuals to execute legal directives clearly defining the extent of extraordinary medical procedures to be taken in the event they are in a persistent vegetative state.

incompetent persons have the same right to refuse extraordinary measures as competent persons and that family members or guardians may exercise such rights on their behalf. *John F. Kennedy Memorial Hosp., Inc. v. Bludworth*, 452 So.2d 921 (Fla. 1984).

Judicial opinions vary as to when, under what circumstances, and by whom discontinuance of medical treatments may be ordered for minors and incompetents. Statutes in several states now address many of the problems in this area, yet there is no statutory or judicial consensus on the procedures to effect discontinuance. However, courts have been cautious not to allow criminal prosecutions where life-sustaining medical procedures have been discontinued in good faith based on competent medical advice and consent of a competent patient or the patient's family. See, for example, *Barber v. Superior Court*, 195 Cal. Rptr. 484 (Cal. App. 1983).

Prosecutorial Burdens in Homicide Cases

To obtain a conviction in a homicide case, the prosecution bears several burdens peculiar to homicide cases. The victim of the crime must have been alive; the defendant's actions must be the cause of the victim's death; and, in some jurisdictions, death of the victim must occur within a stated period of time. Although these might appear to be matters easily proven, sometimes they pose problems for prosecutors.

The Requirement That the Victim was Alive Before the Homicidal Act

By definition, a criminal homicide consists of someone taking another person's life. It follows that before the accused can be found guilty of a homicidal crime, the prosecution must establish that the victim was alive before the accused's criminal act. In *People v. Dlugash*, 363 N.E.2d 1155 (NY 1977), the New York Court of Appeals reviewed a case where a defendant (Dlugash) had been convicted of murder after he had fired shots into a body that had been shot by another person (Bush) several minutes earlier:

> While the defendant admitted firing five shots at the victim approximately two to five minutes after Bush had fired three times, all three medical expert witnesses testified that they could not, with any degree of medical certainty, state whether the victim had been alive at the time the latter shots were fired by the defendant. Thus, the People failed to prove beyond a reasonable doubt that the victim had been alive at the time he was shot by the defendant. Whatever else it may be, it is not murder to shoot a dead body. Man dies but once. 363 N.E.2d at 1158–1159.

The *Corpus Delicti* Requirement

In addition to establishing that a human being was alive before a killing took place, the prosecution must always establish the **corpus delicti**, or body of the crime. The *corpus delicti* consists of the fact that a human being is dead and that the death was caused by the criminal act or agency of another person. In most jurisdictions the *corpus delicti* rule requires independent evidence beyond a defendant's confession. Some argue that this requirement is simply a technicality that impedes the search for truth. They argue that modern constitutional protections of confessions render the rule unnecessary. Others contend that by requiring some independent evidence to link a defendant to the crime charged ensures that no one is convicted based on a mistake or a coerced or fabricated confession. This rule is firmly implanted in American law, although several states have modified the rule in the last few decades. To prove the *corpus delicti*, the prosecution must show by either direct or circumstantial evidence, independent of the accused's statements, that the victim died as a result of a criminal act. Usually, the victim's body is available for medical examination, and a physician can testify about the cause of death. If the deceased's body is not recovered and the victim's death cannot be determined to have resulted from a criminal act, a conviction cannot be lawfully obtained. Consider the case of *Ex parte Flodstrom*, 277 P.2d 101 (Cal. 1954). There, it could not be determined if a baby died from the mother's alleged homicidal act or if death occurred as a result of natural causes. Consequently, because there was no evidence available to establish the *corpus delicti*, the appellate court discharged the accused mother from custody on the ground that she was being held to answer charges of murder without probable cause.

To hold a defendant responsible for the death of a victim, the prosecution must also establish that the defendant's act was the **proximate cause** of the victim's death. This means that the victim's death must have been the natural and probable consequence of the defendant's unlawful conduct. Where A shoots or physically beats B, A pushes B out of a window or overboard from a boat, or A administers poison to B, medical evidence can usually establish the cause of the victim's death. However, killings can be accomplished in hundreds of ways. For example, death can be precipitated by fright, shock, or other means not involving physical contact with the victim. The accused's acts or omissions need not be the immediate cause of the victim's death as long as the death results naturally from the accused's conduct.

Some situations present perplexing issues for medical experts and courts. For example, a defendant fired a shot into the water about six feet from a boat occupied by two boys. When a second shot struck nearer to the boat than the first, one of the boys leaped out of the boat into the water. The boat capsized with the remaining boy in it. Both boys drowned. The defendant argued that he could not be guilty of causing the death of the boy who drowned when the boat overturned. The Tennessee Supreme Court rejected his contention and upheld the defendant's conviction for involuntary manslaughter, concluding that it was his shots, not the act of the boy who caused the boat to capsize, that caused the decedent's death. *Letner v. State*, 299 S.W. 1049 (Tenn. 1927).

In another instance, a wife who had been severely beaten by her husband in the past was impelled by fear of another beating at his hands to jump from a moving automobile. She died from injuries sustained. Her husband was charged with her murder and was found guilty of the lesser offense of manslaughter. On appeal, the Florida Supreme Court upheld the conviction. *Whaley v. State*, 26 So.2d 656 (Fla. 1946).

In a recent prosecution for several counts of attempted murder, the evidence revealed that the defendant was aware that he had tested positive for human immunodeficiency virus (HIV). The defendant's probation officer had even informed him that if he passed HIV to another person, "he would be killing someone." Nevertheless, he repeatedly and intentionally engaged in sexual activity with multiple partners and refused to take "safe sex" precautions. The defendant was convicted and appealed. He argued that he meant only to satisfy himself sexually and such was insufficient to prove intent to cause death. The Oregon Court of Appeals rejected his appeal and held that the defendant did not act impulsively merely to satisfy his sexual desire; rather, he acted deliberately to cause his victims serious bodily injury and death. *State v. Hinkhouse*, 912 P.2d 921 (Or. App. 1996).

Prosecutions of HIV-positive defendants under statutes proscribing attempted murder pose difficult problems for prosecutors. For example, proof of the element of intent is problematic, and proof of causation can pose great difficulty when the victim has had sexual relations with multiple partners. In *Smallwood v. State*, 680 A.2d 512 (Md. 1996), an HIV-positive defendant who pled guilty to attempted first-degree rape and robbery was then convicted of assault with intent to murder and attempted murder. On appeal, the Maryland Court of Appeals reversed the defendant's convictions for assault with intent to murder and attempted murder. The court held that evidence that the defendant knew he was HIV positive when he raped three women was insufficient to prove that he had an intent to kill.

Some states allow for the prosecution of persons who are HIV positive under reckless endangerment statutes, thus eliminating proof of intent and causation. A number of states have adopted statutes that proscribe a person who has been diagnosed with HIV from engaging in sexual activity with another person without first informing that person of the HIV diagnosis.

When Death Occurs

Just as it is necessary to determine that a homicide victim was alive before the injury that caused death, it is also necessary to establish that death has occurred. In most instances, the classic definition will suffice: death occurs when the heart stops beating and respiration ends. However, technological advances have rendered this definition obsolete as the sole means of determining when death occurs. Many state legislatures have now adopted a definition of **brain death** that specifies that irreversible cessation of total brain functions constitutes death. For example, North Carolina law states,

> Brain death, defined as irreversible cessation of total brain function, may be used as a sole basis for the determination that a person has died, particularly when brain death occurs in the presence of artificially maintained respiratory and circulatory functions. This specific recognition of brain death as a criterion of death of the person shall not preclude the use of other medically recognized criteria for determining whether and when a person has died. N.C.G.S.A. § 90-323.

All states and the District of Columbia, either by statute or judicial decision, now recognize brain death as a criterion for death.

The "One-Year-and-a-Day" Rule

Another obstacle to the prosecution of homicide cases can be the **one-year-and-a-day rule**. Although the rule originated during the early development of the English common law, in 1894 the U.S. Supreme Court acknowledged its applicability to criminal prosecutions in this country, stating,

> In cases of murder the rule at common law undoubtedly was that no person should be adjudged "by any act whatever to kill another who does not die by it within a year and a day thereafter. . . ." And such is the rule in this country in prosecutions for murder, except in jurisdictions where it may be otherwise prescribed by statute. *Louisville, Evansville, & St. Louis R.R. Co. v. Clarke*, 152 U.S. 230, 239, 14 S.Ct. 579, 581, 38 L.Ed. 422, 424 (1894).

This inflexible rule continued because of uncertainties of medical science in establishing the cause of a victim's death after a lengthy period had elapsed. But in an age of advancing medical technology, the "one-year-and-a-day" rule has little relevance.

Either by statute or judicial decision the vast majority of states have abolished the rule; a few have modified it. California amended its statute in 1969 to stipulate that "[i]f death occurs beyond the time of three years and a day, there shall be a rebuttable presumption that the killing was not criminal." West's Ann. Cal. Penal Code § 194. Tennessee was one of the latest states to abolish the rule by judicial decision. In *State v. Rogers*, 992 S.W.2d 393 (Tenn. 1999), the Tennessee Supreme Court concluded that the reasons that prompted common-law courts to recognize the rule no longer exist, observing, "Modern pathologists are able to determine the cause of death with much greater accuracy than was possible in earlier times." *Id*. at 400. The U.S. Supreme Court upheld the Tennessee Supreme Court's retroactive abolition of the one-year and-a-day rule. Justice Sandra Day O'Connor, writing for the majority of the Court, pointed out that the rule was an outdated relic of the common law and that modern medicine no longer necessitated the rule. Further, her opinion held that judicial abrogation of the year-and-a-day rule was not unexpected, and thus Rogers had fair warning that the rule may be abolished and there was no violation of the Ex Post Facto Clause of the Constitution. *Rogers v. Tennessee*, 532 U.S. 451, 121 S.Ct. 1693, 149 L.Ed.2d 697 (2001).

Defenses to Homicide Charges

Defendants charged with murder or manslaughter frequently plead either self-defense or insanity. These defenses are discussed in detail in Chapter 14. Where an accused defends against a charge of murder, the heat-of-passion defense discussed earlier may be available in some instances, as would be the defense of reasonable care or accidental killing in others.

Suicide and Assisted Suicide

The early English common law defined the offense of suicide as the intentional taking of a person's life by self-destruction. Suicide was not only regarded as being contrary to nature; it was regarded as an offense against the biblical commandment "Thou shalt not kill." Suicide was a species of felony punishable by forfeiture of the decedent's goods and chattels because it deprived the king or queen of one of his or her subjects.

In the United States, the thrust of the criminal law has been to make it an offense to cause or aid another person to commit suicide, with many states making **assisted suicide** a crime. New York law provides that a person who "intentionally causes or aids another person to commit suicide" is guilty of manslaughter in the second degree. McKinney's N.Y. Penal Law § 125.15. In Texas, a person who, with intent to promote or assist in the commission of suicide, aids or attempts to aid another to commit suicide is guilty of a misdemeanor. If the actor's conduct causes a suicide or an attempted suicide that results in serious bodily injury, the offense becomes a felony. Vernon's Tex. Penal Code Ann. § 22.08. Until recently, the validity of laws of this character went unchallenged. As we explain in the following sections, this is no longer the case.

Oregon's Death with Dignity Act

On November 8, 1994, Oregon voters adopted a Death with Dignity Act that allows terminally ill adult patients to obtain a physician's prescription for a lethal dose of medication. Two doctors must determine that the patient has less than six months to live and is mentally competent. The patient must request a lethal dose of medicine both orally and in writing and must wait at least fifteen days to obtain it. Although a federal district court originally enjoined the enforcement of the act, the U.S. Court of Appeals vacated the injunction. *Lee v. State of Oregon*, 107 F.3d 1382 (9th Cir. 1997). The U.S. Supreme Court declined to review the case. 522 U.S. 927, 118 S.Ct. 328, 139 L.Ed.2d 254 (1997).

On November 6, 2001, U.S. Attorney General John Ashcroft advised the Drug Enforcement Administration that assisting suicide was not a "legitimate medical purpose" and that the use of controlled substances to do so would violate the Controlled Substances Act (CSA). He pointed out that prescribing controlled substances for assisting suicide would make a physician's license subject to suspension or revocation. The State of Oregon filed suit, arguing that the Attorney General's actions exceeded his authority under the CSA. A federal court issued a permanent injunction against enforcement of the Attorney General's directive on the ground that the directive exceeded authority delegated to the Attorney General by the CSA. *Oregon v. Ashcroft*, 192 F. Supp.2d 1077 (D. Or. 2002). The Ninth Circuit Court of Appeals agreed. The U.S. Supreme Court granted review and held that the CSA did not authorize the Attorney General to prohibit doctors from prescribing regulated drugs for use in physician-assisted suicide, as authorized by the Oregon Death with Dignity Act. *Gonzales v. Oregon*, 546 U.S 243, 126 S.Ct. 904, 163 L.Ed.2d 748 (2006).

The Michigan Experience

Over the past several years, a series of judicial decisions have held that physicians may withhold or withdraw medical treatment at a patient's request. But the courts recognized a sharp distinction between such activity and administering drugs to assist a person to take his or her own life. Michigan, and several other states, had no laws against assisted suicide. This was dramatized on June 4, 1990, when a fifty-four-year-old woman suffering from Alzheimer's disease took her life by pressing a button that injected a lethal substance into her system through use of a suicide machine developed by Dr. Jack Kevorkian, a retired Michigan pathologist. Murder charges filed against the doctor were dismissed on the grounds that Michigan had no law against assisted suicide and that the prosecutors failed to show that the doctor tripped the device used to effect the death. After additional instances of assisted suicide of terminally ill patients, the Michigan legislature enacted a bill banning assisted suicide. It became effective on April 1, 1993.

In succeeding years, the media reported numerous instances of alleged participation by Kevorkian in assisting terminally ill persons to commit suicide. After several unsuccessful attempts to prosecute Kevorkian, in 1999 a Michigan jury found him guilty of second-degree murder in the death of a man suffering from Lou Gehrig's disease. The court sentenced him to serve ten to twenty-five years in prison. The Michigan Court of Appeals affirmed his conviction and sentence. *People v. Kevorkian*, 639 N.W.2d 291 (Mich. App. 2001). The Supreme Court of Michigan denied his request for a further appeal, *People v. Kevorkian*, 642 N.W.2d 681 (Mich. 2002), and the U.S. Supreme Court denied his petition for a writ of certiorari. *Kevorkian v. Michigan*, 537 U.S. 881, 123 S.Ct. 90, 154 L.Ed.2d 137 (2002). Kevorkian was paroled on June 1, 2007, after having served eight years of his sentence. One of the conditions of his parole was that he could not help anyone else die.

During the 1990s, state laws that prohibit assisted suicide were challenged on constitutional grounds in instances where terminally ill patients seek to end their lives with the aid of a physician. Soon the state of Washington became the venue for a direct challenge to a state statute prohibiting assisted suicide, a challenge that would eventually lead to a seminal decision by the U.S. Supreme Court.

The Washington Experience

To prevent assisted suicide in the state of Washington, the legislature enacted a law providing that "[a] person is guilty of promoting a suicide attempt when he knowingly causes or aids another person to attempt suicide." Wash. Rev. Code § 9A.36.060(1) (1994). "Promoting a suicide attempt" is a felony, punishable by up to five years' imprisonment and up to a $10,000 fine. § 9A.36.060(2). However, Washington's Natural Death Act, enacted in 1979, as amended in 1992, states that the "withholding or withdrawal of life sustaining treatment" at a patient's direction "shall not, for any purpose, constitute a suicide or a homicide." Wash. Rev. Code § 70.122.070(1).

In 1996 in *Compassion in Dying v. Washington*, 79 F.3d 790, the U.S. Court of Appeals for the Ninth Circuit, in an en banc decision, found a substantive due process right to physician-assisted suicide and held unconstitutional the Washington statute. In *Vacco v. Quill*, 80 F.3d 716 (2d Cir. 1996), the U.S. Court of Appeals for the Second Circuit addressed a similar New York statute and found that the Equal Protection Clause rendered it unconstitutional.

Go to the companion website for an edited version of the Supreme Court's decision in *Washington v. Glucksberg*.

The U.S. Supreme Court granted certiorari and heard the two cases in tandem. In *Washington v. Glucksberg*, 521 U.S. 702, 117 S.Ct. 2258, 138 L.Ed.2d 772 (1997), the U.S. Supreme Court reversed the Ninth Circuit's decision. Writing for a unanimous Court, Chief Justice William Rehnquist pointed out that in almost every state it is a crime to assist in a suicide and that the statutes banning assisted suicide are longstanding expressions of the states' commitment to the protection and preservation of all human life. Rehnquist analyzed the interests that come into play in determining whether a statute banning assisted suicide passes constitutional muster. In doing so, the Court rejected any parallel between a person's right to terminate medical treatment and the "right" to have assistance in committing suicide. In *Vacco v. Quill*, 521 U.S. 793, 117 S.Ct. 2293, 138 L.Ed.2d 834 (1997), the Court held that New York's assisted-suicide ban did not violate the Equal Protection Clause of the Fourteenth Amendment.

Competing Values in Suicide Laws

Laws against assisted suicide bring into play significant policy issues and require legislatures to balance carefully competing claims of individual liberty, ethics, and the interest of society. Some proponents of allowing assisted suicide argue that it simply enables a person who has a rational capacity to make a choice. Those who reject this view argue that the state has an interest in the preservation of life and that some individuals may elect to die needlessly as a result of misdiagnosis. Moreover, opponents of legalizing assisted suicide argue that allowing it leads to an indifference to the value of life. As a result of the Supreme Court's 1997 decision in *Washington v. Glucksberg*, supra, the states may enforce statutory bans on assisted suicide with

CASE-IN-POINT

Assisted Suicide

In 1997 Charles E. Hall, a mentally competent but terminally ill patient, and his physician, Cecil McIver, M.D., sought to have a Florida court declare that section 782.08, Florida Statutes, which prohibits assisted suicide, violated the Privacy Clause of the Florida Constitution and the Due Process and Equal Protection Clauses of the Fourteenth Amendment to the U.S. Constitution. They sought an injunction to keep the state attorney from prosecuting the physician for giving deliberate assistance to Hall in committing suicide. Basing its conclusion on Florida's privacy provision and the federal Equal Protection Clause, the trial court held that the Florida law could not be constitutionally enforced against Hall and McIver. The Florida

Supreme Court granted an expedited review. By the time it rendered its decision on July 17, 1997, the U.S. Supreme Court had ruled that state laws prohibiting assisted suicide pass muster under the federal constitution. On the basis of that decision, the Florida Supreme Court summarily disposed of the contention that the Florida law violated the U.S. Constitution. The court then proceeded to find that the explicit privacy provision in the Florida constitution was not violated by the state's 129-year-old statute prohibiting assisted suicide. In concluding its opinion, the court opted to leave "social policy" to the state legislature when it observed that "[w]e do not hold that a carefully crafted statute authorizing assisted suicide would be unconstitutional."

Krischer v. McIver, 697 So.2d 97 (Fla. 1997).

more assurance, yet as the terminally ill population continues to increase, the debate is destined to continue. The Supreme Court's decision places that debate in the state legislatures and the state judicial tribunals.

Public opinion would seem to support the legalization of doctor-assisted suicide, at least in some instances. In a series of national surveys conducted between 1996 and 2005, the Gallup Organization asked, "When a person has a disease that cannot be cured and is living in severe pain, do you think doctors should or should not be allowed by law to assist the patient to commit suicide if the patient requests it?" In 1996, 52 percent of respondents said yes; in 2005, 58 percent answered in the affirmative. The Gallup Organization, Inc., The Gallup Poll, December 29, 2005.

Less than one month after the Supreme Court's decision in *Washington v. Glucksberg*, the Florida Supreme Court ruled that the state statute prohibiting assisted suicide did not offend the state constitution. *Krischer v. McIver*, 697 So.2d 97 (Fla. 1997). (See the Case-in-Point on assisted suicide.) In 2001 the Alaska Supreme Court held that the state constitution's guarantees of privacy and liberty do not afford terminally ill patients the right to a physician's assistance in committing suicide. *Sampson v. State*, 31 P.3d 88 (Alaska 2001).

A lengthier excerpt from the Florida Supreme Court's decision in *Krischer v. McIver* is reproduced on the companion website.

The Abortion Controversy

Abortion has been legally defined as the willful bringing about of the miscarriage of a pregnant woman. Under English common law, **abortion** was a misdemeanor, but only after quickening (that point in the pregnancy where the mother can feel the movement of the fetus inside her). As the Supreme Court recognized in *Roe v. Wade*, 410 U.S. 113, 132, 93 S.Ct 705, 716, 35 L.Ed 2d 147, 165 (1973), "It is undisputed that at common law, abortion performed before 'quickening'—the first recognizable movement of the fetus *in utero*, appearing usually from the 16th to the 18th week of pregnancy—was not an indictable offense." This was based on the belief that the soul entered the fetus at the time of quickening, thus making it alive.

In the late nineteenth century most states adopted statutes increasing the penalties for abortion and abolishing the quickening distinction. However, there was a tendency to provide that abortion was justified if physicians found it essential to save the mother's life. More-liberal statutes allowed abortions to be performed when one or two physicians advised that it was necessary to preserve the life or health of the mother. By 1970, a few states had even repealed criminal penalties for abortions where they were performed under medical supervision in the very early stages of a woman's pregnancy.

The 1960s and 1970s, a period of liberalized views on sexual practices, witnessed a clamor for liberalization of abortion laws. But before significant reforms occurred in most states, the U.S. Supreme Court entertained a challenge to the constitutionality of a Texas law that made it a felony to procure or attempt an abortion except one "procured or attempted by medical advice for the purpose of saving the life of the mother." Texas Rev. Crim. Stat., Arts. 1071–1076 (1911). In *Roe v. Wade*, supra, the Court held that this statute impermissibly interfered with a woman's constitutional right of privacy, which the Court determined to be "broad enough to encompass a woman's decision whether or not to terminate her pregnancy." 410 U.S. at 153, 93 S.Ct at 727, 35 L.Ed 2d at 177. Moreover, the Court held that the fetus is not a person and therefore has no constitutional right to life. At the same time the Court recognized the state's interest in protecting the unborn, an interest that becomes compelling at the point of **fetal viability**. The Court summarized its holding as follows:

(a) For the stage prior to approximately the end of the first trimester, the abortion decision and its effectuation must be left to the medical judgment of the pregnant woman's attending physician.

(b) For the stage subsequent to approximately the end of the first trimester, the State, in promoting its interest in the health of the mother, may, if it chooses, regulate the abortion procedure in ways that are reasonably related to maternal health.

(c) For the stage subsequent to viability, the State in promoting its interest in the potentiality of human life may, if it chooses, regulate, and even proscribe, abortion except where it is necessary, in appropriate medical judgment, for the preservation of the life or health of the mother. 410 U.S. at 164–165, 93 S.Ct at 732, 35 L.Ed 2d at 183–184.

The Court's decision had the effect of invalidating most state laws proscribing or regulating abortions, giving rise to an intense national debate that rages on today. As part of the national debate, Congress in the early 1980s considered but rejected a constitutional amendment to restrict abortions. In the 1980s and early 1990s, a more conservative Supreme Court modified *Roe* to allow states greater leeway in regulating abortions in such areas as waiting periods and required counseling. In the wake of one of these decisions, *Planned Parenthood v. Casey*, 505 U.S. 833, 112 S.Ct. 2791, 120 L.Ed.2d 674 (1992), supporters of abortion rights clamored for Congress to adopt a statute that would codify the holding in *Roe v. Wade*. In January 2004, supporters of abortion rights introduced into Congress the Freedom of Choice Act (FOCA), the express intent of which is to "prohibit, consistent with *Roe v. Wade*, the interference by the government with a woman's right to choose to bear a child or terminate a pregnancy, and for other purposes." Despite support from the Obama Administration, the bill did not pass Congress in 2009–10 and was not reintroduced in 2011.

Partial-Birth Abortion

In 1995 and 1997, Congress passed bills banning the medical procedure known as intact dilation and extraction, commonly referred to as **partial-birth abortion**. In each instance President Clinton vetoed these measures. Several states, however, enacted laws proscribing partial-birth abortion; they were usually declared unconstitutional by federal courts. The Nebraska Legislature enacted a statute defining partial-birth abortion as "an abortion procedure in which the person performing the abortion partially delivers vaginally a living unborn child before killing the unborn child and completing the delivery." Neb. Rev. Stat. Ann. Sec. 28-326(9). In *Stenberg v. Carhart*, 530 U.S. 914, 120 S.Ct. 2597, 147 L.Ed.2d 743 (2000), the U.S. Supreme Court, in a 5–4 decision, invalidated the Nebraska law because it lacked an exception for the preservation of the health of the mother and imposed an undue burden on a woman's right to choose to have an abortion.

In November 2003 Congress enacted a new statute proscribing partial-birth abortions. Lower federal courts found the law unconstitutional, primarily because it contained no exception for performing the procedure where necessary for preserving the health of the mother. But the Supreme Court, dividing 5–4, reversed and upheld the statute. *Gonzales v. Carhart*, 550 U.S. 124, 127 S.Ct. 1610, 167 L.Ed.2d 480 (2007). Justice Anthony Kennedy, writing for the majority, explained that the government has a legitimate and substantial interest in preserving and promoting fetal life and in banning abortions that involve partial delivery of a living fetus. Relying on Congress's findings that the partial-birth abortion procedure is not necessary to protect the health of a pregnant woman, he further found there had been no showing that the act imposes an undue burden on a woman's right to abortion based on a lack of a "health-of-the mother" exception. Dissenting, Justice Ruth Bader Ginsburg (joined by Justices Stephen Breyer, John Paul Stevens, and David Souter) viewed the decision as alarming in that the law contains no provision safeguarding a woman's health.

Abortion rights advocates see *Gonzales v. Carhart* as being harmful to a woman's health and interfering with a woman's decision making. Moreover, many view it as "chipping away" at women's rights under the Court's landmark 1973 decision in *Roe v. Wade*. On the other hand, pro-life supporters herald the new decision as a recognition of the rights of the unborn and one that may open the door for state legislatures to enact further restrictions on abortion procedures.

Laws Criminalizing Other Acts Resulting in the Death of a Fetus

Under common law a child was not considered born until the umbilical cord had been severed and the child's circulation became independent of its mother's. In the highly publicized case of *Keeler v. Superior Court*, 470 P.2d 617 (Cal. 1970), the California Supreme Court held that in enacting its homicide statute, the legislature intended it to follow the common-law rule that in order for there to be a homicide, the victim must be "born alive." Consequently, the court overturned a murder conviction where the defendant stomped on a pregnant woman's abdomen, thereby causing the death of her fetus. As a result, California amended section 187(a) of its penal code, which defines murder, to include the present language, *"the unlawful killing of a human being, or a fetus, with malice aforethought"* [emphasis added].

Nearly all states have laws criminalizing intentional acts other than medical abortion that result in death to a fetus. Some statutes explicitly limit the offense to instances where the fetus is "viable." See, e.g., Tenn. Code. Ann. § 39-13-214. Other states, such as Michigan, prohibit the killing of an "unborn quick child." See, e.g., Mich. Stat. Ann. § 28.554. The Michigan Supreme Court has said that this law applies only those fetuses that are viable. *Larkin v. Cahalan*, 208 N.W.2d 176 (Mich. 1973). Other state courts have generally followed the same approach in defining the term "unborn quick child."

In Tennessee, the killing of a viable fetus can be first-degree murder, second-degree murder, voluntary manslaughter, vehicular homicide, reckless homicide, or criminally negligent homicide, depending on the mental state of the perpetrator. Tenn. Code Ann. § 39-13-201 *et seq.*

The California Supreme Court has held that "viability is not an element of fetal homicide," but the state must demonstrate "that the fetus has progressed beyond the embryonic stage of seven to eight weeks." *People v. Taylor*, 86 P.3d 881 (Cal. 2004). Thus, under California state law, when a defendant commits murder of a pregnant woman, the prosecution can also charge the defendant with murder of an unborn child only if fetal development has progressed beyond the embryonic stage.

In some of the more conservative states, the killing of a fetus (other than through abortion) is a crime throughout pregnancy. For example, in South Carolina,

- (A)(1) A person who commits a violent crime . . . that causes the death of, or bodily injury to, a child who is *in utero* at the time that the violent crime was committed, is guilty of a separate offense under this section.
    - (2)(a) Except as otherwise provided in this subsection, the punishment for a separate offense . . . is the same as the punishment provided for that criminal offense had the death or bodily injury occurred to the unborn child's mother. S.C. Code Ann § 16-3-1083.

The South Carolina statute is controversial inasmuch as it does not require the unborn child to be viable. Under the South Carolina statute, the killing of a woman who is in the earliest stage of pregnancy can result in two counts of first-degree murder. In Virginia, by contrast, one "who unlawfully, willfully, deliberately and maliciously kills the fetus of another" is guilty of a Class 2 felony, which is punishable by five to forty years in prison. Va. Code. § 18.2-32.2.

Conclusion

The English common law provides the starting point for study of the law of homicide. But unlike England, America insisted that homicidal offenses be precisely defined. Crimes involving homicide bring into play separate categories of public opinion, which are represented by legislative judgments. While the public may disagree to some extent on definitions and degrees of culpability, there is near-universal support for proscribing murder, manslaughter, and vehicular homicide. Although courts and legislatures have restricted, and in some instances abolished, the felony murder rule, application of the rule remains controversial. Finally, ethical and religious opinions and secular views evoke considerable controversy on issues of suicide and abortion. These reactions are apparent in legislative proscriptions and in litigation involving the constitutionality of statutes proscribing suicide and abortion.

Chapter Summary

- **LO1** Modern American laws on homicide are based on the English common law, which classified murder and manslaughter as criminal homicide, and classified non-criminal homicide as justifiable or excusable.

- **LO2** Modern statutes generally classify taking another's life with either malice aforethought or premeditation as first-degree murder. To obtain a conviction the prosecution must establish the defendant's specific intent to take the life of the accused. Comments made by a defendant before and after killing, use of grossly excessive force or infliction of lethal blows, and a history of altercations or ill will between the parties all bear on establishing malice aforethought or premeditation. Second-degree murder is now frequently defined as "an unlawful killing of a human being by a person having a depraved mind or heart." It often becomes a residual classification applied to unlawful homicides not evidenced by malice aforethought or premeditation, not occurring in conjunction with other felonies, and not falling within the statutory definitions of manslaughter. Convictions often reflect a "jury pardon" where a jury concludes that circumstances surrounding the killing do not justify the penalty for first-degree murder, which is often death.

- **LO3** The common law developed a doctrine under which, where an accused was engaged in the commission of a felony and a homicide occurred, the felonious act substituted for proof of malice aforethought. Thus it became felony murder when an accused unintentionally killed a human being while committing, or attempting to commit, such common-law felonies as burglary, arson, rape, or robbery. Today federal law and statutes in many states define felony murder, often limiting its applicability to specified felonies. A few states have abolished felony murder; in other jurisdictions the doctrine poses numerous questions and is subject to considerable criticism.

- **LO4** Today statutes often define manslaughter as the "unlawful killing of a human being without malice." Some abolish the common-law distinction between voluntary and involuntary manslaughter, but federal law and the laws of many states preserve the common-law distinction. Irrespective of whether a killing is classified as voluntary or involuntary, certain scenarios typify manslaughter. These include death resulting from mutual combat, use of excessive force in defense of a family member or property, criminal negligence, and parental failure to provide medical attention for their children. Taking the life of another in a hot-blooded fury may lower the blameworthiness of an accused from murder to the manslaughter level.

- **LO5** Vehicular homicide is a common statutory offense often defined as "killing of a human being, or the killing of a viable fetus by any injury to the mother, caused by operation of a motor vehicle (or boat or other vehicle) in a reckless manner likely to cause the death of, or great bodily harm to, another."

- **LO6** Homicide is justifiable when a person takes another's life in obedience to a court judgment or when necessarily committed in overcoming actual resistance to execution of legal process. It is excusable when a person kills someone while resisting the decedent's attempts to murder or to inflict great bodily injury upon another; in defense of a person's home under certain circumstances; or in some instances of self-defense where there is a reasonable ground to apprehend imminent danger of great bodily harm to another.

- **LO7** The prosecution bears several burdens unique to homicide cases: First, it must establish the *corpus delicti*, or body of the crime. This requires proof that a person's death was caused by the criminal act or agency of another person. Ordinarily death occurs when the heart stops beating and respiration ends; however, all jurisdictions have now adopted laws that specifying that irreversible cessation of total brain functions constitutes death. Second, the victim must have been alive before a killing took place and that the defendant's act was the proximate cause of the victim's death. Finally, some jurisdictions follow the common-law rule that death of the victim must occur "within a year and a day." But today this rule has little relevance and most jurisdictions have abolished the rule by statute or judicial decision.

- **LO8** Common law imposed harsh penalties on the body and the estate of a person who committed suicide and against a person who assisted another in committing suicide. Modern criminal laws make it an offense to cause or aid another person to commit suicide. In 1997, the Supreme Court reversed federal appellate courts and held that statutes banning assisted suicide are long-standing expressions of the states' commitment to the protection and preservation of all human life. On the other hand, in 2006, the Court held that the federal Controlled Substances Act did not authorize the Attorney General to prohibit doctors from prescribing regulated drugs for use in physician-assisted suicide as authorized by Oregon's Death with Dignity Act, which allows terminally ill adult patients to obtain a physician's prescription for a lethal dose of medication.

- **LO9** Judicial opinions vary as to when, under what circumstances, and by whom discontinuance of medical treatments may be ordered for minors and incompetents. Statutes in several states now address many of the problems in this area. Yet there is no statutory or judicial consensus on the procedures to effect discontinuance, and courts are cautious not to allow criminal prosecutions where life-sustaining procedures are removed based on medical advice and patient and family consent.

- **LO10** Under English common law, abortion was a misdemeanor, but only after quickening (that point in the pregnancy where the mother can feel the movement of the fetus inside her). In its landmark decision in *Roe v. Wade* in 1973, the Supreme Court held that a woman's constitutional right to privacy allows her to obtain an abortion, effectively invalidating most state laws proscribing or regulating abortions.

- **LO11** After *Roe v. Wade*, several states enacted laws proscribing a procedure commonly referred to as "partial-birth abortion" and these laws were declared unconstitutional by lower federal courts. But relying on Congress's findings that the partial-birth abortion procedure is not necessary to protect the health of a pregnant woman, in 2007 the Supreme Court, in a 5–4 decision, upheld a 2003 act of Congress that bans abortions that involve partial delivery of a living fetus. Dissenting justices argued that the act is unconstitutional because it does not include an exception for the mother's health.

- **LO12** Nearly all states now have laws criminalizing intentional acts (other than medical abortions) that result in death to a fetus. Some limit the offense to instances where the fetus is "viable." In some of the more conservative states, the killing of a fetus (other than through medical abortion) is a crime throughout pregnancy.

Key Terms

homicide The killing of a human being.

murder At common law, the unlawful killing of one person by another with malice aforethought (premeditation).

manslaughter The crime of unlawfully killing another person without malice.

malice aforethought The mental predetermination to commit an illegal act.

heat of passion A violent and uncontrollable rage resulting from a provocation that would cause such a response by a reasonable person.

suicide The intentional taking of a person's own life.

premeditation Deliberate decision or plan to commit a crime.

voluntary manslaughter The intentional killing of a human without malice or premeditation and usually occurring during a sudden quarrel or in the heat of passion.

involuntary manslaughter The unintentional killing of another person as the result of gross or wanton negligence.

justifiable homicide Killing another in self-defense or defense of others when there is serious danger of death or great bodily harm to self or others or when authorized by law.

excusable homicide A death caused by accident or misfortune.

doctor-assisted suicide The commission of suicide with the aid of a physician.

right to die Controversial "right" to terminate one's own life under certain circumstances.

provocation Refers to conduct that prompts another person to react through criminal conduct.

first-degree murder The highest degree of unlawful homicide, usually defined as "an unlawful act committed with the premeditated intent to take the life of a human being."

felony murder A homicide committed during the course of committing another felony other than murder (for example, armed robbery). The felonious act substitutes for the malice aforethought ordinarily required in murder.

second-degree murder A killing perpetrated by any act imminently dangerous to another and evincing a depraved mind regardless of human life, although without any premeditated design to effect the death of any particular individual.

depraved mind or heart A serious moral deficiency; a high level of malice often linked to second-degree murder.

vehicular homicide Homicide resulting from the unlawful and negligent operation of a motor vehicle.

corpus delicti "The body of the crime." The material thing upon which a crime has been committed.

proximate cause The cause that is nearest a given effect in a causal relationship.

brain death The complete cessation of activity of the central nervous system.

one-year-and-a-day rule A common-law rule that to convict a defendant of homicide, not more than a year and a day can intervene from the defendant's criminal act to the death of the victim.

assisted suicide The act of aiding or assisting a person to take his or her life. An offense in some jurisdictions.

abortion The intentional termination of a pregnancy.

fetal viability That point in pregnancy at which the fetus is capable of prolonged life outside the mother's womb.

partial-birth abortion A method of abortion in which the fetus is partially delivered before its life is terminated and it is removed from the mother's body.

Questions for Thought and Discussion

1. What circumstances are usually presented by the prosecution to bear on the issue of whether a killing was premeditated or with malice aforethought?
2. Describe some scenarios that might typify a conviction for second-degree murder.
3. Is it legitimate for a jury to find a defendant guilty of manslaughter in a case where there is evidence of premeditation, simply because members of the jury feel that the defendant was somewhat justified in taking the life of the victim?
4. How can the prosecution establish the *corpus delicti* in a murder case when the body of the victim cannot be found?
5. Compare the U.S. Supreme Court's 1997 opinion holding that there is no constitutional right to have assistance in committing suicide with the constitutional right of privacy discussed in Chapter 3. Can these views be logically reconciled?
6. Why has the common-law doctrine of felony murder become controversial among courts and legal scholars in recent years?
7. Is a state law making it a felony to kill an unborn child at any stage of development constitutional, notwithstanding the Supreme Court's decision in *Roe v. Wade*?

Problems for Discussion and Solution

1. During a domestic quarrel, a wife continually taunted her husband by degrading him and telling him he was a "lousy lover" and that she wanted to be rid of him. When the husband tried to persuade her to relent she continued to taunt him in a louder voice. Finally, he grabbed a kitchen knife and stabbed her. As a result she died. The husband was convicted of second-degree murder. On appeal he argues his actions were taken during a "fit of passion" and seeks to have his conviction reduced from second-degree murder to manslaughter. Is he likely to succeed? Why or why not?
2. Shortly before midnight, a man is driving through a residential area in an attempt to get his wife, who is in labor, to the hospital. The posted speed limit is 30 mph, but the anxious husband is driving 50 mph. In a dark area, the car strikes and kills a ten-year-old boy who is playing in the middle of the street. Can the driver be convicted of (a) manslaughter or (b) vehicular homicide?
3. A male who is aware that he has been diagnosed with acquired immunodeficiency syndrome (AIDS) engages in sexual intercourse with a female. He does not inform the female that he has AIDS. As a result, the female contracts AIDS and dies from the disease two years later. Under the laws of your state, could the male be convicted of a homicidal act?
4. An intoxicated driver recklessly drove his vehicle into a car being driven by a woman who was seven months pregnant. As a result of the accident, the woman's baby was born prematurely, suffered from extensive brain damage, and died two days later. The state law defines a "person" as an individual "who has been born and is alive." Nevertheless, the state prosecuted the intoxicated driver, and a jury found him guilty of manslaughter. Do you think an appellate court should uphold the defendant's conviction? Why or why not?

CHAPTER 7

Other Offenses against Persons

In 1982 David W. Lanier was elected judge of the Chancery Court in the small town of Dyersburg, Tennessee. Soon he developed a reputation for taking liberties with women who appeared before him as litigants or worked with him in the courthouse. Because Judge Lanier's family was prominent and because his brother was district attorney, the women whom Lanier victimized were reluctant to come forward. Eventually, federal authorities in Memphis heard of the allegations and launched an investigation. Five women agreed to appear before a federal grand jury. They testified that Judge Lanier had sexually assaulted them in his chambers and in his courtroom. One woman, a litigant in a child custody dispute, told the grand jury how Lanier threatened to deny her custody of her children in order to extort sexual favors from her.

Judge Lanier was indicted on eleven counts of violating 18 U.S.C.A. § 242, a civil rights law enacted after the Civil War. Had the case been prosecuted in state court, the charge would have been straightforward—sexual assault. But that option was not available to federal prosecutors. In a somewhat novel theory of the scope of 18 U.S.C.A. § 242, the indictment alleged that the judge, acting willfully and under color of state law, had deprived his victims of their federal constitutional right to be free from sexual assault. After trial, Lanier was convicted and sentenced to twenty-five years in prison and a $25,000 fine. The U.S. Supreme Court upheld the conviction and in so doing signaled the breadth of conduct that is susceptible to prosecution under the federal civil rights laws. *United States v. Lanier*, 520 U.S. 259, 117 S.Ct. 1219, 137 L.Ed.2d 432 (1997). After the Supreme Court's decision, Judge Lanier was apprehended in Mexico, where he had fled to avoid imprisonment. He is currently serving his sentence in federal prison. The Lanier case shows how crimes against persons have evolved well beyond the common-law foundations of our legal system.

Introduction

As with homicide offenses, the English common law provided the basis for other crimes against persons. But by the 1800s America's quest for representative government and its penchant for definiteness and certainty, combined with the standards of written constitutions, resulted in legislative definitions of crimes. Defining offenses against persons became primarily a state rather than a federal legislative function, and the new states followed the common-law themes, making variations deemed necessary in the new social, economic, and political environment. As the United States became urbanized, more densely populated, and increasingly mobile, the areas of conduct initially defined as criminal offenses against persons required revision and, in many instances, enlargement.

Under modern statutes, assault and battery are classified according to their seriousness, the character of the victim, and the environment in which these crimes are committed, and legislatures have created new crimes against persons such as stalking and, more recently, "cyberstalking." Conduct that constituted the offense of mayhem at common law is now often prosecuted under various forms of assaultive crimes.

In recent years contemporary moral standards have caused the offense of rape to be expanded into a more comprehensive, gender-neutral offense of sexual battery, with new emphasis on the victim's age and vulnerability. And laws prohibiting consensual sodomy between adults, a felony at common law, have been found unconstitutional by the U.S. Supreme Court. *Lawrence v. Texas*, 539 U.S. 558, 123 S.Ct. 2472, 156 L.Ed.2d 508 (2003).

The offense of false imprisonment is essentially the same as at common law, but the crime of kidnapping, which today focuses on child abduction, serves a much different role in American society than it did under the English common law.

As noted in Chapter 4, common-law crimes required proof of a criminal intent. In contrast, many statutory crimes—for example, the sale of intoxicants to minors and consensual sexual relations between an adult and a minor—now fall in the category of strict liability offenses. In contemporary society there is a new emphasis on enforcement of civil rights laws that originated in the post–Civil War environment and have been supplemented by modern enactments. Finally, in an effort to curb intimidation, many states now proscribe certain conduct as "hate crimes."

Assaultive Offenses

Assault and **battery**, though commonly referred to together, were separate misdemeanor offenses at common law. An assault was basically an attempted battery. It consisted of an attempt to do bodily harm to another using force and violence, while a battery was a completed or consummated assault. Although an actual touching was not required, words alone did not constitute an assault. The common law made no distinction between classes or degrees of assault and battery, but dealt more severely with aggravated cases.

Modern Statutory Developments

Today all jurisdictions make assault a crime, and most make battery a crime as well. Assault is defined by statute, as is battery, and sometimes the term "assault and battery" is used to indicate one offense. Simple assaults and batteries generally remain misdemeanors, whereas those perpetrated against public officers (for example, fire and police personnel) are frequently classified as felonies. Legislatures commonly classify as felonies more-egregious assaultive conduct such as **aggravated assault**, **aggravated battery**, and assault with intent to commit other serious crimes.

The California Penal Code defines an assault as "an unlawful attempt, coupled with a present ability, to commit a violent injury on the person of another." West's Ann. Cal. Penal Code § 240. It imposes increased penalties for an assault committed on a person engaged in performing the duties of a peace officer, firefighter, lifeguard, process server, paramedic, physician, or nurse. West's Ann. Cal. Penal Code § 241(c). Like most states, California makes it a felony to commit an assault with a deadly weapon or with force likely to produce great bodily injury. West's Ann. Cal. Penal Code § 245. Many states classify this latter offense as aggravated assault. For example, under Florida law, a person who commits an assault with a deadly weapon without intent to kill or an assault with intent to commit a felony is guilty of aggravated assault, a felony offense. West's Fla. Stat. Ann. § 784.021.

The California Penal Code defines as battery "any willful and unlawful use of force or violence upon the person of another." West's Ann. Cal. Penal Code § 242. The code also specifies increased punishment for batteries committed

Assault with a Deadly Weapon

CASE-IN-POINT

Rasor, a police officer, stopped a vehicle and attempted to arrest the driver, Jackson, for driving while intoxicated. As he did, a fight broke out between the officer and Jackson. At that point, the defendant, Lloyd Gary, a passenger in Jackson's car, approached the two combatants, removed the officer's pistol, and pointed it at Rasor and Jackson. Gary was convicted of assault with a deadly weapon. On appeal, he argued that the trial judge erred in not directing the jury to return a verdict of not guilty because the evidence showed no attempt to commit a physical injury. The Arizona Supreme Court rejected Gary's argument, saying that "[t]he pointing of a gun may constitute 'an assault' . . . and it is not necessary to show in addition that there was an intent to do physical harm to the victim."

State v. Gary, 543 P.2d 782, 783 (Ariz. 1975).

against specific classes of officers, West's Ann. Cal. Penal Code § 243.6, or those committed on school property, park property, or hospital grounds, West's Ann. Cal. Penal Code § 243.2. Consistent with its handling of aggravated assaults, Florida law classifies a battery resulting in great bodily harm, permanent disability, or permanent disfigurement, or one committed with a deadly weapon, as an aggravated battery, an even more serious felony than aggravated assault. West's Fla. Stat. Ann. § 784.045.

Although most assault and battery prosecutions occur under state laws, the federal government also has a role in this area. Federal statutes proscribe assault within the maritime and territorial jurisdiction of the United States. 18 U.S.C.A. § 113. Interestingly, federal courts have held that the statute covers the entire range of assaults, *United States v. Eades*, 615 F.2d 617 (4th Cir. 1976), and that the word "assault" includes acts that would constitute batteries under most state laws. *United States v. Chaussee*, 536 F.2d 637 (7th Cir. 1976). Additional federal statutes proscribe assaults on federal officers, including members of the uniformed services engaged in the performance of official duties, 18 U.S.C.A. § 111, and assaults on foreign diplomatic and other official personnel, 18 U.S.C.A. § 112.

Common Illustrations of Simple and Aggravated Assault and Battery

Statutory definitions vary, but under most statutes a simple assault would include a threat to strike someone with the fist or a small stone, or simply a missed punch. Firing a shot in the direction of a person or threatening someone with a weapon would probably qualify as aggravated assault. A battery, on the other hand, involves some physical contact with the victim. Common illustrations of simple battery include hitting or pushing someone, a male hugging and kissing a female—or even an offensive touching—if against her will; using excessive force in breaking up a fight; intentionally tripping another individual; or using excessive force (by a parent or teacher) in disciplining a child. The acts referred to above as constituting aggravated assault, if completed, would most likely be prosecuted as aggravated batteries. When courts must determine whether an assault or battery is "aggravated," two questions commonly arise: first, what constitutes a "deadly weapon," and second, whether the defendant's conduct results in "great bodily harm." For example, the South Carolina Supreme Court observed,

Circumstances of aggravation include the use of a deadly weapon, the intent to commit a felony, infliction of serious bodily injury, great disparity in the ages or physical conditions of the parties, a difference in gender, the purposeful infliction of shame and disgrace, taking indecent liberties or familiarities with a female, and resistance to lawful authority. *State v. White*, 605 S.E.2d 540 (S.C. 2004).

Courts have no difficulty in finding that a gun, a knife, a club, or an axe is a deadly weapon. Other objects such as a pocketknife, hammer, rock, or walking cane, while not dangerous instruments per se, may under certain circumstances cause death or serious bodily injury.

What constitutes great or serious bodily injury is a factual determination not subject to a precise definition; however, the Indiana Supreme Court has stated that the term "great bodily harm" means "great as distinguished from slight, trivial, minor or moderate harm, and as such does not include mere bruises as are likely to be inflicted in a simple assault and battery." *Froedge v. State*, 233 N.E.2d 631, 636 (Ind. 1968). In making factual determinations of whether an injury constitutes a "serious" or "great" bodily injury, courts consider the type of injury the victim has suffered, as well as the instrument by which the injury was inflicted, and any disability that the victim will suffer. In many instances courts make the determination of whether the use of one's body can be a "deadly weapon" by focusing on the manner in which such body parts are used in committing an assault or battery. For example, in *Jefferson v. State*, 974 S.W.2d 887 (Tex. App. 1998), the court upheld a defendant's conviction for aggravated assault where the defendant struck the victim in the face four times with his fist and the victim suffered a broken nose, lacerations, and bleeding. In *State v. Bolarinho*, 850 A.2d 907, 910 (R.I. 2004), the Rhode Island Supreme Court noted that it is the object's capability and manner of use that is determinative of whether an object qualifies as a dangerous weapon. The court held that a person's foot can qualify as a dangerous weapon, particularly when employed with karate-like precision. Many other courts have considered hands and fists to be deadly weapons for purposes of assault with a deadly weapon, given the manner in which they were used and the relative size and condition of the parties involved. See, for example, West's N.C.G.S.A. § 14-33; *State v. Yarrell*, 616 S.E.2d 258 (N.C. App. 2005).

In *State v. Flemming*, 19 S.W.3d 195, 197 (Tenn. 2000), the Tennessee Supreme Court took a contrary view and held that feet and fists are not deadly weapons under Tennessee Code Annotated section 39-11-106(a)(5). The court commented, "Were we to interpret the statute to be written broadly enough to include one's fists and feet within the statutory definition of 'deadly weapon,' it would lead to an absurd result—the merger of simple and aggravated offenses—which would contradict the expressed intent of the General Assembly."

The Burden of the Prosecution

The proof required to establish assaultive offenses depends on the statutory language of the offense. To convict a defendant of simple assault or battery, the prosecution generally needs only to prove the act and the defendant's general, not specific, intent. In aggravated assault and aggravated battery prosecutions, courts have arrived at different interpretations of the intent requirement, but proof of the defendant's general intent is usually sufficient. In contrast, if a defendant is prosecuted for committing an assault or battery "with the intent to do great bodily harm" or "with the intent to commit a specific felony, for example, murder," courts generally require the prosecution to prove the defendant's specific intent to accomplish those results.

An excerpt from *State v. Towers*, in which the Supreme Court of Maine upholds a conviction for aggravated assault and battery, is reproduced on the companion website.

Defenses to Charges of Assault and Battery

Many forms of conduct involving intentional use of physical force do not constitute batteries. In many instances, there is an express or implied consent of the person against whom the physical force is exerted. Reasonableness is the test applied in sports contests and friendly physical encounters. Everyday examples include such contact sports as football, in which the participants obviously consent to forceful bodily contact. The physician who performs surgery with consent of the patient provides another example of physical contact that, if properly applied, does not constitute a battery. Reasonableness is also the test applied to interpersonal relationships. Thus, although a person might imply consent to a friendly kiss or caress, seldom could a person imply consent to an act of violence, even when done under the guise of affection.

Statutory law regulates the degree of force that can be used by teachers, police officers, and correction officials, and an excessive use of force may constitute a battery. Likewise, parents, guardians, and those standing *in loco parentis* have a right to impose reasonable punishment when disciplining a child but must consider the child's age, health, size, and all other relevant circumstances. Parents who inflict injury on a child or who impose excessive punishment may be guilty of committing a simple or even an aggravated battery. They may also be subject to prosecution under modern statutes proscribing child abuse.

A person charged with battery can defend the action by showing that the touching or hitting was unintentional, that the physical force used was reasonable, or that the action was taken in self-defense. Self-defense is subject to qualifications, as we explain in Chapter 14. Defenses applicable to the offense of battery generally apply as well to a charge of assault. The theory is that a person who fails to make physical contact with another can defend on the same basis of reasonableness or self-defense as a person who successfully commits a battery.

Mayhem

At common law, **mayhem** consisted of willfully and maliciously injuring another so as to render the victim less able in fighting. Mayhem became a statutory crime in most states, with some statutes extending the common law definition to include injuries that disfigure a person. In most instances it is a general-intent offense; however, some statutes require proof of the actor's specific intent to maim or disfigure the victim. Mayhem statutes are less common today because many of the acts formerly prosecuted under these laws are now prosecuted under such statutory crimes as aggravated battery and attempted murder.

Hazing

Hazing consists of intentional or reckless physical or mental harassment, abuse, or humiliation. It frequently occurs in the process of initiation into clubs, fraternities, sororities, athletic teams, and other groups. Hazing sometimes merely consists of foolish pranks, but too often it has resulted in serious injuries to the initiate. In recent years state legislatures in the great majority of states have enacted statutes making hazing in all schools and colleges either a misdemeanor or felony, depending on the degree of injury to the initiate. The objective of anti-hazing statutes is to prevent or severely curtail the practice of hazing. Currently many national fraternities and sororities have adopted prohibitions or restrictions on the hazing activities of local chapters. Likewise, many colleges and universities have explicit prohibitions on hazing. See, for example, *Buttny v. Smiley*, 281 F. Supp. 280 (D. Colo. 1968) (upholding anti-hazing rule at University of Colorado). Hazing is also prohibited in the armed forces academies. See 10 U.S.C.A. §§ 4352, 6964, 6965, 9352. Moreover, anti-hazing statutes do not restrict prosecutions, and, in some instances, egregious conduct can be prosecuted under other statutes as a felony, for example, aggravated battery.

The Maryland legislature has enacted a rather typical anti-hazing statute. MD Code, Criminal Law, § 3-607 provides:

(a) A person may not recklessly or intentionally do an act or create a situation that subjects a student to the risk of serious bodily injury for the purpose of an initiation into a student organization of a school, college, or university.

(b) A person who violates this section is guilty of a misdemeanor and on conviction is subject to imprisonment not exceeding 6 months or a fine not exceeding $500 or both.

(c) The implied or express consent of a student to hazing is not a defense under this section.

In rejecting an attack on the constitutionality of the statute, the Maryland Court of Special Appeals held that the state has a compelling interest in preventing violent or dangerous initiation activities on campuses and found that the law is not vague and does not violate freedoms of association and assembly guaranteed by the First Amendment. The court further observed that the statute "does not reach students' rights to participate in fraternities, sororities, or other organizations, does not reach such conduct as yelling at or insulting pledges, and does not reach such conduct as requiring pledges to don matching tee shirts, memorize silly songs, or run errands for and serve meals to regular members. . . ." *McKenzie v. State*, 748 A.2d 67, 72 (Md. App. 2000).

Stalking

By the late 1980s, persons who were being continually followed, threatened, or harassed by others were beginning to file complaints with law enforcement officers. Most complainants were women targeted by former suitors or celebrities who were being constantly followed by obsessive fans. Police began to refer to this type of behavior as **stalking**, which consists of repeatedly following, watching or harassing another person, often to enforce a relationship. But they were hampered in taking action to protect victims until after harm occurred to them. Police and prosecutors who felt that the traditional protections of the criminal law were not always sufficient to protect victims from stalking urged legislators to adopt statutes to help them combat the problem.

In California an obsessed fan shot and killed actress Rebecca Schaeffer after stalking her for two years. In 1990 this led the California legislature to enact the first law making stalking a crime. By 1994 all states and the District of Columbia had enacted laws defining stalking and making it either a misdemeanor or a felony. Some stalking statutes require proof of a stalker's specific intent, while in others proof of a general intent suffices. Some require that stalking must have frightened the victim; others require only that the stalking would cause a reasonable person to experience fear.

In 1996 Congress enacted a law to protect persons against stalking when the perpetrator has crossed state lines to commit the crime. The federal statute was amended as part of the Violence against Women Act (VAWA) of 2000. It makes it a crime to stalk someone across state or tribal lines where the stalker has the intent to kill, injure, harass, or intimidate a victim. 18 U.S.C.A. § 2261A(1). In a report entitled *Stalking Victimization in the United States* (January 2009), the Bureau of Justice Statistics noted that during 2006 an estimated 3.4 million persons age eighteen or older were victims of stalking.

In what is often considered to be one of the toughest laws on stalking, the Illinois Criminal Code makes stalking another person a felony and provides that a person guilty of aggravated stalking is guilty of an even more serious felony. As amended, Illinois law now provides:

(a) A person commits stalking when he or she, knowingly and without lawful justification, on at least two separate occasions follows another person or places the person under surveillance or any combination thereof and:

(1) at any time transmits a threat of immediate or future bodily harm, sexual assault, confinement or restraint and the threat is directed towards that person or a family member of that person; or

(2) places that person in reasonable apprehension of immediate or future bodily harm, sexual assault, confinement or restraint; or

(3) places that person in reasonable apprehension that a family member will receive immediate or future bodily harm, sexual assault, confinement, or restraint.

(a-5) A person commits stalking when he or she has previously been convicted of stalking another person and knowingly and without lawful justification on one occasion:

(1) follows that same person or places that same person under surveillance; and

(2) transmits a threat of immediate or future bodily harm, sexual assault, confinement or restraint; and

(3) the threat is directed towards that person or a family member of that person.

Subsection (d) of the statute states that a defendant "places a person under surveillance" by: (1) remaining present outside the person's school, place of employment, vehicle, other place occupied by the person, or residence other than the residence of the defendant; or (2) placing an electronic tracking device on the person or the person's property. Subsection (e) stipulates that the words "follows another person" mean "(i) to move in relative proximity to a person as that person moves from place to place or (ii) to remain in relative proximity to a person who is stationary or whose movements are confined to a small area." However, subsection (e) points out that following another person does not include following within the residence of the defendant. Subsection (g) defines "transmit[ting] a threat" as giving a "verbal or written threat or a threat implied by a pattern of conduct or a combination of verbal or written statements or conduct." Finally, subsection (h) broadly defines "family member." ILL. ST. 720 ILCS 5/12-7.3.

In Illinois a person commits aggravated stalking when he or she, in conjunction with committing the offense of stalking, also does any of the following:

(1) causes bodily harm to the victim;

(2) confines or restrains the victim; or

(3) violates a temporary restraining order, an order of protection, or an injunction prohibiting the behavior described in subsection (b)(1) of Section 214 of the Illinois Domestic Violence Act of 1986. Ill. ST. 720 ILCS 5/12-7.4(a).

During the 1990s a number of defendants attacked stalking laws on grounds that the laws violated the First Amendment to the U.S. Constitution. In *People v. Bailey*,

657 N.E.2d 953 (Ill. 1995), the Illinois Supreme Court upheld its stalking laws against challenges that the statutes were unconstitutionally vague and overbroad and that they intruded on the right to freedom of speech. As pointed out in *People v. Baer*, 973 P.2d 1225 (Colo. 1999), the majority of courts have upheld the constitutionality of stalking laws in various states. In 2007 a Colorado appellate court upheld a defendant's conviction for harassment and stalking where he repeatedly contacted a victim through letters and phone calls and threatened to overwhelm her with lawsuits to bring her to financial ruin if she would not communicate with him. *People v. Richardson*, 181 P.3d 340 (Colo. App. 2007).

Nevertheless, in some instances defendants have prevailed in such attacks. For example, in *Commonwealth v. Kwiatkowski*, 637 N.E.2d 854 (Mass. 1994), the Massachusetts Supreme Judicial Court held that state's stalking statute to be unconstitutional because the uncertain meaning of "repeated patterns of conduct" and "repeated series of acts" rendered the statute vague, thereby failing to give a person of ordinary intelligence fair notice of what conduct is forbidden. Where appellate courts have found infirmities in statutory language, state legislatures usually have made necessary changes in wording to avoid such further challenges. For example, litigation over what constitutes a "credible threat" caused some state legislatures to eliminate that term from their stalking statutes.

Cyberstalking

Following the increased use of computers, many people complained of being victims of relentless e-mail messages. **Cyberstalking,** sometimes referred to as "stalking by proxy," often involved some prankster or disappointed suitor placing a female's name online with suggestive data directed to third parties. But today cyberstalking is not limited to female victims; often males complain. The anonymity of the Internet makes it extremely difficult for law enforcement agencies to track down cyberstalkers. The problem is exacerbated by the availability of personal data on the Internet and, in addition to e-mail messages, cyberstalking often includes such electronic forms as blogs, bulletin boards, chat rooms, and Internet sites.

Title 18 U.S.C.A. § 2261A(2) makes it a federal crime to stalk someone across state, tribal, or international lines using regular mail, e-mail, or the Internet with the intent to kill or injure the victim, or to place the victim, a family member, or a spouse or intimate partner of the victim in fear of death or serious bodily injury.

Illinois has now specifically criminalized cyberstalking as a felony. Illinois Statutes, Ch. 720, Sec. 5/12-7.5 provides:

(a) A person commits cyberstalking when he or she, knowingly and without lawful justification on at least 2 separate occasions, harasses another person through use of electronic communication and:

(1) at any time transmits a threat of immediate or future bodily harm, sexual assault, confinement, or restraint and the threat is directed toward that person or a family member of that person, or

(2) places that person or a family member of that person in reasonable apprehension of immediate or future bodily harm, sexual assault, confinement, or restraint.

Several other states have amended their statutory definitions of stalking to include cyberstalking. For example, in 2004 the Florida legislature amended West's Fla. Stat. Ann. §784.048 to define cyberstalking as "to engage in a course of conduct to communicate, or to cause to be communicated, words, images, or language by or

Evidence Sufficient to Affirm Defendant's Conviction for Menacing by Stalking

Christopher G. Schwab appealed his conviction for "menacing by stalking" in violation of R.C. 2903.211, which prohibits a person from engaging in a pattern of conduct causing mental distress to another person. In his appeal Schwab argued that the evidence did not show he caused the victim mental distress and did not establish his guilt beyond a reasonable doubt.

The evidence at the defendant's trial disclosed that Schwab and his female victim had lived together in a romantic relationship for about two years. On March 5, 1996, she moved out of their apartment and moved in with her parents. When the defendant phoned her the next day at her parents' home she informed him they were "broken up" and that she did not love him or want to be with him or talk to him. She told Schwab not to call her because the calls were upsetting her and her family. Between the time she moved out and April 1, 1996, Schwab sent the victim a number of unwanted letters and flowers. He followed the victim on more than one occasion and tried to obtain information about her college class schedule from the university she attended. These actions, the victim testified, caused her to become frightened. The court found that the evidence was sufficient to establish that the defendant's actions caused the victim mental distress and to support the defendant's conviction for menacing by stalking.

State v. Schwab, 695 N.E.2d 801 (Ohio App. 1997).

through the use of electronic mail or electronic communication, directed at a specific person, causing substantial emotional distress to that person and serving no legitimate purpose."

Rape and Sexual Battery

There are early biblical accounts of the offense of rape; however, the law of rape, as it exists today, has its roots in the early English common law. It was a felony for a male to have unlawful **carnal knowledge** of (that is, sexual intercourse with) a female by force and against her will. This is usually referred to as **common-law rape** or **forcible rape**. In later stages of the English law, it became a statutory offense for a man to have carnal knowledge of a female child less than ten years of age with or without the child's consent. This latter offense came to be known as **statutory rape.**

The common-law offenses required penetration, however slight, of the female's sexual organ by the male sexual organ; no emission of seed was required. At common law, there was a conclusive presumption that a male under age fourteen could not commit the crime of rape.

Common-law rape contemplated unlawful intercourse; therefore, a husband could not be guilty of raping his wife. Although this **marital exception** is of somewhat dubious judicial origin, it is generally referred to as **Hale's Rule** and is credited to the writings of Sir Matthew Hale, who served as Lord Chief Justice in England from 1671 to 1676. Of course, in egregious cases the husband could be charged with assault or battery of his wife. Furthermore, a husband or even another woman could be charged as an aider or abettor if he or she assisted or procured another man to rape his wife.

More than two centuries after Hale's demise, in March 1991, England's Court of Appeal dismissed an appeal by a man who was convicted of an attempted rape of his estranged wife. In delivering the opinion of the five-judge court, the Lord Chief

Justice observed that a rapist remains a rapist irrespective of his relationship with his victim. Further, the court observed that the centuries-old legal doctrine that a husband could not be guilty of raping his wife no longer represented the law, considering the position of a wife in contemporary society.

The American Approach

The new American states followed the common-law scheme in statutorily defining rape; however, two principal changes soon occurred. First, many states explicitly rejected the common-law presumption that males under age fourteen could not commit the offense. Second, legislatures in most states made consensual intercourse with a young female an offense (statutory rape) if the female was younger than sixteen or eighteen, rather than ten. Some, however, added the qualification that the female must have been "of previous chaste character."

American courts disagreed on the intent required for a defendant to be guilty of rape, and most held that no intent other than that evidenced by the act of intercourse was needed. See, for example, *Walden v. State*, 156 S.W.2d 385 (Tenn. 1941).

Courts in American jurisdictions struggled with the requirements of **force** and **consent** in the law of rape. Some judges instructed juries that "for the defendant to be found guilty of rape, you must find that the woman resisted to her utmost." Later cases recognized degree of resistance as a relative matter dependent on all the circumstances surrounding the incident. Yet courts continued to recognize that resistance generally had to be more than a mere negative verbal response by a female.

All courts recognized that to constitute common-law rape, intercourse had to be without the female's consent. However, consent by a woman who was asleep, unconscious, or mentally deficient and consent obtained by fraud or impersonation or through pretext were invalid. Thus, if a man impersonated a woman's husband and caused her to submit to sexual intercourse, he would be guilty of rape. Likewise, a physician who had intercourse with female patients who were not conscious of the nature of the doctor's acts because of the treatments being administered was properly found guilty of rape. *People v. Minkowski*, 23 Cal. Rptr. 92 (Cal. App. 1962).

Statutory Rape Laws

In America, state legislatures enacted laws to protect young women from sexual intercourse. These statutory rape laws usually stipulate that carnal knowledge (sexual intercourse) with a female under age sixteen, seventeen, or eighteen is a crime. In contrast with common-law rape, the elements of force and consent are irrelevant in statutory rape laws. In effect, underage females are deemed unable to validly consent to sexual relations. A few states have allowed a male to defend against a charge of statutory rape on the basis that he was mistaken about the female's age, but most hold a male defendant strictly liable even if he made a reasonable inquiry in good faith to determine the victim's age. (The concept of a strict liability offense is explained in Chapter 4.)

Statutory rape laws are now gender-neutral in most states, and some impose penalties only if there is at least a two- to five-year disparity between the ages of the perpetrator and the underage party. Obviously, it would be inconceivable to prosecute every minor who has a consensual sexual relationship. The original objective of statutory rape laws was to protect the chastity of young females; however, those who support these laws now emphasize both the psychological effects and the threat of disease that accompany sexual encounters involving minors. They also point out that it is adult males who impregnate most teenage mothers and that, when vigorously enforced, statutory rape laws that focus on sexual relationships involving age discrepancies of several years are one solution to the problem of teenage pregnancy. Some states have graded voluntary sexual battery offenses by considering the age of a perpetrator who engages in sex with a minor. For example, in 1996 the Florida legislature made it a second-degree felony for a person age twenty-four or older to engage in sex with a person age sixteen or seventeen. West's Fla. Stat. Ann. § 794.05.

There is universal agreement that very young children should be protected from sexual predators, but there is considerable opposition to statutory rape laws. Opponents argue that these laws are out of touch with present-day sexual mores. Some see statutory rape laws as depriving women in their late teens of exercising a personal choice; others point out that these laws are largely unobserved and lend themselves to selective enforcement along the lines of race and social class. Despite the conflict in views, it appears that for the foreseeable future statutory rape laws, now often termed "voluntary sexual assault or battery" laws, will remain on the American legal scene.

Reform in the American Law of Rape

During the late 1970s and the 1980s, protests led to several statutory and judicial reforms in the law of rape. As societal awareness increased, legislatures and courts came to realize that marriage in contemporary society is regarded as a partnership and should not be deemed a license to enjoy sex on demand by a forcible encounter with one's spouse.

Legislative reforms focused on revising statutes by

- Defining rape as a **gender-neutral offense**, whereby the offender and victim may be of either sex
- Criminalizing forced sexual relations between spouses or cohabitants. For example, Connecticut law defines "sexual intercourse" very broadly and states, "No spouse or cohabiter shall compel the other spouse or cohabiter to engage in sexual intercourse by the use of force against such other spouse or cohabiter, or by the threat of the use of force against such other spouse or cohabiter which reasonably causes such other spouse or cohabiter to fear physical injury." C.G.S.A. § 53a-70b.
- Expanding common-law definitions to include anal, oral, or vaginal penetrations by a sex organ or another object, excepting acts performed for *bona fide* medical purposes.
- Dividing the offense of sexual battery into classifications and degrees, and providing punishment based on the type of sexual conduct or contact, the force used, and the age and vulnerability of the victim.
- Enacting **rape shield laws**, which preclude presentation of evidence of a victim's prior sexual activity with anyone other than the defendant.

Rape Shield Laws

Rape shield laws are designed "to protect the victims of sexual assault from humiliating and embarrassing public fishing expeditions into their sexual conduct; to overcome victims' reluctance to report incidents of sexual assault; and to protect victims from psychological or emotional abuse in court as the price of their cooperation in prosecuting sex offenders." *State v. Guthrie*, 518 S.E.2d 83, 96 (W.Va. 1999). Even where the defendant seeks to introduce evidence of prior relations with a victim, statutes commonly require such evidence to be first presented to the court *in camera* (in the judge's private chambers) for the court to determine whether the evidence of the defendant's prior relationship with the victim is relevant to the victim's consent. For example, New Jersey law provides:

> In prosecutions for the crime of rape, assault with intent to commit rape, and breaking and entering with intent to commit rape, evidence of the complaining witness's previous sexual conduct shall not be admitted nor reference made to it in the presence of the jury except as provided in this act. N.J.S.A. 2A:84A-32.1.

The New Jersey statute goes on to state that before permitting evidence of a complaining witness's sexual history, the court must first conduct a hearing *in camera* to determine whether such evidence is relevant and whether its probative value is not outweighed by the prejudice or confusion it will create or by its unwarranted invasion of the complaining witness's privacy.

Rape shield laws are based on the theory that a victim's prior sexual activity is not probative of whether the victim has been violated in the instance for which the defendant stands accused. Thus, in *State v. Madsen*, 772 S.W.2d 656 (Mo. 1989), the Missouri Supreme Court held that neither evidence of a victim having a live-in boyfriend nor of having two illegitimate children was relevant in a prosecution for rape. But can a female victim offer testimony of a prior rape to explain her conduct in failing to resist an attacker? In *Raines v. State*, 382 S.E.2d 738 (Ga. App. 1989), the appellate court found this to be appropriate.

In interpreting the applicability of rape shield laws to some unusual factual situations, courts have faced some difficult judgments. In a Massachusetts decision, the court ruled that a defendant charged with rape should have been allowed to question the complainant as to whether she had sexual intercourse with anyone else on the night of the attack. The court concluded that such evidence would not constitute an attack on the complainant's credibility. Rather, the court held that such evidence tended to support the defendant's theory that someone else had attacked the complainant and that she had wrongly accused him. *Commonwealth v. Fitzgerald*, 590 N.E.2d 1151 (Mass. 1992).

A Virginia appellate court ruled that evidence that a victim did not report her alleged rape until a month after the incident, when she learned that she had contracted gonorrhea, was admissible to show ill will of the complainant. The court found that such evidence did not relate to the sexual conduct of the victim and therefore was not barred by the Virginia rape shield statute. *Evans v. Commonwealth*, 415 S.E.2d 851 (Va. App. 1992).

Judicial Reforms

Significant judicial reforms have also occurred in the law of rape, as courts

- No longer instruct juries that the uncorroborated testimony of a victim of sexual battery deserves more scrutiny than the testimony of other crime victims.
- No longer insist that a woman must "resist to the utmost" to establish that her sexual privacy has been violated. (This is consistent with the advice of law enforcement officers, who frequently caution women that violent resistance to a rapist's attack can result in the victim's serious injury or death.) Now, in

considering whether a victim's resistance has been overcome, courts consider such factors as the extent of the offender's force, the physical capacity of the victim to resist, and the psychological and emotional stress of a victim whose sensibilities are outraged by fear of violation of her bodily integrity.

- Have generally disavowed the unity concept of marriage, abrogating Hale's Rule, discussed previously, which American courts generally followed until the 1970s. By the mid 1990s, about half the states had abolished the marital exception completely; the majority of the remaining states had abolished the exception where the spouses were living apart from each other. In 1981 the New Jersey Supreme Court held that the state's rape statute, which used the language "any person who has carnal knowledge of a woman forcibly against her will," did not except from its operation a husband who was living apart from his wife. *State v. Smith*, 426 A.2d 38 (N.J. 1981). In *People v. Liberta*, 474 N.E.2d 567 (N.Y. 1984), New York's highest court termed the notion of a wife's implied consent to intercourse as "irrational and absurd" and emphasized that a married woman should have the same right to bodily autonomy as a single woman. Either statutes or judicial decisions in many states now provide that a husband may be charged with rape of his wife.

A Contemporary Statutory Treatment of Sexual Offenses

Michigan has modern, comprehensive laws that classify criminal sexual conduct by various degrees, depending on whether it involves sexual penetration or sexual contact with another person as well as other factors. Mich. Comp. Laws Ann. Sexual contact is defined as including the intentional touching of the victim's intimate parts or the intentional touching of the clothing covering the immediate area of the victim's intimate parts, if that intentional touching can reasonably be construed as being for the purpose of sexual arousal or gratification (§ 750.520a(q)). **Sexual penetration** is defined as sexual intercourse, cunnilingus, fellatio, anal intercourse, or any other intrusion, however slight, of any part of a person's body or of any object into the genital or anal openings of another person's body, but emission of seed is not required. § 750.520a(r).

CASE-IN-POINT

Does Asking an Attacker to Wear a Condom Constitute Consent to Sex?

In May 1993, in Travis County, Texas, Joel Valdez, a twenty-eight-year-old defendant who was charged with rape, claimed that the female with whom he admittedly had sexual intercourse had asked him to wear a condom. Valdez testified that he complied with the woman's request and that accordingly they were simply "making love." But the twenty-six-year-old complainant explained that she pleaded with her attacker to wear a condom only to protect herself from acquired immunodeficiency syndrome (AIDS). The jury in Austin, Texas, found Valdez guilty of rape, implicitly finding that asking the attacker to wear a condom does not constitute consent to sexual intercourse.

Sec. 720.520(b) deals with first-degree criminal sexual conduct and provides:

1. A person is guilty of criminal sexual conduct in the first degree if he or she engages in sexual penetration with another person and if any of the following circumstances exists:

(a) That other person is under 13 years of age.

(b) That other person is at least 13 but less than 16 years of age and any of the following:

(i) The actor is a member of the same household as the victim.

(ii) The actor is related to the victim by blood or affinity to the fourth degree.

(iii) The actor is in a position of authority over the victim and used this authority to coerce the victim to submit.

(iv) The actor is a teacher, substitute teacher, or administrator of the public or nonpublic school in which that other person is enrolled.

(c) Sexual penetration occurs under circumstances involving the commission of any other felony.

(d) The actor is aided or abetted by 1 or more other persons and either of the following circumstances exists:

(i) The actor knows or has reason to know that the victim is mentally incapable, mentally incapacitated, or physically helpless.

(ii) The actor uses force or coercion to accomplish the sexual penetration. Force or coercion includes but is not limited to any of the circumstances listed in subdivision (f).

(e) The actor is armed with a weapon or any article used or fashioned in a manner to lead the victim to reasonably believe it to be a weapon.

(f) The actor causes personal injury to the victim and force or coercion is used to accomplish sexual penetration. Force or coercion includes but is not limited to any of the following circumstances:

(i) When the actor overcomes the victim through the actual application of physical force or physical violence.

(ii) When the actor coerces the victim to submit by threatening to use force or violence on the victim, and the victim believes that the actor has the present ability to execute these threats.

(iii) When the actor coerces the victim to submit by threatening to retaliate in the future against the victim, or any other person, and the victim believes that the actor has the ability to execute this threat. As used in this subdivision, "to retaliate" includes threats of physical punishment, kidnapping, or extortion.

(iv) When the actor engages in the medical treatment or examination of the victim in a manner or for purposes which are medically recognized as unethical or unacceptable.

(v) When the actor, through concealment or by the element of surprise, is able to overcome the victim.

(g) The actor causes personal injury to the victim, and the actor knows or has reason to know that the victim is mentally incapable, mentally incapacitated, or physically helpless.

(h) The other person is mentally incapable, mentally disabled, mentally incapacitated, or physically helpless, and any of the following:

(i) The actor is related to the victim by blood or affinity to the fourth degree.

(ii) The actor is in a position of authority over the victim and uses this authority to coerce the victim to submit.

Second-degree criminal sexual conduct follows substantially along the lines of the preceding section, but instead of penetration it makes sexual contact with a victim unlawful. Third-degree criminal sexual conduct includes two of the same elements as a first-degree offense (that is, penetration and use of force or coercion) but does not include the element that the defendant was aided or abetted in the act by one or more persons. § 750.520(d). Fourth-degree criminal sexual conduct involves **sexual contact** with another person involving force or coercion; an actor who knows or has reason to know that the victim is mentally incapable, mentally incapacitated, or physically helpless; or a victim who is under jurisdiction of the department of corrections and an actor who is associated with that department.

Note that the Michigan law makes no distinction as to the sex of the actor or victim. In other words, it is gender neutral. It broadly defines sexual penetration and sexual contact and divides the offense of criminal sexual conduct into degrees considering the conduct of the actor and the vulnerability of the victim. Thus, it is a comprehensive sexual battery statute that embodies many of the reforms discussed earlier.

Violations of the Michigan law for first-, second-, and third-degree sexual conduct constitute felonies; fourth degree sexual conduct that involves contact is a serious misdemeanor.

In *State v. Studham*, which is reproduced on the companion website, the Utah Supreme Court explains how force in committing sexual assault can be psychological as well as physical.

Prosecutorial Burdens

As in all criminal cases, the prosecution must prove the *corpus delicti*—that is, the fact that the crime has been committed. Proof that an act of sexual intercourse (or other sexual imposition, depending on the statutory definition of the offense) has taken place with the victim is usually sufficient in a sexual battery case. In addition, in a statutory rape case, proof must be offered of the age of the victim (usually the female) and, in some instances, the age of the offender (usually the male). In sexual battery prosecutions, proof of the defendant's general intent is usually sufficient, absent a statute requiring proof of the defendant's specific intent.

One common problem in sexual battery prosecutions is the lack of independent eyewitness testimony. Consequently, it frequently becomes the victim's word against the defendant's word. Thus, police and prosecutors place paramount importance on a "fresh complaint" by a victim. Preservation of semen, photographs of bruises, torn clothing, and even pubic hairs become valuable evidence to corroborate a victim's testimony. Seldom is the credibility of a complaining witness as vital as in sexual battery prosecutions. To appear in court and testify concerning a sexual assault is a traumatic experience for a victim of sexual assault. This is particularly true for young children. To assist youngsters, many courts permit them to illustrate their testimony through the use of anatomically detailed dolls.

Rape Trauma Syndrome

In 1974, to describe a recurring pattern of physical and emotional symptoms experienced by rape victims, psychiatrists coined the term **rape trauma syndrome**, which refers to a set of psychological manifestations (for example, fear, depression, and a sense of guilt) of victims usually following a sexual assault. Since then, prosecutors

The Connecticut Supreme Court's decision in *State v. Rothenberg* is reproduced on the companion website.

have sought to introduce expert testimony at rape trials to establish that a victim's symptoms are consistent with those of the syndrome. This type of evidence has particular relevance to prosecutions where the defendant claims consent of the victim as a defense. On review of convictions, appellate courts have disagreed on whether such evidence is admissible. The Kansas Supreme Court was the nation's first appellate court to address the question of the admissibility of expert testimony concerning rape trauma syndrome. The court allowed the introduction of psychiatric testimony that a rape victim suffered from rape trauma syndrome, noting that such expert evidence is relevant where the defendant claims consent. *State v. Marks*, 647 P.2d 1292 (Kan. 1982). Other state supreme courts have reached a similar conclusion. *State v. Liddell*, 685 P.2d 918 (Mont. 1984); *State v. Huey*, 699 P.2d 1290 (Ariz. 1985). An Ohio appellate court held that such expert psychiatric testimony is admissible but only where its value outweighs its prejudicial impact. The court noted that expert opinions of this type assist laypersons in interpreting reactions of a victim, especially in child rape cases. *State v. Whitman*, 475 N.E.2d 486 (Ohio App. 1984).

There is respectable judicial authority to the contrary. In 1982 the Minnesota Supreme Court ruled that the diagnosis of rape trauma syndrome is not a fact-finding tool but rather a therapeutic tool and that admission of expert testimony on the subject at a rape trial is erroneous. *State v. Saldana*, 324 N.W.2d 227 (Minn. 1982). Several other appellate courts have held that expert testimony concerning the syndrome is not admissible to prove that a rape in fact occurred. For example, in *People v. Pullins*, 378 N.W.2d 502 (Mich. App. 1985), the court held evidence of rape trauma syndrome inadmissible to establish that a rape occurred. This came the year after the Missouri Supreme Court, in *State v. Taylor*, 663 S.W.2d 235 (Mo. 1984), concluded that such testimony was beyond the proper basis of expert opinion.

In 1990 New York's highest court concluded that the scientific community has now generally accepted that rape is a highly traumatic event that triggers the onset of certain identifiable symptoms. The court agreed that expert testimony of the rape trauma syndrome may be admitted to aid the jury's understanding of the victim's behavior after the assault. Nevertheless, the court observed that identifiable symptoms in rape victims do not indicate whether an incident did or did not occur; thus,

CASE-IN-POINT

Sufficiency of Evidence to Support a Conviction for Sexual Assault

Rothenberg met the complainant in a bar. After dancing with her, Rothenberg asked the complainant to accompany him to a party at a friend's condominium. The complainant agreed and drove to the condominium in her own car. When she arrived at the condo, there appeared to be no one there except Rothenberg. The complainant and Rothenberg sat on a couch in the living room where they kissed and exchanged back massages. The complainant then told Rothenberg that she wanted to leave, but he refused to let her go. She ran to the front door and attempted to open it, but Rothenberg closed the door and prevented her from leaving. The complainant then locked herself in the bathroom where she remained for thirty minutes. Rothenberg promised to let the complainant leave if she would come out of the bathroom. When she came out, Rothenberg forced her onto the couch. At that point the complainant submitted to sexual intercourse. In sustaining Rothenberg's conviction for sexual assault, the Connecticut Supreme Court noted that "the complainant's unambiguous request to leave the condominium disabused the defendant of any misinterpretation of her wishes" and that "the defendant's conduct thereafter was knowingly coercive."

State v. Rothenberg, 487 A.2d 545 (Conn. 1985).

trial judges cannot allow such testimony to be introduced for this purpose. *People v. Taylor*, 552 N.E.2d 131 (N.Y. 1990). In *People v. Nelson*, 837 N.Y.S.2d 697 (N.Y.S.2d 2007), the court held that expert testimony regarding rape trauma syndrome was properly admitted, in a prosecution for sexual abuse, to aid the jury in understanding the victim's unusual behavior.

Appellate courts still disagree on the admissibility of evidence of the rape trauma syndrome. Much of the controversy focuses on the purpose of the evidence and the qualifications of experts. Yet the trend is to allow such evidence. As the New Mexico Court of Appeals recently pointed out, an expert's testimony on victimization and impact of trauma on victims is relevant in a trial for sex offenses. *State v. Maestas*, 112 P.3d 1134 (N.M. App. 2005).

Can a defendant charged with rape introduce expert testimony concerning the rape trauma syndrome to establish that a rape did not occur? In *Henson v. State*, 535 N.E.2d 1189 (Ind. 1989), the defense presented a witness who testified to seeing the victim dancing and drinking at a bar on the evening after the alleged rape. The defense then sought to introduce expert testimony on the subject, but the trial judge would not allow it. The state supreme court ruled that the testimony must be permitted because it would be unfair to allow the prosecution to present expert testimony on rape trauma syndrome but deny a defendant the same opportunity.

Sex Offender Registration Laws

On June 20, 1997, a Trenton, New Jersey, court sentenced Jesse Timmendequas to death for the rape and murder of seven-year-old Megan Kanka in 1994. The case attracted national attention after it was revealed that Timmendequas had a record of committing sex offenses against children. Public outrage led the New Jersey legislature to enact a law requiring convicted sex offenders who are released from prison, move into the state, or simply change their address to register with local law enforcement agencies. Registration must include the individual's address, description, and other personal data along with a complete criminal history. These agencies in turn must make this information available to the public. The New Jersey statute became widely known as **Megan's Law** in memory of Megan Kanka. Failure to comply with the registration requirement is itself a criminal offense. After fifteen years with no violations, an offender may request a court to terminate sex offender status. See, generally, N.J.S.A. 2C: 7-1 *et seq*.

Similar laws have been enacted in most states, and most of these laws have survived constitutional attack. In 1996 Congress enacted a federal version of Megan's Law. 42 U.S.C.A. § 14071. The federal statute sets forth guidelines for state programs and encourages states to adopt such programs by threatening them with the loss of federal funds. All states and the District of Columbia have adopted variations of Megan's Law.

It remains to be seen how effective the various versions of Megan's Law will be in protecting children from sexual predators. There is also concern that these laws may be too inclusive, in that persons convicted in the past of minor sexual offenses are subjected to undeserved community scorn. Megan's Law and similar laws are also subject to the criticism that they impose penalties based on status rather than on wrongful acts. However, the public has demanded that the justice system do more to protect people from sexual predators, and such individuals often remain a serious threat to the community even after they have paid their debt to society.

The U.S. Supreme Court's decision in *Smith v. Doe* is excerpted on the companion website.

State registration laws modeled after Megan's Law have survived constitutional attacks based on double jeopardy, vagueness, equal protection, the right to privacy, and cruel and unusual punishment. For example, in Cutshall v. Sundquist, 193 F.3d 466 (6th Cir. 1999), a federal appeals court rejected a challenge to Tennessee's sex offender registration law based on the Double Jeopardy Clause of the Fifth Amendment.

In March 2003 the U.S. Supreme Court upheld Alaska's version of Megan's Law against an attack based on the constitutional prohibition against *ex post facto* laws. *Smith v. Doe*, 538 U.S. 84, 123 S.Ct. 1140, 155 L.Ed.2d 164 (2003). The majority found that although the act was retroactive, it was nonpunitive in nature; therefore, the *Ex Post Facto* Clause did not apply. In dissent, Justice Ruth Bader Ginsburg (joined by Justice Stephen Breyer) asserted that the legislative intent behind the act was ambiguous but that its effect was punitive. In her view, the act was an unconstitutional *ex post facto* law. Justice John Paul Stevens also dissented, noting the severe stigma that sex offender registration places on the convicted sex offender. In Stevens's view, it was "clear beyond peradventure that these unique consequences of conviction of a sex offense are punitive." 538 U.S. at 112, 123 S.Ct. at 1157, 155 L.Ed.2d at 189.

Defenses to Charges of Sexual Battery

Beyond a general denial of the charges, the most common defense asserted in a rape case is that the victim consented. For consent to be a defense, it must be voluntarily given before the sexual act. As we pointed out previously, the defense of consent is not available where the victim is unconscious, asleep, or mentally deficient.

The defense of consent would not be valid in a case of voluntary sexual battery (that is, statutory rape) because persons under a certain age are legally incapable of consent. Moreover, it is usually not a defense to a charge of voluntary sexual battery that the defendant believed the victim was older than the prohibited age. In the majority of states this is true despite the victim's appearance or misrepresentation of his or her age. The Model Penal Code allows a defense when the victim is over the age of ten, but it requires the actor "to prove by a preponderance of the evidence that he reasonably believed the child to be above the critical age." M.P.C. § 213.6. Legislatures in about one-third of the states have enacted statutes allowing a mistake-of-age defense, often with variations such as the age of the victim and in instances when a mistake is based on declarations of age by the victim.

Impotency (that is, the inability to engage in sexual intercourse) can be asserted as a defense to a charge of rape. The majority of cases where the defense of impotency is asserted involve charges against young males and men of an advanced age. However, this defense is seldom successful. Modern laws have so broadened the definition of sexual battery as to render impotency irrelevant in many sexual impositions.

Finally, if the statute under which the defendant is prosecuted requires proof of a specific intent, the defendant may be able to show an inability to form such intent due to voluntary intoxication (see Chapter 14).

Sodomy

Sodomy refers to oral or anal sex between humans and sexual intercourse between humans and animals (the latter is often termed bestiality). In his landmark commentaries on the English common law, Sir William Blackstone defined sodomy as "the infamous crime against nature" and asserted that it was an offense of "deeper malignity" than rape. Sodomy can be consensual or nonconsensual. Nonconsensual sodomy is considered a crime against a person and is often charged along with rape in states with older, narrower statutory definitions of rape. (Of course, in jurisdictions with more modern rape statutes, any nonconsensual sexual penetration is considered rape.) Consensual sodomy, on the other hand, was viewed traditionally as an offense against public morality. Prior to 2003, many states had abolished the offense either through legislative or judicial action. In June 2003 the U.S. Supreme Court found a Texas law that proscribed private, consensual sodomy between same-sex partners to be unconstitutional. *Lawrence v. Texas*, 539 U.S. 558, 123 S.Ct. 2472, 156 L.Ed.2d 508 (2003). The Supreme Court's decision sounded the death knell for state laws prohibiting consensual sodomy.

Go to the companion website for an edited version of the Supreme Court's decision in *Lawrence v. Texas*.

Abusive Offenses

Laws proscribing abuse of one person by another are modern concepts. Many of these laws have been proposed by social agencies that bear the responsibility of coping with problems of members of society who require protection from abusive behavior. Increasingly, legislatures and, even more recently, Congress have responded by enacting laws designed to protect children, spouses and other intimate partners, and, in some instances, the elderly.

Child Abuse

Since the 1980s, complaints of **child abuse** have increased dramatically. Many cases involve commission of assault, battery (or aggravated categories thereof), or some category of sexual assault or sexual battery and are prosecuted under one or more of such statutes. Nevertheless, with the rise of neglect and abuse of and violence against children, many states have enacted specific child abuse laws to cover a broader range of abusive behavior. These laws often refer to **endangering the welfare of a child**, and they hold a parent or guardian responsible for abuse of a child regardless of the source of the mistreatment. These concerns appear to be reflected in McKinney's N.Y. Penal Law § 260.10. That law makes endangering the welfare of a child a misdemeanor and provides that a person is guilty of endangering the welfare of a child when

1. He knowingly acts in a manner likely to be injurious to the physical, mental or moral welfare of a child less than seventeen years old or directs or authorizes such child to engage in an occupation involving a substantial risk of danger to his life or health; or
2. Being a parent, guardian or other person legally charged with the care or custody of a child less than eighteen years old, he fails or refuses to exercise reasonable diligence in the control of such child to prevent him from becoming an "abused child," a "neglected child," a "juvenile delinquent," or a "person in need of supervision," as those terms are defined in articles ten, three and seven of the family court act.

Because of the age and vulnerability of minors, statutes proscribing child abuse are strict liability crimes in many states. Since 2000, several states have enacted statutes making it a misdemeanor to allow young children to remain unattended in a vehicle. For example, a defendant's actions in leaving a three-week-old child locked in a van on a hot summer day posed substantial risk of harm to the child and thus was a violation of an Ohio child endangerment statute that provided that "[n]o person, who is the parent . . . or person *in loco parentis* of a child under eighteen years of age . . . shall create a substantial risk to the health or safety of the child, by violating a duty of care, protection, or support." *State v. Morton*, 741 N.E.2d 202 (Ohio App. 2000).

The prosecution of parents for leaving a child unattended in a vehicle has engendered some debate. Some argue that parents should not be punished criminally for their lack of judgment. But the more prevalent view is that punishing parents for such lapses of judgment forces parents to face the consequences of their actions. Moreover, such statutes raise public awareness as to the danger of leaving children alone in vehicles. In other instances, a parent has been charged with endangering a child's welfare by transporting a child in an auto while the parent was driving under the influence of intoxicating beverages.

Statutes now commonly require medical professionals and social workers to report instances of suspected child abuse to the enforcement authorities. When such cases of child abuse reach the courts, they often involve legal issues as to whether parents, social workers, and others who discuss these matters with an abused child are to be permitted to testify in court concerning communications with the child. Moreover, expert testimony of physicians, psychologists, and social workers is often relied on to explain a child's sometimes-curious behavior that might be a result of certain types of abuse.

The widespread drug problem has led to prosecutions of women for child abuse when, during pregnancy, they ingested cocaine or other controlled substances and demonstrable adverse medical effects were present in their children at birth. Courts have generally declined to hold that such action constitutes child abuse, often based on their interpretation of statutes proscribing child endangerment or delivery of controlled substances. For example, Kentucky Revised Statute § 508.110 criminalizes abuse of "another person of whom [the offender] has actual custody" which "places him in a situation that may cause . . . serious physical injury" to a person twelve years of age or less or who is physically helpless or mentally helpless.

In a leading decision on the subject, the Kentucky Supreme Court held the statute does not apply to a mother whose baby suffered injuries as the result of the mother's ingestion of drugs during her pregnancy. *Commonwealth v. Welch*, 864 S.W.2d 280 (Ky. 1993). In reaching its decision, the court cited *Johnson v. State*, 602 So.2d 1288 (Fla. 1992). There, the Florida Supreme Court held that cocaine passing through a baby's umbilical cord after birth but before the cord was cut did not violate a Florida law making it a crime for an adult to deliver a controlled substance to a minor.

In *Reinesto v. Superior Court*, 894 P.2d 733 (Ariz. App. 1995), the state prosecuted a mother for having knowingly caused injury to her unborn child under circumstances likely to produce death or serious physical injury in violation of A.R.S. § 13-3623.B. The statute makes it a felony for "any person" who "[u]nder circumstances likely to produce death or serious physical injury . . . causes a child . . . to suffer physical injury. . . ." The statute defines a child as "an individual who is under eighteen years of age" and physical injury as "the impairment of physical condition . . . or any physical condition which imperils health or welfare." A.R.S. § 13-3623.A. The defendant challenged the right of the state to bring charges against her. The appellate court granted her petition and held,

> The plain language of section 13-3623 indicates that the legislature intended to proscribe conduct by any person that causes physical harm to a child. Applying the ordinary meaning of these words leads us to conclude that the statute refers to conduct that directly endangers a child, not to activity that affects a fetus and thereby ultimately harms the resulting child. *Id*. at 735–736.

Because it concluded that Arizona's child abuse statute does not reach the defendant's conduct, the court declined to reach the constitutional issue of whether the statute violated her right of privacy.

Many court decisions hold that maternal conduct before the birth of the child does not give rise to criminal prosecution under state child abuse/endangerment or drug distribution statutes. However, in *Whitner v. State*, 492 S.E.2d 777 (S.C. 1997), the South Carolina Supreme Court held that a mother of a newborn infant could be criminally prosecuted on the statutory theory of child abuse or endangerment for injuries to her child resulting from prenatal substance abuse.

Spousal Abuse

In recent years, legislatures and courts have given increased attention to **spousal abuse**. Many of these abuses constitute criminal violations of one or more traditional statutes of the types previously discussed. Nevertheless, laws have been enacted in many states to provide for issuance of court injunctions to protect spouses from domestic violence and provide for the arrest of those who violate these orders. In many instances, courts issue protective orders of this character during litigation. In *Cole v. Cole*, 556 N.Y.S.2d 217 (Fam. Ct. 1990), a wife petitioned the court to have her husband held in contempt for violating such an order. A question arose about the effectiveness of such order when the wife voluntarily seeks reconciliation with her husband. The court explained that a victim of domestic violence who has procured such an order is entitled to the court's protection from violence throughout the duration of the order, even if the victim is desirous of pursuing a goal of voluntary reconciliation with the offending spouse.

Prosecutions for spousal abuse are sometimes hindered by the difficulty of showing which instances of domestic violence have occurred in which legal jurisdiction. Recognizing this, Congress included in the Violent Crime Control and Law Enforcement Act of 1994 (commonly referred to as the "federal crime bill") an offense of "interstate domestic violence." Section 40221 of the act inserts a new chapter titled "Domestic Violence" after Chapter 110 in 18 U.S.C.A. Title 18 U.S.C.A. § 2261 now provides:

> (a) Offenses.—
>
>> (1) Travel or conduct of offender.—A person who travels in interstate or foreign commerce or enters or leaves Indian country or within the special maritime and territorial jurisdiction of the United States with the intent to kill, injure, harass, or intimidate a spouse, intimate partner, or dating partner, and who, in the course of or as a result of such travel, commits or attempts to commit a crime of violence against that spouse or intimate partner, shall be punished as provided in subsection (b).
>>
>> (2) Causing travel of victim.—A person who causes a spouse, intimate partner, or dating partner to travel in interstate or foreign commerce or to enter or leave Indian country by force, coercion, duress, or fraud, and who, in the course of, as a result of, or to facilitate such conduct or travel, commits or attempts to commit a crime of violence against that spouse or intimate partner, shall be punished as provided in subsection (b).

Shortly after the new act took effect, Christopher Bailey was charged with violating it for assaulting his spouse and driving her around West Virginia and Kentucky until he finally carried her into an emergency room. A jury found Bailey guilty of kidnapping and interstate domestic violence under the new federal act. The U.S. Court

of Appeals for the Fourth Circuit affirmed his convictions for violating 18 U.S.C.A. §
1201(a)(1), kidnapping, and 18 U.S.C.A. § 2261(a)(2), the new act. The court rejected
Bailey's constitutional argument that the new federal statute was beyond the power
of Congress to enact. *United States v. Bailey*, 112 F.3d 758 (4th Cir. 1997). The court
in *United States v. Lankford*, 196 F.3d 563 (5th Cir. 1999), held that the enactment of
the Violence Against Women Act, 18 U.S.C.A. § 2261(a)(1), did not exceed the scope
of Congress's authority under the Commerce Clause, U.S. Const. Art. 1, § 8.

Abuse of the Elderly

Abuse of the elderly is often handled through state and local regulatory agencies. Frequently, this has involved resorting to civil court processes, but in recent
years some state legislatures have created criminal offenses to punish caregivers who
abuse, neglect, or exploit elderly persons. Generally these statutes define caregivers
broadly to include adults who are close relatives and persons appointed by agencies
or otherwise employed to assist the elderly and disabled. New York and Illinois have
been leaders in enacting legislation that provides criminal sanctions for endangering
the welfare of a vulnerable elderly person.

McKinney's N.Y. Penal Law, Chapter 260, makes it a felony for a caregiver to endanger the welfare of a vulnerable elderly person. A "caregiver" is defined as one who
assumes responsibility for the care of a vulnerable elderly person pursuant to a court
order or who receives monetary or other valuable consideration for providing care
for a vulnerable elderly person. A "vulnerable elderly person" is one sixty years of
age or older who is suffering from a disease or infirmity associated with advanced age
and manifested by demonstrable physical, mental, or emotional dysfunction to the
extent that the person is incapable of adequately providing for his or her own health
or personal care. It is endangering in the second degree (and a felony) for a caregiver
for a vulnerable elderly person to recklessly cause physical injury to such person or
subject the person to sexual contact without that person's consent (§ 260.32). It is
endangering in the first degree (and a felony) for a caregiver to intentionally or recklessly cause injury to a vulnerable elderly person (§ 260.34).

Under Illinois law, the caregiver of an elderly or disabled person commits a felony if he or she knowingly

(1) performs acts which cause the elderly or disabled person's life to be endangered,
health to be injured, or pre-existing physical or mental condition to deteriorate; or
(2) fails to perform acts which he knows or reasonably should know are necessary to
maintain or preserve the life or health of the elderly or disabled person and such failure causes the elderly or disabled person's life to be endangered, health to be injured
or pre-existing physical or mental condition to deteriorate; or
(3) abandons the elderly or disabled person. 720 ILCS 5/12-21 (West 1994).

In *People v. Simester*, 678 N.E.2d 710 (Ill. App. 1997), Janice and Dale Simester,
husband and wife, were convicted of two counts of criminal neglect of an elderly
person and sentenced to thirty months probation and one thousand hours of community service. The victim, Stanley Pierzga, the wife's seventy-four-year-old uncle,
had lived with the couple for several years. At trial the evidence revealed that when
paramedics responded to a call to the home they found Mr. Pierzga lying on the floor
in a coma in a fetal position. An emergency room physician found him covered with
dried urine and crusted feces. Medical evidence further revealed the victim had had
no nutritional intake for at least one week, that his rigid fetal position took at least

two weeks to develop, and that his deep coma had to have existed for several days before his hospitalization.

On appeal the defendants argued that the statute (quoted above) presumptively imposes medical and psychiatric knowledge on a layperson for diagnosing and correctly treating the pre-existing ailments of the elderly or disabled and that by making it an offense to fail to give adequate care to the victim on the basis that one "should reasonably know" the proper care, the statute "impermissibly adopts a civil negligence standard and enforces it as a criminal felony." The appellate court rejected their contentions and, in affirming their convictions, observed that both defendants should have reasonably known of the victim's condition long before the paramedics were summoned.

False Imprisonment and Kidnapping

In recognition of the need to protect an individual's freedom of movement, the common law developed two misdemeanor offenses: **false imprisonment** and **kidnapping**. False imprisonment consisted of confining someone against the person's will, whereas kidnapping involved forcibly abducting and taking a person to another country.

The Statutory Offense of False Imprisonment

Not all states have adopted statutes making false imprisonment an offense. Those that have generally classify it as a misdemeanor and define it much as did the common law, which defined the offense as the unlawful detention of a person.

One typical example, the Texas statute, states that "[a] person commits an offense if he intentionally and knowingly restrains another person." Vernon's Tex. Penal Code Ann. § 20.02(a). Texas law declares the offense to be a misdemeanor but provides that it becomes a felony if the offender recklessly exposes the victim to a substantial risk of serious bodily injury. Vernon's Tex. Penal Code Ann. § 20.02(c). Usually, a prosecution for false imprisonment requires only proof of a defendant's general intent, although this depends on the language of the particular statute.

Four hypothetical situations illustrate the crime of false imprisonment:

- A police officer takes a person into custody under an unlawful arrest.
- A prison warden fails to release a prisoner who has served his or her term.
- A storekeeper detains a customer when the storekeeper has a hunch the customer has shoplifted but has no reasonable basis for such suspicion.
- An overzealous male refuses to allow his female companion to leave his apartment without yielding to his sexual demands.

In *State v. Snider*, which is reproduced on the companion website, the Court of Appeals of Iowa reversed a defendant's conviction for false imprisonment on the ground that the facts did not show the victim's freedom was substantially restricted.

In recent years, false imprisonment has not been a commonly charged offense. Three reasons chiefly account for this: (1) Serious charges involving restraint of a person frequently reveal elements constituting the statutory offense of kidnapping; (2) persons claiming to have been falsely imprisoned often seek to recover damages in a civil suit rather than press criminal charges; and (3) on close investigation, many restraints undoubtedly are determined to have been imposed based on authority, or at least a reasonable belief that there was authority to have restrained the complaining party.

Modern Statutory Treatment of Kidnapping

Unlike false imprisonment, the crime of kidnapping is a serious felony proscribed by all state and federal jurisdictions. It plays a far greater role in our society than it did at common law, where kidnapping required taking the victim to another country.

Under modern legislation the elements of the crime necessarily depend on the precise wording of the statute in a particular jurisdiction but, in general, for an act to constitute kidnapping, there must be an unlawful taking and forcible carrying away (sometimes called **asportation**) of a victim without that person's consent. Intimidation and coercion can substitute for the required force, and even where consent has been given, a person who has the capacity to consent must have voluntarily given it. Therefore, young children and incompetent persons cannot legally consent to an act of asportation.

Most states classify kidnapping as **simple kidnapping** and **kidnapping for ransom**. Others classify the offense by degrees. In New York, kidnapping in the second degree is a felony that merely involves the abduction of another person. McKinney's N.Y. Penal Law § 135.20. Kidnapping in the first degree is a more serious felony, and the statute proscribing it states,

> A person is guilty of kidnapping in the first degree when he abducts another person and when:
>
> 1. His intent is to compel a third person to pay or deliver money or property as ransom, or to engage in other particular conduct, or to refrain from engaging in particular conduct; or
>
> 2. He restrains the person abducted for a period of more than twelve hours with intent to:
>> (a) Inflict physical injury upon him or violate or abuse him sexually; or
>> (b) Accomplish or advance the commission of a felony; or
>> (c) Terrorize him or a third person; or
>> (d) Interfere with the performance of a governmental or political function; or
>
> 3. The person abducted dies during the abduction or before he is able to return or to be returned to safety. McKinney's N.Y. Penal Law § 135.25.

The Requirement of Asportation in Kidnapping

The asportation or movement of the victim distinguishes the crime of kidnapping from the offense of false imprisonment. One of the more commonly litigated issues in kidnapping prosecutions concerns the extent of movement of the victim required to meet this element of the crime. In *People v. Martinez*, 973 P.2d 512 (Cal. 1999), the California Supreme Court noted that there are two requirements under the asportation standard. First, the movement of the victim must not be merely incidental to the commission of the underlying crime, and second, it must increase the risk of harm to the victim over and above that necessarily present in the underlying crime itself. See West's Ann. Cal. Penal Code § 209(b)(2).

In recent years, courts have tended to limit the scope of kidnapping statutes by deciding that the required movement of a victim must be something more than that inherent in or incidental to the commission of another felony. The proliferation of court decisions on this subject might be the result of prosecutors' tendencies to levy multiple charges against a criminal defendant for conduct arising from a single criminal episode.

When is the offender's movement of a victim in conjunction with an independent offense such as assault, rape, or robbery sufficient to constitute an independent offense of kidnapping? If the movement is merely incidental to a crime and does not involve an additional significant risk to the victim, courts generally will not sustain a conviction for kidnapping in addition to the other offense. Appellate court decisions are instructive. The New Hampshire Supreme Court has held that a defendant was properly convicted for kidnapping as an accomplice of a defendant who forced a woman into a car and drove her to an apartment where the principal defendant assaulted her. *State v. Goodwin*, 395 A.2d 1234 (N.H. 1978). In the same vein, two years later, the North Carolina Supreme Court sustained a kidnapping conviction where a handyman forced a woman off the street and into her home for purposes of sexually assaulting her. *State v. Adams*, 264 S.E.2d 46 (N.C. 1980).

Two 1983 appellate court decisions addressed the extent of movement required to meet the asportation element of kidnapping. The Florida Supreme Court held that the statutory requirement of "confining, abducting, or imprisoning another person . . . with intent to commit or facilitate commission of any felony" does not include movement or confinement that is inconsequential or inherent in the nature of the felony. *Faison v. State*, 426 So.2d 963 (Fla. 1983). In applying this rationale, a California appellate court held that moving a robber's victim across a room or from one room to another was an insufficient movement to meet the requirement for kidnapping. *People v. John*, 197 Cal. Rptr. 340 (Cal. App. 1983).

Federal Kidnapping Laws

Perhaps the most notorious kidnapping to have occurred in the United States was the abduction of the infant son of Charles A. Lindbergh, the "Lone Eagle" who, in 1927, made the first nonstop solo flight across the Atlantic Ocean. The Lindbergh baby was abducted from the family home in New Jersey in 1932. Bruno Richard Hauptmann was convicted of the crime after a spectacular trial and was executed in 1936. The Lindbergh kidnapping led to a demand for federal laws to enable the FBI to become involved in apprehending kidnappers. This, in turn, led to sweeping changes in state and federal laws on kidnapping. The Federal Kidnapping Act, commonly called the Lindbergh Law, provides, "Whoever unlawfully seizes, confines, inveigles, decoys, kidnaps, abducts, or carries away and holds for ransom or reward or otherwise any person, except in the case of a minor by a parent thereof . . . shall be punished by imprisonment." 18 U.S.C.A. § 1201(a). Subsection (b) of the statute raises a presumption that if the kidnapped victim is not returned within twenty-four hours after the taking, then the defendant did, in fact, take the victim across state lines. This presumption effectively allows the federal government to act promptly to bring federal agents into the investigation of an alleged kidnapping.

A recent federal statute makes **hostage taking** an offense. 18 U.S.C.A. § 1203. Other federal statutes make it a crime to knowingly receive, possess, or dispose of any money or property that has been delivered as ransom for a victim of a kidnapping, 18 U.S.C.A. § 1202, or for a bank robber to avoid apprehension by forcing someone to accompany him, 18 U.S.C.A. § 2113(e).

Defenses to Charges of False Imprisonment and Kidnapping

It is not false imprisonment for a person to detain another under authority of the law. Thus, an officer, or even a private citizen, who makes a lawful arrest or a jailer who detains a prisoner lawfully committed to custody is not guilty of an offense. Likewise, a parent who reasonably disciplines a child or a teacher who reasonably restrains a pupil would not be guilty of false imprisonment.

Consent can also be a defense to false imprisonment or kidnapping. Of course, the consent must not have been induced by threat, coercion, or misrepresentation and must have been given by a person competent to give consent. A person who relies on consent as a defense has the burden of establishing the validity of such consent.

Finally, as we have noted, a defendant may challenge whether there was sufficient movement of the victim to constitute the asportation element of kidnapping.

Child Snatching

In recent years, marital disputes have given rise to many serious problems concerning the custody of children of divorced or separated parents. It has been estimated that in excess of 300,000 children are abducted by family members each year. The term **child snatching** is now commonly applied to situations in which one parent deliberately retains or conceals a child from the other parent. The problem has resulted partly from the ability of one parent to seize a child from the custodial parent, travel to another state, and petition the court in the latter state for custody of the child.

In 1995 the Supreme Judicial Court of Maine affirmed the conviction of a father who took his children from their home, where their mother had equal legal custody rights. The evidence revealed the defendant's purpose was to keep the children away from their mother and to hold them in a place where they were not likely to be found. The court found this evidence sufficient to support the conviction of the father for violating a statute defining criminal restraint to include taking a child "from the custody of his other parent." *State v. Butt*, 656 A.2d 1225 (Me. 1995).

Most states have made child snatching a felony, thereby subjecting violators to extradition for prosecution in the state where the offense occurred. In addition, child snatching is now being curbed by several approaches:

- In many states, trial judges include a provision in a divorce judgment requiring court approval to remove a child from the state where the divorce is granted. Violation may subject the offending party to being held in contempt of court or, in some states, to be prosecuted for a felony.
- The **Uniform Child Custody Jurisdiction and Enforcement Act (UCCJEA)**, proposed in 1968 and now in force in all fifty states, generally continues jurisdiction for custody in the home or resident state of the child. Cooperation between the courts in the different states is becoming increasingly effective in preventing "judge shopping."
- In 1980 Congress enacted the **Parental Kidnapping Prevention Act (PKPA)**. The federal act is designed to prevent jurisdictional conflicts over child custody, and it takes precedence over any state law, including the UCCJA. Its primary goal is to reduce any incentive for parental child snatching.

CASE-IN-POINT

Rape and Kidnapping: Required Resistance in the Face of Threats

Late one night after leaving work, a woman responded to a request by two men to assist them in getting their car off the road. When she began to leave, both men grabbed her, ordered her into the back seat of the car, and threatened to kill her unless she cooperated. The men told her that they had escaped from prison and were holding her as a hostage. They then drove their victim to a tent, disrobed her, and forced her to submit to sexual acts with each of them. When they drove her back to her car the next morning, they told her that they would kill her if she reported the incident to the police.

The defendants were convicted of rape, kidnapping, and several other offenses. On appeal, they argued that the victim had cooperated in their endeavors; hence, they were not guilty of either rape or kidnapping. The Indiana Supreme Court rejected their contentions and explained that the resistance necessary to protect against sexual attack is dependent on all circumstances. Further, the court noted that a victim need not physically resist after being confronted with threats and being in fear of injury.

Ballard v. State, 385 N.E.2d 1126 (Ind. 1979).

- Federal and state governments, as well as religious and civic organizations and the media, have initiated programs for identifying children and for collecting and disseminating information on missing children.

Prosecuting international parental kidnapping presents additional problems, most notably the difficulties encountered in dealing with a foreign legal system.

Civil Rights Offenses

A category of offenses unknown to the common law involves injuries to the **civil rights** of individuals. After the Civil War, Congress adopted a series of laws designed to protect the civil rights of the newly freed former slaves. Today, these statutes as amended can be used to initiate federal prosecutions against individuals who conspire or use their official positions to deprive persons of rights guaranteed by the U.S. Constitution or the laws of the United States. The relevant provisions are as follows:

18 U.S.C.A. § 241. Conspiracy against rights

If two or more persons conspire to injure, oppress, threaten, or intimidate any inhabitant of any State, Territory, Commonwealth, Possession, or District in the free exercise or enjoyment of any right or privilege secured to him by the Constitution or laws of the United States, or because of his having so exercised the same; or

If two or more persons go in disguise on the highway, or on the premises of another, with intent to prevent or hinder his free exercise or enjoyment of any right or privilege so secured—

They shall be fined under this title or imprisoned not more than ten years, or both; and if death results from the acts committed in violation of this section or if such acts include kidnapping or an attempt to kidnap, aggravated sexual abuse or an attempt to commit aggravated sexual abuse, or an attempt to kill, they shall be fined under this title or imprisoned for any term of years or for life, or both, or may be sentenced to death.

18 U.S.C.A. § 242. Deprivation of rights under color of law

Whoever, under color of any law, statute, ordinance, regulation, or custom, willfully subjects any person in any State, Territory, or District to the deprivation of any rights, privileges, or immunities secured or protected by the Constitution or laws of the United States, or to different punishments, pains, or penalties, on account of such person being an alien, or by reason of his color, or race, than are prescribed for the punishment of citizens, shall be fined under this title or imprisoned not more than one year, or both; and if bodily injury results from the acts committed in violation of this section or if such acts include the use, attempted use, or threatened use of a dangerous weapon, explosives, or fire, shall be fined under this title or imprisoned not more than ten years, or both; and if death results from the acts committed in violation of this section or if such acts include kidnapping or an attempt to kidnap, aggravated sexual abuse, or an attempt to commit aggravated sexual abuse, or an attempt to kill, shall be fined under this title, or imprisoned for any term of years or for life, or both, or may be sentenced to death.

These statutes are used most frequently to prosecute in federal court individuals who engage in criminal acts that are racially motivated. Thus, although a conspiracy to commit arson may be prosecuted as such under state law, if it is racially motivated, it may also constitute a federal civil rights violation under 18 U.S.C.A. § 241. Instances of police brutality are sometimes prosecuted under 18 U.S.C.A. § 242. Increasingly, section 242 is being used to prosecute state officials who engage in other types of egregious conduct. See, e.g., *United States v. Lanier*, 520 U.S. 259, 117 S.Ct. 1219, 137 L.Ed.2d 432 (1997), the case described at the beginning of the chapter.

> The U.S. Supreme Court's decision in *United States v. Lanier* is excerpted on the companion website.

To be guilty of willfully depriving a person of constitutional rights under this section, the defendant's actions must be done under color of law; where use of force is involved, the force used must be unreasonable and unnecessary. *United States v. Stokes*, 506 F.2d 771 (5th Cir. 1975). As a result of judicial interpretation, federal civil rights laws now protect individuals from a wide range of injurious conduct by public officials or other persons acting under the authority of the government.

Among the most common types of civil rights offenses is the excessive use of force by police. In a highly publicized case in March 1991, four Los Angeles police officers were charged with the beating of Rodney King, an African American motorist who was stopped by the police after a high-speed automobile chase. After the officers were acquitted in a state court trial, highly destructive riots erupted in South Central Los Angeles. Federal authorities then prosecuted the officers under 18 U.S.C.A. § 242 for violating King's civil rights, in particular, his Fourth Amendment right to be free from an unreasonable seizure. In April 1993, two of the officers, Stacey Koon and Laurence Powell, were convicted and sentenced to prison; the two other officers were found not guilty. Their convictions were upheld by the U.S. Court of Appeals, *United States v. Koon*, 34 F.3d 1416 (9th Cir. 1994). (Later review by the Supreme Court was limited to issues regarding sentencing. *Koon v. United States*, 518 U.S. 81, 116 S.Ct. 2035, 135 L.Ed.2d 392 [1996].)

Hate Crimes

Hate crimes are offenses motivated by bias against a person's race, religion, nationality, gender, disability, or sexual orientation. Hate crimes can be offenses against property—for example, an instance of synagogue vandalism that is motivated by anti-Semitism. But most hate crimes are violent crimes against persons. In recent years there have been a number of highly publicized homicides where the only apparent motive was animus based on the victim's race, religion, gender, or sexual orientation. One of the most grisly such crimes was the racially motivated murder of James Byrd, Jr., in Jasper, Texas in 1998. Byrd, an African American, was chained by his ankles to the back of a pickup truck and dragged for three miles. He died when he was decapitated when his body struck a culvert. A Texas court sentenced two of the three white males convicted of Byrd's murder to death; the third was sentenced to life in prison.

Concerned about an apparent rise in hate crimes, Congress in 1990 enacted the Hate Crime Statistics Act, 28 U.S.C.A. § 534, which requires the U.S. Justice Department to acquire data on such offenses. In 2004 the Justice Department recorded 9,035 hate crimes nationwide. These included crimes against persons and property motivated by race, ethnicity, religion, sexual orientation, and disability. U.S. Department of Justice, Federal Bureau of Investigation, *Hate Crime Statistics*, 2004, FBI Uniform Crime Reports (Washington, D.C.: U.S. Department of Justice, 2005), p. 10. Interestingly, victims of hate crimes are most likely to be white and male (see Table 7.1).

Until recently, federal law limited federal prosecution of hate crimes to civil rights offenses under 18 U.S.C.A. § 245, which criminalizes interference with "federally protected activities" such as voting. But in 2009 Congress enacted the Matthew Shepard and James Byrd, Jr. Hate Crimes Prevention Act, 18 U.S.C.A. § 249, which eliminated the requirement that the victim be engaging in a federally protected activity. The new law also expanded federal hate crimes to include those motivated by a victim's actual or perceived gender, sexual orientation, gender identity, or disability.

Hate crimes are also subject to state legislation. For example, New Jersey Statutes section 16-1 provides, "A person is guilty of the crime of bias intimidation if he commits, attempts to commit, conspires with another to commit, or threatens the immediate commission of an offense specified [in certain chapters of New Jersey Statutes] (1) with a purpose to intimidate an individual or group of individuals because of race, color, religion, gender, handicap, sexual orientation, or ethnicity. . . ." The law goes on to provide for a grading of the offense and specifies that "the court shall impose separate sentences upon a conviction for bias intimidation and a conviction of any underlying offense."

Most states now have laws permitting courts to enhance criminal penalties when defendants are convicted of hate crimes. The Supreme Court has upheld hate crime laws of the penalty enhancement variety—see *Wisconsin v. Mitchell*, 508 U.S. 476, 113 S.Ct. 2194, 124 L.Ed.2d 436 (1993)—but it has also said that the factual question of whether a crime was motivated by animus against a particular group is an element

TABLE 7.1	Characteristics of Victims of Hate Crimes, 2000–2003	
Gender		
Male	55.4%	
Female	44.6%	
Race		
White	85.0%	
Blace	9.5%	
Other	5.8%	
Age		
Under 18	18.8%	
18–29	27.4%	
30–49	37.3%	
50 or older	16.5%	

Source: Adapted from Bureau of Justice Statistics Special Report, "Hate Crime Reported by Victims and Police," Table 13. U.S. Department of Justice, Office of Special Programs, November 2005, NCJ 209911.

of the crime that must be proved beyond a reasonable doubt. In a jury trial, this question must be submitted to the jury. *Apprendi v. New Jersey*, 530 U.S. 466, 120 S.Ct. 2348, 147 L.Ed.2d 435 (2000).

Conclusion

Over the centuries the assaultive, sexual, and detention crimes have been a stable base for prosecuting persons whose antisocial conduct offended the basic norms of civilized people. Yet laws must change to cope with the economic, social, and cultural needs of a dynamic society. In addition to the well-known offenses involving persons, in this chapter we have attempted to broaden the scope of the usual coverage of crimes against persons by explaining the impact of newer offenses such as stalking; abuse of children, spouses, and the elderly; and child snatching, as well as federal laws concerning violations of civil rights, which have become integral parts of the criminal justice system.

Chapter Summary

- **LO1** The common law treated assault and battery as separate misdemeanors with an assault consisting of an offer to do bodily harm to another by using force and violence and a battery consisting of a completed assault. Today all jurisdictions make assault an offense; most classify simple assaults and batteries as misdemeanors, while grading as felonies those perpetrated against public officers or involving more egregious conduct (aggravated assault, aggravated battery, and assault with intent to commit a serious crime). Most prosecutions occur under state laws, but federal statutes proscribe assaults within the maritime and territorial jurisdiction of the United States and assaults on federal officers, military personnel engaged in official duties, and foreign diplomatic personnel.
- **LO2** At common law, mayhem consisted of willfully and maliciously injuring another so as to render the victim less able in fighting. Mayhem became a statutory crime in most states, but most of the acts formerly prosecuted under mayhem statutes now result in prosecutions for aggravated battery and attempted murder.
- **LO3** Hazing consists of intentional or reckless physical or mental harassment, abuse, or humiliation and frequently occurs in initiations into clubs, fraternities, sororities, athletic teams, and other groups. Although most hazing involves foolish pranks and seldom results in serious injuries, most states have laws make hazing in all schools and colleges either a misdemeanor or felony, depending on the degree of injury to the initiate. Hazing laws usually stipulate that implied or express consent by the initiate is not a defense. Statutes in all states now proscribe the offense of stalking. It is usually defined as consisting of repeatedly following, watching, or harassing another person. Federal law proscribes interstate stalking. Generally, stalking is a misdemeanor while aggravated stalking involving physical injury to a victim is a felony. Most statutes either proscribe electronic forms of stalking or include it in their statutory definitions of stalking. Where courts have found constitutional infirmities in stalking statutes, legislatures have revised laws to make definitions more precise.
- **LO4** Under early English common law it was a felony for a male to have unlawful carnal knowledge of a female by force and against her will. Rape required *unlawful* intercourse; consequently, a husband could not be guilty of raping his

wife. The law of rape required penetration, however slight, of the female's sexual organ by the male's sexual organ; no emission of seed was required. During the late 1970s and the 1980s, protests led to reforms that focused on making rape a gender-neutral offense embracing all anal, oral, or vaginal penetrations by a sex organ or by another object, excepting acts performed for *bona fide* medical purposes, and dividing the offense of sexual battery into categories. In many states, either by statutes or judicial decisions, a husband may be charged with rape of his wife. A significant reform was the enactment of rape shield laws that preclude presentation of evidence of a victim's prior sexual activity with anyone other than the defendant. Even where the defendant seeks to introduce evidence of prior relations with a victim, such evidence must usually be first presented to the court *in camera* to determine its relevancy to the victim's consent. Appellate courts still disagree on the admissibility of evidence of expert evidence regarding the rape trauma syndrome. Courts no longer insist that a woman must "resist to the utmost" to establish that her sexual privacy has been violated. Neither do they instruct juries to scrutinize a victim's testimony. Marriage in contemporary society is regarded as a partnership and not as a license to enjoy sex on demand by a forcible encounter. Because a prosecution for rape frequently involves the victim's word against the defendant's word, police and prosecutors place paramount importance on a "fresh complaint" by a victim. Preservation of semen, photographs of bruises, torn clothing, and even pubic hairs become valuable evidence to corroborate a victim's testimony. Beyond a general denial of the charges, the most common defense asserted in a rape case is that the victim consented. Impotency is sometimes asserted but it is rarely accepted as a defense.

- **LO5** At common law a male under age fourteen was conclusively presumed not to be able to commit rape. It later became statutory rape for a male to have carnal knowledge of a female child under age ten with or without the child's consent. American courts generally followed the English common law but early on states explicitly rejected the common law presumption that males under age fourteen could not commit rape and determined that consensual intercourse with a female younger than sixteen or eighteen, rather than ten, was statutory rape. A few states have allowed a male to defend against a charge of statutory rape on the basis that he was mistaken about a female's age, but most hold a male defendant strictly liable. Most statutory rape laws are now gender neutral. Some impose penalties only if there is at least a two- to five-year disparity between the ages of the perpetrator and the underage victim. There is universal agreement that very young children should be protected from sexual predators, but there is considerable opposition to statutory rape laws. Opponents argue that these laws are out of touch with present-day sexual mores, deprive women in their late teens of exercising a personal choice, and lend themselves to selective enforcement along the lines of race and social class.

- **LO6** Sodomy refers to oral or anal sex between humans and sexual intercourse between humans and animals. (The latter is often termed bestiality.) Consensual sodomy was formerly viewed as an offense against public morality, but in 2003 the U.S. Supreme Court found unconstitutional a Texas law that proscribed private, consensual sodomy between same-sex partners. This sounded the death knell for laws prohibiting consensual sodomy. Nonconsensual sodomy is considered a crime against a person and is often charged under statutes proscribing sexual battery.

- **LO7** To protect children from sexual predators, states now require sexual offenders who are released from prison, move into a state, or simply change their address to register with local law enforcement agencies. These laws have survived a variety of constitutional attacks.

- **LO8** Recently, Congress and state legislatures have enacted laws designed to protect from abuse children, spouses, other intimate partners, and, in some instances, the elderly. Many offenses against children are subject to traditional crimes against persons, yet many states have enacted specific child abuse laws to cover a broader range of abusive behaviors and violence against children, which are prosecuted as strict liability offenses. Prosecutions for maternal conduct before a birth—for example, ingestion of harmful drugs—are problematical under child abuse/endangerment or drug distribution statutes. Many states have enacted laws to provide for issuance of court injunctions to protect spouses and intimate partners from domestic violence and provide for the arrest of violators. Federal courts have upheld the constitutionality of the federal crime bill, which criminalizes interstate abuses of spouses and intimate partners. Abuse of the elderly is usually handled through regulatory agencies, but some state legislatures have made it a felony in order to punish caregivers who abuse, neglect, or exploit elderly persons.

- **LO9** In recognition of the need to protect an individual's freedom of movement, the common law developed two misdemeanor offenses: false imprisonment and kidnapping. False imprisonment consisted of confining someone against his or her will, whereas kidnapping involved forcibly abducting and taking a person to another country. Today, most cases of false imprisonment involve civil litigation, but where states make it a misdemeanor they generally define it, as did the common law, as "the unlawful detention of a person."

- **LO10** Kidnapping is a serious felony proscribed by all states and by federal law. Unlike the common law, where kidnapping required that the victim be taken to another country, federal and state statutes generally require that there be "an unlawful taking and forcible carrying away (asportation) of a victim without that person's consent." Intimidation and coercion can substitute for force. Consent must be voluntarily given. Young children and incompetents cannot legally consent to an act of asportation. Courts generally do not allow movement incidental to another crime that does not involve additional significant risk to the victim to fulfill the asportation requirement. The Federal Kidnapping Act criminalizes interstate kidnapping for ransom. A recent federal statute makes hostage taking an offense. Most defenses to false imprisonment or kidnapping contend the acts were done as authorized by law. Defendants charged with kidnapping often challenge whether there has been proper asportation.

- **LO11** A category of offenses unknown to the common law involves injuries to the civil rights of individuals. After the Civil War, Congress adopted a series of laws designed to protect the civil rights of the newly freed former slaves. As a result of judicial interpretation, federal civil rights laws now protect individuals from a wide range of injurious conduct by public officials or other persons acting under the authority of the government. Today, these statutes are also used to prosecute individuals who conspire to use their official positions to deprive persons of rights guaranteed by the U.S. Constitution or federal laws and to prosecute individuals who engage in criminal acts that are racially motivated and police who use excessive force.

- **LO12** Hate crimes are motivated by bias against members of certain groups. Until recently, federal law limited federal prosecution of hate crimes to interference with "federally protected activities." In 2009 Congress enacted the Matthew Shepard and James Byrd, Jr., Hate Crimes Prevention Act, which eliminated this requirement and expanded federal hate crimes to include those motivated by a victim's actual or perceived gender, sexual orientation, gender identity, or disability. Hate crimes are also subject to state legislation, which often takes the form of enhancing criminal penalties for persons convicted of crimes motivated by bias.

Key Terms

assault The attempt to inflict bodily injury upon another person.

battery The unlawful use of force against another person that entails some injury or offensive touching.

aggravated assault An assault committed with a dangerous weapon or with intent to commit a felony.

aggravated battery A battery committed by use of an instrument designed to inflict great bodily harm on the victim.

mayhem At common law, the crime of injuring someone so as to render that person less able to fight.

hazing Intentional or reckless physical or mental harassment, abuse, or humiliation, often as part of an initiation.

stalking Following or placing a person under surveillance and threatening that person with bodily harm, sexual assault, confinement, or restraint, or placing that person in reasonable fear of bodily harm, sexual assault, confinement, or restraint.

cyberstalking Harassing and threatening a person through persistent online contact so that the person is placed in fear for his or her safety.

carnal knowledge An antiquated term for sexual intercourse.

common-law rape Rape as it was defined by the English common law, i.e., sexual intercourse by a male with a female, other than his wife, by force and against the will of the female.

forcible rape Sexual intercourse by force and against the will of the victim.

statutory rape The strict liability offense of having sexual intercourse with a minor, irrespective of the minor's consent.

marital exception The traditional common-law principle that a husband could not be guilty of raping his wife.

Hale's Rule English common law doctrine credited to Sir Matthew Hale, Lord Chief Justice in the seventeenth century, holding that a husband could not be charged with the rape of his wife

force The element of compulsion in such crimes against persons as rape and robbery.

consent Voluntarily yielding to the will or desire of another person.

gender-neutral offense A crime that may be committed by members of either sex against members of either sex.

rape shield laws Statutes that protect the identity of a rape victim and/or prevent disclosure of a victim's sexual history.

sexual penetration Sexual intercourse, cunnilingus, fellatio, anal intercourse, or any other intrusion, however slight, of any part of a person's body or any object into the genital or anal openings of another person's body.

sexual contact The intentional touching of the victim's intimate parts or the intentional touching of the clothing covering the immediate area of the victim's intimate parts, if that intentional touching can reasonably be construed as being for the purpose of sexual arousal or gratification.

rape trauma syndrome A recurring pattern of physical and emotional symptoms experienced by rape victims.

Megan's Law Name applied to statutes that require convicted sex offenders, upon release from prison, to register with local law enforcement agencies. (The statute was named in memory of Megan Kanka, who died in 1994 at the hands of a released offender.)

impotency Lacking in power; in reference to a male, the inability to achieve an erection.

sodomy Oral or anal sex between persons or sex between a person and an animal. The latter act is commonly referred to as bestiality.

child abuse Actions that physically, mentally, or emotionally endanger the welfare of a child.

endangering the welfare of a child Knowingly acting in a manner likely to be injurious to the physical, mental, or moral welfare of a child.

spousal abuse Physical, emotional, or sexual abuse of one's husband or wife.

abuse of the elderly Infliction of physical or mental harm on elderly persons.

false imprisonment Also known as false arrest, this is the tort or crime of unlawfully restraining a person.

kidnapping The forcible abduction and carrying away of a person against that person's will.

asportation The carrying away of something; in kidnapping, the carrying away of the victim; in larceny, the carrying away of the victim's property.

simple kidnapping The abduction of another person without a demand for ransom.

kidnapping for ransom The offense of unlawfully taking and confining a person until a specified payment is made to the offender.

hostage taking The act in which the perpetrator of a robbery or some other crime forcibly detains innocent bystanders.

child snatching Action taken by one parent to deliberately retain or conceal a child from the other parent.

Uniform Child Custody Jurisdiction and Enforcement Act (UCCJEA) A law in force in all fifty states that generally continues jurisdiction for custody of children in the home or resident state of the child.

Parental Kidnapping Prevention Act (PKPA) A federal act adopted in 1980 designed to prevent jurisdictional conflicts over child custody matters. The primary goal of the statute is to reduce any incentive for parental child snatching.

civil rights In general, this term refers to all the rights protected by the federal and state constitutions and statutes. The term is often used to denote the right to be free from unlawful discrimination.

hate crimes Crimes in which the victim is selected on the basis of race, ethnicity, religion, gender, or sexual orientation.

Questions for Thought and Discussion

1. What elements, in addition to those required for assault or battery, must the prosecution prove to convict a defendant of aggravated assault or battery?
2. What interests does the law seek to protect in proscribing (a) forcible rape and (b) statutory rape?
3. Which statutory and judicial reforms of the 1970s and 1980s in the law of rape were the most significant from a female victim's standpoint? Are there other biases against female victims of sexual assault that should be addressed?
4. Does Hale's Rule, which creates a marital exception in the law of rape, apply in your state?
5. What role do the Uniform Child Custody Jurisdiction and Enforcement Act (UCCJEA) and the Parental Kidnapping Prevention Act (PKPA) play in controlling child snatching?
6. Do the federal statutes that make it unlawful to deprive persons of their civil rights under color of law have a significant deterrent effect on misconduct of law enforcement personnel? Or do these statutes hamper effective police action?
7. Explain the necessity for the prosecution to prove asportation in order to establish the offense of kidnapping.
8. Why have most state courts rejected prosecution of a mother whose child suffers adverse medical effects from the mother's ingestion of cocaine during her pregnancy?
9. Assume you are a staff member of a state criminal justice agency. The director asks you to compose a draft of a statute to prohibit endangerment to children. What key points would you include in your draft?

Problems for Discussion and Solution

1. Daniel grabbed a large stick and in a threatening manner advanced toward William. Before he came within striking distance of William, a third party stopped him. Based on this evidence is it likely that Daniel will be found guilty of assault?
2. A state law defines false imprisonment as "the intentional restraint of another person without lawful authority." Alan drove his girlfriend, Olivia, to the shopping mall. He insisted she wait in the car while he shopped. When she protested he locked the car and was gone for forty-five minutes. Olivia filed a complaint with the police. Is it likely that the state will prosecute Alan for false imprisonment?
3. A store manager observes Lucy Grabit stuffing a pair of nylon hose into her purse before going through the checkout counter in a supermarket. The manager detains her and promptly directs his employee to call the police. Is the store manager guilty of false imprisonment? Why or why not?
4. Several college freshmen enter the dean's private office and remain there for several hours. They refuse to let the dean leave until he yields to their demands to allow unrestricted visitation in all dormitories. Under contemporary criminal statutes, what offense, if any, have the students committed? Explain.
5. The defendant was convicted of battery under a statute that provides that "a person commits a battery who either intentionally or knowingly, and without legal justification, makes physical contact of an insulting or provoking nature with an individual." The evidence disclosed that one morning the male defendant picked up a female friend whom he had invited to have breakfast with him. En route to the restaurant he unbuttoned her blouse and placed his hand on her breast; after

she removed his hand and asked him to stop, he again placed his hand on her breast. On appeal, the defendant argues that his conviction should be reversed because his acts were not insulting, there was no struggle, and the female did not testify that she was traumatized or disturbed by his acts. Moreover, he points out that the evidence disclosed that after the incident the female complainant accompanied him to a restaurant where they had breakfast together. Should the appellate court reverse this conviction on the ground that the evidence is insufficient? Why or why not?

6. The defendant and her husband have two sons, ages five and three. Without notifying her husband, the defendant left the family home with both children. At that time, no court proceedings were pending concerning either their marriage or custody of their children. Two weeks later, and without the wife's knowledge, the husband obtained a court order granting him custody of the two children. An arrest warrant was eventually issued for the wife. She was arrested in another state and brought back to her home state, where she now faces prosecution under a statute that provides, "Whoever, being a relative of a child . . . without lawful authority, holds or intends to hold such a child permanently or for a protracted period, or takes or entices a child from his lawful custodian . . . shall be guilty of a felony." The wife's attorney stipulates that the facts are correct as stated but contends the wife cannot be convicted of parental kidnapping under the quoted statute. What result do you think should occur? Why?

7. A nineteen-year-old woman returns home from an evening at the beach. She tells her mother that she has been raped and sodomized by an attacker she does not know. Some hours later, the woman identifies her attacker to her mother, and they notify the police. At trial, the prosecution seeks to admit expert testimony on rape trauma syndrome to explain the victim's reticence in promptly identifying her attacker. The defense objects. Should the court allow expert testimony on this subject to explain the reactions of the female victim in the hours following her attack and to explain why she may initially have been unwilling to report the defendant who attacked her? Why or why not?

CHAPTER 8

Property Crimes

LEARNING OBJECTIVES

After reading this chapter, you should be able to explain . . .

1. how the common-law theft offenses have evolved under modern statutory law to include sophisticated forms of theft
2. why robbery is considered more heinous than other property crimes
3. why Congress created the offense of carjacking
4. how extortion differs from robbery
5. how forgery differs from passing a worthless check
6. how and why burglary is defined more broadly today than it was under the common law
7. why arson is no longer merely an offense against habitation
8. how malicious mischief can be either a misdemeanor or a felony
9. the defenses against prosecution for property crimes

Key Terms

Questions for Thought and Discussion

Problems for Discussion and Solution

In March 2010, Robert Halderman pleaded guilty in a New York courtroom to the crime of extortion. His was far from a run-of-the-mill property crime. Halderman, who worked as a producer at CBS, apparently uncovered information about the private life of late-night comic David Letterman. Halderman then demanded $2 million from Letterman in exchange for not revealing the information. Halderman presented the extortion threat under the guise of a "treatment," which is industry jargon for an idea for a television program. Appearing to give in to the threat, Letterman's attorney delivered a bogus $2 million check to Halderman. Reading from a prepared statement in court, Halderman acknowledged that the treatment he presented "was just a thinly veiled threat to ruin Mr. Letterman if he did not pay me a lot of money." He also admitted, "I knew throughout this time that I was not engaged in a legitimate business transaction with Mr. Letterman and that what I was doing was against New York law."

The statute under which Halderman was convicted, N.Y. Penal Law §155.05(2), provides, in relevant part, that a person commits extortion when "he compels or induces another person to deliver . . . property to himself or to a third person by means of instilling in him a fear that, if the property is not so delivered, the actor or another will . . . expose a secret or publicize an asserted fact, whether true or false, tending to subject some person to hatred, contempt or ridicule. . . ." Like most of the property crimes discussed in this chapter, extortion is rooted in the English common law, but it has become a broader offense under modern statutes.

As part of a plea bargain with prosecutors, Robert Halderman agreed to plead guilty to extortion and publicly admit responsibility for the crime. He was sentenced to six months in jail and one thousand hours of community service. Under New York law, he could have faced a prison term of up to fifteen years.

Introduction

Private property is a basic value of American society and a fundamental tenet of American law. In early America, property interests beyond raw land were often meager, consisting primarily of possessions necessary for survival. Most people's dwellings were modest. At that time, enforcement of the law largely depended on "self-help." As the nation developed, property interests became a vital part of the American economy, and professional law enforcement became the rule rather than the exception. The law recognized the need to deter people from infringing on the property interests of others and to punish transgressors. In today's affluent society and with the rapid technological advances of the past few decades, crimes against property have assumed even greater significance. In this chapter we examine the background of basic common-law property and habitation offenses and provide a sampling of the present-day statutory crimes in this area.

The Common-Law Background

When the common law emerged, England was an agrarian country with relatively little commercial activity. Possession of private property was an important concept, but beyond the right to occupy a dwelling, the property interests of most people consisted largely of what the law refers to as **tangible property** (such things as animals, cooking implements, and tools). Today, in addition to tangible property (such as automobiles, household goods, and books), a majority of households own some intangible property, such as bank accounts, stocks, bonds, and notes. Thus, in contrast to the early common-law period, intangible assets are now of great economic importance.

The common-law offenses involving property reflect the environment in which they matured. It was a very serious offense for someone to permanently deprive another of the possession of personal property, whether through stealth or through force, violence, or intimidation. However, it was of far less consequence to cheat someone by the use of false tokens or false weights and measures. When it came to such breaches of ethics as misrepresentations and violations of trust, the common law generally left victims to their civil remedies. This view gave rise to such early maxims as *caveat emptor*, meaning, "let the buyer beware." Because commercial transactions were not a major concern, forgery remained a misdemeanor. Likewise, extortion and malicious mischief were misdemeanors, because the conduct involved in these offenses did not qualify for the severe punishment meted out for felonies. Finally, offenses concerning the rights of landholders were dealt with largely through the civil law.

The Common-Law Theft Offenses

By 1776 the English common law recognized two offenses dealing with theft: larceny and false pretenses. Theft offenses of embezzlement and receiving stolen property were later created by statutes passed by the English Parliament.

Larceny

The basic common-law offense against infringement of another's personal property was **larceny**, the crime from which all other theft offenses developed. Larceny was a felony that consisted of (1) the wrongful taking and carrying away of (2) the personal property of another (3) with the intent to permanently deprive the other person of the property. The taking was called the "caption," the carrying away was called the "asportation," and the personal property had to have a "corporeal" (that is, a physical) existence. The wrongful act of taking was described as a "trespass," and the intent to permanently deprive the victim of the property was known as the *animus furundi*. Although many of these terms are not in common use today, the reader will find that courts frequently use them in judicial opinions when interpreting modern-day theft statutes.

To constitute common-law larceny, the taking had to be a deprivation of the owner or possessor's interest in personal property. Real estate and the property attached to it were not subject to larceny; neither were trees nor crops wrongfully severed from the land. But if the owner of property had already severed crops and a thief carried them away, it was larceny because the thief was carrying away personal property rather than merely infringing on the owner's real property.

These distinctions are difficult to appreciate today, but they were significant in the development of the common law, where wrongs concerning a person's land gave rise to civil, as opposed to criminal, remedies. Also, at common law, anyone wrongfully deprived of possession of personal property was entitled to recover damages based on the tort (civil wrong) of conversion. Thus, there was overlap between the crime of larceny and the tort of conversion.

As the common law developed, personal property consisted largely of tools, household items, and domestic animals. Items such as promissory notes were not subject to larceny because they represented intangible legal rights; however, coins and bills were, because they had a physical existence.

A taking by a person who had a lawful right to possession was not larceny. As we will discuss later, this led Parliament to legislatively create the crime of embezzlement. Because the property had to be taken from another, a co-owner or partner did not commit larceny by taking jointly owned property. Nor did a spouse commit larceny by taking the other spouse's property, because at common law, both spouses were considered one entity.

To find an accused guilty of larceny, it was necessary to prove that the taker carried the property away. This element was usually satisfied by even a slight removal of the property. It was also essential to prove the taker's intent to permanently deprive the owner or possessor of the property. A person could not be convicted for borrowing property, or for using property under a reasonable belief of a right of possession. Consequently, a person who temporarily took another's horse would not be guilty of larceny because there was no intent to permanently deprive the owner of the horse. Furthermore, had someone taken a horse that reasonably appeared to be the taker's own, the taker would likely have been acting under a *bona fide* mistake of fact and hence would not have been guilty of larceny. (See Chapter 14 for a discussion of the mistake-of-fact defense.) Yet a person who secured possession of goods through trickery could be found guilty of larceny if there was proof that the trickster intended to permanently deprive the owner of the goods.

False Pretenses, Embezzlement, and Receiving Stolen Property

Many technical and often subtle distinctions developed in the common-law crime of larceny. Perhaps one reason for this was that courts were reluctant to find a thief guilty of larceny because the penalty at early common law was death. As commerce became more significant in England, the crime of larceny was not adequate either to deal with those who obtained financial advantage through false pretenses or to deter or punish servants who fraudulently appropriated property that rightfully came into their possession. Consequently, by the late 1700s, the English Parliament created two supplemental misdemeanor offenses: **false pretenses** and embezzlement. The offense of false pretenses came into being in 1757, before the American Revolution. The offense thereby became a part of the common law of those states that adopted it with the statutory modifications made by Parliament before the American Revolution. **Embezzlement**, on the other hand, did not become a statutory crime until an enactment by Parliament in 1799. Although as early as 1691 a receiver of stolen goods could be prosecuted as an accessory after the fact to larceny, not until 1827 did Parliament enact a statute making receiving stolen property a misdemeanor. Thus, embezzlement and receiving stolen property became English laws too late to become part of the common law adopted by the new American states. By subsequent enactments, the English Parliament broadened the scope of embezzlement.

A charge of false pretenses (actually, "obtaining property by false pretenses") usually involves (1) the accused obtaining wares or merchandise of another (2) by false pretenses and (3) with the intent to cheat or defraud the other person.

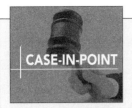

CASE-IN-POINT

Receiving Stolen Property: Sufficient Evidence to Convict

Defendant Lynn Belt was convicted of receiving stolen property in violation of Utah Code Ann. 76–6–408 (1) (Supp. 1989), which makes it a crime for a person to receive property of another "knowing that it has been stolen or believing that it probably has been stolen . . . with a purpose to deprive the owner thereof." Belt appealed, contending the evidence was legally insufficient to support his conviction. The evidence revealed that the defendant purchased videocassette recorders from Sgt. Illsley of the Metro Major Felony Unit during an undercover operation involving the purchase and sale of stolen property. Defendant met Illsley at an empty parking lot, where Illsley offered the new recorders to the defendant at a very low price, explaining that the store name and serial numbers had been cut off. Defendant replied, "I don't want to hear about the serial number or store names—just do our business." Illsley testified that at one point the defendant said, "I wish you wouldn't cut the serial numbers off. That makes it look hot." The Court of Appeals of Utah held that the evidence was sufficient for the jury to have found that the defendant believed the goods he purchased were stolen and affirmed Belt's conviction.

State v. Belt, 780 P.2d 1271 (Utah App. 1989).

Parliament's enactment of the offense of false pretenses during the Industrial Revolution represented an important development in the English criminal law. Because false pretenses became an offense just before the American Revolution, few English court decisions interpreting this offense became a part of the common law adopted by the new American states. Even so, the English law in this area influenced both American legislation and judicial decisions.

In contrast with larceny, embezzlement occurred where an accused who had lawful possession of another's property (for example, a servant or employee) wrongfully appropriated the property. A series of enactments by the English Parliament brought not only servants but also brokers, bankers, lawyers, and trustees within the scope of embezzlement. Thus, an embezzlement occurred when someone occupying a position of trust converted another's property to his or her own use, whereas larceny required proof of a wrongful taking and carrying away of the personal property of another. Nevertheless, to convict a defendant of embezzlement, it was necessary to prove that the accused intended to defraud the victim. **Receiving stolen property** consisted of receiving possession and control of another's personal property knowing it was stolen and with the intent to permanently deprive the owner of possession of such property.

The Modern Approach to Theft Offenses

A review of the various technical distinctions that developed in the common-law offenses of larceny, receiving stolen property, and false pretenses and the early statutory offenses of embezzlement and receiving stolen property makes it obvious that significant reforms were needed. A redefinition of these basic property offenses was required to cope with the various aspects of theft in American society. Modern theft includes not only forms of larceny known to the common law but also theft of vehicles, shoplifting, looting, carjacking, extortion, and other sophisticated forms of theft (see Figure 8.1). We deal with the more sophisticated forms of larceny in Chapter 9 under the heading of "white-collar crimes."

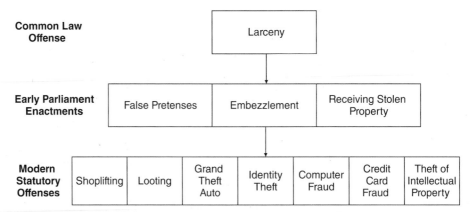

FIGURE 8.1 Evolution of Theft Offenses.

Federal Approaches

Congress has enacted a series of statutes comprehensively proscribing theft and embezzlement. The first, 18 U.S.C.A. § 641, provides,

> Whoever embezzles, steals, purloins, or knowingly converts to his use or the use of another, or without authority, sells, conveys or disposes of any record, voucher, money, or thing of value of the United States or any department or agency thereof, or any property made or being made under contract for the United States or any department or agency thereof; or
>
> Whoever receives, conceals, or retains the same with intent to convert it to his use or gain, knowing it to have been embezzled, stolen, purloined or converted; . . .
>
> Shall be fined. . . .

The purpose of 18 U.S.C.A. § 641 is to place in one part of the criminal code crimes so kindred as to belong in one category. The Supreme Court has said that despite the failure of Congress to include expressly the common-law intent requirement for larceny, section 641 should not be construed to eliminate that intent requirement. The statute has been held to apply not only to larceny and embezzlement, but also to all instances in which a person may obtain wrongful advantage from another's property. *Morissette v. United States*, 342 U.S. 246, 72 S.Ct. 240, 96 L.Ed. 288 (1952).

Another federal statute, 18 U.S.C.A. § 659, provides penalties for embezzling or unlawfully taking the contents of any vehicle moving in interstate or foreign commerce or from any passenger therein. Federal appellate courts have characterized the intent requirement under this statute as the intent to appropriate or convert the property of the owner. Furthermore, the federal appellate courts have said that a simultaneous intent to return the property or make restitution does not make the offense any less embezzlement. See, for example, *United States v. Waronek*, 582 F.2d 1158 (7th Cir. 1978).

A variety of other federal statutes define embezzlement and theft by public officers or employees of the United States, custodians of federal funds, bank examiners, and bank officers and employees. See 18 U.S.C.A. §§ 641–665. During the 1990s Congress added statutes creating new offenses involving theft. These included theft from programs involving federal funds, theft of livestock and artwork, and theft or embezzlement in connection with health care. 18 U.S.C.A. §§ 666–669.

State Approaches

All states have enacted statutes expanding the common-law concept of larceny to include all types of tangible and intangible property. Historically, the states maintained numerous statutes that adopted the basic concepts of common-law larceny and false pretenses as well as the later English statutes proscribing embezzlement and receiving stolen property. As new problems developed, legislative bodies attempted to fill the gaps by creating new offenses. This resulted in the legislative creation of numerous statutory offenses proscribing various forms of stealing and dishonest dealings. These statutes often were confusing and in many instances were contradictory.

In recent years, many states have replaced their various theft statutes with a consolidated theft statute that proscribes stealing in very broad terms. These new statutes make it unlawful for a person to commit any of the common-law theft offenses mentioned, as well as other crimes, and impose penalties based on the amount and character of the property stolen.

Florida, for example, passed the Florida Anti-Fencing Act in 1977. Despite its narrow title, the act defines theft as including all the common-law theft offenses, several former statutory offenses, possession of property with altered or removed identifying features, and dealing in stolen property (that is, fencing). As do other modern theft statutes, the statute defines theft by degrees based on the seriousness of the offender's conduct. West's Fla. Stat. Ann. § 812.012–037. Section 812.014(1) provides,

> A person commits theft if he or she knowingly obtains or uses, or endeavors to obtain or to use, the property of another with intent to, either temporarily or permanently:
> (a) Deprive the other person of a right to the property or a benefit from the property.
> (b) Appropriate the property to his or her own use or to the use of any person not entitled to the use of the property.

Under the comprehensive Florida theft statute, the phrase "obtains or uses" replaces the old common-law requirement of "taking and carrying away." The law defines "obtains or uses" as

> any manner of (a) taking or exercising control over property; (b) making any unauthorized use, disposition, or transfer of property; (c) obtaining property by fraud, willful misrepresentation of a future act, or false promise; or (d) by conduct previously known as stealing, larceny, purloining, abstracting, embezzlement, misapplication, misappropriation, conversion, or obtaining money or property by false pretenses, fraud, or deception; or (e) other conduct similar in nature. § 812.012(1)(2).

"Property" is broadly defined to include "(a) Real property, including things growing on, affixed to, and found in land; (b) Tangible or intangible personal property, including rights, privileges, interests, and claims; and (c) Services." § 812.012(4).

"Property of another" means "property in which a person has an interest upon which another person is not privileged to infringe without consent, whether or not the other person has an interest in the property." § 812.012(5).

"Services" means "anything of value resulting from a person's physical or mental labor or skill, or from the use, possession, or presence of property, and includes: (a) Repairs or improvements to property. (b) Professional services. (c) Private, public, or government communication, transportation, power, water, or sanitation services. (d) Lodging accommodations. (e) Admissions to places of exhibition or entertainment." § 812.012(6).

The value and type of property stolen categorize the seriousness of the offense. **Grand theft** in the first degree is the most serious felony. It includes stealing property valued at $100,000 or more or cargo valued at $50,000 or more, as well as committing any grand theft in the course of which the offender uses a motor vehicle as an instrumentality, other than merely as a getaway vehicle, to assist in committing the offense and thereby damages the real property of another or causes damage to the real or personal property of another in excess of $1,000. § 812.014(2)(a)(b).

Grand theft in the second degree, a somewhat less serious felony, involves theft of property valued at $20,000 or more but less than $100,000, cargo valued at less than $50,000, or emergency medical equipment or law enforcement equipment valued at $300 or more. § 812.014(2)(b). It is grand theft in the third degree, and a lesser felony, if the property stolen is valued at $300 or more but less than $20,000, or if the property stolen is a will, codicil, or other testamentary instrument; firearm; motor vehicle; livestock; fire extinguisher; 2,000 or more pieces of citrus fruit; a stop sign; property taken from an identified construction site; or anhydrous ammonia. § 812.014(2) (c). If the property stolen is valued at $100 or more but less than $300 and is taken from a dwelling or from the unenclosed curtilage of a dwelling, the offense is also classified as a third-degree felony. § 812.014(2)(d). Otherwise, except for the specified articles, theft of property having a value under $300 is petit theft, a misdemeanor. § 812.014 (2)(e).

Finally, a person previously convicted of theft who commits **petit theft** is guilty of a more serious misdemeanor, § 812.014(3)(b). One who has been convicted of theft two or more times commits a felony of the third degree, § 812.014(3)(c). Special penalties include suspension of the driver's license of a person who drives away from a filling station without paying for gasoline, § 812.014(5). Penalties are also upgraded where the victim of theft is over age 65. § 812.0145.

Theft remains a specific-intent crime, but like many newer theft statutes, the Florida statute simply refers to the **intent to deprive**. The Florida Supreme Court has said this means the "intent to steal" and not necessarily the intent to permanently deprive the owner of the property. *State v. Dunmann*, 427 So.2d 166 (Fla. 1983). Because the statutory definition of theft includes an endeavor to commit theft, the crime is fully proved when an attempt, along with the requisite intent, is established. *State v. Sykes*, 434 So.2d 325 (Fla. 1983) (see Chapter 5).

An excerpt from *State v. Richard*, a decision of the Nebraska Supreme Court dealing with shoplifting, is reproduced on the companion website.

CASE-IN-POINT

Larceny Committed through a Phony Night-Deposit Box

A Massachusetts jury convicted Brian Donovan and Robert Grant of larceny. Evidence introduced at trial showed that they had constructed a phony night-deposit box and attached it to the wall of a bank building. The box was constructed of heavy-gauge steel just like a real depository. Seven depositors lost an estimated $37,000 by making deposits to the phony box. Although the phony box was never recovered, a witness testified that he overheard the defendants in a bar talking about the phony deposit box as "a helluva'n idea." Another witness stated that Grant had admitted to her that he had robbed a bank using a phony deposit box. On appeal, the Massachusetts Supreme Court rejected the defendants' contentions that certain testimony had been improperly admitted into evidence and that the evidence produced at trial was legally insufficient to prove the crime of larceny.

Commonwealth v. Donovan, 478 N.E.2d 727 (Mass. 1985).

A Unique Prosecutorial Burden in Theft Offenses

Except where statutorily specified articles are stolen, theft offenses are usually classified as grand theft or petit theft. Statutes commonly grade the felony and misdemeanor offenses based on ranges of market value of goods stolen. Therefore, the prosecution must establish the market value of goods or services stolen. The determining factor is generally the market value at the time and in the locality of the theft. *State v. Kimbel*, 620 P.2d 515 (Utah 1980). This may be shown by proof of the original market cost, the manner in which the property stolen has been used, and its general condition and quality. *Negron v. State*, 306 So.2d 104 (Fla. 1974). Judges customarily instruct juries that if the value of the property cannot be ascertained, they must find the value to be less than that required for grand theft. However, consider the theft of a credit card. Usually, these cards have set credit limits that are only available to the holder on proper signature. Therefore, a credit card has no market value to a third person in lawful channels. In *Miller v. People*, 566 P.2d 1059 (Colo. 1977), the Colorado Supreme Court held that the amount that could be purchased on the stolen card in the "illegitimate" market could be considered in determining whether a defendant was guilty of felony theft. In *Owolabi v. Commonwealth*, 428 S.E.2d 14 (Va. App. 1993), a Virginia appellate court disagreed. Where there was no evidence of the value of the credit cards stolen, but only of the lines of credit they represented, the evidence did not support a finding that the card had a value greater than $200. Thus, the court held the defendant could be convicted only of petit larceny, not grand larceny.

Proof of value is very important in a theft case because it can often mean the difference between a misdemeanor conviction and a felony conviction, or even between felonies of various degrees. For this reason, courts often receive expert testimony on this issue.

Robbery

At common law, **robbery** was a felony that consisted of (1) a taking of another's personal property of value (2) from the other person's possession or presence (3) by force or placing the person in fear and (4) with the intent to permanently deprive the other person of that property. In reality, robbery was an aggravated form of larceny where the taking was accomplished by force or threats of force and had the same specific-intent requirement as common-law larceny. The intent to steal (*animus furundi*), for example, was the same as in larceny and the taking of property had to be from the victim's actual or constructive possession. To constitute robbery, the violence or intimidation had to overcome the victim's resistance and precede or accompany the actual taking of property. Property in the victim's dwelling or vicinity was regarded as being in the victim's possession. To illustrate a significant difference between larceny and robbery, a person who spirited a person's wallet from his pocket would be guilty of larceny, but if the victim resisted and the thief took the wallet by force or violence, the offense constituted robbery.

Statutory Approaches to Robbery

In some respects, robbery is an offense against the person because it usually involves an assault or battery. See, for example, *State v. Shoemake*, 618 P.2d 1201 (Kan. 1980). Yet it also involves a taking of property and is generally classified as an offense against property.

Robbery

CASE-IN-POINT

On the morning of July 26, 1984, Lamont Julius McLaughlin and a companion, both wearing masks, entered a bank in Baltimore. McLaughlin brandished a handgun and told those in the bank to put up their hands and not to move. While McLaughlin held the gun, his companion leaped over the counter and stuffed several thousand dollars into a brown paper bag. Police officers were waiting outside and promptly arrested the pair. It was then determined that McLaughlin's gun was not loaded.

McLaughlin was found guilty in federal court of bank robbery "by the use of a dangerous weapon." 18 U.S.C.A. § 2113(d). On appeal, McLaughlin argued that his unloaded gun did not qualify as a "dangerous weapon" under the federal bank robbery statute. The U.S. Supreme Court rejected the argument and upheld McLaughlin's conviction. Justice John Paul Stevens opined,

Three reasons, each independently sufficient, support the conclusion that an unloaded gun is a 'dangerous weapon.' First, a gun is an article that is typically and characteristically dangerous; the use for which it is manufactured and sold is a dangerous one, and the law reasonably may presume that such an article is always dangerous even though it may not be armed at a particular time or place. In addition, the display of a gun instills fear in the average citizen; as a consequence, it creates an immediate danger that a violent response will ensue. Finally, a gun can cause harm when used as a bludgeon.

McLaughlin v. United States, 476 U.S. 16, 106 S.Ct. 1677, 90 L.Ed.2d 15 (1986).

Federal Laws

A federal statute makes it an offense to take, or attempt to take, by force and violence or intimidation from the person or presence of another any property or money belonging to or in the care of a bank, credit union, or savings and loan association. 18 U.S.C.A. § 2113(a). In addition, 18 U.S.C.A. § 1951 (Hobbs Act) defines the obstruction of interstate commerce in the context of robbery.

Federal jurisdiction is established where the bank is a federally chartered institution or where its deposits are federally insured. *United States v. Harris*, 530 F.2d 576 (4th Cir. 1976). The statutory offense varies from the common-law crime of robbery in that the government need only establish the defendant's general intent. *United States v. Klare*, 545 F.2d 93 (9th Cir. 1976).

State Laws

Robbery is an offense in every state. Many states have enacted statutes simply defining it as did the common law, a practice sometimes referred to as *codifying the common law*. Other states classify robbery according to degree, with the seriousness of the offense usually based on whether the assailant is armed, the degree of force used, and, in some instances, on the vulnerability of the victim. The value of the property taken does not usually affect the degree of the crime of robbery, as it does that of theft.

The Colorado Criminal Code provides a good illustration of classification of robbery offenses: "A person who knowingly takes anything of value from the person or presence of another by the use of force, threats, or intimidation commits robbery." West's Colo. Rev. Stat. Ann. § 18-4–301(1). Property is taken from the "presence of another" under Colorado law when it is so within the victim's reach, inspection, or observation that he or she would be able to retain control over the property but for the force, threats, or intimidation directed by the perpetrator. *People v. Bartowsheski*, 661 P.2d 235 (Colo. 1983). This is "simple robbery," in contrast with the statutory offense of **aggravated robbery**. The Colorado statute further provides:

(1) A person who commits robbery is guilty of aggravated robbery if during the act of robbery or immediate flight therefrom:

(a) He is armed with a deadly weapon with intent, if resisted, to kill, maim, or wound the person robbed or any other person; or

(b) He knowingly wounds or strikes the person robbed or any other person with a deadly weapon or by the use of force, threats, or intimidation with a deadly weapon knowingly puts the person robbed or any other person in reasonable fear of death or bodily injury; or

(c) He has present a confederate, aiding or abetting the perpetration of the robbery, armed with a deadly weapon, with the intent, either on the part of the defendant or confederate, if resistance is offered, to kill, maim, or wound the person robbed or any other person, or by the use of force, threats, or intimidation puts the person robbed or any other person in reasonable fear of death or bodily injury; or

(d) He possesses any article used or fashioned in a manner to lead any person who is present reasonably to believe it to be a deadly weapon or represents verbally or otherwise that he is then and there so armed.

West's Colo. Rev. Stat. Ann. § 18-4-302.

In *Jones v. Commonwealth*, reproduced on the companion website, the Virginia Court of Appeals considers the sufficiency of the evidence to support a defendant's conviction for robbery.

The Colorado Supreme Court has said that the gist of the crime of robbery under the Colorado statutes is "the putting in fear and taking of property of another by force or intimidation." *People v. Small*, 493 P.2d 15 (Colo. 1972). Aggravated robbery is distinguished from simple robbery by the fact that an accomplice or confederate is armed with a dangerous weapon with intent, if resisted, to maim, wound, or kill. The Colorado Supreme Court has observed that simple and aggravated robbery are but two degrees of the same offense. *Atwood v. People*, 489 P.2d 1305 (Colo. 1971).

The Temporal Relationship of Force to the Taking

Is it essential to the crime of robbery that the element of violence or intimidation occur before or at the same time as the taking of the victim's property? State appellate courts are divided on this issue, often based on the specific statutory language. Note that the Colorado statute in addressing aggravated robbery includes the language "if during the act of robbery or immediate flight therefrom." The Colorado Supreme Court has said that force used in robbery need not occur simultaneously with the taking. *People v. Bartowsheski*, supra. Other courts have agreed. In *Hermann v. State*, 123 So.2d 846 (Miss. 1960), a defendant, after stealthily obtaining gasoline, made a getaway from a filling station by pointing a deadly weapon at the attendant. The attendant stuck his hand through the window of the vehicle but was pushed away by the offender. The Mississippi Supreme Court held that this act of pushing the victim away constituted the force element of robbery. Again, in *People v. Kennedy*, 294 N.E.2d 788 (Ill. App. 1973), the court held that while the taking may be without force, the offense is robbery if the departure with the property is accomplished by the use of force. Likewise, a Utah appellate court noted that if force or fear is used at any time prior to or concurrent with the victim actually losing the ability to control his chattel (personal property), then a robbery has occurred. *State in Interest of D.B.*, 925 P.2d 178 (Utah App. 1996).

In 1986 the Florida Supreme Court held that defendants who used force while fleeing a retail store after committing theft in the store could not be convicted of robbery. The court followed the traditional common-law view that the use of force must occur before or at the same time as the taking of property. *Royal v. State*, 490 So.2d 44 (Fla. 1986). The state legislature promptly amended the statutory definition of robbery to add "an act shall be deemed 'in the course of committing the robbery' if it occurs in an attempt to commit robbery or in flight after the attempt or commission." West's Fla. Stat. Ann. § 812.13(3)(a). The statute also added that "an act shall be deemed 'in the course of taking' if it occurs either prior to, contemporaneous with, or subsequent to the taking of the property and if it and the act of taking constitute a continuous series of acts and events." § 812.13(3)(b). See *Perry v. State*, 801 So.2d 78 (Fla. 2001) (recognizing the change under the revised statute).

Carjacking

Depending on the circumstances, a person who forcibly takes another's vehicle may be subject to prosecution for grand larceny and robbery. Recognizing the serious national threat that forcible auto theft poses to persons and their motor vehicles, and after a nationwide spree of **carjacking**, in 1992 Congress enacted the Anti-Car Theft Act of 1992. 18 U.S.CA. § 2119. As originally enacted, the statute made it a crime for anyone who "takes a motor vehicle that has been transported, shipped, or received in interstate or foreign commerce from the person or presence of another by force and violence or by intimidation, or attempts to do so." The Ninth Circuit interpreted the 1992 statute as creating a general-intent offense. *United States v. Martinez*, 49 F.3d 1398 (9th Cir. 1995).

In 1994 Congress amended section 2119 to provide:

Whoever, *with the intent to cause death or serious bodily harm* [emphasis added] takes a motor vehicle that has been transported, shipped, or received in interstate or foreign commerce from the person or presence of another by force and violence or by intimidation or attempts to so shall

(1) be fined under this title or imprisoned not more than 15 years, or both,

(2) if serious bodily injury (as defined in section 1365 of this title, including any conduct that, if the conduct occurred in the special maritime and territorial jurisdiction of the United States, would violate section 2241 or 2242 of this title) results, be fined under this title or imprisoned not more than 25 years, or both, and

(3) if death results, be fined under this title or imprisoned for any number of years up to life, or both, or sentenced to death.

Thus, the amended statute describes three offenses with different statutory elements: (1) a carjacking (or attempted carjacking), § 2119(1); (2) a carjacking (or attempted carjacking) resulting in a serious bodily injury, § 2119(2); and (3) a carjacking (or attempted carjacking) resulting in a death, § 2119(3).

In 1999, the Supreme Court reconciled the views of lower federal courts and held that section 2119 merely requires proof of an unconditional intent to seriously harm or kill the driver if necessary to steal the car or a conditional intent to kill or seriously harm the driver if necessary to steal the car. *Holloway aka Ali v. United States*, 526 U.S. 1, 119 S.Ct. 966, 143 L.Ed.2d 1 (1999).

In recent years the Supreme Court has indicated that there are limits to congressional authority to create new federal crimes under the auspices of the Commerce Clause of the U.S. Constitution. See *United States v. Lopez*, 514 U.S. 549, 115 S.Ct.

1624, 131 L.Ed.2d 626 (1995). Some critics have suggested that the Court might also invalidate the federal carjacking statute, but this seems unlikely inasmuch as the automobile is a major article of interstate commerce and a primary vehicle of interstate transportation. In fact, lower federal courts have upheld the constitutionality of the act as a valid expression of congressional power under the Commerce Clause. See, for example, *United States v. Coleman*, 78 F.3d 154 (11th Cir. 1996).

Extortion

In describing common-law **extortion**, William Blackstone said it was "the taking by color of an office of money or other thing of value, that is not due, before it is due, or more than is due." Under most modern statutes, extortion has been extended beyond acts by public officers. As the California law provides, extortion is "the obtaining of property from another, with his consent, or the obtaining of an official act of a public officer, induced by a wrongful use of force or fear, or under color of official right." West's Ann. Cal. Penal Code § 518.

In the vignette at the beginning of the chapter, we recounted a high-profile extortion case prosecuted by the state of New York. Robert Halderman, who attempted to extort $2 million from David Letterman, was convicted of violating the following statute:

A person obtains property by extortion when he compels or induces another person to deliver such property to himself or to a third person by means of instilling in him a fear that, if the property is not so delivered, the actor or another will:

(i) Cause physical injury to some person in the future; or

(ii) Cause damage to property; or

(iii) Engage in other conduct constituting a crime; or

(iv) Accuse some person of a crime or cause criminal charges to be instituted against him; or

(v) Expose a secret or publicize an asserted fact, whether true or false, tending to subject some person to hatred, contempt or ridicule; or

(vi) Cause a strike, boycott or other collective labor group action injurious to some person's business; except that such a threat shall not be deemed extortion when the property is demanded or received for the benefit of the group in whose interest the actor purports to act; or

(vii) Testify or provide information or withhold testimony or information with respect to another's legal claim or defense; or

(viii) Use or abuse his position as a public servant by performing some act within or related to his official duties, or by failing or refusing to perform an official duty, in such manner as to affect some person adversely; or

(ix) Perform any other act which would not in itself materially benefit the actor but which is calculated to harm another person materially with respect to his health, safety, business, calling, career, financial condition, reputation or personal relationships.

N.Y. Penal Law § 155.05(2).

Extortion Distinguished from Robbery

There are both similarities and distinctions between the offenses of extortion and robbery. As explained by a California appellate court,

The crime of extortion is related to and sometimes difficult to distinguish from the crime of robbery. . . . Both crimes have their roots in the common law crime of larceny. Both crimes share the element of an acquisition by means of force or fear. One distinction between the robbery and extortion frequently noted by courts and commentators is that in robbery property is taken from another by force or fear "against his will" while in extortion property is taken from another by force or fear "with his consent." The two crimes, however, have other distinctions. Robbery requires a "felonious taking" which means a specific intent to permanently deprive the victim of the property. . . . Robbery also requires the property be taken from the victim's "person or immediate presence." . . . Extortion does not require proof of either of these elements. . . . Extortion does, however, require the specific intent of inducing the victim to consent to part with his or her property. *People v. Torres*, 39 Cal. Rptr. 2d 103, 110–111 (Cal. App. 1995).

Extortion under Federal Law

In many instances, the statutory offense of extortion has become synonymous with the common understanding of **blackmail**. In fact, 18 U.S.C.A. § 873—a federal statute that provides that "[w]hoever, under a threat of informing, or as a consideration for not informing, against any violation of any law of the United States, demands, or receives any money or other valuable thing, shall be fined . . ."—is often referred to as the "blackmail statute." Another federal statute, 18 U.S.C.A. § 876, makes it a crime to mail using the U.S. Postal Service a demand for ransom or a threat to injure a person's property or reputation. The only specific intent required to support a conviction under § 876 is that the defendant knowingly deposited a threatening letter in the mail, not that he or she intended to carry out the threat. *United States v. Chatman*, 584 F.2d 1358 (4th Cir. 1978). Finally, 18 U.S.C.A. § 879 makes it a felony to "knowingly and willfully threaten to kill, kidnap, or inflict bodily harm upon . . . persons protected by the Secret Service."

Forgery and Uttering a Forged Instrument

Blackstone defined common-law **forgery** as "the fraudulent making or alteration of a writing to the prejudice of another man's right." The early cases reveal that such writings as wills, receipts, and physicians' certificates were subject to forgery. To convict a defendant of forgery under common law, it was essential to establish the accused's intent to defraud. **Uttering a forged instrument** was also a common-law offense, but one separate and distinct from forgery. "Utter," a term of art synonymous with "publish," distinguishes the actual forgery from the act of passing a forged instrument to someone. As an indication of the lesser importance of commercial matters in early English society, the common law classified both forgery and uttering a forged instrument as misdemeanors.

Statutory Expansion of Forgery Offenses

Unlike the common law, federal and state statutes generally classify forgery as a felony. Reflecting the importance of written and printed documentation in our modern economy, statutes in all American jurisdictions have extended the crime of forgery to almost every type of public or private legal instrument.

Federal Statutes

Under federal law, "[w]hoever, with intent to defraud, falsely makes, forges, counterfeits, or alters any obligation or other security of the United States" commits the crime of forgery. 18 U.S.C.A. § 471. Federal courts have stated that the manifest purpose of these laws is to protect all currency and obligations of the United States, *United States v. LeMon*, 622 F.2d 1022 (10th Cir. 1980), and that the prosecution must prove not only the passing but also the defendant's "intent to pass the bad money," *United States v. Lorenzo*, 570 F.2d 294, 299 (9th Cir. 1978).

Title 18, § 472 provides that "[w]hoever, with intent to defraud, passes, utters, publishes, or sells, or attempts to pass, utter, publish, or sell, or with like intent brings into the United States or keeps in possession or conceals any falsely made, forged, counterfeited, or altered obligation or other security of the United States, shall be fined under this title or imprisoned. . . ." In *United States v. Drumright*, 534 F.2d 1383 (10th Cir. 1976), a defendant seeking a reversal of his conviction under section 472 argued that the Federal Reserve bill he uttered was not of an appearance calculated to deceive an unsuspecting person of ordinary observation. The court disagreed, pointing out that the bill was "a falsely made and altered obligation of the United States because it was composed of parts of three genuine bills which had been fastened together with transparent tape. When folded with the right half of the obverse side showing, it has the appearance of a good $50 bill. . . . Although the workmanship on the bill was crude, it was of such character that under favorable circumstances it could be uttered and accepted as genuine." *Id.* at 1385. The court concluded that the circumstances presented in the case's peculiar facts were sufficient to establish a violation of the statute.

Several other federal statutes relate to forgery and the **counterfeiting** of federal securities, postage stamps, postage meters, money orders, federal and state securities, public records, judges' signatures, and court documents. See 18 U.S.C.A. §§ 472–520. Many prosecutions are brought under 18 U.S.C.A. § 495, which provides that

> Whoever falsely makes, alters, forges, or counterfeits any deed, power of attorney, order, certificate, receipt, contract, or other writing, for the purpose of obtaining or receiving, or of enabling any other person, either directly or indirectly, to obtain or receive from the United States or any officers or agents thereof, any sum of money; or
>
> Whoever utters or publishes as true any such false, forged, altered, or counterfeited writing, with intent to defraud the United States, knowing the same to be false, altered, forged, or counterfeited; or
>
> Whoever transmits to, or presents at any office or officer of the United States, any such writing in support of, or in relation to, any account or claim, with intent to defraud the United States, knowing the same to be false, altered, forged, or counterfeited—
>
> Shall be fined under this title or imprisoned. . . .

To convict someone under this statute, the government must establish the defendant's specific fraudulent intent. *United States v. Sullivan*, 406 F.2d 180 (2d Cir. 1969).

State Statutes

Most states have substantially adopted the common-law definition of forgery but have expanded the types of instruments that can be forged to include a lengthy list of public and private documents. For example, the Arizona Criminal Code makes forgery a felony and provides the following:

A. A person commits forgery if, with intent to defraud, the person:

1. Falsely makes, completes or alters a written instrument; or

2. Knowingly possesses a forged instrument; or

3. Offers or presents, whether accepted or not, a forged instrument or one which contains false information. (Ariz. Rev. Stat. § 13-2002.)

Under this section, the offenses of forgery and uttering have been coupled under the term "forgery," but their status as separate offenses must still be observed because the elements of the offenses are not the same and the proof required can differ. *State v. Reyes*, 458 P.2d 960 (Ariz. 1969). Thus, under Arizona law the crime of forgery has three elements: (1) signing the name of another person, (2) intending to defraud, and (3) knowing that there is no authority to sign. *State v. Nettz*, 560 P.2d 814 (Ariz. App. 1977). On the other hand, uttering is the passing or publishing of a false, altered, or counterfeited paper or document. *State v. Reyes*, supra. Proof of the intent to defraud is essential to obtain a conviction of forgery, *State v. Maxwell*, 445 P.2d 837 (Ariz. 1968), but such intent may be inferred from circumstances in which the false instrument is executed or issued, *State v. Gomez*, 553 P.2d 1233 (Ariz. App. 1976). Note that based on the wording of the Arizona statute proscribing forgery, a conviction for "attempt to pass" is a conviction of forgery, not of an attempt. *Ponds v. State*, 438 P.2d 423 (Ariz. App. 1968) (see Chapter 5).

The Arizona Court of Appeals' opinion in *State v. Gomez* is reproduced on the companion website.

Common Examples of Forgery and Uttering a Forged Instrument

Among the more common examples of forgery today are the following:

- Signing another's name to an application for a driver's license
- Printing bogus tickets to a concert or sports event
- Signing another's name to a check on his or her bank account without authority

CASE-IN-POINT

Forgery

The state prosecuted defendant Donald E. Hicks for forgery. At trial, the evidence revealed that on August 4, 1984, Hicks went to see Edmond Brown to make a payment on a debt. Hicks told Brown he could pay him $100 on his debt if Brown could cash a two-party check for him. Hicks presented Brown with a check for $349 made out to Hicks on the account of Gott, Young, and Bogle, PA., a Wichita law firm. The check was signed "Gott Young." The defendant told Brown that the check was a partial payment of a settlement of a claim stemming from an automobile accident. Hicks assured Brown that the check was good and endorsed it over to him. Brown accepted the check and returned $249 to Hicks. When the check was returned by the bank, Brown contacted the law firm. He was told that there was no one by the name of Gott Young at the firm and that the firm had never represented Hicks. He further learned that some twenty-five checks from the firm's petty cash account were missing. Hicks was found guilty by a jury, and his conviction was affirmed on appeal.

State v. Hicks, 714 P.2d 105 (Kan. App. 1986).

- Altering the amount of a check or note
- Signing another's name without authority to a certificate transferring shares of stock
- Signing a deed transferring someone's real estate without authorization
- Making an unauthorized change in the legal description of property being conveyed under a deed
- Altering the grades or credits on a college transcript

Uttering a forged instrument commonly occurs when a person knowingly delivers a forged check to someone in exchange for cash or merchandise, knowingly sells bogus tickets for an event, or submits a deed with forged signatures for official recording.

Falsification of computerized records such as college credits and financial records poses new challenges to laws proscribing forgery. The increasing use of computers gives rise to the need for new applications of statutes proscribing forgery and uttering a forged instrument.

Worthless Checks

As commercial banking developed, the passing of "bad checks" became a serious problem. A person who writes a worthless check on his or her bank account does not commit a forgery. In early cases, some courts referred to issuance of checks without funds in the bank as use of a "false token." These cases were prosecuted under statutes making it unlawful to use false pretenses to obtain property.

States have now enacted a variety of statutes making it unlawful to issue checks with insufficient funds to cover payment. Earlier statutes often provided that to be guilty of false pretenses for issuing a worthless check, a person had to fraudulently obtain goods. This proved to be an impracticable method to control issuance of checks by depositors who misgauged their checking account balances. The widespread use of commercial and personal banking led legislatures to enact **worthless-check statutes** to cope with the problem. These statutes usually classify such an offense as a misdemeanor, and legislatures have increasingly opted to allow offenders to make restitution of losses caused by worthless checks. State laws often allow a recipient of a bad check to assess a fee against one who issues or transfers a bad check. Many retail stores have signs posted notifying customers of such fees.

Ohio R.C. § 2913.11(B) makes it an offense to "issue or transfer or cause to be issued or transferred a check or other negotiable instrument, knowing that it will be dishonored." The statute further provides that one who issues or transfers such a negotiable instrument is presumed to know that it will be dishonored if either (1) the drawer had no account with the drawee bank, or (2) the negotiable instrument was properly refused payment for insufficient funds upon presentment within thirty days and the liability of any person liable on the instrument was not discharged by payment or satisfaction within ten days after receiving notice of dishonor. See Ohio R.C. § 2913.11(C)(1–2). If a bad check is for less than $500, the offense is a misdemeanor; beyond that amount it becomes a felony, the degree of which is dependent on the amount of the check, with a check for $100,000 or more becoming a felony of the third degree. See Ohio R.C. § 2913.11(F). Ohio courts have held that where the payee of a check knows that the check is not collectible at the time it is tendered, there is no criminal violation of passing a bad check. *State v. Edwards*, 751 N.E.2d 510 (Ohio App. 2001).

Burglary

English common law emphasized the sanctity of one's dwelling, as reflected in the well-known dictum, "A man's home is his castle." According to Blackstone, common-law **burglary** consisted of (1) breaking and entering of (2) a dwelling of another (3) during the nighttime (4) with intent to commit a felony therein. The "breaking" at common law could be either "actual" or "constructive." An actual breaking could be merely technical, such as pushing open a door or opening a window. An entry gained through fraud or deception was considered a "constructive" breaking. Even the slightest entry was deemed sufficient; for instance, a hand, a foot, or even a finger within the dwelling was regarded as a sufficient entry. Proof of the defendant's intent to commit a felony was essential: A breaking and entering did not constitute burglary at common law unless the perpetrator had a specific intent to commit a felony (for example, murder, rape, or larceny); however, it was not necessary to prove that any felony was committed. "Dwelling" was defined as the house or place of habitation used by the occupier or member of the family "as a place to sleep in." Finally, to constitute burglary at common law, it was essential that the offense be committed at nighttime, generally defined as the period between sunset and sunrise.

Statutory Revisions of Burglary

Many states have enacted statutes proscribing **breaking and entering**, thereby placing a new label on the common-law crime of burglary. At a minimum, these statutes expand the offense of burglary beyond dwelling houses and eliminate the requirement that the offense take place in the nighttime. Most states retain the common-law requirement that the accused break and enter with intent to commit a felony, and others include the language "or theft." Even where the offense is still labeled burglary, legislatures have made significant changes in the common-law definition. In addition to eliminating the nighttime requirement, they have broadened the offense to include buildings and structures of all types. Today, most criminal codes include vehicles, aircraft, and vessels either in the definition of burglary or by a separate statute. Finally, modern statutes frequently provide that a person who enters a structure with consent but who remains therein with intent to commit a felony may be found guilty of burglary notwithstanding an original lawful entry. An example of this would be someone intentionally remaining in a department store with the intent to commit an offense therein after the store closes for the day.

Mich. Comp. Laws Ann. § 750.110 deals with breaking and entering and provides:

> A person who breaks and enters with intent to commit any felony, or any larceny therein, a tent, hotel, office, store, shop, warehouse, barn, granary, factory or other building, structure, boat or ship, shipping container, or railroad car shall be guilty of a felony.

Increasingly, state statutes recognize **home invasion** as a more heinous form of burglary in that the perpetrator is armed with a dangerous weapon or persons are present in the home at the time of the break-in. Mich. Comp. Laws Ann. § 750.110(a) stipulates:

> (2) A person who breaks and enters a dwelling with intent to commit a felony, larceny, or assault in the dwelling, a person who enters a dwelling without permission

with intent to commit a felony, larceny, or assault in the dwelling, or a person who breaks and enters a dwelling or enters a dwelling without permission and, at any time while he or she is entering, present in, or exiting the dwelling, commits a felony, larceny, or assault is guilty of home invasion in the first degree if at any time while the person is entering, present in, or exiting the dwelling either of the following circumstances exists:

(a) The person is armed with a dangerous weapon.

(b) Another person is lawfully present in the dwelling.

(3) A person who breaks and enters a dwelling with intent to commit a felony, larceny, or assault in the dwelling, a person who enters a dwelling without permission with intent to commit a felony, larceny, or assault in the dwelling, or a person who breaks and enters a dwelling or enters a dwelling without permission and, at any time while he or she is entering, present in, or exiting the dwelling, commits a felony, larceny, or assault is guilty of home invasion in the second degree.

(4) A person is guilty of home invasion in the third degree if the person does either of the following:

(a) Breaks and enters a dwelling with intent to commit a misdemeanor in the dwelling, enters a dwelling without permission with intent to commit a misdemeanor in the dwelling, or breaks and enters a dwelling or enters a dwelling without permission and, at any time while he or she is entering, present in, or exiting the dwelling, commits a misdemeanor.

(b) Breaks and enters a dwelling or enters a dwelling without permission and, at any time while the person is entering, present in, or exiting the dwelling, violates any of the following ordered to protect a named person or persons:

CASE-IN-POINT

What Constitutes "Entry" Within the Meaning of a Burglary Statute?

On February 4, 1998, a man later identified as the defendant was seen removing a screen from a bathroom window of the Floreas's house and unsuccessfully attempting to open the window itself. Then, after unsuccessfully attempting to open the front door of the house, the defendant banged on the wall and drove away. Shortly thereafter he was arrested and charged with burglary under California law, which provides that the crime of burglary is committed when a person "enters any . . . building," including a "house," "with intent to commit. . . larceny or any felony." A jury found the defendant guilty of burglary in the first degree because the crime involved an inhabited dwelling house. The trial court sentenced him to four years in prison. In 2001, a California appellate court reversed his conviction on the ground that penetration into the area behind a window screen did not constitute an entry as required by the burglary statute.

The California Supreme Court granted review, and in reversing the court of appeals' decision, opined, "We recognize that penetration into the area behind a window screen without penetration of the window itself usually will effect only a minimal entry of a building in terms of distance. But it has long been settled that '[a]ny kind of entry, complete or partial . . . will' suffice." *Id.* at 927. A dissenting judge argued that the defendant committed attempted burglary because he tried, but failed, to enter the house.

People v. Valencia, 46 P.3d 920 (Cal. 2002).

(i) A probation term or condition.

(ii) A parole term or condition.

(iii) A personal protection order term or condition.

(iv) A bond or bail condition or any condition of pretrial release.

Home invasion of the first, second, and third degrees is a felony, the imprisonment and fine varying in severity based on the degree of the offense.

Courts tend to construe liberally the terms "breaking" and "entering" commonly found in burglary statutes. In *State v. Jaynes*, 464 S.E.2d 448, 466 (N.C. 1995), the North Carolina Supreme Court said that for purposes of burglary, "any force, however slight, employed to effect entrance through any usual or unusual place of ingress, whether open, partly open, or closed . . . by any use of force, however slight, . . . will suffice as the 'breaking' required for burglary." A New York appellate court has said that a defendant "enters" a building within the meaning of that state's burglary statute when a defendant's person or any part of a defendant's body intrudes. *People v. Jackson*, 638 N.Y.S.2d 140 (1996).

In *State v. Feldt*, reproduced on the companion website, the Supreme Court of Montana considers an appeal by a convenience store employee who was convicted of burglary.

Possession of Burglar's Tools

Michigan, like most states, makes **possession of burglar's tools** a felony if the possessor has the intent to use the tools for burglarious purposes. Michigan law provides,

> Any person who shall knowingly have in his possession any nitroglycerine, or other explosive, thermite, engine, machine, tool or implement, device, chemical or substance, adapted and designed for cutting or burning through, forcing or breaking open any building, room, vault, safe or other depository, in order to steal therefrom any money or other property, knowing the same to be adapted and designed for the purpose aforesaid, with intent to use or employ the same for the purpose aforesaid, shall be guilty of a felony. Mich. Comp. Laws Ann. § 750.116.

Many years ago, the Michigan Supreme Court emphasized that to obtain a conviction, the state must prove the accused knowingly had possession of burglar's tools, knew the tools could be used for a criminal purpose, and intended to use them for such purpose. *People v. Jefferson*, 126 N.W. 829 (Mich. 1910).

Arson

Like burglary, **arson** was a felony at common law designed to protect the security of the dwelling place. The crime consisted of (1) the willful and malicious burning (2) of a dwelling (3) of another. There was no requirement that the dwelling be destroyed or even that it be damaged to a significant degree. In fact, a mere charring was sufficient, but scorching or smoke damage did not constitute arson at common law. The common law gave the term "dwelling" the same meaning as in burglary. Consequently, the burning of buildings within the curtilage constituted arson. The common law regarded arson as a general-intent crime, with the required malice being presumed from an intentional burning of someone's dwelling. Setting fire to one's own home was not arson at common law. Yet some early English cases indicate that under circumstances where burning one's own house posed a danger to others, "houseburning" was a misdemeanor offense.

Statutory Revision of Arson

Modern statutes have extended the offense of arson to include the intentional burning of buildings, structures, and vehicles of all types. Frequently, this even includes a person's own property. Several states have enacted statutes that provide that the use of explosives to damage a structure constitutes arson. As in burglary, the modern offense of arson is designed to protect many forms of property. Therefore, arson can no longer be considered strictly a habitation offense. By categorizing arson, legislatures can make appropriate distinctions and provide penalties accordingly.

Michigan law embraces four categories of arson. Mich. Comp. Laws Ann. § 750.72 provides,

> Any person who willfully or maliciously burns any dwelling house, either occupied or unoccupied, or the contents thereof, whether owned by himself or another, or any building within the curtilage of such dwelling house, or the contents thereof, shall be guilty of a felony.

In *People v. Williams*, 318 N.W.2d 671 (Mich. App. 1982), the court held that to establish the *corpus delicti* of arson of a dwelling house, the state must show not only a burning of the house but also that it resulted from an intentional criminal act. The court explained that where only a burning is shown, a presumption arises that it was accidentally caused.

Section 750.73 makes it a lesser felony for anyone to willfully or maliciously burn any building or other real property or contents thereof, other than a dwelling house, while § 750.74 makes it a misdemeanor or felony to willfully and maliciously burn personal property, the level of offense being determined by the value of the property involved. For a fire to be "willfully" set by the accused requires that the defendant commit such act stubbornly and for an unlawful purpose. Mere proof of carelessness or accident is not sufficient to establish guilt. *People v. McCarty*, 6 N.W.2d 919 (Mich. 1942).

In contrast with Michigan's law, many state statutes broaden the scope of the offense by referring to "damage caused by fire" rather than "burning." In further contrast with the common law, under many modern statutes proof of damage by smoke or scorching is sufficient to constitute arson. See, for example, *State v. McVeigh*, 516 P.2d 918 (Kan. 1973).

CASE-IN-POINT

Proving the Crime of Arson

Early on the morning of September 23, 1981, a fire destroyed a log cabin belonging to Henry Xavier Kennedy. Investigators determined the fire was incendiary in origin. A hot plate with its switch in the "on" position was found in the most heavily burned area of the cabin. Investigators also determined that kerosene poured around the area of the hot plate had accelerated the fire.

Five days before the fire, Kennedy had renewed a $40,000 insurance policy on the cabin. Evidence was also presented that Kennedy's building business was slow. Kennedy introduced evidence of an alibi from midnight until 4:00 A.M. Although the fire was reported at 3:42 A.M., investigators testified that the incendiary device could have been set before midnight.

Kennedy was convicted of arson, and his conviction was upheld on appeal.

Kennedy v. State, 323 S.E.2d 169 (Ga. App. 1984).

Burning Property with the Intent to Defraud an Insurance Company

Most jurisdictions have enacted statutes making it a crime to burn any property with the intent to defraud an insurance company, usually requiring the prosecution to prove the defendant's specific intent to defraud. In this respect, Mich. Comp. Laws Ann. § 750.75 stipulates the following: "Any person who shall willfully burn any building or personal property which shall be at the time insured against loss or damage by fire with intent to injure and defraud the insurer, whether such person be the owner of the property or not, shall be guilty of a felony."

Malicious Mischief

A mere trespass to land or personal property was not a crime at common law unless it was committed forcibly or maliciously. However, it was a common-law misdemeanor called **malicious mischief** for a person to damage another's real or personal property. Modern statutes usually define the offense much as did the common law, often referring to the offense as **vandalism** and imposing penalties based on the extent of damage inflicted on the victim's property.

In *State v. Tonnisen*, reproduced on the companion website, the Appellate Division of the New Jersey Superior Court rejects an appeal by a defendant who was found guilty of malicious mischief.

Section 806.13(1)(a), West's Florida Statutes Annotated, is a good illustration of present-day statutes. It provides that "[a] person commits the offense of criminal mischief if he or she willfully and maliciously injures or damages by any means any real or personal property belonging to another, including, but not limited to, the placement of graffiti thereon or other acts of vandalism thereto." The offense is a misdemeanor, and the value of property determines the punishment. But if the damage is $1,000 or greater, or if there is interruption or impairment of a business operation or public communication; transportation; supply of water, gas or power; or other public service which costs $1,000 or more in labor and supplies to restore, or the defendant has had one or more previous convictions, the offense is a felony of the third degree. Florida appellate courts have held that to be found guilty of the offense, the actor must possess the specific intent to damage the property of another. *In Interest of J.G.*, 655 So.2d 1284 (Fla. App. 1995).

Defenses to Property Crimes

At common law, the offenses of larceny and robbery were specific-intent crimes. This intent requirement has been carried over in statutes proscribing theft, either comprehensively or in various descriptive crimes, but the intent requirement in modern robbery statutes varies. Therefore, in a prosecution for theft, a defendant may raise the defense of mistake of fact, but this does not necessarily follow when defending a charge of robbery (see Chapter 14). This means that a defendant who takes items of property from another person in the good-faith belief that they belong to the defendant may have a defense. A classic example: Sherry leaves a jacket on a coat rack, and later Mary does also. The jackets are similar, and Sherry mistakenly walks away with Mary's jacket. The problem becomes more acute if Mary has left a wallet in her jacket with hundreds of dollars of currency in it. These mistakes justify requiring the prosecution to prove a defendant's specific intent in theft offenses. Have you ever opened the door of a car like yours in a shopping center parking lot, thinking the car was your own?

In some theft prosecutions, mistake of law has been held to be a defense. This is limited to situations where there are exceedingly technical questions concerning ownership rights (see Chapter 14).

In a prosecution for forgery, an accused can defend by proving that he or she was authorized to sign another's name. Under certain circumstances, a person accused of forgery can also assert the defense of "mistake of fact" (see Chapter 14).

In some instances, a person charged with burglary can also assert mistake of fact as a defense. For example, an intoxicated person who enters a "row house" identical to his or her own may have a defense. And, of course, the requirement that the prosecution prove "an intent to commit a felony" would make it difficult to prove that a person who took refuge from a storm on the porch of an unoccupied dwelling did so with intent to commit a felony therein (see Chapter 14). Arson, on the other hand, is usually a general-intent crime. This imposes a limitation on defenses beyond consent, where a person intentionally commits the proscribed acts. Because statutes proscribing the commission of arson with the intent to defraud an insurer usually require proof of the defendant's specific intent to defraud, the lack of such intent can be shown in defense. As we point out in Chapter 14 the defenses of alibi, insanity, duress, and, in some instances, intoxication may be defenses to property crimes.

Conclusion

Most statutory property crimes parallel the basic common-law scheme but have been broadened to meet the demands of our changing society. Although the common-law crimes against property and habitation provide a good starting point for legislating against offenses involving property, there is a need for continuing statutory revision to consolidate the laws proscribing certain property offenses that have proliferated over the years.

Consumers are no longer willing to acquiesce in outmoded doctrines such as *caveat emptor*. Thus, laws concerning representations made in commercial transactions assume an important role in today's society. Consumer fraud, intentional false advertising, credit card fraud, and a variety of other scams need to be specifically proscribed or included in omnibus definitions in theft and forgery statutes and in statutes specifically addressing computer fraud and access device fraud.

The laws proscribing burglary and arson must protect more than homes. These offenses pose serious threats to lives and property, regardless of whether they are committed in a residential or business property; whether the structure involved is private or public; and whether it is a vehicle, vessel, building, or other structure. These offenses have changed from crimes against habitation to crimes against property. Modern statutes tend to make these offenses crimes against persons as well. With the almost-universal dependence on insurance to protect against casualty losses, the need for a close look at statutes proscribing insurance fraud is also essential.

Chapter Summary

- **LO1** At the time the United States was founded, the common law recognized two theft offenses: larceny and false pretenses. Larceny was a felony that consisted of the wrongful taking and carrying away of the personal property of another with intent to permanently deprive the owner of the property. Obtaining property by false pretenses was a misdemeanor that involved obtaining wares or merchandise of another with the intent to cheat or defraud the other person.

Later, the English Parliament created the misdemeanor offenses of embezzlement and receiving stolen property. Whereas larceny required proof of a wrongful taking and carrying away of another's personal property, embezzlement made it unlawful for servants and others with a fiduciary relationship to wrongfully convert assets. The common law that America inherited included larceny and false pretenses but left matters involving real property and commercial transactions to the civil law. As America matured, most households acquired intangible property, and commercial transactions assumed a role of greater importance. Congress enacted statutes comprehensively proscribing theft and embezzlement and expanding larceny to include all types of tangible and intangible property. A proliferation of statutes addressing various forms of theft led many states to adopt comprehensive theft statutes that proscribe all types of theft and make temporary as well as permanent deprivation of all classes of property subject to theft laws. Theft remains a specific-intent crime. Because penalties are graded according to the value of items stolen, prosecutors must produce evidence to prove the value of goods or services stolen.

- **LO2** At common law, robbery was a felony that consisted of taking another's personal property from the other person's possession or presence by force or by placing the person in fear, with the intent to permanently deprive the other person of that property. Force had to occur at the time of taking of property. Because robbery can result in injury to a victim, it is considered a more serious felony than theft and is sometimes referred to as "aggravated theft." Many states simply define robbery as did the common law; others classify it according to degree, with the seriousness of the offense usually based on whether the assailant is armed, the degree of force used, and the vulnerability of the victim. Where courts have followed the common-law view that the use of force must occur before or at the same time as the taking of property, legislatures have amended their robbery statutes to provide that the force can occur at or after the criminal act. Federal statutes make it an offense "to take, or attempt to take, by force and violence or intimidation from the person or presence of another any property or money belonging to or in the care of a bank, credit union, or savings and loan association."

- **LO3** The Federal Anti-Car Theft Act of 1992, as amended, makes carjacking a crime by stipulating that "[w]hoever, with the intent to cause death or serious bodily harm, takes a motor vehicle that has been transported, shipped, or received in interstate or foreign commerce from the person or presence of another by force and violence or by intimidation or attempts to so. . ." is guilty of a felony.

- **LO4** Extortion is the obtaining of property from another, with his or her consent, induced by a wrongful use of force or fear, or under color of official right or the obtaining of an official act of a public officer, induced by a wrongful use of force or fear, or under color of official right. Today extortion has often become synonymous with the common understanding of blackmail. It differs from robbery because of its consensual nature.

- **LO5** At common law, forgery was a felony defined as "the fraudulent making or alteration of a writing to the prejudice of another man's right." Federal law provides that "[w]hoever, with intent to defraud, falsely makes, forges, counterfeits, or alters any obligation or other security of the United States" commits the crime of forgery and that "Whoever, with intent to defraud, passes, utters, publishes, or sells, or attempts to pass, utter, publish, or sell, or with like intent brings into the United States or keeps in possession or conceals any falsely made, forged, counterfeited, or altered obligation or other security of the United States" commits the offense of "uttering." Most states have substantially adopted the common-law definition of forgery (in some instances coupling it with the offense of uttering) and make if a felony. But states have expanded the number of instruments that can be forged to include a lengthy list of public and private documents. Uttering a forged instrument is commonly a felony and occurs when a person knowingly delivers a forged check to someone in exchange for cash or merchandise, knowingly sells bogus tickets for an event, or submits a deed with forged signatures for official recording. The widespread use of commercial and personal banking led state legislatures to enact worthless-check statutes that usually classify issuing a worthless check as a misdemeanor. These statutes frequently allow offenders to make restitution of losses caused by worthless checks.

- **LO6** The common-law offenses of burglary and arson gave credence to the old English saying "A man's home is his castle." These offenses protected the dwelling house and buildings within the curtilage, an enclosed area around the dwelling. At common law, burglary consisted of breaking and entering a dwelling of another during the nighttime with intent to commit a felony. In America, state laws soon eliminated the nighttime requirement and extended the coverage to include buildings and structures of all types. Today these laws usually include vehicles, aircraft, and vessels either in the definition of burglary or by a separate statute. Moreover, modern statutes frequently provide that a person who enters a structure with consent but who remains therein with intent to commit a felony may be found guilty of burglary notwithstanding an original lawful entry. State statutes usually provide for greater penalties for those who break and enter a dwelling. Most states also have statutes that make possession of burglar's tools a felony.

- **LO7** Arson at common law consisted of the willful and malicious burning of another's dwelling. Early on, states broadened the scope of arson laws to include the intentional burning of buildings, structures, and vehicles of all types. Frequently, this includes burning a person's own property. Several states have enacted statutes that provide that the use of explosives to damage a structure constitutes arson. Most jurisdictions also have statutes making it a crime to burn any property with the intent to defraud an insurance company, usually requiring the prosecution to prove the defendant's specific intent to defraud.

- **LO8** A mere trespass to land or personal property was not a crime at common law unless it was committed forcibly or maliciously. Malicious mischief was a common-law misdemeanor consisting of damaging another's real or personal property. Modern statutes usually define the offense much as did the common law, often calling the offense "vandalism" and imposing penalties based on the extent of damage inflicted on the victim's property.

- **LO9** At common law, the offenses of larceny and robbery were specific-intent crimes. This intent requirement has been carried over to statutes proscribing theft; by contrast, the intent requirement in modern robbery statutes varies. Therefore, in a prosecution for theft and burglary (and under some robbery statutes), a defendant may raise the defense of mistake of fact. In some instances consent may apply as a defense to forgery.

Key Terms

tangible property Property that has physical form, substance, and value in itself.

larceny A synonym for theft. At common law, larceny was defined as the unlawful taking of property with the intent of permanently depriving the owner of same.

false pretenses The crime of obtaining money or property through misrepresentation.

embezzlement The crime of using a position of trust or authority to transfer or convert the money or property of another to oneself.

receiving stolen property Knowingly receiving possession and control of personal property belonging to another with the intent to permanently deprive the owner of possession of such property.

grand theft Major form of larceny; theft of a sufficient value of property to make the crime a felony.

petit theft Minor form of larceny; theft of property of sufficiently small value that the offense is classified as a misdemeanor.

intent to deprive The willful design to take goods or services from another without permission or authority of law.

robbery The crime of taking money or property from a person against that person's will by means of force or intimidation.

aggravated robbery A robbery made worse by one or more aggravating factors, such as the perpetrator being armed with a dangerous weapon or actually inflicting harm on the victim.

carjacking Taking a motor vehicle from someone by force and violence or by intimidation.

extortion Also known as blackmail; the crime of obtaining money or property by threats of force or the inducement of fear.

blackmail The vernacular term for extortion.

forgery The crime of making a false written instrument or materially altering a written instrument with the intent to defraud.

uttering a forged instrument The crime of passing a false or worthless instrument, such as a check, with the intent to defraud or injure the recipient.

counterfeiting Making an imitation of something with the intent to deceive—for example, making imitations of U.S. coins and currency.

worthless check statutes Laws making it an offense to knowingly pass a worthless check.

burglary At common law, breaking and entering a dwelling of another during the nighttime with the intent to commit a felony therein. Modern statutes typically expand the offense beyond dwellings and eliminate the "nighttime" element.

breaking and entering Forceful, unlawful entry into a building or conveyance.

home invasion A more heinous form of burglary, in which the perpetrator is armed with a dangerous weapon or persons are present in the home at the time of the break-in.

possession of burglar's tools The knowing control of instruments, machines, or substances designed to enable one to forcefully break into buildings or vaults in order to carry out the intent to steal or destroy property.

arson The crime of intentionally burning someone else's house or building; now commonly extended to other property as well.

malicious mischief Synonym for vandalism; the willful destruction of the property of another person.

vandalism Synonym for malicious mischief; the willful destruction of the property of another person.

Questions for Thought and Discussion

1. What advantages do you see for a state that adopts a comprehensive theft statute?
2. How does the criminal law of your state distinguish between grand theft and petit theft?
3. How does the crime of burglary as it is typically defined under modern statutes differ from the definition of this offense under English common law?
4. Is it more important for theft offenses to be classified as specific-intent crimes or for robbery to be so classified? Why?
5. What provisions would you include in a model statute making arson a crime? Would you provide for separate degrees of the offense?
6. Should the offense of forgery be divided into degrees based on the importance of the forged documents? If so, what criteria would you propose for the various degrees of the crime?
7. Give some examples of actions that would probably fall within the conduct proscribed by (a) extortion statutes and (b) vandalism or malicious mischief statutes.
8. Identify some important similarities and distinctions between the offenses of robbery and extortion.
9. What is the rationale for courts to require that to obtain a conviction for possession of burglar's tools the state must prove the accused knowingly had possession of burglar's tools, knew the tools could be used for a criminal purpose, and intended to use them for such purpose?
10. Assume you are working as a staff assistant to a legislator who desires to introduce a bill to assist merchants who are experiencing losses from bad checks. What types of provisions and penalties would you recommend?

Problems for Discussion and Solution

1. Larry Lightfingers steals a package of filet mignon priced at $19.99 from the meat counter in a supermarket. As he leaves the store, he is approached by a security guard. Lightfingers kicks and injures the security guard in his attempt to leave with the meat he has stolen. In your state, would Mr. Lightfingers be charged with petit theft, grand theft, or robbery? Why?
2. Sally Spendthrift has an established bank account at a local bank. She gives a check to a merchant for the purchase of a new stereo. Her bank returns the check to the merchant because Spendthrift's account has insufficient funds to cover payment. Do you think Spendthrift should face criminal charges or simply be required to compensate the bank and anyone else who suffered a loss?
3. Phillip, a jilted boyfriend, demanded that Michelle, his ex-girlfriend, reimburse him for expenses incident to their dating experiences. When she refused, Phillip threatened to distribute to patrons of a local bar copies of explicit videos of Michelle engaged in sexual activity along with her phone number and a suggestion to contact her for sex. What offense does this scenario suggest?

CHAPTER 9

White-Collar and Organized Crime

LEARNING OBJECTIVES

After reading this chapter, you should be able to explain . . .

1. what is meant by "white-collar crime"
2. the nature of organized crime and racketeering
3. the major federal statutes dealing with white-collar crime
4. how and why a corporation can be found guilty of a crime
5. how federal antitrust laws define certain conduct as criminal
6. how contemporary criminal law proscribes computer crimes
7. how the USA PATRIOT Act expanded the scope of federal computer crimes
8. how the law protects "access devices" such as credit and debit cards
9. why identity theft is a major problem today and how the criminal law deals with it
10. the various offenses involving intellectual property
11. money laundering and related offenses
12. different species of fraud, including tax fraud, bankruptcy fraud, securities fraud, and mail and wire fraud
13. insider trading, churning, Ponzi schemes, and other forms of securities fraud
14. the relation of federal tax laws to white-collar crime
15. the development of federal laws dealing with organized crime
16. the importance of the federal RICO law in the prosecution of racketeering
17. how RICO has been expanded beyond traditional organized crime syndicates into other aspects of white-collar crime

CHAPTER OUTLINE

Introduction
Legal Principles Governing White-Collar Crimes
Antitrust Violations

Bernie Madoff was a major player on Wall Street for decades. His investment firm, Bernard L. Madoff Investment Securities, had numerous high-profile clients, including banks, foundations, and universities. Madoff was widely sought after as an expert on stock markets and had close ties to the Securities and Exchange Commission (SEC). In March 2009, Madoff pleaded guilty to eleven federal crimes, including securities fraud, mail fraud, wire fraud, and money laundering, all of which are offenses discussed in this chapter. In pleading guilty, Madoff admitted to a massive Ponzi scheme that defrauded billions of dollars from thousands of investors. A Ponzi scheme is one in which money from new investors is used to provide bogus returns to earlier investors. Investors are attracted by the promise of exceptional returns on their investments. When someone of Madoff's résumé and reputation is running the scam, it proves to be irresistible to many. Madoff's Ponzi scheme started as far back as the 1980s. The SEC had investigated Madoff on several occasions, but those investigations never bore fruit. In December 2008, Madoff's sons came to the SEC with information that their father had confessed to them that he was perpetrating a fraud. Investigators subsequently found that more than $65 billion was missing from client accounts. A court-appointed trustee determined that actual losses to investors were in the vicinity of $18 billion. In June 2009, Madoff was sentenced to 150 years in prison, the maximum sentence for his offenses. Today Madoff resides in a medium-security facility at the Federal Correctional Complex in Butner, North Carolina. He is, without question, America's most notorious white-collar criminal.

Introduction

In the previous chapter we delineated what might be called "traditional" property crimes. In this chapter we examine a set of distinctly modern economic offenses. Some of these offenses can be viewed as extensions of the ancient common-law offense of larceny. But most of them are decidedly modern creations—the products of statutes enacted by Congress or the state legislatures. These offenses are often referred to as **white-collar crimes** because perpetrators typically come from the middle and upper socioeconomic strata of society, whereas the offenses described in the previous chapter are often termed "street crimes." However, it is important to understand that anyone, regardless of his or her social status, can commit any of the crimes described in this chapter, just as anyone can commit larceny, robbery, burglary, or any of the other traditional property crimes. While crimes such as burglary, robbery, and carjacking are often associated with violence, white-collar crimes are almost always nonviolent. Instead, they are characterized by deception or abuse of trust and often involve the use of computers or other modern technologies.

The rapid growth of the Internet has opened up new vistas of opportunity for criminals. Identity theft, theft of intellectual property, and numerous types of fraudulent schemes have been propelled to unprecedented levels by means of the Internet. Indeed, in March 2009, the FBI, the investigative division of the U.S. Department of Justice, reported that Internet-based crime increased by 33 percent over the previous year, making 2008 the worst year on record for reported **cybercrimes**.

Organized crime involves offenses committed by persons or groups who conduct their business through illegal enterprises. Organized crime figures, or "racketeers," often attempt to gain political influence through graft and corruption, and they frequently resort to threats and acts of violence in the commission of white-collar offenses. Organized crime gained its greatest foothold during the Prohibition era, when the Eighteenth Amendment to the U.S. Constitution, prohibiting the sale and distribution of alcoholic beverages, was in effect. By the time Prohibition was repealed in 1933, organized crime had become involved in many phases of our economy, often pursuing its interests through such illegal activities as **loan-sharking**, gambling, prostitution, and drug trafficking. Protection rackets and other forms of **racketeering** have become the methodology of organized crime as it has infiltrated many legitimate business operations.

White-collar crime is responsible for the loss of billions of dollars annually by government, businesses, and citizens nationwide. The FBI has special units that handle investigations of economic crimes, financial institution fraud, government fraud, and public corruption. In addition, the Internal Revenue Service, the Secret Service, the Environmental Protection Agency, and the Securities and Exchange Commission are active in the enforcement of federal white-collar crime legislation. In recent years the states have become more active in establishing agencies to enforce state laws in this area.

The U.S. Department of Justice also has an Organized Crime and Racketeering Section (OCRS), which coordinates the department's program to combat organized crime. OCRS coordinates with other investigative agencies such as the FBI and the Drug Enforcement Administration and works with the Attorney General's Organized Crime Council. OCRS also reviews all proposed federal prosecutions under the Racketeer Influenced and Corrupt Organizations (RICO) statute and provides advice to prosecutors.

Legal Principles Governing White-Collar Crimes

The principles discussed in relation to the elements of crimes and parties generally also apply to white-collar offenses. Requirements under both state and federal laws for an *actus reus*, *mens rea*, their concurrence, and causation of harm, as well as the definition of principals and accessories, are explained in Chapter 4. In prosecuting white-collar crimes in federal court, the government is usually required to prove that the accused committed the prohibited act "knowingly and willfully." Frequently, federal prosecutors charge white-collar defendants with conspiracy, either under 18 U.S.C.A. § 371 or under one of the conspiracy provisions pertaining to substantive offenses. As pointed out in Chapter 5, the prosecution enjoys certain procedural advantages in using conspiracy as a basis for criminal charges.

Most white-collar crimes prosecuted as federal violations are based on statutes enacted by Congress under the authority of Article I, Section 8 of the U.S. Constitution, which grants Congress power over postal, bankruptcy, and taxing matters and authority to regulate interstate domestic and foreign commerce. Of course, state legislatures have broad authority to proscribe such offenses as contrary to the public welfare.

While the most notable prosecutions of white-collar crimes involve large-scale corporate frauds, white-collar offenses more frequently entail telephone, mail, and e-mail solicitations by those who commit frauds and swindles as they furnish their victims with "opportunities" to buy unregistered securities, obtain undeserved diplomas, participate in phony contests, and the like. Also common are scams involving fraudulent home-improvement schemes, bogus land sales, and spurious investments.

Many statutes defining offenses that have become known as white-collar crimes also provide civil remedies designed to compensate those who have suffered pecuniary losses as a result of a defendant's activities. These laws provide an example of the overlap between the civil and criminal law discussed in Chapter 1. In instances where a civil proceeding and a criminal proceeding are conducted at the same time, courts often stay the civil proceeding pending resolution of the criminal action.

Prosecution of Corporate Defendants

Under common law, a corporation was not held criminally responsible for its acts. This was because a corporation is an artificial being that cannot form the mental element necessary for imposition of criminal liability and cannot be imprisoned. Nevertheless, its members could be held responsible. As strict liability offenses not requiring proof of a *mens rea* developed, corporations were held criminally responsible. Eventually, courts began to interpret the words "person" and "whoever" in criminal statutes to include corporations. Where statutes prescribed punishment other than death or incarceration, courts began to impose criminal liability based on acts of the corporation's agents and to punish corporations by imposing fines. In some jurisdictions, however, a corporation cannot be held criminally liable for crimes against persons unless the offense is one based on the corporation's negligence rather than a crime based on specific intent. The rationale for this is that the corporation cannot form the necessary *mens rea*.

Acts by Corporate Agents

Today, prosecutions of white-collar crime are frequently directed against **corporate defendants**, and corporations are held criminally liable for the acts of their agents committed within the **scope of an agent's authority**. In 1909 the U.S. Supreme Court first held that a corporation could be held criminally liable based on acts of its agents attributed to the corporation. *N.Y. Cent. & Hudson River R.R. Co. v. United States*, 212 U.S. 481, 29 S.Ct. 304, 53 L.Ed. 613 (1909). Today, corporations are held criminally liable for the unlawful acts of their agents, provided that such conduct is within the scope of the agent's actual or apparent authority. *United States v. Bi-Co*

Pavers, Inc., 741 F.2d 730 (5th Cir. 1984). An agent's knowledge is imputed to the corporation where the agent is acting within the scope of his or her authority and where the knowledge relates to matters within the scope of that authority. See *In re Hellenic, Inc.*, 252 F.3d 391, 395 (5th Cir. 2001). State and federal courts tend to define broadly what constitutes scope of authority, generally holding that the agent's acts must be intended to benefit the corporation in some way.

A few states have adopted section 2.07 of the Model Penal Code or some version of it. Section 2.07(1) provides that a corporation may be convicted of an offense under the following guidelines:

(a) the offense is a violation defined by a statute in which a legislative purpose to impose liability on corporations plainly appears and the conduct is performed by an agent of the corporation acting in behalf of the corporation within the scope of his office or employment, except that if the law defining the offense designates the agents for whose conduct the corporation is accountable or the circumstances under which it is accountable, such provisions shall apply; or

(b) the offense consists of an omission to discharge a specific duty of affirmative performance imposed on corporations by law; or

(c) the commission of the offense was authorized, requested, commanded, performed or recklessly tolerated by the board of directors or by a high managerial agent acting in behalf of the corporation within the scope of his office or employment.

In other jurisdictions, courts simply seek to determine whether the corporate agent or employee was acting within the scope of his or her authority. If so, the courts impute that action to the corporation. Although a corporation may be prosecuted for crimes, that does not exonerate individuals who commit unlawful acts. In fact, in prosecutions for white-collar crimes committed by or on behalf of a corporation, it is not uncommon for corporate executives to be individually punished, generally by the imposition of large fines.

Antitrust Violations

The **Sherman Antitrust Act**, 15 U.S.C.A. § 1 *et seq.*, makes it a crime to enter into any contract or engage in any combination or conspiracy in restraint of trade or to monopolize or attempt to monopolize trade. The act is designed to protect and preserve a system of free and open competition. Its scope is broad and reaches individuals and entities in for-profit and nonprofit activities as well as local governments and educational institutions. The act includes civil remedies as well as criminal sanctions. The criminal provisions are enforced by the Antitrust Division of the U.S. Justice Department.

To prove a criminal violation of the act, the government must establish that (1) two or more entities formed a combination or conspiracy; (2) the combination or conspiracy produces, or potentially produces, an unreasonable restraint of trade or commerce; (3) the restrained trade or commerce is interstate in nature; and (4) the defendant's general intent is to violate the law.

Principles outlined in Chapter 5 concerning conspiracies come into play in prosecutions for **antitrust violations**. The antitrust statutes are unclear regarding whether intent must be proven to convict a defendant. In *United States v. U.S. Gypsum Co.*, 438 U.S. 422, 98 S.Ct. 2864, 57 L.Ed.2d 854 (1978), a case involving alleged price-fixing, the Supreme Court rejected any idea that criminal violations of the act were intended to be strict liability crimes. Rather, the Court observed that intent is an indispensable element of a criminal antitrust case, just like any other criminal offense.

The essence of a Sherman Antitrust Act violation is a combination and conspiracy in restraint of trade. For example, in 1998 the Tenth Circuit Court of Appeals held that the NCAA's rules restricting earnings of a class of coaches to an annual salary of $16,000 was an unreasonable restraint of trade that had an anticompetitive effect. *Law v. National Collegiate Athletic Ass'n.*, 134 F.3d 1010 (10th Cir. 1998).

Among the more common violations are **price-fixing** and **bid rigging**. As previously suggested, price-fixing occurs when sellers unlawfully enter into agreements to control the prices of products or services. Bid rigging involves interference with competitive bidding for the award of a contract. Illustrative convictions are the following:

- Parties made an agreement not to bid competitively at a bankruptcy auction and to hold a later auction and then split the profits. *United States v. Seville Industrial Machinery Corp.*, 696 F. Supp. 986 (D.N.J. 1988).
- An agent for a public contractor agreed to rig bids with another on a county construction project. *United States v. Bi-Co Pavers, Inc.*, 741 F.2d 730 (5th Cir. 1984).
- Parties entered into a conspiracy to submit collusive noncompetitive bids on a project. *United States v. Mobile Materials, Inc.*, 881 F.2d 866 (10th Cir. 1989).
- Defendant corporations conspired to fix prices for fiberglass materials. *United States v. Therm-All, Inc.*, 373 F.3d 625 (5th Cir. 2004).

The U.S. Justice Department alone is authorized to enforce the criminal sanctions of the act. Criminal violations are felonies; the act provides that those convicted shall be punished by a fine not exceeding $100,000,000 if a corporation; or, if any other person, $1,000,000; or by imprisonment not exceeding ten years; or by both punishments, in the discretion of the court. 15 U.S.C.A. § 1.

Corporate defendants often seek to avoid liability for violations committed by their agents. But courts have generally held that as long as an agent acts within the scope of employment or apparent authority, the corporation may be held legally responsible.

Most state legislatures have enacted statutes under which intrastate violations of securities laws are prosecuted. The text of state statutes and their judicial interpretations often parallel the federal ones.

Computer Crimes

Once computers became common in society, criminals began to employ them to commit a variety of offenses. Indeed, the pervasiveness of computers poses some unique challenges to federal and state law enforcement agencies and prosecutors. In 1984 Congress enacted the **Computer Fraud and Abuse Act**, 18 U.S.C.A. §. 1030. The statute has been amended several times, most recently in 2008. The act proscribes crimes involving "protected computers"— those used in interstate commerce or communications—including computers connected to the Internet. As amended in 1996, 18 U.S.C. A. § 1030(a)(5)(A) makes it a crime to "knowingly cause the transmission of a program, information, code, or command" in interstate commerce with intent to cause damage to a computer exclusively used by a financial institution or the U.S. government. In addition, the act prohibits "knowingly and with intent to defraud, trafficking in passwords to permit unauthorized access to a government computer, or to affect interstate or foreign commerce." 18 U.S.C.A. § 1030(a)(6)(A)(B). Subsection 1030(a)

A Federal Computer Crime

CASE-IN-POINT

The federal government charged John Larking Trotter with intentionally causing damage to a Salvation Army computer without authorization in violation of the Computer Fraud and Abuse Act, 18 U.S.C.A. § 1030(a)(5)(A)(i). Trotter admitted that the Salvation Army's computer that he accessed was a protected computer, but on appeal he argued that the statute was unconstitutional as applied to him because "the statute cannot possibly be so broad as to cover the computer network of a not-for-profit organization like the Salvation Army." The federal appellate court rejected his argument, explaining that the Salvation Army's computers are intertwined with interstate commerce and thus are within the realm of Congress's power to regulate interstate commerce. The court further observed, "The Salvation Army's status as a not-for-profit entity has no bearing on our analysis; it is the characteristics of the computer or computer network, not the entity using the network, that is the focus of the statutes."

United States v. Trotter, 478 F.3d 918 (8th Cir. 2007).

(7) makes it illegal to transmit in interstate or foreign commerce any threat to cause damage to a protected computer with intent to extort something of value.

It is also a federal crime to "knowingly with intent to defraud" produce, use, or traffic in counterfeit **access devices**. 18 U.S.C.A. § 1029(a). Access devices include cards, plates, codes, electronic serial numbers, mobile identification numbers, personal identification numbers, telecommunications services, equipment, instrument identifiers, or other means that can be used to obtain goods or services. 18 U.S.C.A. § 1029(e). To obtain a conviction for unauthorized access devices, the government must prove that a defendant acted knowingly and with intent to defraud, but proof of such intent may be established with circumstantial evidence. *United States v. Ismoila*, 100 F.3d 380 (5th Cir. 1996).

The USA PATRIOT Act

After the terrorist attacks of September 11, 2001, Congress hastily passed important legislation officially known as the Uniting and Strengthening America by Providing Appropriate Tools Required to Intercept and Obstruct Terrorism Act of 2001. Better known by its acronym, the **USA PATRIOT Act** was signed into law by President George W. Bush on October 25, 2001. This 342-page statute was designed to deter and punish terrorist acts in the United States and around the world and to enhance the federal government's law-enforcement investigatory tools. On March 9, 2006, President Bush signed legislation essentially renewing the USA PATRIOT Act. Section 814 of the act makes a number of changes in federal statutes designed to strengthen the Computer Fraud and Abuse Act, 18 U.S.C.A. § 1030.

Section 814 of the PATRIOT Act amends the definition of "protected computer" to include computers outside of the United States that affect "interstate or foreign commerce or communication of the United States." 18 U.S.C.A. § 1030(e)(2)(B). Section 814 of the act raises the maximum penalty for violations for damaging a protected computer to ten years for first-time offenders and twenty years for repeat offenders. 18 U.S.C.A. § 1030(c)(4). Under previous law, first-time offenders who violate section 1030(a)(5) by damaging a protected computer could be punished by no more than five years' imprisonment, while repeat offenders could receive up to ten years.

Section 814 of the act added 18 U.S.C.A. 1030(c)(2)(C) and (e)(8), which clarify that a hacker need only intend to damage a protected computer or the information on it, not to cause a specific dollar amount of loss or other special harm.

State Laws Proscribing Computer Offenses

Since 1978 nearly every state has enacted laws specifically defining computer crimes. These laws define *access, computer program, software, database, hacking, financial instrument,* and other terms used in modern computer parlance and address such activities as computer manipulation, theft of intellectual property, telecommunications crimes, and software piracy. They also create such offenses as **theft of computer services**, **computer fraud**, and **computer trespass**. The Virginia legislature has addressed each of these offenses by enacting the Virginia Computer Crimes Act, § 18.2–152.3 of which provides:

> Any person who uses a computer or computer network without authority and with the intent to:
>
> 1. Obtain property or services by false pretenses;
>
> 2. Embezzle or commit larceny; or
>
> 3. Convert the property of another is guilty of the crime of computer fraud.

Depending on the value of property or services actually obtained, the offense is either a felony or a serious misdemeanor.

Section 18.2–152.4 provides:

> A. It shall be unlawful for any person, with malicious intent, to:
>
> 1. Temporarily or permanently remove, halt, or otherwise disable any computer data, computer programs or computer software from a computer or computer network;
>
> 2. Cause a computer to malfunction, regardless of how long the malfunction persists;
>
> 3. Alter, disable, or erase any computer data, computer programs or computer software;
>
> 4. Effect the creation or alteration of a financial instrument or of an electronic transfer of funds;
>
> 5. Use a computer or computer network to cause physical injury to the property of another; or
>
> 6. Use a computer or computer network to make or cause to be made an unauthorized copy, in any form, including, but not limited to, any printed or electronic form of computer data, computer programs or computer software residing in, communicated by, or produced by a computer or computer network.

Depending on the damages caused, an offense under this statute is either a felony or a serious misdemeanor.

Anti-Spam Laws

As everyone who uses e-mail knows, "spam" refers to unsolicited e-mail messages sent to thousands, even millions, of e-mail accounts. Spam is a nuisance to e-mail users and causes real problems for Internet service providers. A number of states have enacted laws regulating commercial spam. Arizona law, for example, provides:

A person shall not knowingly transmit commercial electronic mail if any of the following apply:

1. The person falsifies electronic mail transmission information or other routing information for unsolicited commercial electronic mail.

2. The mail contains false or misleading information in the subject line.

3. The person uses a third party's internet address or domain name without the third party's consent for the purpose of transmitting electronic mail in a way that makes it appear that the third party was the sender of the mail.

Ariz. Rev. Stat. § 44-1372.01(A).

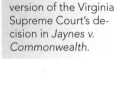

Go to the companion website for an edited version of the Virginia Supreme Court's decision in *Jaynes v. Commonwealth*.

In enacting regulations of unsolicited bulk e-mail, states must be aware of First Amendment considerations. Virginia's anti-spam law was declared unconstitutional by the Virginia Supreme Court because it prohibited transmission of any unsolicited e-mails, including those containing political, religious, or other protected speech. *Jaynes v. Commonwealth*, 666 S.E.2d 303 (Va. 2008); *Jaynes v. Commonwealth*, 657 S.E.2d 478 (Va. 2008). On March 31, 2009, the U.S. Supreme Court refused to take the case, thus allowing the Virginia Supreme Court decision to stand. *Virginia v. Jaynes*, 08-765.

International Efforts to Combat Cybercrime

Because of its global reach, Internet crime poses an especially difficult challenge to domestic law enforcement agencies. In 2006, the United States joined more than forty other countries by ratifying the Convention on Cybercrime, a treaty designed to harmonize national laws and strengthen international cooperation in this area.

CASE-IN-POINT

Unauthorized Access to a Voice Mailbox

Andrea M. Gerulis was convicted in a bench trial of two counts of unlawful use of a computer and two counts of violating a statute that criminalized intentionally obtaining various electronic services "available only for compensation" by deception, unauthorized connection, etc. Gerulis was ordered to make restitution. The evidence revealed that Gerulis had deposited and retrieved information from voice mailboxes (VMBs) of a hospital and a telephone message company without authority from either to do so. By altering passwords, she thereby prevented authorized users from using their VMBs. Gerulis appealed, contending the evidence was insufficient to sustain her convictions.

The appellate court found that VMBs are "computers" within the meaning of the statute, and Gerulis's disruption of normal use of the VMBs violated the statute. The court then addressed Gerulis's convictions for theft of services. The court observed that the prosecution had charged Gerulis under a statute that makes it an offense if a person "intentionally obtains services for himself or for another which he knows are available only for compensation." Because the evidence revealed that the VMBs that Gerulis accessed were provided by the hospital and message company without charge for their employees, the court found that Gerulis's mere intent to obtain free services did not violate that statute. Accordingly, the court affirmed Gerulis's convictions for unlawful use of a computer, reversed her convictions for theft of services, and remanded the case to the trial court to modify the restitution order imposed as Gerulis's sentence.

Commonwealth v. Gerulis, 616 A.2d 686 (Pa. Super. 1992).

In addition to its provisions dealing with sexual exploitation of children, terrorism, and "hate crimes," the treaty addresses several problems in the area of international white-collar crime, including computer-related fraud, "hacking," the dissemination of computer viruses, and electronic attacks on financial institutions.

Access Device Fraud

Debit cards and credit cards, automated teller machine (ATM) cards, account numbers, personal identification numbers (PINs), and other means are now commonly available to named persons who assume the obligation of their use. Because of their widespread use, state legislatures have realized the necessity to enact comprehensive statutes proscribing the fraudulent use of devices to secure cash, goods, and services through means beyond the traditional credit card.

In 1998 Pennsylvania rewrote its statute titled "Credit Card Fraud" to proscribe a variety of means of gaining fraudulent access to money, goods, and services. As amended, the revised section of Purdon's Pennsylvania Consolidated Statutes Annotated now provides:

Section 4106. Access device fraud

(a) Offense defined.—A person commits an offense if he:

(1) uses an access device to obtain or in an attempt to obtain property or services with knowledge that:

(i) the access device is counterfeit, altered or incomplete;

(ii) the access device was issued to another person who has not authorized its use;

(iii) the access device has been revoked or canceled; or

(iv) for any other reason his use of the access device is unauthorized by the issuer or the device holder; or

(2) publishes, makes, sells, gives, or otherwise transfers to another, or offers or advertises, or aids and abets any other person to use an access device knowing that the access device is counterfeit, altered or incomplete, belongs to another person who has not authorized its use, has been revoked or canceled or for any reason is unauthorized by the issuer or the device holder; or

(3) possesses an access device knowing that it is counterfeit, altered, incomplete or belongs to another person who has not authorized its possession.

(a.1) Presumptions.—For the purpose of this section as well as in any prosecution for theft committed by the means specified in this section:

(1) An actor is presumed to know an access device is counterfeit, altered or incomplete if he has in his possession or under his control two or more counterfeit, altered or incomplete access devices.

(2) Knowledge of revocation or cancellation shall be presumed to have been received by an access device holder seven days after it has been mailed to him at the address set forth on the access device application or at a new address if a change of address has been provided to the issuer.

(b) Defenses.—It is a defense to a prosecution under subsection (a)(1)(iv) if the actor proves by a preponderance of the evidence that he had the intent and ability to meet all obligations to the issuer arising out of his use of the access device.

Subsection (c) of the Pennsylvania statute stipulates that if the value involved is $500 or more, the offense constitutes a felony; if less than $500, the offense constitutes a misdemeanor. The degree of felony or misdemeanor depends on the value involved.

Subsection (d) includes the following definitions:

- "Access device." Any card, including, but not limited to, a credit card, debit card and automated teller machine card, plate, code, account number, personal identification number or other means of account access that can be used alone or in conjunction with another access device to obtain money, goods, services or anything else of value or that can be used to transfer funds.
- "Altered access device." A validly issued access device which after issue is changed in any way.
- "Counterfeit access device." An access device not issued by an issuer in the ordinary course of business.
- "Device holder." The person or organization named on the access device to whom or for whose benefit the access device is issued by an issuer.

Because of the widespread use of access devices, many states have adopted statutes prohibiting **access device fraud**. Offenses proscribed by the above statute could likely be prosecuted under modern comprehensive theft or forgery statutes; however, given such statutes, an issue has arisen as to whether the existence of a statute proscribing credit card use (more recently included in statutes proscribing access device fraud) precludes prosecution under a theft or forgery proscribing more severe penalties. Several courts have held that such specific statutes did not preclude prosecution under a statute based on theft or forgery. See, for example, *People v. James*, 497 P.2d 1256 (Colo. 1972); *Garcia v. State*, 669 S.W.2d 169 (Tex. App. 1984).

In *Commonwealth v. Sargent*, 823 A.2d 174 (Pa. Super. 2003), a Pennsylvania appellate court rejected a defendant's argument that, because he obtained property valued at $450 through fraudulent use of a credit card, he could not be convicted under a statute making forgery a felony. He argued that because of the existence of section 4106, his offense would be a misdemeanor because he obtained property valued at only $450. The court held that the defendant's action of signing the victim's name to credit card receipts was a felony of the third degree because the receipts constituted documents within the meaning of a statute providing that forgery is a felony of the third degree. The court concluded, "We find meritless Appellant's argument that the Legislature did not intend the fraudulent signing of credit card receipts to constitute a felony of the third degree under the facts in this case since the Legislature specifically provided for the unauthorized use of credit cards in 18 Pa. C.S.A. § 4106." *Id.* at 177.

Many states have adopted statutes similar to the Pennsylvania law. Courts have generally held that the existence of a statute specifically addressing access devices does not preclude the state from prosecution of an access device offense as forgery, where the facts warrant it, under a forgery statute proscribing more severe penalties. See, for example, *Garcia v. State*, 669 S.W.2d 169 (Tex. App. 1984); *People v. James*, 497 P.2d 1256 (Colo. 1972).

Identity Theft

The theft or misappropriation of personal identifying information and documents, commonly referred to as **identity theft**, has become a theft offense of major proportions in the United States. In April 2006, the *Bureau of Justice Statistics*

Bulletin reported that in 2004, 3.6 million households, representing 3 percent of the households in the United States, discovered that at least one member of the household had been the victim of identity theft during the previous six months.

A person's identity is closely tied to personal and numerical identification of bank accounts; credit cards; Social Security, Medicare, telephone, insurance, and utility accounts; and many other identifying documents. Thieves obtain information about a person through many means. These include such obvious means as theft of wallets and purses, mail, and computer data, and gathering information from home and car burglaries. They also obtain information from such less obvious means as "shoulder surfing" when someone is paying by check or credit card, and "dumpster diving" into trash to obtain discarded identifying documents such as unused preapproved credit card applications. Information obtained from e-mail and other computer transactions, including responses to requests for passwords and other information, is increasingly becoming a source of identifying information. Armed with such information, a thief can then assume the victim's identity, change the victim's address, open new accounts, buy a car, borrow money, and otherwise injure the victim's assets, credit standing, and reputation. Most victims of identity theft are unaware of how a thief obtained their personal information. Often the victim is unaware of the fraud until substantial damage has been inflicted. Victims often incur large expenses and expend considerable time in opening new accounts and repairing their credit ratings.

Federal Legislation

To address the growing problem of identity theft, Congress enacted the Identity Theft and Assumption Deterrence Act of 1998 (ITADA), which amends 18 U.S.C.A. § 1028 by adding subsection (a)(7). This subsection makes it a felony to "knowingly transfer, possess or use, without lawful authority, a means of identification of another person with the intent to commit, or to aid or abet, any unlawful activity that constitutes a violation of Federal law, or that constitutes a felony under any applicable State or local law." Conduct involving identity theft or fraud may in some instances also be a violation of 18 U.S.C.A. § 1341 (credit card fraud); 18 U.S.C.A. § 1030 (computer fraud); 18 U.S.C.A. § 1341 (mail fraud); 18 U.S.C.A. § 1343 (wire, radio and television fraud); or 18 U.S.C.A. § 1344 (financial institution fraud).

The Federal Trade Commission maintains a website (www.consumer.gov/ idtheft) that furnishes considerable information about identity theft. It explains how the crime occurs, what steps can be taken to prevent it, and what measures should be taken when people discover that they have been victimized by identity theft. The site also features a comprehensive survey of federal and state legislation criminalizing identity theft.

State Legislation

By 2003 most states had enacted specific statutes criminalizing identify theft and fraud, but even without specific statutes such activity could be prosecuted under statutes proscribing theft and fraud. Section 943.201(2) of the Wisconsin Statutes, as recently amended, provides that

> (2) Whoever, for any of the following purposes, intentionally uses or attempts to use or possess with intent to use any personal identifying information or personal identification document of an individual, including a deceased individual, without the authorization or consent of the individual and by representing that he or she is the

Georgia Supreme Court Affirms a Conviction for Identity Theft

Nohe Gomes Hernandez, an illegal immigrant, was convicted under a Georgia statute that makes it a crime to access the resources of a person unlawfully through the use of identifying information. The evidence at trial revealed that Hernandez misappropriated Jason Smith's social security number to obtain a social security card and a driver's license in Smith's name. Next, posing as Smith, Hernandez used these means of identification to obtain a job at a poultry processing plant. Hernandez's wages, under Smith's name, were reported to the Internal Revenue Service. In 2005, when Smith contacted the IRS to inquire about a tax refund he was expecting, an IRS agent informed him that he owed approximately $12,000 in back taxes. This led to the discovery that Hernandez had assumed Smith's identity.

On appeal, Hernandez argued that although he used Smith's identifying information to obtain a job there was no evidence that he used the information to access any of Smith's resources. In rejecting his contention the court pointed out that OCGA Sec. 16-9-120(f)(F), which states that a person's resources includes "[a]ny account, . . . including a national bank . . . is sufficiently broad to include the U.S. Treasury, the nation's foremost banking institution." The appellate court affirmed Hernandez's conviction.

Hernandez v. State, 639 S.E.2d 473 (Ga. 2007).

individual, that he or she is acting with the authorization or consent of the individual, or that the information or document belongs to him or her is guilty of a Class H felony:

> (a) To obtain credit, money, goods, services, employment, or any other thing of value or benefit.
>
> (b) To avoid civil or criminal process or penalty.
>
> (c) To harm the reputation, property, person, or estate of the individual.

In *State v. Ramirez*, 633 N.W.2d 656 (Wis. App. 2001), the court upheld the conviction of a defendant found guilty under Wis. Stat. § 943.201(2) for misappropriating the personal identifying information of another. The defendant had used someone else's social security number without authorization to obtain employment.

In 2005, the Washington Court of Appeals rejected a defendant's contention that the state's choice to prosecute him for the felony of identity theft rather than the misdemeanor offense of use of a false name or a false identity denied him his constitutional right to equal protection of the laws. The court rejected his contention because the misdemeanor offense did not require assuming the identity of an actual person. *State v. Presba*, 26 P.3d 1280 (Wash. App. 2005).

In *People v. Montoya*, 868 N.E.2d 389 (Ill. App. 2007), defendant Montoya used another person's name and social security number to get a job with Terra Harvest Foods. Over more than three years she received over $50,000 in wages and approximately $31,000 in medical insurance benefits under the name and social security number of her victim. The Illinois appellate court found the evidence of identity theft sufficient to support her conviction.

Intellectual Property Offenses

The term **intellectual property** refers to products of the human intellect such as patents, copyrights, trademarks, and trade secrets. In the information age, intellectual property is as important as real estate or tangible personal property. The U.S.

Constitution, Article 1, Section 8, clause 8, grants Congress the power to secure for a limited time to authors and inventors the exclusive rights to their writings and discoveries. Congress has legislated pursuant to such authority and has granted federal courts exclusive jurisdiction over civil and criminal actions based on federal statutes. See 28 U.S.C.A. §§ 1338, 1355. While most disputes involving intellectual property are civil matters, there are several important criminal prohibitions in this area, most notably patent infringement, copyright infringement, trademark counterfeiting, and theft of trade secrets.

Patent Infringement

A **patent** is a federal government grant of the right to exclude others from producing or using a discovery or invention. Patents are issued by the U.S. Patent and Trademark Office for inventions and discoveries that are novel, useful, and not something of an obvious nature. See 35 U.S.C.A. §§ 101–103. Patents are issued for a period of twenty years. 35 U.S.C.A. § 154.

Patent infringements are generally remedied through civil litigation. Indeed, there are few instances of criminal penalties being imposed. The Patent Act, however, establishes criminal liability of $500 per infringement for falsely affixing or marking in connection with sales or advertising of any imitation the name of the patentee or the patent number, or using the words "patent," "patentee," "patent applied for," or "patent pending" to falsely convey the status of a patent. To prove any of the above violations, the prosecution must show the deceitful intent of the defendant. 35 U.S.C.A. § 292. Title 18 U.S.C.A. § 497 makes it an offense for "[w]hoever passes, utters, or publishes, or attempts to pass, utter, or publish as genuine, any such letters patent, knowing the same to be forged, counterfeited or falsely altered." The statute calls for a fine or imprisonment.

Copyright Infringement

A **copyright** is a form of legal protection that is provided to the authors of original works. Congress has enacted statutes to expand the protection of literary work to include musical, artistic, and architectural works as well as videos, computer software, and databases. Copyrights are registered in the Copyright Office in the Library of Congress, and a copyright for a work created after January 1, 1978, is given statutory protection for the life of the author plus seventy years after the author's death. 17 U.S.C.A. § 302(a). Section 506 of the Copyright Act provides for the criminal prosecution of certain types of infringement.

Section 506(a) of the Copyright Act, 17 U.S.C.A. § 506(a), provides that anyone "who infringes a copyright willfully either (1) for purposes of commercial advantage or private financial gain, or (2) by the reproduction or distribution, including by electronic means of one or more copies or phonorecords . . . shall be punished as provided in 18 U.S.C.A. § 2319." (The term "willfully" distinguishes the crime from infringement in civil litigation.) Under this latter statute the determination of whether such violation is a felony or misdemeanor depends on the quantity and value of items distributed in a specified period of time. Penalties are also provided for fraudulent removal of copyright notices and for false representations in copyright applications. 17 U.S.C.A. § 506(d) & (e).

Knowingly trafficking in counterfeit labels affixed or designed to be affixed to a phonorecord or copy of a computer program, motion pictures, or other audiovisual works is **bootlegging**, an offense punishable by fine or imprisonment under 18 U.S. C.A. § 2318.

Section 506(b) of the Copyright Act provides for the "forfeiture and destruction . . . of all infringing copies or phonorecords and all implements, devices, or equipment used in the manufacture of such infringing copies or phonorecords." 17 U.S.C. A. § 506(b).

It is a misdemeanor to fraudulently place a copyright notice on an article, to distribute such an article, to fraudulently remove the copyright notice from a validly copyrighted article, or to knowingly make false representations in an application for copyright. 17 U.S.C.A. § 506(c), (d), & (e). Some states have also enacted laws making bootlegging of copyrighted materials an offense.

In 1994 Congress adopted 18 U.S.C.A. Sec. 2319A, which, as amended, provides:

> Whoever, without the consent of the performer or performers, knowingly and for commercial advantage or private financial gain
> (1) fixes the sounds or sounds and images of a live musical performance in a copy or phonorecord, or reproduces copies or phonorecords of such a performance from an unauthorized fixation;
> (2) transmits or otherwise communicates to the public the sounds or sounds and images of a live musical performance; or
> (3) distributes or offers to distribute, sells or offers to sell, rents or offers to rent, or traffics in any copy or phonorecord fixed as described in paragraph (1) shall be imprisoned for up to five years and for up to ten years for a second offense.

Internet-Based Copyright Infringement

In 1997, Congress enacted the No Electronic Theft (NET) Act, 111 STAT. 2678, Public Law 105-147, specifically to address Internet-based copyright infringement. Prior to this legislation, copyright infringement could be prosecuted only where the

---

CASE-IN-POINT

Criminal Copyright Infringement

In August of 1999, Jeffrey G. Levy, a twenty-two-year-old senior at the University of Oregon, pleaded guilty to criminal copyright infringement. According to a statement issued by the U.S. Attorney's Office in Oregon, Levy admitted that he illegally posted computer software, music files, and digitally recorded movies on the Internet, which allowed anyone accessing his site to download and copy these products. Officials at the University of Oregon brought the matter to the attention of the FBI after noting an unusually large volume of bandwidth traffic being generated from Levy's website, which was hosted on the University's file server. The FBI's investigation confirmed that thousands of computer programs, movies, and musical recordings had been made available for downloading from Levy's site. Although Levy faced a possible $250,000 fine and three years in prison, his negotiated guilty plea led to a sentence of two years' probation. As a condition of probation, Levy was ordered not to access the Internet from his home computer.

Source: United States Attorney's Office, District of Oregon, "Defendant Sentenced for First Criminal Copyright Conviction Under the 'No Electronic Theft' (NET) Act for Unlawful Distribution of Software on the Internet," November 23, 1999.

defendant derived a financial benefit from the infringement. The proliferation of file sharing via the Internet prompted Congress to change the law. The NET Act amended 17 U.S.C.A. § 506 and 18 U.S.C.A. § 2319 to make it unlawful to reproduce or distribute copyrighted works even where a defendant lacks a commercial or financial motive. One who reproduces or distributes ten or more copyrighted works that have a total value of more than $2,500 can be charged with a felony punishable by up to three years in prison and a fine of up to $250,000. A defendant who reproduces or distributes one or more copies of copyrighted works with a value of more than $1,000 can be charged with a misdemeanor punishable by up to one year in prison and a fine of up to $100,000.

Trademark Counterfeiting

A **trademark** is a distinctive word, phrase, or graphic symbol used to distinguish a product. To be protected by federal law, trademarks used in interstate or foreign commerce maybe registered with the U.S. Patent and Trademark Office. Once registered, a trademark has nationwide protection. See 15 U.S.C.A. §§ 1051–1072. Trademark disputes are generally resolved in civil courts, but federal law does provide criminal penalties for **trademark counterfeiting**. The Trademark Counterfeiting Act of 1984 provides:

> Whoever intentionally traffics or attempts to traffic in goods or services and knowingly uses a counterfeit mark on or in connection with such goods or services shall, if an individual, be fined not more than $2,000,000 or imprisoned not more than ten years, or both, and, if a person other than an individual, be fined not more than $5,000,000. 18 U.S.C.A. § 2320.

The statute defines "counterfeit mark" to mean "a spurious mark . . . that is identical with, or substantially indistinguishable from, a mark registered in the United States Patent and Trademark Office . . . and the use of which is likely to cause confusion, to cause mistake, or to deceive. . . ." 18 U.S.C.A. § 2320(e). When a genuine trademark is affixed to a counterfeit product, it becomes a "spurious mark" within the meaning of the statutory prohibition against trafficking in counterfeit goods. To establish a violation of the statute, the government must prove that the mark is counterfeit and that the defendant knew the mark was counterfeit. Section 2320 requires the government to establish, beyond a reasonable doubt, four elements: (1) that the defendant trafficked or attempted to traffic in goods or services; (2) that such trafficking, or the attempt to traffic, was intentional; (3) that the defendant used a "counterfeit mark" on or in connection with such goods or services; and (4) that the defendant "knew" that the counterfeit mark was so used. *United States v. Sultan*, 115 F.3d 321, 325 (5th Cir. 1997).

Theft of Trade Secrets

A **trade secret** is generally a formula, pattern, physical device, idea, process, compilation of information, or other information that provides a business with a competitive advantage. Trade secrets include "all forms and types of financial, business, scientific, technical, economic, or engineering information . . . whether tangible or intangible, and whether or how stored, compiled, or memorialized physically, electronically, graphically, photographically, or in writing." 18 U.S.C.A. § 1839(3). Controversies concerning the use and misuse of trade secrets are frequently handled in civil courts where state statutes and the common law provide remedies. However, Congress enacted the Economic Espionage Act of 1996 (EEA), creating the first national criminal penalty for theft of trade secrets. The EEA prohibits foreign governments from stealing trade secrets (18 U.S.C.A. § 1831) and criminalizes domestic trade secret theft (18 U.S.C.A. § 1832). Title 18 U.S.C.A. § 1832, provides that

(a) Whoever, with intent to convert a trade secret, that is related to or included in a product that is produced for or placed in interstate or foreign commerce, to the economic benefit of anyone other than the owner thereof, and intending or knowing that the offense will, injure any owner of that trade secret, knowingly—

(1) steals, or without authorization appropriates, takes, carries away, or conceals, or by fraud, artifice, or deception obtains such information;

(2) without authorization copies, duplicates, sketches, draws, photographs, downloads, uploads, alters, destroys, photocopies, replicates, transmits, delivers, sends, mails, communicates, or conveys such information;

(3) receives, buys, or possesses such information, knowing the same to have been stolen or appropriated, obtained, or converted without authorization;

(4) attempts to commit any offense described in paragraphs (1) through (3); or

(5) conspires with one or more other persons to commit any offense described in paragraphs (1) through (3), and one or more of such persons do any act to effect the object of the conspiracy, shall, except as provided in subsection (b), be fined under this title or imprisoned not more than 10 years, or both.

(b) Any organization that commits any offense described in subsection (a) shall be fined not more than $5,000,000. 18 U.S.C.A. § 1832.

Title 18 U.S.C.A. § 1834 provides for forfeiture to the United States of any profits and proceeds derived from violation of section 1832.

In July 2006 the media reported that three people had been arrested for allegedly violating the EEA. An employee of the Coca-Cola Company and two others were charged with stealing the confidential files and a sample of a new drink product and offering to sell these items to Coca-Cola's main rival, PepsiCo. Reportedly, the plot was foiled when Coca-Cola learned of the crime and reported it to the FBI. On February 2, 2007, a federal jury in Atlanta convicted Joya Williams, a former executive assistant at Coca-Cola, of conspiracy to steal trade secrets.

CASE-IN-POINT

Violation of the Economic Espionage Act

Dr. Victor Lee was employed by Avery Dennison Inc. to conduct scientific research on adhesives. In 1989, while making a presentation in Taiwan, Lee was introduced to Pin-Yen Yang, the head of Four Pillars Enterprise Company, Ltd., a competing firm. According to the indictment, Yang and Lee agreed that Lee would receive $25,000 to serve as a secret consultant to Four Pillars. Some time later Lee provided Yang with confidential materials belonging to Avery Dennison, including information regarding a new adhesive product. After learning of Lee's activities, the FBI confronted him and persuaded him to participate in a "sting" operation in which the FBI videotaped a meeting between Lee and Yang at which Lee provided Yang with confidential Avery Dennison materials. After a jury trial, Yang was convicted of attempt and conspiracy to commit theft of a trade secret. The U.S. Court of Appeals for the Sixth Circuit upheld the conviction.

United States v. Yang, 281 F.3d 534 (6th Cir. 2002).

False Statements, Bankruptcy Fraud, and False Claims

The federal **False Statements Act** (18 U.S.C.A. § 1001) prohibits knowingly and willfully making a false statement that is material to a matter within the jurisdiction of any department or agency of the United States. "Congress intentionally drafted § 1001 in an expansive fashion in order that it be accorded the broadest possible interpretation regarding the situations in which it would come into play." *Moser v. United States*, 18 F.3d 469, 473 (7th Cir. 1994).

When proceeding under the False Statements Act, the government must prove that the accused knowingly and willfully submitted to a government agency or department a statement that was false and material. The issue of materiality is one for the court to consider. *United States v. Rodgers*, 466 U.S. 475, 104 S.Ct. 1942, 80 L.Ed.2d 492 (1984). (A false statement in any matter within the jurisdiction of any department or agency of the United States encompasses criminal investigations conducted by the FBI and Secret Service.)

Federal statutes criminalize **bankruptcy fraud**, which is defined as the knowing and fraudulent concealment of assets, avoiding distribution of nonexempt assets, taking false oaths, and related conduct in connection with bankruptcy proceedings. 18 U.S.C.A. § 152. To convict, the government must prove the defendant acted willfully; however, one who acts with "willful blindness" can be found to have acted with the requisite criminal intent. Although the statute does not expressly state a materiality requirement, 18 U.S.C.A. § 152 has been construed "to require that [a] false oath be given in relation to some material matter." *United States v. O'Donnell*, 539 F.2d 1233, 1237 (9th Cir. 1976).

Medicare and Medicaid provide health care benefits to millions of Americans. Medicare is designed to provide medical care primarily to older citizens, whereas Medicaid is a program that furnishes health care services to the needy. Historically, criminal violations of the federal statutes providing these benefits, as well as other false claims to federal entitlements, have been prosecuted under the **False Claims Act**, 18 U.S.C.A. § 287, and the False Statements Act. To prove Medicare or Medicaid fraud under the False Claims Act, the government must prove that (1) the defendant presented a claim seeking reimbursement from the government for medical

Criminal Prosecution under the False Claims Act

CASE-IN-POINT Evidence at trial disclosed that the defendant had submitted false claims to Pennsylvania Blue Shield and the Travelers Insurance Company but not to any federal agency or official. These insurance companies processed and paid the claims and were reimbursed by the federal government for their payments and costs of processing the claims. The defendant was convicted and appealed. A question arose whether the insurance carriers could be considered "agencies" of the United States for purposes of criminal prosecution. The court

doubted that the insurance carriers were agencies of the United States; however, it cited another federal statute, 18 U.S.C.A. § 2(b), which provides that "[w]hoever willfully causes an act to be done which if directly performed by him or another would be an offense against the United States, is punishable as a principal." Finding the proof established that the defendant "caused" the private carriers to submit false claims to the government, the court affirmed the defendant's conviction.

United States v. Catena, 500 F.2d 1319 (3d Cir. 1974).

Criminal Prosecution under the Health Insurance Portability and Accountability Act

Three defendants participated in staged automobile accidents and fabricated personal injury claims to take advantage of the operation of the New York No-Fault Act. They contended that they were not subject to prosecution under 18 U.S.C.A. § 1347 because they were not health professionals. The court rejected their contention and held that

> [W]hether that person is a medical professional, a patient, or otherwise—who purposefully endeavors to defraud a health care benefit program

may be found guilty of health care fraud, if his or her conduct otherwise conforms to the elements of the offense. The broad language of section 1347 shows that Congress intended for this statute to include within its scope a wide range of conduct so that all forms of health care fraud would be proscribed, regardless of the kind of specific schemes unscrupulous persons may concoct.

United States v. Lucien, 347 F.3d 45, 51, (2d Cir. 2003).

services or goods, (2) the claim was false or fraudulent, and (3) the accused knew of the claim's falsity. See *United States v. Upton*, 91 F.3d 677 (5th Cir. 1996), where the court, after reciting these elements of proof, affirmed the defendants' convictions under 18 U.S.C.A. § 287 for filing a false claim with the U.S. Air Force for reimbursement of unpaid bond premiums.

The Health Insurance Portability and Accountability Act (HIPAA)

In 1996 Congress enacted the Health Insurance Portability and Accountability Act of 1996, Public Law 104–191. Section 244 of the act, codified at 18 U.S.C.A. § 1035, establishes a new false-statement offense that prohibits making material false or fraudulent statements or entries in connection with delivery of or payment for health care benefits. This new section covers statements and concealments made to private insurers that could not be prosecuted under the False Statements Act. The new act also includes several other criminal provisions. Section 242 makes it an offense for any person to knowingly and willfully execute or attempt to execute a scheme or artifice to defraud any health care benefit program or to fraudulently obtain money or property of such programs in connection with the delivery of or payment for health care benefits, items, or services. 18 U.S.C.A § 1347. Section 243 proscribes knowingly and willfully embezzling assets of a health care benefit program. 18 U.S.C.A. § 669. Section 245 creates a new crime that prohibits willfully obstructing, misleading, or delaying communication of information or records to a criminal investigator relating to a violation of a federal health care offense. 18 U.S.C.A. § 1518.

Mail and Wire Fraud

The Federal Mail Fraud Statute, 18 U.S.C.A. § 1341, makes it a crime to use the mail to defraud. **Mail fraud** consists of (1) a scheme devised or intended to defraud or to obtain money or property by fraudulent means and (2) the use of or causing to use the mails in furtherance of the fraudulent scheme. Courts have held that to obtain a conviction, the government must prove the existence of a scheme committed by

Mail Fraud

CASE-IN-POINT

Wayne T. Schmuck, a used-car distributor, purchased used cars, rolled back their odometers, and then sold the automobiles to Wisconsin retail dealers for prices artificially inflated because of the low mileage readings. The dealers, in turn, mailed the title applications to the state transportation department. Finding that the mailings by the dealers were essential to the defendant distributor's fraudulent acts, the Supreme Court upheld Schmuck's conviction under 18 U.S.C.A. § 1341, observing that the mailings were "part of the execution of the scheme as conceived by the perpetrator at the time."

Schmuck v. United States, 489 U.S. 705, 109 S.Ct. 1443, 103 L.Ed.2d (1989).

the defendant with a specific intent to defraud through use of the U.S. Postal Service or some other interstate commercial carrier. The government is not required to prove that the scheme to defraud was successful. It is sufficient for the government to prove that a scheme existed in which use of the mails was reasonably foreseeable and that an actual mailing occurred in furtherance of the scheme. *United States v. Dick*, 744 F.2d 546, 550 (7th Cir. 1984).

A companion statute, the Federal Wire Fraud Statute, 18 U.S.C.A. § 1343, parallels the mail fraud statute and criminalizes fraudulent schemes that use interstate television, radio, or wire communications. Although the U.S. Constitution grants Congress jurisdiction over the postal service, Congress enacted the **wire fraud** statute under its authority to regulate interstate commerce. U.S. Const., Art. I, § 8. Therefore, a violation of this statute exists only if the communication crosses state lines.

Shortly after the tragedy of September 11, 2001, Americans were again shocked by allegations of fraud affecting the rights of employees and shareholders of once–highly regarded corporations. One of the most highly publicized was that involving the Enron Corporation, an energy company that had become one of the largest corporations in America. In July 2004, a federal jury convicted a former Enron financial executive and four former investment brokers of conspiracy and fraud. On May 25, 2006, a federal jury convicted former Enron chief executive Jeffrey Skilling and founder Kenneth Lay of conspiracy to commit securities and wire fraud. Lay died before sentencing. Because his demise occurred before the sentencing and appeal process was completed, on October 17, 2006 the U.S. District Judge in Houston, Texas, vacated the proceedings against Lay. See *United States v. Moehlenkamp*, 557 F.2d 126, 127–128 (7th Cir. 1977) (Defendant's death pending appeal from final judgment of conviction deprives the defendant of the right to an appellate decision and requires vacating of a conviction). At a sentencing hearing on October 23, 2006, the court sentenced Skilling to serve twenty-four years and four months in confinement.

Money Laundering and Currency Violations

Money laundering is the crime of disguising illegal income to make it appear legitimate and is prohibited by the Money Laundering Control Act of 1986, 18 U.S.C.A. §§ 1956, 1957. Section 1956 (a)(1) provides as follows:

> Whoever, knowing that the property involved in a financial transaction represents the proceeds of some form of unlawful activity, conducts, or attempts to conduct such a financial transaction which in fact involves the proceeds of specified unlawful activity

(A)(i) with the intent to promote the carrying on of specified unlawful activity; or (ii) with intent to engage in conduct constituting a violation of section 7201 or 7206 of the Internal Revenue Code of 1986; or

(B) knowing that the transaction is designed in whole or in part (i) to conceal or disguise the nature, the location, the source, the ownership, or the control of the proceeds of specified unlawful activity; or (ii) to avoid a transaction reporting requirement under State or Federal law, shall be sentenced to a fine of not more than $500,000 or twice the value of the property involved in the transaction, whichever is greater, or imprisonment for not more than twenty years, or both.

Thus, crimes under section 1956 fall into three categories: (1) acts committed with intent to promote unlawful activity; (2) those committed with knowledge that a transaction is to conceal ownership, control, or source of funds; and (3) those designed to avoid certain currency reporting laws.

Section 1957 makes it a crime to engage in or attempt to engage in a transaction involving criminally derived property. To convict a defendant of money laundering, the government must show that (1) the defendant took part in a financial transaction and knew that the property in the transaction involved proceeds of illegal activity; (2) the property involved was in fact proceeds of illegal activity; and (3) the defendant knew that the transaction was designed in whole or part to conceal or disguise the nature, source, location, ownership, or control of illegal proceeds. The government bears a heavy burden to establish that a defendant is guilty of money laundering. It must show the accused has "actual knowledge" or is guilty of "willful blindness" to the criminal acts; simply showing that a defendant "should have known" is insufficient to establish guilt.

Often, federal appellate courts have had to determine whether certain acts constitute a financial transaction within the meaning of the statute. In *United States v. Jackson*, 935 F.2d 832 (7th Cir. 1991), the defendant appealed his conviction on three counts of money laundering in violation of section 1956(a) and other violations. The evidence revealed the defendant had deposited funds derived from both legitimate and illegal activities in a local savings and loan institution and had written checks on the account. After first pointing out that writing a check on an account in a financial institution is a "transaction" within the money laundering statute, the court of appeals rejected the defendant's argument that the prosecution failed to establish that the financial transactions involved the proceeds of unlawful activity within the meaning of the statute, because the checks involved were written on an account that contained both legitimate funds and drug profits. The court held that it was sufficient for the government to show that the transaction in question involved the proceeds of one of the types of criminal conduct specified. Federal courts have also held that the term "financial transaction" includes making a deposit into an account. See *United States v. Reynolds*, 64 F.3d 292 (7th Cir. 1995). But the Fifth Circuit has held that transportation of drug proceeds by car does not constitute a financial transaction within the meaning of section 1956. *United States v. Puig-Infante*, 19 F.3d 929 (5th Cir. 1994).

Structuring Cash Transactions to Avoid Reporting Requirements

Federal statutes require financial institutions to file currency transaction reports with the Secretary of the Treasury for cash transactions in excess of $10,000. 31 U.S.C.A. § 5313. A related provision, 31 U.S.C.A. § 5324, prohibits a person from causing or attempting to cause a financial institution from making the required reports or from **structuring** or assisting in structuring a transaction with one or more institutions to evade the requirement, and provides penalties for persons who willfully conduct a transaction to evade this structuring requirement.

On October 20, 1988, Waldemar Ratzlaf ran up a debt of over $100,000 playing blackjack at a casino in Reno, Nevada. The casino gave him one week to pay. On the due date, Ratzlaf returned to the casino with cash totaling $100,000 in hand. When Ratzlaf offered to pay $100,000 on his gambling debt, the casino informed him that payment by a check in that amount would trigger the currency reporting requirements under federal law. Ratzlaf then proceeded to obtain a series of $10,000 cashier's checks from various banks to pay his debt. The government charged him with "structuring transactions" in violation of 31 U.S.C.A. § 5322 and § 5324. Section 5324 provides that it is illegal to "structure" financial transactions "for the purpose of evading" a financial institution's reporting requirements. Section 5322(a) established that "a person willfully violating" the anti-structuring provision (section 5324) is subject to criminal penalties. A jury found him guilty.

On review, the U.S. Supreme Court, in a 5–4 decision, interpreted "willfully" in 31 U.S.C.A. § 5322 to require the government to prove that a defendant acted with knowledge that his conduct was unlawful, and reversed his conviction. *Ratzlaf v. United States*, 510 U.S. 135, 114 S.Ct. 655, 126 L.Ed.2d 615 (1994). The Court based its holding upon a strict reading of the statutory language of the two sections. Section 5324 provides that it is illegal to "structure" financial transactions "for the purpose of evading" a financial institution's reporting requirements. Section 5322(a) establishes that a person "willfully violating" the anti-structuring provision (section 5324) is subject to criminal penalties.

After *Ratzlaf*, Congress amended section 5324 to no longer include the requirement that the defendant acted "willfully." See 31 U.S.C.A. § 5324. Apparently the only mental state now required is a purpose to evade the reporting requirement. See *United States v. Vazquez*, 53 F.3d 1216, 1218 n. 2 (11th Cir. 1995).

Securities Fraud

A variety of federal and state statutes criminalize conduct involving misrepresentations, omissions, **insider trading**, and other aspects of fraud in securities dealing. The most significant federal acts are the Securities Act of 1933, 15 U.S.C.A. § 77a *et seq.*, and the **Securities and Exchange Act** of 1934, 15 U.S.C.A. § 78a *et seq.* Again, these statutes provide for civil remedies as well as criminal sanctions. The Securities and Exchange Commission (SEC) refers most criminal prosecutions to the Department of Justice. Convictions can result in fines in the millions of dollars and imprisonment.

SIDEBAR | **Ponzi Schemes**

A "Ponzi scheme," also known as a "pyramid scheme," is a form of securities fraud in which investors are paid abnormally high rates of return using money from new investors. The funds are never really invested, so the scheme must constantly bring in new money in order to pay the initial investors the promised high returns. The scheme is named for Charles Ponzi, who ran a notorious pyramid scheme in the early twentieth century. In 2008, Wall Street icon Bernard Madoff was charged by federal authorities with operating a Ponzi scheme that defrauded investors of more than $50 billion. The scheme collapsed when, during the financial panic of late 2008, Madoff's clients began to withdraw their funds. In March 2009, after waiving an indictment, Madoff pleaded guilty to all eleven counts he was charged with, including fraud, perjury, and theft from an employee benefit plan and two counts of international money laundering.

Not all misrepresentations or omissions involving securities give rise to criminal violations. Rather, the government must prove the accused's *willful* intent to commit a substantive fraud in connection with the purchase or sale of a security or in the offering or sale of a security involving interstate commerce or through use of the mails. Courts uniformly hold that to sustain a conviction, the omission or misrepresentation must be material and be made in reckless disregard for the truth or falsity of the information provided. See, for example, *United States v. Farris*, 614 F.2d 634 (9th Cir. 1979). The specific intent that must be proven to sustain a criminal prosecution can be found in a defendant's deliberate and intentional acts or reckless disregard for the facts. *United States v. Boyer*, 694 F.2d 58 (3d Cir. 1982).

Churning and Insider Trading

In recent years, many financial executives and securities brokers have been prosecuted under the Securities and Exchange Act for fraudulent conduct known as churning and insider trading. **Churning** is a term applied to transactions made in a customer's account without regard to the customer's investment objectives; rather, they are made simply to generate commissions for the broker. When determining whether a broker is guilty of churning, courts often focus on whether the trading by a broker was disproportionate to the size of the customer's account. Insider trading usually occurs when a person who operates within a corporation has access to material, nonpublic information and uses that information to trade securities without first disclosing that information to the public.

Securities and Exchange Commission rule 10(b) proscribes (1) using any "deceptive device" (2) "in connection with the purchase or sale of any security," in contravention of rules promulgated by the SEC. Insider trading qualifies as a "deceptive device" because the insider occupies a position of trust and confidence with regard to the corporation's shareholders. This position of trust requires the insider to abstain from trading based on information he or she has acquired by virtue of the insider status. *Chiarella v. United States*, 445 U.S. 222, 100 S.Ct. 1108, 63 L.Ed.2d348 (1980). (See Case-in-Point.)

The late 1980s witnessed sensational cases involving insider trading by prominent Wall Street financiers. Since then, the SEC has secured indictments under rule 10(b) against numerous prominent individuals and corporations for securities violations.

Is Anyone Who Profits from Inside Information an "Insider"?
During 1975–76, Vincent Chiarella worked as a "markup man" for a company that printed announcements of corporate takeover bids. From the copy submitted for printing, he discerned information that enabled him to purchase stock in companies targeted for takeover before this information was disclosed to the general public. Chiarella made a profit in excess of $30,000 from the purchase, and later sale, of stock in the targeted companies. He was convicted in the U.S. District Court for violating section 10(b) of the Securities Exchange Act of 1934. 15 U.S.C.A. §§ 78b, 78j(b). In 1978 the U.S. Court of Appeals for the Second Circuit affirmed his conviction.

On review, the Supreme Court recognized that a corporate insider must not trade in shares of a corporation without having first disclosed all material insider information. But the Court ruled that the obligation to disclose is based on having the "duty to disclose arising from a relationship of trust and confidence between parties

CASE-IN-POINT

Domestic Diva Investigated for Insider Trading

In one of the most highly publicized insider trading cases in history, "domestic diva" Martha Stewart was investigated by the Securities and Exchange Commission in 2002 for selling 4,000 shares of stock in a company called ImClone after allegedly receiving insider information that the company's new cancer drug was going to be rejected by the Food and Drug Administration (FDA). The day after Stewart sold her stock, the FDA announced its rejection of the cancer drug and ImClone stock declined 16 percent. The SEC charged Stewart with insider trading via a civil complaint; additionally, she was charged criminally with conspiracy, obstructing an agency proceeding, making false statements to investigators, and securities fraud. Although Stewart was acquitted of securities fraud, a federal jury found her guilty of the other offenses. On July 16, 2004, a federal district judge sentenced Stewart to five months in prison followed by two years of supervised release (including five months of house arrest and electronic monitoring). On January 6, 2006, a federal appeals court upheld Stewart's conviction.

United States v. Stewart, 433 F.3d 273 (2d Cir. 2006).

to a transaction." Thus, the Court held that the trial court erred when, in effect, it instructed the jury that Chiarella owed a duty to everyone, including all sellers—indeed, to the market as a whole. Accordingly, the Court reversed his conviction. *Chiarella v. United States*, 445 U.S. 222, 100 S.Ct. 1108, 63 L.Ed.2d 348 (1980).

Tax Fraud

Prosecutions for white-collar crime often include charges of violating federal tax statutes. Although the government can employ a wide variety of federal criminal statutes to prosecute those who commit **tax fraud**, most prosecutions are based on the Internal Revenue Code, 26 U.S.C.A. § 7201 *et seq.* Some of the more common violations include deliberately underreporting or omitting income and overstating the amount of deductions. Whether violations are felonies or misdemeanors, to obtain a conviction the government must prove the defendant's willfulness to commit the proscribed act. *United States v. Bishop*, 412 U.S. 346, 93 S.Ct. 2008, 36 L.Ed.2d 941 (1973). To establish "willfulness," the government must prove the defendant's "intentional violation of a known legal duty." *United States v. Pomponio*, 429 U.S. 10, 97 S.Ct. 22, 50 L.Ed.2d 12 (1976). In reaffirming this standard of proof, the Supreme Court observed in *Cheek v. United States*, 498 U.S. 192, 111 S.Ct. 604, 112 L.Ed.2d 617 (1991), that the term "willfully" as used in federal criminal tax statutes serves to "carve out an exception to the traditional rule [that ignorance of the law or mistake of law is no defense to prosecution]." 498 U.S. at 200, 111 S.Ct. at 609, 112 L.Ed.2d at 628.

Many prosecutions for tax evasion occur under section 7201, which makes it a felony to willfully attempt to evade or to evade federal taxes. A successful prosecution requires that the government prove willfulness, the existence of a tax deficiency, and an affirmative act of evasion or attempted evasion of the tax. *Sansone v. United States*, 380 U.S. 343, 85 S.Ct. 1004, 13 L.Ed.2d 882 (1965).

Section 7202 also makes it a crime to willfully fail to collect, account truthfully for, or pay over taxes. Although most employers do not fail to collect taxes, a more common violation is the employer's failure to pay over those taxes to the Internal Revenue Service (IRS).

Section 7203 makes it a misdemeanor to willfully fail to pay an estimated tax, file a tax return, keep records, or supply information required by law. To successfully prosecute an accused, the government must establish that the accused had knowledge of a duty to file a return and willfully failed to file.

Section 7206 makes it a felony to commit fraud or make false statements in conjunction with tax obligations. To convict a person of "tax perjury," under section 7206 the government must prove the defendant (1) acted willfully, (2) filed a return containing a written declaration (3) made under penalty of perjury, (4) did not believe that the return was true and correct as to every material matter, (5) and exercised willfulness with the specific intent to violate the law. The defendant's willfulness may be inferred from the existence of unreported or misreported tax information. In *United States v. Tarwater*, 308 F.3d 494 (6th Cir. 2002), the court pointed out that section 7206 is an anti-perjury statute that criminalizes lying on any document filed with the IRS and that "the government need only prove that a defendant willfully made and subscribed a return, that the return contained a written declaration that it was made under penalties of perjury, and that the defendant did not believe the return to be true and correct as to every material matter." *Id.* at 504.

Section 7206(2) makes it a felony to willfully aid and assist another in a material falsity. To convict, the government must prove (1) an act of aiding and assisting in the preparation of a return or other document, (2) material falsity, and (3) willfulness. Tax preparers are sometimes prosecuted under this provision of the statute.

Additional sections of 26 U.S.C.A. criminalize the furnishing of false and fraudulent statements to the IRS, interfering with the administration of the tax laws, and delivering a fraudulent tax return.

Criminal Prosecution of Tax Violations

In April 2006, the U.S. Department of Justice (DOJ) announced that during 2005, the department's Tax Division authorized prosecutions against 1,256 defendants for tax crimes, an increase of more than 43 percent over the 877 defendants authorized for prosecution in 2001 (see "Justice Department and IRS Highlight Tax Enforcement Efforts," U.S. Department of Justice, April 11, 2006, at www.usdoj.gov/tax/txdv06212.htm). According to the DOJ's press release, the Tax Division's criminal enforcement priorities include investigating and prosecuting schemes that involve the following:

- Using trusts or other entities to conceal control over income and assets
- Shifting assets and income to hidden offshore accounts
- Claiming fictitious deductions
- Using frivolous justifications for not filing truthful tax returns
- Failing to withhold, report, and pay payroll and income taxes
- Failing to report income
- Failing to file tax returns

Racketeering and Organized Crime

During the Prohibition era, organized gangs trafficked in liquor and became involved in prostitution and other vices. After the repeal of the Eighteenth Amendment in 1933, these **crime syndicates** expanded into loan-sharking, gambling, narcotics, and extortion. As they did, they infiltrated legitimate businesses and conducted widespread illegal operations through their own complex and secretive structures.

As we have pointed out in other chapters, the common-law development of crimes and the legislative acts defining crimes focused on particular acts of wrong-doing and on inchoate activities. This approach did not cover the ongoing criminal activity by organized groups. To that extent, the traditional definitions of crime left a void in the criminal justice system.

The Hobbs Act

Congress enacted the Anti-Racketeering Act of 1934 in an effort to control rack-eteering activities. However, the act did not specifically mention racketeering, and as a result of certain judicial interpretations, in 1946 Congress enacted the **Hobbs Act**. 18 U.S.C.A. § 1951. Subsection (a) provides:

> Whoever in any way or degree obstructs, delays, or affects commerce or the movement of any article or commodity in commerce, by robbery or extortion or attempts or conspires so to do, or commits or threatens physical violence to any person or property in furtherance of a plan or purpose to do anything in violation of this section shall be fined under this title or imprisoned not more than twenty years, or both.

Note that the act includes the inchoate offenses of attempt and conspiracy. Other subsections define "robbery," "extortion," and "commerce." The Hobbs Act was enacted under the power of Congress to regulate interstate commerce; however, the courts have held that it is sufficient if the government simply proves that an act has an effect on interstate commerce. Courts allow this to be established by proof of an actual impact, however small, or, in the absence of actual impact, by proof of a probable or potential impact.

Originally, most prosecutions under the Hobbs Act were based on extortion by public officials using force, violence, or fear. Now prosecutors frequently rely on the act as a basis to prosecute state and local officials based on extortion "under color of official rights."

Go to the companion website for an edited version of the Supreme Court's decision in *Evans v. United States*.

In *Evans v. United States*, 504 U.S. 255, 112 S.Ct. 1881, 119 L.Ed.2d 57 (1992), Evans, a commissioner in DeKalb County, Georgia, was approached by an undercover FBI agent who posed as a real estate developer seeking assistance with a re-zoning petition. The agent gave Evans a $1,000 check payable to a campaign fund and $7,000 in cash. Evans reported the $1,000 campaign contribution but failed to report the cash payment of $7,000 on either his campaign disclosure form or his income tax return. In upholding his conviction for extortion under the Hobbs Act, the U.S. Supreme Court stated that "[w]e hold today the Government need only show that a public official has obtained a payment to which he was not entitled, knowing that the payment was made in return for official acts." 504 U.S. at 268, 112 S.Ct. at 1889, 119 L.Ed.2d at 72.

In 1961 Congress enacted three statutes to combat the growing problem of organized crime. These acts gave the FBI jurisdiction over gambling violations and interstate and foreign travel or transportation in aid of racketeering, 18 U.S.C.A. § 1952; interstate transportation of wagering paraphernalia, 18 U.S.C.A. § 1953; prohibition of illegal gambling, 8 U.S.C.A. § 1955; and laundering of monetary instruments, 18 U.S.C.A. § 1956. In 1968 Congress passed the Omnibus Crime Control and Safe Streets Act. This act provided for the conduct of court-authorized electronic surveillance. 18 U.S.C.A. §§ 2510–2521.

The Organized Crime Control Act of 1970

Notwithstanding the FBI's increased attention to organized crime, the problem continued to grow. Congress found that organized crime had weakened the stability of the nation's economy through infiltration of legitimate businesses and labor unions and threatened to subvert and corrupt democratic processes. Under its power to regulate foreign and interstate commerce, Congress enacted the **Organized Crime Control Act of 1970**. Title IX of the act, titled **Racketeer Influenced and Corrupt Organizations (RICO)**, prohibits the infiltration of legitimate organizations by racketeers where foreign or interstate commerce is affected. 18 U.S.C.A. §§ 1961–1963. In addition to increased criminal penalties, RICO provided for forfeiture of property used in criminal enterprises and permitted the government to bring civil actions against such enterprises.

RICO created new crimes and a new approach to criminal prosecution. First, it makes it a crime for any person "who has received any income derived, directly or indirectly, from a pattern of racketeering activity or through collection of an unlawful debt . . . to use or invest [in] any enterprise which is engaged in interstate or foreign commerce." 18 U.S.C.A. § 1962(a). Second, RICO makes it unlawful for any such person to participate, directly or indirectly, in the conduct of the enterprise's affairs through a "pattern of racketeering." 18 U.S.C.A. § 1962(b). Third, it is a crime for any person "employed by or associated with any enterprise engaged in, or the activities of which affect, interstate or foreign commerce, to conduct or participate, directly or indirectly, in the conduct of such enterprise's affairs through a pattern of racketeering activity or collection of unlawful debt." 18 U.S.C.A. § 1962(c). This last subsection has become the provision most frequently used by prosecutors. Finally, the act prohibits conspiracies to violate any of these proscriptions. 18 U.S.C.A. § 1962(d).

The Expansive Scope of RICO

RICO broadly defines racketeering activity to include a variety of federal offenses as well as nine state crimes that are characteristically felonies. 18 U.S.C.A. § 1961(1). Establishing a **pattern of racketeering** activity requires proof of at least two of these acts of racketeering having occurred within a period of ten years, excluding any period of imprisonment. 18 U.S.C.A. § 1961(5). Courts frequently refer to these acts as **predicate acts**, and any combination of two or more can constitute a pattern of racketeering. To obtain a conviction under RICO, the government must establish the defendant's involvement in a "pattern of racketeering or collection of an unlawful debt." A pattern of racketeering is not established merely by proving two predicate acts. Rather, to form a pattern of racketeering activity, predicate acts must be related to each other and to the enterprise. Therefore, to establish a RICO violation requires proof of a specified relationship between racketeering acts and a RICO enterprise. *United States v. Indelicato*, 865 F.2d 1370 (2d Cir. 1989). There is no requirement that a state conviction be obtained before the state offense can be used as a predicate act of the racketeering activity charged. *United States v. Malatesta*, 583 F.2d 748 (5th Cir. 1978). RICO provides for a maximum of twenty years' imprisonment, a heavier penalty than many of the predicate offenses on which a RICO conviction can be based.

RICO does not criminalize a person for being a racketeer—it criminalizes that person's conduct of an enterprise through a pattern of racketeering. Therefore, a jury that finds a defendant has committed the required predicate acts must still find that these acts were committed in connection with a pattern of racketeering or collection of an unlawful debt.

Court Holds that Predicate Acts Satisfy Relatedness under RICO

CASE-IN-POINT

Louis Daidone was found guilty of racketeering, racketeering conspiracy, witness tampering by murder, conspiracy to make extortionate loans, and conspiracy to collect extensions of credit by extortionate means. On appeal Daidone argued that the government failed to prove that the three predicate acts alleged in the racketeering counts formed a unitary "pattern of racketeering activity as required by 18 U.S.C.A. § 1962(c)" because these acts "were committed years apart, by different people and for entirely different reasons." He contended that instead of independently establishing the requirements for proving a pattern of racketeering activity—which requires proving both horizontal and vertical relatedness—the government improperly used what was essentially the same evidence to prove both avenues of relatedness.

In rejecting his contention, the court pointed out that racketeering Act One was the murder and the conspiracy to murder Thomas Gilmore; racketeering Act Two was the murder and conspiracy to murder Bruno Facciolo; and racketeering Act Three was the loansharking business. The court found that sufficient evidence established that as a member of an organized crime family Daidone orchestrated predicate acts of murdering two associates and participating in loansharking operations. The court concluded that each of the defendant's three predicate acts were related to the organized crime family's enterprise, as well as to each other, as required to satisfy the relatedness requirement in defendant's RICO prosecution, and affirmed his conviction.

United States v. Daidone, 471 F.3d 371 (2d Cir. 2006).

What Constitutes an Enterprise?

In RICO, Congress defined **enterprise** broadly to include "any individual, partnership, corporation, association, or other legal entity, and any union or group of individuals associated in fact although not a legal entity." 18 U.S.C.A. § 1961(4). The Supreme Court has said that the term encompasses both legitimate and illegitimate entities and groups. *United States v. Turkette,* 452 U.S. 576, 101 S.Ct. 2524, 69 L.Ed.2d 246 (1981). Lower federal courts have held the term includes both private and public entities such as corporations, banks, and decedents' estates, as well as state agencies, police departments, traffic courts, and prostitution rings.

Extension of RICO beyond Its Original Scope

RICO was conceived as a weapon for prosecution of organized crime, but it has become the basis of prosecution against white-collar criminals as well. Prosecutors have long experienced difficulty in securing convictions of organized crime leaders for violating specific criminal statutes. In part, this occurs because the evidence of a specific statutory violation might be unconvincing to a judge or jury. The reaction of a judge or jury is likely to be different when the prosecution parades before the court evidence of a series of violations that reveal a pattern of criminal behavior.

RICO has been justified because the harm that organized crime inflicts on society is far greater than the harm inflicted by those who commit statutory crimes. It can be an effective tool to help prosecutors fight against crime syndicates. Yet membership in organized crime is not a necessary element for a conviction under RICO. Unlike conventional criminal statutes, which historically have been narrowly construed, Congress provided that RICO is to be liberally interpreted to effect its remedial purposes. The liberal construction of the enterprise requirement and the fact that the pattern requirement of racketeering activity is cast in numerical terms

Defendant's Conspiracy Conviction Upheld Despite Acquittal of Substantive RICO Charge

The federal government charged Mario Salinas, a deputy sheriff of Hidalgo County, Texas, with one count of violating RICO, 18 U.S.C.A. § 1962(c); one count of conspiracy to violate RICO, section 1962(d); and other offenses. The government alleged that Deputy Salinas accepted two watches and a truck in exchange for permitting women to make "contact visits" to a federal prisoner housed in the county jail. A jury acquitted Salinas of the substantive RICO count but convicted him on the conspiracy charge. The U.S. Court of Appeals for the Fifth Circuit affirmed, and the Supreme Court granted review.

Salinas contended he could not be convicted of conspiracy under the RICO statute because he was found not guilty of the substantive RICO offense. In rejecting his contention, Justice Anthony Kennedy, writing for the Court, noted that the RICO conspiracy statute provides, "It shall be unlawful for any person to conspire to violate any of the provisions of subsection (a), (b), or (c) of this section." 18 U.S.C.A. § 1962(d). Kennedy stated, "There is no requirement of some overt act or specific act in the statute before us, unlike the general conspiracy provision applicable to federal crimes, which requires that at least one of the conspirators have committed an 'act to effect the object of the conspiracy'." 18 U.S.C.A. § 371. "The RICO conspiracy provision, then, is even more comprehensive than the general conspiracy offense in § 371."

Salinas v. United States, 522 U.S. 52, 118 S.Ct. 469, 139 L.Ed.2d 352 (1997).

have engendered some criticism. Critics contend that RICO is a catchall statute that gives prosecutors too much discretion to expand the range of indictable offenses. Examples of RICO prosecutions include the following:

- Several members of the Outlaws Motorcycle Club were prosecuted for a RICO violation based on narcotics and prostitution offenses. *United States v. Watchmaker*, 761 F.2d 1459 (11th Cir. 1985).
- A U.S. Customs Service Officer accepted payment for information that was used to facilitate a drug smuggling operation. The bribe money was invested in foreign bank accounts, thus constituting a money laundering enterprise. *United States v. Vogt*, 910 F.2d 1184 (4th Cir. 1990).
- A gambler and a police officer were convicted for their involvement in a police protection racket. *United States v. Sanders*, 962 F.2d 660 (7th Cir. 1992).
- Gang members were convicted of racketeering offenses for extorting protection money from local Chinese businesses; committing robberies; and kidnapping and murdering rival gang members, potential witnesses, and business owners who refused to pay protection money. *United States v. Wong*, 40 F.3d 1347 (2d Cir. 1994).
- An attorney was convicted of violating RICO based on participating in a scheme involving bribery of judges, where evidence revealed that the defendant had agreed to seek to use the court system corruptly by bribing judges to appoint attorneys as special assistant public defenders. *United States v. Massey*, 89 F.3d 1433 (11th Cir. 1996).

RICO has been extended beyond its original purpose to target non–organized criminals such as white-collar criminals and corrupt government officials. Thus, through RICO a prosecutor can circumvent statutes of limitation and seek to inflict multiple punishments for the same offenses.

Most states have adopted RICO-type statutes. Some closely parallel the federal act, whereas others have varying provisions concerning prohibited acts, sanctions, forfeitures of property, and the procedures involved.

CASE-IN-POINT

RICO, Predicate Offenses, and Double Jeopardy

Sixty members of the Nicodemo Scarfo crime family allegedly controlled Mafia operations in parts of Pennsylvania and New Jersey. The government alleged that over the course of eleven years the family's activities included a number of felony offenses. All the defendants were found guilty of conspiring to participate and participating in an enterprise through a pattern of racketeering in violation of 18 U.S.C.A. § 1962.

On appeal, Scarfo contended that the use of his former convictions as predicate offenses on which to base the RICO prosecution violated his constitutional right not to be placed in jeopardy twice for the same offense. In rejecting Scarfo's claims, the U.S. Court of Appeals pointed out the following: (1) As to state convictions used as predicate offenses, there could be no double jeopardy because different sovereigns were involved; and (2) as to federal convictions used as predicate offenses, the court in previous cases has ruled that a RICO offense "is not, in a literal sense, the 'same' offense as one of the predicate offenses" because a RICO violation requires proof of a "pattern of racketeering" and is intended to deter continuous criminal conduct, whereas the predicate offenses are intended to deter discrete criminal acts. Accordingly, the court rejected Scarfo's contentions.

United States v. Pungitore, 910 F.2d 1084 (3d Cir. 1990).

Despite criticism, RICO is firmly established as a weapon in the arsenal of federal and, in many instances, state prosecutors. It has proved to be a useful tool in the war against racketeering and corruption, both private and public, whether organized or not.

Constitutional Assaults on Rico

Since its enactment in 1970, RICO has withstood a number of constitutional assaults. In *United States v. Martino*, 648 F.2d 367 (5th Cir.1981), the Fifth Circuit found that RICO does not violate the *ex post facto* prohibition of the U.S. Constitution, nor does it violate the Ninth and Tenth Amendments by intruding on state sovereignty. Prior to that the Ninth Circuit had rejected a contention that the RICO term "pattern of racketeering" is vague and ambiguous, concluding that any ambiguity was cured by the definitions of "pattern" and "racketeering activity" in section 1961. *United States v. Campanale*, 518 F.2d 352, 364 (9th Cir. 1975). Perhaps a more serious challenge to RICO has been the allegation that it violates the Double Jeopardy Clause of the Constitution. But because a RICO violation involves a separate criminal proceeding, courts have generally denied such contentions. For example, the Fifth Circuit has held that the Double Jeopardy Clause of the Fifth Amendment does not prohibit the government from prosecuting a defendant for a RICO charge where the defendant has been previously prosecuted for a substantive offense used as one of the predicate crimes. *United States v. Smith*, 574 F.2d 308 (5th Cir. 1978).

Defenses In White-Collar and Organized Crime Cases

Many of the defenses available to defendants charged with white-collar and organized crime offenses are similar to those available to defendants generally. The most common defense to prosecutions involving fraud is that the defendant had a good-faith belief that allegedly "fraudulent" representations were, in fact, true. In a prosecution under a statute that requires the government to prove the defendant acted willfully, an effective defense is one that negates the defendant's willfulness. In tax prosecutions, a defendant who in good faith relied on the advice of a professional tax preparer can assert such reliance as a defense, provided the taxpayer disclosed all relevant information to the tax preparer.

In prosecutions under RICO, the defenses of entrapment, double jeopardy, and selective prosecution appear more frequently than in other situations (see Chapter 14). In organized crime prosecutions, the defense often attacks the validity of the underlying predicate offenses. Moreover, the complexities involved in many federal statutes aimed at organized crime raise more issues of statutory construction and legislative intent than do the more traditionally defined crimes.

Conclusion

Unlike transactional criminal offenses, white-collar crime and organized crime are not easily defined, and the conduct involved is often elusive and not readily quantifiable. We know that white-collar crimes are usually characterized by deception or abuse of trust and often involve the use of computers or other modern technologies. But we lack the accurate data and statistical information that is available on the traditional defined offenses. Some conduct criminalized today as white-collar crimes might have been considered mere unethical business practices in our earlier history. Other behavior, although long recognized as offensive, did not fit into the molds developed at common law and has become statutorily forbidden only in recent years. In today's society, so dependent on electronic transactions, the computer criminal might become as significant a danger to our well-being as is the street criminal who robs, burglarizes, and steals.

Organized crime syndicates cater to people's desire for goods and services that cannot be legally supplied but that can be made available to them at minimal risks to the providers. Organized crime gained its greatest foothold during the Prohibition era, and by the time Prohibition was repealed in 1933, organized crime had permeated many phases of the American economy. On the positive side, today there is an increased awareness of organized crime operations and an increased emphasis, particularly at the federal level, on investigation and prosecution. RICO has introduced a new dimension to the criminal law and has provided the legal system with effective tools to prosecute criminal enterprise activity and those who engage in racketeering. If the public demands increased efforts in this area, we should see considerable progress in ferreting out and punishing those who threaten the safety and economic well-being of society.

Chapter Summary

- **LO1** The substantive criminal offenses described in previous chapters are frequently associated with violence and are often termed "street crimes." In contrast, white-collar crimes typically come from the middle and upper socioeconomic strata of society and are usually nonviolent offenses characterized by deception or abuse of trust. Today they often involve the use of computers or other modern technologies.
- **LO2** Organized crime involves offenses committed by persons or groups who often attempt to gain political influence through graft and corruption. Organized crime figures, sometimes called "racketeers," frequently conduct their business through illegal enterprises. They often resort to threats and acts of violence in the commission of white-collar offenses. Organized crime gained its greatest

foothold during the Prohibition era, when the Eighteenth Amendment to the U.S. Constitution, prohibiting the sale and distribution of alcoholic beverages, was in effect. By the time Prohibition was repealed in 1933, organized crime had become involved in many phases of the economy, often pursuing its interests through such illegal activities.

- **LO3** White-collar crimes often are prosecuted based on federal statutes enacted by Congress under its constitutional power over postal, bankruptcy, and taxing matters and its authority to regulate interstate domestic and foreign commerce. State legislatures have broad authority to proscribe other offenses as contrary to the public welfare. Prosecutions involve not only large-scale corporate frauds but also unlawful telephone, mail, and e-mail solicitations; sales of unregistered securities and undeserved diplomas; phony contests; fraudulent home improvement schemes; and bogus land sales. In some instances statutes also provide civil remedies.

- **LO4** Under common law, a corporation (as opposed to its members) was not held criminally responsible for its acts. Eventually courts imposed criminal liability based on acts of the corporation's agents; however, a corporation cannot be held criminally liable for crimes against persons unless the offense is one based on the corporation's negligence as opposed to a crime based on specific intent. Prosecutions of white-collar crime are frequently directed against corporate defendants, with corporations held criminally liable for the acts their agents commit within the scope of their actual or apparent authority. State and federal courts broadly define "scope of authority" to include an agent's acts intended to benefit the corporation. The fact that a corporation is prosecuted for crimes does not exonerate the individuals who commit the unlawful acts. In fact, it is not uncommon for corporate executives to be punished, generally by imposition of fines.

- **LO5** The Sherman Antitrust Act is a federal statute that makes it a crime to enter any contract or engage in any combination or conspiracy in restraint of trade or to monopolize or attempt to monopolize trade. The act reaches individuals and entities in for-profit and nonprofit activities as well as local governments and educational institutions. Price-fixing and bid rigging are among the most common violations. To prove a criminal violation of the act, the government must establish that two or more entities formed a combination or conspiracy that produces, or potentially produces, an unreasonable restraint of interstate in trade or commerce with intent to violate the law. The act includes civil remedies as well as criminal sanctions. Criminal violations are felonies. The U.S. Department of Justice alone is authorized to enforce the criminal sanctions of the act. Corporations may be fined as much as $100,000,000; individuals may be fined as much as $1,000,000, sentenced to imprisonment, or both.

- **LO6** In 1984 Congress enacted the Computer Fraud and Abuse Act. As amended in 1996, it makes it a crime to "knowingly cause the transmission of a program, information, code, or command" in interstate commerce with intent to cause damage to a computer exclusively used by a financial institution or the U.S. government. In addition, the act prohibits "knowingly and with intent to defraud, trafficking in passwords to permit unauthorized access to a government computer, or to affect interstate or foreign commerce" or to transmit in interstate or foreign commerce any threat to cause damage to a protected computer with intent to extort something of value.

- **LO7** In 2001 President George W. Bush signed the USA PATRIOT Act and in 2006 he signed legislation essentially renewing the Act. As amended, the USA

PATRIOT Act defines "protected computer" to include computers outside of the United States that affect "interstate or foreign commerce or communication of the United States" and increases the penalty for violations for damaging a protected computer. In 2006, the United States ratified the Convention on Cybercrime, a treaty designed to harmonize national laws and strengthen international cooperation in this area. The treaty addresses several problems in the area of international white-collar crime, including computer-related fraud, "hacking," the dissemination of computer viruses, and electronic attacks on financial institutions. Federal and state statutes now proscribe theft of computer programs, computer fraud, and computer trespass.

- **LO8** The widespread use of debit and credit cards, automated teller machine cards, account numbers, personal identification numbers, and other access devices caused states to enact comprehensive statutes proscribing the fraudulent use of devices to secure cash, goods, and services through means beyond the traditional credit card. A person who without authority uses an access device or one who uses a revoked access device to obtain or attempt to obtain property or services commits the offense. The offenses are usually classified as misdemeanors or felonies depending on the amount involved.

- **LO9** To address the growing problem of identity theft, Congress enacted the Identity Theft and Assumption Deterrence Act of 1998 making it a felony to "knowingly transfer, possess or use, without lawful authority, a means of identification of another person with the intent to commit, or to aid or abet, any unlawful activity that constitutes a violation of Federal law, or that constitutes a felony under any applicable State or local law." By 2003 most states had also enacted specific statutes making identify theft and fraud a felony.

- **LO10** Intellectual property comprises patents, copyrights, trademarks, and trade secrets. Patents are issued for a period of twenty years by the U.S. Patent and Trademark Office for inventions and discoveries that are novel, useful, and not something of an obvious nature. A copyright affords legal protection to authors of original works, which now include musical, artistic, and architectural works as well as videos, computer software, and databases. For a work created after January 1, 1978, statutory protection is given for the life of the author plus seventy years after the author's death. A trademark is a distinctive word, phrase, or graphic symbol used to distinguish a product. To be protected by federal law, trademarks used in interstate or foreign commerce may be registered with the U.S. Patent and Trademark Office. Disputes involving intellectual property are mostly civil matters, but there are criminal prohibitions for patent and copyright infringement, trademark counterfeiting, and theft of trade secrets. The Economic Espionage Act of 1996 prohibits foreign governments from stealing trade secrets and criminalizes domestic trade-secret theft.

- **LO11** The federal Money Laundering Control Act of 1986 makes it a crime to disguise illegal income to make it appear legitimate. Federal statutes require financial institutions to file currency transaction reports with the Secretary of the Treasury for cash transactions in excess of $10,000 and to cause or attempt to cause a financial institution from making the required reports or from structuring or assisting in structuring a transaction to evade the reporting requirements.

- **LO12** The federal False Statements Act prohibits knowingly and willfully making a false statement that is material to a matter within the jurisdiction of any department or agency of the United States. Federal bankruptcy statutes criminalize fraudulent concealment of assets, avoiding distribution of nonexempt assets, taking false oaths, and related conduct in bankruptcy proceedings. The Health

Insurance Portability and Accountability Act of 1996 (HIPPA) prohibits making material false or fraudulent statements or entries in connection with delivery of or payment for health care benefits. The Federal Mail Fraud Statute makes it a crime to use the mail to obtain money or property by fraudulent means and to use the mails in furtherance of the fraudulent scheme. The Federal Wire Fraud Statute, which parallels the mail fraud statute, criminalizes fraudulent schemes that use interstate television, radio, or wire communications.

- **LO13** A variety of federal and state statutes criminalize conduct involving misrepresentations, omissions, insider trading, and other aspects of fraud in securities dealing. The most significant federal acts are the Securities Act of 1933 and the Securities and Exchange Act of 1934. These statutes provide for civil remedies as well as criminal sanctions. In recent years, many financial executives and securities brokers have been prosecuted under the Securities and Exchange Act for fraudulent conduct known as "churning" and "insider trading." Churning is a term applied to transactions made to generate commissions for the broker without regard to the customer's investment objectives. Insider trading refers to buying or selling a security by someone who is in possession of material, nonpublic information about the security.

- **LO14** Prosecutions for white-collar crime often include charges of willfully violating federal tax statutes. Although most federal tax violations are resolved through civil proceedings, the Internal Revenue Code criminalizes a host of offenses including deliberately failing to file tax returns, underreporting or omitting income, and overstating the amount of deductions. Most violations are felonies. To establish "willfulness," the government must prove the defendant's "intentional violation of a known legal duty."

- **LO15** After the Eighteenth Amendment was repealed in 1933 crime syndicates expanded into loan-sharking, gambling, narcotics, and extortion and infiltrated legitimate businesses. Common-law and statutory crimes focus on specific acts of wrongdoing and were not too effective in controlling ongoing criminal activity by organized groups. To combat this, Congress enacted the Anti-Racketeering Act of 1934; to increase its effectiveness it enacted the Hobbs Act in 1946. Prosecutions under the Hobbs Act originally focused on extortion by public officials using force, violence, or fear; now prosecutors frequently rely on the act to prosecute state and local officials based on extortion "under color of official rights." In 1961 Congress enacted statutes to combat organized crime by giving the FBI jurisdiction over various interstate gambling and interstate and foreign travel in aid of racketeering.

- **LO16** A gigantic legal step in fighting organized crime occurred in 1970 when Congress enacted the Organized Crime Control Act, which includes the Racketeer Influenced and Corrupt Organizations (RICO) Act. RICO prohibits infiltration of legitimate organizations by racketeers where foreign or interstate commerce is affected. RICO created a new approach to criminal prosecution. It makes it a crime for any person "who has received any income derived, directly or indirectly, from a pattern of racketeering activity or through collection of an unlawful debt . . . to use or invest [in] any enterprise which is engaged in interstate or foreign commerce." Further, RICO makes it unlawful for any such person to participate, directly or indirectly, in the conduct of the enterprise's affairs through a "pattern of racketeering." It broadly defines racketeering activity to include a variety of federal offenses as well as nine state crimes that are characteristically felonies, and it defines "enterprise" to include "any individual, partnership, corporation, association, or other legal entity, and any union or group of individuals associated in fact although not a legal entity." Establishing a pattern of racketeering activity requires the government to prove at least two acts of racketeering (called predicate acts) that have occurred within a period of ten years, excluding any period of imprisonment. The predicate acts must be related to each other and to the enterprise. RICO also provides for forfeiture of property used in criminal enterprises and permits the government to bring civil actions against such enterprises.

- **LO17** RICO was conceived as a weapon for prosecution of organized crime, but it has become the basis for prosecution of white-collar criminals as well. Unlike other criminal statutes that historically have been narrowly construed, Congress provided that RICO is to be liberally interpreted. RICO has withstood a number of constitutional challenges. The most serious challenge was that it violates the Double Jeopardy Clause of the Constitution. Because a RICO violation involves a separate criminal proceeding, courts have generally denied such contentions.

Key Terms

white-collar crimes Economic offenses characterized by deception or abuse of trust and often involving the use of computers or other modern technologies.

cybercrimes Crimes committed using computers and the Internet.

organized crime Syndicates involved in racketeering and other criminal activities.

loan-sharking The practice of lending money at illegal rates of interest.

racketeering A system of organized crime traditionally involving the extortion of money from businesses by intimidation, violence, or other illegal methods.

corporate defendants Corporations charged with criminal offenses.

scope of an agent's authority In white-collar crime cases, the scope of an agent's authority depends on whether the commission of the offense was authorized, requested, commanded, performed, or recklessly tolerated by the board of directors or by a high managerial agent acting in behalf of the corporation within the scope of his or her office or employment.

Sherman Antitrust Act A federal statute prohibiting any contract, combination, or conspiracy in restraint of trade. The act is designed to protect and preserve a system of free and open competition. Its scope is broad and reaches individuals and entities in for-profit and nonprofit activities as well as local governments and educational institutions.

antitrust violations Violations of laws designed to protect the public from price-fixing, price discrimination, and monopolistic practices in trade and commerce.

price-fixing Sellers unlawfully entering into agreements as to the price of products or services.

bid rigging Illegally manipulating the submission of bids to obtain a contract, usually from a public body.

Computer Fraud and Abuse Act Federal law criminalizing fraud and related activity in connection with computers.

access devices Cards, plates, codes, electronic serial numbers, mobile identification numbers, personal identification numbers, and telecommunications services, equipment, instrument identifiers, and other means that can be used to obtain goods or services.

USA PATRIOT Act Controversial act of Congress enacted in 2001 to strengthen the federal government's efforts to combat terrorism.

theft of computer services Stealing software, data, computer access codes, computer time, and so on.

computer fraud An offense consisting of obtaining property or services by false pretenses through use of a computer or computer network.

computer trespass An offense consisting of the unauthorized copying, alteration, or removal of computer data, programs, or software.

access device fraud The crime of knowingly producing, using, or trafficking in counterfeit credit cards, personal identification numbers, access codes, account numbers, etc. with the intent to fraudulently obtain money, goods, or services.

identity theft The crime of using someone else's personal information—such as their name, social security number, or credit card number—without their permission to commit fraud or other crimes.

intellectual property Products of the human intellect, such as inventions, plays, stories, films, music, and trade secrets.

patent A government grant of the right to exclude others from producing or using a discovery or invention for a certain period of time.

copyright A form of legal protection provided to the authors of original literary, musical, artistic, and architectural works as well as videos and computer software and databases.

bootlegging The crime of knowingly trafficking in counterfeit labels affixed or designed to be affixed to copies of musical recordings, computer programs, motion pictures, etc.

trademark A distinctive word, phrase, or graphic symbol used to distinguish a commercial product.

trademark counterfeiting The offense of using a registered trademark to falsely market a product or service.

trade secret A formula, pattern, physical device, idea, process, compilation of information, or other information that provides a business with a competitive advantage.

False Statements Act A federal statute making it a crime for a person to knowingly make a false and material statement to a U.S. government agency to obtain a government benefit or in connection with performing work for the government.

bankruptcy fraud Dishonest or deceitful acts committed by one who seeks relief under laws designed to protect honest debtors from their creditors.

False Claims Act A federal statute that makes it unlawful for a person to knowingly present a false or fraudulent claim to the U.S. government.

mail fraud A scheme devised or intended to defraud or to obtain money or property by fraudulent means, or using or causing the use of the mails in furtherance of the fraudulent scheme.

wire fraud A fraudulent scheme that uses interstate television, radio, or wire communications.

money laundering The offense of disguising illegal income to make it appear legitimate.

structuring Engaging in multiple smaller transactions to avoid currency reporting requirements.

insider trading Transactions in securities by a person who operates inside a corporation and, by using material nonpublic information, trades to his or her advantage without first disclosing that information to the public.

Securities and Exchange Act The 1934 act of Congress regulating the sale of securities in interstate commerce.

churning Making purchases and sales of securities in a client's account simply to generate commissions for the broker.

tax fraud False or deceptive conduct performed with the intent of violating revenue laws, especially the Internal Revenue Code.

crime syndicates An association or group of people that carries out organized crime activities.

Hobbs Act A 1946 act of Congress authorizing criminal penalties for whoever in any way or degree obstructs, delays, or affects commerce or the movement of any article or commodity in commerce by robbery or extortion or attempts or conspires so to do, or commits or threatens physical violence to any person or property in furtherance of a plan or purpose to do anything in violation of the act.

Organized Crime Control Act of 1970 Federal law dealing with organized crime. Title IX of the act is entitled "Racketeer Influenced and Corrupt Organizations" and is commonly referred to by the acronym RICO.

Racketeer Influenced and Corrupt Organizations (RICO) A federal law enacted in 1970 imposing civil and criminal liability where two or more acts of racketeering show a pattern of criminal activity carried on by an enterprise. (Many states now have adopted RICO laws.)

pattern of racketeering To obtain a conviction under the federal RICO statute, the government must establish the defendant's involvement in a "pattern of racketeering" that requires proof of the occurrence of at least two predicate acts of racketeering within a period of ten years, excluding any period of imprisonment.

predicate acts Prior acts of racketeering used to demonstrate a pattern of racketeering in a RICO prosecution.

enterprise An individual, partnership, corporation, association, or other legal entity; a union or group of individuals that is not a legal entity.

Questions for Thought and Discussion

1. Why do federal criminal statutes figure so prominently in the context of white-collar offenses?
2. Under what circumstances can a corporation be held legally responsible for a white-collar offense committed by one of its agents or employees?
3. Is it a crime to share digital music files with friends if one receives no payment for the files?
4. What is the federal constitutional authority for enacting (a) antitrust and wire fraud laws? (b) postal offenses? (c) securities laws? (d) bankruptcy laws?
5. What is the extent of prohibitions under the Sherman Antitrust Act? Give some examples of violations of the act.
6. Why does the rationale for federal antitrust and securities laws require the availability of both civil and criminal sanctions?

7. Describe a factual scenario that could occur in the operation of a municipal or county government in your state and that could likely result in a person's being prosecuted under the Hobbs Act.
8. What led Congress to the realization that the traditional common-law transactional approach to crime was inadequate to deal with organized crime?
9. What is required to establish a "pattern of racketeering activity" under RICO?
10. How does RICO define "enterprise," and what is its significance in prosecution of RICO offenses?

Problems for Discussion and Solution

1. Ima Hacker is a skilled computer operator at a business office. Through stealthy operation of her computer, she successfully obtains a list of names and addresses of a competitor's customers without the knowledge or consent of the competitor. For what offense would Ms. Hacker most likely be prosecuted in your state?
2. Men's Fashions, a clothing store, was an incorporated business that was experiencing financial problems. Some of the principals of the business organized a new corporation and sold a substantial portion of the inventory of Men's Fashions to the new corporation for considerably less than the wholesale cost of the merchandise. A few weeks after the sale, Men's Fashions filed a bankruptcy petition, listing as assets a greatly diminished inventory without disclosing the recent sale of inventory to the new corporation. Does this scenario suggest bankruptcy fraud? Why or why not?
3. An elderly widow whose income was derived primarily from Social Security and a small pension owned $100,000 in government bonds that she inherited from her late husband. Other than her home and a modest checking account, her bonds constituted her estate. On advice of A. Brokero, a licensed securities broker, she converted the bonds into cash and deposited the proceeds with Brokero to manage. She explained her financial situation and investment objectives. She and Brokero agreed that her funds should be invested in conservative, income-producing investments. Instead, Brokero, who had trading authorization from the widow, bought and sold numerous issues of aggressive stocks for the account, and at the end of two years the account had dwindled to $28,500. During the two-year period, Brokero had earned thousands of dollars in commissions for buying and selling the investments. What, if any, criminal violation is suggested by this scenario?
4. At a state peace officers' convention, two police officers from Sedateville, a small rural community, developed a friendship with two officers from Trendville, a metropolitan city. Gambling, except for a state lottery, was prohibited in the state. As their friendship developed, they enjoyed "a friendly game of poker" with modest betting. They all agreed that "after all, gambling is really not all bad" and probably should not be prohibited. As the rural officers began to lament their modest salaries, the Trendville officers introduced them to some "prominent businessmen." They all agreed that "it would hurt no one" to allow these businessmen to conduct some private gambling operations in Sedateville. But, of course, the operation would require some protection by the local police. With cooperation of the officers, the businessmen opened a bar where gambling was conducted in a back room. The new operation also accommodated male patrons seeking prostitutes by transporting the men to Trendville for a weekend "sports event."

Through the cooperation of the officers, the new operation was "overlooked" by the Sedateville police. In turn, the officers from Trendville and Sedateville enjoyed some of the profits from the gambling and prostitution activities. The four officers' gains eventually exceeded their salaries as police officers, and as they later said, "No one was hurt in this operation—people were just allowed to have a good time." Under what circumstances would this scenario present a basis for a RICO prosecution?

CHAPTER 10

Vice Crimes

LEARNING OBJECTIVES

After reading this chapter, you should be able to explain . . .

1. how the law traditionally sought to protect societal morality and why this notion has become controversial today
2. how and why common-law offenses involving consensual sexual conduct have largely disappeared from the criminal law
3. how the criminal law treats indecent exposure and voyeurism
4. how nude dancing in places of public accommodation is viewed by the criminal law
5. why courts and prosecutors have struggled with obscenity cases
6. why child pornography is viewed differently from other forms of pornography
7. why Congress and the courts have struggled over efforts to restrict pornography on the Internet
8. why prosecutions for public profanity are increasingly rare
9. how the laws regarding gambling have changed and why enforcement of gambling laws is so difficult
10. how the law protects domestic animals from abandonment, neglect, and abuse
11. the various offenses that still exist with respect to the use of alcohol
12. why the criminal law has evolved with respect to the use of alcohol by drivers of motor vehicles
13. the origin and development of the "war on drugs"
14. how the marijuana laws have evolved and are moving in the direction of decriminalization
15. how and why specialized drug courts have been developed to deal with drug offenders

CHAPTER OUTLINE

Introduction

Criminal Prohibitions of Consensual Sexual Conduct

Bigamy and Polygamy

Prostitution

Indecent Exposure and Voyeurism

Obscenity and Pornography

Lindsey Lohan was already an established model when she made her acting debut at age eleven, starring in the 1998 Disney film *The Parent Trap*. From there her career took off and she appeared in numerous films, television programs, and magazines and even recorded several music CDs Like so many celebrities, Lohan developed problems with substance abuse. A May 2007 traffic accident led to her arrest for driving under the influence of alcohol (DUI). Later that year she was arrested again for DUI and possession of cocaine. A plea agreement required her to spend one day in jail, perform ten days of community service, and undergo drug and alcohol treatment as conditions of the three-year term of probation. In October 2009 Lohan's probation was extended another year after the judge learned that she had not completed her alcohol treatment program. In the summer of 2010 Lohan was jailed for thirty days for violating the terms of her probation. In September 2010 the judge revoked Lohan's probation and issued a bench warrant for her arrest after learning that Lohan had failed a court-ordered drug test. Lohan served a day in jail and then checked into another treatment facility. The Lohan case, although tragic, is all too common. For centuries people have struggled with addictions to drugs and alcohol, as well as many other vices discussed in this chapter. The question is, "What is the appropriate role of the criminal law in dealing with such vices?"

Introduction

The word "vice" comes from the Latin *vitium*, meaning "fault" or "defect." In the criminal justice system, the term **"vice"** is associated with a number of crimes traditionally classified as offenses against public decency or morality. Some of these offenses, such as indecent exposure, bigamy, and obscenity, have their roots in English common law. Others, like prostitution, gambling, and alcohol and drug offenses, were created legislatively at various times in our nation's history. All of these offenses have evolved substantially in recent decades, reflecting tremendous changes in our society.

It is not uncommon today for critics to question whether the furtherance of decency and morality is a legitimate goal of the criminal justice system. Many believe that morality, like religion, is a personal matter and that the state should be neutral in matters of morality, much as it is with respect to religion. Others, stressing the practical aspect of the problem, cite the aphorism "you can't legislate morality." However, critics must realize that the moral basis of the law extends far beyond the prohibition of vice. Many proscriptions of the criminal law, from animal cruelty to insider stock trading, are based on collective societal judgments about what is right and what is wrong. Writing for the U.S. Supreme Court in *Bowers v. Hardwick*, 478 U.S. 186, 106 S.Ct. 2841, 92 L.Ed.2d 140 (1986), Justice Byron White observed that "the law . . . is constantly based on notions of morality, and if all laws representing essentially moral choices are to be invalidated . . . , the courts will be very busy indeed." 478 U.S. at 196, 106 S.Ct. at 2846, 92 L.Ed.2d at 149. It should also be pointed out that many of the crimes discussed in this chapter can be viewed as threats to other societal interests beyond morality. For example, prostitution is often seen as a public health issue. Alcohol- and drug-related offenses are often real threats to the public safety and order.

Criminal Prohibitions of Consensual Sexual Conduct

Reflecting its common-law origins, American criminal law traditionally proscribed a wide range of consensual sexual conduct, including fornication, adultery, seduction, sodomy, prostitution, and, incest. Today the prevalent view is that such behavior is, or at least ought to be, private in character and thus beyond the reach of the law. However, many people still subscribe to the classical conservative view that such prohibitions are necessary to maintain a proper moral climate. In any event, changes in attitudes about such matters have led state legislatures to abolish many of these offenses. Others have been invalidated by courts of law on the basis of the constitutional **right of privacy**. Judicial decisions in this area have given rise to the constitutional principle that competent adults have the right to make their own decisions in matters of sex and reproduction (see Chapter 3).

Fornication, Adultery, and Seduction

Fornication is sexual intercourse between unmarried persons. **Adultery** is generally defined as sexual intercourse between a male and female, at least one of whom is married to someone else. Fornication and adultery were regarded as offenses against morality and were punishable in the ecclesiastical courts in England. Neither was considered a common-law crime unless committed openly. In such instances the act was prosecuted as a public nuisance. Historically, the rationale for criminalizing these acts was threefold: (1) to avoid disharmony in family relationships, (2) to prevent illegitimate births, and (3) to prevent the spread of sexually transmitted diseases.

Because of changing societal attitudes, these offenses are rarely prosecuted today. Indeed, as suggested above, many states have eliminated these offenses altogether. Adultery and fornication might be widespread, but they generally occur under the most private of circumstances. Consequently, complaints about these sexual encounters are seldom reported to the authorities. In instances where sexual conduct is the subject of a complaint by a participant, it may fall under the classification of sexual battery (see Chapter 7). As we noted in Chapter 3 , in 2005 the Virginia Supreme Court struck down that state's prohibition of fornication as a violation of the liberty guaranteed by the Fourteenth Amendment. *Martin v. Ziherl*, 607 S.E.2d 367 (Va. 2005).

Seduction was not a crime at common law; hence, it exists only by statute. The essence of the offense is that a male obtains sexual intercourse with a virtuous female on the unfulfilled promise of marriage. Historically, prosecution for seduction served the role of persuading a recalcitrant suitor to marry the woman he seduced. Most states have repealed their seduction statutes, and where such laws remain on the books, prosecution is rare.

Sodomy: The Demise of a Historic Offense

The word "sodomy" is derived from the biblical account of Sodom, the city that was destroyed because of its vices. **Sodomy** consists of committing acts that were once commonly referred to as "crimes against nature." Sodomy was originally an ecclesiastical offense but became a felony in 16th century England, the later stages of the common law. In general, the offense includes oral or anal sex between humans and sexual intercourse between humans and animals. (The latter is often termed *bestiality*.) Until 1961 all states had statutes outlawing sodomy; however, during the 1970s and 1980s many of these statutes were either repealed or invalidated by courts. The few that remained on the books were not actively enforced.

In *Lawrence v. Texas*, 539 U.S. 558, 123 S.Ct. 2472, 156 L.Ed.2d 508 (2003), the Supreme Court struck down one of the few remaining sodomy laws, saying that it "furthers no legitimate state interest which can justify its intrusion into the personal and private life of the individual." 539 U.S. at 578, 123 S.Ct. at 2484, 156 L.Ed.2d at 526. The *Lawrence* decision signaled the demise of consensual sodomy as a criminal offense in the United States. However, as we pointed out in Chapter 7, forcible sodomy can be prosecuted as a species of rape or sexual battery.

Incest

Incest is sexual intercourse within or outside the bonds of marriage between persons related within certain prohibited degrees. *Haller v. State*, 232 S.W.2d 829 (Ark. 1950). Incest was not a crime at common law but was punishable by the ecclesiastical courts.

There are strong religious and moral taboos against incest. Furthermore, it has been almost universally believed that incest not only disrupts family relationships but also leads to genetically defective offspring. For these reasons, all states prohibit marriage or sexual relations between certain close relatives. Once the prosecution establishes the defendant's knowledge of the prohibited relationship, proof of the act of sexual intercourse is sufficient to show violation of the statute.

Statutes that prohibit intermarriage or sexual relations between persons within certain degrees of kinship usually refer to relationship by consanguinity (that is, blood relationships). But some went further and classified as incestuous close relationships between persons related by affinity (that is, marriage) as well as relationships by the bloodline.

There is little support for repealing laws forbidding incest. The practice of incest among those related by consanguinity is widely condemned in Western civilization, and laws forbidding it will undoubtedly remain intact. Those who do advocate the repeal of these laws advance the same arguments as those advanced for legalizing fornication, adultery, and sodomy. Others who see incest as a genuine concern urge that government should approach the problem through counseling and by furnishing psychiatric assistance to transgressors, rather than by making incest a penal offense.

Bigamy and Polygamy

Like most sexual offenses, **bigamy** was originally a canonical offense punishable by the ecclesiastical courts in England; later it became a common-law offense. All American jurisdictions prohibit bigamy (that is, marriage between two persons when one is already legally married to another). Usually these statutes require the prosecution

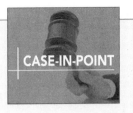

Criminal Prosecution of a Polygamist

CASE-IN-POINT

In what was described in the press as the country's first major polygamy case in nearly five decades, Thomas Arthur Green was found guilty on four counts of bigamy and one count of child rape in May of 2001. Green, a fundamentalist Mormon polygamist, had five wives and thirty children by them.

Upon conviction, Green was sentenced to five years in prison. In reviewing the case in 2004, the Utah Supreme Court rejected Green's argument that the state bigamy statute violated the federal constitutional right to free exercise of religion. It also held that the bigamy statute was not unconstitutionally vague as applied.

State v. Green, 99 P.3d 820 (Utah 2004).

to prove that the defendant had knowledge of the prior marital status of the person whom he or she married. Since everyone is presumed to know the consequences of his or her acts, no further intent need be shown.

During the 1800s arguments were advanced that **polygamy**—the practice of one person being married to several spouses at the same time—was a religious practice protected by the First Amendment. The U.S. Supreme Court soundly rejected these contentions when it held that a religious belief cannot be made a justification for commission of an overt act made criminal by the state. *Reynolds v. United States*, 98 U.S. (8 Otto) 145, 25 L.Ed. 244 (1878). The *Reynolds* case involved a Mormon polygamist who challenged the constitutionality of the federal statute prohibiting polygamy in federal territories. Subsequently the Church of Jesus Christ of Latter-day Saints disavowed the practice of polygamy, but the practice continues to this day in some fundamentalist Mormon communities in the western United States. Prosecutions for bigamy or polygamy are rare (but see Case-in-Point above).

Prostitution

A prostitute is a person who indulges in indiscriminate sexual activity for hire. Although **prostitution** was not a crime at common law, statutes proscribing prostitution have been part of the laws directed against public immorality since the early history of the United States. Lawmakers have officially deplored the existence of prostitution, and law enforcement authorities have long linked the activity with other forms of vice, including narcotics offenses, as well as the exploitation of women.

Today, prostitution is illegal in all states except Nevada, where it exists by local option in some counties, although it is strictly regulated by law. See Nev. Rev. Stat., Chapter 201, Crimes Against Public Decency and Good Morals. Despite the limited legalization in Nevada, arrests for prostitution are still quite numerous in that state, as shown in Table 10.1. This is largely explained by the fact that prostitution is rampant in Las Vegas, where it remains illegal.

Historically, statutes prohibiting prostitution have been directed at females who have sexual intercourse with males for compensation, but in recent years, as prostitution by males has increased, enforcement has come to be directed at males as well.

Historically, laws prohibiting prostitution were directed almost exclusively at the prostitute. However, newer statutes provide for conviction of customers as well as prostitutes. Indeed, if the statutes are not so construed, they might be vulnerable to constitutional attack as a denial of equal protection under the law.

TABLE 10.1	Prostitution Arrests in the United States by State, 2005		
California	13,911	Connecticut	493
Texas	5,999	Oklahoma	456
Florida	5,715	Louisiana	447
Illinois	4,931	Utah	344
Nevada	4,633	Hawaii	341
Pennsylvania	2,552	Arkansas	301
New Jersey	2,342	New Mexico	300
Minnesota	2,133	Iowa	215
Tennessee	2,025	West Virginia	163
Maryland	1,861	Nebraska	148
Indiana	1,809	Delaware	140
Michigan	1,776	Alabama	124
New York	1,743	Alaska	123
Georgia	1,681	Wisconsin	121
Arizona	1,611	Rhode Island	110
Washington	1,567	New Hampshire	74
North Carolina	1,370	Mississippi	63
Ohio	1,282	Maine	18
Missouri	1,271	Kansas	8
Colorado	869	Idaho	3
South Carolina	742	South Dakota	3
Virginia	737	Wyoming	3
Massachusetts	672	Montana	2
Oregon	635	North Dakota	1
Kentucky	509	Vermont	1

Source: U.S. Department of Justice, Federal Bureau of Investigation, *Uniform Crime Reports* 2005.

In addition to making prostitution an offense, most states make it an offense to solicit for a prostitute or to live off the earnings of a person engaged in prostitution. Statutes also commonly declare brothels and houses of prostitution as public nuisances.

Texas statutes provide that a person who offers or agrees to engage or engages in sexual conduct for a fee, or who solicits another in a public place to engage in such conduct, commits the misdemeanor offense of prostitution. Vernon's Tex. Penal Code Ann. § 43.02. Texas also makes promotion of prostitution a misdemeanor offense. § 43.03. One who owns or manages a prostitution enterprise that uses two or more prostitutes commits a felony. § 43.04. Finally, Texas law makes it a serious felony for a person to knowingly cause another by force, threat, or fraud or to cause by any means a person younger than seventeen years to commit prostitution. § 43.05.

Prostitution has been dealt with primarily at the state and local levels, but the federal government has also shown an interest in coping with the problem. The Mann Act, 18 U.S.C.A. § 2421 *et seq.*, prohibits interstate transportation of an individual for purposes of prostitution or with the intent to compel an individual to become a prostitute or to engage in any other immoral practice. The Supreme Court has held that the act applies to transporting persons for immoral purposes even if commercial vice is not involved. *Cleveland v. United States*, 329 U.S. 14, 67 S.Ct. 13, 91 L.Ed. 12 (1946).

Those who oppose the prostitution laws now extant in the United States point to the fact that the so-called oldest profession has survived many centuries of condemnation yet exists as a cultural institution. Thus, they argue, it fulfills a socially desirable function because it furnishes an outlet for sexual impulses and tends to lessen the incidence of sexual attacks on women. In addition to the need to conserve scarce resources to fight serious crime and the futility of trying to eradicate an ingrained institution, reformers contend that legalization of prostitution would lead to needed regulation. This, they point out, could provide for medical inspections to diminish the spread of sexually transmitted diseases. Finally, many critics of the present laws concerning prostitution contend that legalization would allow the police to take this activity from the grips of organized crime and control more effectively many of the vices that now accompany prostitution.

Austin v. State, a Texas appellate court decision dealing with prostitution, is reproduced on the companion website.

Despite the cries for reform, any decriminalization of prostitution will most likely be in selected locations only and will confine activities to prescribed areas. The inherent privacy of the scene of offenses makes it very difficult to apprehend prostitutes and their customers. Therefore, enforcement is more effective when it is focused on procurers of prostitutes and solicitors for their services, and not merely on those who render or buy those services.

Indecent Exposure and Voyeurism

At common law, it was a misdemeanor for persons to expose their "private parts" intentionally in a public place. Today, statutes and local ordinances in most jurisdictions make it a misdemeanor to expose one's private parts to the view of another under offensive circumstances. However, such laws have been generally interpreted not to prohibit public exposure of the buttocks. See, for example, *Duvallon v. District of Columbia*, 515 A.2d 724 (D.C. App. 1986). Frequently state statutes and local ordinances specify that the prohibited exposure must be in public or visible to the public. Questions are often raised as to what constitutes being "in public" or "visible to the public."

Some statutes proscribing indecent exposure do not include the requirement that the exposure must be open to the public. For example, in *People v. Neal*, 702 N. W.2d 696 (Mich. App. 2005), the defendant exposed his erect penis to a minor victim while they were in his home and not in a public place. The court held that the Michigan statute providing that "[a]ny person who shall knowingly make any open or indecent exposure of his or her person or of the person of another is guilty of a misdemeanor . . ." does not require that the offending act take place in public.

Several state courts have upheld laws criminalizing **indecent exposure** against a variety of constitutional challenges. See, for example, *Keller v. State*, 738 P.2d 186 (Okl. Crim. App. 1987); *State v. Ludwig,* 468 So.2d 1151 (La. 1985).

Frequently, the offense of indecent exposure is termed **lewd and lascivious conduct**. Because a person can expose himself or herself either accidentally or of necessity, laws generally provide that indecent exposure must be done willfully and in an offensive manner. See, for example, *People v. Randall*, 711 P.2d 689 (Colo. 1985).

Often, statutes require that offensive exposure must be in the *presence* of another person. Interpreting the term "presence" has become problematic. In 1992, the Florida Supreme Court ruled that presence "encompasses sensory awareness as well as physical proximity." Consequently, the court reversed the conviction of a man who admitted to masturbating in the presence of his thirteen-month-old child. In the court's view, the child did not have "sensory awareness" of the act in question. *State v. Werner*, 609 So.2d 585 (Fla. 1992). The Supreme Court of Kansas took a contrasting view. In *State v. Bryan*, 130 P.3d 85 (Kan. 2006), the court held that there is no awareness requirement associated with the offense of publicly exposing a sex organ in the presence of a person.

CASE-IN-POINT

Indecent Exposure

A man exposing himself in a second-story apartment in New Orleans was seen from below by persons in the apartment parking lot. He was prosecuted for indecent exposure under a statute that had been interpreted as criminalizing indecent exposure if it was viewable from any location open to the public. In upholding his conviction, the Louisiana Supreme Court noted that the parking lot from which the victims observed the man exposing himself was not enclosed, nor was it posted as private property, and was open to any visitors to the apartment complex.

State v. Clark, 372 So.2d 1218 (La. 1979).

Exotic Dancing in Places of Public Accommodation

Generally, laws against indecent exposure are applied in situations where individuals expose themselves in public or in private to unwilling viewers. But what if the exposure takes place by mutual consent, such as in a nightclub that features nude dancing? Often regulation of "exotic dancing" is accomplished through local ordinances aimed at places of public accommodation that serve alcohol. The Supreme Court has recognized that exotic dancing is entitled to First Amendment protection under certain circumstances, but has also expressed a willingness to uphold reasonable regulations, especially involving establishments that serve alcoholic beverages. *Doran v. Salem Inn*, 422 U.S. 922, 95 S.Ct. 2561, 45 L.Ed.2d 648 (1975). In *Barnes v. Glen Theatre, Inc.*, 501 U.S. 560, 111 S.Ct. 2456, 115 L.Ed.2d 504 (1991), the Court upheld an Indiana statute requiring that nightclub dancers wear "pasties" and "G-strings" when they dance. In an opinion expressing the view of three justices, Chief Justice William H. Rehnquist observed that "Indiana's requirement that the dancers wear at least pasties and a G-string is modest, and the bare minimum necessary to achieve the state's purpose. . ." 501 U.S. at 571, 111 S.Ct. at 2463, 115 L.Ed.2d at 515.

After the Supreme Court's decision in *Barnes v. Glen Theatre*, the city of Erie, Pennsylvania, adopted an ordinance making it an offense for anyone to "knowingly or intentionally appear in public in a state of nudity." To comply with the ordinance, erotic dancers were required to wear pasties and G-strings. The owners of Kandyland, a club that featured all-nude erotic dancers, filed suit in a state court to challenge the constitutionality of the new ordinance. The Court of Common Pleas declared the ordinance unconstitutional under the First Amendment, and the Pennsylvania Supreme Court agreed, concluding that the unstated purpose of the ordinance was the suppression of expression. On certiorari, the U.S. Supreme Court reversed and upheld the ordinance. Writing for a plurality of justices, Justice Sandra Day O'Connor concluded that the requirement that dancers wear pasties and G-strings was "a minimal restriction" that left dancers "ample capacity" to convey their erotic messages. *City of Erie et al. v. Pap's A. M.*, 529 U.S. 277, 120 S.Ct. 1382, 146 L.Ed.2d 265 (2000).

Go to the companion website for an edited version of the Supreme Court's decision in *Barnes v. Glen Theatre*.

Nudity and Seminudity on Public Beaches

Historically, public nudity has been taboo in Western societies. Yet only a few states have imposed outright bans. Many states maintain that public nudity on beaches and other recreational areas violates laws proscribing lewd and lascivious conduct or indecent exposure. For example, in Florida, where public beaches are popular attractions, signs are commonly posted notifying beachgoers that nude sunbathing is a violation of Florida Statutes section 877.03. Actually, that law prohibits "such acts as are of a nature to corrupt the public morals, or outrage the sense of public decency, or affect the peace and quiet of persons who may witness them." In 1976 the Florida Supreme Court held that the legislative intent of the statute prohibits adult females from openly exposing their breasts on public beaches. *Moffett v. State*, 340 So.2d 1155 (Fla. 1976). Arrests under this provision are not common. In fact, Miami Beach and other Florida cities that attract large numbers of tourists have set aside specified areas where topless or nude sunbathing is permitted. In 2001 a Florida appellate court held that a state statute and a county ordinance that prohibited exposure of the female breast in circumstances where the exposure of the male breast would not be prohibited did not violate the equal protection guarantee of the state constitution because the classification served an important governmental objective. *Frandsen v. County of Brevard*, 800 So.2d 757 (Fla. App. 2001). The Florida Supreme Court denied review. 828 So.2d 386.

Voyeurism

Voyeurism refers to obtaining sexual gratification from seeing another person's sexual organs or sexual activities. Historically voyeurism has been addressed under "Peeping Tom" statutes and ordinances based on a trespass theory. Modern photography and the availability to publish photos on the Internet have caused some states to revisit such prohibitions in order to protect the privacy of persons, not only in their homes but also in public where a person would ordinarily expect a reasonable degree of privacy.

Although most state statutes defining voyeurism prohibit nonconsensual viewing only in "private" places, Florida statutes now take a modern approach to prohibiting voyeurism. Section 810.14 provides, "A person commits the offense of voyeurism when he or she, with lewd, lascivious, or indecent intent, secretly observes, photographs, films, videotapes, or records another person when such other person is located in a dwelling, structure, or conveyance and such location provides a reasonable expectation of privacy." Another recently enacted statute makes it unlawful for any merchant to directly observe or make use of video cameras or other visual surveillance devices to observe or record customers in the merchant's dressing room, fitting room, changing room, or restroom when such room provides a reasonable expectation of privacy. West's Fla. Stat. Ann. § 877.26.

"Up-skirt" Video Voyeurism

CASE-IN-POINT

Tony O. Morris was convicted of "interference with privacy" under Minnesota Statutes § 609.746 (2000). The evidence showed that Morris carried a bag containing a concealed video camera into a J.C. Penney department store and surreptitiously positioned the lens underneath a sales clerk's skirt so as to photograph her underwear. Morris was sentenced to ninety days in jail and fined $1,000. On appeal, the conviction was affirmed. The appellate court concluded that "[b]ecause appellant surreptitiously positioned a video camera lens underneath [the victim's] skirt, a place where [the victim] had a reasonable expectation of privacy, so as to photograph the clothing covering the immediate area of the intimate parts of her body, with the intent to intrude upon or interfere with her privacy, he was lawfully found guilty of interference with privacy . . . ."

State v. Morris, 644 N.W.2d 114 (Minn. App. 2002).

Obscenity and Pornography

At common law, vulgar and obscene language and indecent public exhibitions were considered public nuisances, punishable as misdemeanors. Historically, federal and state governments in the United States passed laws banning various forms of obscenity. By the late 1800s, Congress had made it an offense to mail any "obscene, lewd or lascivious paper or writing" and provided that the word "obscene" should be given fully as broad a significance as it had at common law. The states and many municipalities also passed laws making the sale or distribution of obscene materials a crime, but seldom did these laws attempt to define obscenity. As questions arose, the courts tended to define obscenity as sexual or erotic speech or conduct. The word "obscene" came to mean something offensive to the senses—that is, repulsive, disgusting, foul, or filthy.

The Emerging Constitutional Standards

As mass communications developed, laws banning obscene speech, materials, and performances became subject to scrutiny under the First Amendment. The Supreme Court's first direct encounter with regulating obscenity came in *Roth v. United States*, 354 U.S. 476, 77 S.Ct. 1304, 1 L.Ed.2d 1498 (1957). Roth was found guilty of sending erotic materials through the mail, and his conviction was affirmed on appeal. The Supreme Court granted review and held that obscenity was not constitutionally protected; rather, the Court viewed it as "utterly without redeeming social importance." After observing that "sex and obscenity are not synonymous," the Court said the test for determining obscenity was whether "to the average person applying contemporary community standards, the dominant theme of the material taken as a whole, appeals to the prurient interest." 354 U.S. at 489, 77 S.Ct. at 1311, 1 L.Ed.2d at 1509 (1957).

By the late 1950s, there was a flood of erotic materials on the market. *Roth* effectively made the definition of obscenity a matter of federal constitutional law. It also evidenced the Court's concern for First Amendment freedoms and for protecting the free flow of expression from local interpretations of what constituted obscenity. But under the *Roth* standards, law enforcement officers experienced great difficulty in enforcing obscenity laws.

From 1957 to 1973, the Supreme Court granted review of several lower court decisions determining that particular books, plays, and movies were obscene, often explicating due process guidelines to be followed by lower courts in determining what constitutes obscenity. In 1964, Justice Potter Stewart, in expressing the view that obscenity is limited to **hard-core pornography**, made his oft-quoted remark on obscenity: "I know it when I see it." *Jacobellis v. Ohio*, 378 U.S. 184, 197, 84 S.Ct. 1676, 1683, 12 L.Ed.2d 793 (1964) (Stewart, J. concurring).

The *Miller* Test

When the Supreme Court decided the seminal case of *Miller v. California*, 413 U.S. 15, 93 S.Ct. 2607, 37 L.Ed.2d 419 (1973), it referred to "the intractable obscenity problem." 413 U.S. at 16, 93 S.Ct. at 2610, 37 L.Ed.2d at 426. In *Miller*, the defendant had mailed unsolicited material containing explicit sexual drawings in violation of a California law. A jury found him guilty, and an appellate court upheld the judgment without opinion. At the outset, Chief Justice Warren Burger reiterated that obscene materials were unprotected by the Constitution. Then the Court suggested that local juries could base their judgments on local and not national standards. Most significantly, the Court redefined the standards for determining obscenity, saying that the

> basic guidelines for the trier of fact must be: (1) whether "the average person, applying contemporary community standards" would find that the work, taken as a whole, appeals to the **prurient interest**; (b) whether the work depicts or describes, in a **patently offensive** way, sexual conduct specifically defined by the applicable state law; and (c) whether the work, taken as a whole, lacks serious literary, artistic, political, or scientific value. 413 U.S. at 24, 93 S.Ct. 2614, 37 L.Ed.2d at 431.

Finally, the Court expressly rejected any requirement that the challenged materials be found to be "utterly without redeeming social importance." 413 U.S. at 24, 93 S.Ct. at 2614, 37 L.Ed.2d at 431. The Court gave examples of "patently offensive" by saying it meant "representations or descriptions of ultimate sexual acts, normal or perverted, actual or simulated . . . , representations or descriptions of masturbation, excretory functions, and lewd exhibition of genitals." 413 U.S. at 25, 93 S.Ct. at 2615, 37 L.Ed.2d at 431. The Court made it clear that no one would be subject to prosecution unless the materials alleged to be obscene described patently offensive, "hard-core" sexual conduct.

Go to the companion website for an edited version of *Miller v. California*.

In a companion case, *Paris Adult Theatre I v. Slaton*, 93 S.Ct. 2628, 37 L.Ed.2d 446 (1973), the Court observed that the states have a right to "maintain a decent society" and may challenge obscene material even if it is shown only to consenting adults.

Significant Post-*Miller* Developments

Miller may have clarified the tests for obscenity, but it did not satisfy those who sought to ban pornographic materials. For example, *Carnal Knowledge*, a very successful movie in the early 1970s, was held not obscene under the *Miller* test. There were scenes in which "ultimate sexual acts" were understood to be taking place; however, the camera did not focus on the bodies of the actors, nor was there any exhibition of genitals during such scenes. The Court said that the film was not a "portrayal of hard core sexual conduct for its own sake, and for the ensuing commercial gain" and did not depict sexual conduct in a patently offensive way. *Jenkins v. Georgia*, 418 U.S. 153, 161, 94 S.Ct. 2750, 2755, 41 L.Ed.2d 642, 650 (1974).

Go to the companion website for an edited version of *Jenkins v. Georgia*.

In *Pope v. Illinois*, 481 U.S. 497, 107 S.Ct. 1918, 95 L.Ed.2d 439 (1987), the Supreme Court said that the application of "contemporary community standards" is

CASE-IN-POINT

Obscenity

In the first federal appeals court decision applying the *Miller v. California* obscenity test to a musical composition, the Eleventh Circuit Court of Appeals ruled that the recording *As Nasty as They Wanna Be* by 2 Live Crew was not obscene. The Eleventh Circuit ruled that even assuming the work was "patently offensive" and appealed to a "prurient interest," the trial judge erred in concluding, simply on the basis of his own listening to a tape recording, that the work lacked "serious artistic value."

Luke Records, Inc. v. Navarro, 960 F.2d 134 (11th Cir. 1992).

appropriate in evaluating the first two prongs of the *Miller* test for obscenity—that is, the work's appeal to the prurient interest and its patent offensiveness. However, the Court concluded that the third prong must be determined on an objective basis, with the proper inquiry being not whether an ordinary member of any given community would find serious literary, artistic, political, or scientific value in allegedly obscene material, but whether a reasonable person would find such value in the material taken as a whole. 481 U.S. at 500, 107 S.Ct. at 1921, 95 L.Ed.2d at 445.

Noting that the First Amendment protection extends to rap music and is not weakened because the music takes on an unpopular or even dangerous viewpoint, in 2000 a federal district court in Louisiana found that "gangsta rap" did not lack serious artistic value so as to constitute obscene speech devoid of First Amendment protection. *Torries v. Hebert*, 111 F. Supp.2d 806 (W.D. La. 2000).

State and Local Regulation of Obscenity

Radey v. State, an Ohio Court of Appeals decision dealing with obscenity, is reproduced on the companion website.

States, of course, may interpret their own constitutions to allow greater freedom of expression than is allowed under the current federal constitutional interpretations. In that vein, in 1987 the Oregon Supreme Court held that "any person can write, print, read, say, show or sell anything to a consenting adult even though that expression may be generally or universally condemned as 'obscene'." *State v. Henry*, 732 P.2d 9, 18 (Or. 1987).

Some states classify violations of their obscenity statutes by degree. For example, in New York a person is guilty of obscenity in the third degree when, knowing its content and character, he or she

1. Promotes, or possesses with intent to promote, any obscene material; or
2. Produces, presents or directs an obscene performance or participates in a portion thereof which is obscene or which contributes to its obscenity.

McKinney's N.Y. Penal Law § 235.05.

A person is guilty of obscenity in the second degree "when he commits the crime of obscenity in the third degree . . . and has been previously convicted of obscenity in the third degree." § 235.06. A person is guilty of obscenity in the first degree "when, knowing its content and character, he wholesale promotes or possesses with intent to wholesale promote, any obscene material." § 235.07. New York law makes third-degree obscenity a misdemeanor, whereas second-degree or first-degree obscenity is a felony.

States generally set higher penalties for exposing juveniles to pictures or shows where obscenity or even pornography is involved, and some state laws have been updated to proscribe disseminating indecent material to minors through computers. For example, McKinney's N.Y. Penal Law § 235.22 provides that disseminating indecent material to minors in the first degree is a class D felony. In *People v. Foley*, 731 N.E.2d 123 (N.Y. 2000), the New York Court of Appeals, the state's highest court, upheld the constitutionality of section 235.22 against challenges that it is vague and that, by its content-based restrictions, it violates the First Amendment. The court distinguished its decision from the U.S. Supreme Court's decision in *Reno v. American Civil Liberties Union*, 521 U.S. 844, 117 S.Ct. 2329, 138 L.Ed.2d 874 (1997). In *Reno*, the Court struck down the Communications Decency Act (47 U.S.C.A. § 223), which prohibited the knowing transmission of "obscene or indecent" comments to any person under the age of eighteen. (We discuss the *Reno* decision in a later topic in this chapter.)

Defenses to Charges of Obscenity

New York law provides a defense for those charged with obscenity if they can establish that the allegedly obscene material was disseminated to or performed for an audience of persons having scientific, educational, governmental, or other similar justification for possessing or viewing the material. McKinney's N.Y. Penal Law § 235.15. Moreover, it is a defense for disseminating indecent material to minors if the defendant had reasonable cause to believe that the minor involved was seventeen years old or older and exhibited official documentation to the defendant to establish that fact. McKinney's N.Y. Penal Law § 235.23. This latter provision was undoubtedly inserted to protect theater personnel from conviction on a strict liability basis.

Problems of Enforcement

Police and prosecutors often experience difficulty in determining what is to be considered obscene based on "contemporary community standards." Juries in most instances now determine the issue of obscenity simply by reviewing the material. As a result, it is not unusual for a given work to be determined obscene by a jury in one locality and not obscene by another jury in a different locality. For example, the rock musical stage production *Hair* was found not to be obscene by a federal court in Georgia. *Southeastern Promotions, Ltd. v. Atlanta*, 334 F. Supp. 634 (N.D. Ga. 1971). The following year, it was found to be obscene by another federal court in Tennessee, but this decision was reversed by the Supreme Court. *Southeastern Promotions, Inc. v. Conrad*, 341 F. Supp. 465 (E.D. Tenn. 1972), aff'd., 486 F.2d 894 (6th Cir. 1973), rev'd., 420 U.S. 546, 95 S.Ct. 1239, 43 L.Ed.2d 448 (1975).

Legal problems incident to searches and seizures of allegedly obscene materials can be very technical. Because books, movies, and even live performances are presumptively protected by the First Amendment, the Supreme Court has held that police must obtain a search warrant before conducting searches and seizures of such materials. *Roaden v. Kentucky*, 413 U.S. 496, 93 S.Ct. 2796, 37 L.Ed.2d 757 (1973). However, the Court has explained that the Fourth Amendment does not prohibit undercover police officers from purchasing allegedly obscene materials, because such a purchase would not constitute a "seizure." *Maryland v. Macon*, 472 U.S. 463, 105 S.Ct. 2778, 86 L.Ed.2d 370 (1985).

Pornography on the Internet

Amid growing public concerns about the prevalence of sexually explicit material on the Internet, and especially the relatively easy access of children to such material, Congress enacted the Communications Decency Act of 1996 (CDA). One provision, codified at 47 U.S.C.A. § 223(a) (Supp. 2000), prohibited the knowing transmission of obscene or indecent messages to any recipient under eighteen years of age. In *Reno v. American Civil Liberties Union*, 521 U.S. 844, 117 S.Ct. 2329, 138 L.Ed.2d 874 (1997), the Supreme Court struck down this provision on First Amendment grounds. Focusing on the statute's proscription of "indecent" transmissions, the Court concluded that the CDA presented a real threat of censoring expression entitled to First Amendment protection. Thus, the Court held that the statute was unconstitutionally overbroad.

In an attempt to overcome some of the constitutional defects of the CDA, in 1998 Congress passed the Child Online Protection Act (COPA). 47 U.S.C.A. § 231. COPA states,

Go to the companion website for an edited version of *Reno v. ACLU*

Whoever knowingly and with knowledge of the character of the material, in interstate or foreign commerce by means of the World Wide Web, makes any communication for commercial purposes that is available to any minor and that includes any material that is harmful to minors shall be fined not more than $50,000, imprisoned not more than 6 months, or both.

Go to the companion website for an edited version of the Supreme Court's 2004 decision in *Ashcroft v. ACLU*.

Subsection (6) of COPA relies on "community standards" to determine whether materials are harmful to minors. Lower federal courts enjoined enforcement of COPA on the ground that it improperly relied on community standards to identify what material is harmful to minors and was unconstitutionally overbroad in violation of the First Amendment. The Supreme Court then held COPA's reliance on community standards did not by itself render the statute substantially overbroad for First Amendment purposes; however, it remanded the case to the Third Circuit Court of Appeals to determine whether COPA suffers from substantial overbreadth for other reasons. *Ashcroft v. American Civil Liberties Union*, 535 U.S. 564, 122 S.Ct. 1700, 152 L.Ed.2d 771 (2002). On March 6, 2003, the Third Circuit found the plaintiffs established a substantial likelihood of prevailing on their claim that COPA is unconstitutionally overbroad and continued a preliminary injunction against enforcement of the act. 322 F.3d 240 (3rd Cir. 2003). The Supreme Court granted review and held the District Court did not abuse its discretion when it entered the preliminary injunction. However, the Court remanded the case to enable the District Court to consider whether recent technological developments in the Internet and recent Congressional enactments might enable the government to meet its constitutional burden of showing that COPA is the least restrictive alternative available to accomplish Congress's goal. *Ashcroft v. American Civil Liberties Union*, 542 U.S. 656, 124 S.Ct. 2783, 159 L.Ed.2d 690 (2004).

On March 22, 2007, a federal district judge in Philadelphia again struck down COPA, finding it to be impermissibly vague and overbroad and not narrowly tailored to the compelling interest of the government in protecting children. In his final order, Judge Lowell A. Reed, Jr. concluded that COPA "is facially violative of the First and Fifth Amendments of the United States Constitution" and ordered that the government is "PERMANENTLY ENJOINED from enforcing or prosecuting matters premised upon 47 U.S.C. § 231 at any time for any conduct." *American Civil Liberties Union v. Gonzales*, 478 F. Supp. 2d 775 (E.D. Pa. 2007). On July 22, 2008 the U.S. Court of Appeals for the Third Circuit upheld the district court, *American Civil Liberties Union v. Mukasey*, 532 F.3d 181 (2008). When the Supreme Court denied review on January 21, 2009, 555 U.S. ____, 129 S.Ct. 1032, 173 L.Ed.2d 293, the decade-long battle over COPA finally ended in defeat for the federal government.

Child Pornography

Go to the companion website for an edited version of *New York v. Ferber*.

In *New York v. Ferber*, 458 U.S. 747, 102 S.Ct. 3348, 73 L.Ed.2d 1113 (1982), the Supreme Court unanimously held that **child pornography**, like obscenity, is unprotected by the First Amendment to the Constitution. The Court upheld a New York law prohibiting persons from distributing materials that depict children engaging in lewd sex. The Court found such laws valid even if the material does not appeal to the prurient interest of the average person and is not portrayed in a patently offensive manner. The Court found a compelling state interest in protecting the well-being of children and perceived no value in permitting performances and photo reproductions of children engaged in lewd sexual conduct.

Most states have also criminalized the possession of child pornography. For example, Ohio law makes it a crime to "possess or view any material or performance that shows a minor who is not the person's child or ward in a state of nudity." Ohio Rev. Code Ann. 2907.323(A)(3) (Supp. 1989). In 1990, the Supreme Court upheld this prohibition against a constitutional challenge that the statute was overbroad. *Osborne v. Ohio*, 495 U.S. 103, 110 S.Ct. 1691, 109 L.Ed.2d 98 (1990). Together, the *Ferber* and *Osborne* decisions suggested that the Supreme Court would not be sympathetic to any First Amendment claim that would protect from criminal prosecution those who produce, distribute, or consume child pornography.

Having determined that virtual child pornography is as destructive as pornography using real children, and in an effort to keep up with developing technology, Congress enacted the Child Pornography Prevention Act of 1996 (CPPA). 18 U.S.C.A. § 2252A. The Act prohibited any type of virtual or simulated child pornography, even if real children were not involved. In *Ashcroft v. Free Speech Coalition*, 535 U.S. 234, 122 S.Ct. 1389, 152 L.Ed.2d 403 (2002), the Supreme Court surprised some observers in striking down the prohibition of virtual child pornography. The Court noted that in upholding the ban on child pornography *Ferber* focused on how the depictions of child pornography were made, not on what was communicated, and held that *virtual* child pornography is distinguishable from *real* child pornography, which, under *New York v. Ferber*, supra, may be banned without regard to whether it depicts works of value. The Court found that the ban on virtual child pornography in the CPPA abridges the freedom to engage in a substantial amount of lawful speech, and thus is overbroad and therefore unconstitutional under the First Amendment. Three justices dissented from this ruling.

Profanity

Historically states and local communities enacted laws prohibiting public profanity. In many instances these prohibitions were incorporated into broader prohibitions of offensive or disorderly conduct (see Chapter 12). In recent decades, the courts have often invalidated such laws for vagueness (see Chapter 3). In other instances, courts have upheld their validity but ruled that such laws can be applied only where the defendant's language consisted of "fighting words" or the defendant's conduct threatened a breach of the peace (see Chapter 12).

Go to the companion website for an edited version of *Cohen v. California*.

In *Cohen v. California*, 403 U.S. 15, 19, 91 S.Ct. 1780, 1785, 29 L.Ed.2d 284, 290 (1971), the Supreme Court invalidated the "offensive conduct" conviction of a man who entered a courthouse wearing a jacket emblazoned with the slogan "Fuck the Draft." Writing for the Court, Justice John M. Harlan noted that "while the particular four-letter word being litigated here is perhaps more distasteful than others of its genre, it is nevertheless often true that one man's vulgarity is another's lyric." 403 U.S. at 25, 91 S.Ct. at 1788, 29 L.Ed.2d at 294.

Despite the Supreme Court's decision in *Cohen v. California*, a number of jurisdictions retain laws proscribing **profanity**. Such laws are seldom enforced and even more rarely challenged in court. A notable exception occurred in 1999 in the widely publicized case of the "cussing canoeist" (see the Case-in-Point below).

CASE-IN-POINT

The Case of the Cussing Canoeist

When Timothy Boomer, age twenty-five, fell out of his canoe and into the Rifle River in Michigan, he let loose a three-minute tirade of profanity. Two sheriff's deputies patrolling the river heard Boomer and ticketed him. Boomer was charged with violating an 1897 Michigan statute that provides, "Any person who shall use any indecent, immoral, obscene, vulgar or insulting language in the presence or hearing of any woman or child shall be guilty of a misdemeanor." M.C.L. § 750.337

Standing before the Arenac County Circuit Court, Boomer said, "[I]f my words offended anyone, I'm sorry. I've said from the beginning that I did not know that there were children in the area and I would not have said what I said if I had known there were children around." A jury found Boomer guilty, and the court sentenced him to four days' community service and imposed a $75 fine.

On appeal the Michigan Court of Appeals reversed Boomer's conviction, noting, "Allowing a prosecution where one utters 'insulting' language could possibly subject a vast percentage of the populace to a misdemeanor conviction, M.C.L. § 750.337 fails to provide fair notice of what conduct is prohibited, and it encourages arbitrary and discriminatory enforcement. . . . Here, it would be difficult to conceive of a statute that would be more vague than M.C.L. § 750.337. There is no restrictive language whatsoever contained in the statute that would limit or guide a prosecution for indecent, immoral, obscene, vulgar, or insulting language."

People v. Boomer, 655 N.W.2d 255 (Mich. App. 2002).

Gambling

Traditionally, to gamble has meant to risk money on an event, chance, or contingency in the hope of realizing a gain. See *State v. Stripling*, 21 So. 409 (Ala. 1897). The common law did not regard gambling as an offense. However, many of the new American states, by either constitution or statute, made all or certain forms of **gambling** illegal. Today, federal laws and a variety of state statutes and local ordinances prohibit gambling. Laws regulating gambling come under the police power of the state. The U.S. Supreme Court has recognized that there is no constitutional right to gamble. *Lewis v. United States*, 348 U.S. 419, 75 S.Ct. 415, 99 L.Ed. 475 (1955).

Bingo, craps, baccarat, poker, raffles, bookmaking, and slot machines are just a few common forms of gambling. Gambling also includes betting on sports events and card games. Many forms of gambling are legal; therefore, when considering gambling, we must separate the legal from the illegal. For example, those who pay something of value to take a chance to win a prize in a **lottery** are gambling. In many jurisdictions, this is a criminal offense. Yet in several states, lotteries are not only legal—they are an important source of public revenue. In effect, it is only unregulated gambling that is illegal. A common form of unregulated gambling is "numbers." To play, you place a bet on a number with the hope that it will correspond to a preselected number. The **numbers racket** is widespread and, along with prostitution, is a major source of income for organized crime.

What Constitutes Gambling?

To constitute gambling, gaming activity must generally include three elements: **consideration, prize, and chance**. Retail stores conduct a variety of promotional schemes; local carnivals and fairs offer opportunities to play a variety of games for

What Constitutes an Illegal Gaming Machine?

CASE-IN-POINT

The Michigan Liquor Control Commission imposed a $250 fine on the Sanford Eagles Club for having a "video poker" machine on its premises. The machine had five windows, and when a quarter was deposited, a playing card appeared in each window. Essentially, the contestant played a game of five-card draw against the machine. A "winner" could gain credits entitling the player to free replays based on a random "reshuffling" of the cards. After administrative and judicial hearings, the court of appeals held that the machine was not an illegal gaming device because there was no monetary payoff. The Michigan Supreme Court reversed. The court based its decision on a provision of the statute addressing gambling devices that exempted mechanical amusement devices that reward a player with replays as long as the device is not allowed to accumulate more than fourteen replays at one time. Because the video poker machine at issue in this case permitted the player to accumulate more than fourteen replays, it did not fall within the statutory exemption.

Automatic Music and Vending Corp. v. Liquor Control Comm., 396 N.W.2d 204 (Mich. 1986).

prizes. When are they gambling, and when are they games of skill? And if they are games of skill, are they exempt from laws prohibiting gambling? Some statutes regulating gambling provide the answer. In other instances, courts may be called on to determine whether a particular activity offends a statutory prohibition against gambling.

Most statutes prohibiting gambling are interpreted to exclude athletics or other contests in which participants pit their physical or mental skills against one another for a prize. Courts tend to be practical in their interpretations. For example, an Ohio appellate court found that a pinball machine that allowed the outcome of its operation to be determined largely by the skill of the user was not "a game of chance," and the pinball operators were not in violation of the Ohio gambling statute. *Progress Vending, Inc. v. Department of Liquor Control*, 394 N.E.2d 324 (Ohio App. 1978).

Statutory Regulation of Gambling

A federal statute called the Travel Act, 18 U.S.C.A. § 1952, prohibits interstate travel in aid of gambling. The act is not aimed at local criminal activity; rather, its purpose is to attack crime that has a definite interstate aspect. *United States v. O'Dell*, 671 F.2d 191 (6th Cir. 1982).

Many states broadly proscribe gambling much the same as Florida law, which provides:

> Whoever plays or engages in any game at cards, keno, roulette, faro or other game of chance, at any place, by any device whatever, for money or other thing of value, shall be guilty of a misdemeanor of the second degree. West's Fla. Stat. Ann. § 849.08.

Typically, Florida law creates certain exemptions. Nonprofit organizations are permitted to conduct bingo games under strict regulations, § 849.0931, and charitable and nonprofit organizations are allowed to conduct certain drawings by chance, § 849.0935. Subject to specific restrictions, certain retail merchandising promotions with prizes awarded to persons selected by lot are permitted. § 849.092. Another exception allows penny-ante card games with participants age eighteen or older provided that the games are conducted in a dwelling in which the winnings of any player in a single round or game do not exceed $10 in value. Section 849.085.

Where gambling is prohibited, states customarily make it unlawful to possess gambling devices and provide for their confiscation. See, for example, West's Fla. Stat. Ann. §§ 849.231, 849.232.

Prosecutorial Problems and Defenses

Because of the consensual nature of gambling, apprehension of violators largely depends on the use of informants by police. Procedures for obtaining search and arrest warrants are technical and require close adherence to Fourth Amendment standards. In most instances, the prosecution must prove a consideration, a prize, and a chance; however, some statutes have eliminated the consideration requirement. If the statute prohibiting gambling makes intent an element of the offense, the prosecution must prove the defendant's intent; otherwise, it is sufficient merely to prove the act of gambling.

Texas law makes it an offense to bet on results of games, contests, political nominations, or elections or to play games with cards and dice. See Vernon's Tex. Penal Code Ann. § 47.02(a). The Texas legislature has taken a pragmatic approach by providing that it is a defense to prosecution under that section of the statute if

> (1) the actor engaged in gambling in a private place; (2) no person received any economic benefit other than personal winnings; and (3) except for the advantage of skill or luck, the risks of losing and the chances of winning were the same for all participants. Vernon's Tex. Penal Code Ann. § 47.02(b).

Section 47.02(c) provides that it is a defense to prosecution if the actor reasonably believed that the gambling conduct was permitted under bingo or a charitable raffle or occurred under a lottery approved by a parks and wilderness agency for determination of hunting privileges.

In some instances a defendant charged with gambling might succeed in establishing entrapment, a defense discussed in Chapter 14 .

The Paradox of Gambling Laws

The law on gambling seems paradoxical. Some laws authorize nonprofit organizations to conduct certain forms of gambling that are otherwise forbidden. In some states, people can legally bet at dog tracks and horse tracks, yet may still be prosecuted for betting in their own homes on the World Series or the Kentucky Derby. Many reformers contend that present laws are ineffective to suppress gambling. Instead, they claim these laws actually lend support to the activities of organized crime.

Certain forms of legalized gambling, particularly state lotteries and state-franchised dog and horse tracks, have become increasingly acceptable. Yet unregulated forms of gambling will most likely continue to be prohibited in most instances. In any event, if inroads are to be made in controlling unregulated gambling, enforcement efforts must be directed primarily toward gambling activity that is under the control of organized crime syndicates.

United States v. Pinelli, a federal circuit court decision dealing with gambling, is reproduced on the companion website.

Today, gambling via the Internet is widespread and very easily accessible. Because gambling websites tend to be hosted on servers located in foreign countries, prosecution of those who operate the sites is not possible. And it is very difficult to obtain the identities of persons in this country who use the sites. Thus, prosecutions for Internet-based gambling are extremely rare.

Animal Cruelty

Today there are a number of interest groups advocating the cause of "animal rights." Domestic animals do not have rights as such under American law. Nevertheless they can be, and in many instances are, protected by law. For example, the Tennessee Code provides:

(a) A person commits an offense who intentionally or knowingly:

(1) Tortures, maims or grossly overworks an animal;

(2) Fails unreasonably to provide necessary food, water, care or shelter for an animal in the person's custody;

(3) Abandons unreasonably an animal in the person's custody;

(4) Transports or confines an animal in a cruel manner; or

(5) Inflicts burns, cuts, lacerations, or other injuries or pain, by any method, including blistering compounds, to the legs or hooves of horses in order to make them sore for any purpose including, but not limited to, competition in horse shows and similar events.

(b) It is a defense to prosecution under this section that the person was engaged in accepted veterinary practices, medical treatment by the owner or with the owner's consent, or bona fide experimentation for scientific research. T.C.A. § 39-14-202

Violation of these animal cruelty laws is a misdemeanor; however, a second or subsequent conviction for cruelty to animals is a felony.

Tennessee law also proscribes cockfighting, dog fighting, and other forms of animal fighting, T.C.A. § 39-14-203, as well as the intentional killing of animals belonging to other persons, except where necessary to protect oneself, T.C.A. § 39-14-205. There is also a statute governing offenses involving farm animals and animal research facilities. T.C.A. § 39-14-803. Tennessee law classifies all of these offenses as crimes against property, but these behaviors are prohibited because people are repulsed by the wanton or unnecessary infliction of suffering on animals.

When Atlanta Falcons star quarterback Michael Vick was arrested and charged by federal authorities with conspiracy for his alleged role in a commercial dog-fighting operation during the summer of 2007, the nation became aware that Congress has also enacted legislation prohibiting animal fighting. The statute, codified at 7 U.S.C.A. § 2156, makes it a crime "for any person to knowingly sponsor or exhibit an animal in an animal fighting venture, if any animal in the venture was moved in interstate or foreign commerce." 7 U.S.C.A. § 2156(a)(1). Vick, who ultimately pleaded guilty to conspiracy and other related charges, was sentenced to twenty-three months in federal prison.

Alcohol-Related Offenses

Alcohol is the oldest and most widely abused drug known to mankind. Nearly 2000 years B.C., the Code of Hammurabi regulated commercial establishments where alcoholic beverages were consumed. In Judeo-Christian culture, consumption of alcoholic beverages was tolerated, even encouraged, and wine took on a ceremonial importance in Judaism and a sacramental importance in Christianity. However, Judeo-Christian culture frowned upon drunkenness. Islam, which dates from the seventh century A.D., has from its inception prohibited the consumption of alcohol.

In England, the common law had little to say about alcohol, except that drunkenness was not regarded as a defense to a criminal prosecution (see Chapter 14).

However, in 1603 an English court took the view that not only was intoxication no defense, but it was a wrong in itself in the sense that it aggravated a crime committed. *Beverly's Case*, 4 Co. Rep. 125 (1603).

In colonial America, alcohol use was very widespread, the favorite libations being beer, ale, and rum. In 1697 New York adopted the first law requiring that drinking establishments be closed on Sundays. The sale of alcohol was prohibited altogether by the State of Georgia in 1735, but this early experiment in "prohibition" proved unsuccessful and was repealed after only seven years. The rise of evangelical Protestantism in the early nineteenth century led to the temperance movement, which condemned the use of alcohol, and by the mid-1800s, thirteen states had enacted laws prohibiting the sale of alcohol. The Civil War dealt a setback to the temperance movement, but the movement was revitalized in the early twentieth century as women became politically active and acquired the right to vote.

"Prohibition"

In response to growing, but far from unanimous, public sentiment, Congress proposed the Eighteenth Amendment to the U.S. Constitution, which was ratified by the states in 1919. This amendment, widely referred to as "Prohibition," made unlawful the "manufacture, sale, or transportation of intoxicating liquors" within the United States. Prohibition actually began with the passage of the National Prohibition Act of 1920, 41 Stat. 305, better known as the Volstead Act, which implemented the Eighteenth Amendment to the Constitution.

Prohibition was widely violated and contributed greatly to the development of organized crime syndicates in this country. Rates of murder and other violent crimes rose dramatically during Prohibition—and then declined steadily after Prohibition was repealed. Many commentators believe that Prohibition also weakened public respect for the law, the courts, and law enforcement agencies. Jury nullification was common during Prohibition, as citizens were reluctant to convict people for doing something (albeit illegal) they themselves did on a regular basis. By the beginning of the 1930s, public opinion demanded that Prohibition be repealed.

Ultimately, Prohibition was repealed by the Twenty-First Amendment, ratified in 1933. Under the Twenty-First Amendment, however, state and local governments retain the authority to ban or regulate the manufacture, sale, and use of alcohol within their borders. As the U.S. Supreme Court recognized in *California Retail Liquor Dealers Assn. v. Midcal Aluminum, Inc.*, 445 U.S. 97, 110, 100 S.Ct. 937, 946, 63 L.Ed.2d 233, 246 (1980), the "Twenty-First Amendment grants the States virtually complete control over whether to permit importation or sale of liquor and how to structure the liquor distribution system." Indeed, there are still a number of so-called "dry counties" throughout the United States, mainly in the South and Midwest, where the sale of all or some alcoholic beverages is prohibited. Although no state has chosen to ban the sale of alcohol altogether, all states regulate the sale and use of alcoholic beverages and retain a number of alcohol-related offenses.

Offenses Related to the Consumption of Alcohol by Minors

All states prohibit minors from purchasing, possessing, and consuming alcoholic beverages and also make it an offense for an adult to sell, serve, or otherwise provide alcohol to a minor. Such offenses are misdemeanors, but the recent trend is to punish these offenses severely. For example, Texas law makes furnishing alcohol to a minor a class A misdemeanor punishable by up to one year in jail and a fine of up to $4,000. Texas Alcoholic Beverages Code § 106.03(c). However, it is not a strict liability offense; an adult who furnishes alcohol to a minor is not guilty of a crime if the minor uses a plausible but false identification card to represent himself or herself as an adult. Texas Alcoholic Beverages Code §106.03(b).

Although states are free to set their own drinking ages, Congress has used its considerable fiscal power to induce states to raise the drinking age to twenty-one. Under 23 U.S.C.A. § 158, the Secretary of Transportation is required to withhold a percentage of a state's otherwise allocable federal highway funds if the state does not establish a minimum age of twenty-one for "the purchase or public possession" of alcoholic beverages. The act has effectively established twenty-one as the minimum age for drinking. In *South Dakota v. Dole*, 483 U.S. 203, 107 S.Ct. 2793, 97 L.Ed.2d. 171 (1987), the Supreme Court upheld this measure as a valid exercise of congressional spending power.

Public Intoxication

Laws and ordinances making **public drunkenness** an offense have long been enforced by all jurisdictions, with most states and municipalities simply providing that whoever shall become intoxicated from the voluntary use of intoxicating liquors shall be punished. The offense merely involves a person being found in a public place in a state of intoxication. This offense is usually classified as a minor misdemeanor. A common police practice has been to take offenders into custody and release them once they have sobered up, a practice sometimes described as a "revolving door." In a great many cases, people who are repeatedly arrested for public intoxication suffer from alcoholism and are in need of treatment. For such individuals, the application of a criminal sanction is not likely to curb their unlawful behavior.

There is a growing awareness that alcoholism is a disease, and many have argued that the criminal law is an inappropriate mechanism to deal with it. In addition, some reformers have contended that criminalizing the public presence of an intoxicated person is contrary to the Eighth Amendment's prohibition of cruel and unusual punishments. However, the Supreme Court has declined to accept such a view. Instead, in *Powell v. Texas*, 392 U.S. 514, 88 S.Ct. 2145, 20 L.Ed.2d 1254 (1968), the Court upheld a public intoxication law. In effect, the Court ruled that the defendant, Powell, was not being punished for his status as an alcoholic but rather for his presence in a public place in an inebriated condition.

In recent years, some states have enacted statutes directing police officers to take persons found intoxicated in public places to treatment facilities rather than to incarcerate them. Consistent with this approach, many statutes now criminalize only **disorderly intoxication**. This newer offense involves the offender's being intoxicated in a public place or on a public conveyance and endangering the safety of others, not merely being in a state of intoxication in public. See, for example, Vernon's Tex. Penal Code § 49.02. In 1992 a Texas appellate court ruled that a police officer had sufficient probable cause for a warrantless arrest for public intoxication. The officer believed that the defendant could have fled from the scene, posing a danger to himself and others. Witnesses testified that the defendant ran into a parked car while intoxicated. *Segura v. State*, 826 S.W.2d 178 (Tex. App. 1992).

Driving Under the Influence

The carnage on the American highways attests to the urgent need for states to take stern measures to keep drunk drivers off the road, and all states have enacted laws attempting to accomplish this goal. Perhaps these measures contributed to the decline from over 1.5 million arrests for driving while under the influence of intoxicants in 1985 to approximately 871,000 in 2000, a decrease of 41 percent (U.S. Department of Justice, Bureau of Justice Statistics, *Sourcebook of Criminal Justice Statistics* 2001, p. 358).

The "classic" offense in this area is **driving while intoxicated (DWI)** or, more accurately, operating a motor vehicle while intoxicated. In the 1950s the laws in many states stipulated that a level of 0.15 percent or more alcohol in the bloodstream evidenced intoxication. In the 1960s and 1970s, many jurisdictions expanded the offense to prohibit **driving under the influence (DUI)** of intoxicating liquors or drugs. DWI and DUI laws sometimes allowed a defendant to avoid conviction because of the ambiguity of his or her subjective behavior. In response to this problem, most states have modified their statutes to prohibit **driving with an unlawful blood-alcohol level (DUBAL).** For many years most states defined "an unlawful blood-alcohol level" as 0.10 percent or more alcohol in the bloodstream. Today, as a result of federal fiscal incentives, all fifty states have lowered the prohibited blood-alcohol level to 0.08 percent. Moreover, most states now impose harsher penalties on DUBAL offenders whose blood-alcohol levels are especially high, typically defined as 0.15 to 0.20 percent.

CASE-IN-POINT

Public Intoxication

Joseph W. Findlay, Jr. was convicted of the offense of public intoxication and was fined $25.00. At trial in Tulsa Municipal Court, the arresting officer testified that he had been called to a Seven-Eleven store at approximately 3:00 A.M. There he observed Findlay "leaning against a food counter . . . eating Fritos with a can of dip opened beside him; he was staring with a dazed look on his face; his eyes were dilated and very bloodshot; his face was dirty; and, he had an odor of alcohol on his breath." The officer also testified that the defendant's speech was slurred and that he staggered when he attempted to walk. Testifying in his own defense, Findlay admitted to having consumed three double scotches between 11:00 P.M. and 2:30 A.M. and three beers earlier in the evening. He also testified that he took a prescription drug to control stomach pains and that the drug made him "kind of woozy." The defense also called to the stand a pharmacist who testified that the drug Findlay had taken was known to cause stupor, which might account for the staggering and slurred speech.

On appeal, Findlay claimed, among other things, that the ordinance under which he was convicted was unconstitutionally vague. That ordinance provided, "It shall be an offense for any person to be drunk or in a state of intoxication in any street, avenue, alley, park or other place open to the public." The Oklahoma Court of Criminal Appeals affirmed the conviction and upheld the ordinance. In rejecting the constitutional challenge the court opined, "The condition of being in a state of intoxication is a matter of general knowledge, the meaning of which is sufficiently 'settled and commonly understood' so that definite and sensible definition may be made of the words of the ordinance in question." The court observed, "This is true whether the term "intoxication" is used in reference to intoxication as a result of consumption of intoxicating liquor or any other intoxicating substance."

Findlay v. City of Tulsa, 561 P.2d 980 (Okla. Cr. App. 1977)

Most states now require mandatory minimum jail terms (usually twenty-four or forty-eight hours) for first-time DWI, DUI, or DUBAL offenders. Jail terms increase with subsequent offenses. Other penalties include monetary fines, suspension, or revocation of driving privileges, and alcohol education or treatment programs. In several states, repeat offenders may have their vehicles confiscated. A number of states allow judges to require repeat offenders to install devices that measure the driver's blood-alcohol level before the vehicle can be started.

Zero Tolerance for Juveniles

In 1996 Kentucky enacted a "**zero tolerance law**," also known as the juvenile DUI law, which makes it an offense for a person under age twenty-one to drive with a blood-alcohol content of 0.02 percent or higher. In *Commonwealth v. Howard*, 969 S.W.2d 700 (Ky. 1998), the Kentucky Supreme Court upheld the law as being rationally related to the legitimate legislative purpose of reducing teenage traffic fatalities and protecting all members of the public. Therefore, the court held that it does not violate the equal protection rights of those who are prosecuted. By 2003, all fifty states had followed Kentucky's lead in establishing a lower permissible blood-alcohol level for juveniles (in most states, 0.02 percent).

Prosecution of DWI, DUI, and DUBAL Charges

To obtain a conviction for DWI, DUI, or DUBAL, the prosecution must first establish that the defendant charged with driving while intoxicated or driving under the influence was operating the vehicle. This may be accomplished by either eyewitness testimony or circumstantial evidence. In *State v. Harrison*, 846 P.2d 1082 (N.M. App. 1992), the court reviewed a DUI conviction where the defendant's only contention was that the prosecution failed to prove he was driving a vehicle. Evidence at the defendant's trial revealed that he was found asleep behind the steering wheel of his car parked on the roadway with the key in the ignition, the motor running, and the transmission in drive. The court determined that this evidence established that the defendant was in actual physical control of the vehicle and therefore was sufficient to prove that the defendant was driving the automobile.

Next, the prosecution must establish the intoxication. Statutes, it should be noted, often refer to intoxication occurring as a result of alcohol or from ingestion of **contraband** substances. Intoxication is often a difficult state to articulate. Therefore, in addition to frequently offering evidence of a defendant's blood and urine alcohol content, law enforcement officers who observed the defendant are permitted to testify as to the defendant's appearance, speech, or conduct and whether the officer detected the odor of an alcoholic beverage on the defendant's person. These factors are relevant evidence of the defendant's mental and physical impairment.

In *Berkemer v. McCarty*, 468 U.S. 420, 104 S.Ct. 3138, 82 L.Ed.2d 317 (1984), the U.S. Supreme Court held that an officer's roadside questioning and administration of a **field sobriety test** to an individual stopped for irregular driving was not a "custodial interrogation" that required giving the suspect the *Miranda* warnings. However, the Court cautioned that the *Miranda* warnings apply once the suspect is under arrest.

Evidence indicates that field sobriety tests can be somewhat unreliable, and courts are beginning to scrutinize cases that rely solely on field sobriety tests without supporting chemical testing of the blood, urine, or breath of the suspect. Still, most courts permit persons to be convicted of DUI without chemical tests, especially when multiple sobriety tests have been performed by more than one officer.

Increasingly, police videotape suspects' performance on field sobriety tests and make audiotape recordings of suspects' speech. Many police agencies today have mobile blood-alcohol testing units ("Batmobiles") equipped with **breathalyzer** testing machines, videotape equipment, and voice recorders. These vans, available at the call of the arresting officer, give the police the opportunity to collect evidence promptly at or near the scene of the arrest.

One of the most sophisticated methods of alcohol detection is measuring the grams of alcohol in a volume of breath by use of a spectrophotometer, which measures the absorption of infrared light by a sample of a gas. The sampled gas is human breath, and the absorption of infrared light by a sample of the gas is affected by the concentration of alcohol in the gas. A formula can be used to determine the concentration of alcohol. An instrument called the Intoxilyzer, which performs this calculation electronically and provides a printout of the results, is increasingly used by law enforcement.

Although generally regarded as superior to field sobriety tests from an evidentiary standpoint, chemical tests are not devoid of problems. We mention some of these problems in the following topic. Ideally, to obtain a conviction, a prosecutor would like to have evidence that the defendant was driving abnormally, smelled of alcohol, exhibited slurred speech, failed a battery of field sobriety tests administered by several officers, and registered an impermissibly high blood-alcohol level on one or more chemical tests performed by a trained technician. Of course, in the real world of law enforcement, such thorough evidence is seldom obtained.

Defense of DWI, DUI, and DUBAL Charges

Historically, counsel who represent a defendant charged with DWI, DUI, or DUBAL have challenged the methodology of an officer's administration of field sobriety tests, particularly where the defendant suffers from any physical impairment or has been taking medication that might make it difficult to perform these tests. Today defense counsel must have a basic knowledge of scientific evidence and also be prepared to challenge the reliability and validity of chemical testing equipment and the operator's level of competence. Defense counsel may present expert testimony challenging the chemicals that breath analysis machines measure and offer evidence of a defendant's illnesses and the medications a defendant was taking at the time of the tests.

States have administrative rules that specify the procedure to be followed in administering a breath test. Defense counsel often seeks to suppress the results of Intoxilyzer tests on grounds that the prosecution has not established a proper predicate for their admissibility. For example, in *Davis v. State*, 712 So.2d 1115 (Ala. Crim. App. 1997), the defense objected to the introduction of the results of the Intoxilyzer tests on the ground that the instrument was not properly calibrated at the time the blood-alcohol test was performed. The trial court denied the motion. On appeal, the Alabama Criminal Appeals Court agreed with the defense. The court held there was no evidence the equipment used to perform the tests had been inspected as required by rules of the Alabama Department of Forensics.

State administrative rules usually require an observation period before administration of a breath test to ensure that no substance enters the defendant's mouth that might affect the validity of the test results. For example, an Illinois administrative rule governing alcohol breath tests stipulated that the test was valid only if the driver did not regurgitate within an observation period of twenty minutes before the test. In *People v. Bonutti*, 817 N.E.2d 489 (2004), defense counsel had objected to the introduction of the tests, asserting what has become known as the "acid reflux defense." The Illinois Supreme Court reversed the lower court's ruling and suppressed the results of the breath alcohol test because the evidence revealed the defendant suffered an acid reflux episode while waiting to take the breath test.

Defense counsel often challenge the results of breath tests made by the Intoxilyzer 5000 or 8000 instruments referred to above. The manufacturer of these instruments has been unwilling to release their source codes, claiming that this information does not satisfy the "materiality" requirement and that they are protected as trade secrets. Several trial courts in Florida have found that non-disclosure of the source codes denies defendants material evidence in support of their defense and that the instruments are not an "approved test" as required by the Florida implied consent statute. Thus, in some cases non-disclosure of the source codes has resulted in exclusion of all Intoxilyzer evidence at trial or in denying the prosecution the presumptions and shortened predicate for admissibility of the breath test results allowed under Florida law.

Implied Consent Statutes

To facilitate chemical testing in DWI, DUI, and DUBAL cases, California and most other jurisdictions have enacted **implied consent statutes**. Under these laws, a person who drives a motor vehicle is deemed to have given consent to a urine test for drugs and to blood, breath, or urine testing to determine blood-alcohol content. The testing is made incident to a lawful arrest of a driver. See, for example, West's Ann. Cal. Vehicle Code § 23612. In most instances, refusal to submit to the tests required by an implied consent law will result in an administrative suspension of licensing privileges. The Supreme Court has upheld the validity of the Massachusetts implied consent law, which provides for suspension of the driver's license of a person who refuses to take a breathalyzer test. *Mackey v. Montrym*, 443 U.S. 1, 99 S.Ct. 2612, 61 L.Ed.2d 321 (1979).

Go to the companion website for an edited version of *Mackey v. Montrym*.

Drug Offenses

Though not as widespread as alcohol, drugs like marijuana and opium have been used by people in various parts of the world for thousands of years. The indigenous peoples of South America knew of the stimulating properties of coca leaves, although cocaine was not invented until the nineteenth century. In that century, cocaine and opium derivatives were widely used by Americans with no legal prohibitions or regulations. Opium derivatives were routinely used to treat diarrhea, sleeplessness, and anxiety. In 1875, the City of San Francisco prohibited the smoking of opium, a common practice among Chinese immigrants. But the city did not criminalize other means of ingesting opium that were popular among white citizens, such as in the liquid preparation called laudanum. As the twentieth century dawned, Americans were becoming more aware of the addictive nature of narcotics, and people began to call for governmental restrictions on such products.

The Harrison Act

The Harrison Act of 1914, 38 Stat. 785, was the first attempt by the federal government to regulate the sale and use of opium and cocaine. Ostensibly a revenue measure, the act levied criminal penalties on those who distributed cocaine or opium and failed to register and pay the requisite taxes. Although the act allowed doctors to prescribe cocaine and opiates for legitimate medical reasons, it criminalized their prescription merely to satisfy the cravings of addicts. The Supreme Court upheld the Harrison Act against the challenge that it was not a valid revenue measure and usurped the police powers of the states. *United States v. Doremus*, 249 U.S. 86, 39 S.Ct. 214, 63 L.Ed. 493 (1919). In the wake of the Harrison Act, state legislatures enacted statutes criminalizing the sale and possession of opiates and cocaine. By the 1930s, these prohibitions were nearly universal among the states. During this period, rates of cocaine and opium use declined, but the country also saw the emergence of an underground drug economy that persists to this day.

Prohibition of Marijuana

Marijuana or hemp, which has been used in parts of the world for thousands of years, was widely cultivated in the United States in the nineteenth century. Used primarily as a source of fiber for making rope, marijuana was also used as medicine, both for people and animals. Smoking marijuana for "recreational" purposes was not widespread in the United States until the early twentieth century, when an influx of immigrants from Mexico brought the practice to this country. During Prohibition, many people turned to marijuana as a cheap and legal alternative to alcohol. After Prohibition was repealed in 1933, federal and state authorities turned their attention to marijuana.

By 1937, forty-six of the forty-eight states had banned the cultivation, sale, possession, and use of the cannabis plant. Marijuana use declined dramatically during the 1940s and 1950s, at least partly due to the new criminal prohibitions, but rose again in the 1960s.

The Marihuana Tax Act of 1937 was the federal government's first attempt to control marijuana. Not a direct prohibition, the act criminalized the failure to pay a tax on the transfer of cannabis. Of course, compliance with the law exposed a person to criminal prosecution under state laws, which is why the U.S. Supreme Court declared the statute unconstitutional in 1969. *Leary v. United States*, 395 U.S. 6, 16, 89 S.Ct. 1532, 1537, 23 L.Ed.2d 57, 70 (1969).

Go to the companion website for an edited version of *Leary v. United States*.

Modern Federal Drug Laws

In the 1960s, the United States saw a resurgence of illicit drug use. Whereas illegal drug use had previously been concentrated in big cities, among ethnic minorities, and among the lower socioeconomic strata, in the 1960s drug use proliferated within the middle-class white population, especially young people. During the 1960s marijuana use increased dramatically and new hallucinogenic drugs like LSD came on the scene. The use of such drugs was encouraged by a "counterculture" movement that eschewed middle-class conventions and encouraged young people to experiment with alternative lifestyles.

Responding to concern over the rise in drug use, Congress enacted the Comprehensive Drug Abuse Prevention and Control Act of 1970. 21 U.S.C.A. § 801 *et seq.* The act, commonly referred to as the **Controlled Substances Act**, establishes the criteria for classification of substances and lists controlled substances according to their potential for abuse. Offenses involving the manufacture, sale, distribution, and possession with intent to distribute are defined and the penalties are prescribed in 21 U.S.C.A. § 841. Penalties for simple possession of controlled substances are prescribed in 21 U.S.C.A. § 844. Provision is made in 21 U.S.C.A. § 823 for registered practitioners to dispense narcotics for approved purposes.

Modern State Drug Laws

In 1972 the Uniform Controlled Substances Act was drafted by the Commission on Uniform Laws, whose purpose was to achieve uniformity among state and federal laws. There are three versions of the Uniform Controlled Substances Act: 1970, 1990, and 1994. Provisions within each version are similar. All fifty states and the Virgin Islands have adopted one of the three versions. Like the federal statute, the uniform act classifies controlled substances according to their potential for abuse. For example, opiates are included in Schedule I because they are unsafe for use even under medical treatment, whereas Schedule II includes drugs that have a high potential for abuse but may be medically acceptable under certain conditions. The remaining schedules include controlled substances that have lesser potential for abuse and dependency. The range of controlled substances includes such well-known drugs as cocaine, amphetamines, tranquilizers, and barbiturates (see Table 10.2).

Go to the companion website for an edited version of *Robinson v. California*.

All states make the manufacture, sale, and possession of **controlled substances** illegal. Offenses involving drugs that have a high potential for abuse (for example, heroin and cocaine) are usually very serious felonies. Although it is constitutionally permissible to enact such laws, the U.S. Supreme Court has ruled that states may not criminalize the mere status of being addicted to such drugs. *Robinson v. California*, 370 U.S. 660, 82 S.Ct. 1417, 8 L.Ed.2d 758 (1962).

Like most states, California statutes proscribe possession or purchase for sale of designated controlled substances and provide penalties according to the harmfulness

TABLE 10.2	Schedule of Controlled Substances under Tennessee Law	
Schedule I	High potential for abuse; no accepted medical use in treatment or lacks accepted safety for use in treatment under medical supervision.	This includes certain opiates (e.g., heroin); hallucinogens (e.g., LSD); depressants (e.g., methaqualone); and stimulants (e.g., MDMA).
Schedule II	High potential for abuse; has currently accepted medical use in treatment, or currently accepted medical use with severe restrictions; abuse of the substance may lead to severe psychic or physical dependence.	Examples: Cocaine, morphine, amphetamines, amobarbital.
Schedule III	Potential for abuse less than the substances listed in Schedules I and II; has currently accepted medical use in treatment; and may lead to moderate or low physical dependence or high psychological dependence.	Examples: Anabolic steroids.
Schedule IV	Low potential for abuse relative to substances in Schedule III; has currently accepted medical use in treatment; and may lead to limited physical dependence or psychological dependence relative to the substances in Schedule III.	Example: Phenobarbital.
Schedule V	Low potential for abuse relative to the controlled substances listed in Schedule IV; has currently accepted medical use in treatment in the United States; and has limited physical dependence or psychological dependence liability relative to the controlled substances listed in Schedule IV.	Example: A medicine containing not more than two hundred (200) milligrams of codeine per one hundred (100) grams.
Schedule VI	Tetrahydrocannabinols.	Marijuana; hashish; synthetic equivalents.
Schedule VII	Butyl nitrite and any isomer thereof.	

Source: Tennessee Drug Control Act of 1989, T.C.A § 39-17-401 *et seq.*

of the substance. See West's Ann. Cal. Health & Safety Code §§ 11350–11352. In most states offenses involving the mere possession of less harmful substances are often classified as lesser-degree felonies or, where a very small quantity of marijuana is involved, are frequently classified as misdemeanors.

During the 1970s several states decriminalized their anti-marijuana laws by removing the threat of a jail sentence for possession offenses. In Nebraska, where the legislature amended its laws in 2008, possession of less than one ounce of marijuana is considered an "infraction" for which a first-time offender may be fined no more than three hundred dollars and assigned to attend a drug education course. Neb. Rev. Stat. § 28–416 (13)(a). Possession of more than one ounce but less than one pound of marijuana is a misdemeanor, see Neb. Rev. Stat. § 28-416 (11); possession of more than one pound is a felony. Neb. Rev. Stat. § 28-416 (12).

The Marijuana Controversy

Marijuana violations lead to nearly half of all drug arrests in the United States. Despite aggressive law enforcement, marijuana remains widely available, a situation that exemplifies the difficulty of enforcing a law that has less-than-universal public support. Nevertheless, courts have generally declined to reassess legislative judgments in this area, and statutes making it a criminal offense to possess marijuana have withstood numerous constitutional challenges. For example, in *State v. Smith*, 610 P.2d 869 (Wash. 1980), the Supreme Court of Washington held that criminal penalties for possession of marijuana did not violate the constitutional prohibition against cruel and unusual punishments. More recently, in *State v. Harland*, 556 So.2d 256 (La. App. 1990), a Louisiana appellate court rejected the contention that such penalties violated a state constitutional provision protecting the right of privacy.

Go to the companion website for an edited version of the Alaska Supreme Court's decision in *Ravin v. State*.

Perhaps the most notable court ruling dealing with marijuana use is an Alaska Supreme Court decision in 1975. In *Ravin v. State*, 537 P.2d 494 (Alaska 1975), the court held that the explicit right to privacy contained in the Alaska state constitution protects the possession and personal use of marijuana by an adult in the home. In interpreting the right to privacy under the Alaska Constitution, the court took note of the individualistic nature of Alaska's political culture. The court concluded that, given the relatively innocuous nature of marijuana, the state had an insufficient basis for criminalizing its use in the home. The court recognized that the distribution of marijuana could still be criminalized.

Responding to the *Ravin* decision, the Alaska legislature in 1982 decriminalized the possession by an adult of up to four ounces of marijuana for personal use. However, in 1990 Alaska voters approved a ballot initiative that stated,

> Under Alaska law it is currently legal for adults over 18 years old to possess less than four ounces of marijuana in a home or other private place. The penalty for adults over 18 years old for possessing less than one ounce in public is a fine of up to $100. This initiative would change Alaska's laws by making all such possession of marijuana criminal, with possible penalties of up to 90 days in jail and/or up to a $1000 fine.

In *Noy v. State*, 83 P.3d 545 (Alaska App. 2003), the Alaska Court of Appeals struck down the statute adopted by voter initiative in 1990. The court noted that the voters are bound, as is the legislature, to respect the provisions of the state constitution as interpreted by the state's highest court. The court determined that the legislature had acted properly in its 1982 enactment decriminalizing possession of up to four ounces of marijuana for personal use. Unless and until the Alaska Supreme Court says otherwise, or the people of Alaska amend their state constitution, Alaskans have a constitutional right to possess up to four ounces of cannabis in their homes for personal use. As noted in *State v. Crocker*, 97 P.3d 93, 95 (Alaska App. 2004), "Not all marijuana possession is a crime in Alaska. Under *Ravin* and *Noy*, an adult may possess any amount of marijuana less than four ounces in their home, if their possession is for personal use."

Marijuana for Medicinal Use

As we noted earlier in the chapter, marijuana was sometimes used in the nineteenth century for medicinal purposes. Today, there is a growing demand that marijuana be made legal for medical use, especially for the relief of nausea experienced by persons undergoing chemotherapy for cancer or acquired immunodeficiency syndrome (AIDS). In 1991 a Florida appellate court permitted a husband and wife suffering from AIDS to assert a medical necessity defense (see Chapter 14) in a marijuana possession case. *Jenks v. State*, 582 So.2d 676 (Fla. App. 1991). That decision and similar decisions in other states helped to give rise to a national movement to legalize marijuana for medicinal use. Between 1996 and 2008, thirteen states (Alaska, California, Colorado, Hawaii, Maine, Michigan, Montana, Nevada, New Mexico, Oregon, Rhode Island, Vermont, and Washington) passed laws legalizing marijuana for medical uses. Most of these laws resulted from referenda.

Opponents of medical marijuana initiatives claim that they are a cleverly disguised first step toward drug legalization rather than a genuine effort to alleviate suffering due to cancer or AIDS. Indeed, in California today it is easy for people suffering from stress to obtain a prescription so that they can legally purchase and use cannabis. Some might say California has already legalized marijuana on a *de facto* basis.

The federal authorities have thus far taken the position that marijuana has no legitimate medical use. In *United States v. Oakland Cannabis Buyers' Cooperative*, 532 U.S. 483, 121 S.Ct. 1711, 149 L.Ed.2d 722 (2001), the Court refused to recognize a "medical necessity exception" to the Controlled Substances Act. As yet, Congress has not amended the act to create a medical necessity exception.

Go to the companion website for an edited version of *Gonzales v. Raich*.

The legalization of marijuana for medical use creates a conflict between state and federal law. As we noted in Chapter 3 , in *Gonzales v. Raich*, 545 U.S. 1, 125 S.Ct. 2195, 162 L.Ed.2d 1 (2005), the Supreme Court held that Congress does have the power under the Commerce Clause to prohibit the mere possession of small quantities of marijuana, even if it is solely for personal medicinal use authorized by state law. Thus, a person using marijuana with a doctor's prescription pursuant to a state "compassionate use" statute is still subject to arrest and prosecution by federal authorities, although it is safe to say that the enforcement of the marijuana prohibition against such individuals is not a high priority for federal prosecutors or law enforcement agencies.

The Crystal Meth Crisis

In the 1980s, cocaine (especially "crack") emerged as the leading drug problem in this country. Today, law enforcement agencies are confronting a new epidemic—that of homemade methamphetamines. Also known as "crystal meth" or "crank," this powerful stimulant can be easily made by amateur chemists with products readily available in the marketplace. However, the making of the drug is itself extremely dangerous, as it involves highly volatile, explosive, and noxious chemicals.

The process also produces highly toxic by-products that, when disposed of, present a serious threat to the natural environment. Meth labs tend to be located in rural areas where they can operate without detection. Often the authorities become aware of them only after a fire, explosion, or serious environmental contamination has occurred. Prosecutors have begun to take a new and dramatic approach to the meth lab problem. They have begun to charge operators of labs with environmental crimes (see Chapter 11).

The Combat Methamphetamine Epidemic Act

In 2005, Congress passed an important measure to address the crystal meth crisis. In addition to increasing penalties for smuggling and selling methamphetamine, the Combat Methamphetamine Epidemic Act of 2005, now codified in various sections of Title 21 of the U.S. Code, is designed to make it more difficult to acquire the precursor chemicals used to make meth. The new law limits purchases of ephedrine, pseudoephedrine, and phenylpropanolamine, which are commonly found in over-the-counter cold and sinus products as well as appetite suppressants. The law requires stores to keep products containing these ingredients behind the counter or in locked display cases. Vendors are prohibited from selling more than 3.6 grams per day or 9 grams per month of these chemicals to any customer, regardless of the number of transactions. Of course, those who are intent on acquiring large quantities of these products can go from store to store. That is why vendors are required to keep a logbook in which they record the names and addresses of purchasers, who must show valid identification in order to purchase the regulated products. These logbooks must be made available on demand to state and federal authorities investigating meth production.

Prohibition of Drug Paraphernalia

Under federal law, it is a crime to import, export, sell, offer for sale, or use the mails to transport any **drug paraphernalia**. 21 U.S.C.A. § 863(a). Violation of this prohibition is punishable by a fine and imprisonment up to three years. 21 U.S.C.A. § 863(b). Federal law defines drug paraphernalia to include "any equipment, product, or material of any kind which is primarily intended or designed for use in manufacturing, compounding, converting, concealing, producing, processing, preparing, injecting, ingesting, inhaling, or otherwise introducing into the human body a controlled substance, possession of which is unlawful under this subchapter." 21 U.S.C.A. § 863(d). Under federal law, drug paraphernalia is subject to confiscation. 21 U.S.C.A. § 863(c). In *United States v. Janus Industries*, 48 F.3d 1548 (10th Cir. 1995), a federal appeals court upheld the federal prohibitions and penalties associated with drug paraphernalia. Possession of drug paraphernalia is also commonly a criminal offense under state laws and many local ordinances.

Problems of Drug Enforcement and Prosecution

Federal and state laws on controlled substances mirror one another in many respects. Federal enforcement is usually directed against major interstate or international drug traffickers; states usually concentrate on those who possess or distribute controlled substances. Many drug-trafficking violations of federal law involve prosecution for conspiracy. Unlike many state laws, the federal law proscribing conspiracy to violate the Controlled Substances Act does not require proof of an overt act. 21 U.S.C.A. § 846; *United States v. Pulido*, 69 F.3d 192 (7th Cir. 1995); *United States v. Wilson*, 657 F.2d 755 (5th Cir. 1981).

Because those involved in narcotics transactions are usually willing participants, enforcement often depends on the use of confidential informants by police. Obtaining search warrants and making arrests based on probable cause often present difficult Fourth Amendment problems.

The level of intent that the prosecution must establish in contraband cases can vary according to the particular statutory offense (see Chapter 4). However, courts have generally held that statutes making possession, distribution, or trafficking of contraband unlawful require the prosecution to prove only the defendant's general intent. See, for example, *State v. Williams*, 352 So.2d 1295 (La. 1977) (Intent established by mere proof of voluntary distribution); *State v. Bender*, 579 P.2d 796 (N.M. 1978).

Actual and Constructive Possession

In drug possession cases, a critical problem is proving that the defendant was in possession of a controlled substance. The prosecution may prove either actual or constructive possession of contraband to satisfy the possession requirement. Proof of actual possession is established by evidence that the contraband was found on the accused's person or that the accused was in exclusive possession of the premises or vehicle where the contraband was discovered. Where the accused is not in actual possession, however, or where the accused and another person jointly occupy a dwelling or automobile where contraband is discovered, the prosecution must attempt to prove what the law calls *constructive possession*.

A person has constructive possession of contraband if he or she has ownership, dominion, or control over the contraband itself or over the premises in which it is concealed. *United States v. Schubel*, 912 F.2d 952 (8th Cir. 1990). The prosecution usually attempts to establish constructive possession by evidence of incriminating statements and circumstances from which the defendant's ability to control the contraband may be inferred. This can pose a formidable difficulty.

In *State v. Somerville*, 572 A.2d 944 (Conn. 1990), the defendant appealed his conviction for possession of cocaine with intent to sell sixty-nine vials of crack cocaine. He argued that no evidence was presented at his trial to establish that he possessed the drugs in question. He pointed to the fact that no drugs and no large sums of money were found on his person. The evidence revealed that the police found the sixty-nine vials of cocaine underneath a garbage can at the defendant's neighbor's house. Witnesses had seen the defendant selling crack cocaine in small vials before his arrest. They testified that he had been stooping near the garbage can under which the police found the vials of cocaine. The Connecticut Supreme Court rejected the defendant's contention and found the evidence sufficient to establish that the defendant had dominion and control over the cocaine and had knowledge of the character of the contraband and its presence.

Proof of Intent to Sell or Distribute Drugs

Intent to distribute controlled substances may be proved by either direct or circumstantial evidence. It may be inferred from the presence of equipment to weigh and measure narcotics and paraphernalia used to aid in their distribution. Large sums of

Constructive Possession of Drugs

After Minneapolis police obtained a tip that crack cocaine was being sold out of cars parked in front of a certain duplex, an officer observed a blue Cadillac parked in front of the building. A female later identified as the defendant, Nina Knox, made several trips between the car and the duplex. At one point she drove the car from the scene, but she returned shortly and sat in the car for a period of time while a number of men approached the car and walked away after brief encounters. The officer, who was experienced in dealing with drug offenses, believed the activities he witnessed to be drug transactions, although he was unable to observe money and drugs being exchanged. Knox was arrested, and a search of the car produced 14.3 grams of crack cocaine and $2,200 in cash. A search of Knox's purse produced a large amount of money and food stamps. Knox was convicted in federal court of possession with intent to distribute a controlled substance.

On appeal, Knox argued that the evidence failed to establish that she was in physical control of the cocaine and was intending to sell it. The U.S. Court of Appeals rejected Knox's contention, concluding that the evidence supported a finding that Knox had exercised "dominion over the premises in which the contraband [was] concealed" since she was observed driving the car, sitting in the car, and entering it on several occasions. The court further concluded that intent to distribute could be inferred from the fact that sizable amounts of cash and cocaine were found at the scene. Knox's conviction was affirmed.

United States v. Knox, 888 F.2d 585 (8th Cir. 1989).

cash and narcotics are common indicia of circumstantial evidence of intent to distribute illegal drugs. See, for example, *United States v. Brett*, 872 F.2d 1365 (Mo. 8th Cir. 1989).

Defenses in Drug Cases

Defendants on trial for drug offenses sometimes assert that they were entrapped by the police, a defense discussed in Chapter 14 . More frequently, defense counsel attempt to suppress the contraband seized by police on the ground that it was obtained in violation of the Fourth Amendment prohibition against unreasonable searches and seizures. In some instances, a defendant presents an expert witness to contest the type of contraband introduced in evidence, and frequently defendants challenge the chain of custody of the contraband from the time it was seized until the time it was introduced into evidence. Because the gravity of the offense is often based on the amount of contraband seized, defendants sometimes challenge the weight of the contraband being introduced into evidence. Possession with intent to deliver drugs within a certain proximity of a school is a more serious offense that can carry severe penalties. Defendants charged with this offense often challenge the measurement of the distance between the school and the place where the offense allegedly occurred.

In a number of cases, courts have rejected such defenses as economic coercion and duress, but, as we noted above, in some instances courts have accepted the defense of "medical necessity" in possession of marijuana cases.

The "War on Drugs"

President Richard Nixon first "declared war" on illegal drugs in 1973. President Ronald Reagan "redeclared" the war in 1982, as did the first President Bush in 1988. Since 1973 the war on drugs has been waged on numerous fronts, from elementary schools to Colombian coca farms, and law enforcement agencies have employed a number of controversial weapons and tactics. Federal and state drug laws have been made more stringent; budgets for drug enforcement activities have been increased dramatically, teachers, police officers and other public employees have been subjected to random drug testing; and constitutional restrictions on searches and seizures have been relaxed. Millions of dollars have been spent on public information campaigns on the dangers of drug abuse. To supporters of the drug war, it is a war for national survival, nearly as important as the current war on terrorism. Its detractors see it as a war on people or, alternatively, a war on the Constitution.

The Drug Enforcement Administration

In 1973, President Nixon issued an executive order creating the Drug Enforcement Administration (DEA) within the Department of Justice to concentrate federal drug enforcement responsibilities within one agency of government. Since then, the DEA has been involved in all facets of the drug war, including joint operations with state and local law enforcement agencies as well as agencies in other countries. The DEA has even worked in tandem with the Coast Guard in an effort to interdict smuggling operations into the United States. The DEA has employed a number of controversial tactics, including **drug courier profiling**, in which a set of behavioral characteristics believed to typify drug smugglers is employed to identify, monitor and sometimes detain suspected drug couriers. Such tactics have generated considerable litigation—with disparate results. See, for example, *Reid v. Georgia*, 448 U.S. 438, 100 S.Ct. 2752, 65 L.Ed.2d 890 (1980); *United States v. Sokolow*, 490 U.S. 1, 109 S.Ct. 1581, 104 L.Ed.2d 1 (1989).

The DEA employs more than 9,000 people, including more than 4,500 special agents. Its annual budget exceeds $1.8 billion. Yet according to a Performance and Management Assessment released by the White House in February 2003, the DEA "is unable to demonstrate its progress in reducing the availability of illegal drugs in the U.S." The report cited a lack of cooperation with other law enforcement agencies, misplaced priorities, and a lack of internal evaluation and accountability mechanisms, all of which may be valid criticisms. The reality may well be that the problem that DEA is tasked with solving is beyond the capabilities of any government agency.

Mandatory Minimum Sentences

In 1969, amidst public outcry over drugs and street crime, the New York legislature enacted the first of the so-called Rockefeller Drug Laws, which required mandatory prison terms for persons convicted of serious drug crimes. In 1973, the legislature strengthened these laws by establishing more severe penalties and by restricting plea bargaining in drug cases. By and large, these laws remain in effect today. As an example of the harshness of the laws, a person convicted of selling two ounces or possessing four ounces of cocaine or heroin is required to serve at least fifteen years in prison before being eligible for parole. While their effect on deterring illegal drug use is debatable, the Rockefeller Drug Laws have certainly had the effect of dramatically increasing the size of the prison population in New York. In 1998 the prison population in New York State stood at roughly 70,000 inmates, nearly three times as many prisoners as in 1979. By 1998, non-violent drug offenders accounted for 30 percent of the state prison population. (See Spiros A. Tsimbinos, *Is It Time to Change the Rockefeller Drug Laws?*, 13 St. John's J. Legal Comment 613–34, Spring 1999.)

In the late 1970s and 1980s, other states and the federal government followed New York's example. Beginning in 1986, Congress required mandatory minimum prison terms for drug felonies. For example, a person charged with possession with the intent to distribute more than five kilograms of cocaine is subject to a mandatory minimum sentence of ten years in prison. See 21 U.S.C.A. § 841(b)(1)(A). Consequently, the federal prison population has swelled with drug offenders who theretofore received probation. In 1991, 58 percent of federal prisoners were convicted of drug offenses; by 1997 the proportion had risen to 63 percent. (U.S. Department of Justice, Bureau of Justice Statistics, *Sourcebook of Criminal Justice Statistics*, 2001, p. 499). As of November 2004 there were 143,864 federal offenders sentenced to prison. Of these, 77,867 or 54.1 percent were sentenced for drug offenses. (*Sourcebook of Criminal Justice Statistics*, 2003, p. 519). As a result of mandatory sentencing under federal law, a significantly higher percentage of federal drug defendants are sentenced to prison than are state drug defendants.

Drug Testing of Public Employees and Public School Students

As a means of reducing drug use among public employees, numerous local, state, and federal government agencies in the 1980s adopted **drug-testing requirements** for their employees. In 1989 the U.S. Supreme Court sustained a Customs Service policy requiring drug tests for persons seeking positions as customs inspectors. *Treasury Employees Union v. Von Raab*, 489 U.S. 656, 109 S.Ct. 1384, 103 L.Ed.2d 685 (1989). As yet, the Supreme Court has not addressed the issue of general, random drug testing of public employees. However, it has invalidated a policy under which all political candidates were required to submit to drug testing as a condition of qualifying for the ballot. *Chandler v. Miller*, 520 U.S. 305, 117 S.Ct. 1295, 137 L.Ed.2d 513 (1997). Several state courts have addressed the question of random drug testing of public employees, and at least one state appellate court has found such a policy to be unconstitutional. *City of Palm Bay v. Bauman*, 475 So.2d 1322 (Fla. App. 1985).

Go to the companion website for an edited version of *Treasury Employees Union v. Von Raab*.

In many school districts around the country, teachers and students are subjected to drug testing. Teachers are required to submit to drug testing as a condition of employment, and this requirement has generally been upheld by the courts. See, for example, *Knox County Education Association v. Knox County Board of Education*, 158 F.3d 361 (6th Cir. 1998). With respect to students, most policies require drug testing as a condition of participation in sports or other extracurricular activities. One such policy established by the City of Tecumseh, Oklahoma, was upheld by the U.S. Supreme Court in 2002. See *Board of Education v. Earls*, 536 U.S. 822, 122 S.Ct. 2559, 153 L.Ed.2d 735 (2002). Writing for the Court, Justice Clarence Thomas concluded, "Given the nationwide epidemic of drug use, and the evidence of increased drug use in Tecumseh schools, it was entirely reasonable for the School District to enact this particular drug testing policy." 536 U.S. at 836, 122 S.Ct. at 2568, 153 L.Ed.2d at 748.

Asset Forfeiture

In passing the Comprehensive Drug Abuse Prevention and Control Act of 1970, Pub.L. No. 91-513, 84 Stat. 1276, Congress for the first time provided for forfeiture of property used in connection with federal drug crimes. Today federal law authorizes forfeiture of illegal drugs themselves, drug paraphernalia, money and other assets furnished or intended to be furnished in drug exchanges, proceeds from illegal drug transactions, real estate used or intended to be used in illegal drug transactions, as well as aircraft, vessels, and vehicles used to transport or otherwise facilitate illegal drug transactions. Most states have enacted similar laws. See, for example, Oklahoma's Uniform Controlled Dangerous Substances Act, 63 Okl. St. Ann. § 2-503.

Federal asset forfeitures can be criminal or civil. In a **criminal forfeiture**, a person convicted of a federal drug offense is ordered to forfeit property involved in that offense. However, in order for that to occur, the property sought by the government must be specifically identified in the indictment so that the owner has the opportunity to contest the forfeiture. Furthermore, the standard of proof with respect to the forfeiture is lower than that required to convict the defendant. As in any criminal prosecution, the government must prove the defendant's guilt beyond a reasonable doubt. But the standard of proof with respect to the associated forfeiture of property is merely "by a preponderance of the evidence." The two principal statutes governing criminal forfeiture in federal drug cases are 18 U.S.C.A. § 982 and 21 U.S.C.A. § 853.

In contrast to a criminal forfeiture, a **civil forfeiture** (see 18 U.S.C.A. § 983) does not require a criminal conviction, or even prosecution of the owner, because the legal action is brought against the property itself in what is known as an *in rem* action. Thus, a civil forfeiture case is likely to be styled something like *United States v. 2003 Porsche 911 Carrera Cabriolet*. Property may be seized as long as agents have probable cause to believe it is subject to forfeiture. A subsequent civil proceeding determines whether the property is to be forfeited or returned to the owner. Civil forfeiture thus rests on the legal fiction that the property itself is in violation of the law and can be the target of legal action. Of course, the real target of the action is the property owner, who may or may not be simultaneously defending against a criminal prosecution.

The Supreme Court has held that civil forfeitures are neither punishment nor criminal for purposes of the Double Jeopardy Clause. *United States v. Ursery*, 518 U.S. 267, 116 S.Ct. 2135, 135 L.Ed.2d549 (1996).

Go to the companion website for an edited version of *United States v. Ursery*.

Criticism and Reform

In the 1980s, the federal government became much more aggressive in the use of civil forfeitures as part of the war on drugs. The Comprehensive Crime Control Act of 1984, Pub. L. 98-473, 98 Stat. 1976, directed that proceeds of forfeitures be disbursed to law enforcement agencies that made seizures, thus creating a powerful incentive for the seizure of assets in connection with drug arrests. As a result, civil forfeitures increased dramatically. Critics charged that the practice was being abused and called on Congress and the courts to limit the government's power in this area.

The Supreme Court limited civil forfeitures in several important decisions handed down in 1993. In *United States v. A Parcel of Land*, 507 U.S. 111, 113 S.Ct. 1126, 122 L.Ed.2d 469 (1993), the Court ruled that although proceeds traceable to an unlawful drug transaction are subject to forfeiture, an owner's lack of knowledge that her home had been purchased with proceeds of illegal drug transactions constitutes a defense to a forfeiture proceeding under federal law. In *United States v. Good Real Property*, 510 U.S. 43, 114 S.Ct. 492, 126 L.Ed.2d 490 (1993), the Court held that due process requires government to provide property owners adequate notice and a meaningful opportunity to be heard before seizing real estate that is subject to civil forfeiture. And in *Austin v. United States*, 509 U.S. 602, 113 S.Ct. 2801, 125 L.Ed.2d 488 (1993), the Court ruled that civil *in rem* forfeitures, although not technically criminal proceedings, are subject to the Excessive Fines Clause of the Eighth Amendment. However, the Court declined to establish any test for determining when a forfeiture is constitutionally excessive.

Responding to continuing criticism of civil forfeitures, Congress enacted the Civil Asset Forfeiture Reform Act (CAFRA) of 2000, Pub. L. No. 106-185, 114 Stat. 202. Previously, the property owner carried the burden of proving by a preponderance of the evidence that the property seized by the government is not subject to forfeiture. CAFRA reversed the burden of proof so that it now rests on government. 18 U.S.C.A. § 983(c). It also established a uniform "innocent owner defense" applicable to all federal forfeiture statutes. To prevail in this defense, owners must prove either that they did not know of the unlawful activity associated with their property or that they did all they could reasonably be expected to do to prevent or halt it. 18 U.S.C.A. § 983(d). The new law also provides counsel to indigent property owners who have standing to challenge forfeitures. 18 U.S.C.A. § 983(b)(2). While CAFRA represents a serious attempt to reform civil forfeitures, it does not severely retard the government's ability to use this powerful weapon in the war on drugs.

The Office of National Drug Control Policy

In 1988, Congress enacted the Anti-Drug Abuse Act, which established the Office of National Drug Control Policy (ONDCP) within the Executive Office of the President to coordinate federal and state drug control policies. The ONDCP spends considerable time, effort, and money on public relations and advertising in an attempt to persuade people not to use illicit drugs and to defeat efforts by various interest groups to ease existing drug laws. The director of the ONDCP is known colloquially as the "drug czar." To emphasize the importance of the war on drugs, President Reagan made the drug czar a member of his cabinet, and subsequent presidents have followed suit. As the official responsible for coordinating federal drug policy, the drug czar deals with every federal agency involved in the war on drugs, including the FBI, the Customs Service, the DEA, the Department of Transportation, the Department of Health and Human Services, the State Department, and even the Department of Defense. But the role is more than one of coordinator. The drug czar helps set the tone for national policy on illicit drug use, including the use of criminal prohibitions. By rhetoric and directive, the drug czar is in a position to greatly influence whether the war on drugs continues along its present course.

Assessing the War on Drugs

Some commentators, believing that the national "war on drugs" has failed, have argued for the legalization of such drugs as marijuana, cocaine, and heroin. These commentators would prefer to see the use of these drugs legalized, although highly regulated, with increased efforts directed toward educational and treatment programs. Advocates of legalization contend that criminal prohibition of drug use has led to a vast underground economy and that the war on drugs has debased the rule of law by ineffective attempts to alter personal conduct. They argue that imprisonment of nonviolent drug offenders is excessive, unjust, and ruinous to lives that might otherwise be productive. They also object to what they perceive to be the curtailment of individual rights that has accompanied the drug war. Although the number of Americans who are sympathetic to such arguments may be increasing, there remains substantial public support for maintaining criminal prohibitions in this area. Although the attitude toward legalization appears to be more favorable toward marijuana than other drugs, in 2000 only 32 percent of Americans thought its use should be made legal (U.S. Department of Justice, Bureau of Justice Statistics, *Sourcebook of Criminal Justice Statistics*, 2001, pp. 158–159).

Despite widespread criticism, the war on drugs continues. There were more than 1.7 million drug arrests in the United States in 2008. (See 2008 Crime in the United States," FBI Uniform Crime Reports, Washington, DC: US Dept. of Justice, September 2009.)

Libertarians argue that drug use should be strictly a moral question, where each person is free to decide his or her own limits. Yet drug abuse affects more than just the individual user. Drug abuse creates many dramatic economic, social, and health problems in our society. Illegal trafficking in drugs has led to many violent crimes as well as to instances of official corruption. Moreover, many violent crimes are committed by people under the influence of illicit drugs. The correlation between drug abuse and crime is demonstrated by the fact that in twenty-three of the largest cities in the United States, between 50 and 77 percent of male arrestees test positive for drugs. In 2009, anywhere from 56 percent (Charlotte) to 82 percent (Chicago) of arrestees . . . tested positive for the presence of some substance at the time of arrest." Office of National Drug Control Policy, ADAM II 2009 Annual Report, p. 23. Most Americans want their government to continue to fight the war on drugs, although citizens and officials are often frustrated with the rate of progress.

Drug Courts: A New Approach to an Old Problem

By the late 1980s, judges began to recognize that traditional court processes were neither deterring substance abusers nor addressing the medical, social, and economic problems associated with drug abuse. In an effort to use the court's authority to divert certain offenders to closely monitored programs, courts began to develop the concept of a drug court. Rather than sending nonviolent defendants to jail, a **drug court**—in collaboration with prosecutors, defense counsel, and other professionals— would monitor their progress through status hearings and prescribe sanctions and rewards and thus reduce substance abuse, rehabilitate participants, and thereby reduce recidivism.

The first drug court was implemented in 1989 in Miami, Florida. Since then there has been a continual expansion in the number of drug courts. The Bureau of Justice Assistance Drug Court Clearinghouse Project, February 11, 2009, listed 2,018 drug courts operating in all fifty states, the District of Columbia, Northern Mariana Islands, Puerto Rico, and Guam, with another 257 drug court programs in the planning stages. Drug court procedures vary from standard post-arrest processes. After an individual who has not committed a violent crime is arrested for possession of a controlled substance, a background check is made. If the arrestee meets the drug court eligibility requirements and the prosecuting attorney agrees, the defendant may opt to be diverted to a drug court program. Prosecution is deferred as long as the participant progresses. Once in the program, the participant must obtain a sponsor, attend certain meetings and counseling sessions, give frequent urine samples, and attend required court status hearings. The participant signs a "contract" to complete the program within a specified period, usually twelve months. The treatment phases consist of detoxification, counseling sessions, and often assistance in job training or obtaining employment. In some programs a participant who agrees is given acupuncture treatments to aid in detoxification and to make the participant more receptive to counseling sessions.

The status hearings before the drug court are central to the program. They are held in open court with all participants present. The judge may begin with a short orientation emphasizing the need for sobriety and gainful employment. The judge then reviews each participant's progress file and commends those whose urine samples are "clean" and who are in complete compliance with their contract. Participants applaud those with outstanding records of performance. The judge encourages those who have minor deviations in their performance and admonishes those who have relapsed. Often the court prescribes additional counseling, treatment, community service, or a short stay in jail for those who have seriously relapsed in their efforts.

Most programs countenance some relapse; however, positive urine tests, additional arrests, or failure to attend status hearings or treatment sessions may cause a participant to be terminated and prosecution resumed. Successful completion of a drug court program usually results in the charges against the participant being dropped or the plea of guilty being stricken from the record.

There are many variations on the drug court model. Some focus on women or juveniles; others handle both male and female adults. Some provide support services such as health and housing assistance and job placement; others do not. Some operate with a professional staff; in other instances, the assigned judge might have minimal professional assistance. These factors, along with the relative newness of the programs and the problem of comparing a given group of drug court participants with a control group of those whose offenses are handled in the traditional manner, make it difficult to evaluate the success of the drug court program. Nevertheless, the relapse rate of the participants and the frequency of new arrests are criteria that can be used to assess the program's effectiveness. And, though still new and innovative institutions, drug courts appear to hold considerable promise to deter repetitive criminal behavior of drug abusers. They also hold a promise to relieve courts and other functionaries in the criminal justice system of the burden of repetitive arrests and overloaded trial and sentencing dockets of criminal cases where drugs play an important role.

Conclusion

The criminal law proscribes certain forms of conduct that offend the norms of societal morality. Chief among these prohibitions are laws prohibiting certain forms of sexual activity, public indecency, obscenity, profanity, and gambling. As societal consensus changes—as it surely has with respect to sexual activities, pornography, and gambling—the prohibitions of the criminal law must, and do, change as well. But offenses involving the use of alcohol and drugs, although sometimes categorized as offenses against public morality, can also be viewed as threats to public order, safety, and peace.

The American public is committed to strict enforcement of laws proscribing drunk driving, where positive results are being achieved through education and through law enforcement officers' use of sophisticated technological methods. In other areas the control of the use of illegal drugs has been less promising. The widespread abuse of drugs is a serious social problem with many undesirable consequences. Society has responded to this problem largely through the criminal justice system, and the American public has generally supported this approach. However, there are those who believe that criminalizing drug possession is undesirable public policy. Because efforts to control the supply of illegal drugs has proved extremely difficult, the public now appears to place primary emphasis on criminal enforcement against drug dealers while being receptive to increasing education designed to control demand by educating the public of the consequences of drug abuse, minimizing penalties for the possession of small amounts of marijuana, and rehabilitating minor nonviolent offenders through treatments administered by drug courts.

Chapter Summary

- **LO1** Vice crimes are offenses against public morality. Bigamy and obscenity have their roots in English common law, but prostitution, gambling, and alcohol and drug offenses were created legislatively in America. The criticism that "you can't legislate morality" overlooks that many offenses against morality have a strong basis in public health and safety.

- **LO2** Fornication, adultery, seduction, and consensual sodomy, which were prohibited at common law, are today generally regarded as private matters, and statutes prohibiting such conduct either have been repealed or are seldom enforced. But there remains strong support for prohibiting bigamy and incest (intermarriage or sexual relations between persons within certain degrees of consanguinity). Attitudes vary on whether prostitution should be a criminal offense, but almost every state continues to prohibit prostitution, with newer statutes providing for conviction of customers as well as prostitutes. Federal law prohibits interstate transportation of an individual for purposes of prostitution or with the intent to compel an individual to become a prostitute.

- **LO3** It was a common-law misdemeanor for persons intentionally to expose their "private parts" in public. Today, state statutes and local ordinances make it a misdemeanor, often called "lewd and lascivious conduct," intentionally to expose one's private parts under offensive circumstances. Courts vary as to whether such exposure must be in the presence of another. Some state courts have upheld laws that require female beachgoers to cover their breasts against constitutional challenges that such laws do not apply equally to both sexes. Voyeurism, which refers to obtaining sexual gratification from viewing another person's sexual organs or sexual activities, has been addressed under "Peeping Tom" statutes and ordinances that make it a misdemeanor. Publication of photos on the Internet has caused some states to enact laws to protect the privacy of persons not only in their homes, but also in public where they would ordinarily expect a reasonable degree of privacy.

- **LO4** The Supreme Court has upheld laws that prohibit totally nude dancing in places of entertainment as passing muster under the First Amendment. Typically such conduct is regulated by local ordinances, which often are limited to places of public accommodation that serve alcohol.

- **LO5** At common law, vulgar and obscene language and indecent public exhibitions were public nuisances and punishable as misdemeanors. In America federal and state governments enacted laws banning various forms of obscenity, but questions arose as to the definition of obscenity. As mass communications developed, laws banning obscene speech, materials, and performances were scrutinized under First Amendment standards. In a series of landmark decisions the Supreme Court ruled that obscenity is not entitled to First Amendment protection. By 1973 the Court defined obscenity as "whether the average person, applying contemporary community standards (1) would find that the work, taken as a whole, appeals to the prurient interest; (2) whether it depicts or describes, in a patently offensive way, sexual conduct specifically defined by the applicable state law; and (3) whether the work, taken as a whole, lacks serious literary, artistic, political, or scientific value. The Court made it clear that no one would be subject to prosecution unless the materials alleged to be obscene described "hard-core" sexual conduct, but also ruled that states can challenge obscenity even if materials are viewed by consenting adults. In 1987, the Court held that the third prong defining obscenity must be based on whether a "reasonable person" (not the average person) would find serious literary, artistic, political, or scientific value in allegedly obscene material. Because books, movies, and even live performances are presumptively protected by the First Amendment, the Supreme Court has held that police must obtain a search warrant before conducting searches and seizures of such materials.

- **LO6** Most states make it a crime to "possess or view any material or performance that shows a minor who is not the person's child or ward in a state of nudity." In 1982 the Supreme Court unanimously held that child pornography, like obscenity, is unprotected by the First Amendment and upheld state laws prohibiting persons from distributing materials that depict children engaging in lewd sex. Congress then enacted the Child Pornography Prevention Act of 1996 (CPPA) prohibiting any type of virtual or simulated child pornography, even if real children were not involved. But in 2002, with three justices dissenting, the Court distinguished virtual from real child pornography and struck down the prohibition of virtual child pornography in CPPA, finding that it abridges freedom of speech under the First Amendment.

- **LO7** Public concern about the prevalence of sexually explicit material on the Internet, and especially the easy access of children to such material, caused Congress, in 1997, to enact the Communications Decency Act of 1996 (CDA). After the Supreme Court held the statute unconstitutionally overbroad, Congress passed the Child Online Protection Act of 1998 (COPA), which makes it an offense to "knowingly and with knowledge of the character of the material, in interstate or foreign commerce by means of the World Wide Web, make any communication for commercial purposes that is available to any minor and that includes any material that is harmful to minors . . ." Lower federal courts found COPA "facially violative of the First and Fifth Amendments of the United States Constitution" and enjoined the government from enforcing or prosecuting any conduct premised upon the law. The Supreme Court denied review and on January 21, 2009, the decade-long battle over COPA finally ended in defeat for the federal government.

- **LO8** Historically, many states and prohibited public profanity. Since the Supreme Court, on First Amendment grounds, invalidated a conviction of a man wearing a jacket with an offensive four-letter word emblazoned upon it, profanity laws have seldom been enforced.

- **LO9** The common law did not regard gambling as an offense. However, many of the new American states, by either constitution or statute, made all or certain forms of gambling illegal. Today, the Federal Travel Act prohibits interstate travel in aid of gambling. The Supreme Court has recognized that there is no constitutional right to gamble and has upheld a variety of state statutes and local ordinances that prohibit gambling. Gambling must generally include three elements: consideration, prize, and chance. Gambling laws present a paradox. In many jurisdictions it is a criminal offense to buy a chance in a lottery; yet many states sponsor lotteries as a source of public revenue. Most laws prohibiting gambling either include exceptions for, or are interpreted to exclude, contests in which participants pit their physical or mental skills against one another for a prize, retail promotions that award prizes by lot, and penny-ante card games played in dwellings. Where gambling is prohibited, states customarily make it unlawful to possess gambling devices, and provide for their confiscation. Today, gambling via the Internet is widespread, but because these websites tend to be hosted on servers in foreign countries, prosecution is rare and usually not possible.

- **LO10** Every state today has laws protecting animals from unnecessary harm. State laws also proscribe cockfighting, dog fighting, and other forms of animal fighting, as well as the intentional killing of animals belonging to other persons, except where necessary to protect oneself. There also are laws governing offenses involving farm animals and animal research facilities.

- **LO11** Until 1603, when an English court viewed drunkenness as aggravating a crime, the common law had little to say about alcohol. In America, when alcohol use became widespread, public sentiment caused the states in 1919 to ratify the Eighteenth Amendment to the U.S. Constitution, making unlawful the "manufacture, sale, or transportation of intoxicating liquors" within the United States. Prohibition was widely disregarded, and contributed to increased criminal activity and a lack of respect for the law. Ultimately, it was repealed by the Twenty-First Amendment, ratified by the states in 1933. State and local governments retain the authority to ban or regulate the manufacture, sale, and use of alcohol, and while no state has completely banned the sale of alcohol, states regulate the sale and use of alcoholic beverages. Laws usually make it a misdemeanor to sell alcoholic beverages to minors or for minors to purchase or consume alcoholic beverages. Federal incentives to states have effectively established twenty-one as the minimum age for drinking. Historically, states and cities prohibited public drunkenness. After the Supreme Court ruled in 1968 that a person convicted of public drunkenness could be punished for being in public in an inebriated condition, many states began to criminalize only disorderly intoxication.

- **LO12** Most early driving while intoxicated (DWI) laws stipulated that a level of 0.15 percent or more alcohol in the bloodstream of a driver evidenced intoxication. But in the 1970s, many states expanded the offense to prohibit driving under the influence (DUI) of intoxicating liquors or drugs. Most states modified their statutes to prohibit driving with an unlawful blood-alcohol level (DUBAL), and as a result of federal fiscal incentives, all fifty states have lowered the prohibited blood-alcohol level to 0.08 percent. Most states now require mandatory minimum jail terms (usually twenty-four or forty-eight hours) for first-time DWI, DUI, or DUBAL offenders. Other penalties include fines, suspension or revocation of driving privileges, and alcohol education or treatment programs. Some states allow judges to require repeat offenders to install devices that measure the driver's blood-alcohol level before the vehicle can be started; in others repeat offenders may have their vehicles confiscated. By 2003, all fifty states had followed Kentucky's lead in establishing a lower permissible blood-alcohol level for juveniles (in most states, 0.02 percent). The Supreme Court has held that an officer's roadside questioning and field sobriety test are not "custodial interrogation" that requires giving the suspect the *Miranda* warnings. To facilitate chemical testing in DWI, DUI, and DUBAL cases most jurisdictions have enacted implied consent statutes stipulating that a person who drives a motor vehicle is deemed to consent to a urine test for drugs and to blood, breath, or urine testing to determine blood-alcohol content incident to the arrest of a driver. Many police agencies today have "Batmobiles" equipped with breath testing machines, videotape equipment, and voice recorders that allow police to collect evidence at or near the scene of the arrest. One sophisticated method of alcohol detection is

measuring the grams of alcohol in a volume of breath by use of a spectrophotometer, which measures the absorption of infrared light by a sample of a gas.

- **LO13** In the 1960s drug use proliferated within the middle-class white population, especially young people. Responding, Congress enacted the Comprehensive Drug Abuse Prevention and Control Act of 1970 (the Controlled Substances
Act), which defines offenses involving the manufacture, sale, distribution, and
possession with intent to distribute, sets penalties, and establishes criteria for
classification of controlled substances according to their potential for abuse.
Congress also provided for forfeiture of property used in connection with federal
drug crimes. Federal asset forfeitures can be criminal or civil. In a criminal forfeiture, a person convicted of a federal drug offense is ordered to forfeit property
involved in that offense; however, the owner has the opportunity to contest the
forfeiture. Federal and state laws on controlled substances mirror one another in
many respects. Federal enforcement is usually directed against major interstate
or international drug traffickers; states usually concentrate on those who possess
or distribute controlled substances. Under federal law, it is a crime to import,
export, sell, offer for sale, or use the mails to transport any drug paraphernalia.
Possession of drug paraphernalia is also commonly a criminal offense under state
laws.

- **LO14** During the 1970s several states decriminalized their anti-marijuana laws
by removing the threat of a jail sentence for possession offenses. Between 1996
and 2008, thirteen states passed laws (usually resulting from referendums) legalizing marijuana for medical uses. But legalization creates a conflict between state
and federal law because in 2005 the Supreme Court held that Congress has the
power under the Commerce Clause to prohibit the mere possession of small
quantities of marijuana, even if it is solely for personal medicinal use authorized
by state law. Thus, a person using marijuana, even one with a doctor's prescription pursuant to a state "compassionate use" statute, is still subject to arrest and
prosecution by federal authorities. In 1973, President Nixon issued an executive order creating the Drug Enforcement Administration (DEA) within the
Department of Justice to concentrate federal drug enforcement responsibilities
within one agency of government. Since then, the DEA has been involved in
all facets of the drug war. Yet the DEA has been unable to demonstrate much
progress in reducing the availability of illegal drugs in the U.S. Beginning in
1986, Congress required mandatory minimum prison terms for drug felonies,
and many states did the same. In 1988, Congress enacted the Anti-Drug Abuse
Act, which established the Office of National Drug Control Policy (ONDCP)
within the Executive Office of the President to coordinate federal and state drug
control policies. The ONDCP spends considerable time, effort, and money on
public relations and advertising in an attempt to persuade people not to use
illicit drugs. The Supreme Court has ruled that states may not criminalize the
mere status of being addicted to such drugs. Some employees, and teachers
and students in many school districts, are subjected to drug testing, and these
programs have been upheld by the courts. Advocates of legalization contend
that criminal prohibition of drug use has led to a vast underground economy
and that the war on drugs has debased the rule of law by ineffective attempts to
alter personal conduct.

- **LO15** The establishment of drug courts has been an important development in
the criminal justice system. Rather than sending nonviolent defendants to jail,
a drug court—in collaboration with prosecutors, defense counsel, and other
professionals—monitors their progress through status hearings and prescribes

sanctions and rewards. There is evidence that this approach can reduce substance abuse, rehabilitate participants, and thereby reduce recidivism.

- Because those involved in narcotics transactions are usually willing participants, enforcement often depends on the use of confidential informants by police. Obtaining search warrants and making arrests based on probable cause often present difficult Fourth Amendment problems. In drug possession cases, a critical problem is proving that the defendant was in actual or constructive possession of a controlled substance. Defendants on trial for drug offenses sometimes assert that they were entrapped by the police, a defense discussed in Chapter 14 . More frequently, defense counsel attempt to suppress the contraband seized by police on the ground that it was obtained in violation of the Fourth Amendment prohibition against unreasonable searches and seizures.

Key Terms

vice Immoral conduct such as prostitution, gambling, and the use of narcotics.

right of privacy Constitutional right to engage in intimate personal conduct or make fundamental life decisions without interference by the government.

fornication Sexual intercourse between unmarried persons; an offense at common law.

adultery Voluntary sexual intercourse between a married person and someone other than that person's spouse.

seduction The common-law crime of inducing a woman to have sexual intercourse outside of wedlock on the promise of marriage.

sodomy Oral or anal sex between persons or sex between a person and an animal; the latter is commonly referred to as bestiality.

incest Sexual intercourse with a close blood relative or, in some cases, a person related by affinity.

bigamy The crime of being married to more than one person at the same time.

polygamy The state or practice of having more than on spouse simultaneously.

prostitution The practice of selling sexual favors.

indecent exposure The intentional exposure in public of private areas of a person's body.

lewd and lascivious conduct Indecent exposure of a person's private parts in public; indecent touching or fondling of a child.

voyeurism The practice of seeking sexual gratification by observing the naked bodies or sexual acts of others, usually from a hidden vantage point.

hard-core pornography Material that is extremely graphic in its depiction of sexual conduct.

prurient interest An excessive or unnatural interest in sex.

patently offensive That which is obviously offensive or disgusting.

child pornography Material depicting persons under the age of legal majority in sexual poses or acts.

profanity Irreverence toward sacred things; foul language.

gambling Operating or playing a game for money in the expectation of gaining more than the amount played.

lottery A drawing in which prizes are distributed to winners selected by lot from among those who have participated by paying consideration.

numbers racket A common form of illegal gambling in which one places a bet on a number with the hope that it will correspond to a preselected number.

consideration, prize, and chance The legal elements that constitute gambling under most statutes that make it an offense to gamble.

public drunkenness The offense of appearing in public while intoxicated.

disorderly intoxication An offense consisting of misbehavior by a person who is drunk that results in disturbing the public peace or safety.

driving while intoxicated (DWI) The crime of driving while intoxicated by alcohol or drugs.

driving under the influence (DUI) The crime of driving under the influence of alcohol or drugs.

driving with an unlawful blood-alcohol level (DUBAL) The offense of operating a motor vehicle while one's blood-alcohol level is higher than allowed by law.

zero tolerance law A statute that the enacting authority claims will be enforced zealously and without exception.

contraband Any property that is inherently illegal to produce or possess.

field sobriety test A test administered by police to people suspected of driving while intoxicated. Usually consists of requiring the suspect to demonstrate the ability to perform such physical acts as touching one's finger to one's nose or walking backward.

breathalyzer A device that detects the amount of alcohol in a sample of a person's breath.

implied consent statutes Laws providing that by accepting a license, a driver arrested for a traffic offense consents to urine, blood, and breath tests to determine blood-alcohol content.

Controlled Substances Act A federal law listing controlled substances according to their potential for abuse. States have similar statutes.

controlled substances Drugs designated by law as contraband.

drug paraphernalia Items closely associated with the use of illegal drugs.

drug courier profiling Occurs when police employ a set of characteristics thought to typify people engaged in drug smuggling in order to identify such persons.

drug-testing requirements Laws, regulations, or policies that require students or employees to undergo chemical testing of their urine to determine whether they are free of illicit drugs.

criminal forfeiture Government confiscation of private property obtained through or otherwise involved in criminal activity pursuant to a criminal conviction of the owner of said property.

civil forfeiture Taking of property used in or obtained through unlawful activity pursuant to a civil proceeding in which the property itself is named as the defendant.

drug court A specialized court or division of a court designed to deal specifically with defendants charged with violating laws proscribing the possession and use of controlled substances. Drug courts emphasize rehabilitation of offenders.

Questions for Thought and Discussion

1. Assume you are a legislative assistant for a member of the state house of representatives. Your representative intends to introduce a bill to prohibit up-skirt videography in public shopping areas. She asks you to prepare a memo suggesting language for the bill. What suggestions would you offer to be included in the text of the bill?
2. Would prostitution be more injurious or less injurious to the public health, welfare, and morality if it were legalized and regulated?
3. Is "mooning," a common adolescent prank, a form of indecent exposure in your state?
4. How are laws proscribing obscenity susceptible to the overbreadth and vagueness challenges discussed in Chapter 3?
5. Given the fact that there are millions of Internet users throughout the United States, is it appropriate for courts to apply the "contemporary community standards" test in making determinations concerning obscenity on the Internet?
6. Do you think Congress can devise a law that will pass constitutional muster to protect children from Internet pornography? What suggestions do you have in this area?
7. What, if any, constitutional objections could be raised against a city ordinance making it a criminal offense "to use profane language in a public place"?
8. What forms of gambling are legal and illegal in your state? Are there any particular games that fall into a gray area between permitted and prohibited activity? Is church bingo legal in your state?
9. Should chronic alcoholism be a defense to intoxication offenses such as public drunkenness or driving under the influence?
10. Is requiring a person suspected of driving while intoxicated to submit to a blood-alcohol test a violation of the Fifth Amendment prohibition against compulsory self-incrimination?
11. Is it sensible to maintain the criminal prohibitions against illicit drugs, or should these substances be legalized and carefully regulated, and their abuse dealt with through other means?
12. What are the typical difficulties facing prosecutors in drug possession cases?
13. Why, according to *Robinson v. California*, may a person not be held criminally liable for being addicted to illicit narcotics? Is this decision distinguishable from *Powell v. Texas*?
14. Is the drug court method of dealing with nonviolent drug offenders superior to the traditional methods of imposing a fine or jail term or placing the defendant on probation? Should drug courts limit eligibility to participate to first-time offenders?
15. How does the prosecution establish that a defendant is in constructive possession of illicit drugs?
16. To what extent have the federal courts approved drug testing of students in public institutions?
17. To what extent has the U.S. Supreme Court placed restrictions on forfeiture of real estate involved in drug trafficking operations?

Problems for Discussion and Solution

1. Gerald N. runs a video game arcade. One of his most popular games is called Video Blackjack. Essentially, the game is a computerized form of blackjack in which the contestant plays against the computer. The cost of playing the game is

fifty cents. The contestant who wins the game is issued a token that can be used to play any other game in the arcade. Suppose your state gambling statute prohibits all "games involving valuable consideration, chance, and a possible prize." If you were the prosecutor, would you be concerned about the legality of this game?

2. YourSpot.com is a popular social networking website on the Internet. The site targets teenage users and is supported solely by advertising revenue. Users create accounts, share music clips, post announcements about their interests and activities, and communicate with their peers through the site. In recent months, several pedophiles have been caught using YourSpot to solicit young victims across the country. In response to public outcry against YourSpot, the Sylvania state legislature passed a law making it illegal for children under the age of eighteen to visit YourSpot. Violators will be fined $100 and compelled to attend a six-hour diversionary program on Internet safety. Two challenges to the new law are pending in the courts. Sylvania resident Rachel Rebel (age sixteen) was caught maintaining a YourSpot account to promote her band, the Pop Tarts, and soliciting performance gigs. Ms. Rebel was adjudged delinquent by her county's juvenile court system. She is now appealing that decision. Does she have a case? What would be her contentions on appeal?

3. Suppose you were elected to the state assembly. In your first week on duty, a colleague asks you to cosponsor a bill she plans to introduce that would decriminalize all drug possession offenses in your state, as long as the quantity of drugs possessed is relatively small. The bill would require offenders to complete a drug education and treatment program in lieu of payment of a substantial civil fine, but it would not permit the state to incarcerate anyone for drug possession. Would you be willing to cosponsor the bill? Why or why not? If not, are there amendments you might propose that would engender your support for the legislation?

4. Late one night, a deputy sheriff found Ronald Rico in his car parked on the side of a road in a rural area of the county. Rico was at the wheel, the headlights were on, and the radio was playing at a loud volume. The motor was not running. No one else was in the vehicle. A field sobriety test and a later chemical test indicated that Rico had a 0.14 blood alcohol concentration level. Under these circumstances, should Rico be prosecuted for driving under the influence of alcohol? What defenses would a lawyer representing Rico likely raise?

5. Police were called to quell a disturbance at a motel where the management had reported some disorderly conduct and apparent drug use. Outside the motel, the police observed Henry Egad standing by a tree. About eighteen inches from Egad's feet, the police discovered a matchbox on the ground. Their examination revealed that the matchbox contained a substance that later proved to be PCP, an illegal drug. Police placed Egad under arrest and charged him with possession of a controlled substance. Based on these facts alone, do you think the prosecutor can establish that Egad was in possession of the PCP?

CHAPTER 11

Offenses against Public Health and the Environment

LEARNING OBJECTIVES

After reading this chapter, you should be able to explain . . .

1. why government has criminalized offenses against the public health and the natural environment and why most offenses in this area do not have antecedents in the English common law
2. why many offenses in this area are strict liability crimes and why laws carrying more severe penalties are apt to include a *mens rea* requirement
3. the importance of the federal Food, Drug, and Cosmetic Act in criminalizing offenses to the public health
4. why violations of zoning ordinances seldom result in criminal prosecutions
5. the range of federal environmental laws and the agencies involved in the enforcement of those laws
6. the Clean Air Act and Clean Water Act as bases for prosecution of environmental crimes involving air and water pollution, respectively
7. the Resource Conservation and Recovery Act as a basis for criminal enforcement with respect to hazardous waste violations
8. the Toxic Substances Control Act as a basis for criminal enforcement with respect to manufacture, distribution, and use of toxic chemicals
9. the Comprehensive Environmental Response, Compensation and Liability Act as a basis for imposing criminal penalties on those who are in a position to detect, prevent, or abate the release of hazardous substances into the environment
10. how and why corporations and responsible corporate officers can be held criminally liable for offenses against the public health and the natural environment
11. how Congress and local governing bodies have addressed the problem of noise pollution
12. why states and cities are prohibiting smoking in certain places
13. how federal and state laws protect wildlife

CHAPTER OUTLINE

When BP's Deepwater Horizon offshore drilling rig exploded and burned on April 20, 2010, it touched off the largest oil spill in the history of the United States. Oil gushed from the severed wellhead 5,000 feet below the surface of the Gulf of Mexico at a rate of more than a million gallons per day. It was not until mid-July that BP was able to stop the flow of oil, and not until mid-September that the well was permanently sealed. By then, more than 200 million gallons of oil had leaked into the Gulf. Despite efforts by BP, the government, and others to mitigate the effects of the spill and begin the cleanup of the Gulf, wetlands, and beaches, much of the ecology and economy of the Gulf Coast had been devastated. Without a doubt, the oil spill of 2010 was the worst environmental disaster in American history. Most economists agreed that the economic cost of the spill was far greater than the $20 billion that BP agreed to place in a fund to compensate victims of the disaster. On June 1, 2010, Attorney General Eric Holder announced that the Department of Justice had opened a criminal investigation of the BP oil spill. Holder mentioned that several laws may have been broken: the Clean Water Act, the principal federal statute dealing with water pollution; the Migratory Bird Act, a federal law making it a crime to kill migratory birds; and the Refuse Act, which prohibits illegal dumping in the nation's waterways. In this chapter we discuss all three of these important environmental statutes. In contemplating criminal prosecution under these and other environmental laws, one must consider carefully the culpable mental state (*mens rea*) required for criminal violations. Obviously, BP and the company that operated the Deepwater Horizon did not intentionally spill millions of barrels of oil into the Gulf of Mexico. What, then, would be the basis for holding BP criminally liable? Think about this question as you read this chapter.

Introduction

In the wake of the Industrial Revolution, people recognized the need for government to protect the public health. In the latter decades of the twentieth century, society became aware of the need for governmental action to protect the natural environment as well. Obviously, these two societal interests are closely related, as public health is greatly dependent on a healthy natural environment. Increasingly, governments at all levels (i.e., federal, state, and local) are making use of criminal sanctions as means of protecting the public health and the environment.

In addition to offenses involving the adulteration or misbranding of foods, medicines, and cosmetics and the unlawful exposure of others to germs or toxins, this chapter examines **environmental crime**, which includes, among other things, the unlawful pollution of the air and water; unlawful transportation, handling, or storage of hazardous materials; and unlawful destruction of protected animal and plant species or their habitats.

SIDEBAR   **Tennessee's Littering Statute**

Tenn. Code Ann § 39-14-502. Offense of littering.—
(a) A person commits littering who:
   (1) Knowingly places, drops or throws litter on any public or private property without permission and does not immediately remove it;
   (2) Negligently places or throws glass or other dangerous substances on or adjacent to water to which the public has access for swimming or wading, or on or within fifty feet (50′) of a public highway; or
   (3) Negligently discharges sewage, minerals, oil products or litter into any public waters or lakes within this state.
(b) Whenever litter is placed, dropped, or thrown from any motor vehicle, boat, airplane, or other conveyance in violation of this section, the trier of fact may, in its discretion and in consideration of the totality of the circumstances, infer that the operator of the conveyance has committed littering.
(c) Whenever litter discovered on public or private property is found to contain any article or articles, including, but not limited to, letters, bills, publications, or other writings that display the name of a person in such a manner as to indicate that the article belongs or belonged to that person, the trier of fact may, in its discretion and in consideration of the totality of the circumstances, infer that the person has committed littering.

Beyond protecting natural resources and public health, the criminal law seeks to promote aesthetic values. Laws forbidding **littering** (see Tennessee statute in the following Sidebar) or dumping of refuse along the roadside are based on aesthetic considerations as well as environmental and public health concerns. **Antismoking laws**, which we discuss later in this chapter, are motivated by aesthetic as well as public health concerns. **Noise ordinances** also seek to protect the aesthetic quality of the living environment that people share.

Sources of Law Defining Crimes against the Public Health and the Environment

As we have seen throughout the foregoing chapters, common-law crimes were originally recognized by courts and later revised and expanded by legislatures. But crimes against public health and the environment do not have their origin in the English common law. Rather, these offenses originated directly from Congress and state legislatures in response to the needs of a changing society. Offenses relating to public health originated in the late nineteenth and early twentieth centuries as a result of the widespread distribution of food, drugs, and cosmetics and the need to control communicable diseases. By the early 1900s, municipalities perceived the need for zoning to control nuisances and to regulate land use. Since the middle of the twentieth century, pollution of the ground, water, and air has been recognized as a major threat to the health and welfare of the people and, indeed, to the ecological balance of the Earth.

Enforcing regulations in these fields is accomplished largely through regulatory agencies and measures imposing civil liability. Nevertheless, legislatures have found it necessary to impose criminal sanctions to enforce standards effectively and to deter violators. Although not faced with the severe environmental problems of our age, the common law did regard wildlife, game, and fish as resources to be preserved by government. In the United States, the state and federal governments have for many years imposed criminal sanctions against **poaching** to protect these resources for the benefit of the public.

In contrast with the typical common-law crimes, many offenses against the public health and environment consist of an offender's neglect to comply with required standards or failure to take action required by law. These offenses are *mala prohibita*, and statutes criminalizing conduct in these areas generally contemplate a lower level of intent, frequently imposing a standard of **strict liability** (a concept we introduced in Chapter 4). For example, in *State v. Budd Co.*, 425 N.E.2d 935 (Ohio App. 1980), the defendant was convicted under a state law that made it a criminal offense to dispose of garbage or other pollutants in any ditch, pond, stream, or other watercourse. On appeal, the court rejected the appellant's argument that it was necessary for the state to prove his criminal intent. The court observed that the law did not require proof of intent and that "the destruction of wildlife through pollution will occur whenever the waterways are intentionally or accidentally polluted." 425 N.E.2d at 938.

Public Health Legislation

The authority of government to enact laws to protect the public health is a basic component of the police power of the state. Statutes delegating to public health agencies the power to declare quarantines, and later to require inoculations to control communicable diseases, were among the earliest applications of this police power. At the turn of the century, the U.S. Supreme Court reviewed a defendant's sentence to pay a fine for refusing to be vaccinated for smallpox as required by a Cambridge, Massachusetts, ordinance. The defendant argued that a compulsory vaccination law invaded his liberty under the Constitution. Rejecting this contention, the Court observed that "persons and property are subjected to all kinds of restraints and burdens in order to secure the general comfort, health, and prosperity of the state." *Jacobson v. Massachusetts*, 197 U.S. 11, 26, 25 S.Ct. 358, 361, 49 L.Ed. 643, 650 (1905). Today all states require vaccinations of public school students; however, some states provide exemptions where parents show that vaccinations are contrary to their religious beliefs.

Today, numerous federal, state, and local laws address health concerns, providing criminal penalties for serious violations. Modern statutes address a variety of contemporary problems. California, like other states, has a comprehensive collection of laws concerning prevention and control of communicable disease and sexually transmitted disease. Section 120600 of the California Health and Safety Code stipulates the following:

> Any person who refuses to give any information to make any report, to comply with any proper control measure or examination, or to perform any other duty or act required by this chapter, or who violates any provision of this chapter or any rule or regulation of the state board issued pursuant to this chapter, or who exposes any person to or infects any person with any venereal disease; or any person infected with a venereal disease in an infectious state who knows of the condition and who marries or has sexual intercourse, is guilty of a misdemeanor.

In *Reynolds v. McNichols*, 488 F.2d 1378 (10th Cir. 1973), a federal appeals court upheld a Denver, Colorado, "hold and treat" ordinance authorizing detention and treatment, if necessary, of a woman arrested for prostitution who was reasonably suspected of having a venereal disease. Indeed, many states now have statutes imposing criminal penalties on health care professionals who fail to report communicable diseases. See, for example, West's Colo. Stat. Ann. § 25-4-402. A California appellate court has held that under the "special needs" doctrine, the state, without individualized suspicion, may require that a person convicted of prostitution be tested for AIDS. *Love v. Superior Court*, 276 Cal. Rptr. 660 (Cal. App. 1990). In *Fosman v.*

State, 664 So.2d 1163 (Fla. App. 1995), the court held that a court order requiring a defendant charged with sexual battery to submit to an HIV test did not constitute an unreasonable search and seizure. Florida has also enacted laws criminalizing intentional sexual transmission of HIV without a partner's consent and making it a felony for a person who knows that he or she is HIV-positive to donate blood or organs. West's Fla. Stat. Ann. §§ 381.0041(11), 384.24(1). In Nevada, a licensed prostitute who practices with knowledge of a positive HIV test result is guilty of a felony. Nev. Rev. Stat. § 201.358. Most public health laws that impose criminal penalties create strict liability offenses ion that they do not include any intent requirement. In those instances the government need only prove the defendant violated the statute.

The Federal Food, Drug, and Cosmetic Act

In 1848 Congress first enacted legislation to prevent the importation of adulterated drugs and medicines. Today, numerous federal acts relate to foods and drugs, but the basic **Food, Drug, and Cosmetic Act (FDCA)** dates back to 1906. It was comprehensively amended in 1938 and subsequently amended many times. 21 U.S.C.A. §§ 301–392. The present law prohibits traffic in food, drugs, and cosmetics being prepared or handled under unsanitary circumstances or under conditions that render them injurious to health. Included in its broad sweep are prohibitions against misbranding and adulteration of food, drugs, and cosmetics, as well as requirements for truthful labeling.

The U.S. Supreme Court has declared that the purpose of the FDCA is "to safeguard the consumer by applying the act to articles from the moment of their introduction into interstate commerce all the way to the moment of their delivery to the ultimate consumer." *United States v. Sullivan*, 332 U.S. 689, 696, 68 S.Ct. 331, 336, 92 L.Ed. 297, 303 (1948).

Violations of the FDCA are punishable by criminal penalties, civil fines, and injunctive relief, and, in some instances, by seizure of the articles found to be adulterated or misbranded.

Specifically, the FDCA prohibits

(a) The introduction or delivery for introduction into interstate commerce of any food, drug, device, or cosmetic that is adulterated or misbranded.

(b) The adulteration or misbranding of any food, drug, device, or cosmetic in interstate commerce.

(c) The receipt in interstate commerce of any food, drug, device, or cosmetic that is adulterated or misbranded, and the delivery or proffered delivery thereof for pay or otherwise. 21 U.S.C.A. § 331.

The FDCA defines adulterated food, 21 U.S.C.A. § 342; sets out standards for considering whether drugs and devices are adulterated, 21 U.S.C.A. § 351; and sets out criteria for adulterated cosmetics, 21 U.S.C.A. § 361. In general an item is considered adulterated if its ingredients are poisonous, filthy, putrid, or otherwise unsanitary or if it has come into contact with unsanitary substances.

Misbranding includes false or misleading labels, packaging, and containers. Specifically, 21 U.S.C.A. § 343 defines misbranded foods; 21 U.S.C.A. § 352 classifies misbranded drugs and devices; and 21 U.S.C.A. § 362 defines misbranded cosmetics.

In 1952, the Eighth Circuit declared that "It is not necessary that [food] actually become contaminated. . . . [T]he statute is designed to prevent adulterations 'in their incipiency' by condemning unsanitary conditions which may result in contamination." *Berger v. United States*, 200 F.2d 818, 821 (8th Cir. 1952). Numerous federal court decisions have interpreted what constitutes adulteration and misbranding under the FDCA. Illustrative decisions include:

- *United States v. Kohlback*, 38 F.3d 832 (6th Cir. 1994), where the court found that orange juice had been adulterated by adding beet sugar, other additives, and preservatives in order to extend the product's shelf life.
- *United States v. Bhutani*, 175 F.3d 572 (7th Cir. 1999), where the court noted the jury had found that a manufacturer adulterated a liver drug by "spiking" it with sodium hydroxide and repacking it with falsified expiration dates.
- *United States v. Haas*, 171 F.3d 259 (5th Cir. 1999), where the court upheld a conviction for aiding and abetting the illegal delivery of misbranded drugs into interstate commerce by sale of non-FDA-approved drugs.

In addition to provisions prohibiting adulteration and misbranding, the FDCA proscribes

The alteration, mutilation, destruction, obliteration, or removal of the whole or any part of the labeling of, or the doing of any other act with respect to, a food, drug, device, or cosmetic, if such act is done while such article is held for sale (whether or not the first sale) after shipment in interstate commerce and results in such article being adulterated or misbranded. 21 U.S.C.A. § 331(k).

The Supreme Court has held that section 331(k) defines two distinct offenses with respect to products held for sale after interstate shipment: (1) acts relating to misbranding and (2) acts relating to adulteration of the product. *United States v. Wiesenfeld Warehouse Co.*, 376 U.S. 86, 84 S.Ct. 559, 11 L.Ed.2d 536 (1964).

Strict Liability Offenses

As do most public health laws, violations of federal food and drug laws fall in the category of **regulatory offenses**. Therefore, unless the statute criminalizing conduct or failure to act requires an intent element, criminal liability can attach without proof of the defendant's intent. *United States v. Park*, 421 U.S. 658, 670, 95 S.Ct. 1903, 1910, 44 L.Ed.2d 489, 500 (1975).

In *United States v. Dotterweich*, 320 U.S. 277, 64 S.Ct. 134, 88 L.Ed. 48 (1943), the U.S. Supreme Court established a standard of strict liability for violations of the FDCA by holding that proof of the defendant's intent to commit a violation was not required to obtain a misdemeanor conviction. In felony prosecutions, however, the government must prove the defendant's intent. Moreover, in prosecutions under certain sections of the FDCA, lower federal courts have held that to obtain a felony conviction, the government must establish the defendant's specific intent. See, for example, *United States v. Mitcheltree*, 940 F.2d 1329 (10th Cir. 1991), where the defendant was prosecuted for violating 21 U.S.C.A. §§ 331(a) and 333(a) (2) for introducing a misbranded drug into interstate commerce with the intent to mislead or defraud.

Many legal scholars criticize the imposition of strict liability in regulatory offenses, such as violations of food, drug, and health laws. They contend that it brands as criminals people who are without moral fault. Arguing against making the violation of such laws punishable by incarceration, critics suggest decriminalization, with liability predicated on a **negligence standard** rather than on strict liability, or punishment by only a monetary fine. These criticisms notwithstanding, Congress has determined that the interest of society requires a high standard of care and has been unwilling to eliminate either the strict liability standard or incarceration. The courts follow *United States v. Park*, supra, and hold that a corporate agent who bears a responsible relationship to the operation of the enterprise, and has power to take measures necessary to ensure compliance, can be found guilty of violating such regulatory statutes.

Criminal Liability of Responsible Corporate Officers

Food, drugs, and cosmetics are usually produced and distributed by corporate enterprises. To enforce regulatory laws imposing criminal sanctions in these areas effectively, government agencies must be able to affix responsibility on individuals in supervisory positions as well as on corporate entities. The Supreme Court first recognized the concept of a **responsible corporate officer** in *United States v. Dotterweich*, 320 U.S. 277, 64 S.Ct. 134, 88 L.Ed. 48 (1943). There, a pharmacy company and Dotterweich, its president and general manager, were charged with shipping misbranded and adulterated drugs in violation of the FDCA. The jury declined to find the company guilty but did find Dotterweich guilty. A federal appellate court reversed his conviction. The U.S. Supreme Court granted review, upheld Dotterweich's conviction, and held that a "responsible corporate officer" could be held accountable for corporate violations of the FDCA. The Court reasoned that Dotterweich was in a responsible position to prevent any public danger.

Until 1975 there were conflicting federal court decisions about whether a corporate officer who failed to take measures to prevent violations of the food and drug laws from occurring could be held criminally liable. Recognizing this conflict, the Supreme Court again addressed the standard of liability of corporate officers under the FDCA in *United States v. Park,* 421 U.S. 658, 95 S.Ct. 1903, 44 L.Ed.2d 489 (1975). There, a national retail food chain and its president and chief executive officer were charged with causing food shipped in interstate commerce to be held in a building accessible to rodents and exposed to contamination. The food chain pled guilty, but its president contested the charges against him. He argued that although he retained authority over corporate affairs, he delegated "normal operating duties," including sanitation, to lower-level personnel. In rejecting his contention as a basis of nonliability, the Court explained that the prosecution established a *prima facie* case of the guilt of the accused when it established that the defendant had, by reason of his position in the corporation, responsibility and authority either to prevent in the first instance or promptly to correct the violation complained of and that he failed to do so. The Court left open a means for a defendant to establish that he or she was powerless to prevent or correct a violation but noted that "If such a claim is made, the defendant has the burden of coming forward with evidence, but this does not alter the Government's ultimate burden of proving . . . the defendant's guilt, including his power, in light of the duty imposed by the Act, to prevent or correct the prohibited condition." *United States v. Park,* 421 U.S. at 673, 95 S.Ct. at 1912, 44 L.Ed.2d at 502. The Court agreed with the government that Park was subject to strict criminal liability because he failed to use his authority in operating the company to prevent the storage of food in an area where it could be contaminated by rodents.

Defenses under the FDCA

Defendants charged with violations of the FDCA have challenged warrantless inspections, but in most cases this has not proved to be successful because the courts have ruled that the Fourth Amendment allows considerable latitude in inspection of commercial establishments. A corporate officer charged with a violation of the act may assert the defense of objective impossibility. In *United States v. Gel Spice Co., Inc.,* 773 F.2d 427 (2d Cir. 1985), the court noted that to establish the impossibility defense, the corporate officer must introduce evidence that he or she exercised extraordinary care but was nevertheless powerless to prevent or correct violations of the act. The defense is very difficult to establish and fails in most

Responsibility Follows Authority

CASE-IN-POINT

Dean Starr, secretary-treasurer of Cheney Brothers Food Corporation, was convicted of violating the Federal Food, Drug, and Cosmetic Act, 21 U.S.C.A. §§ 301–391, for allowing contamination of food stored in a company warehouse over which he had operational responsibility. After an inspector from the Food and Drug Administration (FDA) pointed out the problem, the janitor for the warehouse was instructed to make corrections, but no action was taken. A month later, a second inspection by the FDA disclosed that the problem had not been corrected. On appeal, Starr contended that he was not responsible because the janitor in charge had failed to comply with instructions to clean up the warehouse. The court rejected his argument, noting that Starr was aware of the problem after the first inspection and had ample time to remedy the situation. In affirming his conviction, the court also observed that supervisory officers have a duty to anticipate the shortcomings of their delegates.

United States v. Starr, 535 F.2d 512 (9th Cir. 1976).

situations. In cases where the government prosecutes for misbranding of articles, the defense will sometimes rely on experts to establish the validity of the defendant's branding.

Planning and Zoning Laws

Although sometimes used interchangeably, the terms "zoning" and "planning" are not synonymous. Zoning is primarily concerned with the use and regulation of buildings and structures, whereas planning is a broader term embracing the systematic and orderly development of a community. *State ex rel. Kearns v. Ohio Power Co.*, 127 N.E.2d 394, 399 (Ohio 1955).

In *Village of Euclid, Ohio v. Ambler Realty Co.*, 272 U.S. 365, 47 S.Ct. 114, 71 L.Ed. 303 (1926), the Supreme Court first upheld the concept of **zoning**, which allows local governments to divide areas of the community and to designate the permitted and prohibited land uses in the respective districts. Today land-use zoning has become widespread and sophisticated. For example, newer concepts such as the "planned unit development" (PUD) may permit a mixture of land uses on the same tract of land. See, for example, *Rouse-Fair-wood Development Ltd. Partnership v. Supervisor of Assessments for Prince George's County*, 773 A.2d 535 (Md. App. 2001). Comprehensive planning has evolved into complex land-use management that guides the development of a community. Such planning is implemented to a large degree by local zoning ordinances (their enactment usually preceded by studies and recommendations of professional consultants). Building codes are generally encompassed within the overall local zoning requirements. Local citizens are enlisted to sit on planning and zoning boards that make recommendations to the governing body. Any comprehensive zoning ordinance must provide for a board of adjustment to act in a quasi-judicial capacity. The board must have the power to grant variances where strict enforcement of an ordinance would cause an undue hardship to property owners. It may also be empowered to approve special exceptions based on criteria specified in a zoning ordinance.

As with other regulatory measures, enforcement of local zoning codes is accomplished administratively in most instances. Failing this, local governments often resort to civil court actions, commonly seeking injunctive relief against violators. Most zoning ordinances classify violations as misdemeanors and provide for a fine and a jail term on conviction. Zoning ordinances, like most health regulations, generally do not include an intent requirement. Prosecution of violators is usually undertaken only as a last resort. But once a state or local government commences prosecution of a defendant for violating a zoning ordinance, it must meet all burdens placed on the prosecution in criminal proceedings. *People v. St. Agatha Home for Children,* 389 N.E.2d 1098 (N.Y. 1979).

Numerous federal statutes and agencies play a part in regulating and enforcing the laws affecting our environment. Among the older agencies are the Army Corps of Engineers, the Coast Guard, and the Departments of the Interior, Commerce, Transportation, and Justice. A newer agency, the **Environmental Protection Agency (EPA)**, acts under the authority of major congressional enactments and has significant responsibilities in numerous areas, including hazardous wastes, toxic substances, and air and water pollution. State environmental agencies became active in the 1970s, and planning and coordinating councils now function at state, regional, and local levels. They play an important part in environmental regulation by establishing pollution controls, water management programs, and wastewater and solid-waste disposal programs.

The Scope of Federal and State Environmental Statutes

The Commerce Clause found in Article I, Section 8 of the U.S. Constitution provides the authority for Congress to enact laws protecting the environment. Environmental regulation at the federal and state levels has become a vast undertaking. Laws enacted by federal and state governments are enforced by regulatory agencies, by civil suits, and by criminal prosecutions. At the federal level, the EPA, which came into being in 1970, coordinates national efforts to reduce environmental risks and enforce federal laws protecting health and the environment. During the 1970s government agencies relied almost exclusively on civil penalties as an enforcement tool. The concept changed in the 1980s and 1990s, when criminal enforcement of environmental laws became prominent, particularly in instances of egregious waste disposal, water pollution, and air pollution.

The trend toward prosecution of violators, particularly at the federal level, is shown by the increase in prosecutions. According to the Transactional Records Access Clearinghouse (TRAC) at Syracuse University, the EPA referred 139 cases to the U.S. Department of Justice (DOJ) for criminal prosecution during the 1992 fiscal year. During fiscal year 2001, the EPA referred 328 criminal cases to the DOJ. The high-water mark in EPA criminal referrals was fiscal year 1998, when 486 criminal cases were referred to the DOJ.

Most states now have environmental agencies that coordinate with the EPA in the enforcement of national environmental laws as well as in supervising the enforcement of state environmental laws. The California Environmental Protection Agency is a good example. In 1991 the governor, by executive order, established the agency as a cabinet-level position in order to restore, protect, and enhance the environment and to ensure public health, environmental quality, and economic vitality.

Some environmental crimes (usually punishable as misdemeanors) require only proof that the defendant committed a proscribed act or failed to comply with a required standard. In prosecutions of these strict liability offenses, the government may establish the defendant's guilt in a manner similar to that used in prosecuting many crimes against the public health. Other statutes (usually those that impose felony punishment) require the government to establish the defendant's negligent conduct or a willful or knowing violation, and many court decisions in environmental prosecutions turn on whether the evidence is sufficient to meet the required statutory standard.

Major Federal Environmental Legislation Providing Criminal Sanctions

Congress enacted its first major environmental law, the **Rivers and Harbors Act**, 33 U.S.C.A. §§ 401–467, in 1899. Most of the Act deals with improvements to and regulation of the navigable waters of the country. But a section of the statute, 33 U.S.C.A. § 407, known commonly as the **Refuse Act**, act makes it a misdemeanor to "throw, discharge, or deposit, or cause, suffer, or procure to be thrown, discharged, or deposited either from or out of . . . the shore (or) . . . manufacturing establishment . . . any refuse matter of any kind or description . . . into any navigable water of the United States." Courts have held that the Refuse Act does not require government to prove any culpable mental state. See, e.g., *United States v. White Fuel Corp.*, 498 F.2d 619 (1st Cir.1978). A violation of the Act is thus a strict liability offense. Courts have interpreted "refuse" broadly to include oil. See, e.g., *United States v. White Fuel Corp.*, supra, where a company was prosecuted and fined after oil from its onshore tanks leaked into Boston Harbor. Thus, the Refuse Act provided a statutory basis for the federal government's criminal investigation into the calamitous BP oil spill of 2010.

In recent years, the following acts of Congress have provided significant means to enforce criminal violations of environmental laws and regulations.

- **Clean Air Act** of 1970, 42 U.S.C.A. §§ 7401–7642.
- **Federal Water Pollution Control Act** of 1972 (Clean Water Act), 33 U.S.C.A. §§ 1251–1376.
- **Resource Conservation and Recovery Act** of 1976 (RCRA), 42 U.S.C.A. §§ 6901–6992.
- **Toxic Substances Control Act** of 1976 (TSCA), 15 U.S.C.A. §§ 2601–2692.
- **Comprehensive Environmental Response, Compensation and Liability Act** of 1980 (CERCLA), 42 U.S.C.A. §§ 9601–9675.

The Clean Air Act

The Clean Air Act sets federal standards designed to enhance the quality of the air by deterring air polluters. In 1977 Congress passed a series of amendments establishing stricter standards for air quality. As amended, the act provides criminal sanctions for the violation of any provisions for which civil penalties apply and for any person who knowingly makes any false representation in a document filed under the act.

The Clean Air Act recognizes that the prevention and control of air pollution at its source is the primary responsibility of states and local governments. It provides that enforcement may be delegated to the states pursuant to the State Implementation Plan (SIP), 42 U.S.C.A. § 7410, but the states are not required to enact minimum criminal provisions to receive EPA approval of their implementation plans. Nevertheless, states are increasingly toughening criminal penalties in this area. State penalties for violations of air pollution laws vary. For example, violation of Oklahoma's Clean Air Act entails a fine of $25,000 or up to one year in jail per day for misdemeanor violations and a fine of $250,000 or up to ten years' imprisonment for violations classified as felonies. 27A Okl. Stats. Ann. § 2–5–116. Rhode Island law provides for substantial fines and imprisonment for violations of air pollution laws and regulations, yet it stipulates:

> No person shall be convicted or found liable in any criminal prosecution . . . brought by or on behalf of the state, the director or the public to enjoin, suppress, prohibit, or

punish air pollution unless he or she knowingly violated a rule or regulation or order of the director, issued under the authority conferred upon him or her by [Ch. 23]. R.I. Gen. Laws.

There have been fewer criminal prosecutions for violation of air pollution laws than for violations of hazardous waste and water pollution laws. Two reasons have been advanced: first, the cost of criminal enforcement in this area is apparently great; second, the problems of enforcement are made exceedingly difficult for states because air pollution is a less stationary category of pollution.

The Clean Water Act

The Federal Water Pollution Control Act of 1972 (Clean Water Act, or CWA), 33 U.S.C.A. §§ 1251–1376, is designed to control water pollution and regulate industrial and other discharges into navigable waters. What constitutes "navigable waters" under the CWA is important because it defines the extent of EPA jurisdiction. The term has been subject to debate. In *Rapanos v. United States*, 547 U.S. 715, 126 S.Ct. 2208, 165 L.Ed.2d 159 (2006), a plurality opinion of the Supreme Court said that navigable waters under the CWA includes only relatively permanent standing or flowing bodies of water and does not cover transitory puddles or ephemeral flows of water. The CWA prohibits the discharge of pollutants from any **point source** into the navigable waters of the United States unless such discharge complies with a permit issued by the EPA pursuant to the National Pollutant Discharge Elimination System (NPDES) or by an EPA-authorized state agency. See 33 U.S.C.A. §§ 1311(a) and 1342. Although the CWA is enforced primarily through civil means, criminal sanctions have been imposed for willful or negligent violations of certain provisions concerning permits and the making of false statements. Amendments in 1987 substituted the term "knowingly" for the earlier intent requirement of "willfully" and imposed

---

CASE-IN-POINT

The *Exxon Valdez* Prosecution and Subsequent Civil Suit

In March 1989, the supertanker *Exxon Valdez* ran aground and ruptured, spilling more than 240,000 barrels of oil into Alaska's Prince William Sound and wreaking havoc on the natural environment. Subsequently, the federal government brought criminal charges against the Exxon Shipping Co. and its parent, Exxon Corporation, under the Clean Water Act, the Migratory Bird Act, the Ports and Waterway Safety Act, and the Dangerous Cargo Act. In October 1991, one week before the case was scheduled to go to trial, Exxon accepted a plea bargain under which it agreed to plead guilty and pay $25 million in federal fines and another $100 million in restitution, split between the federal and state governments. The $125 million fine was the largest environmental criminal fine in U.S. history.

In 1994, a federal district court in Anchorage, Alaska, ordered Exxon to pay roughly $287 million in compensatory damages to commercial salmon and herring fishermen, plus $5 billion in punitive damages. However, the Ninth Circuit Court of Appeals remanded the case to the district court to reconsider the punitive damages. *In re Exxon Valdez*, 270 F.3d 1215 (9th Cir. 2001). On remand, the district court concluded the $5 billion in punitive damages was still fair, but in compliance with the Ninth Circuit mandate, it reduced the award to $4 billion. *In re Exxon Valdez*, 236 F. Supp.2d 1043 (2002). After further litigation, on December 22, 2006, the Ninth Circuit Court of Appeals ordered the district court to reduce the punitive damage award against Exxon to $2.5 billion.

In re Exxon Valdez, 472 F.3d 600 (9th Cir. 2006).

more stringent penalties for negligent violations and even more severe penalties for knowing violations of the act's criminal provisions. 33 U.S.C.A. § 1319(c)(2).

Courts have construed the term "knowingly" to find that a defendant's acts violate the CWA if those acts are proscribed, even if the defendant was not aware of the proscription. Thus, courts have held the government need only prove the defendant performed acts intentionally; it is not required to prove the defendant knew those acts violated the CWA. *United States v. Hopkins*, 53 F.3d 533 (2d Cir. 1995).

Courts tend to construe the penal provisions of the CWA broadly and generally hold supervisory personnel vested with authority to a high standard of compliance. The trend in the federal courts is to hold responsible corporate officers criminally liable in environmental offenses despite their lack of "consciousness of wrongdoing."

In *United States v. Hanousek*, 176 F.3d 1116 (9th Cir. 1999), Edward Hanousek Jr., a roadmaster for a railroad company, was convicted under a *respondeat superior* (supervisory responsibility) theory for the negligent discharge of oil into navigable waters, a violation of 33 U.S.C.A. § 1319(c)(1). The accident occurred due to a backhoe's puncture of a high-pressure oil line and resulted in the release of up to 5,000 gallons of oil directly into the Skagway River. Although Hanousek held a supervisory position of responsibility for construction and maintenance of the railroad track, he was home at the time of the accident. On appeal, he argued that the trial judge had violated his right to due process of law by failing to instruct the jury that the government had to prove that he acted with *criminal* and not ordinary negligence. The U.S. Court of Appeals for the Ninth Circuit rejected his argument, observing, "The criminal provisions of the CWA constitute public welfare legislation. . . . Public welfare legislation is designed to protect the public from potentially harmful or injurious items . . . and may render criminal 'a type of conduct that a reasonable person should know is subject to stringent public regulation and may seriously threaten the community's health or safety.'" The court then noted that "a public welfare statute may subject a person to criminal liability for ordinary negligence without offending due process." *Id.* at 1121–1122. The Ninth Circuit's decision sends a message to those who occupy supervisory roles that a supervisor can be held criminally liable for ordinary negligence in failing to take precautions to prevent another person from committing a violation of the CWA. Thus, in *United States v. Ortiz*, 427 F.3d 1278 (10th Cir. 2005), the Tenth Circuit Court of Appeals upheld the conviction of an operator of a chemical distillation facility for negligently discharging propylene glycol wastewater by pouring it into a toilet where the storm drain led to a navigable river.

A majority of the states have programs approved by the EPA. Although states vary somewhat in their approaches, many provide penalties similar to those in the federal act for either willful or negligent violations of water pollution provisions.

The Government's Requirement of Proof of Violation of the Clean Water Act

In *United States v. Wilson*, 133 F.3d 251, 264 (4th Cir. 1997), the court stated:

> To establish a felony violation of the Clean Water Act, we hold [the government] must prove:
>
> 1) that the defendant knew that he was discharging a substance, eliminating a prosecution for accidental discharges;
> 2) that the defendant correctly identified the substance he was discharging, not mistaking it for a different, unprohibited substance;

3) that the defendant knew the method or instrumentality used to discharge the pollutants;
4) that the defendant knew the physical characteristics of the property into which the pollutant was discharged that identify it as a wetland, such as the presence of water and water-loving vegetation;
5) that the defendant was aware of the facts establishing the required link between the wetland and waters of the United States; and
6) that the defendant knew he did not have a permit.

The Point Source Problem

As noted, the CWA prohibits the discharge of pollutants from any point source into the navigable waters of the United States unless such discharge complies with a permit issued by the EPA. The CWA states:

> The term "point source" means any discernible, confined and discrete conveyance, including but not limited to any pipe, ditch, channel, tunnel, conduit, well, discrete fissure, container, rolling stock, concentrated animal feeding operation, or vessel or other floating craft, from which pollutants are or may be discharged. This term does not include agricultural storm water discharges and return flows from irrigated agriculture. 33 U.S.C.A. 1362 (14)

Courts generally have interpreted "point source" broadly. For example, in *Froebel v. Meyer*, 217 F.3d 928, 938 (7th Cir. 2000), the court noted that several circuit courts have even considered that a dam can act as point sources if an artificial mechanism introduces pollutants. In *Avoyelles Sportsmen's League, Inc. v. Marsh*, 715 F.2d 897 (5th Cir. 1983), the U.S. Court of Appeals for the Fifth Circuit held that bulldozers and backhoes are point sources within the meaning of the CWA.

The issue of whether a human being can be a point source came into sharp focus in 1988 after schoolchildren on a field trip discovered glass vials of blood in the Hudson River. The vials were traced to Plaza Health Laboratories, Inc. (Plaza Health), a blood-testing laboratory in Brooklyn, New York. In 1989 a federal grand jury handed down a four-count indictment against Plaza Health and its co-owner and vice president, Geronimo Villegas, for violating the CWA. At Villegas's trial the evidence revealed that Villegas had thrown the vials into water with his hands. The court instructed the jury that under the CWA, the act of physically throwing the pollutants into the water constituted a discharge from a point source. The jury found Villegas guilty on all four counts. On appeal by Villegas, the U.S. Court of Appeals for the Second Circuit found that the language and legislative history of the CWA and the case law interpreting the term "point source" supported a conclusion that "the statute was never designed to address the random, individual polluter like Villegas." Rather, the court noted the term "point source" in the CWA was defined to include a "pipe, ditch, channel, tunnel, conduit, well, [and] discrete fissure" and to "evoke images of physical structures and instrumentalities that systematically act as a means of conveying pollutants from an industrial source to navigable waterways." Thus, applying the rule of lenity (a rule often applied in criminal prosecutions), the court found the CWA did not clearly proscribe Villegas's conduct and therefore did not give him fair warning that he was violating the law. *United States v. Plaza Health Laboratories, Inc.*, 3 F.3d 643, 646 (2d Cir. 1993). A dissenting judge pointed out "the discharge was directly into the water, and came from an identifiable point," *Id.* at 653, and concluded that Villegas had fair warning that his actions were illegal and proscribed by the CWA. At the time this book was written, Congress had not acted to indicate that under the intent of the CWA a discharge of pollutants into the water by an individual is illegal, although many observers had expected that it would do so.

The Resource Conservation and Recovery Act

Enactment of the Resource Conservation Recovery Act (RCRA) in 1976 was a significant step in environmental control. It establishes detailed provisions for the regulation of hazardous wastes. Its objective is to encourage the states—through grants, technical assistance, and advice—to establish standards and provide for civil and criminal enforcement of state regulations. The EPA sets minimum standards requiring the states to enact criminal penalties against any person who knowingly stores or transports any hazardous waste to an unpermitted facility, who treats such waste without a permit, or who makes false representations to secure a permit. All states have enacted criminal statutes pursuant to the criteria specified in the RCRA.

The RCRA proscribes a comprehensive list of illegal actions and imposes criminal penalties on any person who

1. knowingly transports or causes to be transported any hazardous waste to an unpermitted facility, 42 U.S.C.A. § 6928(d)(1);
2. knowingly treats, stores, or disposes of any hazardous waste without a permit, in knowing violation of any material condition or requirement of the interim status, 42 U.S.C.A. § 6928(d)(2)(A)—(C); or one who
3. knowingly omits material information or makes any false statement or representation in any record or document required to be maintained under the regulations or submitted to the [EPA] or any state which is authorized to run RCRA programs. 42 U.S.C.A. § 6928(d)(3).

CASE-IN-POINT

Criminal Prosecution under the Clean Water Act

David W. Boldt was the chemical engineering manager for Astro Circuit Corporation, a Massachusetts company that manufactured circuit boards using an electroplating process. Boldt's duties included supervising the company's pretreatment process, a part of the pollution control system. He was charged with six counts of violating the Clean Water Act. He was convicted on two counts: one for knowingly aiding and abetting the discharge of pollutants into a municipal sewer in 1987, when the copper level in Astro's effluent greatly exceeded the federal standards, and another for ordering a subordinate in 1988 to dump 3,100 gallons of partially treated industrial wastewater containing excessive metals into the municipal sewer. At trial, Boldt asserted the defense of impossibility to the first incident, arguing he was only a mid-level manager who was not responsible for the discharge. Boldt acknowledged responsibility for the second discharge but pleaded the defense of necessity, arguing it was necessary to authorize the discharge to avoid a worse harm.

In upholding both convictions, the appellate court observed that the evidence showed that pollution control was part of Boldt's area of responsibility and that, regarding the 1987 violation, he was aware of the practice of bypassing the pollution control system and had condoned it on the occasion at issue. Regarding the 1988 incident, the court found the evidence undisputed that Boldt directly ordered his subordinate to dump the copper wastewater, a conclusion bolstered by his subordinate's testimony that Boldt attempted to cover up the incident. Finally, the appellate court observed that the record of the trial disclosed that the president of Astro testified that Boldt was authorized to shut down the plant.

United States v. Boldt, 929 F.2d 35 (1st Cir. 1991).

RCRA contains criminal penalties of up to five years' imprisonment and $50,000 per day in fines, or both. In addition, section 6928(e), often referred to as the "knowing endangerment" provision, makes it a criminal offense knowingly to place another person in imminent danger of death or serious bodily injury in conjunction with the transportation, storage, or disposal of hazardous wastes. This provision carries fines of up to $250,000 and up to fifteen years' imprisonment, or both. A defendant that is an organization is subject to a fine of not more than $1,000,000.

RCRA has become an important tool for enforcement, and prosecutors frequently rely on it when prosecuting persons who illegally dispose of hazardous wastes. In *United States v. Johnson & Towers, Inc.*, 741 F.2d 662, 664 (3d Cir. 1984), the court held that the term "person" in RCRA section 6928(d) includes employees as well as owners and operators, but that employees can be subject to criminal prosecution only if they knew or should have known that there had been no compliance with the permit requirement of section 6925. Proof of the knowledge element required may be inferred for those individuals holding responsible corporate positions.

In *United States v. Hayes International Corp.*, 786 F.2d 1499 (11th Cir. 1986), the court affirmed a conviction under section 6928(d)(1) for unlawfully transporting hazardous waste materials to an unpermitted facility and ruled that neither a lack of knowledge that paint waste was a hazardous material nor ignorance of the permit requirement was a defense.

Conviction for the treatment, storage, or disposal of hazardous waste without an RCRA permit has been more problematic. In *United States v. Hoflin*, 880 F.2d 1033 (9th Cir. 1989), the court held that the government is not required to prove the defendant's knowledge of the lack of a permit to secure a conviction in either transport or storage cases; nevertheless, a person who does not know that the waste material he or she is disposing of is hazardous cannot be guilty of violating section 6928(d)(2)(a).

One of the most serious cases brought under the RCRA involved section 6928(e) (the knowing endangerment provision), which makes it a criminal violation to knowingly place employees "in imminent danger of death or serious bodily injury." *United*

CASE-IN-POINT

Prosecution of a "Responsible Corporate Officer" under the Clean Water Act

During 1996, Avion Environmental employees discharged untreated wastewater directly into the Richmond, Virginia, sewer system in violation of Avion's discharge permit. Based on these activities, the government charged James Hong, as a responsible corporate officer of Avion, with thirteen counts of negligently violating pretreatment requirements under the CWA, 33 U.S.C.A. § 1319(c)(1)(A) (West Supp. 2000). Hong, the sole shareholder of Avion Environmental, was convicted. Although he played a substantial role in the corporation's operations, Hong was not identified as an officer or as having direct oversight responsibility for operations from which the releases occurred. On appeal, Hong contended the government failed to prove he was a formally designated officer of Avion Environmental. Alternatively, he argued that there was no proof that he had sufficient control over the operations of Avion to be liable for violations of the CWA. The U.S. Fourth Circuit Court of Appeals rejected his arguments. The court held that the government was not required to prove that Hong was formally designated an officer of Avion. Rather, the court stated, "[T]he pertinent question is whether the defendant bore such a relationship to the corporation that it is appropriate to hold him criminally liable for failing to prevent the charged violations of the CWA." Holding that he did not prevent the violations, the court affirmed his convictions.

United States v. Hong, 242 F.3d 528, 531 (4th Cir. 2001).

States v. Protex Industries, Inc., 874 F.2d 740 (10th Cir. 1989), involved a company that operated a drum-recycling facility and, in connection with its business, purchased drums that previously contained toxic chemicals. The evidence revealed that the company's safety provisions were inadequate to protect its employees and, as a result, certain company employees suffered from solvent poisoning and exhibited serious maladies. The court upheld a conviction of Protex for placing employees in an industrial environment without sufficient protection against exposure to toxic chemicals.

The Government's Requirement of Proof of RCRA Offenses

Actions that violate the RCRA are often quite evident, yet proof of an offending person's intent is often the key to successful prosecution under the RCRA. To successfully prosecute a defendant charged with illegally transporting hazardous materials to a facility that lacks a permit, the government must prove that the substance being transported fit within the parameters of the definition of "hazardous waste," not that the defendant had knowledge that the material was hazardous and waste. *United States v. Kelly*, 167 F.3d 1176 (7th Cir. 1999). A corporate officer who does not "directly" cause the violations may still be culpable. *United States v. Hansen*, 262 F.3d 1217, 1243 (11th Cir. 2001).

It is not necessary that the government prove that the defendant knew a chemical waste had been defined as a "hazardous waste" by the EPA. *United States v. Goldsmith*, 978 F.2d 643, 646 (11th Cir. 1992). The government need only prove that a defendant had knowledge of "the general hazardous character" of the chemical. *United States v. Dee*, 912 F.2d 741, 745 (4th Cir. 1990).

CASE-IN-POINT

Criminal Prosecution under the RCRA: No Requirement that Defendant Knew Waste Would Be Harmful if Improperly Disposed

James Ralph Sellers was convicted of knowingly and willfully disposing of methylethylketone (M.E.K.), a hazardous waste, without obtaining a permit, a violation of 42 U.S.C.A. § 6928(d)(2)(A) (RCRA). At his jury trial the evidence revealed that residents discovered sixteen 55-gallon drums of hazardous paint waste on the embankment of a creek that flows into the Leaf River. These drums contained paint waste and M.E.K., a paint solvent. The evidence further revealed that Sellers did not have a permit for disposing of hazardous waste, nor did he take the waste to a licensed disposal area.

The trial court instructed the jury that the government must prove (1) that the defendant knowingly disposed of, or commanded and caused others to dispose of, wastes as charged in the indictment; (2) the defendant knew what the wastes were; (3) the wastes were listed or identified or characterized by the EPA as a hazardous waste pursuant to the RCRA; and (4) the defendant had not obtained a permit from either the EPA or the state of Mississippi authorizing the disposal under the RCRA.

On appeal, Sellers argued that the jury charge should have required the government to prove that Sellers knew that the paint waste could be hazardous or harmful to persons or the environment. The U.S. Court of Appeals rejected Sellers's contention and held that in a prosecution for knowingly and willfully disposing of methylethylketone (M.E.K.), a hazardous waste, without obtaining a permit, there was no requirement that defendant knew that waste would be harmful if improperly disposed of.

United States v. Sellers, 926 F.2d 410 (5th Cir. 1991).

The Toxic Substances Control Act

Go to the companion website for a more complete version of the Fifth Circuit's decision in *United States v. Sellers*.

The Toxic Substances Control Act (TSCA) of 1976 authorizes the EPA to require testing of, and to prohibit the manufacture, distribution, or use of, certain chemical substances that present an unreasonable risk of injury to health or the environment and to regulate their disposal. Section 14 of TSCA prohibits the commercial use of substances that the user knew or had reason to know were manufactured, processed, or distributed in violation of any provision of TSCA. 15 U.S.C.A. § 2614(2). Although the act depends primarily on civil penalties, a person who knowingly or willfully fails to maintain records or submit reports as required violates the criminal provisions of the act. 15 U.S.C.A. §§ 2614, 2615(b). There have been relatively few criminal prosecutions under TSCA; however, in 1982 a court upheld the conviction of Robert Earl Ward Jr., the chairman of the board of Ward Transformer Company, on eight counts of the unlawful disposal of toxic substances (PCB-containing oils from used transformers) and the willful aiding and abetting of the unlawful disposal of toxic substances. The evidence at trial revealed that although the defendant himself did not dispose of the toxic substances, the company's employees performed the task while he was kept advised of the progress. *United States v. Ward*, 676 F.2d 94 (4th Cir. 1982). In 1995 the U.S. Court of Appeals for the First Circuit found sufficient evidence to uphold a conviction of a defendant who allowed others to take PCB-laden transformers, knowing they would dump them unlawfully. *United States v. Catucci*, 55 F.3d 15 (1st Cir. 1995).

The Comprehensive Environmental Response, Compensation, and Liability Act

In 1980 Congress enacted the Comprehensive Environmental Response, Compensation, and Liability Act (CERCLA), commonly known as the Superfund Law. Its purpose is to finance cleanup and provide for civil suits by citizens. As revised in 1986, the act requires notice to federal and state agencies of any "release" of a "reportable quantity" of a listed hazardous substance. "Release" is broadly defined, and "reportable quantity" is related to each of the several hundred "hazardous substances." CERCLA also allows the EPA to promulgate regulations for the collection and disposal of solid wastes. The act imposes criminal sanctions against those who fail to report as required or who destroy or falsify records. 42 U.S.C.A. § 9603(d) (2).

Standard of Liability of Corporate Officers

Many violations in the public health area are caused by corporate entities; therefore, courts often focus on whether an accused, by reason of his or her position in the corporate enterprise, had sufficient responsibility and authority to either prevent or correct the violation charged. Courts hold responsible corporate officers liable in environmental crimes just as in prosecutions under the FDCA. In fact, Congress has adopted the "responsible corporate officer" doctrine in the Clean Air Act, 42 U.S.C. A. § 7413(c)(6), and the Clean Water Act, 33 U.S.C.A. § 1319(c)(3)(6). The doctrine has been upheld by federal appeals courts in CERCLA cases. For example, in *United States v. Carr*, 880 F.2d 1550 (2d Cir. 1989), the court rejected a maintenance supervisor's argument that he could not be guilty because he was a relatively low-level employee. The court explained that CERCLA imposes criminal responsibility on a person "even of relatively low rank" who acts in a supervisory capacity and is "in a position to detect, prevent, and abate a release of hazardous substances." 880 F.2d at 1554. Thus, a responsible corporate officer not only cannot avoid criminal liability by delegating tasks to others but also must remedy any violations that occur. At the state level, corporate executives have been charged with criminally negligent homicide and manslaughter where employees' deaths have resulted from the improper use of hazardous substances. See, for example, *State ex rel. Cornellier v. Black*, 425 N.W.2d 21 (Wis. App. 1988).

Lack of Uniformity in Environmental Laws

Disparate environmental standards, enforcement policies, and sanctions in the areas of water and air pollution and disposal of hazardous wastes can lead industrial companies to "shop" for locations that will enable them to be more competitive by not having to comply with stringent environmental standards. Significant differences exist among the fifty states in the standards of proof required and in the sanctions imposed for criminal violations of hazardous waste, water pollution, and air pollution laws.

Compare the differences between the statutory language in the Kentucky and Vermont offenses set out in Tables 11.1 and 11.2. What level of proof should be required for establishing a defendant's guilt under the "knowingly" standard of the

TABLE 11.1	Kentucky Environmental Laws Imposing Criminal Penalties Concerning Hazardous Wastes, Water Pollution, and Air Pollution	
	Unlawful Acts	**Penalties**
Hazardous Wastes	Knowingly engaging in the generation, treatment, storage, transportation, or disposal of hazardous wastes in violation of this chapter, or contrary to a permit, order, or administrative regulation issued or promulgated under the chapter; or knowingly making a false statement, representation, or certification in an application for, or form pertaining to, a permit, or in a notice or report required by the terms and conditions of an issued permit. Ky. Rev. Stat. Ann. § 224.99-010(6).	Imprisonment between one and five years or a fine up to $25,000 per day of violation, or both. § 224.99-010(6).
Water Pollution	Knowingly violating any of the following: § 224.70-110 (water pollution) § 224.73-120 (monitoring and reporting) § 224.40-100 (waste disposal) § 224.40-305 (unpermitted waste disposal facilities) Or violating any determination, permit, administrative regulation, or order of the Cabinet promulgated pursuant to those sections which have become final; or knowingly providing false information in any document filed or required to be maintained under this chapter; or knowingly rendering inaccurate any monitoring device or method required to be maintained. § 224.99-010(4).	Imprisonment between one and five years or a fine up to $25,000 per day of violation, or both. § 224.99-010(4).
Air Pollution	Knowingly violating § 224.20-110 (air pollution), or any determination, permit, administrative regulation, or order of the Cabinet promulgated pursuant to those sections which have become final; or knowingly providing false information in any document filed or required to be maintained under this chapter; or knowingly rendering inaccurate any monitoring device or method required to be maintained. § 224.99-010(4).	Imprisonment between one and five years or a fine up to $25,000 per day of violation, or both. § 224.99-010(4).

Source: Kentucky Revised Statutes Annotated.

TABLE 11.2	Vermont Environmental Laws Imposing Criminal Penalties Concerning Hazardous Wastes, Water Pollution, and Air Pollution	
	Unlawful Acts	Penalties
Hazardous Wastes	Violating any provision of the waste management chapter (transportation, storage, disposal, or treatment of hazardous waste; permit and manifest requirements), rules promulgated therein, or terms or conditions of any order of certification. Vt. Stat. Ann., Title 10, § 6612(a).	Imprisonment up to six months or a fine up to $25,000 per day of violation, or both. Title 10, § 6612(a).
	Violating any provision of the waste management chapter by the knowing or reckless (1) transport, treatment, storage or disposal of any hazardous waste; (2) transport, treatment, storage or disposal of more than one cubic yard of solid waste or more than 275 pounds of solid waste; or release of any hazardous material. Title 10, § 6612(d).	Imprisonment up to five years; or a fine not to exceed $250,000 or both. Title 10, § 6612(d).
Water Pollution	Violating any provision of the water pollution control subchapter, or failing, neglecting, or refusing to obey or comply with any order or the terms of any permit issued under this subchapter. Title 10, § 1275(a).	Imprisonment up to six months or a fine up to $25,000 per day of violation, or both. Title 10, § 1275(a).
	Knowingly making any false statement, representation, or certification in any document filed or required to be maintained under the water pollution control subchapter, or by any permit, rule, regulation, or order issued thereunder; or falsifying, tampering with, or knowingly rendering inaccurate any monitoring device or method required to be maintained under this subchapter, or by any permit, rule, regulation, or order issued thereunder. Title 10, § 1275(b).	Imprisonment up to six months or a fine up to $10,000 or both. Title 10, § 1275(b).
Air Pollution	Violating a provision of the air pollution control chapter (discharge of air contaminants without a permit or in violation of pollution standards) except § 563 and § 567 (relating to motor vehicles and confidential records), or any rule issued thereunder. Title 10, § 568(a).	Imprisonment up to five years, a fine up to $100,000 per violation, or both. Title 10, § 568(a).
	Knowingly making any false statement, representation or certification in any application, record, report, plan or falsifying, tampering with, or knowingly rendering inaccurate any monitoring devices required to be maintained under chapter or by permit, rule, regulation, or order issued under chapter. Title 10, § 568(b).	Imprisonment up to one year, a fine up to $50,000 per violation, or both. Title 10, § 568(b).

Source: Vermont Statutes Annotated.

Kentucky laws? Would a different standard of proof be required under Vermont's laws concerning hazardous wastes and air pollution?

Unfortunately, fines imposed on violators of environmental laws are too often regarded as "costs of doing business" because in reality these costs can be passed on to the ultimate consumer. The threat of imprisonment, on the other hand, is one cost that cannot be passed on to consumers; therefore, it is a powerful deterrent to those who would pollute the environment. As states more aggressively prosecute environmental crimes, more uniformity of criminal sanctions will undoubtedly develop, much as it has for the more common criminal offenses.

Defenses to Environmental Crimes

Defendants' attacks on most environmental statutes, alleging them to be vague and ambiguous, have largely failed. Defenses asserting that a criminal prosecution constitutes double jeopardy (see Chapter 14) because the government has previously exacted a civil fine against the defendant have also been unsuccessful. Nevertheless, courts must provide an opportunity for assertion of defenses. In *United States v. Pa. Industrial Chemical Corp.*, 411 U.S. 655, 93 S.Ct. 1804, 36 L.Ed.2d 567 (1973), a manufacturing corporation was convicted under the Rivers and Harbors Act of discharging refuse into navigable waters without a permit. The Court reversed the defendant's conviction after the trial court failed to allow the defendant to present evidence at trial that he had been misled deliberately by the government about required permits, and thus deprived of presenting a defense.

Environmental cases can be very technical. Frequently they involve challenging the government's test results that form the basis of the charges. Some prosecutions under the CWA where defendants have eventually prevailed provide illustrations of defenses under environmental statutes. For example, in *United States v. Borowski*, 977 F.2d 27 (1st Cir. 1992), the First Circuit reversed a conviction where company officers had directed employees to pour toxic chemicals into a drain that led to a public treatment plant. While observing that the defendants' conduct was reprehensible, the court held that they did not violate the CWA because prosecution for knowing endangerment under the CWA cannot be premised upon danger that occurs before a pollutant reaches publicly owned sewer or treatment works. As noted in *United States v. Plaza Health Labs* earlier in this chapter, in a prosecution under the CWA, defense counsel succeeded in establishing a restrictive application of what constitutes a discharge from a point source.

In *Village of Oconomowoc Lake v. Dayton Hudson Corp.*, 24 F.3d 962 (7th Cir. 1994), the Seventh Circuit held that a six-acre artificial retention pond that discharged only to groundwater did not constitute "waters of the United States," a predicate for conviction under the CWA's proscription on discharges of pollutants into navigable waters. In *Solid Waste Agency of Northern Cook County v. United States Army Corps of Engineers*, 531 U.S. 159, 121 S.Ct. 675, 148 L.Ed.2d576 (2001), the U.S. Supreme Court held that isolated ponds, some used only seasonally as a habitat by migratory birds, did not fall within the CWA's definition of "navigable waters" merely because these waters served as a habitat for migratory birds. The Court's decision has caused speculation as to the viability of the so-called Migratory Bird Rule.

Noise Pollution

Congress enacted the **Quiet Communities Act** of 1978, 42 U.S.C.A. §§ 4901–4918, to protect the environment against noise pollution, which has become perceived as a growing danger to the health and welfare of the population. Section 4909 details prohibited acts, and section 4910 provides criminal penalties for those who knowingly or willfully import, manufacture, or distribute products that fail to comply with noise standards specified in the statute. However, the act recognizes that the primary responsibility for protecting communities against noise pollution lies with state and local governments.

Historically, local governments have adopted ordinances that prohibit excessive noise. In the twentieth century, ordinances have reflected concern about amplified sound equipment. Noise control ordinances often prohibit the use of loud audio equipment in an apartment building where residents live in close quarters. These ordinances are directed at loud late-night parties that disturb neighbors or against persons whose car stereos are played so loudly as to be an annoyance or even a safety hazard.

Most persons charged with violations of noise ordinances do not choose to contest the charges. Instead, they pay a small fine or agree to abate the violation. Those who do choose to contest the charge often attack the constitutionality of the ordinance. As we pointed out in Chapter 3, the vagueness doctrine requires that a statute that defines a criminal offense must be definite so that ordinary persons can understand what conduct is prohibited. Local ordinances that vaguely prohibit unnecessary noise are subject to constitutional challenge. In 1991 the Supreme Court of Mississippi held that Gulfport's noise control ordinance, by prohibiting "unnecessary or unusual noises . . . which either annoys, injures or endangers the comfort, repose, health or safety of others . . . fails to provide clear notice and sufficiently definite warning of the conduct that is prohibited." As a result, the court said that persons of "common intelligence must necessarily guess at its meaning and differ as to its application." *Nichols v. City of Gulfport,* 589 So.2d 1280, 1282 (Miss. 1991). Likewise the Supreme Court of Georgia invalidated a county ordinance that prohibited "any . . . unnecessary or unusual sound or noise which . . . annoys . . . others." The court held that the ordinance failed to provide the requisite clear notice and sufficiently definite warning of the conduct that is prohibited. *Thelen v. State,* 526 S. E.2d 60, 62 (Ga. 2000).

The city of Sarasota, Florida adopted an ordinance that amended its zoning code by prohibiting all amplified sound in non-enclosed structures in an area zoned "Commercial Business–Newtown" during specified times of day. Daley, who owned a restaurant that provided both live and recorded musical entertainment for its customers, challenged the ordinance's validity. A Florida appellate court invalidated the ordinance. *Daley v. City of Sarasota,* 752 So.2d 124 (Fla. App. 2000). The court recognized that music, as a form of expression and communication, is protected under the First Amendment and observed,

> The goal of regulating unreasonable sound is unquestionably a matter within the city's province. However, that goal, no matter how laudable, cannot be achieved by the overbroad regulation of activities protected by the First Amendment. As currently written, the city's ordinance can be used to suppress First Amendment rights far more severely than can be justified by the city's interest in regulating unreasonable sound. 752 So.2d at 126.

Narrowly drafted noise control ordinances fare better before judicial tribunals. In *City of Janesville v. Garthwaite,* 266 N.W.2d 418 (Wis. 1978), the city charged the defendant with violation of an ordinance that states, "No person shall make unnecessary and annoying noise with a motor vehicle by squealing tires, excessive acceleration of engine or by emitting unnecessary and loud muffler noises." The Supreme Court of Wisconsin held the ordinance was a valid exercise of the city's police power to manage and control its streets.

In 2001 the Ohio Court of Appeals upheld the village of Kelleys Island's antinoise ordinance, which provides:

> No person shall generate or permit to be generated noise or loud sound which is likely to cause inconvenience or annoyance to persons of ordinary sensibilities by means of a live performance, radio, phonograph, television, tape player, compact disc player, loudspeaker or any other sound amplifying device which is plainly audible at a distance of 150 feet or more from the source of the noise or loud sound.

The owner of a bar that featured karaoke or live bands on an outdoor patio was cited for violation of the ordinance. The owner contended the ordinance was vague and therefore unconstitutional under the First Amendment to the U.S. Constitution. The court, however, found the ordinance was sufficiently definite to allow a person to determine what conduct violated the ordinance and prevent arbitrary enforcement. Addressing concerns as to the ordinance's constitutionality, the court explained that the "noise or loud sound" is made definite by adding that it must be "plainly audible" or "clearly heard" by a person using his or her "normal hearing faculties." Also, the noise or sound must be inconvenient or annoying to persons of "ordinary sensibilities." "Time and distance limitations also aid in providing fair warning of the nature of the unlawful conduct." The distance requirement puts "an objective quantifiable number into the ordinance, thus narrowing the scope of its operations." Thus, it held the ordinance was a valid exercise of police power and not unconstitutionally vague. *Kelleys Island v. Joyce,* 765 N.E.2d 387, 393 (Ohio App. 2001).

Antismoking Legislation

As society has become more aware of the ill effects of smoking and, in particular, the hazards of "secondhand smoke," governments have restricted smoking in public buildings and places of public accommodation and transportation. Perhaps the best-known example is the Federal Aviation Administration regulation prohibiting all smoking on domestic passenger airline flights. The last few years have witnessed enactment of no-smoking laws by states; by 2003 most states had laws restricting smoking in public places, and several have laws restricting smoking in private workplaces. In some instances state laws have preempted the subject, and local communities have been prevented from enacting conflicting ordinances. In other instances local communities have acted where the states have not. Often antismoking laws carry minor civil penalties, and local ordinances frequently impose penalties analogous to parking fines.

The Florida Initiative

In November 2002 Florida voters, by a margin in excess of 70 percent, adopted a state constitutional amendment that required the state legislature to enact a comprehensive ban on smoking in restaurants and other public places. The state legislature promptly enacted laws that require proprietors to implement policies regarding smoking prohibitions in indoor workplaces and generally prohibit smoking in restaurants, with exceptions that allow smoking in "stand-alone" bars that serve incidental snacks, on outdoor patios at restaurants, at membership associations, in designated smoking rooms at public lodging establishments, and at designated smoking areas at airports. The new laws make violations noncriminal and impose civil fines for violators. West's Fla. Stat. Ann., Ch. 386.

New York's Comprehensive Smoking Ban

In 2003 the New York legislature enacted a comprehensive antismoking law. Effective July 24, 2003, McKinney's Public Health Law § 1399-o provides that smoking shall not be permitted and no person shall smoke in places of employment, indoor areas of bars and restaurants, subways, and numerous other enclosed areas. Smoking is permitted in private automobiles and homes, unless the home is used to provide day care. This far-ranging and controversial statute is enforced through administrative fines, not criminal penalties. The statute is praised by public health authorities and antismoking groups and severely criticized by "smokers' rights" organizations.

The Future of Smoking Bans

As noted, the clear trend is to prohibit or restrict smoking in public places. Thus, the great majority of the other states have enacted laws prohibiting or restricting smoking in a variety of areas—for example, public transportation vehicles, hospitals, medical offices, public offices and meeting rooms, schools, child care centers, libraries, motion picture theaters, stage performance theaters, restaurants, waiting and meeting rooms owned or operated by the executive and judicial branches of the state and local governments, and specified areas of sports arenas. Many smokers resent laws that they see as infringements on their freedom and often assert that their decision to smoke is no one else's business. But because smoking negatively affects others who are in close proximity, there is little question that government has a legitimate basis upon which to restrict smoking in public places. How far government chooses to go in this area is a political issue, not a constitutional one, as most constitutional attacks on nonsmoking regulations based on equal protection and due process grounds and the right of privacy have failed.

Wildlife Protection Laws

Since the early common law, fish and game have been viewed as *ferae naturae* (wild animals), meaning that the state as sovereign owns them in trust for the people. *Bayside Fish Flour Co. v. Gentry*, 297 U.S. 422, 56 S.Ct. 513, 80 L.Ed. 772 (1936). As trustee, the state has the duty to preserve and protect wildlife by regulating fishing in public and private streams and by controlling the taking of game. *Shively v. Bowlby*, 152 U.S. 1, 14 S.Ct. 548, 38 L.Ed. 331 (1894). Federal courts have said that under the public trust doctrine, the U.S. and state governments have the right and the duty to protect and preserve the public's interest in natural wildlife resources. See, for example, *Toomer v. Witsell*, 334 U.S. 385, 68 S.Ct. 1156, 92 L.Ed. 1460 (1948). Owners of private property retain a qualified interest, so those seeking to take fish or game from the confines of private property must secure the owner's permission.

The Migratory Bird Act

Although it is generally within the jurisdiction of the states to regulate wildlife, fish, and game, the federal government has jurisdiction to enact statutes to carry out treaties for migratory birds. The jealous regard that the states have over wildlife within their borders led Missouri to challenge the constitutionality of the **Migratory Bird Act**, 16 U.S.C.A. §§ 703–712, a statute Congress enacted to enforce the provisions of the Migratory Bird Treaty entered into by the United States in 1916. Missouri claimed the federal statute infringed rights reserved to the states by the Tenth Amendment to the U.S. Constitution. The Supreme Court rejected that challenge, thereby settling the issue of federal control. The Court held that Article II, Section 2 of the Constitution grants the president the power to make treaties, and Article I, Section 8 gives Congress the power to enact legislation to enforce those treaties. *Missouri v. Holland*, 252 U.S. 416, 40 S.Ct. 382, 64 L.Ed. 641 (1920). Of course, the federal government retains jurisdiction to protect all wildlife, game, and fish within national game preserves. *Hunt v. United States*, 278 U.S. 96, 49 S.Ct. 38, 73 L.Ed. 200 (1928).

Enforcement of the Migratory Bird Act (MBA) remains a viable part of the federal environmental enforcement program. In *Humane Society v. Glickman*, 217 F.3d

882 (D.C. Cir. 2000), the U.S. Court of Appeals for the D.C. Circuit held that federal agencies are subject to the provisions of the MBA. Its broad proscription makes it

> unlawful . . . to pursue, hunt, take, capture, kill, attempt to take, capture, or kill, possess, offer for sale, sell, offer to barter, barter, offer to purchase, purchase, deliver for shipment, ship, export, import, cause to be shipped, exported, or imported, deliver for transportation, transport or cause to be transported, carry or cause to be carried, or receive for shipment, transportation, carriage, or export birds protected under the treaty. 16 U.S.C.A. §§ 703–712.

A violation of a regulation issued under the MBA is a misdemeanor, but a person guilty of knowingly taking a migratory bird with intent to sell or offer for sale or barter is guilty of a felony and subject to up to two years' imprisonment and a substantial fine. 16 U.S.C.A. § 707.

In 1986 Congress inserted the word "knowingly" into the section of the act providing criminal sanctions, thus requiring the prosecution to prove the defendant's *mens rea* as well as *actus reus* to establish a violation (see Chapter 4). Although section 707 requires the government to prove a knowing act, it does not require it to establish that a defendant's act is willful. Thus, in *United States v. Pitrone*, 115 F.3d 1 (1st Cir. 1997), in upholding the defendant's conviction for unlawfully selling a Harlequin duck, the appellate court rejected the defendant's contention that the government was required to prove his specific intent in order to establish that he knowingly violated the law. In effect, the government must show that the defendant's actions were intentional but need not show that the defendant knew they were illegal.

In an appeal from conviction for possessing more migratory game birds than the daily bag limit imposed under 16 U.S.C.A. § 703, another defendant argued that his hunting dog had simply picked up birds from other hunters. Thus, he contended, he had no intent to violate the law. But the U.S. Court of Appeals for the Fifth Circuit rejected his argument, holding that a misdemeanor violation of the MBA for possessing more migratory game birds than the daily limit allowed is a strict liability offense. *United States v. Morgan*, 283 F.3d 322 (5th Cir. 2002).

The Endangered Species Act

Modern efforts of the federal government to preserve the environment through protection of wildlife is illustrated by the Federal **Endangered Species Act** of 1973 (ESA), 16 U.S.C.A. §§ 1531–1544. This act is designed to conserve ecosystems by preserving wildlife, fish, and plants. And although enforcement is largely through civil penalties, criminal liability is imposed against any person who knowingly violates regulations issued under the act. 16 U.S.C.A. § 1540(b). The ESA prohibits several specific acts regarding endangered species, and the Secretary of the Interior is further authorized to prohibit any of those acts with regard to threatened species.

The powerful role the ESA plays in the preservation of endangered species was dramatized in 1978 when the U.S. Supreme Court upheld a permanent injunction against construction of the Tellico Dam and Reservoir, a nearly complete $100 million water project in Tennessee. According to the plaintiffs in the case, the project would have eradicated or destroyed the remaining habitat of the only known population of an endangered species of fish, the snail darter. In upholding an injunction against the continuance of the project, the Court held that "the plain intent of Congress in enacting this statute was to halt and reverse the trend toward species extinction, whatever the cost." 437 U.S. 153, 184, 98 S.Ct. 2279, 2297, 57 L.Ed.2d

117 (1978). Subsequently, Congress enacted legislation restarting the project and the Tellico Dam was completed in 1979.

Under the ESA, criminal liability is imposed for the knowing violation of one of the specific prohibitions listed in the act, a regulation issued to implement those prohibitions, or a permit or certificate issued pursuant to the act. Violators may be fined up to $50,000 or imprisoned for up to a year, or both. ESA also authorizes fines of up to $25,000 or imprisonment for up to six months, or both, for violations of any other regulation promulgated under the act.

In *United States v. Billie*, 667 F. Supp. 1485 (S.D. Fla. 1987), the defendant was charged with killing a Florida panther, an endangered species. He argued that the prosecution had to prove his specific intent—that is, that he knew the animal he shot was a Florida panther, as opposed to a species of panther not on the list of "endangered species." The U.S. District Court rejected his argument and held that the government "need prove only that the defendant acted with general intent when he shot the animal in question." 667 F. Supp. at 1493. The court discussed the fact that the defendant was charged with violating a regulatory statute enacted to conserve and protect endangered species and that its purposes would be eviscerated if the government had to prove that a hunter who killed an animal recognized the particular subspecies as being protected under the act. 667 F. Supp. at 1492–1493. The following year a defendant was convicted for illegally taking a grizzly bear. The court held that the government had to establish that the defendant knowingly took the bear without a permit, but the government was not required to prove the defendant knew he was shooting at a grizzly bear. *United States v. St. Onge*, 676 F. Supp. 1044 (D. Mont. 1988).

CASE-IN-POINT

A Federal Appellate Court Grants Protection to Nesting Sea Turtles

In 1978 the U.S. Fish and Wildlife Service listed the loggerhead sea turtle as a threatened species and the green sea turtle as an endangered species. In the spring, the female sea turtles come ashore on the beaches in Volusia County, Florida, deposit their eggs in the sand, and return to the ocean. Nesting females avoid bright lights. Months later, the hatchlings break out of their shells at night and instinctively crawl toward the brightest light on the horizon, which on an undeveloped beach is the moon's reflection off the surf. But on a developed beach, the brightest light can be artificial and can lead to disorientation of the turtles. Citizens acting on behalf of the endangered turtles sought an injunction against the county's refusal to ban beach driving and beachfront artificial light sources that adversely impact sea turtles during sea turtle nesting season, arguing that the county had violated the "take" prohibition of 16 U.S.C.A. section 1538(a)(1)(B). The county responded that it had implied permission to "take" federally protected sea turtles through artificial beachfront lighting because it had a federal permit conditioned on its implementation of detailed lighting-related mitigatory measures. The district court enjoined the county from permitting beach driving during the nesting season but denied relief as to the beachfront lighting. The turtles appealed.

In a case of first impression, the U.S. Court of Appeals for the Eleventh Circuit held that the ESA's incidental-take permit exception to its "take prohibition" did not apply to an activity performed as a purely mitigatory measure upon which the permit is conditioned, and thus did not authorize the county to take protected sea turtles through measures associated with artificial beachfront lighting.

Turtles v. Volusia County, 148 F.3d 1231 (11th Cir. 1998).

Despite the existence of criminal penalties for the violation of environmental laws, often the most effective means of enforcement is to secure an injunction against actual or threatened violations. This is illustrated by an action against Volusia County, Florida, filed under the citizen-suit provision of the ESA, 16 U.S.C.A. § 1540(g)(1)(A), discussed in the 1998 decision from the Fifth Circuit Court of Appeals in *Turtles v. Volusia County*, illustrated in the Case-in-Point.

State Regulation of Wildlife

State legislatures may make it a strict liability offense to take or possess fish and game in violation of regulations. *Cummings v. Commonwealth*, 255 S.W.2d 997 (Ky. 1953). Most states have done so, usually imposing strict liability for taking quantities of game or fish in excess of permitted allowances and for hunting and fishing during closed seasons. But it can be quite difficult to determine whether a given law that imposes a criminal penalty for violating a fishing or game regulation is a strict liability statute. If a wildlife penal statute includes language incorporating a *mens rea* requirement, it is clear that the prosecution must prove the defendant's intent. Although it is difficult to generalize, if a wildlife penal law does not explicitly require intent by including such words as "willfully" or "knowingly," only proof of the *actus reus* of the offense is required. The courts have tended to make an exception to imposing strict liability where the offense is of a more serious criminal character (for example, smuggling and chemical trafficking) or where the offense is designated as a felony or otherwise carries a severe punishment.

In *State v. Rice*, 626 P.2d 104 (Alaska 1981), the court considered a game regulation that lacked any requirement for criminal intent. As we have noted, this type of regulation is generally treated as a strict liability offense, much like a traffic law. The Alaska Supreme Court took a different approach, saying, "strict liability is an exception to the rule that requires criminal intent" and that criminal statutes will be "strictly construed to require some degree of *mens rea* absent a clear legislative intent to the contrary." *Id.* at 108.

Statutes also commonly make it a strict liability offense to use improper types of fishing nets, to hunt with artificial lights, and to shoot over baited fields. In addition, statutes provide for forfeiture of illegal equipment used to hunt or fish in violation of laws. See, for example, *State v. Billiot*, 229 So.2d 72 (La. 1969), where the Louisiana Supreme Court upheld the forfeiture of seines and other devices used in trawling for shrimp during a closed season.

Irrespective of whether a penal statute imposes strict liability or requires proof of intent, the prosecution is not required to establish that a person accused of fishing in a closed season actually caught fish, *State v. Parker*, 167 A. 854, 855 (Me. 1933), nor is it a defense that a hunter has failed to kill any game, *Key v. State*, 384 S.W.2d 22 (Tenn. 1964).

What Constitutes Possession?

Recall that in Chapter 10 we discussed the difference between actual and constructive possession and the elements of joint possession, concepts that often come into play in regard to possession of illegal drugs and drug paraphernalia. These same concepts become important in wildlife laws where proof of violation of game and fish laws can be based on constructive possession, and even constructive joint possession, as well as actual possession of game and fish.

The concept of constructive possession of wildlife is illustrated by the Vermont Supreme Court's decision in *State v. Letourneau*, 503 A.2d 553 (Vt. 1985). There, the defendants appealed their convictions for illegal possession of moose where a game warden had searched their premises and found packages of moose meat in the defendants' freezers. The trial judge had instructed the jury that if a person deposited unlawful property in a place of concealment on his own premises or otherwise, he nevertheless had possession of the property even though he might have been absent from the place he was using for its concealment. The court rejected the defendants' contention that the instruction was improper and held the instruction was consistent with statutory and case law.

In *Ford v. State*, 344 S.E.2d 514 (Ga. App. 1986), a Georgia appellate court reviewed a conviction for possession of a wild turkey with the knowledge that it had been taken in violation of Ga. Code Ann. § 27-1-31. The court reversed the defendant's conviction because there was no evidence that the defendant knew or reasonably should have known that the turkey was taken in violation of the law. Nevertheless, the court took the occasion to explain the law of constructive possession of the turkey. The court observed that the jury could have inferred the defendant's joint constructive possession of a turkey where the defendant waited for a companion who shot a wild turkey. The court found the defendant knew her companion was to hunt for turkey on the morning in question; she waited for him during the hunt and cooked and ate the game he killed.

Defenses Rejected

Defendants have attacked certain wildlife regulations as being vague and ambiguous, but in most cases such challenges have failed. In other cases defendants have challenged warrantless searches as violations of the Fourth Amendment to the U.S. Constitution. Historically, a "subsistence" defense—that is, a contention that game or fish was taken as a means of subsistence—may have been allowed, but this defense generally fails today. See *State v. Eluska*, 742 P.2d 514 (Alaska 1986). In *State v. Gibbs*, 797 P.2d 928 (Mont. 1990), a defendant charged with illegal possession of a bobcat pelt claimed he had killed the bobcat in defense of his son, whom the animal had attacked. (We discuss defense of another person in Chapter 14.) He based his defense on Mont. Code Ann. § 87-3-112, which provided there was no criminal liability for the taking of wildlife that was molesting or threatening to kill a person. The trial court refused to submit the issue of defense of another person to the jury, noting the statute that the defendant relied upon required notification to the Department of Fish, Wildlife, and Parks within seventy-two hours and that the defendant failed to comply with the statutory reporting requirement. The Montana Supreme Court upheld the trial court's action in refusing to submit the defense to the jury and affirmed the defendant's conviction.

The Florida appellate court's decision in *State v. Billie* is reproduced on the companion website.

In *State v. Billie*, 497 So.2d 889 (Fla. App. 1986), a Florida appellate court held that the state of Florida had jurisdiction to charge a member of the Seminole tribe with unlawfully killing a panther pursuant to Florida Statutes § 372.671. The court rejected claims that the ESA preempted state law, finding that the state law in this area was more protective than the federal ESA.

Conclusion

The authority of state governments to enact laws to protect the public health is a basic component of their police powers. The federal government has acquired a virtual police power through an expansive interpretation of the Commerce Clause of Article I,

Section 8 of the U.S. Constitution and has exercised this power to legislate extensively with respect to the public health and environmental protection. The Food, Drug, and Cosmetic Act, the Clean Air Act, the Clean Water Act, and the Endangered Species Act are some of the more prominent manifestations of this power.

Many of the offenses in this area are strict liability crimes. Formerly, governmental agencies relied almost exclusively on civil penalties to punish violators of environmental laws, but the regulatory climate has changed. The coming years will continue to witness an increased reliance by federal and state authorities on criminal sanctions, often with greatly increased penalties. As this trend continues, legislatures (or, in their absence, courts of law) will most likely include a *mens rea* requirement in regulatory statutes that subject violators of environmental laws to severe punishment.

Strict liability is also applied to transgressors of wildlife regulations, although—whenever a violation rises to the level of a felony or involves a substantial penalty—courts are inclined to require proof of the defendant's intent before upholding a conviction that visits serious consequences on the offender.

Noise pollution and smoking in public places are increasingly viewed by society as detrimental. Increased concern about the deleterious effects of secondhand smoke has caused the public to demand restrictions on smoking in public buildings, restaurants, bars, and workplaces.

Chapter Summary

- **LO1** Crimes against public health and the environment originate from Congress and state legislatures, which have responded to public concerns about. States exercise this authority through their police powers; the Commerce Clause in the U.S. Constitution has been interpreted to grant similar authority to the federal government. Although enforcement is accomplished largely through regulatory agencies, Congress and state legislatures impose criminal sanctions to enforce standards and deter violators.

- **LO2** Many of the offenses in this area are *mala prohibita*, usually strict liability misdemeanor offenses that consist of neglect to comply with required standards. In felony prosecutions, however, the government must generally prove the defendant's intent.

- **LO3** First passed in 1905, the Food, Drug, and Cosmetic Act (FDCA), was comprehensively amended in 1938 and has since been amended many times. The FDCA defines adulterated food, sets standards for determining whether drugs and devices are adulterated, and defines misbranding by false or misleading labels and packaging. Violations are punishable by criminal penalties, civil fines, injunctive relief, and, in some instances, by seizure of adulterated or misbranded articles. Misdemeanor offenses are generally strict liability, but in felony prosecutions the government must usually prove the defendant's intent. Because food, drugs, and cosmetics are usually produced and distributed by corporate enterprises, government agencies affix responsibility on supervisory personnel as well as corporate entities for violations and for failure to prevent violations from occurring.

- **LO4** In 1926 the Supreme Court upheld the concept of land use zoning, which allows local governments to designate permitted and prohibited land uses. Today land-use zoning is widespread. Enforcement is usually accomplished administratively or by civil law proceedings. Most zoning ordinances classify violations as misdemeanors and provide for a fine and a jail term on conviction. Zoning ordinances, like most health regulations, generally do not include an intent requirement. Prosecution of violators is usually undertaken only as a last resort.

- **LO5** Since the early 1980s Congress has enacted various laws affecting control of the environment. The Army Corps of Engineers, the Coast Guard, and the Departments of the Interior, Commerce, Transportation, and Justice enforce these laws and regulations. The Environmental Protection Agency (EPA) has significant responsibilities involving hazardous wastes, toxic substances, and air and water pollution. States became active players in the 1970s, and planning and co-ordinating councils now function at state, regional, and local levels. Governments formerly relied on civil penalties for enforcement, but since the 1980s criminal enforcement of environmental laws in instances of egregious waste disposal and air and water pollution have become became prominent. Most misdemeanors are strict liability offenses, and the government may establish the defendant's guilt by proof of a proscribed act or failure to comply with a standard, but to convict a violator of a felony the government must generally establish the defendant's negligence or a willful or knowing statutory violation.

- **LO6** The Clean Air Act sets federal standards to enhance the quality of the air and provides criminal sanctions for violations. Enforcement may be delegated to the states pursuant to the State Implementation Plan (SIP). The Clean Water Act prohibits the discharge of pollutants from any *point source* (pipe, ditch etc.) into navigable waters unless such discharge complies with a permit issued by the EPA or by an EPA-authorized state agency. Although enforced primarily through civil means, criminal sanctions are imposed for *knowingly* discharging pollutants, for violations concerning permits and for making false statements.

- **LO7** The Resource Conservation and Recovery Act (RCRA) imposes criminal penalties on those who knowingly transport or cause any hazardous waste to be transported to an unpermitted facility, or who treat, store, or dispose of hazardous waste without a permit. It also makes it a crime to omit material information or make false statements in any record or document required under the regulations or submitted to the EPA or to any state authorized to run RCRA programs.

- **LO8** The Toxic Substances Control Act (TSCA) authorizes the EPA to require testing of and to prohibit the manufacture, distribution, or use of certain chemical substances that present an unreasonable risk of injury to health or the environment, and to regulate their disposal. The TSCA also prohibits commercial use of substances that the user knew or had reason to know were manufactured, processed, or distributed in violation of any provision of the TSCA. Most enforcement is by civil means but one who knowingly or willfully fails to maintain records or submit reports as required violates the criminal provisions of the act.

- **LO9** The Comprehensive Environmental Response, Compensation, and Liability Act (CERCLA), the "Superfund Law," finances environmental cleanup and provides for civil suits by citizens. The act now requires notice to federal and state agencies of any "release" of a "reportable quantity" of a listed hazardous substance. CERCLA imposes criminal penalties on supervisors who are in a position to detect, prevent, and abate a release of hazardous substances. The fifty states vary in the standards of proof required and the sanctions imposed for criminal violations of hazardous waste, water pollution, and air pollution laws.

- **LO10** Many violations in the public health area are caused by corporate entities; therefore, courts often focus on whether an accused, by reason of his or her position in the corporate enterprise, had sufficient responsibility and authority to either prevent or correct the violation charged. Courts hold responsible corporate officers liable for environmental crimes as well. Congress has adopted the "responsible corporate officer" doctrine in the Clean Air Act and the Clean Water Act, the doctrine has been upheld in CERCLA cases by federal appeals courts.

- **LO11** The Quiet Communities Act of 1978 protects against noise pollution and provides criminal penalties for knowingly or willfully importing, manufacturing, or distributing products that do not comply with specified noise standards. But it recognizes that states and local communities have primary responsibility in these areas. Local governments often enact ordinances prohibiting the use of loud audio equipment and loud and annoying car stereos. Ordinances attacked on First Amendment grounds have met with mixed success.
- **LO12** States have adopted laws restricting smoking in public transportation vehicles, hospitals, medical offices, public offices and meeting rooms, schools, child care centers, libraries, theaters, restaurants, and specified areas of sports arenas. Anti-smoking laws and ordinances often carry minor civil penalties.
- **LO13** To protect and preserve the public's interest in natural wildlife resources, states regulate the taking of wildlife and fish, but the federal government has jurisdiction to enforce the Migratory Bird Act (MBA) and migratory bird treaties. In 1986 Congress inserted the word "knowingly" into the act, providing criminal sanctions. Most wildlife and fish statutes proscribe strict liability offenses, but if a law includes terms such as "willfully" or "knowingly," the prosecution must prove the defendant's intent. The Federal Endangered Species Act of 1973 (ESA) is designed to conserve ecosystems by preserving wildlife, fish, and plants. The law prohibits specific acts regarding endangered species. Enforcement is largely through civil penalties, but criminal liability is imposed against anyone who knowingly violates regulations issued under the act.

Key Terms

environmental crime A violation of a criminal provision of an environmental statute such as the Clean Water Act, the Clean Water Act, the Refuse Act, and so forth.

littering The crime of disposing of garbage or other waste material along a public street or road, or in public parks, beaches, or waterways.

antismoking laws State statutes or local ordinances prohibiting or restricting smoking in all or specified public places.

noise ordinances Local laws restricting the making of excessive noise.

poaching Taking of game illegally, either by hunting protected species, hunting out of season, hunting in areas in which hunting is prohibited, or violating restrictions as to the number or size of animals that may be taken.

strict liability Criminal responsibility based solely on the commission of a prohibited act.

Food, Drug, and Cosmetic Act (FDCA) Federal law that prohibits traffic in food, drugs, and cosmetics prepared or handled under unsanitary circumstances or under conditions that render them injurious to health.

regulatory offenses Criminal offenses of statutory origin dealing with public health and the environment. The term is also used to denote noncriminal violations of regulations promulgated by government agencies in the executive branch.

negligence standard The basic standard for liability in civil cases: the failure to exercise ordinary care or caution.

responsible corporate officer A person who holds a supervisory position in an organization, and may be subject to criminal liability for regulatory offenses committed by subordinates.

zoning Local laws regulating the use of land.

Environmental Protection Agency (EPA) Independent agency within the executive branch of the national government with principal responsibility for the enforcement of federal environmental laws, promulgation of environmental regulations, and administration of environmental programs.

Rivers and Harbors Act The first major environmental statute enacted by Congress. The Act authorizes the Army Corps of Engineers to regulate the use of the navigable waters of the United States.

Refuse Act A section of the Rivers and Harbors Act that makes it unlawful to discharge refuse matter of any kind into any navigable water of the United States.

Clean Air Act A federal statute designed to enhance the quality of the air by regulating, deterring, and penalizing polluters.

Clean Water Act A federal statute designed to enhance the quality of bodies of public water by regulating, deterring, and penalizing polluters.

Resource Conservation and Recovery Act (RCRA) The major federal law dealing with the transportation, storage, and disposal of hazardous waste.

Toxic Substances Control Act Federal statute authorizing the Environmental Protection Agency to prohibit the manufacture, distribution, or use of chemicals that present unreasonable risks to the environment and to regulate the disposal of such chemicals.

Comprehensive Environmental Response, Compensation, and Liability Act (CERCLA) Federal statute commonly known as the Superfund Law. Its purpose is to finance cleanup and provide for civil suits by citizens. The act also imposes reporting requirements for the collection and disposal of solid wastes. CERCLA imposes criminal penalties on those who act in a supervisory capacity and who are in a position to detect, prevent, and abate a release of hazardous substances.

point source Any discernible, confined, and discrete conveyance from which pollutants are or may be discharged.

Quiet Communities Act Federal law enacted in 1978 to protect the environment against noise pollution.

Migratory Bird Act Federal law protecting certain species of migratory birds from hunting within the United States and its territories.

Endangered Species Act Federal statute designed to conserve ecosystems by preserving wildlife, fish, and plants. The act imposes criminal penalties against any person who knowingly violates regulations issued under the act.

Questions for Thought and Discussion

1. Are criminal sanctions essential to the effective enforcement of food, drug, and cosmetic laws?
2. Should the term "responsible corporate officer" be explicitly defined by statute, or should courts make this determination on a case-by-case basis?
3. Does your community impose criminal penalties for violations of zoning regulations? If so, are violations treated as strict liability offenses? Why is it often more effective for a local governmental body to seek injunctive relief against zoning violators?

4. Should efforts be made to formulate a model state code of environmental regulations?

5. Should environmental crimes that carry major penalties be strict liability offenses, or should prosecutors be required to prove that a defendant knowingly or willfully committed an offense?

6. Do you think hunting and fishing violations should be decriminalized and treated as civil infractions in the way that many states treat less serious traffic offenses? Give reasons for your view.

7. Can you describe some instances where it is advisable to seek injunctive relief rather than impose criminal penalties for violations of environmental laws?

8. Where smoking is prohibited by law in workplaces, restaurants, and bars, should violations be treated as civil or criminal infractions? What, if any, exceptions should be provided in such laws?

Problems for Discussion and Solution

1. Two boys died of asphyxiation after playing in a dumpster in which a toxic solvent was disposed of improperly. The solvent was placed in the dumpster by workers at a nearby industrial plant. Under which, if any, federal statute can the plant manager be prosecuted?

2. After purchasing an old automobile repair shop, Jerry Huxley hires a crew to clean up the shop. The crew finds numerous rusty unmarked cans containing unknown liquids. These cans, along with various other junk and garbage, are loaded onto the bed of Huxley's pickup truck and hauled to the county landfill. At the landfill, Huxley signs a form certifying that none of the cans contains any hazardous waste. Subsequently, Huxley is indicted under 42 U.S.C.A. § 6928(d)(1) for "knowingly transporting hazardous wastes, including various industrial solvents and petrochemicals, to an unpermitted facility." What will be Huxley's defense? Is that defense likely to be successful?

3. Mal Hocus decides to go bass fishing. Before putting his boat in the lake, he stops at a nearby fish camp to renew his fishing license. The proprietor informs him that she is out of license forms, but that a camp across the lake has them. Mal puts his boat in the water and heads across the lake. En route, he notices a group of boats anchored at a spot where he has had good luck in the past. Mal stops his boat but does not anchor. At the very moment he casts his lure for the first time, a state wildlife officer approaches in another boat. Upon discovering that Mal has no current license, the officer cites him for fishing without a license, a misdemeanor punishable by a $50 fine. When Mal protests that he was just about to obtain his license at the camp across the lake, the officer responds, "Tell it to the judge." Does Mal have a defense, or would he be better advised to simply mail in the fine?

4. Hoss Tile is arrested after police are called to the scene of a private social club where Tile is a member. The police are called because Tile refuses to extinguish his cigarette in the dining room and is becoming belligerent. He is charged with a misdemeanor under a new ordinance that prohibits smoking in "restaurants and other places of public accommodation other than those in which alcoholic beverages are sold for consumption on the premises." The club in which he was arrested does not sell or serve alcohol. How might Tile defend himself in this case?

5. The Acme Oil Refining Corporation operates several oil refineries along the Gulf Coast. For the last decade, Acme officials have known that a pipeline bringing crude oil into one of its refineries has been leaking and that as a result thousands of gallons of crude oil have leached into the ground and have contaminated the groundwater. During this time Acme took no action to rectify the problem, nor did it report the problem to the Environmental Protection Agency or any other regulatory agency. Now that the EPA has learned of the problem from a corporate "whistleblower," Acme is taking steps to repair the pipeline. In addition to announcing fines against Acme for violating its regulations, EPA is considering referring the matter to the Department of Justice for prosecution. Under what statute(s) could Acme Corporation or its corporate officers be prosecuted?

CHAPTER 12

Offenses against Public Order, Safety, and National Security

LEARNING OBJECTIVES

After reading this chapter, you should be able to explain . . .

1. how the common law defined breaches of the peace
2. how local, state, and federal laws define breaches of the peace today
3. why the common law criminalized vagrancy and why vagrancy laws have been declared unconstitutional
4. why laws governing loitering and panhandling and laws imposing curfews are controversial
5. why many jurisdictions have decriminalized traffic offenses
6. how gun control laws comport with the Second Amendment to the U.S. Constitution
7. why treason and sedition pose constitutional problems
8. how the modern criminal law has attempted to combat various forms of terrorism
9. why immigration offenses pose a serious problem for law enforcement today

CHAPTER OUTLINE

Key Terms

Questions for Thought and Discussion

Problems for Discussion and Solution

On the night of May 1, 2010, New York City police received a call from a street vendor about a vehicle parked in Times Square and emitting smoke. Upon arriving on the scene, police discovered a Nissan Pathfinder containing a crude bomb consisting of fireworks, cans of gasoline, and propane tanks. Times Square was evacuated while the bomb squad defused the device. Had the bomb exploded, as many as fifty people might have been killed and many more injured. After attempting to detonate the device, the perpetrator had escaped on foot, leaving behind his getaway car with the keys still in the ignition. It did not take long for the FBI to catch up to the would-be bomber. They arrested him two days later at JFK Airport as he was boarding a plane to the Middle East.

In June 2010, a thirty-year-old Pakistani American named Faisal Shahzad pleaded guilty in federal court to an indictment that charged, among other things, attempted use of a weapon of mass destruction, transportation of an explosive device, and conspiracy to commit an act of terrorism. Shahzad, the son of a Pakistani air force officer, had come to the United States when he was eighteen. After graduating from college, he worked as a financial analyst and lived what seemed to be a normal middle-class life in suburban Connecticut. But he became disillusioned with the West and angry at the United States for its actions in the Islamic world. He travelled to Pakistan for a year and affiliated with the Taliban. While in Pakistan he received weapons training and made a video in which he proclaimed, "You will see the Muslim war has just started, until Islam spreads war over the whole world." Upon returning to America, he began his efforts to commit a bombing in Times Square. On October 5, 2010, Shahzad was sentenced to life in prison

The Shahzad case is one of a string of terrorism cases in the United States in the decade since September 11, 2001. Terrorism-related offenses are crimes against public order, safety, and national security and thus are examined in this chapter along with many other much more prosaic offenses. Since 9/11 there have been a number of developments in the substantive criminal law relative to terrorism, including the controversial USA PATRIOT Act. Obviously, terrorism presents a formidable challenge to law enforcement, and combating terrorism strains our national commitment to civil rights and liberties. It is a problem that is likely to remain with us for decades to come.

Introduction

Government has a fundamental obligation to protect the public order and safety. The criminal law is one means by which government performs this function—by criminalizing acts that threaten society's interests in order and safety. Government is also obligated to protect the security of the nation itself. It does this primarily through its military capabilities and intelligence agencies, but the criminal law also plays a role in the protection of national security. Since September 11, 2001, protection of the homeland against acts of terrorism has become a high priority for the criminal law.

As with most basic criminal offenses, the crimes against public order and safety are rooted in the English common law. The common law recognized the right of the people to assemble peaceably for lawful purposes. Nevertheless, maintaining public order was given a high priority. To maintain order, the common law developed three misdemeanors: **unlawful assembly, rout,** and **riot**. If three or more persons met together with the intention of cooperating to disturb the public peace by doing an unlawful act, their gathering was considered an unlawful assembly. If they took steps to achieve their purpose, it was a rout, and if they actually executed their plans, they committed a riot.

Modern statutes have modified these common-law crimes somewhat. Today, the category of offenses known as **breaches of the peace** includes unlawful assembly, riot, **inciting a riot**, and **disorderly conduct**, as well as violations of noise ordinances. While these offenses are very important in carrying out the day-to-day peacekeeping function of the police, they do raise constitutional problems in certain instances. The First Amendment guarantees the rights of free expression and assembly. Of course, the exercise of these freedoms sometimes poses a threat to public order and safety. The line between what the Constitution protects and what the criminal law legitimately forbids can sometimes be difficult to perceive (see Chapter 3).

To discourage idleness, the common law also developed the offense of **vagrancy**, which was the crime of "going about without visible means of support." Historically, this offense allowed the police tremendous discretion in dealing with suspicious persons. Accordingly, it has been the subject of considerable controversy. Today, the offense of vagrancy has been largely supplanted by the modern offense of **loitering**, although it too is subject to criticism. Numerous vagrancy and loitering laws have been attacked as being excessively vague and therefore in violation of the constitutional requirement that criminal laws provide fair notice as to what specific conduct is prohibited.

Offenses against public order and safety also include **motor vehicle violations** and **weapons offenses,** which, while unknown to the common law, exist by virtue of modern legislation aimed at protecting the public safety. While there is little constitutional debate over traffic safety laws, weapons offenses are sometimes challenged under the Second Amendment to the Constitution, which protects the right to keep and bear arms. Today, there is a strident political debate taking place in this country on both the desirability and constitutionality of **gun control laws**.

In the wake of the horrific terrorist attacks of September 11, 2001, offenses against national security have taken on renewed importance. Many offenses that were far less prominent before 9/11, such as sabotage, espionage, and sedition, are receiving renewed attention. So too are immigration offenses, not only due to the threat of terrorists entering the country illegally but also because in the last two decades the country has experienced an enormous wave of unlawful immigrants, primarily coming across the Mexican border.

The USA PATRIOT Act, enacted shortly after 9/11 and essentially reauthorized in 2006, has updated many federal criminal laws by relating new technologies to new terrorist threats. In interpreting these laws, the courts will bear the responsibility of balancing the need to effectively combat terrorism against the need to preserve the freedoms and due process of law guaranteed by the U.S. Constitution.

Breaches of the Peace

In the United States, the responsibility for maintaining public order and peace rests primarily with state and local governments, although the federal government has a significant role as well. A variety of state statutes and local ordinances prohibit unlawful assemblies, riots, and disorderly conduct. Control of unlawful assemblies and riots is aimed at group behavior, whereas laws proscribing disorderly conduct are aimed at both group and individual behavior. By enforcing laws prohibiting disorderly conduct, state and local governments attempt to prevent such undesirable conduct as violent and tumultuous behavior, excessive noise, offensive language and gestures, actions impeding movement of persons on public sidewalks and roads, and disturbances of lawfully conducted meetings.

On the other hand, the First Amendment to the U.S. Constitution guarantees citizens the rights of free speech and free assembly in the public forum. Courts must carefully weigh the community's interests in maintaining order and peace against these fundamental freedoms. The exercise of freedom of speech and assembly in the public forum may be restricted only where necessary to achieve a compelling public interest. *United States v. Grace*, 461 U.S. 171, 103 S.Ct. 1702, 75 L.Ed.2d 736 (1983).

Unlawful Assembly and Riot

In *State v. Mast*, reproduced on the companion website, a Missouri appellate court upholds a defendant's conviction for unlawful assembly and refusal to disperse.

Most states have enacted statutes proscribing unlawful assemblies and riots. For example, the Indiana Code defines unlawful assembly as "an assembly of five or more persons whose common object is to commit an unlawful act, or to commit a lawful act by unlawful means." West's Ann. Ind. Code § 35-45–1–1. It further defines tumultuous conduct as "conduct that results in, or is likely to result in, serious bodily injury to a person or substantial damage to property." West's Ann. Ind. Code § 35-45-1-1. Under the Indiana Code, a person who is a "member of an unlawful assembly who recklessly, knowingly, or intentionally engages in tumultuous conduct commits rioting." Under Indiana law, the offense is punishable as a misdemeanor unless committed while armed with a deadly weapon, in which case it becomes a felony. West's Ann. Ind. Code § 35-45-1-2.

The Federal Anti-Riot Act

Historically, federal statutes have made it a crime to riot. However, the controversy over the Vietnam War, racial unrest, poverty, and a host of other social ills during the1960s became catalysts for riotous behavior beyond proportions previously experienced. To cope better with riots, Congress enacted the **Federal Anti-Riot Act** of 1968. The act applies to persons who travel in or use any facility of interstate and foreign commerce. It proscribes interstate travel and use of the mail, telegraph, telephone, radio, or television with intent to incite, encourage, participate in, or carry on a riot; or to aid or abet any person in inciting or participating in a riot or committing any act of violence in furtherance of a riot. 18 U.S.C.A. § 2101(a). The act comprehensively defines riot by stating that

> the term "riot" means a public disturbance involving (1) an act or acts of violence by one or more persons part of an assemblage of three or more persons, which act or acts shall constitute a clear and present danger of, or shall result in, damage or injury to the property of any other person or to the person of any other individual or (2) a threat or threats of the commission of an act or acts of violence by one or more persons part of an assemblage of three or more persons having, individually or collectively, the ability of immediate execution of such threat or threats, where the performance of the threatened act or acts of violence would constitute a clear and present danger of, or would result in, damage or injury to the property of any other person or to the person of any other individual. 18 U.S.C.A. § 2102(a).

The federal law defines "to incite a riot" by explaining that

Evidence Sustaining a Conviction for Inciting a Riot

A jury convicted Powell of inciting a riot. He appealed, challenging the sufficiency of the evidence. The jury heard evidence that after fourteen-year-old Anderson rejected Powell's request to have sex with him, Powell threatened to have his eighteen-year-old girlfriend, Johnson, beat her. Powell then informed Johnson that Anderson had been talking about her and suggested that Johnson go up the street to meet Anderson. As Anderson and her friends Lattimore and Faust walked down the street, Johnson cursed them, and at Powell's direction, Johnson jumped on Lattimore's back and began pulling her hair and punching her. When Lattimore's sister attempted to break up the fight, Powell insisted on keeping the fight going and shoved away everyone who tried to stop it. Before Faust returned with Lattimore's mother and uncle, who ended the fight, between twenty-five and sixty onlookers had gathered.

In affirming Powell's conviction, the Georgia Court of Appeals noted that the essential elements of inciting a riot are (1) engaging in conduct which urges, counsels, or advises others to riot; (2) with intent to riot; and (3) at a time and place and under circumstances which produce a clear and present danger of a riot. OCGA § 16–11–31(a). The court observed that Powell encouraged Johnson to confront Anderson and that after Johnson attacked Lattimore, Powell directed Johnson's moves and yelled, "You ought to be beating this bitch" and "Don't stop the fight, the bitch got too much mouth." Further, Powell shoved and bullied several people in the gathering crowd in order to prevent any interference with the fight.

Powell v. State, 462 S.E.2d447 (Ga. App. 1995).

the term "to incite a riot," or "to organize, promote, encourage, participate in, or carry on a riot," includes, but is not limited to, urging or instigating other persons to riot, but shall not be deemed to mean the mere oral or written (1) advocacy of ideas or (2) expression of belief, not involving advocacy of any act or acts of violence or assertion of the rightness of, or the right to commit, any such act or acts. 18 U.S.C.A. § 2102(b).

In 1972 the U.S. Court of Appeals for the Seventh Circuit held that the Anti-Riot Act is not unconstitutionally vague or overbroad in relation to the First Amendment. *United States v. Dellinger*, 472 F.2d 340 (7th Cir. 1972).

Disorderly Conduct

Closely related to statutes prohibiting unlawful assembly and riot are laws making disorderly conduct an offense. The Indiana Code concisely, yet comprehensively, proscribes disorderly conduct by providing that

[a] person who recklessly, knowingly or intentionally: (1) engages in fighting or in tumultuous conduct; (2) makes unreasonable noise and continues to do so after being asked to stop; (3) disrupts a lawful assembly of persons; commits disorderly conduct.... West's Ann. Ind. Code § 35-45-1-3.

In *Commonwealth v. Young*, which is reproduced on the companion website, a Pennsylvania court upholds a defendant's conviction for disorderly conduct.

Statutes and ordinances similar to those in Indiana are found in virtually every state. There is no constitutional problem when such laws are applied to conduct that is violent or threatens to produce imminent lawless action. *Brandenburg v. Ohio*, 395 U.S. 444, 89 S.Ct. 1827, 23 L.Ed.2d 430 (1969). Nor is there any constitutional barrier against applying such statutes to the utterance of fighting words. *Chaplinsky v. New Hampshire*, 315 U.S. 568, 571, 62 S.Ct. 766, 769, 86 L.Ed. 1031, 1035 (1942). However, the Constitution "does not permit a State to make criminal the peaceful expression of unpopular views." *Edwards v. South Carolina*, 372 U.S. 229, 237, 83 S.Ct. 680, 684, 9 L.Ed.2d 697, 703 (1963). (For more discussion of these First Amendment concepts, see Chapter 3.)

In *Edwards v. South Carolina*, supra, the Supreme Court reviewed a set of convictions that stemmed from a civil rights protest. On the morning of March 2, 1961, a large group of black students congregated on the lawn of the statehouse in Columbia, South Carolina, to protest the state's segregation laws. Speeches were made; songs were sung. The students responded by clapping and stamping their feet. A large crowd of onlookers gathered nearby. Nobody among the crowd caused or threatened any trouble, and there was no obstruction of pedestrian or vehicular traffic. A contingent of thirty or more police officers was present to meet any foreseeable possibility of disorder. After refusing to obey a police order to disperse, many of the students were arrested and found guilty of breach of the peace. In reversing their convictions, the U.S. Supreme Court said the following:

> These petitioners were convicted of an offense as to be, in the words of the South Carolina Supreme Court, 'not susceptible of exact definition.' And they were convicted upon evidence which showed no more than that the opinions which they were peaceably expressing were sufficiently opposed to the views of the majority of the community to attract a crowd and necessitate police protection. . . . The Fourteenth Amendment does not permit a State to make criminal the peaceful expression of unpopular views. 372 U.S. at 237, 83 S.Ct. at 684, 9 L.Ed.2d at 703.

The U.S. Supreme Court's decisions in *Edwards v. South Carolina* and *Adderley v. Florida* are excerpted on the companion website.

It is instructive to compare *Edwards v. South Carolina* with *Adderley v. Florida*, 385 U.S. 39, 87 S.Ct. 242, 17 L.Ed.2d 149 (1966). Here the Supreme Court affirmed the convictions of African American student protesters who blocked a driveway to the local jail. Emphasizing the use of the driveway for vehicles providing service to the jail, the Supreme Court observed, "The State, no less than a private owner of property, has power to preserve the property under its control for the use to which it is lawfully dedicated." 385 U.S. at 47, 87 S.Ct. at 247, 17 L.Ed.2d at 156.

In *People v. Barron*, 808 N.E.2d 1051 (Ill. App. 2004) the defendant was convicted of disorderly conduct for violating an Illinois statute proscribing specific categories of conduct, 720 ILCS 5/26-1(a)(3, which provided:

> A person commits disorderly conduct when he knowingly . . . [t]ransmits or causes to be transmitted in any manner to another a false alarm to the effect that a bomb or other explosive of any nature . . . is concealed in such place that its explosion or release would endanger human life, knowing at the time of such transmission that there is no reasonable ground for believing that such bomb . . . is concealed in such place.

The evidence at the defendant's trial disclosed that although the defendant was not actually in possession of a concealed explosive device, he informed two airline ticket agents that he had a bomb in his shoe. He claimed the ticket agents knew he was joking; however, one of the agents called the police, who used bomb-searching dogs and arrested the defendant. On appeal, the defendant argued that section 26-1(a)(3) requires that, once transmitted, the alarm must cause actual fear in the mind of the listener. In a case of first impression, the court rejected his arguments and held that the crime of disorderly conduct is complete upon the transmission of a false alarm to another person, regardless of the effect the false alarm has upon the individual who receives it. The court affirmed the defendant's conviction.

In *Colten v. Kentucky*, 407 U.S. 104, 92 S.Ct. 1953, 32 L.Ed.2d 584 (1972), the Supreme Court upheld a conviction for disorderly conduct arising from a confrontation between a police officer and a student protester. After conducting a political demonstration, several students got into their cars and formed an entourage. A police officer stopped one of the vehicles after noting that its license plate had expired. The other cars in the group were also pulled over. One of the students approached the officer to find out what was wrong. After explaining the situation, the officer asked the student to leave. The student refused to do so and was arrested for violating section 437.016(1)(f) of the Kentucky Revised Statutes, which provided that a person was guilty of disorderly conduct "if, with intent to cause public inconvenience, annoyance or alarm, or recklessly creating a risk thereof," he "congregates with other persons in a public place and refuses to comply with a lawful order of the police to disperse." A conviction for disorderly conduct was upheld by the Kentucky Court of Appeals. *Colten v. Commonwealth*, 467 S.W.2d 374 (Ky. 1971). In upholding the conviction, the U.S. Supreme Court said this:

> As the Kentucky statute was construed by the state court, . . . a crime is committed only where there is no *bona fide* intention to exercise a constitutional right—in which event, by definition, the statute infringes no protected speech or conduct—or where the interest so clearly outweighs the collective interest sought to be asserted that the latter must be deemed to be insubstantial. . . . Individuals may not be convicted under the Kentucky statute merely for expressing unpopular or annoying ideas. The statute comes into operation only when the individual's interest in expression, judged in the light of all relevant factors, is 'minuscule' compared to a particular public interest in preventing that expression or conduct at that time and place. 407 U.S. at 111, 92 S.Ct. at 1958, 32 L.Ed.2d at 590.

In a similar case, *Hess v. Indiana*, 414 U.S. 105, 94 S.Ct. 326, 38 L.Ed.2d 303 (1973), the Supreme Court reversed a conviction of a student protester who had been arrested after the sheriff heard him shout, "We'll take the fucking street later." The Supreme Court found that the defendant's language did not amount to fighting words or represent imminent lawless action.

In *Cavazos v. State*, 455 N.E.2d 618 (Ind. App. 1983), an Indiana appellate court found that a defendant calling a police officer an "asshole" and continuing to debate

CASE-IN-POINT

Allegations of Disorderly Conduct and Inciting a Riot

Reggie Upshaw was charged with disorderly conduct and inciting a riot. He moved to dismiss the charges, contending the complaint failed to allege facts from which it could be inferred that he intended to cause a riot or disturbance or to present a clear and present danger of creating unrest. The court found the complaint was supported by sworn allegations that shortly after the September 11, 2001, terrorist attacks on the World Trade Center, the defendant and several accomplices confronted a gathering street crowd in the vicinity of Times Square in New York City. They allegedly boasted that they supported the attacks and were disappointed the carnage had not been greater, yelling in the faces of the crowd, "We've got something for your asses." The complaint further alleged that the defendant and his accomplices refused to disperse after police officers asked them to do so. In ruling against the motion to dismiss, the court concluded that the defendant's remarks went beyond speech protected by the First Amendment and constituted a real threat of violence.

People v. Upshaw, 741 N.Y.S.2d 664 (N.Y. City Crim. Ct. 2002).

with him about the arrest of her brother was insufficient to support her conviction for disorderly conduct. The court reasoned that the defendant's words to the police officer did not constitute fighting words or fall within any of the other unprotected classes of speech.

In 1999 a Georgia appellate court reversed a defendant's conviction for disorderly conduct. The court held that although the defendant's statement to a female medic that she had "nice tits" was crude and socially unacceptable, such words were not such as to incite a breach of the peace. *Lundgren v. State*, 518 S.E.2d 908 (Ga. App. 1999). But vulgar language, when combined with physical action, may constitute disorderly conduct. In 1999 the Supreme Judicial Court of Maine affirmed a defendant's conviction for disorderly conduct where, in addition to the use of foul and vulgar language, the defendant, an emergency room patient, "head butted" a physician. *State v. McKenzie*, 605 A.2d 72 (Me. 1999).

Excessive Noise

Local governments often use disorderly conduct ordinances to control **excessive noise**. To sustain a conviction based on unreasonable noise, the prosecution must show that the speech at issue infringed on the peace and tranquility enjoyed by others. *Hooks v. State*, 660 N.E.2d 1076 (Ind. App. 1996). For example, the noise produced by a late-night party with a live band might be actionable under a breach of the peace ordinance, but only if the party is in fact disturbing the peace of the neighborhood. Courts are inclined to uphold the application of ordinances that proscribe making excessive noise in areas such as hospitals and nursing homes. Police officers responding to complaints about excessive noise usually first request that the offending party "turn it down." If this fails, the offender may be charged with a breach of the peace.

Vagrancy, Loitering, Curfews, and Panhandling

Elites in feudal England placed great emphasis on able-bodied serfs performing labor and not straying from their assigned tasks. This was motivated by both the need for laborers and the desire to prevent idle persons from becoming public charges. With the breakup of feudal estates, England found it necessary to prevent workers from moving from one area to another in search of improved working conditions. Thus, to regulate the economics of the populace, the common law developed the misdemeanor offense of vagrancy. The offense comprised three elements: (1) being without visible means of support, (2) being without employment, and (3) being able to work but refusing to do so. *Fenster v. Leary*, 229 N.E.2d 426 (N.Y. 1967). In sixteenth-century England, persons who loitered idly for three days were subject to punishment under the Enslavement Acts.

Eventually the emphasis shifted from merely punishing idleness toward the prevention of crime, as England enacted statutes defining vagrancy. The objective then became to protect the people and their property from persons considered potential criminals or simply regarded as undesirables. Thus, by the time the American colonists settled in their new environment, the concept of punishing vagrants had become firmly implanted, and the colonists found it to be a desirable way to prevent idleness and to outlaw conduct offensive to their social mores.

The American Approach to Vagrancy

During the 1800s, virtually all American states and most cities enacted statutes and ordinances punishing a wide variety of conduct as vagrancy. Statutory language was intentionally rather vague, presumably to allow police broad discretion to arrest persons they deemed undesirable to the community. Vagrancy laws not only proscribed such acts as disorderly conduct, begging, and loitering; they also criminalized the conditions of being poor, idle, or of bad reputation, or simply "wandering around without any lawful purpose." By 1865, Alabama's vagrancy statute included "runaways" and "stubborn servants." By making a person's status an offense, these laws ran counter to the historical concept that a crime consisted of the commission of an unlawful act or the failure to perform a required act. Frequently, vagrancy laws were directed against persons without the means to contest their validity or to challenge the application of such laws to them. Moreover, the U.S. Supreme Court had sanctioned these laws in 1837 by saying that

> [w]e think it [is] as competent and as necessary for a state to provide precautionary measures against the moral pestilence of paupers, vagabonds, and possibly convicts; as it is to guard against . . . physical pestilence. . . . *City of New York v. Miln*, 36 U.S. (11 Pet.) 102, 142, 9 L.Ed. 648, 664 (1837).

In the first half of the 1900s, arrests and convictions for vagrancy were common, as were appellate court decisions upholding convictions in a variety of circumstances. For example, in Minnesota a defendant's conviction for wandering about the streets with no place of abode and without giving a good account of himself was affirmed. *State v. Woods*, 163 N.W. 518 (Minn. 1917). In Virginia, an appellate court held that a defendant's conduct in consorting with gamblers and idlers constituted the offense of vagrancy. *Morgan v. Commonwealth*, 191 S.E. 791 (Va. 1937). Even a defendant's conduct as part of "a group of 4 or 5 suspicious men" at a saloon was, under the particular circumstances, held to be vagrancy. *State v. Carroll*, 30 A.2d 54 (N.J. 1943).

The wide range of vaguely proscribed conduct in vagrancy laws made them susceptible to arbitrary enforcement by law enforcement agencies. In their efforts to prevent crime and control "undesirables," these laws became somewhat of a catchall of the criminal justice system. Police commonly used them as a basis to arrest a suspect, who was then held pending investigation, or as a method of getting the suspect to confess. Vagrancy laws also furnished a convenient basis for police to justify a search incident to arrest as an exception to the warrant requirement of the Fourth Amendment.

By the 1950s, the vagrancy laws were enforced primarily against alcoholics and derelicts when they left the environs of "skid row" and ventured into the more respectable neighborhoods, where residents found their presence offensive. The constitutionality of the vagrancy laws was frequently challenged on grounds that they were vague, violated due process of law requirements, and exceeded the police power of the states. Such challenges were rejected by state and federal courts, which generally upheld the right of the legislature to define what constitutes being a vagrant. During the 1960s, however, a number of statutes defining a vagrant as a person "without visible means of support," who "wanders around the streets at late hours," or who "fails to give account of himself" were declared unconstitutional.

The Death Knell of Vagrancy Laws

In 1972 the U.S. Supreme Court issued an opinion that had a profound effect on the enforcement of vagrancy laws in the United States. *Papachristou v. City of Jacksonville*, 405 U.S. 156, 92 S.Ct. 839, 31 L.Ed.2d 110 (1972).

In Jacksonville, Florida, eight defendants were convicted under a municipal ordinance that broadly defined vagrancy and levied criminal penalties on violators of as many as ninety days in jail, a $500 fine, or both. The ordinance included language common to many of the statutes and ordinances extant at the time:

> Rogues and vagabonds, or dissolute persons who go about begging, common gamblers, persons who use juggling or unlawful games or plays, common drunkards, common night walkers, thieves, pilferers or pickpockets, traders in stolen property, lewd, wanton and lascivious persons, keepers of gambling places, common railers and brawlers, persons wandering or strolling around from place to place without any lawful purpose or object, habitual loafers, disorderly persons, persons neglecting all lawful business and habitually spending their time by frequenting houses of ill fame, gaming houses, or places where alcoholic beverages are sold or served, persons able to work but habitually living upon the earnings of their wives or minor children shall be deemed vagrants. . . . Quoted in *Papachristou*, 405 U.S. at 158–159, n. 1, 92 S.Ct. at 841, 31 L.Ed.2d at 112.

The Supreme Court's decision in *Papachristou v. City of Jacksonville* is excerpted on the companion website.

Speaking for a unanimous Supreme Court, Justice William O. Douglas said that the Jacksonville ordinance was void for vagueness, both in the sense that it "fails to give a person of ordinary intelligence fair notice that his contemplated conduct is forbidden by the statute and because it encourages arbitrary and erratic arrests and convictions." 405 U.S. at 162, 92 S.Ct. at 843, 31 L.Ed.2d at 115.

Despite the Supreme Court's ruling in *Papachristou*, the effects of the vagrancy ordinances lingered on. In 1968 a Nevada police officer arrested Lloyd Powell under a Henderson, Nevada, vagrancy ordinance. In a search incident to the arrest, the officer discovered a .38-caliber revolver with six spent cartridges in the cylinder. Laboratory analysis determined that the weapon had been used in a recent murder. Powell was convicted of second-degree murder, and although a federal court later declared the vagrancy ordinance unconstitutional, the use of the evidence against Powell, and his conviction for murder, were ultimately sustained. *Stone v. Powell*, 428 U.S. 465, 96 S.Ct. 3037, 49 LEd.2d 1067 (1976).

State legislatures and local governments continued to enact ordinances in an attempt to control conduct they deemed objectionable; however, courts have invalidated such laws when they criminalize a person's status (for example, homelessness or intoxication) as opposed to proscribing a person's actions, frequently on the ground that such laws are vague and lead to arbitrary enforcement. One state supreme court took the view that a vagrancy statute that made it an offense to be a habitual drunkard violated the constitutional prohibition against cruel and unusual punishment for punishing a person's status. *State v. Pugh*, 369 So.2d 1308 (La. 1979).

Loitering

After the Supreme Court's decision in *Papachristou*, a new generation of laws making loitering a crime came on the scene. These new laws are narrower and often focus on preventing such crimes as prostitution and drug dealing. Courts scrutinize these ordinances carefully because they often prohibit or restrict constitutionally protected activities. Some have met the same fate as the traditional vagrancy ordinances.

One such ordinance enacted by Akron, Ohio, made it an offense to loiter "for the purpose of engaging in drug-related activity." The ordinance then listed eleven factors that may be considered in determining whether such purpose is manifested. The Ohio Supreme Court found the ordinance to be unconstitutionally vague under both the federal and state constitutions because it did not give persons of ordinary intelligence a reasonable opportunity to know what conduct was prohibited. Moreover, the court held that the enumerated factors to be considered—for example, looking like a drug user, being in an area known for unlawful drug use, and so on—could well be innocent and constitutionally protected conduct. Finally, the court pointed out that the ordinance was flawed because it delegated matters to enforcement authorities without providing necessary objective standards. *Akron v. Rowland*, 618 N.E.2d 138 (Ohio 1993).

In 1992 the Nevada Supreme Court held that the Nevada statute and Las Vegas Municipal Code provision criminalizing "loitering" on private property when the person has "no lawful business with owners or occupant thereof" lacked guidelines to avoid arbitrary and discriminatory enforcement and were unconstitutionally vague under the Due Process Clauses of the federal and state constitutions. *State v. Richard*, 836 P.2d 622 (Nev. 1992).

Any ordinance that proscribes loitering without clearly defining the activities prohibited and without providing objective guidelines for enforcement is vulnerable to constitutional objections; however, courts have upheld loitering ordinances with a more narrow scope. For example, in 1989 the Oregon Supreme Court rejected a defendant's argument that the phrase "loiter in a manner and under circumstances manifesting the purpose of soliciting prostitution" did not meet the required constitutional standard of certainty. *City of Portland v. Levi*, 779 P.2d 192 (1989).

Police often use loitering ordinances and statutes to remove suspected drug dealers from the streets. At least one appellate court has approved this approach. See *Griffin v. State*, 479 S.E.2d 21 (Ga. App. 1996), where the court held that the sale of drugs on the streets violated a state loitering statute.

Chicago's Gang Loitering Ordinance

In 1992 the Chicago City Council enacted the "Gang Congregation Ordinance," which made it a criminal offense for gang members to loiter with one another in any public place "with no apparent purpose." The ordinance required police to order a group of people who were standing around "with no apparent purpose" to move along if an officer believed that at least one of them belonged to a street gang. Those who disregarded an order to disperse were subject to arrest. Some 45,000 people were arrested in the three years the ordinance was enforced before the Illinois Supreme Court struck down the ordinance as violating due process of law by giving the police too much discretion and impermissibly restricting personal liberty. *City of Chicago v. Morales*, 687 N.E.2d 53 (Ill. 1997).

On review, the Supreme Court agreed with the Illinois Supreme Court. Writing for a divided Court, Justice John Paul Stevens criticized the ordinance for requiring police to tell people without inquiring about their purpose for standing around. He wrote that the ordinance "affords too much discretion to the police and too little notice to citizens who wish to use the public streets." *City of Chicago v. Morales*, 527 U.S. 41, 119 S.Ct. 1849, 144 L.Ed.2d 67 (1999).

The Supreme Court's decision in *Chicago v. Morales* is excerpted on the companion website.

To withstand constitutional attack, it appears that any ordinance proscribing loitering must, at a minimum, focus on a person's conduct and not a person's status or association, give fair notice as to what is proscribed, and afford a person an opportunity to explain his or her presence before being ordered to disperse.

Homeless Persons Sleeping On Public Property—The Florida Experience
In recent years Florida municipalities have attempted to control the problem of homeless persons sleeping on public property in attempts to remove such persons from the streets and parks. These attempts were preceded by a history of courts invalidating ordinances. In *State v. Penley*, 276 So.2d 180 (Fla. App. 1973), the court invalidated a city ordinance that provided, "No person shall sleep upon or in any street, park, wharf or other public place." The appellate court determined the ordinance was unconstitutional in that it might result in arbitrary and erratic arrests and convictions.

A decade later, in *City of Pompano Beach v. Capalbo*, 455 So.2d 468 (Fla. App. 1984), another Florida appellate court reviewed a municipal ordinance that provided, "It shall be unlawful for any person to lodge or sleep in, on, or about any automobile, truck, camping or recreational vehicle or similar vehicle in any public street, public way, right of way, parking lot or other public property, within the limits of the city." The court found the ordinance void for vagueness "because it leaves in the unbridled discretion of the police officer whether or not to arrest one asleep in a motor vehicle on a public street or way or in a parking lot. A wide range of persons may violate [the ordinance] from the tired child asleep in his car-seat while a parent drives or while the car is parked, to the alternate long-distance driver asleep in the bunk of a moving or parked tractor-trailer, to the tired or inebriated driver who has . . . chosen to go to sleep in his parked car rather than take his life or others' lives in his hands." 455 So.2d at 470.

Against this background, section 43.52 of the city of Orlando's Code prohibited "camping" on public property, which was defined to include, among other things, "sleeping out-of-doors." After James Joel, a homeless person, was arrested for violating the ordinance, he filed suit against the city, contending the ordinance violated his rights under the Fifth, Eighth, and Fourteenth Amendments to the U.S. Constitution. He contended the ordinance (1) encouraged discriminatory, oppressive, and arbitrary enforcement, (2) was unconstitutionally vague, (3) bore no rational relationship to a legitimate governmental purpose, (4) violated his right to travel, and (5) violated his right to be free from cruel and unusual punishment. He sought a declaratory judgment, injunctive relief, and monetary damages under 42 U.S.C.A. § 1983. The federal district court ruled in favor of the city, and Joel appealed. On appeal, the U.S. Court of Appeals affirmed, noting the ordinance was rationally related to the city's interest in promoting aesthetics, sanitation, public health, and safety and did not violate equal protection rights of the homeless, notwithstanding that it may have had disproportionate impact on homeless persons. *Joel v. City of Orlando*, 232 F.3d 1353 (11th Cir. 2000).

Curfews

In an attempt to combat juvenile crime and protect children by keeping them off the streets at night, most large cities and many counties have enacted **curfew ordinances**. While restrictions vary considerably, most curfew laws define juveniles as unmarried persons under age eighteen and prohibit them from being on public streets or in other public places from midnight to 6:00 A.M. unless accompanied by a parent or guardian or another adult approved by the juvenile's parent or guardian. Many curfew ordinances provide that parents and guardians violate the ordinance if they knowingly allow their child to commit a violation. Curfew laws often provide exceptions concerning work, school and civic events, travel, and emergencies.

Considerable litigation has ensued concerning the validity of curfews. Those who seek to sustain them argue that a juvenile curfew is a valid exercise of the government's police power. They liken the curfew regulations to requirements that minors are required to attend school, are prohibited from purchasing alcoholic beverages, and are subject to restrictions on operation of motor vehicles. Challengers contend that curfew regulations are vague and violate First Amendment rights of association, abridge Fourth Amendment rights to be free from unreasonable detention, deny juveniles the equal protection of the law, and interfere with parental rights.

In *City of Wadsworth v. Owens*, 536 N.E.2d 67 (Ohio 1987), a city ordinance prohibited anyone under age eighteen from being on the streets, sidewalks, or other public places during certain nighttime hours unless accompanied by a parent or some other responsible adult having the parent's permission. The court found the ordinance unconstitutionally overbroad, pointing out that it contained no exceptions, thereby restricting a minor's church, school, and work activities. Courts in New Jersey, Ohio, Hawaii, and the state of Washington have also found curfew ordinances unconstitutional. On the other hand, in *Panora v. Simmons*, 445 N.W.2d 363 (Iowa 1989), the Iowa Supreme Court upheld an ordinance making it unlawful for any minor to be or remain upon any street or in any public place between 10:00 P.M. and 5:00 A.M. The ordinance provided exceptions for a minor accompanied by a parent or other adult custodian and for a minor traveling between home and places of employment, and to church, civic, or school functions.

More recent curfew ordinances that have been upheld have included an expanded number of exceptions. For example, in May 1997, Pinellas Park, Florida, adopted a curfew ordinance along the lines described above. In addition to permitting a juvenile to be accompanied by a parent or an adult authorized by a custodial parent, the ordinance includes numerous exceptions such as when a juvenile is exercising First Amendment rights to attend religious, political, and governmental meetings or events sponsored by civic and governmental groups, during or going to and from lawful employment and school-sponsored or theme-park events, when on the sidewalk at home or at a neighbor's home with the neighbor's permission, or when involved in interstate travel. The trial court, applying a strict scrutiny test (see Chapter 3), invalidated the ordinance on the basis that it violates a juvenile's parents' fundamental right to raise their children without governmental intrusion. On appeal, the court applied a "heightened scrutiny" test and reversed the trial court's ruling, noting that the ordinance includes adequate exceptions to limit the scope of the curfew. *State v. T.M.*, 761 So.2d 1140 (Fla. App. 2000). On review, the Florida Supreme Court ruled that the appellate court had erred in applying "heightened scrutiny" test and remanded the case to the appellate court to apply a "strict standard" in reviewing the ordinance. *T.M. v. State*, 784 So.2d 442 (Fla. 2001). On remand, the district court of appeals held that the city's juvenile curfew ordinance was unconstitutional under the "strict scrutiny test." 832 So.2d 118 (Fla. App. 2002).

Courts in Texas, Virginia, and Washington, D.C., have also upheld curfew ordinances. Those people who oppose curfews recognize the authority of parents to impose restrictions, but they claim the government should not intrude into the parental sphere. They also point to studies showing no correlation between arrests for curfew violations (which are quite common) and the incidence of juvenile crime. The American Civil Liberties Union (ACLU) has been very active in attacking curfew laws in the courts. In excerpts from a March 2009 letter to the Wisconsin Equal Opportunity Commission, explaining its position on juvenile curfews, the ACLU observed,

Juvenile curfew laws inherently discriminate against young people and give police unlimited discretion to give citations or even arrest youth engaged in otherwise noncriminal or constitutionally protected freedoms. Limits on young people's freedom of movement should come from parents, not police.

Despite the controversial nature of juvenile curfews, law enforcement officials and local governing bodies overwhelmingly support these measures. They are likely to remain on the scene as long as juvenile crime continues to plague our nation's cities, although to be upheld the ordinances must recognize reasonable exceptions.

Emergency Curfews

Although most curfews involve restrictions on juveniles, the law recognizes that governments can also impose curfews to cope with emergencies. Curfews restrict a person's right of movement, but the Supreme Court has stated that the constitutional right to travel may be legitimately curtailed when a community has been ravaged by flood, fire, or disease and its safety and welfare are threatened. *Zemel v. Rusk*, 381 U.S. 1, 85 S.Ct. 1271, 14 L.Ed.2d 179 (1965).

State laws usually grant local governments the authority to impose limited curfews during emergencies where floods, fires, riots, looting, and other situations threaten the safety and welfare of a community. West's Ann. Cal. Gov. Code § 8634 is illustrative. It provides:

> During a local emergency the governing body of a political subdivision, or officials designated thereby, may promulgate orders and regulations necessary to provide for the protection of life and property, including orders or regulations imposing a curfew within designated boundaries where necessary to preserve the public order and safety. Such orders and regulations and amendments and rescissions thereof shall be in writing and shall be given widespread publicity and notice.

Courts generally uphold the exercise of emergency powers by local governing bodies or their authorized representatives to declare a curfew where life and property are threatened, as long as the curfew regulations are reasonable. To be reasonable, curfew regulations must not be directed at any one class of persons, must not unduly restrict the right of expression, and must allow necessary exemptions.

In April 1992, widespread rioting, looting, and arson occurred in Los Angeles County following the jury verdict acquitting police officers in the Rodney King beating. Long Beach, California, imposed curfew regulations that prohibited anyone from being on the public streets and in public places between 7:00 P.M. and 6:00 A.M. so long as the emergency existed. The regulations were not directed at any particular class or group, regulated conduct and not the content of speech, exempted law enforcement officers and firefighters, and permitted arrest of only those who refused, after notice, to obey the curfew. A California appellate court upheld the curfew regulations. *In re Juan C*, 33 Cal.Rptr.2d 919 (Cal. App. 1994).

Panhandling

Before the Supreme Court's 1972 seminal decision in *Papachristou v. City of Jacksonville*, supra, vagrancy ordinances commonly included a prohibition on begging on public streets and sidewalks. Once catchall vagrancy ordinances were invalidated, cities began to look for new ways to prohibit begging, often called **panhandling**. Some local ordinances proscribe all begging on public ways; others prohibit "aggressive begging." Prohibitions against begging subordinate a beggar's right of expression on the public ways to a pedestrian's right to be left alone. The issue becomes whether the activity of begging is conduct that can be proscribed under local "police power" or whether such activity constitutes expression protected by the First Amendment. In some instances courts have analyzed the problem based on the "time, place, and manner" doctrine that guides the regulation of expressive conduct in the public forum (see the discussion in Chapter 3). The U.S. Supreme Court has held that government can regulate, but not prohibit, solicitation of funds for charities on public ways. *Village of Schaumburg v. Citizens for a Better Environment*, 444 U.S. 620, 100 S.Ct. 826, 63 L.Ed.2d 73 (1980). But the Court has not yet spoken directly on the issue of begging on public streets and sidewalks. Decisions from lower federal and state courts make it difficult to generalize as to whether such ordinances pass constitutional muster. Federal courts have held that any ordinance that restricts begging must be narrowly drawn to avoid conflict with the First Amendment.

In 1990 the U.S. Court of Appeals for the Second Circuit upheld a prohibition against begging and panhandling in the New York City subway system. The court observed that begging and panhandling in the city subway system was not expression protected by the First Amendment and that the regulations furthered the government's interest in preventing disruption and startling of passengers. *Young v. New York City Transit Authority*, 903 F.2d 146 (2d Cir. 1990). The U.S. Supreme Court denied certiorari. 498 U.S. 984, 111 S.Ct. 516, 112 L.Ed.2d 528 (1990). Seven years later, in *Loper v. New York City Police Dept.*, 999 F.2d 699, 705 (2d Cir. 1993), the same federal appellate court declared unconstitutional a New York statute that provided, "A person is guilty of loitering when he loiters, remains or wanders about in a public place for the purpose of begging. . . ." The court distinguished its 1990 decision in *Young v. New York City Transit Authority*, supra, saying, "[W]e observed that the prohibition on panhandling in the subway did not foreclose begging throughout all of New York City." *Young*, 903 F.2d at 160. The court found the regulation was neither content neutral nor justifiable as a proper time, place, or manner restriction on protected speech. Finally, the court found no compelling state interest served by excluding those who beg in a peaceful manner from communicating their messages of indigency to their fellow citizens.

State courts have commonly struck down local ordinances that prohibit begging on the public streets. For example, in *Ledford v. State*, 652 So.2d 1254 (Fla. App. 1995), a Florida appellate court struck down a St. Petersburg Beach ordinance that provided:

It shall be unlawful for any person to beg for money in the City while about or upon any public way, and it shall be unlawful for any persons to be in or upon any public way in the City for the purpose of begging money for themselves or any other person.

In holding the ordinance unconstitutional, the court stated,

[B]egging is communication entitled to some degree of First Amendment protection. . . . [S]ince the ordinance restricts speech on the 'public ways,' a traditional public forum, the regulation is subject to intense scrutiny. Such regulations survive only if: (1) they are narrowly drawn to achieve a compelling governmental interest; (2) the regulations are reasonable; and (3) the viewpoint is neutral. *Id.* at 1256.

In subjecting the ordinance to strict scrutiny, the court pointed out that it was vague and neither defined the terms "beg" or "begging" nor distinguished between "aggressive" and "passive" begging.

In recent years federal appellate courts have approved ordinances that restrict "aggressive panhandling." An Indianapolis ordinance restricting panhandling is illustrative. The ordinance prohibited solicitation of cash on any day after sunset or before sunrise. It also prohibited solicitation at a bus stop, near a public transportation vehicle or facility, at a parked or stopped vehicle, at a sidewalk cafe, or in an area within twenty feet in any direction of an automatic teller machine or entrance to a bank. It also made it unlawful to engage in an act of panhandling in an aggressive manner, which entails blocking the path of a person being solicited or the entrance to any building or vehicle; following behind, ahead, or alongside a person who walks away from the panhandler after being solicited; or using profane or abusive language, either during the solicitation or following a refusal to make a donation. In 2000 the U.S. Court of Appeals for the Seventh Circuit held that the ordinance was narrowly tailored to promote the city's legitimate interest in safety and convenience of its citizens on public streets and that it allowed feasible alternatives to reach both daytime and nighttime downtown crowds. In upholding the ordinance the court pointed out, "Under the ordinance, panhandlers may ply their craft vocally or in any manner they deem fit (except for those involving conduct defined as aggressive) during all the daylight hours on all of the city's public streets." *Gresham v. Peterson*, 225 F.3d 899, 907 (7th Cir. 2000).

Motor Vehicle Violations

States, and many municipalities, have adopted laws defining a wide range of motor vehicle violations. These are generally strict liability offenses; therefore, there is generally no requirement to prove criminal intent to find a defendant guilty of a traffic violation (see Chapter 4). Among other offenses, these laws proscribe speeding; failing to yield the right-of-way; failing to observe traffic officers, signs, and signals; and driving without required equipment.

By the 1980s, many states adopted a number of "model" laws, providing legal uniformity to the **rules of the road**. Such uniformity is highly desirable given the mobility of today's populace and the volume of traffic on the nation's highways. People driving along the nation's highways, often passing through several states on a single trip, would be ill served by variance in state traffic laws.

In *State v. Young*, reproduced on the companion website, the Court of Appeals of Ohio reverses a defendant's conviction for failure to yield the right-of-way.

When a driver is stopped for a traffic violation, police may observe conduct or evidence that gives rise to probable cause to conduct a search or make an arrest. Frequently drugs, alcohol, and weapons are discovered by police officers stopping automobiles for routine traffic violations.

Decriminalization of Traffic Offenses

Historically, traffic offenders were treated like persons committing other misdemeanors: they were arrested and required to post bond to avoid confinement pending the adjudication of their cases. Since the 1960s, most states and municipalities have decriminalized minor traffic offenses, which mean that these offenses are now considered **civil infractions** rather than misdemeanors. For example, consider the following excerpt from the Maine Revised Statutes, Title 29-A:

§ 103. Traffic infraction

1. Traffic infraction. A traffic infraction is not a crime. The penalty for a traffic infraction may not be deemed for any purpose a penal or criminal punishment.
2. Jury trial. There is no right to trial by jury for a traffic infraction.

3. Exclusive penalty. The exclusive penalty for a traffic infraction is a fine of not less than $25 nor more than $500, unless specifically authorized, or suspension of a license, or both.

In Maine and most other states, traffic violators are now commonly issued citations or "tickets" instead of being subject to arrest. Offenders may avoid a court appearance by simply paying a fine according to a predetermined schedule of fines. Of course, offenders may elect to contest the charge by appearing in the appropriate court, often a municipal court or **traffic court**. In addition to fines, most states assess "points" against a driver for traffic violations, and an accumulation of points can lead to suspension or revocation of a driver's license.

The **decriminalization of routine traffic offenses** has proved to be an expeditious and efficient means of maintaining discipline and order on the public thoroughfares. Under most traffic codes, however, the more serious motor vehicle offenses—such as driving while intoxicated, eluding a police officer, and reckless driving—are still defined as misdemeanors, and offenders are subject to arrest.

Seat Belts, Cell Phones, and Text Messaging

During the 1980s and the 1990s many state legislatures enacted **mandatory seat belt laws** and **mandatory child restraint laws**. Such laws usually require a violator to pay a small fine and have generally been accepted by the driving public and upheld by the courts. But it came as a surprise to many observers when the Supreme Court in 2001 upheld a custodial arrest for the violation of a seat-belt law. A police officer in Lago Vista, Texas, arrested Gail Atwater for driving without wearing a seat belt as required by Texas law. The law provided for punishment by payment of a fine, and police officers had discretion to issue citations to violators. Instead of simply issuing a citation, the officer arrested and detained Atwater in jail. The Court held the warrantless custodial arrest did not violate Atwater's Fourth Amendment rights. *Atwater v. City of Lago Vista*, 532 U.S. 318, 121 S.Ct. 1536, 149 L.Ed.2d 549 (2001). Dissenting, Justice Sandra Day O'Connor contended the majority "cloaks the pointless indignity that Gail Atwater suffered with the mantle of reasonableness." 532 U.S. at 373, 3121 S.Ct. at 1567, 149 L.Ed.2d at 589 (2001).

By 2000 state legislatures had begun to express concern that using a cell phone had become a mental and visual distraction from driving. In 2001 New York enacted the first prohibitory law. McKinney's Vehicle and Traffic Law § 1225-c provides:

2. (a) Except as otherwise provided in this section, no person shall operate a motor vehicle upon a public highway while using a mobile telephone to engage in a call while such vehicle is in motion.
(b) An operator of a motor vehicle who holds a mobile telephone to, or in the immediate proximity of his or her ear while such vehicle is in motion is presumed to be engaging in a call within the meaning of this section. The presumption established by this subdivision is rebuttable by evidence tending to show that the operator was not engaged in a call. The law makes exceptions for use of mobile phones in emergency communications; by fire, police, and other persons in the performance of official duties; and for use of a hands-free mobile phone. A violation of the statute is treated as a traffic infraction and is punishable by a fine not to exceed $100.

In an initial assault on the statute, a New York Justice Court upheld its constitutionality. *People v. Neville*, 737 N.Y.S.2d 251 (N.Y. Just. Ct. 2002). But the law has been held not to apply to a parking lot in a public shopping center because such property does not qualify as a "public highway" under the above-quoted statute. *People v. Moore*, 765 N.Y.S.2d 218 (N.Y. Just. Ct. 2003).

In 2004 New Jersey became the second state to ban the use of handheld cell phones while driving, and by 2008 four states had enacted laws making the use of a cell phone while driving a primary offense—an offense where an officer may issue a traffic ticket irrespective of any other traffic violation taking place. Legislators in other states are considering similar proposals. In January 2009, the National Safety Council called on motorists to stop using cell phones and messaging devices while driving, and urged legislators in all fifty states and the District of Columbia to pass laws banning that behavior.

Another recent advance in communications technology is text messaging, which has become extremely popular among young people. But it has also brought problems when drivers of motor vehicles engage in text messaging. Some regulation was inevitable. Washington became the first state to make text messaging by drivers a traffic infraction. Effective January 2, 2008, a person operating a moving motor vehicle in that state who, by means of an electronic wireless communications device, other than a voice-activated global positioning or navigation system, sends, reads, or writes a text message, is guilty of a traffic infraction. West's RCWA 46.61.668. California's Wireless Communications Device Law, effective January 1, 2009, makes it a traffic infraction to write, send, or read a text-based communication on an electronic wireless communications device, such as a cell phone, while driving a motor vehicle. West's Ann. Cal. Vehicle Code § 23123.5. These laws include certain emergency exceptions.

The Governors Highway Safety Association has a useful reference. Its website (http://www.ghsa.org/html/stateinfo/laws/cellphone_laws.html) provides a state-by-state review of laws affecting the use of cell phones and text messaging.

Weapons Offenses

Firearms are commonly used in the perpetration of serious crimes. Although their incidence has receded somewhat in recent years, more than 300,000 murders, robberies, and assaults in the United States were known to have been committed with firearms in 2005 alone (see Figure 12.1). For this reason, governing bodies have enacted laws restricting access to and limiting use of firearms. The Second Amendment to the U.S. Constitution provides that "a well regulated Militia, being necessary to the security of a free state, the right of the people to keep and bear Arms, shall not be infringed." Nevertheless, there are numerous state and federal statutory prohibitions against the manufacture, sale, possession, and use of firearms and other weapons.

The Meaning of the Second Amendment

In 1939 and again in 1980 the Supreme Court said that the Second Amendment protects the keeping and bearing of arms only in the context of a **well-regulated militia**. See *United States v. Miller*, 307 U.S. 174, 59 S.Ct. 816, 83 L.Ed. 1206 (1939); *Lewis v. United States*, 445 U.S. 55, 100 S.Ct. 915, 63 L.Ed.2d 198 (1980). But in *District of Columbia v. Heller*, 554 U.S. 570, 128 S.Ct. 2783, 171 L.Ed.2d 637 (2008), the Court reversed course and declared that the Second Amendment does protect a personal right to possess a firearm for "traditionally lawful purposes" irrespective of one's service in any militia. In *Heller* the Court struck down a District of Columbia ordinance

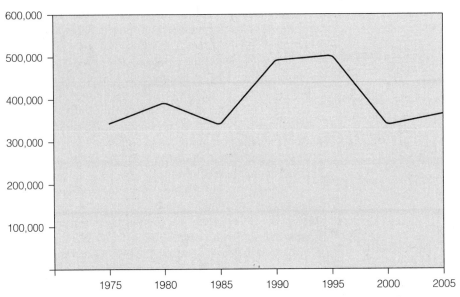

FIGURE 12.1 Number of Murders, Robberies, and Assaults Committed with Firearms, 1975–2005. Source: U.S. Department of Justice, Federal Bureau of Investigation, *Uniform Crime Reports 2005.*

effectively prohibiting the possession of handguns, even in the home. Writing for a sharply divided Court, Justice Antonin Scalia observed,

> Undoubtedly some think that the Second Amendment is outmoded in a society where our standing army is the pride of our Nation, where well-trained police forces provide personal security, and where gun violence is a serious problem. That is perhaps debatable, but what is not debatable is that it is not thé role of this Court to pronounce the Second Amendment extinct. 554 U.S. at 636, 128 S.Ct. at 2822, 171 L.Ed.2d at 684.

However, Justice Scalia noted that "nothing in our opinion should be taken to cast doubt on longstanding prohibitions on the possession of firearms by felons and the mentally ill, or laws forbidding the carrying of firearms in sensitive places such as schools and government buildings, or laws imposing conditions and qualifications on the commercial sale of arms." 554 U.S. at 626, 128 S.Ct. at 2816, 171 L.Ed.2d at 678.

As we mentioned in Chapter 3, the Supreme Court in 2010 reaffirmed its *Heller* decision and also held that the Second Amendment applies to the state and local governments via the Due Process Clause of the Fourteenth Amendment. *McDonald v. Chicago*, 561 U.S. ___, 130 S.Ct. 3020, 177 L. Ed. 2d 894 (2010). This means that state and local gun control laws are now subject to challenge as infringements of the federal constitutional right to keep and bear arms. However, in *McDonald*, as in *Heller*, the Court made clear that the Second Amendment allows for the reasonable regulations of firearms. Clearly, the Court's decisions in *Heller* and *McDonald* have set the stage for widespread legal challenges to federal, state, and local gun control measures.

The Supreme Court's decision in *District of Columbia v. Heller* is excerpted on the companion website.

State Gun Laws

Under Iowa law, any unauthorized person who knowingly possesses an "offensive weapon" commits a class D felony, I.C.A. § 724.3. "Offensive weapons" include machine guns, short-barreled rifles and shotguns, bombs, grenades, mines, poison gases, ballistic knives, bullets, and projectiles containing any explosive mixtures or chemical compounds. Section 724.1. The statute makes exceptions for peace officers and certain other instances. In *State v. Winders*, 366 N.W.2d 193 (Iowa App. 1985), the court held that the term "knowingly" in section 724.3 merely requires that the defendant had knowledge that he or she possessed a weapon within the general meaning of such term, rather than knowledge that he or she possessed an "offensive weapon" as statutorily defined. "To hold otherwise," the court said, "would only serve to undermine the very purpose of the provision in regulating possession of weapons in the interest of public safety." 366 N.W.2d at 196.

States commonly enact statutes making it unlawful to carry a **concealed weapon**. Iowa law stipulates that "A person who goes armed with a dangerous weapon concealed on or about the person, or who, within the limits of any city, goes armed with a pistol or revolver, or any loaded firearm of any kind, whether concealed or not, or who knowingly carries or transports in a vehicle a pistol or revolver, commits an aggravated misdemeanor." I.C.A. § 724.4. "A 'dangerous weapon' is any instrument or device designed primarily for use in inflicting death or injury upon a human being or animal, and which is capable of inflicting death upon a human being when used in the manner for which it was designed." *State v. Mitchell*, 371 N.W.2d 432 (Iowa App. 1985). Exceptions include peace officers whose duties require carrying weapons and members of the armed forces whose members are required to carry weapons.

Most laws define a concealed weapon as one that is carried on or about a person in such a manner as to conceal it from the ordinary sight of another person. It follows that a defendant was properly convicted of carrying a concealed weapon in her purse when it was disclosed by a metal detector at a courthouse. *Schaaf v. Commonwealth*, 258 S.E.2d 574 (Va. 1979). But more often, litigation involves less than absolute concealment. For example, a Georgia appellate court ruled that even though the handle of a pistol tucked in a defendant's pants was visible to some extent through a slit in his shirt, the weapon was concealed. *Marshall v. State*, 200 S.E.2d 902 (Ga. App. 1973). Similarly, in *People v. Charron*, 220 N.W.2d 216 (Mich. App. 1974), a Michigan appellate court held that a knife slightly protruding from a defendant's rear pocket was a concealed weapon.

Many concealed-weapons statutes also make it an offense to carry a concealed weapon in a vehicle, and in numerous cases courts have been asked to rule on the application of these laws. For example, a defendant reached into his automobile and withdrew a revolver from a shelf behind the driver's seat. In affirming the defendant's conviction, the Wisconsin Supreme Court said that "[i]f the weapon is hidden from

Unlawful Possession of a Firearm

CASE-IN-POINT

South Carolina law provides that it is unlawful for any person to carry a pistol about his or her person, regardless of whether the pistol is concealed. S.C. Code § 16-23-20. The statute provides twelve exceptions to the prohibition. Barry Clarke was convicted of violating the statute after he was stopped for a traffic violation and the police officer noticed a gun in a holster next to the driver's seat. On appeal, Clarke argued that the burden of proof should have been on the prosecution to show that he did not qualify to carry the weapon under any of the twelve exceptions to the prohibition. The South Carolina Supreme Court disagreed, saying that "[t]he general rule, when dealing with statutory crimes to which there are exceptions, is that the defendant 'has the burden of excusing or justifying his act; and hence the burden may be on him to bring himself within an exception in the statute or to prove the issuance of a license or permit'." *State v. Clarke*, 396 S.E.2d 827 (S.C. 1990).

ordinary observation, it is concealed." The court noted that "absolute invisibility to other persons" was not "indispensable to concealment." The question was this: "Was [the weapon] carried so as not to be discernible by ordinary observation?" *Mularkey v. State*, 230 N.W. 76, 77 (Wis. 1930). More recently, an Illinois appellate court observed that "[i]t is well settled . . . that a weapon is 'concealed' . . . even though there is some notice of its presence to an alert police officer who can see part of the gun when he approaches the vehicle." *People v. Williams*, 350 N.E.2d 81, 83 (Ill. App. 1976).

Federal Gun Control Laws

In *United States v. Evans*, reproduced on the companion website, the United States Court of Appeals for the Ninth Circuit considers the constitutionality of the federal statute that prohibits possession of unregistered machine guns.

The **Federal Gun Control Act** of 1968, 18 U.S.C.A. § 921 *et seq.*, established a fairly comprehensive regime governing the distribution of firearms. The statute prohibits firearms dealers from transferring handguns to persons who are under twenty-one, nonresidents of the dealer's state, or are otherwise prohibited by state or local laws from purchasing or possessing firearms. 18 U.S.C.A. § 922(b). The law also forbids possession of a firearm by, and transfer of a firearm to, persons in several categories, including convicted felons, users of controlled substances, persons adjudicated as incompetent or committed to mental institutions, persons dishonorably discharged from the military, persons who are illegally in the United States, persons who have renounced their citizenship, and fugitives from justice. 18 U.S.C.A. §§ 922(d) and (g).

In the early 1990s, Congress enacted three important gun control statutes. The **Gun-Free School Zones Act** of 1990, 18 U.S.C.A. § 922, makes it unlawful for any individual knowingly to possess a firearm in a school zone, regardless of whether the school is in session. The 1993 **Brady Bill**, also codified at 18 U.S.C.A. § 922, requires a five-working-day waiting period for the purchase of a handgun. And the 1994 Crime Bill banned the manufacture, transfer, or possession of firearms classified as "assault weapons." 18 U.S.C.A. § 922(v)(1).

In 1995 the U.S. Supreme Court struck down the Gun-Free School Zones Act of 1990 and reversed a student's conviction for carrying a handgun to school. The Court found that the law, in its full reach, was beyond the power of Congress to regulate interstate commerce. *United States v. Lopez*, 514 U.S. 549, 115 S.Ct. 1624, 131 L.Ed.2d 626 (1995).

The Supreme Court's decisions in *United States v. Lopez* and *Printz v. United States* are excerpted on the companion website.

In 1997 the Court dealt another blow to federal gun control efforts when it invalidated a section of the Brady Bill requiring local law enforcement officers to conduct background checks of prospective gun purchasers. The Court held that, absent exigent circumstances, Congress could not commandeer state law enforcement authorities to implement a federal program. *Printz v. United States*, 521 U.S. 898, 117 S.Ct. 2365, 138 L.Ed.2d 914 (1997).

Recent State Developments

After several catastrophic incidents involving firearms, state legislatures began to focus on gun safety legislation. Many states have enacted laws that require background checks of gun buyers at gun shows. Most states require registration or permits to purchase firearms and prohibit sales to persons convicted of serious felonies.

New Jersey has been very active in enacting gun safety laws. Licensing of retail dealers and their employees is strictly regulated. No handgun can be delivered to any person unless such person possesses and exhibits a valid permit to purchase a firearm and at least seven days have elapsed since the date of application for the permit. Applications must be submitted to designated officials. The purchaser of a firearm must be personally known to the seller or present evidence of his or her identity. N.J. Stat. 2C:58-2. Trigger locks are required on handguns. N.J. Stat. 2C:58-2. Sawed-off shotguns and silencers are prohibited. N.J. Stat. 2C:39-3. Further, New Jersey laws strictly regulate the possession and use of handguns. Any person who knowingly has in his or her possession any handgun, including any antique handgun, without having obtained a permit to carry the same as provided in N.J. Stat. 2C:58-4, is guilty of a crime of the third degree. N.J. Stat. 2C:39-5.

Offenses against National Security

The preamble to the U.S. Constitution appropriately refers to the role of the federal government "to promote the common defense." The federal government performs this function by relying on the immense military capabilities of the United States and also upon various agencies devoted to the gathering of foreign intelligence. But it also relies on the criminal justice system to deter and punish violations of national security. While there are a number of specific offenses in this category, the principal crimes against national security are treason, **espionage, sabotage,** and sedition.

Treason

As we discussed in Chapter 3, Article III, Section 3 of the U.S. Constitution provides that treason against the United States "shall consist only in levying War against them, or in adhering to their Enemies, giving them Aid and Comfort." Following this constitutional language, the current federal statute on treason provides:

John Marshall's classic 1807 opinion in *United States v. Burr*, which discusses the crime of treason, is reproduced on the companion website.

> Whoever owing allegiance to the United States, levies war against them or adheres to their enemies, giving them aid and comfort within the United States or elsewhere, is guilty of treason and shall suffer death, or shall be imprisoned not less than five years and fined under this title but not less than $10,000; and shall be incapable of holding any office under the United States. . . . 18 U.S.C.A. § 2381.

No one has been convicted of treason since the Second World War. Many people incorrectly believe that Julius and Ethel Rosenberg, who provided the Soviet Union with top-secret information about the construction of the atomic bomb, were convicted of treason. Prosecutors considered charging the Rosenbergs with treason but concluded that they could not obtain a conviction due to the constitutional two-witness requirement. Instead, they elected to charge the Rosenbergs with espionage. The defendants were convicted in 1951 and sentenced to death.

Some people believed that John Walker Lindh, the so-called American Taliban, was guilty of treason based on his involvement with the Taliban regime in Afghanistan and Osama bin Laden's al-Qaeda terrorist organization. Lindh, an American citizen, was captured by American forces after a battle in Afghanistan in December 2001. As in the Rosenberg case, federal prosecutors elected not to charge Lindh with treason. Rather, he agreed to plead guilty to two lesser offenses and was sentenced to twenty years in prison.

Espionage

Known in the popular parlance as "spying," **espionage** consists of turning over state secrets to a foreign government. First criminalized by the Espionage Act of 1917, 40 Stat. 217, espionage is now covered by a number of federal statutes. 18 U.S.C.A.

§ 793 criminalizes gathering or transmitting defense information "with intent or reason to believe that the information is to be used to the injury of the United States, or to the advantage of any foreign nation." 18 U.S.C.A. § 794(b) prohibits collection or transmission of information about American military activities during time of war "with intent that the same shall be communicated to the enemy."

In recent years there have been a number of high-profile espionage cases in the United States. In 1986, Jonathan Pollard, a former U.S. Navy intelligence analyst, was sentenced to life imprisonment after he was convicted of selling classified information to Israel. Pollard admitted that he provided Israel with American intelligence about weapons programs in Syria, Iraq, Pakistan, and Libya. In 1994, former CIA analyst Aldrich Ames was sentenced to life in prison after he was convicted of selling classified information to the Soviet Union. The investigation revealed that Ames had received $2.7 million from Moscow for exposing covert American operations and betraying fellow CIA agents. In 2001, former FBI agent Robert Hanssen pleaded guilty to fifteen counts of espionage and conspiracy to commit espionage and was sentenced to life in prison. The government's investigation revealed that Hanssen received nearly $1.5 million from Russia in exchange for classified information.

The Intelligence Identities Protection Act of 1982, 50 U.S.C.A. § 421, *et seq.*, prohibits disclosure of the identities of undercover intelligence officers, agents, informants, and their "sources." The public became acutely aware of this law in the fall of 2003 when the FBI began an investigation of the Bush administration after it was alleged that senior administration officials had intentionally exposed an undercover CIA operative as an act of political retaliation. The operative was married to a former ambassador who had accused the Bush administration of selectively using intelligence to exaggerate the threat from Iraq in order to justify making war against Saddam Hussein's regime. A *Washington Post/BBC* News survey reported on October 2, 2003, found that more than eight in ten Americans viewed the allegation as "serious" and more than seven in ten thought it likely that a White House official was behind the leak. Ultimately, after a two-year investigation, it was determined that the leak came from an official in the State Department and not the White House.

Sabotage

Sabotage is the intentional destruction of a country's military infrastructure by an enemy agent or a civilian with the objective of hindering that country's war efforts or reducing its military capabilities. Several federal statutes criminalize particular forms of sabotage, but the broadest of these statutes is found at 18 U.S.C.A. § 2155. It provides:

> (a) Whoever, with intent to injure, interfere with, or obstruct the national defense of the United States, willfully injures, destroys, contaminates or infects, or attempts to so injure, destroy, contaminate or infect any national-defense material, national-defense premises, or national-defense utilities, shall be fined under this title or imprisoned not more than 20 years, or both, and, if death results to any person, shall be imprisoned for any term of years or for life.

18 U.S.C.A. § 2153 prohibits sabotage during time of war or national emergency and carries a thirty-year maximum prison term. Most states have similar laws, many of them enacted during World War II.

Sedition

Sedition is the incitement of insurrection or revolution. At common law there was no offense of sedition per se, but English law did proscribe seditious libel, seditious meetings, and seditious conspiracies. In 1798, the U.S. Congress enacted the infamous Sedition Act, which prohibited "false, scandalous and malicious" utterances and publications against the federal government or any of its officials. Thomas Jefferson and his followers assailed the act as a violation of the First Amendment to the U.S. Constitution. After Jefferson was elected president in 1801 and his party won both houses of Congress, the Sedition Act was promptly repealed.

In 1918, during the First World War, Congress enacted a new Sedition Act aimed primarily at communists, socialists, anarchists, and other radicals. More than 2,000 persons were prosecuted under this prohibition. In *Abrams v. United States*, 250 U.S. 616, 40 S.Ct. 17, 63 L.Ed. 1173 (1919), the Supreme Court upheld the conviction of five Russian immigrants who published leaflets criticizing America's role in World War I and attacking the capitalist system. In dissent, Justice Oliver Wendell Holmes questioned the need for governmental suppression of dissent, saying "the best test of truth is the power of the thought to get itself accepted in the competition of the market. . . ." 250 U.S. at 630, 40 S.Ct. at 22, 63 L.Ed. at 1180.

In 1940, Congress adopted the Smith Act, 54 Stat. 670, 671. The act has been amended several times. In its present form, codified at 18 U.S.C.A. § 2385, the act makes it a crime if a person

> knowingly or willfully advocates, abets, advises, or teaches the duty, necessity, desirability, or propriety of overthrowing or destroying the government of the United States or the government of any State, Territory, District or Possession thereof, or the government of any political subdivision therein, by force or violence, or by the assassination of any officer of any such government.

In *Dennis v. United States*, 341 U.S. 494, 71 S.Ct. 857, 95 L.Ed. 1137 (1951), the Supreme Court upheld the convictions under the Smith Act of eleven officials of the Communist Party, rejecting their First Amendment challenge to the statute. But in *Yates v. United States*, 354 U.S. 298, 77 S.Ct. 1064, 1 L.Ed.2d 1356 (1957), the Court set aside the convictions of another set of Communist Party officials. In so doing, the Court distinguished between "advocacy of abstract doctrine and advocacy directed at promoting unlawful action" and held that the Smith Act prohibited only the latter. In 1969, in *Brandenburg v. Ohio*, 395 U.S. 444, 89 S.Ct. 1827, 23 L.Ed.2d 430, the Court went so far as to hold that mere advocacy could never be criminalized in the absence of "imminent lawless action." Although the *Brandenburg* case did not arise under the Smith Act, but rather under a state law prohibiting "criminal syndicalism," most commentators have concluded that the "imminent lawless action" doctrine applies equally to federal prosecutions under the Smith Act. Today, however, such prosecutions are rare.

The Supreme Court's decision in *Brandenburg v. Ohio* is excerpted on the companion website.

Terrorism and Weapons of Mass Destruction

Before the 1980s some sporadic acts of **terrorism** were committed in the United States by radical political protesters and by persons involved in protests during the fight for racial equality. The 1980s and 1990s witnessed a series of attacks by Theodore Kaczynski, the so-called Unabomber, who sent packages with bombs in his protest against modern technology. Antiabortion extremists committed sporadic acts of terrorism at abortion clinics. During the 1980s and 1990s terrorists attacked several American military bases overseas. Militant Islamists were convicted of damaging the World Trade Center in 1993. Timothy McVeigh and Terry Nichols, who bore extreme hatred for the government, were convicted of the massive bombing of a federal government building in Oklahoma City in 1995. And everyone is familiar with the tragic loss of thousands of lives when hijackers crashed aircraft into the World Trade Center and the Pentagon on September 11, 2001.

Antiterrorism Legislation

The Omnibus Diplomatic Security and Antiterrorism Act of 1986, Pub. L. 99-399, now codified as 18 U.S.C.A. § 2332, makes it a federal offense for a terrorist overseas to kill, attempt to kill, conspire to kill, or engage in physical violence with the intent to cause serious bodily injury to an American citizen. The **Antiterrorism and Effective Death Penalty Act** of 1996, Pub. L. 104-132, 110 Stat. 1214, enacted after the Oklahoma City bombing of 1995, expanded federal jurisdiction with respect to investigation and prosecution of international terrorism. It also made it a crime for persons in the United States or subject to U.S. jurisdiction to provide material support to groups designated as terrorist organizations by the U.S. Department of State. 18 U.S.C.A. § 2339B.

Since terrorists attacked the United States on September 11, 2001, the federal government has responded in new ways in attempts to maintain the security of the country. These include the creation of the Department of Homeland Security; stricter safety measures in mass transportation systems; increased protective measures to safeguard borders, ports, utility systems, and government buildings; and training police, fire, and medical personnel to cope with the potential use of weapons of mass destruction. From a legislative standpoint, the USA PATRIOT Act has become an important part of the criminal justice system.

The USA PATRIOT Act

As we explained in Chapter 10, Congress enacted the **USA PATRIOT Act** shortly after the terrorist attacks of 9/11. Title VIII of the USA PATRIOT Act strengthens numerous federal criminal laws against terrorism. Section 801 creates a detailed new offense for willfully attacking mass transportation facilities. Section 802 defines domestic terrorism as "activities that occur primarily within U.S. jurisdiction, that involve criminal acts dangerous to human life that appear to be intended to intimidate or coerce a civilian population, to influence government policy by intimidation or coercion, or to affect government conduct by mass destruction, assassination, or kidnapping." Section 803 prohibits knowingly harboring persons who have committed or who are about to commit an act of terrorism.

The act establishes federal jurisdiction over crimes committed at U.S. facilities abroad, (§ 804) and, by amending 18 U.S.C.A. § 2339A, applies prohibitions against providing material support for terrorism offenses outside of the United States (§ 805). It also subjects to civil forfeiture all assets, foreign or domestic, of individuals and terrorist organizations that plan or perpetrate domestic or international terrorism against the United States (§ 806).

Section 809 extends the statute of limitations for certain offenses and provides that there shall be no statute of limitations for certain terrorism offenses if the commission of such an offense resulted in, or created a foreseeable risk of, death or serious bodily injury to another person. Section 810 provides for alternative maximum penalties for specified terrorism crimes, while section 811 provides the same penalties for attempts and conspiracies as for terrorist acts and provides for post-release supervision for terrorists whose offenses resulted in foreseeable risk of death or serious bodily injury. Certain acts of terrorism are deemed to be racketeering activity (§ 813), and penalties regarding fraud and related activity in connection with specified cyberterrorism offenses are included (§ 814). Finally, section 817 creates a new offense of possession of biological weapons when not justified for research ok other specified purposes.

On March 9, 2006, President Bush signed legislation making permanent all but two provisions of the USA PATRIOT Act. In signing the USA PATRIOT Improvement and Reauthorization Act of 2005, President Bush stated,

> The law allows our intelligence and law enforcement officials to continue to share information. It allows them to continue to use tools against terrorists that they use against drug dealers and other criminals. It will improve our nation's security while we safeguard the civil liberties of our people. The legislation strengthens the Justice Department so it can better detect and disrupt terrorist threats. And the bill gives law enforcement new tools to combat threats to our citizens from international terrorists to local drug dealers.

Although recognizing the need to protect the security of the United States, critics argue that certain sections of the act unduly restrict personal liberties, thereby offending basic constitutional protections. For example, they cite language in section 802, which defines terrorism to include "activities . . . that appear . . . to influence government policy by intimidation or coercion," as having the potential to chill political dissent. Among the sharpest critics of the PATRIOT Act is the American Civil Liberties Union, which has challenged several of the act's provisions in court. As of 2009 litigation was still ongoing challenging various sections of the USA PATRIOT Act.

Aircraft Piracy and Related Offenses

Among the numerous offenses committed by the 9/11 terrorists was the hijacking of four commercial airliners. Of course, the hijacking of airliners has long been a concern in the United States and around the world. Chapter 46 of Title 49 of the U.S. Code is entitled "Special Aircraft Jurisdiction of the United States." As provided in 49 U.S.C. § 46501, the term "special aircraft jurisdiction of the United States" includes any of the following aircraft in flight:

(A) a civil aircraft of the United States.

(B) an aircraft of the armed forces of the United States.

(C) another aircraft in the United States.

(D) another aircraft outside the United States—

> (i) that has its next scheduled destination or last place of departure in the United States, if the aircraft next lands in the United States;

> (ii) on which an individual commits an offense . . . if the aircraft lands in the United States with the individual still on the aircraft; or

> (iii) against which an individual commits an offense . . . if the aircraft lands in the United States with the individual still on the aircraft.

(E) any other aircraft leased without crew to a lessee whose principal place of business is in the United States or, if the lessee does not have a principal place of business, whose permanent residence is in the United States.

Title 49, Chapter 46 of the U.S. Code contains several criminal prohibitions pertaining to aircraft under the special aircraft jurisdiction of the United States:

§ 46502. Aircraft piracy
§ 46503. Interference with security screening personnel
§ 46504. Interference with flight crew members and attendants
§ 46505. Carrying a weapon or explosive on an aircraft
§ 46506. Application of certain criminal laws to acts on aircraft
§ 46507. False information and threats

Naval Piracy

Article I, Section 8, paragraph 10 of the U.S. Constitution authorizes Congress to make laws to "define and punish Piracies . . . committed on the high Seas. . . ." Thus, 18 U.S.C. § 1651 provides, "Whoever, on the high seas, commits the crime of piracy as defined by the law of nations, and is afterwards brought into or found in the United States, shall be imprisoned for life." In April 2009, the U.S. Navy killed two Somali pirates who had attacked an American vessel, the *Maersk Alabama*, and were holding the ship's captain at gunpoint. Another pirate was captured and brought to the U.S. for prosecution under the aforementioned statute. In May 2009, a federal grand jury indicted Abduwali Abdukhadir Muse for piracy, conspiracy to commit hostage-taking, and other offenses. As the quoted statute indicates, the defendant was facing a life sentence for the piracy offense alone.

Weapons of Mass Destruction

While terrorism using conventional explosives can produce massive destruction and widespread panic, as we saw in New York City on 9/11, the prospect of terrorists using chemical, biological, or nuclear weapons is almost too horrible to contemplate. In recent years Congress has enacted a number of statutes that provide criminal jurisdiction over the use of **weapons of mass destruction** (WMDs). For example, 18 U.S.C. A. § 175(a) provides:

Whoever knowingly develops, produces, stockpiles, transfers, acquires, retains, or possesses any biological agent, toxin, or delivery system for use as a weapon, or knowingly assists a foreign state or any organization to do so, or attempts, threatens, or conspires to do the same, shall be fined under this title or imprisoned for life or any term of years, or both. There is extraterritorial Federal jurisdiction over an offense under this section committed by or against a national of the United States.

Additional provisions found in Title 18 of the U.S. Code impose similar prohibitions with respect to toxic chemicals, § 229, and nuclear materials, § 831.

Title 18 § 2332a criminalizes the use of weapons of mass destruction within the United States or against an American national anywhere in the world. It provides:

§ 2332a. Use of weapons of mass destruction

(a) Offense Against a National of the United States or Within the United States.—A person who, without lawful authority, uses, threatens, or attempts or conspires to use, a weapon of mass destruction—

(1) against a national of the United States while such national is outside of the United States;

(2) against any person or property within the United States, and

Court Affirms Defendants' Convictions for Threats to Use Weapons of Mass Destruction

Johnie Wise and Jack Abbott Grebe were convicted of threatening to use a biological agent and a weapon involving a disease organism in violation of 18 U.S.C.A. § 2332a(a)(2). That statute makes it a crime even to threaten to use a weapon of mass destruction if using such a weapon would affect interstate commerce. On appeal the defendants challenged the sufficiency of the evidence, which disclosed that they sent e-mails to government agencies outside their state of Texas, threatening to use weapons with biological or chemical agents. The defendants argued that this was insufficient to support their convictions because the government failed to present any testimony or documentary evidence that the use of the weapon specified in the threat would have affected interstate commerce. In rejecting their contention, the court pointed out that the statute on its face makes clear that, in the case of a threat, it applies where the results would have affected interstate or foreign commerce and that the trial jury was so instructed. In its opinion the court said, "In any event, the e-mails, which had been sent from Texas, were received by government agencies outside of Texas. For example, the FBI received the e-mails in California; the United States Customs received the e-mails at its website in Virginia; the ATF, the Secret Service, and the Office of Correspondence for the President all received the e-mails in Washington, D.C. The threat itself crossed state boundaries; therefore, it cannot be argued that an effect on interstate commerce is lacking in this case." The U.S. Court of Appeals for the Fifth Circuit affirmed the defendants' convictions.

United States v. Wise, 221 F.3d 140 (5th Cir. 2000).

(A) the mail or any facility of interstate or foreign commerce is used in furtherance of the offense;

(B) such property is used in interstate or foreign commerce or in an activity that affects interstate or foreign commerce;

(C) any perpetrator travels in or causes another to travel in interstate or foreign commerce in furtherance of the offense; or

(D) the offense, or the results of the offense, affect interstate or foreign commerce, or, in the case of a threat, attempt, or conspiracy, would have affected interstate or foreign commerce;

(3) against any property that is owned, leased or used by the United States or by any department or agency of the United States, whether the property is within or outside of the United States; or

(4) against any property within the United States that is owned, leased, or used by a foreign government, shall be imprisoned for any term of years or for life, and if death results, shall be punished by death or imprisoned for any term of years or for life.

Immigration Offenses

Article I, Section 8 of the U.S. Constitution vests in Congress the power "[t]o establish an uniform Rule of Naturalization. . . ." The courts have interpreted this language as giving Congress plenary power over immigration. In exercising this power, Congress has created several **immigration offenses**. Section 1325 of Title 8 U.S.C.A. prohibits improper entry by aliens, while 8 U.S.C.A. § 1326 makes it an offense for an alien who has been removed from the United States to reenter the country. Specific immigration offenses include entering or attempting "to enter the United States at any time or place other than as designated by immigration officers," 8 U.S.C.A. § 1325(a)(1); eluding "examination or inspection by immigration officers," 8 U.S.C.A. § 1325(a)(2); attempting to enter or obtaining entry to the United States "by a willfully false or misleading representation or the willful concealment of a material fact," 8 U.S.C.A. § 1325(a)(3); knowingly entering into a marriage "for the purpose of evading any provision of the immigration laws," 8 U.S.C.A. § 1325(c); and knowingly establishing "a commercial enterprise for the purpose of evading any provision of the immigration laws," 8 U.S.C.A. § 1325(d).

Lax enforcement of immigration laws in the face of massive illegal immigration across the nation's southern border has led to a divisive political battle over "immigration reform." On one hand, there is broad public support for tightening security at the borders and more vigorously enforcing existing laws. The need for greater border control is particularly acute in an age of international terrorism and when Mexican drug cartels carry out violent forays into the United States. On the other hand, it is unrealistic to deport or prosecute the millions of immigrants who have come to this country illegally, most simply looking to improve their lives through hard work at low wages, performing jobs than many Americans are unwilling to do.

In 2006 the president and Congress began to seriously address the problem of illegal immigration. The president sent National Guard troops to augment the U.S. Border Patrol's operations on the southern border, and additional funds were provided to increase measures to protect the border. The U.S. Senate and the U.S. House of Representatives crafted very different approaches to the problems of border protection and the resolution of the status of illegal immigrants. But by 2007 major political differences continued to thwart Congressional action to achieve a unified approach to resolve the numerous issues surrounding immigration and border control.

Conclusion

Offenses against public order, safety, and security present a picture of the dynamic development of the law in a constitutional democracy. The needs to maintain order and protect the public safety are high-priority items for any organized society. Yet the U.S. Constitution mandates that government maintain a delicate balance between these interests and the rights of citizens. Of particular relevance to offenses against public order are the protections of the First Amendment. Today, our society faces a new threat, that of terrorism, which adds more pressure to limit individual rights and freedoms and grant more power to law enforcement agencies. Americans today are engaged in a great debate about where the balance should be struck between freedom on one hand and order, safety, and security on the other.

Chapter Summary

- **LO1** The English common law recognized the right of the people to assemble peaceably for lawful purposes, but made unlawful assemblies, routs, and riots misdemeanor offenses. If three or more persons met together with the intention of cooperating to disturb the public peace by doing an unlawful act, their gathering was considered an unlawful assembly. If they took steps to achieve their purpose, it was a rout, and if they actually executed their plans, they committed a riot.
- **LO2** A variety of state statutes and local ordinances prohibit unlawful assemblies, riots, and disorderly conduct. An unlawful assembly is a group of persons who seek to commit unlawful acts or to use unlawful means to commit lawful

acts. A riot is a public disturbance of three or more persons who threaten or commit acts of violence to persons or property. Inciting a riot involves instigating others to riot. Disorderly conduct laws target individual as well as group behavior and usually make it an offense to engage in fighting or making unreasonable noise. States have primary responsibility for controlling breaches of the peace. Laws applied to violent or threatened conduct, imminent lawless action, or utterance of fighting words seldom invoke constitutional challenges; however, laws proscribing loitering and begging and curfew ordinance require courts to weigh the need to maintain order and peace against First Amendment guarantees of freedom of speech and assembly. The Federal Anti-Riot Act of 1968 proscribes interstate travel and use of the mail or other media to encourage or carry on a riot; or to aid or abet any person in inciting or participating in a riot. In 1972 a federal appellate court held that the act is not unconstitutionally vague or overbroad in relation to the First Amendment.

- **LO3** The common law developed the offense of vagrancy to criminalize idleness. American colonists, and later, states and local governments, found it desirable to punish idleness and offensive conduct and to control alcoholics and derelicts. The wide range of conduct prohibited by vagrancy laws made them susceptible to arbitrary enforcement by police to justify arrests and searches of suspects. In 1972 the U.S. Supreme Court declared unconstitutional a typical vagrancy law because it "fails to give a person of ordinary intelligence fair notice that his contemplated conduct is forbidden by the statute and because it encourages arbitrary and erratic arrests and convictions." Thereafter, states and cities enacted loitering ordinances designed to focus on conduct and not status, to give fair notice as to what is proscribed, and to afford persons an opportunity to explain their presence before being ordered to disperse. Like vagrancy ordinances, those that target homeless persons, such as by making it an offense to sleep in public places, have often been invalidated as being vague and subject to arbitrary enforcement. Others have been upheld as promoting aesthetics, sanitation, public health, or safety. Agreeing with the Illinois Supreme Court, in 1999 the U.S. Supreme Court invalidated Chicago's "gang violence ordinance," which police had used to prevent gang members from loitering in any public place "with no apparent purpose."

- **LO4** Most courts have held unconstitutional curfew laws that prohibit young people unaccompanied by a parent or guardian from being on the streets during nighttime hours. Some courts have upheld such ordinances when they include numerous exceptions. On the other hand, the Supreme Court has stated that the constitutional right to travel may be legitimately curtailed by curfews on an emergency basis when the safety and welfare of a community has been ravaged by flood, fire, or disease. Once vagrancy ordinances were declared unconstitutional local governments began to enact ordinances that prohibit begging (panhandling). That raised the issue of whether begging activity constitutes expression protected by the First Amendment. Courts have frequently declared unconstitutional ordinances that proscribe all begging on public ways, but federal appellate courts have recently approved narrowly drawn ordinances that restrict only "aggressive panhandling."

- **LO5** During the 1960s, most states and municipalities decriminalized minor traffic offenses, with violations considered as civil infractions rather than misdemeanors. Some states have begun to enact legal prohibitions on driving while using a cell phone or text messaging. Drivers are issued citations (tickets) instead of being arrested. In order to provide legal uniformity to the "rules of the road," states, and many municipalities, have adopted "model" laws defining a wide range of more serious motor vehicle (generally strict liability) offenses. Since the 1980s many states have enacted mandatory seat belt and child restraint laws. Violators are usually assessed a small fine, but in 2001 the Supreme Court upheld a custodial arrest for the violation of a Texas seat belt law which gave police officers discretion to issue citations to violators.

- **LO6** The common belief that the Second Amendment protects keeping and bearing of arms only in the context of a well-regulated militia was dispelled in 2008 when the Supreme Court struck down a District of Columbia ordinance that effectively prohibited possession of handguns. The Court held that the Second Amendment protects a personal right to possess a firearm for "traditionally lawful purposes" irrespective of one's service in any militia. The Federal Gun Control Act of 1968 prohibits firearms dealers from transferring handguns to persons who are under twenty-one, nonresidents of the dealer's state, or those who are otherwise prohibited by state or local laws from purchasing or possessing firearms. A variety of state laws prohibit possession of offensive weapons by other than law enforcement personnel. States also commonly proscribe carrying a weapon concealed from ordinary sight on or about a person or in a vehicle. Many states have laws that require background checks of gun buyers at gun shows, require registration of firearms or permits to purchase them, and prohibit sales to persons convicted of serious felonies. A 2010 decision of the U.S. Supreme Court makes state and local laws subject to constitutional challenge under the Second Amendment.

- **LO7** The principal crimes against national security are treason, espionage, sabotage and sedition. The U.S. Constitution provides that treason against the United States "shall consist only in levying War against them, or in adhering to their Enemies, giving them Aid and Comfort." Espionage (spying) consists of turning over state secrets to a foreign government and is covered by a number of federal statutes which criminalize gathering or transmitting defense information "with intent . . . that the information . . . be used to the injury of the United States, or to the advantage of any foreign nation." The Intelligence Identities Protection Act of 1982 prohibits disclosure of the identities of undercover intelligence officers, agents, informants, and their "sources." Sabotage is the intentional destruction of the country's military infrastructure by an enemy agent or civilian and is proscribed by federal and state laws. Sedition is the incitement of insurrection or revolution. In 1940, Congress adopted the Smith Act, which in its present form makes it a crime for a person to knowingly or willfully advocate the overthrow of federal, state, or local government by force or violence, or by assassination of any governmental officer. In 1957, the Supreme Court set aside the convictions of Communist Party officials, distinguishing between "advocacy of abstract doctrine and advocacy directed at promoting unlawful action" and held that the Smith Act prohibited only the latter. In a landmark decision, the Court held that mere advocacy could never be criminalized in the absence of "imminent lawless action."

- **LO8** The Omnibus Diplomatic Security and Antiterrorism Act of 1986 makes it a federal offense for a terrorist overseas to kill, attempt to kill, conspire to kill, or engage in physical violence with the intent to cause serious bodily injury to, an American citizen. The Antiterrorism and Effective Death Penalty Act of 1996 expanded federal jurisdiction with respect to investigation and prosecution of international terrorism. After the attacks on September 11, 2001, the federal government created of the Department of Homeland Security. Since then the federal government has taken stricter safety measures to safeguard ma[...] portation, borders, ports, utility systems, and government buildings. It [...] undertaken to train police, fire, and medical personnel to cope with the [...] tial use of weapons of mass destruction. The USA PATRIOT Act, enacted [...] 9/11, amends various federal statutes; creates new offenses for attacks on [...] transportation facilities and for possession of biological weapons, when not j[...] fied for research; deems certain acts of terrorism to be racketeering activity; a[...] extends statutes of limitations. The act increases the ability of law enforceme[...] agencies to search telephone, e-mail communications, medical, and financial re[...] cords and subjects assets of individuals involved in terrorism to civil forfeiture[...] Critics argue that by restricting personal liberties certain sections of the act of- fend basic constitutional protections. In March 2006, Congress made permanent all but two provisions of the USA PATRIOT Act. Federal law also prohibits air- craft piracy; interference with security screening personnel, flight crew mem- bers, and flight attendants; and carrying weapons or explosives onto an aircraft. Other federal criminal laws forbid the use of weapons of mass destruction within the United States or against an American national anywhere in the world.

- **LO9** The U.S. Constitution vests in Congress the power "[t]o establish an uni- form Rule of Naturalization. . . ." Federal statutes prohibit improper entry by aliens; make it an offense for an alien who has been removed from the United States to reenter the country; and include a variety of offenses that make it un- lawful to enter the country by false and misleading actions, by knowingly en- tering into a marriage, or by establishing a commercial enterprise to evade the immigration laws. Lax enforcement of immigration laws in the face of massive illegal immigration across the nation's southern border has led to a divisive politi- cal battle over "immigration reform." In 2006 the president and Congress began to seriously address the problem, but by 2009 major political differences contin- ued to thwart Congressional action to achieve a unified approach to the numer- ous issues surrounding immigration and border control.

Key Terms

unlawful assembly A group of individuals, usually five or more, assembled to com- mit an unlawful act or to commit a lawful act in an unlawful manner.

rout At common law, a disturbance of the peace that was similar to a riot but failed to carry out the intended purpose.

riot A public disturbance involving acts of violence, usually by three or more persons.

breaches of the peace Crimes that disturb the public tranquility and order; a ge- neric term encompassing disorderly conduct, riot, etc.

inciting a riot The crime of instigating or provoking a riot.

disorderly conduct Illegal behavior that disturbs the public peace or order.

vagrancy The common-law offense of going about without any visible means of support.

loitering Standing around idly; "hanging out."

motor vehicle violations Minor crimes or infractions involving the operation of motor vehicles.

weapons offenses Violations of laws restricting or prohibiting the manufacture, sale, transfer, possession, or use of certain firearms.

control laws Laws regulating the manufacture, importation, sale, distribution, possession, or use of firearms.

Federal Anti-Riot Act A federal law enacted in 1968 that made it a crime to travel or use interstate or foreign commerce facilities in connection with inciting, participating in, or aiding acts of violence.

excessive noise Unnecessarily loud sounds that interfere with the public peace and endanger the public, health, and welfare; sounds emitted that exceed the levels permitted by law or ordinance.

curfew ordinances Ordinances requiring people, typically minors, to be off the streets by a certain time of night.

panhandling Begging for money in public.

rules of the road Rules for the operation of motor vehicles on the public streets.

civil infractions Noncriminal violations of a law; often refers to minor traffic violations.

traffic court Court of limited jurisdiction whose main function is the adjudication of traffic offenses and other minor misdemeanors.

decriminalization of routine traffic offenses The recent trend toward treating minor motor vehicle offenses—for example, speeding—as civil infractions rather than crimes.

mandatory seat belt laws Laws requiring automobile drivers and passengers to wear seat belts.

mandatory child restraint laws Laws requiring that children below a specified age be restrained by approved safety devices when riding in automobiles.

well-regulated militia This phrase, from the Second Amendment to the U.S. Constitution, refers to a citizen army subject to government regulations. In the early history of the United States, the militia was the set of able-bodied men who could be pressed into military service by the governor of the state. The National Guard is its modern counterpart.

concealed weapon A weapon carried on or about a person in such a manner as to hide it from the ordinary sight of another person.

Federal Gun Control Act This 1968 statute prohibits firearms dealers from transferring handguns to people who are younger than twenty-one, nonresidents of the dealer's state, and those who are otherwise prohibited by state or local laws from purchasing or possessing firearms. It also forbids possession of a firearm by, and transfer of a firearm to, people in a number of categories, including convicted felons, users of controlled substances, those adjudicated as incompetent or committed to mental institutions, illegal aliens, those dishonorably discharged from the military, those who have renounced their citizenship, and fugitives from justice.

Gun-Free School Zones Act Federal statute making it a crime "for any individual knowingly to possess a firearm at a place that the individual knows, or has reasonable cause to believe, is a school zone." This law was declared unconstitutional by the U.S. Supreme Court in *United States v. Lopez* (1995).

Brady Bill Legislation passed by Congress in 1993 requiring a five-day waiting period before the purchase of a handgun, during which time a background check of the buyer is conducted.

espionage The crime of turning over state secrets to a foreign government

sabotage The crime of infiltrating and destroying a nation's war-making capabilities.

sedition The crime of advocating or working toward the violent overthrow of ‹ own government.

terrorism The crime of inflicting terror on a population through the indiscrimir. killing of people and destruction of property, often with explosive devices.

Antiterrorism and Effective Death Penalty Act A federal statute designed to effectuate reforms in administration of the death penalty by curtailing successive petitions for habeas corpus by prisoners sentenced to death.

USA PATRIOT Act Controversial act of Congress enacted in 2001 to strengthen the federal government's efforts to combat terrorism.

weapons of mass destruction Weapons designed to kill large numbers of people and/or damage extensive areas. Includes nuclear, radiological, biological, and chemical weapons.

immigration offenses Violations of criminal provisions of the Immigration and Nationality Act, a federal law that relates to immigration.

Questions for Thought and Discussion

1. Why has it been necessary for American courts to interpret laws proscribing breach of peace and vagrancy more strictly than did the English common-law courts?

2. How does the Federal Anti-Riot Act seek to prevent the definition of "to incite a riot" from being applied in such a way that it violates First Amendment guarantees of freedom of expression?

3. Is an ordinance that defines "disturbing the peace" simply as "tumultuous or offensive conduct" sufficiently precise to meet the constitutional standard of giving a person of ordinary intelligence fair notice of what conduct is forbidden?

4. How did the Jacksonville, Florida, vagrancy ordinance invalidated by the Supreme Court in the *Papachristou* case offend the Constitution of the United States? Have the reforms in vagrancy laws at the state and local levels sufficiently removed the threat of criminalizing a person's status? Are they now written with the precision necessary to protect citizens from arbitrary enforcement of the law?

5. Based on the ruling of the Supreme Court in *City of Chicago v. Morales*, what protections of the individual do you think must be included in an ordinance proscribing loitering?

6. Assume you are working as a staff assistant to a state legislator who intends to introduce a law making it an offense to solicit funds by "panhandling" on streets and in parks. You are asked to prepare a memorandum of provisions to be considered in order to avoid the proposed act's being declared unconstitutional. What basic provisions would you recommend?

7. Have traffic offenses been decriminalized in your state? Should drivers who use cell phones for conversing or for text messaging be charged with civil infractions? To what extent? What procedures are available to contest a traffic ticket?

8. Why have the courts refused to interpret the Second Amendment's protection of the "right to keep and bear arms" to prohibit gun control legislation? On what

ses other than the Second Amendment can one make constitutional attacks on federal gun control laws?

9. To what extent does the First Amendment protect the right of citizens to advocate on behalf of groups that have been labeled as terrorist organizations by the federal government?

10. Under what circumstances does the law permit the government to prosecute a person who publicly advocates the violent overthrow of the U.S. government? What constitutional considerations come into play?

11. Evaluate the criticism leveled against the USA PATRIOT Act that the sections quoted in the text unconstitutionally deprive individuals of their civil liberties by such vague terms as "acts intended to influence government policy by intimidation or coercion."

12. Are acts of terrorism perpetrated against the United States by foreign nationals more appropriately viewed as crimes or acts of war? Is the criminal justice system the appropriate means of dealing with foreign terrorists?

13. What should be done about the millions of foreign nationals who have entered the United States illegally? Should they be prosecuted for immigration offenses, deported to their countries of origin, or granted some sort of amnesty whereby they can remain in this country and work legally?

Problems for Discussion and Solution

1. Consider the following hypothetical case: Members of the American Nazi Party announced a demonstration to be held in Pleasant Ridge, a predominantly Jewish suburb of Metropolis. The Pleasant Ridge City Council quickly adopted an ordinance requiring groups planning demonstrations to obtain a permit from the police department. Under the ordinance, to hold a demonstration without a permit was a misdemeanor, punishable by a $1,000 fine and sixty days in jail. The Nazis applied for a permit, which was denied on the grounds that their presence in Pleasant Ridge constituted a "clear and present danger to the public order." The Nazis held their demonstration anyway. Approximately one hundred demonstrators congregated on the city square. Many were dressed in Nazi uniforms, others carried banners emblazoned with swastikas, and others held signs on which were printed anti-Semitic slogans. Pleasant Ridge police arrived at the scene and asked the demonstrators to disperse. When they refused, police arrested some demonstrators; others ran to avoid arrest. The leader of the Nazi group, Adrian Maples, was convicted of a number of offenses, including violation of the new ordinance. On appeal, Maples is challenging the constitutionality of the ordinance. What do you think the court's ruling should be? Explain your reasoning.

2. The City of Dystopia experienced difficulties with groups of rowdy individuals congregating on downtown sidewalks and harassing passersby. When the local police were unable to control the situation by enforcing the disorderly conduct statute, the city council enacted the following ordinance:

> Sec. 1. It shall be unlawful for three or more persons to assemble on any public sidewalk or walkway within the city while conducting themselves in a manner that is annoying or bothersome to surrounding persons.

> Sec. 2. Anyone found guilty of violating this ordinance shall be punished as provided in the city charter.

After the ordinance went into effect, three college students congrega[...] public sidewalk and made loud, obnoxious remarks to passersby. The police a[...] the students and charged them under the ordinance. The students admit tha[...] were rowdy but argue that the ordinance unduly restricts their First Amend[...] rights. What constitutional arguments could they, or their counsel, present to a c[...] in an effort to reverse their convictions? Do you think they would prevail? In y[...] opinion, should they prevail?

13

...ses against Justice
... Public Administration

LEARNING OBJECTIVES

After reading this chapter, you should be able to explain . . .

1. how the common law defined offenses against the administration of justice
2. why the offense of bribery has been extended beyond bribing of judges and other public officials
3. why perjury is in most jurisdictions a difficult offense to prove
4. what it means to suborn perjury
5. how obstruction of justice includes a number of related offenses
6. how compounding a crime differs from misprision of felony
7. the circumstances under which one may lawfully escape from confinement
8. how criminal contempt differs from civil contempt and how a direct contempt differs from an indirect contempt

CHAPTER OUTLINE

Introduction
Bribery
Perjury
Obstruction of Justice
Resisting Arrest
Compounding a Crime
Escape
Contempt
Conclusion
Chapter Summary

On December 9, 2008, federal agents arrested Illinois governor Rod Blagojevich on charges of solic-itation of bribery and conspiracy to commit mail and wire fraud. The arrests came after an investiga-tion by the FBI into whether Blagojevich had attempted to profit from the appointment to fill Barack Obama's vacant U.S. Senate seat. The scandal led the Illinois legislature to impeach the governor and remove him from office in January 2009. In April 2009, a federal grand jury indicted Blagojevich on a variety of federal charges. In February 2010, a superseding indictment charged the former governor with additional federal crimes. On June 3, 2010, Blagojevich went on trial on twenty-four counts, including racketeering, solicitation of bribery, conspiracy to commit bribery, attempted ex-tortion, and conspiracy to commit extortion. On August 17, the jury returned a conviction on only one count—making false statements to the FBI. The jury was deadlocked on the remaining counts, forcing the judge to declare a mistrial on twenty-three counts. Subsequent television interviews with jurors in the case revealed that one juror had held out for acquittal, thus deadlocking the jury on all but the one count. Blagojevich celebrated the mistrial and portrayed himself as the victim of a runaway prosecution launched by an overzealous prosecutor. The prosecution vowed to retry the former governor. The one crime of which he was convicted, though, is a serious offense against the administration of justice, which carries a maximum prison term of five years. The applicable federal statute, 18 U.S.C.A. § 1001, is a controversial one. Critics say it allows prosecutors to pile on criminal charges by making it a crime to simply deny an accusation made by law enforcement agents. Cer-tainly it goes well beyond the common-law offense of perjury.

Introduction

The English common-law judges found it necessary to create a number of offenses to maintain the integrity of the law and the administration of justice. Principally, these offenses were bribery, perjury and subornation of perjury, resisting arrest, obstruc-tion of justice, compounding a crime, and escape. At common law, these offenses were misdemeanors. In addition, the common law developed the concept of criminal contempt to enable judges to maintain the dignity and authority of the courts and the respect due judicial officers. All of these common-law crimes remain an important part of contemporary criminal law in the United States, although they have been expanded and augmented by a variety of modern statutes. The offenses against pub-lic administration and the administration of justice in particular serve as a means to punish those who breach the public trust and whose actions corrupt the orderly pro-cesses of government and the justice system.

Bribery

The concept of **bribery** dates back to biblical times, when it was regarded as sinful to attempt to influence a judge with a gift because the judge represented the divine. Thus, when the common law developed the crime of bribery, it sought to penalize only persons whose actions were designed to improperly influence those identified with the administration of justice. Later, it was considered bribery for anyone to give or receive anything of value or any valuable service or promise with the intent to

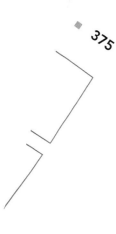

.ce any public officer in the discharge of a legal duty. Bribery is generally a fel-
.nder modern law. The seriousness with which the founders of this country re-
ded bribery is demonstrated by Article 2, Section 4 of the U.S. Constitution, which
pecifically authorizes impeachment of public officials who commit ". . .Treason,
Bribery, or other high Crimes and Misdemeanors" (emphasis added).

The Modern Statutory Offense of Bribery

Today, a variety of federal statutes proscribe bribery of specific public officers and
witnesses as well as of jurors and government employees and functionaries. The most
prominent among these is 18 U.S.C.A. § 201, which makes it a crime if anyone
"directly or indirectly gives, offers, or promises anything of value to any public official, former public official, or person selected to be a public official, for or because
of any official act performed or to be performed by such public official, former public
official, or person selected to be a public official. . . ." 18 U.S.C.A. § 201(c)(1)(A). The
law also makes it a crime if "a public official, former public official, or person selected
to be a public official, otherwise than as provided by law for the proper discharge
of official duty, directly or indirectly demands, seeks, receives, accepts, or agrees to
receive or accept anything of value personally for or because of any official act performed or to be performed. . . ." 18 U.S.C.A. § 201(c)(1)(B). Other subsections of the
statute make it a crime to offer a bribe to a witness or for a witness to solicit or accept
a bribe. 18 U.S.C.A. § 201(c)(2); 18 U.S.C.A. § 201(c)(3).

State statutes generally define bribery in broad terms and frequently address
specific situations as well. The trend has been to enlarge the common-law approach
by extending the offense to new categories of persons and conduct and by making
the punishment more severe. The broad statutory definition of bribery is illustrated
by a Florida law that makes bribery a felony and provides:

> "Bribery" means corruptly to give, offer, or promise to any public servant, or, if a public
> servant, corruptly to request, solicit, accept, or agree to accept for himself or herself or
> another, any pecuniary or other benefit with an intent or purpose to influence the per-
> formance of any act or omission which the person believes to be, or the public servant
> represents as being, within the official discretion of a public servant, in violation of a
> public duty, or in performance of a public duty. West's Fla. Stat. Ann. § 838.015(1).

Section 838.015(2) makes explicit that the person sought to be bribed need not
have authority to accomplish the act sought or represented. Courts generally construe such terms as "public servant" and "benefit" broadly to accomplish the intended
legislative purpose of statutes defining bribery.

Arizona law adds the term "party officer" to its statute proscribing bribery. It
defines that term as "a person who holds any position or office in a political party,
whether by election, appointment or otherwise." Ariz. Rev. Stat. § 13-2601. Section
13-2602 of the Revised Arizona Statutes provides:

> A. A person commits bribery of a public servant or party officer if with corrupt intent:
>
> > 1. Such person offers, confers or agrees to confer any benefit upon a public ser-
> > vant or party officer with the intent to influence the public servant's or party offi-
> > cer's vote, opinion, judgment, exercise of discretion or other action in his official
> > capacity as a public servant or party officer; or
> >
> > 2. While a public servant or party officer, such person solicits, accepts or agrees
> > to accept any benefit upon an agreement or understanding that his vote, opinion,

judgment, exercise of discretion or other action as a public servant or ficer may thereby be influenced.

B. It is no defense to a prosecution under this section that a person sought to fluenced was not qualified to act in the desired way because such person had n assumed office, lacked jurisdiction or for any other reason.

C. Bribery of a public servant or party officer is a class 4 felony.

Although the Florida statute is explicit on the subject, irrespective of statute courts generally hold that where the act intended to be influenced is connected wit a person's public duty, it is immaterial whether the person bribed has, or has not the authority to do a specific act. See, for example, *State v. Hendricks*, 186 P.2d 943 (Ariz. 1947).

The Range of Bribery Offenses

Bribery covers a wide range of conduct and is frequently associated with white-collar and organized crime situations (see Chapter 9). Common examples of bribery include obtaining the release or acquittal of an arrestee, securing an award of a government contract, and even obtaining a favorable vote by a legislator on a pending bill. The Arizona statute just quoted expands the traditional concept of "public servant" by recognizing the potential for bribery within the ranks of political parties. Although we commonly think of money being offered or requested as a bribe, a variety of other things are offered, sought, or exchanged. These not only include cash or its equivalent but also such tangible and intangible benefits as price advantages, use of vehicles, vacation homes, and even sexual favors. Bribes often occur in subtle or disguised ways. For example, a sale of property for less than its true value would likely be considered bribery if the seller's real purpose was to benefit the purchaser to influence his or her official governmental action.

The Burden of the Prosecution

The gist of the crime of bribery is the unlawful offer or agreement to do something under color of office. Ordinarily, the prosecution must prove not only the offer or agreement or the request or acceptance of a benefit but also that the defendant had a false or corrupt intent. One difficulty encountered in prosecuting a bribery charge is establishing the corrupt intent element. For example, it can be extremely difficult

CASE-IN-POINT

Bribery: What Constitutes a Thing of Value?

McDonald, a male trial court judge in Alabama, was prosecuted for solicitation of sexual favors in exchange for affording a female favorable treatment in pending court cases. He was convicted of bribery under a state statute that provided that it was bribery for any public official to accept "any gift, gratuity, or other thing of value." On appeal, McDonald argued that "sexual intercourse, or the promise of sexual intercourse, or the promise of other sexual favors or relationship" did not meet the test of being a "thing of value" under the bribery statute. The Alabama Court of Criminal Appeals rejected the defendant's contention, saying, "The word 'thing' does not necessarily mean a substance. . . . [I]t includes an act, or action."

McDonald v. State, 329 So.2d 583 (Ala. Crim. App. 1975).

...e that a person received employment or was granted a contract as a result of ...be. The difficulty is compounded because, not infrequently, bribes are disguised ...gifts or even as political or charitable contributions.

Offenses Extending the Concept of Bribery

Many states have enacted statutes to extend the offense of bribery to encompass conduct of persons other than public officials and employees. The two principal areas of extension have been commerce and sports. Although **commercial bribery** and **sports bribery** are not offenses against the administration of justice or government, we include them here as they are extensions of the basic offense of bribery beyond its traditional context. For example, the commercial bribery statute quoted in the following section includes bribery in instances of arbitration, an extrajudicial method of settling disputes.

Commercial Bribery

Section 224.8 of the Model Penal Code outlines an offense known as commercial bribery. Some states have classified certain corrupt business practices, for example, fraudulent acts of purchasing agents, as commercial bribery. The New Jersey law making commercial bribery a crime includes many of the provisions outlined in the Model Penal Code. As amended in 1986, the statute provides:

a. A person commits a crime if he solicits, accepts or agrees to accept any benefit as consideration for knowingly violating or agreeing to violate a duty of fidelity to which he is subject as:

(1) An agent, partner or employee of another;

(2) A trustee, guardian, or other fiduciary;

(3) A lawyer, physician, accountant, appraiser, or other professional adviser or informant;

(4) An officer, director, manager or other participant in the direction of the affairs of an incorporated or unincorporated association;

(5) A labor official, including any duly appointed representative of a labor organization or any duly appointed trustee or representative of an employee welfare trust fund; or

(6) An arbitrator or other purportedly disinterested adjudicator or referee.

b. A person who holds himself out to the public as being engaged in the business of making disinterested selection, appraisal, or criticism of commodities, real properties or services commits a crime if he solicits, accepts or agrees to accept any benefit to influence his selection, appraisal or criticism.

c. A person commits a crime if he confers, or offers or agrees to confer, any benefit the acceptance of which would be criminal under this section. N.J. Stat. Ann. § 2C:21–10.

Under the New Jersey statute, the benefit offered, conferred, agreed to be conferred, solicited, accepted, or agreed to determines the degree of the crime and the penalty.

CASE-IN-POINT

A State Supreme Court Upholds a Conviction for Sports Bribery

Following a bench trial, Angelo Trosclair III was convicted of two counts of bribery of sports participants on February 14, 1981, in violation of La. R.S. 14:118.1. That statute defines bribery of a jockey as "the giving or offering to give, directly or indirectly, anything of apparent present or prospective value to any jockey with the intent to influence him to lose or cause to be lost, or corruptly to affect or influence the result of a horse race or to limit his mount or beast's margin of victory in any race." On appeal Trosclair contended the evidence was legally insufficient to support a finding that he was guilty beyond a reasonable doubt.

In rejecting his contention, the Louisiana Supreme Court noted, "The state presented two witnesses who testified that they had been offered, and had actually received, significant sums of money in exchange for their promises not to finish first, second or third in the fourth race at the Fairgrounds on February 14, 1981. The testimony of the two jockeys, Hale and Durousseau, undoubtedly provided an adequate basis for a finding of guilt beyond a reasonable doubt by a rational trier of fact." Despite the defendant's claim that the credibility of these two witnesses was destroyed, the court further noted, "[I]t is not our function to assess credibility or reweigh the evidence. Our review for minimal constitutional sufficiency of evidence is a limited one which ends upon our finding that the rational trier–reasonable doubt standard has been satisfied." The court affirmed the defendant's convictions. *State v. Trosclair*, 443 So.2d 1098 (La. 1983).

Sports Bribery

Because of the increased role of both professional and amateur sports in society, most states now have made sports bribery a crime. Sports bribery statutes generally make it an offense for a person to offer anything of value to a participant or official in an amateur or professional athletic contest to vary his or her performance. Likewise, it is a crime for a participant or official in a sports event to accept a bribe under such circumstances. See, for example, Iowa Code Ann. § 722.3; *State v. Di Paglia*, 71 N.W.2d 601 (Iowa 1955).

Defenses to the Crime of Bribery

An excerpt from *State v. Gustafson*, in which a Minnesota appellate court addresses the offenses of bribery and conspiracy to commit perjury, is reproduced on the companion website.

Of course, the fact that an offer to bribe is not legally enforceable is no defense. The only recognized defense to a charge of bribery, other than denial, is entrapment. See *State v. Harrington*, 332 So.2d 764 (La. 1976). We discuss the defense of entrapment in Chapter 14.

Perjury

Like bribery, the crime of **perjury** has its roots in biblical times. The Mosaic Code included an admonition against the bearing of false witness. At common law, perjury came to consist of willfully giving under oath in a judicial proceeding false testimony material to the issue. Because of the narrow scope of the offense, it was eventually supplemented by the common-law offense of false swearing, a crime committed when an oath was taken in other than a judicial proceeding.

Elements of the Offense of Perjury

The basic elements of the common-law offenses of perjury and false swearing have been codified by a federal statute, 18 U.S.C.A. § 1621, which provides

> Whoever (1) having taken an oath before a competent tribunal, officer, or person, in any case in which a law of the United States authorizes an oath to be administered, that he will testify, declare, depose, or certify truly, or that any written testimony, declaration, deposition, or certificate by him subscribed, is true, willfully and contrary to such oath states or subscribes any material matter which he does not believe to be true; or (2) in any declaration, certificate, verification, or statement under penalty of perjury as permitted under section 1746 of title 28, United States Code, willfully subscribes as true any material matter which he does not believe to be true; is guilty of perjury. . . .

The reference to 28 U.S.C.A. § 1746 covers certifications subscribed under a rule, regulation, or order pursuant to any law where the subscriber signs a document in substantially the following form: "I declare (or certify, verify, or state) under penalty of perjury under the laws of the United States of America that the foregoing is true and correct." Probably the most common example of this is the declaration a taxpayer signs when filing a federal income tax return. 26 U.S.C.A. § 6065.

All states have laws making perjury a criminal offense. For example, the California perjury statute provides that a person who has taken an oath to tell the truth and who "willfully and contrary to the oath, states as true any material matter which he or she knows to be false" is guilty of perjury. West's Ann. Cal. Penal Code § 118. Although section 118 relates to oaths in administrative and judicial proceedings, section 118a makes it perjury for a person to give a false affidavit to be used in those proceedings. Section 118 is applicable whether the statement, testimony, declaration, deposition, or certification is made or subscribed within or without the State of California. As in other jurisdictions, additional California statutes make it unlawful for anyone to give a false statement under oath in various applications, certificates, and reports. Courts have ruled that a grant of immunity (discussed in Chapter 14) will not protect a witness from prosecution for perjury if the witness testifies falsely. The courts reason that although a witness may be compelled to testify, nevertheless the witness is not compelled to testify falsely. See, for example, *DeMan v. State*, 677 P.2d 903 (Alaska App. 1984).

The Burden of the Prosecution

To convict a defendant of perjury, the prosecution must establish that the defendant took an oath to tell the truth and knowingly made a false statement of fact. Statutes usually permit anyone with scruples against taking an oath to affirm that a statement is true. In either event, a person cannot be lawfully convicted of perjury unless there is proof that he or she was administered the oath by, or made an affirmation before, someone with legal authority. *Whitaker v. Commonwealth*, 367 S.W.2d 831 (Ky. 1963). Furthermore, the defendant's statement must have been material. This means that the testimony given by the defendant must have been capable of influencing the tribunal on the issues before it. *United States v. Jackson*, 640 F.2d 614 (8th Cir. 1981).

Historically, courts in many jurisdictions held that the question of whether a witness's statement was material was a matter to be decided by the judge. In the 1990s some courts reasoned that because materiality is an element of the crime of perjury, a jury must determine that such element has been proved beyond a reasonable doubt. See, for example, *State v. Anderson*, 603 A.2d 928 (N.J. 1992). Their view prevailed in 1995, for as the Supreme Court pointed out in *United States v. Gaudin*, 515 U.S. 506, 115 S.Ct. 2310, 132 L.Ed.2d 444 (1995), the Constitution requires that in a perjury prosecution the materiality of the defendant's statements, like all other elements of a crime, is a jury question.

Some statutes that define perjury require the prosecution to prove that the defendant's statement was made with the "intent to deceive." See, for example, Vernon's Tex. Penal Code Ann. § 37.02(a). Irrespective of statutory requirements, most jurisdictions require the prosecution to prove that the defendant's false statement was made "willfully and corruptly" because at common law, perjury was a specific-intent crime. Requiring the prosecution to prove the defendant's specific intent generally eliminates the likelihood of a defendant's being convicted for simply having made a careless or offhanded statement.

Perjury is one of the most difficult crimes to prove. The inherent difficulty of convicting a defendant of this offense is exacerbated by the **two-witness rule** that prevails in most jurisdictions. Under this rule the prosecution must prove the falsity of a defendant's statements by two witnesses. For example, McKinney's N.Y. Penal Code § 210.50 provides:

> In any prosecution for perjury, except a prosecution based upon inconsistent statements pursuant to section 210.20, or in any prosecution for making an apparently sworn false statement, or making a punishable false written statement, falsity of a statement may not be established by the uncorroborated testimony of a single witness.

Most courts have held that the two-witness rule does not require the live testimony of two witnesses. As the Second Circuit Court of Appeals observed in *United States v. Maultasch*, 596 F.2d 19, 25, n. 9 (2nd Cir.1979), "Technically, the 'two witness' rule is a misnomer because the rule requires either the testimony of a second witness or other evidence of independent probative value."

Perjury by Contradictory Statements

Early American cases followed the common-law principle that a defendant could not be convicted of **perjury by contradictory statements** unless the prosecution established which one of the statements was false. Modern statutes make it unnecessary for the prosecution to establish which of two contradictory statements is false. See, for example, McKinney's N.Y. Penal Law § 210.20 (inability of the prosecution to establish specifically which of the two statements is the false one does not preclude a prosecution for perjury).

Subornation of Perjury

An excerpt from *U.S. v. Scott* (1982), in which a federal appeals court discusses perjury by contradictory statements, is reproduced on the companion website.

At common law, **subornation of perjury** consisted of instigating or procuring another person to commit perjury. Statutes now generally define subornation of perjury much as did the common law. To convict a defendant of the offense, the prosecution must first establish that the defendant induced another to testify falsely and that an actual perjury has been committed. *State v. Devers*, 272 A.2d 794 (Md. 1971). Thus, the Tennessee Supreme Court upheld a subornation of perjury conviction of

CASE-IN-POINT

The Perjury Trial of the Twentieth Century

On August 3, 1948, Whitaker Chambers, a magazine editor, acknowledged before a Congressional committee investigating subversive activities of governmental employees that he operated as a spy for the Soviet Union during 1934–1938. Chambers charged that during this time Alger Hiss, a highly respected official of the U.S. Department of State, had turned over U.S. government documents to him in his former role as a spy. Hiss appeared before the committee and categorically denied that he was, or ever had been, a communist or a communist sympathizer. He asserted that he did not know anyone by the name of Whittaker Chambers.

On December 15, 1948, Hiss testified under oath as a witness before a federal grand jury investigating charges of espionage activities by communists in the U.S. government. Hiss stated that he had never, nor had his wife in his presence, turned over any documents of the State Department to Chambers or to any other unauthorized person. He also testified before the same grand jury on the same day that he thought he could definitely say that he did not see Chambers after January 1, 1937. This grand jury indicted Hiss for having committed perjury when he testified that he did not turn over government documents to Chambers and when he denied knowing Chambers. (The statute of limitations had tolled, so the government could not charge Hiss with espionage.)

Hiss was tried by jury twice, the jury at the first trial having failed to agree upon a verdict. At the second trial, in 1950, the government presented Chambers and a witness to corroborate Chambers's testimony. Hiss denied knowing Chambers, denied any involvement with the communists, and branded Chambers a liar. He presented excellent character witnesses and a well-known expert who categorized Chambers as a psychopathic personality given to repetitive lying. But the government also presented evidence of documents evidently prepared for espionage purposes that were typed on a typewriter owned by Hiss.

Hiss was convicted on both counts of perjury and sentenced to five years in prison. On appeal to the U.S. Court of Appeals for the Second Circuit, Hiss contended the evidence was legally insufficient under the law of perjury. The court acknowledged there must be either two witnesses who testify that the accused violated his oath or one witness to that and corroboration by other evidence the jury believes. The court affirmed, however, because in addition to Chambers's direct testimony, there was sufficient independent evidence of the documents of which Chambers produced copies and which were all available to the defendant at the Department of State. Further, the court found that the evidence established the documents were copied on a typewriter when in the defendant's possession. As to count 2, the court noted that both Chambers and his wife testified that the defendant met and saw Chambers after January 1, 1937. Notwithstanding the decisions of the courts, Hiss stoutly maintained his innocence until his death in 1996.

United States v. Hiss, 185 F.2d 822 (2d Cir. 1951). Review denied, 340 U.S. 948, 71 S.Ct. 532 95 L.Ed. 683 (1951).

an attorney for counseling four men charged with illegally selling whiskey to commit perjury. The attorney was prosecuted, however, only after his four clients were convicted. *Grant v. State*, 374 S.W.2d 391 (Tenn. 1964).

Defenses to the Crime of Perjury

Truth, of course, is a complete defense to a charge of perjury; therefore, a defendant who, while under oath, gives an answer that is "literally accurate, technically responsive or legally truthful" cannot lawfully be convicted of perjury. *United States v. Wall*, 371 F.2d 398, 400 (6th Cir. 1967).

After making a false statement under oath, a witness sometimes recants and tells the truth. Federal law provides for a **recantation** defense to a prosecution for

Perjury: The Truth Must Be Unequivocal

CASE-IN-POINT

A police officer was convicted of committing perjury on the basis of his denial of having received money from certain persons while in performance of his police duties. On appeal, he argued that his answer, "No sir. Not for my duties," to the prosecutor's question whether he received any money from any persons while on official duty as a Chicago policeman was literally true and therefore formed no basis for his conviction. The U.S. Court of Appeals for the Seventh Circuit rejected his contention. The court explained that his initial response, "No sir," was directly responsive and false, so that his nonresponsive attempted hedge that followed was not effective.

United States v. Nickels, 502 F.2d 1173 (7th Cir. 1974).

perjury where in the same continuous court or grand jury proceeding in which a declaration is made, the person making the declaration admits such declaration to be false "if the declaration has not substantially affected the proceeding, or it has not become manifest that such falsity has been or will be exposed." 18 U.S.C.A. § 1623(d).

In reviewing a state statute similar to the federal statute, in *Nelson v. State*, 500 So.2d 1308 (Ala. Cr. App. 1986), the court held that retraction of a false statement is a defense if the retraction occurs in the same proceeding and the statement is retracted before it becomes manifest that the fabrication is or will be exposed.

New York courts have held that recantation is a defense provided it occurs promptly, before the body conducting the inquiry (for example, a grand jury) has been deceived or any prejudice has occurred and before the defendant's perjury has most likely become known to the authorities. *People v. Ezaugi*, 141 N.E.2d 580 (N.Y. 1957). The rationale for the recantation defense is that the object of judicial investigations and trials is to ascertain the truth. It follows, therefore, that the law should encourage a witness to correct a false statement without fear of perjury charges as long as the false statement has prejudiced no one.

Federal Statute on Making False Statements to Government Agencies

We have seen that the federal perjury statute, 18 U.S.C.A. § 1621, criminalizes knowingly making false statements under oath. However, another federal statute, 18 U.S.C.A. § 1001, prohibits making false statements to government agencies irrespective of having taken an oath.

(a) Except as otherwise provided in this section, whoever, in any matter within the jurisdiction of the executive, legislative, or judicial branch of the Government of the United States, knowingly and willfully—

(1) falsifies, conceals, or covers up by any trick, scheme, or device a material fact;

(2) makes any materially false, fictitious, or fraudulent statement or representation; or

(3) makes or uses any false writing or document knowing the same to contain any materially false, fictitious, or fraudulent statement or entry;

shall be fined under this title, imprisoned not more than 5 years or, if the offense involves international or domestic terrorism. . ., imprisoned not more than 8 years, or both. . . . 18 U.S.C.A. § 1001(a).

This is the statute under which former Illinois governor Rod Blagojevich was convicted in his high-profile trial in the summer of 2010. Some have criticized this statute as giving prosecutors a means of "piling on" an additional felony charge when a suspect simply denies charges when confronted by investigators. Commenting on this criticism, the Supreme Court in *Brogan v. United States*, 522 U.S. 398, 405, 118 S.Ct. 805, 810, 139 L.Ed.2d 830, 838 (1998), said,

> The supposed danger is that overzealous prosecutors will use this provision as a means of 'piling on' offenses—sometimes punishing the denial of wrongdoing more severely than the wrongdoing itself. The objectors' principal grievance on this score, however, lies not with the hypothetical prosecutors but with Congress itself, which has decreed the obstruction of a legitimate investigation to be a separate offense, and a serious one.

Obstruction of Justice

At common law it was a crime to commit an act obstructing or tending to obstruct public justice. Any act that prevented, obstructed, impeded, or hindered the administration of justice was considered a common-law misdemeanor. This included a host of acts such as obstructing an officer, tampering with jurors or witnesses, preparing false evidence, and secreting or destroying evidence. As statutory law came into being, some offenses that had been prosecuted as **obstructions of justice**, for example, **escape**, rescue and later **resisting arrest**, were dealt with as distinct crimes.

Modern Statutory Developments

Federal statutes proscribe a lengthy list of actions that constitute obstruction of justice. Among the actions made unlawful are assault on a process server; theft or alteration of process; endeavoring to influence or impede grand or petit jurors; obstructing proceedings before departments, agencies, and committees; tampering with or retaliating against a witness, victim, or informant; and obstructing court orders. 18 U.S.C.A. 1501–1518. Postal laws make it an offense to willfully and knowingly obstruct or retard the passage of the mail. 18 U.S.C.A. § 1701. Thus, in *United States v. Upshaw*, 895 F.2d 109 (3d Cir. 1990), a federal appeals court upheld a defendant's conviction for obstructing mail where a postal truck driver took home a package after he signed out from work.

All jurisdictions have statutes proscribing interference with police officers, prosecutors, jurors, and judges in the performance of their duties. Some laws define obstruction to embrace many forms of conduct. Common examples include statutes making it unlawful to

- Give false information to an officer with the intent to interfere with the officer's lawful performance of duties.
- Knowingly give a false fire or emergency alarm.
- Impersonate an officer.
- Intimidate a victim, witness, or juror.
- Destroy or tamper with public records or physical evidence to be offered in official proceedings.

- Fail to appear in court when required to do so by a summons or subpoena.
- Use jamming devices to interfere with radar equipment used by police to detect speeding.

Federal statutes make it an offense for a person to falsely assume or pretend to be an officer or employee acting under the authority of the United States or any department, agency or officer thereof. 18 U.S.C.A. § 912. Likewise, states commonly proscribe impersonation of officers. For example in Tennessee, a person "who pretends to be a law enforcement officer for the purpose of: (1) Engaging in an activity that is ordinarily and customarily an activity established by law as a law enforcement activity; and (2) Causing another to believe that the person is a law enforcement officer" is guilty of criminal impersonation. Tenn. Code 39-16-301(a).

An excerpt from *People v. Brake* is reproduced on the companion website.

Obstruction of justice involves interference with the administration of the justice system. For example, under Illinois law it is obstruction of justice, a felony, to knowingly destroy, alter, conceal, or disguise physical evidence, plant false evidence, or furnish false information with the intent to prevent the apprehension or to obstruct the prosecution or defense of any person, 720 ILCS 5/31-4(a). In 2003, an Illinois appellate court held that a defendant who swallowed a plastic bag containing drugs, of which an arresting officer was aware, was guilty of violating the statute by concealing or destroying evidence of the defendant's possessory offense. *People v. Brake*, 783 N.E.2d 1084 (Ill. App. 2003).

The Citizen's Duty to Assist Law Enforcement Officers

The common law imposed a duty on citizens to assist the sheriff and, on request, to keep the peace and apprehend wrongdoers. Modern statutes impose on citizens the duty to come to the assistance of law enforcement officers on request. Rather typical is the Ohio law that makes it a misdemeanor to fail to aid a law enforcement officer. Ohio Rev. Code Ann. § 2921.23(a) states,

> No person shall negligently fail or refuse to aid a law enforcement officer, when called upon for assistance in preventing or halting the commission of an offense, or in apprehending or detaining an offender, when such aid can be given without a substantial risk of physical harm to the person giving it.

Many states also have comprehensive statutes making it an offense to prevent, hinder, or delay the discovery or apprehension of persons sought by law enforcement.

Resisting Arrest

All jurisdictions make resisting arrest a crime. The common law did not permit a person to resist a lawful arrest by an authorized officer of the law. It did, however, permit a person to use force to resist an unlawful arrest. *United States v. Heliczer*, 373 F.2d 241 (2d Cir. 1967). Until recently this rule of law was applied in most American jurisdictions, but the functioning of the rule in modern society brought about the need to change it. The legality of an arrest may frequently be a close call, and because officers will normally overcome resistance with necessary force, there is a great danger of escalating violence between the officer and the arrestee. Thus, in recent years many courts have reexamined this common-law doctrine and have held that there is no longer authority to use physical force to resist an arrest by a police officer, or by one the arrestee knows or has good reason to believe is an authorized peace officer performing his or her duties, whether such arrest is legal or illegal. See *Miller v. State*, 462 P.2d 421 (Alaska 1969).

Legislatures, too, have reexamined the issue of using physical force in resisting arrest. In 1980, the New York legislature amended its penal law to provide:

> A person may not use physical force to resist an arrest, whether authorized or un-authorized, which is being effected or attempted by a police officer or peace officer when it would reasonably appear that the latter is a police officer or peace officer. McKinney's N.Y. Penal Law § 35.27.

An excerpt from *State v. Blanton*, a 1979 New Jersey appellate deci-sion involving resisting arrest and obstruction of justice, is reproduced on the companion website.

Oregon law now provides, "A person commits the crime of resisting arrest if the person intentionally resists a person known by the person to be a peace officer in making an arrest." Or. Rev. Stat. § 162.315(1). In *State v. Wright*, 799 P.2d 642 (Or. 1990), the Oregon Supreme Court held that a person may not lawfully resist arrest, even if the arresting officer lacks the legal authority to make the arrest, provided that the officer was acting under color of official authority. In addition, the court observed that if a police officer uses excessive force in making an arrest, the arrestee may use only such physical force as is reasonably necessary to defend against such excessive force.

The modern statutory and judicial revisions to the common-law approach make sense. It is not too great a burden today for a person who believes that he or she has been unlawfully arrested to submit to the officer and seek legal remedies in court. The circumstances surrounding an arrest are completely different from those that prevailed at common law. An arrestee today must be promptly taken before a mag-istrate, and legal counsel is readily available. Moreover, today's detention facilities

CASE-IN-POINT

Court Dismisses Assault Charge but Upholds Conviction for Resisting Arrest

Officer Dennis Cole arrested Joshua Deer after witnessing an apparent assault by him in a restaurant parking lot on January 5, 2006. The officer charged Deer with assault and several other misde-meanors. The trial court dismissed the assault charge but found Deer guilty of other misdemeanors, includ-ing resisting arrest, and sentenced him to 217 days in the corrections center. Deer appealed.

The appellate court pointed out that to prove the offense of resisting arrest the prosecution must first show the arrest was lawful. To do so, the court ob-served, "the state must prove not only that there was a reasonable basis to believe an offense was commit-ted, but also that the offense was one for which the defendant could be lawfully arrested." The court fur-ther pointed out that the state must also show that the defendant knew he was under arrest before resisting.

Here the evidence revealed that Officer Cole had a reasonable basis to believe the defendant was assaulting the victim. Officer Cole located the defen-dant in a car, where he was pushing and holding the victim down and screaming at the victim, who was crying. He ordered Deer to release her, and when he refused the officer used his Taser. Deer then raised his hands in a fighting stance and challenged the of-ficer by saying, "Is that all you have?" Officer Cole at-tempted to use the Taser again, but it was ineffective. The officer, who was in uniform, then told Deer that he was under arrest. Another officer arrived, and the two officers handcuffed Deer as he struggled, pushed, and cursed the officers. The court found that the state presented sufficient evidence to find the defendant resisted arrest beyond a reasonable doubt and af-firmed his conviction.

State v. Deer, 2007 Ohio 1866 (Ohio App. 2007).

do not resemble the crude dungeons where arrestees were incarcerated for lengthy periods before trial under the early English common law. The abandonment of the common-law rule is another example of a rule of law ceasing to exist when the rationale for it has ceased to exist.

Compounding a Crime

At common law a person who accepted money or something else of value in exchange for agreeing not to prosecute a felony was guilty of compounding a felony. In the later history of the common law, it became a misdemeanor to compound a misdemeanor if the conduct constituted an offense against public justice and was dangerous to society. To conceal a felony was also a common-law offense known as **misprision of felony**, which was based on the common-law duty to inform authorities about any felony of which one had knowledge. A person who saw someone commit a felony and used no means to prevent the felony or apprehend the felon committed the offense of misprision of felony.

The Modern Statutory Approach

The legal theory underlying the offense of **compounding a crime** is that justice is debased when an offender bargains to escape the consequences of his or her crime. Most states have enacted statutes making it a crime to compound a felony, but some have expanded the common-law rule by making it a crime to compound any offense. To illustrate, New Hampshire law provides that a person is guilty of a misdemeanor who

1. Solicits, accepts, or agrees to accept any benefit as consideration for his refraining from initiating or aiding in a criminal prosecution; or
2. Confers, offers, or agrees to confer any benefit upon another as consideration for such person refraining from initiating or aiding in a criminal prosecution.
3. It is an affirmative defense that the value of the benefit did not exceed an amount which the actor believed to be due as restitution or indemnification for the loss caused, or to be caused by the offense. N.H. Rev. Stat. Ann. § 642:5.

Most states have not made misprision of felony a statutory crime, probably relying on enforcement of statutes making it an offense to become an accessory after the fact to an offense (see Chapter 4). The federal criminal code, however, specifically makes misprision of felony a crime, the gist of the offense being concealment and not merely the failure to report a felony. 18 U.S.C.A. § 4. The U.S. Court of Appeals for the Second Circuit has held that the elements of misprision of felony are that the defendant had full knowledge that the principal committed and completed an alleged felony and that the defendant failed to notify authorities and took steps to conceal the crime. *United States v. Cefalu*, 85 F.3d 964 (2d Cir. 1996).

A Common Scenario of Compounding a Crime

The offense of compounding a crime often appears where a crime victim whose goods have been stolen agrees with the thief to take back the goods in exchange for not prosecuting. Such an action would ordinarily constitute an offense by the victim. But the New Hampshire statute makes it an affirmative defense that the value of the benefit did not exceed that which the victim believed was due as restitution for a loss. In some instances courts will approve dismissal of a prosecution based on an agreement for restitution to the victim, but persons should not reach such an agreement without prior court approval.

Escape

At common law a person who departed from lawful custody committed the crime of *escape*. Where the prisoner used force, the offense came to be known as *prison break*. A person who forcibly freed another from lawful custody was guilty of the offense of *rescue*.

Modern Statutory Approaches to Escape

Statutes proscribing escape are generally broad enough to embrace all three common-law offenses relating to escape. Often the punishment is more severe when force has been used. Federal statutes prohibit a person who has been lawfully arrested or confined from escaping or attempting to escape from custody, 18 U.S.C.A. § 751, or from rescuing or attempting to rescue a federal prisoner, 18 U.S.C.A. § 752.

Most state statutes define escape in rather simple terms. For example, Texas law provides that a person commits the offense of escape "if he escapes from custody when he is: (1) under arrest for, charged with, or convicted of an offense; or (2) in custody pursuant to a lawful order of court." Vernon's Tex. Penal Code Ann. § 38.06.

The Elements of the Offense of Escape

The gist of the offense of escape is the prisoner's unauthorized departure from lawful custody. Lawful custody is generally presumed once the prosecutor establishes that the escapee was confined to an institution specified by law. In other instances it may be essential for the prosecutor to establish proof of lawful custody; however, those who escape from a jail, juvenile detention home, penal institution, or reformatory are usually presumed to have been in lawful custody. Likewise, a person who fails to return to detention following a temporary release or furlough generally falls within the ambit of escape statutes.

Absent an explicit statutory requirement, courts differ on whether the prosecution must prove the defendant's specific intent to avoid lawful confinement. Of course, if a statute requires specific intent, the prosecution must establish this before a conviction can be lawfully obtained. The Supreme Court has held that under the federal statute, the government need only prove that the escapee knew that his or her actions would result in leaving confinement without permission. *United States v. Bailey*, 444 U.S. 394, 100 S.Ct. 624, 62 L.Ed.2d 575 (1980).

State appellate courts differ on whether the prosecution must prove that the escapee intended to leave or be absent from lawful custody. Recognizing that a slim majority of jurisdictions hold that intent is not an element of the crime, a Florida appellate court in 1975 held that the state must prove that a defendant intended to leave or be absent from lawful custody. Despite the lack of such a statutory requirement in Florida law, the court justified its position by raising some interesting "horribles" under which a defendant charged with escape could be improperly convicted if the state were not required to establish the escapee's specific intent to avoid lawful confinement. In one scenario the court hypothesized that a road gang member had

CASE-IN-POINT

Was Defendant Released on Bail "In Custody" Within the Meaning of the Statute?

After Douglas Owen Davis pled guilty to several drug offenses, the trial court released him on bond pending a presentencing investigation. He was ordered to report to jail on August 1, 2003, prior to his sentencing date. When Davis failed to report as ordered, the trial court, in a bench trial, found him guilty of escape under Virginia Statute § 18.2-479(B), which provides that "[I]f any person lawfully confined in jail or lawfully in the custody of any court or officer thereof or of any law-enforcement officer on a charge or conviction of a felony escapes, otherwise than by force or violence or by setting fire to the jail, he shall be guilty of a Class 6 felony."

In reviewing the conviction, the state appellate court framed the issue as whether Davis was in the "the custody of [the] court" within the meaning of Code § 18.2-479(B) when he failed to report to jail after the trial court released him on bond. Noting the case presented an issue of first impression, the court observed, "Appellant in the instant case had been released from the trial court pending sentence and allowed to remain free on bond. At that point he was no longer in the physical custody or even presence of the court. Thus, the sufficient restraint to have physical control over him 'did not presently exist.'" Accordingly, the court ordered the trial court to dismiss the charges against Davis, commenting in a footnote, "We do not preclude by this holding the trial court's other remedies for failure to abide by its orders."

Davis v. Commonwealth, 608 S.E.2d 482 (Va. App. 2005).

fallen asleep under a tree and was left behind by a negligent guard. The prisoner awakened to find that the guards and work detail had returned to the prison. Because of such possibilities, the court opted for requiring the prosecution to establish the defendant's specific intent to escape. *Helton v. State*, 311 So.2d 381 (Fla. App. 1975).

Defenses to the Charge of Escape

Occasionally an innocent person is unlawfully confined. Even if custody was lawful, the fact that a person was innocent is not generally recognized as a defense to a charge of escape. See *Woods v. Commonwealth*, 152 S.W.2d 997 (Ky. 1941). Of course, a person who escapes can always assert the defense of unlawful confinement or custody. *State v. Dickson*, 288 N.W.2d 48 (Neb. 1980).

During the 1970s there was considerable attention to the conditions of prisons, particularly at the state level. This is illustrated by a landmark 1974 California decision. Defendant Marsha Lovercamp was attacked by other inmates demanding sex. Prison authorities failed to provide Lovercamp with adequate protection, and she escaped. She was found guilty of escape, but an appellate court awarded her a new trial because the trial judge had denied her the opportunity to submit evidence of her plight as a justification for her escape. In reversing Lovercamp's conviction, the appellate court enumerated guidelines for asserting the defense of duress or necessity in these situations. *People v. Lovercamp*, 118 Cal. Rptr. 110 (Cal. App. 1974). The court opined that a limited defense is available if the following conditions exist:

(1) The prisoner is faced with a specific threat of death, forcible sexual attack or substantial bodily injury in the immediate future;

(2) There is no time for a complaint to the authorities or there exists a history of futile complaints which make any result from such complaints illusory;

(3) There is no time or opportunity to resort to the courts;

(4) There is no evidence of force or violence used toward prison personnel or other "innocent" persons in the escape; and

(5) The prisoner immediately reports to the proper authorities when he has attained a position of safety from the immediate threat.

In 1991, the Kansas Court of Appeals observed that the great majority of courts now follow the principles outlined in *Lovercamp*. *State v. Pichon*, 811 P.2d 517 (Kan. App. 1991). See, for example, *People v. Unger*, 338 N.E.2d 442 (Ill. App. 1975), affd., 362 N.E.2d 319 (Ill. 1977); *State v. Alcantaro*, 407 So.2d 922 (Fla. App. 1981).

In 1980, the U.S. Supreme Court recognized the defense of necessity as being valid in the context of the crime of escape. To sustain the defense, the Court said a prisoner must demonstrate (1) that because of an imminent threat of harm, escape was the prisoner's only reasonable alternative; and (2) that the prisoner made a *bona fide* effort to surrender or return to custody as soon as the duress or necessity lost its coercive force. *United States v. Bailey*, supra.

Legislatures respond to public opinion, and improvement of prison conditions is not a high priority for most voters. Because courts tend to focus on issues where the legislative process affords no relief, they will undoubtedly continue to give attention to complaints concerning prison conditions. As they do, prisoners will most likely seek to extend the defense of necessity to justify an escape based on the inadequacy of prison conditions. Some have already argued that the denial of needed medical care should be recognized as a defense to escape. See, for example, *People v. Martin*, 298 N.W.2d 900 (Mich. App. 1980) (allowing defendant to present to jury whether lack of medical attention could rise to the defense of necessity). Courts, however, have generally refused to accept either lack of medical care or inhumane living conditions as a defense to escape.

An excerpt from *State v. Ring* (1978), in which the Maine Supreme Court addresses the offense of attempted escape, is reproduced on the companion website.

Contempt

Early in the history of the common law, judges began to exercise the power to punish persons whose conduct interfered with the orderly functioning of the courts in the administration of justice. Federal and state courts exercise the power to hold an offender—sometimes called a **contemnor**—in either civil or criminal contempt.

In *Bessette v. W.B. Conkey Co.*, 194 U.S. 324, 327, 24 S.Ct. 665, 666, 48 L.Ed. 997, 1001 (1904), the U.S. Supreme Court observed,

> The power to punish for contempt is inherent in all courts; its existence is essential to the preservation of order in judicial proceedings, and to the enforcement of the judgments, orders, and writs of the courts, and, consequently, to the due administration of justice. The moment the courts of the United States were called into existence and invested with jurisdiction over any subject, they became possessed of this power.

State courts have universally recognized that the power to punish for contempt is an inherent one that springs from the nature and constitution of a judicial tribunal. See, for example, *Martin v. Waters*, 259 S.E.2d 153 (Ga. App. 1979); *Little v. State*, 90 Ind. 338 (Ind. 1883).

Civil Contempt

Because it is not considered a crime, we will deal very briefly with the concept of **civil contempt**. Usually it is a sanction imposed to coerce a recalcitrant person to obey a court order. For example, a court may hold someone in civil contempt for failing to pay court-ordered support for dependents. Perhaps the best known example of a civil contempt citation occurred in 1999 when Chief Judge Susan Webber Wright of the U.S. District Court in the Eastern District of Arkansas found former president William Jefferson Clinton in civil contempt in a sexual harassment suit filed by Paula Jones because "the President responded to plaintiff's questions by giving false, misleading and evasive answers that were designed to obstruct the judicial process." *Jones v. Clinton*, 36 F. Supp.2d 1118, 1127 (E.D. Ark. 1999). As a result, the court ordered Clinton to pay approximately $90,000 to attorneys and others for expenses they incurred as a result of his actions. *Jones v. Clinton*, 57 F. Supp.2d 719 (E.D. Ark. 1999).

Criminal Contempt

A court imposes **criminal contempt** to punish an offender whose deliberate conduct is calculated to obstruct or embarrass the court or to degrade a judicial officer in the role of administering justice. Intent is always an element in criminal contempt proceedings. Legislative bodies can regulate the power to punish for contempt, and, in recent years, the Supreme Court has referred to 18 U.S.C.A. § 401, where Congress has provided that

> A court of the United States shall have power to punish by fine or imprisonment, or both, at its discretion, such contempt of its authority, and none other, as—
>
> (1) Misbehavior of any person in its presence or so near thereto as to obstruct the administration of justice;
>
> (2) Misbehavior of any of its officers in their official transactions;
>
> (3) Disobedience or resistance to its lawful writ, process, order, rule, decree, or command.

Direct and Indirect Criminal Contempt

Criminal contempt is classified as either direct or indirect. **Direct contempt** is contemptuous behavior committed in the presence of the court or so close to the court

---

CASE-IN-POINT

Defense Counsel Cited for Criminal Contempt

In 1949, after a turbulent trial lasting nine months, eleven officials of the Communist Party were found guilty of violating the Smith Act (now codified at 18 U.S.C.A. § 2385), which prohibits activities aimed at the violent overthrow of the U.S. government (see Chapter 12). When the trial was concluded, the defense counsel were cited for contempt for "their persistent obstructive colloquies, objections, arguments, and many groundless charges against the court. . . . *United States v. Sacher*, 182 F.2d 416, 423 (2d Cir, 1950). On reviewing the case, the Supreme Court upheld the convictions for contempt. Speaking for the Court, Justice Robert Jackson rejected the argument that the lawyers were merely performing their duty by providing a vigorous defense of their clients:

> But that there may be no misunderstanding, we make clear that this Court, if its aid be needed, will unhesitatingly protect counsel in fearless, vigorous and effective performance of every duty pertaining to the office of the advocate on behalf of any person whatsoever. But it will not equate contempt with courage or insults with independence. It will also protect the processes of orderly trial, which is the supreme object of the lawyer's calling.

Sacher v. United States, 343 U.S. 1, 72 S.Ct. 451, 96 L.Ed. 717 (1952).

as to interrupt or hinder the judicial proceedings. Disruptions of the examination of a witness or an assault on a judge or juror are examples of direct contempt. **Indirect contempt**, sometimes called constructive contempt, refers to acts that occur outside the court's presence that tend to degrade the court or hinder the proceedings of the court. One illustration of indirect contempt is an attorney charged with responsibility for a case who is willfully absent from the courtroom; another is a juror who discusses the facts of a case with a news reporter before the trial of that case has been completed.

One reason for classifying contempt as direct or indirect is to determine the processes that must be followed. Direct criminal contempt proceedings are usually handled summarily. The judge must inform the contemnor of the accusation and ask if he or she can show any cause to preclude the court from entering a judgment of contempt. The court then proceeds to enter its judgment accordingly. Courts justify the summary character of these proceedings because the contemptuous act has occurred in the presence of the judge.

The process is more formal in indirect contempt proceedings. The judge is required to issue a written order to the contemnor to show cause as to why he or she should not be held in contempt of court. The order must set forth the essential facts of the charge and allow the contemnor a reasonable time to prepare a defense. The judge tries all issues of law and fact, but the contemnor has the right to counsel, to compulsory process to secure witnesses, and to refuse to testify.

U.S. Supreme Court decisions have established basic due process rights that must be accorded contemnors in these proceedings. Of course, if there are statutes or court rules in a particular jurisdiction that prescribe the method of processing criminal contempt, the judge must not deviate from those rules to the prejudice of the contemnor's rights. In any contempt proceeding, if the contemnor is to be sentenced to a term of imprisonment for more than six months, he or she is entitled to a jury trial. *Baldwin v. New York*, 399 U.S. 66, 90 S.Ct. 1886, 26 L.Ed.2d 437 (1970).

Is Criminal Contempt Really a Crime?

Until the 1960s there was considerable division of thinking on this subject. In 1968, the U.S. Supreme Court, in *Bloom v. Illinois*, 391 U.S. 194, 88 S.Ct. 1477, 20 L.Ed.2d 522 (1968), held that criminal contempt is a crime in the ordinary sense and may be punished by fine, imprisonment, or both. A person charged with criminal contempt is presumed innocent and must be afforded the procedural and substantive benefits of due process of law. Consequently, a contemnor must be proven guilty beyond a reasonable doubt before being held in criminal contempt. In some states, criminal contempt has been made a statutory crime. See, for example, McKinney's N.Y. Penal Law § 215.50–51, which provides that contempt in the second degree includes such misbehavior before the court, a misdemeanor (§ 215.50), while contempt in the first degree is a felony and concerns refusal to be sworn before the grand jury or refusal to answer proper questions after having been sworn in. (§ 215.51).

Legislative Contempt

Legislative bodies also have the power to punish by contempt those persons whose deliberate acts impede legislative activities. Some states have enacted statutes to

Rule 42. Criminal Contempt

(a) Disposition After Notice. Any person who commits criminal contempt may be punished for that contempt after prosecution on notice.

    (1) *Notice*. The court must give the person notice in open court, in an order to show cause, or in an arrest order. The notice must:

        (A) state the time and place of the trial;

        (B) allow the defendant a reasonable time to prepare a defense; and

        (C) state the essential facts constituting the charged criminal contempt and describe it as such.

    (2) *Appointing a Prosecutor*. The court must request that the contempt be prosecuted by an attorney for the government, unless the interest of justice requires the appointment of another attorney. If the government declines the request, the court must appoint another attorney to prosecute the contempt.

    (3) *Trial and Disposition*. A person being prosecuted for criminal contempt is entitled to a jury trial in any case in which federal law so provides and must be released or detained as Rule 46 provides. If the criminal contempt involves disrespect toward or criticism of a judge, that judge is disqualified from presiding at the contempt trial or hearing unless the defendant consents. Upon a finding or verdict of guilty, the court must impose the punishment.

(b) Summary Disposition. Notwithstanding any other provision of these rules, the court (other than a magistrate judge) may summarily punish a person who commits criminal contempt in its presence if the judge saw or heard the contemptuous conduct and so certifies; a magistrate judge may summarily punish a person as provided in 28 U.S.C. sec. 636(e). The contempt order must recite the facts, be signed by the judge, and be filed with the clerk.

---

cover specific instances of criminal contempt in respect to legislative functions. New York, for example, makes criminal contempt of the legislature a misdemeanor. McKinney's N.Y. Penal Law § 215.60 provides:

> A person is guilty of criminal contempt of the legislature when, having been duly subpoenaed to attend as a witness before either house of the legislature or before any committee thereof he:
>
>   1. Fails or refuses to attend without lawful excuse; or
>
>   2. Refuses to be sworn; or
>
>   3. Refuses to answer any material and proper questions; or
>
>   4. Refuses, after reasonable notice, to produce books, papers, or documents in his possession or under his control which constitute material and proper evidence.
>
> Criminal contempt of the legislature is a first-degree misdemeanor.

An edited version of the U.S. Supreme Court's decision in *Watkins v. United States* is reproduced on the companion website.

Courts have been zealous in assuring that legislative bodies afford contemnors due process of law before adjudging them to be in contempt. See, for example, *Watkins v. United States*, 354 U.S. 178, 77 S.Ct. 1173, 1 L.Ed.2d 1273 (1957), where the Supreme Court invalidated a conviction for contempt of Congress because a witness was not adequately advised as to the pertinence of a subcommittee's questions. In practice, the Congress and state legislative bodies frequently make citations for contempt and then turn the matter over to the courts to handle.

CASE-IN-POINT

Direct Criminal Contempt

Attorney Terrence M. Spears represented Gary Kaeding in an indirect criminal contempt proceeding. During the Kaeding proceeding, the judge stated that he would give Spears five days to file a motion for substitution of judge. Thereafter, the following exchange took place between the court and counsel for the parties:

THE COURT: Also I am going to *sua sponte* enter an order ordering Mr. Kaeding to be examined by a psychiatrist of the choice of the Court, because I do not know whether he is competent to stand trial.

MR. SPEARS: You cannot rule since there has been a Motion for Leave—

THE COURT: (Interrupting) I can; anybody can request a psychiatric examination. I am going to do that.

MR. SPEARS: I will be asking for one for you, Judge; have that on the record.

MR. SCHARF: [Prosecutor] Judge, I would ask he be found in contempt for that.

THE COURT: I am going to hold you in contempt, $500 fine.

MR. SPEARS: Praise God, praise the Lord Almighty God. May you—

MR. SCHARF: (Interrupting) I ask for jail.

MR. SPEARS: May you reap what you sow, Judge, by the good book.

THE COURT: You have 24 hours to pay the fine, or you are going to jail.

In affirming the trial court's finding that attorney Spears was in contempt, the appellate court noted, "Direct criminal contempt is contemptuous conduct occurring in the very presence of the judge, making all the elements of the offense matters within his own personal knowledge. Direct criminal contempt may be found and punished summarily without the usual procedural due process rights being followed. Criminal contempt is conduct which is calculated to embarrass, hinder, or obstruct a court in its administration of justice or derogate from its authority or dignity, thereby bringing the administration of law into disrepute.

"We find that Spears' comments were calculated to embarrass the court and to derogate from the court's authority and dignity. Accordingly, we hold that based on this conduct, the trial court's finding of direct criminal contempt was proper."

People v. Kaeding, 607 N.E.2d 580 (Ill. App. 1993).

Conclusion

The fair and impartial administration of justice and the orderly processes of democratic government depend on the honesty and integrity of those who occupy positions of authority. Hence, the basic common-law offenses described in this chapter have endured over the centuries. The offense of bribery seeks to avoid corruption of those in positions of trust, whereas the crime of perjury seeks to maintain the integrity of the judicial system and agencies of government.

To safeguard the security and effectiveness of law enforcement personnel, all jurisdictions make it a crime to resist arrest, even if the arrest is later declared to be unlawful. Society must ensure confinement of those it has chosen to incarcerate, so it is essential to maintain the offense of escape. With increased awareness of inhumane prison conditions and the rights of prisoners, however, courts have recognized that under some circumstances necessity can be a defense to a charge of escape. The abandonment of the common-law principle that allowed a person to forcibly resist an unlawful arrest and the recognition of the necessity defense in the law of escape both demonstrate the dynamic nature of the criminal law in response to societal change.

Finally, to maintain the effectiveness and the dignity of the judicial and legislative processes, courts and legislatures must have the authority to hold persons in contempt, although that authority must be exercised with due regard for the constitutional rights of contemnors.

Chapter Summary

- **LO1** English common-law created several misdemeanor offenses to aid the administration of justice. Bribery involved improper actions identified with the administration of justice. Perjury consisted of willfully giving false and material testimony under oath. Obstruction of justice involved acts that hindered administration of justice. The common law also made it an offense to conceal a felony (misprision) or accept something of value in exchange for not reporting a felony (compounding). It was an offense at common law to resist an arrest. Escape consisted of departing from lawful custody. Assisting someone to escape the consequences of crime was compounding a crime. Finally, to maintain dignity and authority of the courts, the judges developed the offense of criminal contempt.

- **LO2** The gist of bribery is an unlawful to offer or to agree to do something under color of public office, irrespective of whether the person bribed has the authority to do a specific act. Today, federal statutes proscribe bribery of specific public officers and of witnesses, jurors, and government functionaries. State statutes generally define bribery in broad terms and require the prosecution to prove a defendant's false or corrupt intent. This can be difficult, as bribes are often disguised as political or charitable contributions. Many state statutes now criminalize sports and commercial bribery. Other than a denial, the only recognized defense is entrapment.

- **LO3** Federal statutes make it a crime to take false oaths in judicial proceedings or to falsely swear to a variety of certifications—for example, income tax returns. All states make it a crime to take an oath to tell the truth and then to willfully state as true material matter which the oath taker knows to be false. Many courts held that the question of whether a witness's statement was material was to be decided by the judge. But in 1995, the U.S. Supreme Court ruled that the Constitution requires that the materiality of a defendant's statements is an issue for a jury to decide. Perjury was a specific-intent crime at common law, which led most jurisdictions to require the prosecution to prove that the defendant's false statement was made "willfully and corruptly." The "two-witness rule" that prevails in most jurisdictions requires the prosecution to prove the falsity of a defendant's statements by two witnesses; however, testimony of a second witness may be satisfied by evidence of independent probative value. In "perjury by contradictory statements" scenarios, modern statutes make it unnecessary for the prosecution to establish which of two contradictory statements is false.

- **LO4** To prove subornation of perjury the prosecution must establish that the defendant induced another person to testify falsely and that an actual perjury has been committed. Truth is a defense to a charge of perjury. Federal law provides for a recantation defense where in the same continuous court or grand jury proceeding in which a declaration is made, a witness admits such declaration to be false "if the declaration has not substantially affected the proceeding, or it has not become manifest that such falsity has been or will be exposed." Some state courts hold that retraction of a false statement is a defense if the retraction occurs in the same proceeding and the statement is retracted before it becomes manifest that the fabrication is or will be exposed.

- **LO5** Federal statutes proscribe impersonation of federal officers. They also proscribe a lengthy list of acts that influence or impede grand or petit jurors; obstruct proceedings before agencies and committees; tamper with witnesses, victims, or informants; or obstruct court orders. All jurisdictions make resisting arrest a crime. Although the common law allowed a person to use force to resist an unlawful arrest, today many courts hold that a person may not lawfully resist arrest, even if the arresting officer lacks legal authority.

- **LO6** Most states have enacted statutes making it a crime to compound a felony. Some states have expanded the common-law rule by making it a crime to compound any offense. Most states have not made misprision of felony a statutory crime, probably relying on enforcement of statutes that make it an offense to become an accessory after the fact. The federal criminal code, however, specifically makes misprision of felony a crime, with the gist of the offense being concealment and not merely the failure to report a felony.

- **LO7** Federal statutes prohibit a person who has been lawfully arrested or confined from escaping or attempting to escape from custody, or from rescuing or attempting to rescue a federal prisoner. Most state statutes proscribe the offense of "escape" in similar terms. A person who escapes can always assert the defense of unlawful confinement or custody. In 1980, the U.S. Supreme Court recognized the "defense of necessity" if a prisoner can demonstrate that because of an imminent threat of harm, escape was the only reasonable alternative and the prisoner made a *bona fide* effort to surrender or return to custody as soon as the duress or necessity lost its coercive force.

- **LO8** Federal and state courts exercise the power to hold an offender (contemnor) in contempt. Courts impose criminal contempt to punish an offender whose deliberate conduct is calculated to obstruct or embarrass the court or to degrade a judicial officer in the administration of justice. Direct criminal contempt involves behavior committed in the presence of the court or so close to the court as to interrupt or hinder the judicial proceedings. Indirect criminal contempt consists of contemptuous acts that occur outside the court's presence. Contempt procedures must follow strict processes to insure fairness, and a contemnor who is to be punished by more than six months' imprisonment is entitled to a jury trial. Legislative bodies also have the power to punish by contempt those persons whose deliberate acts impede legislative activities. They frequently refer proceedings to a court.

Key Terms

bribery The crime of offering, giving, requesting, soliciting, or receiving something of value to influence a decision of a public official.

commercial bribery Offering, soliciting, or accepting a benefit or consideration in respect to a business or professional matter in violation of a person's duty of fidelity.

sports bribery Offering anything of value to a participant or official in an amateur or professional athletic contest to vary his or her performance.

perjury The crime of making a material false statement under oath.

two-witness rule A requirement that to prove a defendant guilty of perjury, the prosecution must prove the falsity of the defendant's statements either by two witnesses or by one witness and corroborating documents or circumstances.

perjury by contradictory statements Commission of the offense of perjury by a witness who makes conflicting statements under oath.

subornation of perjury The crime of procuring someone to lie under oath.

recantation The withdrawal or repudiation of previous statements. In some instances, a person who has lied under oath is permitted to recant to avoid being charged with perjury.

obstruction of justice The crime of impeding or preventing law enforcement or the administration of justice.

escape Unlawfully fleeing to avoid arrest or confinement.

resisting arrest The crime of obstructing or opposing a police officer making an arrest.

misprision of felony The crime of concealing a felony committed by another.

compounding a crime The acceptance of money or something else of value in exchange for an agreement not to prosecute a person for committing a crime.

contemnor A person found to be in contempt of court.

civil contempt Being held in contempt of court pending the performance of some court-ordered act.

criminal contempt Punishment imposed by a judge against a person who violates a court order or otherwise intentionally interferes with the administration of the court.

direct contempt An obstructive or insulting act committed by a person in the immediate presence of the court.

indirect contempt An act committed outside the presence of the court that insults the court or obstructs a judicial proceeding.

Questions for Thought and Discussion

1. To what extent have contemporary legislative bodies expanded the scope of bribery to cover classes of persons beyond public officials?
2. How does the requirement that the prosecution prove a defendant's specific intent to deceive protect citizens from unwarranted prosecutions for perjury?
3. Contrast the common-law rule allowing a person to resist an unlawful arrest with the modern trend of requiring citizens to submit to unlawful arrests by police officers. Which approach makes more sense in today's society?
4. Is a state statute that makes it a criminal offense "to hinder or delay a law enforcement officer in the performance of his or her duties" likely to be held void for vagueness under the tests outlined in Chapter 3?
5. Would a person who accepts the return of stolen goods from a thief without agreeing to refrain from filing a criminal complaint be guilty of compounding a crime?
6. Name some acts that would likely be considered obstruction of justice under federal and state statutes.
7. Despite the wording of most statutes proscribing the offense of escape, courts increasingly require the prosecution to prove the defendant's specific intent to avoid lawful confinement. Are courts justified in imposing such a requirement on the statutory law?
8. Have courts aided society by allowing escapees from prison to defend their actions on the basis of intolerable prison conditions? Are such conditions likely to be remedied by the legislative process?
9. Should courts allow an escapee from prison to assert as a defense the prison's failure to provide essential medical treatment to the prisoner? If this is to be recognized as a basis for a defense of necessity, what stipulations would you recommend to protect the public?
10. Describe some specific acts that a trial judge could justifiably consider to be in direct contempt of court.
11. Why does the law require more formal proceedings in cases of indirect contempt than in cases of direct criminal contempt?

Problems for Discussion and Solution

1. A pharmaceutical company's agent secretly gives a free three-day ski resort vacation to a hospital purchasing agent, urging the purchasing agent to "to keep in mind the pharmaceutical company's products" when ordering pharmaceuticals for the hospital. What, if any, offense has been committed? By whom?

2. George Fox is a prisoner at a men's reformatory. He is assigned to a work farm enclosed by a fence and instructed to remain inside the fence. On the second day of Fox's imprisonment, a guard discovers that Fox has not returned to his quarters by curfew. Early the next morning, Fox is found walking down a road outside the fence that bounds the work farm. In his trial for escape, Fox contends that this evidence is insufficient to establish his intent to escape. He claims that had he intended to escape he would not have allowed himself to be located so easily. He claims that he got lost on the prison farm and was trying to make his way back to his barracks. What result is likely? Why?

3. Harry Hamilton is arrested for grand theft. He signs a form stating that he has no prior convictions under oath before a deputy court administrator. Based on this representation, he is granted pretrial release on his own recognizance. There is no statute or court rule that authorizes the court administrator to authorize deputies to give oaths. He is prosecuted for perjury and at trial his statement is proven to be false. Based on this evidence, does Hamilton have a good defense to the charge of perjury?

4. The state charges Larcen Inmatio with escape from prison. The court appoints a public defender to represent him. You are assigned to investigate the case and report your findings to the public defender. Your investigation reveals that Inmatio was convicted of burglary of a dwelling and was serving the second year of a five-year sentence in the state prison. He complained to the warden that another inmate had sexually molested him and requested transfer to another prison, or at least another cell block. After confirming that an inmate in Inmatio's cell block had molested him on one occasion, the warden told Inmatio that he would place him in another cell block. During the next three days the warden took no action. On the fourth day, while Inmatio and other prisoners were on a work detail picking up trash from the roadside outside the prison, Inmatio left without permission and caught a ride to a nearby city where he obtained a construction job. He had no contact with the prison until two weeks later, when the local police apprehended him and returned him to prison. Based on your investigation, do you think the public defender can successfully establish the defense of necessity on behalf of Inmatio?

5. Early one evening Alden Dancio was sitting at a table in a tavern with his girlfriend and two other couples. They had been drinking beer and were talking and laughing. A local uniformed police officer, who was patrolling the area, stopped in to have a sandwich. Annoyed by the loud talking and laughing, the officer walked over to the table. There he saw Angela Mellow, a female he occasionally dated, sitting with her arm around Dancio. No one at the table was intoxicated. The officer demanded that Dancio produce some identification and, when he refused, the officer told him he was under arrest for disorderly conduct and ordered him to get in the patrol car. Dancio refused and, after an altercation between the two, the officer handcuffed Dancio and placed him in the patrol car. After reviewing the police file, the prosecutor acknowledged that Dancio should not have been arrested for disorderly conduct. He dismissed that charge. Nevertheless, the prosecutor decided to file charges against Dancio for resisting arrest. Is there a basis for charging Dancio with resisting arrest in the state where you live?

CHAPTER 14

Criminal Responsibility and Defenses

LEARNING OBJECTIVES

After reading this chapter, you should be able to explain . . .

1. the difference between a negative defense and an affirmative defense
2. why the common law recognized "infancy" as a defense and why that defense has become rare today
3. why the distinction between voluntary and involuntary intoxication is important with respect to defenses asserting incapacity to commit a crime
4. the origin of the insanity defense and how the defense has evolved over time
5. why acting under duress can relive one of responsibility for a criminal act
6. the limited application of the defense of necessity
7. why mistake of law is not a criminal defense but mistake of fact can be
8. the unique defense of alibi
9. the degree to which one may use force to defend oneself
10. "battered woman syndrome" and its relationship to self-defense
11. when force may be used to defend other people, and when it may be used to protect property
12. whether one is entitled to use force to resist an unlawful arrest
13. how the Fifth Amendment protects against compulsory self-incrimination
14. the different forms of immunity
15. the constitutionally based defense of double jeopardy
16. why statutes of limitations are important in the criminal law
17. what constitutes entrapment and why it can be a defense
18. the seldom-successful defense of selective prosecution
19. some of the more novel and innovative defenses that have been proposed in recent years

CHAPTER OUTLINE

John W. Hinckley, Jr. watched the 1976 movie Taxi Driver over and over and developed an obsession with the actress Jodie Foster, who portrayed a teenage prostitute in the film. Hinckley moved to New Haven, Connecticut to be close to Foster, who was an undergraduate student at Yale. He never met Foster, but left letters and poems in her mailbox and spoke to her twice by telephone. Hinckley decided that to impress Foster he would assassinate the president of the United States. He followed President Jimmy Carter around the country but never took action against him. On March 30, 1981, Hinckley approached President Reagan's entourage outside the Washington Hilton and fired six shots from a .22 caliber handgun. The President's press secretary, a Secret Service agent, and a Washington, D.C. police officer were struck and wounded. One of the bullets ricocheted off the presidential limousine and struck President Reagan in the chest. Reagan was rushed to George Washington University Hospital, where surgeons removed the bullet and saved the president's life. Federal authorities charged Hinckley with attempted assassination of the president, attempted murder, use of a firearm in the commission of a federal crime, and multiple assault charges, as well as a weapons violation under the D.C. Code. Hinckley was found competent to stand trial but pleaded not guilty by reason of insanity. Although the defense had little difficulty producing evidence of Hinckley's mental illness, the nation was stunned and outraged when the jury returned a not-guilty verdict. Subsequently, Hinckley was committed to a mental institution, where he remains today. As you will see in this chapter, the Hinckley case would have a dramatic impact on the law as it relates to the insanity defense. Still, the insanity defense, which is seldom invoked and rarely successful, continues to evoke popular bewilderment and scorn.

| Introduction

As the English common law developed, the concept of **criminal responsibility** became a significant consideration. As it did, various defenses to criminal conduct emerged. Incapacity to commit a crime because of infancy, insanity, or, under some circumstances, intoxication came to be recognized as defenses. Self-defense, defense of others, and defense of habitation and other property were also recognized as defenses because of justification for a defendant's use of force in those instances. Moreover, the common law allowed a defendant to assert certain matters as an excuse or justification for having committed a criminal act. Mistake of fact that occurred honestly, necessity, duress, and—under limited circumstances—consent were recognized as defenses.

Essentially these defenses have been recognized in various jurisdictions in the United States, although they have been modified over the years. The Fifth Amendment to the U.S. Constitution and corresponding provisions of the state constitutions furnish defendants two additional defenses: immunity and double jeopardy. Legislatures initiated the concept of a statute of limitations on the prosecution of most crimes. Through judicial development, entrapment has become a recognized defense where improper governmental conduct has induced an otherwise innocent person to commit a crime. In rare instances, defendants have successfully asserted the defense of selective prosecution—that is, being singled out for prosecution.

In previous chapters, we have mentioned some defenses applicable to specific substantive crimes. We revisit some of those defenses in this chapter, further examining the scope of common-law, constitutional, and statutory defenses to criminal charges.

Defenses in General

Defendants who plead not guilty to a criminal charge may not only rely on their general denial; they may also offer any defense (sometimes called a **negative defense**) not required to be specifically pled. A defendant merely has the burden of producing evidence of a negative defense. This is sometimes referred to as the defendant's burden of production of evidence; in some instances, however, the prosecution's own evidence might raise the issue. Once such evidence is produced, the prosecution usually has the burden to overcome it. For example, Henry Homeowner is charged with the manslaughter of a person who forced entry into his home one night after Homeowner had gone to bed. Homeowner claims to have acted in self-defense by using deadly force to defend his home. If any evidence discloses that he acted in self-defense, then to establish that Homeowner is guilty of manslaughter, the prosecution must ordinarily prove that he did not act reasonably. But in some jurisdictions, depending on the specific defense, the defendant not only must be required to produce evidence but must also carry the burden of proving the defense by the greater weight of the evidence, usually referred to as the **preponderance of the evidence**.

A defense that must be specifically pled is classified as an **affirmative defense**—that is, one that does not simply negate an element of the crime but, rather, consists of new matters relied on as an excuse or justification for the defendant's otherwise illegal conduct. To illustrate, suppose Larry Boatman is charged with burglary of a vacant beach cottage. He pleads not guilty, raising the affirmative defense of necessity. He argues that although he entered the cottage with the intent to take food from within, it was an act of necessity because he and his starving companions were shipwrecked in a desolate area without other means of obtaining food or drinking water. Ordinarily, a defendant has the burden to prove the matters offered as an affirmative defense. Therefore, it is up to Boatman to prove by the preponderance of the evidence that he acted out of necessity. Courts sometimes vary in their views about whether a defense is a negative or affirmative one.

For purposes of analysis and study, we have divided defenses to crimes (beyond simply negative defenses) into five categories:

1. Those asserting lack of capacity (infancy, intoxication, insanity, automatism)
2. Those asserting excuse or justification (duress, necessity, consent, mistake of law or of fact)
3. Those justifying the use of force (self-defense, defense of others, defense of property and habitation, and using force to resist an arrest)
4. Those relying on constitutional or statutory rights (immunity, double jeopardy, statutes of limitation)
5. Those assailing governmental conduct (entrapment, selective prosecution)

It is difficult to generalize whether a specific defense is or is not an affirmative one. The defenses we categorized are generally classified as affirmative defenses, but this is not always true. The prosecution is always required to prove the defendant guilty beyond any reasonable doubt. Still, the law may constitutionally place the burden on a defendant to establish an affirmative defense as long as that defense is not one that simply negates an element of the crime the prosecution must prove to convict the defendant. *Patterson v. New York*, 432 U.S. 197, 97 S.Ct. 2319, 53 L.Ed.2d 281 (1977). Defenses authorized by statute are often styled as affirmative defenses, but merely labeling a defense an affirmative defense is not sufficient. Courts look to the substance to make certain that an affirmative defense is one that alleges lack of capacity to commit a crime, or seeks to excuse or justify conduct that would otherwise lead to criminal responsibility, rather than one that simply negates an element of the crime.

Defenses Asserting Lack of Capacity to Commit a Crime

In proffering a defense asserting the lack of capacity to commit a crime, the defendant admits the *actus reus* alleged by the prosecution but denies criminal responsibility for that act on the ground that he or she lacked the mental capacity to form the requisite criminal intent. There are four principal defenses asserting the lack of capacity to commit a crime: infancy, intoxication, insanity, and automatism.

Infancy

The common law regarded a child under age seven as incapable of forming criminal intent. Thus, **infancy** gave rise to a conclusive presumption of incapacity for a child younger than seven. This presumption of incapacity was rebuttable regarding a child between seven and fourteen years old, with the prosecution having the burden to demonstrate that a child younger than fourteen was capable of comprehending the wrongdoing involved in commission of an offense. Children over age fourteen were treated as adults. *Commonwealth v. Cavalier*, 131 A. 229 (Pa. 1925).

The rationale for these common-law presumptions was that young children require protection from the harshness of the adversarial processes of the law. Some jurisdictions have abolished these presumptions because legislatures have provided that children under certain ages, usually sixteen to eighteen, are subject to the jurisdiction of the juvenile courts, where the procedures are tailored toward less mature offenders. In establishing juvenile courts, the legislatures frequently intend to eliminate the common-law presumption of incapacity of infants. See *People v. Miller*, 334

CASE-IN-POINT

Court Distinguishes Burden of Establishing Affirmative Defense of Duress from the Prosecution's Burden where a Defendant Raises an Issue of Self-Defense

John New, a prison inmate, was convicted after a jury trial of taking a hostage and carrying a weapon while an inmate. The evidence revealed that New and another inmate, Wesley Floyd, burst into a prison office, where the defendant put a knife to a female prison employee's throat and threatened to harm her unless the building was cleared immediately. At trial, the defendant testified that he had no choice but to do as he was directed by inmate Floyd, a convicted murderer, who had threatened his life several times. Over the defendant's objection, the trial court instructed the jury that it was the defendant's burden to prove his defense of duress by a preponderance of the evidence. On appeal the defendant argued that the State should have the burden of disproving duress, just as it does when a defendant raises an issue of self-defense.

In rejecting New's contention, the South Carolina Supreme Court pointed out that duress excuses the crime but does not negate any element of the offense, whereas self-defense goes to an element of the crime. Generally, affirmative defenses must be established by a preponderance of the evidence. Thus, it was defendant's burden to prove his affirmative defense of duress by a preponderance of the evidence. In a footnote, the court noted that in *Dixon v. United States*, 548 U.S. 1, 126 S.Ct. 2437, 165 L.Ed.2d 299 (2006), the U.S. Supreme Court upheld that a jury instruction that placed the burden on a defendant to establish the defense of duress by preponderance of the evidence. The court affirmed the defendant's conviction.

State v. New, 640 S.E.2d 871 (S.C. 2007)

N.E.2d 421 (Ill. App. 1975), for the court's perception of legislative intent under Illinois law. Under federal law, a juvenile is a person who has not attained age eighteen at the time of the commission of an offense. 18 U.S.C.A. § 5031.

Starting with Illinois in 1899, all states developed juvenile court systems. These courts traditionally handled juvenile offenders separately from adults in nonadversarial proceedings. The theory was that the state acted as *parens patriae*, taking a clinical and rehabilitative, rather than an adversarial or punitive, approach to youthful offenders. Nevertheless, the system suffered from many deficiencies, such as inadequate staffing and substandard facilities, and the results were disappointing. Many youthful offenders were not rehabilitated, nor were they afforded even the most basic constitutional rights accorded adults in the criminal justice system. In the words of the U.S. Supreme Court, "[T]he child receives the worst of both worlds: that he gets neither the protections accorded to adults nor the solicitous care and regenerative treatment postulated for children." *Kent v. United States*, 383 U.S. 541, 556, 86 S.Ct. 1045, 1054, 16 L.Ed.2d 84, 94 (1966). Although juvenile courts remain as part of the judicial scene, statutes commonly provide that for certain offenses a juvenile may be tried as an adult.

Intoxication

Intoxication can result from ingestion of alcohol or drugs. The common law did not excuse from responsibility for criminal conduct a person who voluntarily became intoxicated. In an early English case, the court approved a death sentence for a homicide committed by an extremely intoxicated defendant. *Regina v. Fogossa*, 75 Eng. Rep. 1 (1550).

In evaluating whether intoxication is a defense, **voluntary intoxication** must first be distinguished from **involuntary intoxication**. In most jurisdictions, voluntary intoxication may be considered in determining whether a defendant can formulate the specific intent the prosecution must establish in such crimes as larceny, burglary, and premeditated murder. Most courts reject the defense of voluntary intoxication for general-intent crimes. See, for example, *United States v. Hanson*, 618 F.2d 1261 (8th Cir. 1980) (assault on a federal officer); *Commonwealth v. Bridge*, 435 A.2d 151 (Pa. 1981) (voluntary manslaughter); *State v. Keaten*, 390 A.2d 1043 (Me. 1978) (gross sexual misconduct). These decisions are grounded in the public policy of not excusing conduct by those who voluntarily impair their own judgment. Three decades ago the South Carolina Supreme Court judicially adopted a rule that voluntary intoxication, where it has not produced permanent insanity, is never an excuse for or a defense to a general- or specific-intent crime. *State v. Vaughn*, 232 S.E.2d 328, 330 (S.C. 1977). Recent years have witnessed considerable activity by several state legislatures addressing the issue of voluntary intoxication as a defense.

In 1996 the U.S. Supreme Court, in a 5–4 decision, upheld a Montana law that does not allow a jury to consider a defendant's voluntary intoxication in determining whether the defendant possessed the mental state necessary for the commission of a crime. *Montana v. Egelhoff*, 518 U.S. 37, 116 S.Ct. 2013, 135 L.Ed.2d 361 (1996). In 1999 the Florida Legislature enacted a statute that eliminates voluntary intoxication as a defense. The new law specifies that evidence of voluntary intoxication is not admissible to show a lack of specific intent or to show insanity at the time of the offense. However, the statute makes an exception for controlled substances taken pursuant to a doctor's prescription. West's Fla. Stat. Ann. § 775.051.

Lattimore v. State (1988), where an Alabama appeals court addresses a defendant's contention that his voluntary intoxication should be accepted as a defense to a charge of murder, is excerpted on the companion website.

Florida courts have held that the statute excluding the right to assert the defense does not violate a defendant's constitutional right to due process. *Barrett v. State*, 862 So.2d 44 (Fla. App. 2003); *Cuc v. State*, 834 So.2d 378 (Fla. App. 2003). The trend is for states to disallow the defense of voluntary intoxication, on the theory that a defendant who voluntarily deprives himself or herself of the ability to distinguish between right and wrong is criminally responsible for acts committed. As of 2008, Alabama, Delaware, Florida, Georgia, Hawaii, Idaho, Indiana, Missouri, Montana, Ohio, Oklahoma, Pennsylvania, and Texas had statutes providing that voluntary intoxication is not a defense to crime.

Involuntary intoxication rarely occurs, but when it does, it removes the criminality of an act committed under its influence if, as a result of intoxication, the defendant no longer knows right from wrong. *State v. Mriglot*, 564 P.2d 784 (Wash. 1977). A person can become involuntarily intoxicated through the trickery or fraud of another person—see, for example, *Johnson v. Commonwealth*, 115 S.E. 673 (Va. 1923)—or through inadvertent ingestion of medicine. See *People v. Carlo*, 361 N.Y.S.2d 168 (N.Y. App. Div. 1974). The New Hampshire Supreme Court summarized the law in this area:

> Generally the defense of involuntary intoxication will only be considered when it is shown that the intoxication was the product of external pressures such as fraud, force, or coercion, or when intoxication resulted from a medical prescription. *State v. Plummer*, 374 A.2d 431, 435 (N.H. 1977).

Involuntary intoxication as a defense to criminal liability has been codified in some jurisdictions. Section 939.42 of the Wisconsin Statutes is rather typical:

> An intoxicated or a drugged condition of the actor is a defense only if such condition:

> (1) Is involuntarily produced and renders the actor incapable of distinguishing between right and wrong in regard to the alleged criminal act at the time the act is committed; or

(2) Negatives the existence of a state of mind essential to the crime *except as provided in § 939.24(3).* Wis. Stat. Ann. § 939.42.

The Wisconsin legislature inserted the italicized exception in 1987 to stipulate that a voluntarily produced intoxicated or drugged condition is not a defense to liability for criminal recklessness.

Wisconsin courts have said that to establish the defense of involuntary intoxication, the accused must show the inability to tell right from wrong at the time of the offense.

Insanity

All persons are presumed sane unless previously adjudicated insane. Even a person who has been adjudicated legally insane may still be found guilty of a criminal act if it was committed during a lucid interval. Insanity is a legal concept and is defined differently in various jurisdictions in the United States. A person who meets the requirements of the definition at the time of commission of an offense may plead **insanity** as a defense to criminal conduct.

Few cases have caused as great a concern about how the criminal justice system functions as did the verdict of **not guilty by reason of insanity** in John Hinckley's federal court trial for the 1981 shooting of President Ronald Reagan, his press secretary, and two law officers. The defense of insanity has never been popular with the public. It has sometimes been called "a rich person's defense" because defendants who invoke it frequently expend considerable financial resources to present psychiatric testimony. The Hinckley verdict motivated Congress and several state legislatures to review the status of insanity defenses.

Historical Roots of the Insanity Plea

The concept of mental responsibility has deep roots in Anglo-American law—the common-law crimes included a *mens rea* (mental element). Nevertheless, the common law was slow to develop any standard for a mental condition that would excuse a person from criminal responsibility. By the eighteenth century, some English courts applied what has sometimes been called a "wild beast" test. For example, one English judge opined that "a man . . . totally deprived of his understanding and memory, . . . and doth not know what he is doing, no more than an infant, than a brute, or a wild beast . . . is never the object of punishment." *Rex v. Arnold*, 16 Howell's State Trials 695 (Eng. 1724).

The *M'Naghten* Rule

Little progress occurred in the development of the defense of insanity until 1843, when an event in England caused even greater consternation than the Hinckley verdict caused in the United States. Suffering from delusions that he was being persecuted by government officials, Daniel M'Naghten decided to kill Sir Robert Peel, the British Home Secretary. (Peel was the founder of the British police system; hence, the term "bobbies" is still applied to British law officers.) From outside Peel's home, M'Naghten saw Peel's secretary, Edward Drummond, leave the house. Believing Drummond to be Peel, M'Naghten shot and killed him. At trial, M'Naghten's barristers argued that he was insane at the time of the shooting and therefore should be found not guilty. The jury agreed. Enraged by the verdict, Queen Victoria insisted that the law provide a yardstick for the defense of insanity. The House of Lords responded, and the test they developed is still referred to as the *M'Naghten rule*.

It provides that insanity cannot be a defense to a crime unless "at the time of committing the act, the party accused was labouring under such a defect of reason, from disease of the mind, as not to know the nature and quality of the act he was doing; or, if he did know it, that he did not know what he was doing was wrong." *M'Naghten's Case*, 8 Eng. Rep. 718 (1843).

The *M'Naghten* rule became the test for insanity used in both federal and state courts in the United States. As psychology and psychiatry developed new theories of mental capacity, critics attacked the rule as being based solely on cognition (that is, a process of the intellect) and ignoring a person's emotions. In response, some courts accepted the **irresistible impulse** test, which stressed volition (that is, self-control), as a supplement to the *M'Naghten* rule. See *Parsons v. State*, 2 So. 854 (Ala. 1887). This allowed a person who knew an act was wrong but who acted under an uncontrollable desire or the duress of mental disease to be excused from a criminal act.

The *Durham* Test

Another test for insanity evolved from *Durham v. United States*, where the U.S. Court of Appeals for the District of Columbia held that an accused is not criminally responsible if that person's unlawful act was "the product of mental disease or defect." 214 F.2d 862, 876 (D.C. Cir. 1954). Many psychiatrists applauded the ***Durham* test**, but it gained little judicial support outside of the District of Columbia. It was eventually discarded even there. *United States v. Brawner*, 471 F.2d 969 (D.C. Cir. 1972).

The ALI Standard

In 1962 the American Law Institute (ALI), an association of distinguished lawyers and judges, proposed a new standard combining both cognitive and volitional capacities as a test for insanity. It is sometimes referred to as the **ALI Standard or substantial capacity test** and reads as follows:

> A person is not responsible for criminal conduct if at the time of such conduct, as a result of mental disease or defect, a person lacks substantial capacity either to appreciate the wrongfulness of his conduct or to conform his conduct to the requirements of the law.

An edited version of the Second Circuit's decision in *U.S. v. Freeman* is reproduced on the companion website.

The ALI Standard was adopted by most federal courts and has sometimes been referred to as the *Freeman* rule, stemming from an endorsement of the test by the U.S. Court of Appeals for the Second Circuit in *United States v. Freeman*, 357 F.2d 606 (2d Cir. 1966). State courts, however, remained divided in their approaches to the defense of insanity. Many opted to follow the new substantial capacity test; the remainder adhered to the basic *M'Naghten* **right from wrong test**.

The substantial capacity concept was applied as the test for insanity in the infamous John Hinckley case. Under the ALI criteria, a showing of substantial impairment of a person's mental faculties is enough to meet the test of insanity. In contrast, establishing insanity under a strict *M'Naghten* approach requires a showing of total incapacity, and evidence that does not tend to prove or disprove the defendant's ability to distinguish right from wrong is irrelevant.

The Current Federal Standard

Dissatisfied with the ALI test, Congress decided to eliminate the volitional prong in the federal test for insanity and to revert substantially to the *M'Naghten* rule when it enacted the **Insanity Defense Reform Act of 1984**. This act provides that in federal courts:

It is an affirmative defense to a prosecution under any federal statute that, at the time of the commission of the acts constituting the offense, the defendant, as a result of a severe mental disease or defect, was unable to appreciate the nature and quality or the wrongfulness of his acts. Mental disease or defect does not otherwise constitute a defense. 18 U.S.C.A. § 17(a).

In addition, the act stipulates that "[t]he defendant has the burden of proving the defense of insanity by clear and convincing evidence." 18 U.S.C.A. § 17(b). The **clear and convincing evidence standard** is higher than the usual civil evidentiary standard of preponderance of the evidence but somewhat lower than the standard of **beyond a reasonable doubt**, the evidentiary standard required for criminal convictions. Although there has been some controversy concerning the legitimacy of placing the burden of proof of insanity on the defendant, the U.S. Supreme Court has held that this type of "burden shifting" does not violate the defendant's right of due process of law under the U.S. Constitution. *Patterson v. New York*, supra. Moreover, federal appellate court decisions in 1986 affirmed the constitutionality of this burden shifting under the 1984 federal act. *United States v. Freeman*, 804 F.2d 1574 (11th Cir. 1986); *United States v. Amos*, 803 F.2d 419 (8th Cir. 1986).

On April 4, 1995, a federal jury found Francisco Martin Duran guilty of attempting to assassinate President Bill Clinton. Duran pleaded insanity. His counsel argued that Duran was a paranoid schizophrenic who was shooting at the White House as a symbol of a government he hated. Unlike in the John Hinckley trial, the new federal standard for insanity applied in Duran's trial. The jury rejected Duran's plea of insanity and found him guilty of attempting to assassinate the president, as well as guilty of several other charges.

The Insanity Defense Reform Act: The Effect on the Use of Psychiatric Evidence

Under the Insanity Defense Reform Act, psychiatric evidence of impaired volitional control is inadmissible to support an insanity defense. After passage of the new law, a question arose as to whether Congress also intended to prohibit the use of psychiatric evidence to negate a defendant's specific intent to commit an offense. In 1990 the U.S. Court of Appeals for the Eleventh Circuit addressed the issue: "Both Congress and the courts have recognized the crucial distinction between evidence of psychological impairment that supports an 'affirmative defense,' and psychological evidence that negates an element of the offense charged." The court ruled that the language of the new federal act does not bar the use of psychiatric evidence to negate specific intent where that level of intent is an element of the offense charged by the government. *United States v. Cameron*, 907 F.2d 1051, 1063 (11th Cir. 1990).

Contemporary State Developments

Although Congress has placed the burden on defendants who plead insanity in federal courts to prove their defense, state courts are divided on the issue. In some states, where insanity is classified as an affirmative defense, the defendant bears the burden of proof of insanity, usually by a preponderance of the evidence. See, for example, *State v. Baker*, 424 A.2d 171 (N.H. 1980).

Tennessee is now among the states that place the burden on the defendant to establish the affirmative defense of insanity by clear and convincing evidence. West's TCA § 39-11-501; *State v. Flake*, 114 S.W.3d 487 (Tenn. 2003). In many other states, because of the presumption of insanity, when a defendant pleads insanity and introduces some evidence of insanity, the presumption disappears and the prosecution must then establish the defendant's sanity, usually by proof beyond a reasonable doubt, the standard required for establishing a defendant's guilt. See, for example, *State v. Milam*, 260 S.E.2d 295 (W.Va. 1979). Courts usually permit laypersons as well as expert witnesses to testify about a defendant's sanity.

Unlike a defendant who is simply found not guilty, a defendant who is found not guilty by reason of insanity is committed indefinitely institutionalization and may, in some circumstances, be committed to a mental institution. *Jones v. United States*, 463 U.S. 354, 103 S.Ct. 3043, 77 L.Ed.2d 694 (1983). This is generally accomplished subsequent to the verdict by the trial judge, who determines whether the protection of the public requires that the defendant be confined.

On the premise that a person should not be found not guilty on the basis of insanity, some states have recently resorted to verdicts of **guilty but mentally ill** in cases where the defendant's insanity has been established. For example, in *People v. Sorna*, the court explained that this category of verdict deals with situations "where a defendant's mental illness does not deprive him of substantial capacity sufficient to satisfy the insanity test but does warrant treatment in addition to incarceration." 276 N.W.2d 892, 896 (Mich. App. 1979).

Kansas became the fourth state to abolish the separate defense of insanity when it enacted Kan. Stat. Ann. § 22-3220, effective January 1, 1996. Montana, Idaho, and Utah had previously abolished insanity as a defense. In *State v. Cowan*, 861 P.2d 884 (Mont. 1993), the Montana Supreme Court held that its state law abolishing insanity as a defense did not violate the federal constitution. The defendant, asserting a constitutional right to plead the defense, asked the U.S. Supreme Court to review his case. In March 1994, the Court refused to review the *Cowan* decision. *Cowan v. Montana*, 511 U.S. 1005, 114 S.Ct. 1371, 128 L.Ed.2d 48 (1994). Although the Court declined to definitively settle the issue, its action suggests that the federal constitution does not require that states allow a defendant to plead insanity.

In 1995 the Nevada Legislature enacted a law effectively abolishing insanity as a complete defense to a criminal offense. In *Finger v. State*, 27 P.3d 66 (Nev. 2001), the Nevada Supreme Court held the new statutory scheme to be unconstitutional under both the Nevada and U.S. Constitutions and ordered that the insanity

---

CASE-IN-POINT

Insanity Defense

Joy Ann Robey was charged with involuntary manslaughter and child abuse in connection with the death of her ten-month-old daughter, Christina. At trial, Robey admitted to beating the child severely and repeatedly over a two-month period but pleaded not guilty by reason of insanity. The trial court found that the defendant was temporarily insane each time she beat the child but that she returned to sanity thereafter. Accordingly, the defendant could not be held criminally liable for the beatings, but was responsible for her failure to seek medical care for her child. Robey was convicted of involuntary manslaughter and child abuse and sentenced to three concurrent ten-year terms in prison. Her conviction was upheld on appeal over her contention that the trial court erred in holding her criminally responsible after acknowledging that she was insane at the time of the beatings.

Robey v. State, 456 A.2d 953 (Md. App. 1983).

defense as it previously existed be reinstated. The court noted that "legal insanity is a well-established and fundamental principle of the law of the United States," and "it is therefore protected by the Due Process Clauses of both the United States and Nevada Constitutions." 27 P.3d at 84. The State of Nevada sought review of the court's decision by the U.S. Supreme Court, but the Court denied its request without opinion. *Nevada v. Finger*, 534 U.S. 1127, 122 S.Ct. 1063, 151 L.Ed.2d 967 (2002).

It is sometimes difficult to classify the results that occur from a plea of insanity when a jury acquits the defendant. For example, in 1994 Lorena Bobbitt was charged with severing her husband's penis, a fact that was not in controversy. She relied on insanity as a defense but in a novel way. She testified about her husband's alleged cruel and abusive behavior toward her and characterized herself as a victim. A jury in Manassas, Virginia, acquitted her. Some observers have characterized her acquittal as a jury nullification rather than a finding of not guilty by reason of insanity.

In 1993, the Arizona legislature deleted a reference to the defendant's knowledge of the "nature and quality" of his act, a traditional component of the *M'Naghten* Rule, thereby deleting the cognitive capacity aspect from its statutory test for insanity. Eric Clark, a young man, was charged with first-degree murder for the June 21, 2000, killing of a Flagstaff, Arizona, police officer, Jeff Moritz. Clark, who was suffering from paranoid schizophrenia at the time he shot the officer, pleaded "guilty, but insane" and waived the right to a jury trial. At a bench trial, the judge found Clark did not establish that his schizophrenia distorted his perception of reality so severely that he did not know his actions were wrong. After the Arizona Court of Appeals affirmed his conviction, the U.S. Supreme Court granted review. Clark argued that the Arizona definition of insanity violates due process of law because it does not allow a defendant to be judged insane if he did not understand the "nature and quality of his act," as has historically been an essential part of the *M'Naghten* Rule. Thus, Clark contended that, by not allowing evidence of mental disease or defect, the Arizona law violated his right to due process under the Fourteenth Amendment to the U.S. Constitution. Moreover, Clark's counsel pointed out that at least thirty-eight states, the District of Columbia, and the federal government employ insanity standards under which persons satisfying either part of the *M'Naghten* Rule qualify as legally insane.

In *Clark v. Arizona*, 548 U.S. 735, 126 S.Ct. 2709, 165 L.Ed.2d 842 (2006), the U.S. Supreme Court considered two questions: (1) whether due process prohibits Arizona's use of an insanity test stated solely in terms of the capacity to tell whether an act charged as a crime was right or wrong, and (2) whether the Arizona insanity statute violates due process in restricting the consideration of defense evidence of mental illness and incapacity to its bearing on a claim of insanity, thus eliminating its significance directly on the issue of the mental element of the crime charged. The Court concluded there was no violation of due process in either instance. Thus, the Court upheld Arizona's elimination of the cognitive capacity aspect, not only from its statutory test for insanity, but also in refusing to allow psychiatric testimony short of insanity to negate the *mens rea* element of the crime charged.

Automatism

Older cases treated defendants who claimed that their unlawful acts were committed because of an involuntary condition such as somnambulism (that is, sleepwalking) within the context of the insanity defense. Newer cases tend to classify such involuntary actions as **automatism** and view automatism similarly to unconsciousness as a basis for an affirmative defense independent from insanity. In *State v. Morgan-herring*, 517 S.E.2d 622, 641 (N.C. 1999), the North Carolina Supreme Court stated that "where a person commits an act without being conscious thereof, the act is not a criminal act even though it would be a crime if it had been committed by a person who was conscious." The defense is usually limited to a situation where criminal conduct is beyond a person's knowledge and control. *Sellers v. State*, 809 P.2d 676 (Okla. Cr. App. 1991). In *Fulcher v. State*, 633 P.2d 142 (Wyo. 1981), the court explained that one reason for regarding automatism as a separate defense is that there are generally no follow-up consequences such as institutionalization, which usually occurs in an acquittal by reason of insanity. The defense of sleepwalking is infrequently pled. In November 1994, a defendant in Butler, Pennsylvania, contended that his sleep apnea disorder depleted his oxygen and caused him to shoot his wife. The prosecution countered by arguing the man shot his wife because she had planned to leave him. The jury rejected the defendant's claim and found him guilty of murder.

Defenses Asserting Excuse or Justification

A defendant who asserts an excuse admits the act charged by the prosecution but claims that under the circumstances his or her conduct should not result in punishment. A defendant who asserts a justification for conduct says, in effect, that it was justified under the circumstances. Five principal defenses are based on a defendant's asserting an excuse or justification: duress, necessity, consent, mistake of law, and mistake of fact. For convenience, we also discuss **alibi** under this topic, although rather than offering an excuse, a defendant who pleads alibi simply says that he or she was elsewhere when an offense was committed.

Duress

The common law recognized that duress can be a defense to criminal charges if the coercion exerted involved the use of threats of harm that were "present, imminent, and pending" and "of such nature as to include well-grounded apprehensions of death or serious bodily harm if the act was not done." Nevertheless, no form of **duress**, even the threat of imminent death, was sufficient to excuse the intentional killing of an innocent human being. American courts have generally followed this approach, with both federal and state courts having made it clear that threats of future harm are not sufficient to constitute duress. See, for example, *United States v. Agard*, 605 F.2d 665 (2d Cir. 1979); *State v. Clay*, 264 N.W. 77 (Iowa 1935).

Today jurisdictions recognize the defense of duress, sometimes referred to as coercion or compulsion, by either statute or decisional law. Duress has been asserted most frequently by defendants who have committed robberies and thefts and by prisoners who have escaped from custody. Some courts look to duress as negating an element of the offense charged and classify it as a negative defense. See *People v. Graham*, 129 Cal. Rptr. 31 (Cal. App. 1976) (a defendant who raised a reasonable doubt as to whether he had acted in the exercise of free will did not have the burden of showing duress by a preponderance of evidence). However, most courts classify duress as an affirmative defense and require the defendant to prove the defense by the preponderance of the evidence.

The common-law presumption was that if a wife committed a felony other than murder or treason in her husband's presence, she did so under coercion of her husband. That presumption has little significance in modern America and has been abolished in some jurisdictions either by statute—see, for example, Wis. Stat. Ann. § 939.46(2)—or by judicial decision—see *People v. Statley*, 206 P.2d 76 (Cal. App. 1949).

In November 1992, a California appellate court announced a new development in the law of duress. The court held that evidence of **battered woman syndrome** (BWS) is admissible to support a woman's defense that she committed robbery offenses because she was afraid the man she lived with would kill her if she did not do as he demanded. *People v. Romero*, 13 Cal. Rptr. 2d 332 (Cal. App. 1992). The court compared the situation to California decisions allowing evidence of BWS when a woman is accused of killing a man she lives with who batters her (see the later discussion of self-defense in this chapter).

Prisoners who escape custody frequently plead duress. As pointed out in Chapter 13, the requirement for establishing duress as a defense to escape requires the defendant to show that a *bona fide* effort was made to surrender or return to custody as soon as the claimed duress had ended or lost its coercive force. See *United States v. Bailey*, 444 U.S. 394, 100 S.Ct. 624, 62 L.Ed.2d 575 (1980).

There is a conflict among jurisdictions about whether a threat against persons other than the defendant is a sufficient basis for a defendant to invoke the defense of duress. Kan. Stat. Ann. § 21-3209 provides:

(1) A person is not guilty of a crime other than murder or voluntary manslaughter by reason of conduct which he performs under the compulsion or threat of the imminent infliction of death or great bodily harm, if he reasonably believes that death or great bodily harm will be inflicted upon him or upon his spouse, parent, child, brother or sister if he does not perform such conduct.

(2) The defense provided by this section is not available to one who willfully or wantonly places himself in a situation in which it is probable that he will be subjected to compulsion or threat.

Necessity

Whereas in duress the situation has its source in the actions of others, in the defense of **necessity** forces beyond the actor's control are said to have required a person's choice of the lesser of two evils. Early common-law cases recognized that "a man may break the words of the law . . . through necessity." *Regina v. Fogossa*, supra. Contemporary American judicial authorities hold that if there is a reasonable legal alternative to violating the law, the defense of necessity fails.

Suppose several people are shipwrecked on a cold night. One person swims to shore, breaks into an unoccupied beach cottage, and takes food and blankets to assist the injured until help can be secured. Prosecution in such an event would be unlikely, but if prosecuted, the defendant would properly plead the defense of necessity.

Is the defense of necessity applicable to a person with a suspended license driving a motor vehicle? In South Carolina, a defendant admitted to the offense but justified his actions on the ground that he needed to get help for his pregnant wife, who was suffering. He had no telephone, and his neighbor who did was not at home. The defendant drove to the nearest phone booth to request a relative to take his wife to the hospital. As he left, the police stopped him for having a broken taillight. He was then arrested for driving with a suspended license. At his trial, the judge refused his request to instruct the jury on the defense of necessity. The jury found him guilty, and he appealed. In a 3–2 decision, the Supreme Court of South Carolina ruled that

Rejecting Economic Duress as a Defense

CASE-IN-POINT

The defendant was arrested on board a boat in the Gulf of Mexico just off the coast of Florida and was charged with trafficking in cannabis in excess of ten thousand pounds. He pled not guilty and asserted the defense of duress. At trial, the defendant and his wife testified that economic reasons forced him to participate in trafficking in cannabis by piloting the boat. The trial judge declined to instruct the jury on duress, and the defendant was convicted. On appeal, the court affirmed the conviction and said that such a claim of economic coercion was insufficient to call for a jury instruction on duress.

Corujo v. State, 424 So.2d 43 (Fla. App. 1982), rev. denied, 434 So.2d 886 (Fla. 1983).

under the circumstances the defendant was entitled to plead the defense of necessity. *State v. Cole*, 403 S.E.2d 117 (S.C. 1991).

In 1991 a Florida court of appeals allowed a husband and wife who contracted AIDS to assert the defense of necessity to charges of possession and cultivation of marijuana. *Jenks v. State*, 582 So.2d 676 (Fla. App. 1991). Courts in a few other states have allowed the medical necessity defense. Although Maryland has not legalized the use of medical marijuana, it has enacted legislation that allows a person prosecuted for use or possession of marijuana to have the court consider as a mitigating factor any evidence of medical necessity. If a conviction results, the maximum penalty is a fine not exceeding $100. MD Crim. Law, § 5-601(c)(3).

In November 1996, California voters approved Proposition 215 (Compassionate Use Act of 1996) to make marijuana legally available as a medicine to patients or their caregivers on recommendation of a physician. The Oakland Cannabis Buyers' Cooperative began to distribute marijuana to qualified patients for medical purposes. In 1998, the United States sued to enjoin the cooperative's operation, arguing its activities violated the Controlled Substances Act's prohibitions on distributing, manufacturing, and possessing with the intent to distribute or manufacture a controlled substance. The litigation culminated in 2001 with an 8–0 decision from the U.S. Supreme Court holding there is no implied medical necessity exception to the Controlled Substances Act's prohibitions. Justice Clarence Thomas, writing for the Court, observed, "For purposes of the Controlled Substances Act, marijuana has 'no currently accepted medical use' at all." *United States v. Oakland Cannabis Buyers' Co-op.*, 532 U.S. 483, 491, 121 S.Ct. 1711, 1718, 149 L.Ed.2d 722, 732 (2001). Many commentators predict that Congress will eventually make provision for medical uses of marijuana. In the meantime the Court's decision has tended to thwart the use of medical necessity as a defense by those charged with marijuana offenses.

A number of defendants have attempted to justify actions involving "civil disobedience" on the ground of necessity in instances where they have forcefully asserted their personal or political beliefs. One of the most dramatic of these incidents occurred in 1980 when a group of antinuclear activists entered a factory in Pennsylvania, damaged components of nuclear bombs, and poured human blood on the premises. An appellate court approved of the defendants' pleading a defense of necessity; however, the Pennsylvania Supreme Court reversed the decision. *Commonwealth v. Berrigan*, 501 A.2d 226 (Pa. 1985). Other attempts to plead the necessity defense by antinuclear activists have also failed.

In most, but not all cases, the necessity defense has been unavailing to defendants espousing other social and political causes. In another instance, several defendants

The United States Supreme Court's decision in United States v. Oakland Cannabis Buyers' Co-op is excerpted on the companion website.

were charged with criminal trespass when they refused to leave an abortion clinic in Anchorage, Alaska. They claimed their actions were necessary to avert the imminent peril to human life that would result from abortions being performed. They were convicted, and on appeal they argued that the trial court erred in refusing to instruct the jury on their claim of necessity as a defense. In rejecting their contention, the Alaska Supreme Court outlined three requirements that must be met by a person who pleads the defense of necessity: (1) the act charged must have been done to prevent a significant evil, (2) there must have been no adequate alternative, and (3) the harm caused must not have been disproportionate to the harm avoided. *Cleveland v. Municipality of Anchorage*, 631 P.2d 1073, 1078 (Alaska 1981).

A Wisconsin statute codifies the defense of necessity by providing that

> [p]ressure of natural physical forces which causes the actor reasonably to believe that his or her act is the only means of preventing imminent public disaster, or imminent death or great bodily harm to the actor or another and which causes him or her so to act, is a defense to a prosecution for any crime based on that act, except that if the prosecution is for first-degree intentional homicide, the degree of the crime is reduced to second-degree intentional homicide. Wis. Stat. Ann. § 939.47.

Consent

Because in most instances a victim may not excuse a criminal act, American courts have said that consent is not a defense to a criminal prosecution. See, for example, *State v. West*, 57 S.W. 1071 (Mo. 1900). Yet there are exceptions to this general statement. For example, where lack of consent is an element of the offense, as in larceny, consent is a defense. This can also be true today in a prosecution for rape, but only where competent adults freely consent before having sexual relations. Thus, consent would not be a defense to a charge of statutory rape (the strict liability offense of having sexual intercourse with a minor).

Consent is commonly given to physicians who perform surgery. In contact sports, such as football and boxing, consent is implied and may be a defense to reasonable instances of physical contact that would otherwise be regarded as batteries. Some state legislatures have enacted statutes defining when consent is a defense. For example, section 565.080 of the Missouri Statutes specifies that for consent to be a defense, the physical injury consented to or threatened must result from conduct that is not intended to cause serious physical injury or that the conduct and harm are reasonably foreseeable occupational or athletic event hazards. Nevertheless section 565.080 does not apply to hazing or homicide cases, where consent is no defense.

Of course, a valid consent presupposes that it is voluntarily given by a person legally competent to do so and is not induced by force, duress, or deception. Moreover, a victim cannot ratify a criminal act by giving consent after the offense has been committed. *State v. Martinez*, 613 P.2d 974 (Mont. 1980).

Mistake of Law

One of the oft-quoted maxims of the law is that "ignorance of the law is no excuse." The safety and welfare of society demand that persons not be excused from commission of criminal acts on the basis of their claims that they did not know they committed crimes. Although this is the generally accepted view, in some instances a defendant's honest but mistaken view of the law may be accepted as a defense. One example is where such a mistake negates the specific-intent element of a crime.

CASE-IN-POINT

When a Penalty is Imposed for Failure to Act, Reasonable Notice of a Local Ordinance May Be Required

A Los Angeles, California, ordinance made it unlawful for any "convicted persons" to remain in the city for more than five days without registering with the police, or if they lived outside of the city, to enter the city on five or more occasions during a thirty-day period without registering. Virginia Lambert, a convicted felon, was found guilty of failing to register, fined $250, and placed on probation for three years.

On appeal to the U.S. Supreme Court, Lambert's conviction was reversed. Writing for the Court was Justice William O. Douglas: "Engrained in our concept of due process is the requirement of notice. Notice is sometimes essential so that the citizen has the chance to defend charges. Notice is required in a myriad of situations where a penalty or forfeiture might be suffered from mere failure to act."

Lambert v. California, 355 U.S. 225, 78 S.Ct 240, 2 L.Ed.2d228 (1957).

Thus, a **mistake of law** may be asserted as a defense in a larceny case where there is a technical question of who has legal title to an asset. *State v. Abbey*, 474 P.2d 62 (Ariz. App. 1970). Likewise, a defendant's good-faith but mistaken trust in the validity of a divorce has been held to be a defense to a charge of bigamy. *Long v. State*, 65 A.2d 489 (Del. 1949).

The Illinois Criminal Code lists four exceptions to the general rule that a person's ignorance of the law does not excuse unlawful conduct:

A person's reasonable belief that certain conduct does not constitute a criminal offense is a defense if:

(1) The offense is defined by an administrative regulation which is not known to him and has not been published or otherwise made reasonably available to him, and he could not have acquired such knowledge by the exercise of due diligence pursuant to facts known to him; or

(2) He acts in reliance upon a statute which later is determined to be invalid; or

(3) He acts in reliance upon an order or opinion of an Illinois Appellate or Supreme Court, or a United States appellate court later overruled or reversed; or

(4) He acts in reliance upon an official interpretation of the statute, regulation or order defining the offense, made by a public officer or agency legally authorized to interpret such statute. 720 ILCS 5/4-8(b).

Citing the preceding statutory exceptions, the Illinois Supreme Court held that a taxpayer who contended that she reasonably believed that she would be subject only to civil penalties, not to criminal sanctions, for failure to file an occupational tax return did not present a mistake-of-law defense. *People v. Sevilla*, 547 N.E.2d 117 (Ill. 1989).

In *United States v. Moore*, 627 F.2d 830 (7th Cir. 1980), the court said that "the mistake of law defense is extremely limited and the mistake must be objectively reasonable." 627 F.2d at 833. Furthermore, a court will never recognize a dishonest pretense of ignorance of the law as a defense. *State v. Carroll*, 60 S.W. 1087 (Mo. 1901).

A defendant can always raise the unconstitutionality of a statute as a defense to a prosecution for its violation. But a person who violates a statute thinking it is unconstitutional does so at his or her peril; courts have said that a person's belief that a statute is unconstitutional, even if based on advice of counsel, does not constitute a valid defense for violating the law. *State v. Thorstad*, 261 N.W.2d 899 (N.D. 1978).

Mistake of Fact

In contrast with the ancient common-law maxim that "ignorance of the law is no excuse," at common law, ignorance or **mistake of fact**, guarded by an honest purpose, afforded a defendant a sufficient excuse for a supposed criminal act. American courts have agreed but have generally said that a mistake of fact will not be recognized as a defense to a general-intent crime unless the mistake is a reasonable one for a person to make under the circumstances. However, even an unreasonable mistake may be asserted as a defense to a crime that requires a specific intent. The decisions in recent years have indicated that a mistake of fact may be a defense as long as it negates the existence of the mental state essential to the crime charged. See, for example, *State v. Fuentes*, 577 P.2d 452 (N.M. App. 1978). Some jurisdictions have codified the mistake-of-fact defense. In Indiana, for example, mistake of fact is an affirmative defense by statute:

> It is a defense that the person who engaged in the prohibited conduct was reasonably mistaken about a matter of fact if the mistake negates the culpability required for commission of the offense. West's Ind. Code Ann. § 35-41-3-7.

In strict liability offenses, the defense of mistake of fact is unavailing because these offenses are not based on intent (see Chapter 4). In pointing out that this view represents the weight of authority, the Montana Supreme Court held that neither ignorance nor even a *bona fide* belief that a minor was of legal age constituted a defense to prosecution for selling intoxicating liquor to a minor, unless expressly made so by the statute. *State v. Parr*, 283 P.2d 1086 (Mont. 1955). Likewise, because having consensual sexual relations with a minor is generally considered a strict liability offense, a mistake of fact as to a minor's age is generally not a defense to a charge of statutory rape. Even if a court finds that a statutory rape statute requires proof of a general criminal intent to convict, a defendant's reasonable mistake of fact concerning a female's age is generally not available as a defense. *State v. Stiffler*, 788 P.2d 220 (Idaho 1990). In 1964, however, the California Supreme Court departed from this almost universally accepted rule and held that an accused's good-faith, reasonable belief that a female had reached the age of consent would be a defense to statutory rape. *People v. Hernandez*, 393 P.2d 673 (Cal. 1964).

Other state courts have noted, but not followed, the view of the Supreme Court of California. In 1993 the Court of Appeals in Maryland held that a rape statute prohibiting sexual intercourse with underage persons defines a strict liability offense. The court explained that the statute does not require the prosecution to prove *mens rea* and makes no allowance for a mistake-of-fact defense. *Garnett v. State*, 632 A.2d 797 (Md. App. 1993). A dissenting judge acknowledged the rationale for protecting very young females but challenged such statutes that protect young women: "But when age limits are raised to sixteen, eighteen, and twenty-one, when the young girl becomes a young woman, when adolescent boys as well as young men are attracted to her, the sexual act begins to lose its quality of abnormality and physical danger to the victim. Bona fide mistakes in the age of girls can be made by men and boys who are no more dangerous than others of their social, economic and educational level." *Id.* at 815.

In the past few years, in cases of statutory rape, some trial courts have heard arguments based on a minor's right to privacy. The contention is that because a minor female can consent to an abortion, she should be able to consent to sexual intercourse. Although this argument has generally fallen on deaf ears, some trial judges have questioned the need to continue to employ a strict liability standard in

State v. Freeman (1990), where the Iowa Supreme Court considers the defense of mistake of fact, is excerpted on the companion website.

consensual sexual relationships where the female is a minor but appears to be an adult and represents herself as such.

Writing in the *University of Mississippi Law Journal,* Alexandra Hutton Oglesby has recommended that legislatures should at least provide "the availability of an affirmative defense of reasonable mistake of age when evidence suggests that the defendant honestly and reasonably believed he or she was conducting himself or herself within the boundaries of a constitutional 'safety zone' surrounding private consensual sexual activities engaged in with another legal adult." 76 Miss. L.J. 1067, 1099 (Spring 2007).

Alibi

Alibi means "elsewhere," and the defense of alibi may be interposed by a defendant who claims to have been at a place other than where the crime allegedly occurred. A criminal defendant who relies on an alibi as a defense does not deny that a crime was committed. Rather, he or she denies the ability to have perpetrated such crime because of having been elsewhere at the time.

The Colorado Supreme Court has pointed out that most jurisdictions that have addressed the issue have concluded that an alibi is not an affirmative defense. *People v. Huckleberry,* 768 P.2d 1235 (Colo. 1989). A few, however, characterize the defense as an affirmative one requiring proof of alibi by the defendant. Generally, a defendant who asserts an affirmative defense essentially admits the conduct charged and seeks to excuse or justify it. One who claims an alibi does not so admit. Therefore, it seems logical not to classify alibi as an affirmative defense. As explained by the Missouri Supreme Court,

> The theory of alibi is that the fact of defendant's presence elsewhere is essentially inconsistent with his presence at the place where the alleged offense was committed and, therefore, defendant could not have personally participated. Although the defense is not an affirmative one, the fact of defendant's presence elsewhere is an affirmative fact logically operating to negative his presence at the time and place. *State v. Armstead,* 283 S.W.2d 577, 581 (Mo. 1955).

Statutes or court rules commonly require that to assert alibi as a defense, a defendant must notify the prosecution in advance of trial and furnish the names of witnesses the defendant intends to use to support the alibi. The Supreme Court has said that this requirement does not violate the defendant's right to due process of law. *Williams v. Florida,* 399 U.S. 78, 90 S.Ct. 1893, 26 L.Ed.2d 446 (1970). In 1973, however, the Court held that when the state requires such information, the prosecution must make similar disclosures to the defendant concerning refutation of the evidence that the defendant furnishes. *Wardius v. Oregon,* 412 U.S. 470, 93 S.Ct. 2208, 37 L.Ed.2d 82 (1973). Alibi-notice statutes and court rules now commonly require disclosure by both defense and the prosecution.

Defenses Justifying the use of Force

When offering a defense justifying the use of force, a defendant admits to an offense but claims that his or her conduct was justified under the circumstances. The use of force may be a defense to a criminal charge that the defendant caused injury or death to another. Therefore, the defense of **justifiable use of force** applies to the assaultive and homicidal offenses.

As a starting point, the use of **deadly force** (that is, force likely to cause death or serious bodily injury) must be distinguished from the use of **nondeadly force**. In general, the use of deadly force in self-defense requires that the person using such force (1) be in a place where he or she has a right to be, (2) act without fault, and (3) act in reasonable fear or apprehension of death or great bodily harm. *Lilly v. State*, 506 N.E.2d 23 (Ind. 1987). In evaluating whether the use of deadly force is reasonable, courts consider numerous factors. Among these are the sizes, ages, and physical abilities of the parties; whether the attacker was armed; and the attacker's reputation for violence. Ordinarily, a person may use whatever nondeadly force appears reasonably necessary under the circumstances. *State v. Clay*, 256 S.E.2d 176 (N.C. 1979).

Self-Defense

Defendants frequently admit the commission of acts that constitute an assaultive or homicidal offense but claim to have acted in **self-defense**. Generally, when a defendant raises the issue of self-defense, the prosecution must prove beyond a reasonable doubt that the accused did not act in self-defense. *Wash v. State*, 456 N.E.2d 1009 (Ind. 1983). Variations exist in the law on the permitted degree of force that can be used in self-defense, but the test of reasonableness appears common to all views. In determining the lawfulness of force used in self-defense, courts first look to see if the force used by the aggressor was unlawful. If so, the defender must show there was a necessity to use force for self-protection and that the degree of force used by the defender was reasonable considering the parties and circumstances.

At common law, a person attacked had a duty "to retreat to the wall" before using deadly force in self-defense. *State v. Sipes*, 209 N.W. 458 (Iowa 1926). In *Scott v. State*, 34 So.2d 718 (Miss. 1948), the court explained that to justify the slaying of another in self-defense at common law, there must have been actual danger of loss of life or suffering of great bodily harm. But the court said that the American approach has been that the danger need not be actual but must be "reasonably apparent and imminent."

Most courts reject the common-law doctrine of requiring a person to retreat to the greatest extent possible before meeting force with force. Rather, they say that a person attacked or threatened may stand his or her ground and use any force reasonably necessary to prevent harm. Courts that take this view often state it in positive terms, as did the Oklahoma Court of Criminal Appeals when citing one of its 1912 precedents: "The law in Oklahoma is clear: There is no duty to retreat if one is threatened with bodily harm." *Neal v. State*, 597 P.2d 334, 337 (Okl. Crim. App. 1979).

A substantial minority of courts, however, have adopted the principle that a person who can safely retreat must do so before using deadly force. But courts that follow the **retreat rule** have generally adopted the principle that a person does not have to retreat in his or her own dwelling. *State v. Bennett*, 105 N.W. 324 (Iowa 1905).

The Wisconsin Statutes codify the general law on use of force in self-defense:

> A person is privileged to threaten or intentionally use force against another for the purpose of preventing or terminating what the actor reasonably believes to be an unlawful interference with his or her person by such other person. The actor may intentionally use only such force or threat thereof as he reasonably believes is necessary to prevent or terminate the interference. The actor may not intentionally use force which is intended or likely to cause death or great bodily harm unless the actor reasonably believes that such force is necessary to prevent imminent death or great bodily harm to himself or herself. Wis. Stat. Ann. § 939.48(1).

The Law of Self-Defense

CASE-IN-POINT

Defendant Ernest Young was distributing religious literature on the street when he was approached by George Coleman, who began to harass and swear at him. Later, Coleman again accosted Young, this time at a table in a fast-food restaurant. Coleman began swearing at Young and grabbed his arm. Young pulled out a handgun and shot Coleman three times, killing him. Young was charged with and tried for murder. Notwithstanding his plea of self-defense, the jury returned a verdict of guilty of voluntary manslaughter. As the appellate court reviewing the conviction said, "The jury heard appellant's story and it determined that he acted in the heat of the moment rather than in self-defense. There is ample evidence to support its verdict." The defendant's conviction was affirmed.

Young v. State, 451 N.E.2d 91 (Ind. App. 1983).

The use of deadly force presents the greatest issue in self-defense. As we noted earlier, deadly force may be used only where it reasonably appears necessary to use such force to prevent death or serious injury. In considering whether a defendant is justified in using deadly force, the law has traditionally applied an **objective test for the use of deadly force**. See, for example, *State v. Bess*, 247 A.2d 669 (N.J. 1968). Today, however, there is a conflict in the decisional law. Some courts apply a **subjective standard of reasonableness** to determine whether circumstances are sufficient to induce in the defendant an honest and reasonable belief that force must be used. See, for example, *State v. Wanrow*, 559 P.2d 548 (Wash. 1977). Although the objective test requires the jury to place itself in the shoes of a hypothetical "reasonable and prudent person," the subjective test permits a jury "to place itself in the defendant's own shoes."

Much of the impetus for courts' applying the subjective test to determine whether the use of deadly force is reasonable has resulted from cases where women charged with committing assaultive or homicidal offenses against men have defended their use of force. In *State v. Wanrow*, supra, a woman on crutches was convicted of second-degree murder and first-degree assault in her fatal shooting of a large, intoxicated man who refused to leave her home. In reversing her convictions, the Washington Supreme Court held that the trial judge erred by giving instructions to the jury that did not make it clear that Wanrow's actions were to be judged against her own subjective impressions and not those that the jury might determine to be objectively reasonable.

People v. Greene (1987), where an Illinois appellate court upholds a trial judge's rejection of the defendant's claim of self-defense to a charge of homicide, is excerpted on the companion website.

The Battered Woman Syndrome

Beyond the subjective standard of self-defense, in recent years the concept of self-defense by women has been expanded to include circumstances where a woman claims to have been continually battered by a man. The "battered spouse syndrome" soon became the "battered woman syndrome" (BWS). It describes a pattern of psychological and behavioral symptoms of a woman living with a male in a battering relationship. Some jurisdictions now permit a female in that situation who is charged with assaulting or killing a man to show that even though she did not face immediate harm, her plea of self-defense should be recognized because her actions were her response to constant battering by the man with whom she lived.

Decisional law is in the developing stage on the admissibility of expert testimony concerning the battered woman syndrome, with the trend being to hold that when a woman kills her batterer and pleads self-defense, expert testimony about BWS is admissible to explain how her particular experiences as a battered woman affected her perceptions of danger and her honest belief in its imminence. *State v. Hill*, 339 S.E.2d 121 (S.C. 1986); *People v. Aris*, 264 Cal. Rptr. 167 (Cal. App. 1989). In *Commonwealth v. Rodriquez*, 418 633 N.E.2d 1039 (Mass. 1994), the Supreme Judicial Court of Massachusetts found the trial court erred in refusing to admit evidence of the battered woman syndrome where a defendant who stabbed her boyfriend during an argument claimed she did so in self-defense.

In some instances, legislatures have enacted statutes to provide for admission of such evidence. See, for example, section 563.033 of the Missouri Statutes Annotated, which provides, "Evidence that the actor was suffering from the battered spouse syndrome shall be admissible upon the issue of whether the actor lawfully acted in self-defense or defense of another."

Increasingly, courts are recognizing the role of the battered woman syndrome, not as an independent defense but as furnishing support for a woman's defense where a woman shows that she has been acting under coercion of a male. In *United States v. Brown*, 891 F. Supp. 1501, 1505 (D. Kan. 1995), the court explained that although a woman cannot rely on the syndrome as a complete defense,

> it is some evidence to be considered to support a defense, such as self-defense, duress, compulsion, and coercion. Because women who suffer from the battered woman syndrome do not act in a typical manner as compared with women who do not suffer from it, evidence of the syndrome is used to explain their behavior. Evidence of the syndrome is presented through expert testimony to assist the jury's evaluation of the defendant's state of mind.

In *State v. Haines*, 860 N.E.2d 91 (Ohio 2006), the Ohio Supreme Court agreed that expert testimony regarding the battered woman syndrome can be admitted to help the jury determine whether the defendant had reasonable grounds for an honest belief that she was in imminent danger when considering the issue of self-defense. "Expert testimony on the battered woman syndrome," the court said, "would help dispel the ordinary lay person's perception that a woman in a battering relationship is free to leave at any time." 860 N.E.2d at 98.

The Battered Child Syndrome

Where there is evidence that a child has been abused continually over an extended period, there is a movement now to assert the **battered child syndrome** (BCS) in defense of a child accused of assaulting or killing a parent. Many prosecutors claim that the use of BCS is undermining the law of self-defense, yet there are experts who claim that a child's perceptions of the need to use force are shaped by his or her experience of constant abuse by a parent. These experts argue that when juries hear such evidence, they may be persuaded that a child acted in self-defense and not out of retribution.

In the state of Washington, a boy who killed his stepfather was convicted of second-degree murder and two counts of second-degree assault. At his trial, the court held that evidence of the battered child syndrome could not, as a matter of law, support a finding of self-defense because there was no "imminent threat" to the defendant. In a much-discussed opinion, the appellate court held that this ruling was in error: "Neither law nor logic suggest any reason to limit to women recognition of the impact a battering relationship may have on the victim's actions or perceptions. . . . [T]he rationale underlying the admissibility of testimony regarding the battered women syndrome is at least as compelling, if not more so, when applied to children." *State v. Janes*, 822 P.2d 1238, 1243 (Wash. App. 1992).

In 1993 California charged Erik and Lyle Menendez, ages eighteen and twenty-one, respectively, with the murder of their parents. Although the defendants admitted killing their parents, they claimed to have been victims of parental abuse. Their first two trials ended in mistrials because the jurors could not agree on a verdict. In March 1996, the Menendez brothers were convicted and sentenced to life in prison without the possibility of parole.

Defense of Others

At common law, a defender had the right to use reasonable force to prevent commission of a felony or to protect members of the household who were endangered, a principle that was codified in many jurisdictions. See, for example, *State v. Fair*, 211 A.2d 359 (N.J. 1965). The trend in American jurisdictions is to allow a person "to stand in the shoes of the victim" and to use such **reasonable force** as is necessary to defend anyone, irrespective of relationship, from harm. As the court noted in *State v. Grier*, "What one may do for himself, he may do for another." 609 S.W.2d 201, 203 (Mo. App. 1980). Today a number of states have statutes that permit a person to assert force on behalf of another. To illustrate, the Wisconsin statute provides as follows:

> A person is privileged to defend a third person from real or apparent unlawful interference by another under the same conditions and by the same means as those under and by which the person is privileged to defend himself or herself from real or apparent unlawful interference, provided that the person reasonably believes that the facts are such that the third person would be privileged to act in self-defense and that the person's intervention is necessary for the protection of the third person. Wis. Stat. Ann. § 939.48(4).

Like the quoted Wisconsin statute, statutes in many other states limit a person's right to defend another individual from harm to those persons who "reasonably believe" that force is necessary to protect another. Some courts take a more restrictive view and hold that an intervenor is justified in using force to defend another only if the party being defended would have been justified in using the same force in self-defense. Under either standard, however, the right to go to the **defense of others** does not authorize a person to resort to retaliatory force.

In *People v. Kurr*, 654 N.W.2d 651 (Mich. App. 2002), a Michigan appellate court held that the defense-of-others concept extends to the protection of a nonviable fetus from an assault against the mother. The court concluded that in enacting M.C.L.A. § 750.90a *et seq.* (Fetal Protection Act), which provides penalties for harming a fetus or embryo during an intentional assault against a pregnant woman, the legislature determined that fetuses are worthy of protection as living entities.

Defense of Habitation

The common law placed great emphasis on the security of a person's dwelling and permitted the use of deadly force against an intruder. *Russell v. State*, 122 So. 683 (Ala. 1929). This historical view was chronicled by the Illinois Supreme Court in *People v. Eatman*:

As a matter of history the defense of habitation has been the most favored branch of self-defense from the earliest times. Lord Coke, in his Commentaries, says: "A man's home is his castle—for where shall a man be safe if it be not in his house?" 91 N.E.2d 387, 390 (Ill. 1950).

Referring to a person's **defense of habitation**, the *Eatman* court opined that "he may use all of the force apparently necessary to repel any invasion of his home." 91 N.E.2d at 390. This is sometimes referred to as the **castle doctrine**. Even though a householder may, under some circumstances, be justified in using deadly force, the householder would not be justified in taking a life to repel a mere trespass.

In *State v. McCombs*, 253 S.E.2d 906 (N.C. 1979), the North Carolina Supreme Court addressed the issue of using deadly force to protect one's home. The court said that the use of deadly force is generally justified to prevent a forcible entry into the habitation in circumstances such where the occupant is threatened, or reasonably apprehends death or great bodily harm to self or other occupants, or reasonably believes the assailant intends to commit a felony. Although this decision states the law generally applied by the courts, some statutory and decisional variations exist.

Defense of Property

The right to defend your property is more limited than the right to defend your home or yourself. The common law allowed a person in lawful possession of property to use reasonable, but not deadly, force to protect it. *Russell v. State*, supra. Today, the use of force to protect a person's property is often defined by statute. Typically, Iowa law provides that "[a] person is justified in the use of reasonable force to prevent or terminate criminal interference with his or her possession or other right to property." Iowa Code Ann. § 704.4. The quoted statutory language generally represents contemporary decisional law even in the absence of a statute.

CASE-IN-POINT

Defense of Habitation

Defendant Raines was charged with murder in connection with the death of Stinson. Stinson was the passenger in a car driven by Neese. The evidence showed that Neese had threatened to kill Raines and that Neese had driven past Raines's trailer and fired some shots out the window of his car. Raines was not home at the time, but when he returned, his live-in companion, Quates, told him what had happened. A few minutes later they heard a car approaching and went outside. Quates identified the car as the same one from which the shots had been fired. As the car drove away, Raines fired five shots from a semiautomatic rifle. Quates testified that Raines said that "he'd just shoot the tire out and stop it and we'd go get the law and find out who it was." However, one of the bullets struck Stinson in the head, killing him. Despite his plea that he acted in self-defense and defense of his habitation, Raines was convicted of manslaughter.

The conviction was upheld on appeal, with the appellate court saying that "although Raines may well have been in fear of danger when the . . . car approached, such fear alone did not justify his firing at the car as it drove down the public road past his trailer." As the court further observed, "One assaulted in his house need not flee therefrom. But his house is his castle only for the purposes of defense. It cannot be turned into an arsenal for the purpose of offensive effort against the lives of others."

Raines v. State, 455 So.2d 967 (Ala. Crim. App. 1984).

Some older court decisions hold that a person may oppose force with force, even to the extent of taking a life in defense of his or her person, family, or property against a person attempting to commit a violent felony such as murder, robbery, or rape. However, these decisions focus on preventing a dangerous felony rather than simply on protecting or recapturing property. The prevailing view of the courts is that, in the absence of the felonious use of force by an aggressor, a person must not inflict deadly harm simply for the protection or recapture of property. *State v. McCombs*, supra. This is because the law places higher value on preserving the life of the wrongdoer than on protecting someone's property.

One method of defending property has been through the use of a mechanical device commonly known as a "spring gun" that is set to go off when someone trips a wire or opens a door. In the earlier history of the country, these devices were used on farms, in unoccupied structures, and sometimes in residences at night to wound or kill intruders. Some early court decisions said that use of a spring gun that resulted in the death of an intruder into a person's home was justified in instances where a homeowner, if present, would have been authorized to use deadly force.

Today, if someone is killed or injured as a result of a spring gun or similar mechanical device, the party who set it (and anyone who caused it to be set) generally will be held criminally responsible for any resulting death or injury. This is true even if the intruder's conduct would ordinarily cause a party to believe that the intrusion threatened death or serious bodily injury, conditions that might justify the use of deadly force.

The Model Penal Code § 3.06(5) takes the position that a device for the protection of property may be used only if

(a) the device is not designed to cause or known to create a substantial risk of causing death or serious bodily harm; and
(b) the use of the particular device to protect the property from entry or trespass is reasonable under the circumstances, as the actor believes them to be; and
(c) the device is one customarily used for such a purpose or reasonable care is taken to make known to probable intruders the fact that it is used.

Even courts in jurisdictions that have not adopted the MPC view take a harsh view of the use of such mechanical devices, reasoning that to allow persons to use them can imperil the lives of innocent persons such as firefighters, police officers, and even children at play. Finally, some courts point to another reason: although a deadly mechanical device acts without mercy or discretion, there is always the possibility that a human being protecting property would avoid taking a human life or injuring someone. See *People v. Ceballos*, 526 P.2d 241 (Cal. 1974).

Florida's "Stand Your Ground" Law—A Trendsetter on Self-Defense
In 2005, Florida enacted a new law expanding the right of self-defense for individuals. The law, which amended Florida Statutes section 776.013 effective October 1, 2005, provides:

(1) A person is presumed to have held a reasonable fear of imminent peril of death or great bodily harm to himself or herself or another when using defensive force that is intended or likely to cause death or great bodily harm to another if

(a) The person against whom the defensive force was used was in the process of unlawfully and forcefully entering, or had unlawfully and forcibly entered, a dwelling, residence, or occupied vehicle, or if that person had removed or was attempting to remove another against that person's will from the dwelling, residence, or occupied vehicle; and

(b) The person who uses defensive force knew or had reason to believe that an unlawful and forcible entry or unlawful and forcible act was occurring or had occurred.

(2) [Includes provisions to protect anyone who has a right to be in a residence, those under lawful guardianship, and law enforcement officers]

(3) A person who is not engaged in an unlawful activity and who is attacked in any other place where he or she has a right to be has no duty to retreat and has the right to stand his or her ground and meet force with force, including deadly force if he or she reasonably believes it is necessary to do so to prevent death or great bodily harm to himself or herself or another or to prevent the commission of a forcible felony.

(4) A person who unlawfully and by force enters or attempts to enter a person's dwelling, residence, or occupied vehicle is presumed to be doing so with the intent to commit an unlawful act involving force or violence.

The new law expands the "castle doctrine" discussed above and allows individuals to use deadly force in public places without the duty to retreat. It also forbids the arrest, detention, or prosecution of those covered by the law and prohibits civil suits against them. In *State v. Smiley*, 927 So.2d 1000 (Fla. App. 2006), the defendant was prosecuted for first-degree murder occurring on November 6, 2004; he sought to have the jury instructed based on the expanded right of self-defense under Florida Statutes, section 776.013. When the trial court allowed the instruction the state sought review. Because the defendant was charged with an offense committed prior to the effective date of the new statute, the appellate court held that the new Florida law could not be applied retroactively.

Critics of the new law dubbed it a "shoot first" law and predicted that it would lead to preemptive shootings. But despite such criticism, the trend to expand the right of self-defense continued, and by 2009 twenty-five states had adopted "stand your ground" laws, rejecting the duty to retreat before using deadly force.

Defense to Being Arrested

At common law, a person had the right to use such force as reasonably necessary, short of killing, to resist an unlawful arrest. The common-law rule developed at a time when bail was largely unavailable, arraignments were delayed for months until a royal judge arrived, and conditions in English jails were deplorable. Most American courts followed the English view. See, for example, *State v. Small*, 169 N.W. 116 (Iowa 1918). In some states a person may still forcibly resist an unlawful arrest.

As pointed out in Chapter 13, however, the rationale for the rule has substantially eroded. Increasingly, legislatures and courts recognize that resisting an arrest exposes both the officer and the arrestee to escalating violence. Moreover, defendants are now promptly arraigned, and counsel is generally available to debate the legality of an arrest in court. See *United States v. Ferrone*, 438 F.2d 381 (3d Cir. 1971). Today the majority of states, either by statute or judicial decision, provide that a person may not resist an arrest, even if it is illegal.

Use of Force by Police

Most states have statutes or police regulations that specify the degree of force that may be used to apprehend violators. Officers are usually permitted to use such force as is reasonably necessary to effect an arrest and are not required to retreat from an aggressor. In practice, deadly force is seldom used by modern police forces, yet many states have statutes that authorize the use of deadly force by police in apprehending felons.

The Supreme Court's decision in *Tennessee v. Garner*, 471 U.S. 1, 105 S.Ct. 1694, 85 L.Ed.2d 1 (1985), limits an officer's use of deadly force to situations where it is necessary to prevent the escape of a suspect who poses a significant threat of death or serious injury to the officer or others. A law enforcement officer who injures or kills a person or damages someone's property in the line of duty is sometimes charged with a criminal offense. As long as the officer acted reasonably and not in violation of the Fourth Amendment, a statute, or valid police regulations, the defense of having performed a public function is available to the officer.

> The Supreme Court's decision in *Tenneseee v. Garner* is excerpted on the companion website.

Defenses Based on Constitutional and Statutory Authority

In earlier chapters we mentioned that, subject to certain exceptions, the First Amendment to the Constitution provides a defense for legitimate speech, press, assembly, and religious activities. We also discussed how the Due Process Clauses of the Fifth and Fourteenth Amendments permit one to defend against criminal charges based on statutes that are void for vagueness.

In this section we discuss two significant constitutional defenses asserted by defendants in criminal cases: immunity and double jeopardy. In addition, we mention here the defense provided by statutes of limitations, which are legislative enactments establishing time limits for prosecution of most offenses.

Constitutional Immunity

Everyone is familiar with the scenario of the witness who invokes the constitutional privilege against self-incrimination based on the Fifth Amendment to the Constitution, which provides that "no person . . . shall be compelled in any criminal case to be a witness against himself." The privilege against self-incrimination is applicable to the states through the Fourteenth Amendment, *Malloy v. Hogan*, 378 U.S. 1, 84 S.Ct. 1489, 12 L.Ed.2d 653 (1964), although states have similar protections in their constitutions.

The privilege against self-incrimination guaranteed by the federal constitution is a personal one that applies only to natural persons and not corporations. *United States v. White*, 322 U.S. 694, 64 S.Ct. 1248, 88 L.Ed. 1542 (1944). A strict reading of the clause would limit the privilege to testimony given in a criminal trial. However, the Supreme Court has held that an individual may refuse "to answer official questions put to him in any . . . proceeding, civil or criminal, formal or informal, where the answers might incriminate him in future criminal proceedings." *Lefkowitz v. Turley*, 414 U.S. 70, 77, 94 S.Ct. 316, 322, 38 L.Ed.2d 274, 281 (1973). A classic example is the privilege of suspects in police custody to invoke their *Miranda* rights.

Frequently, when a witness invokes the Fifth Amendment and refuses to testify, the court is requested to compel the witness's testimony. This may be accomplished by conferring **immunity** on the witness, which is a grant of amnesty to protect the witness from prosecution through the use of compelled testimony. A witness compelled to give incriminating testimony thus receives **use immunity** (that is, the testimony given cannot be used against the witness). This form of immunity (sometimes referred to as "derivative immunity") is coextensive with the scope of the privilege against self-incrimination and meets the demands of the Constitution. *Kastigar v. United States*, 406 U.S. 441, 92 S.Ct. 1653, 32 L.Ed.2d 212 (1972).

In some states a witness who testifies under a grant of immunity is given **transactional immunity**, a broader protection than is required under the federal constitution. Transactional immunity protects a witness from prosecution for any activity mentioned in the witness's testimony. An example of requiring broader protection occurred in 1993 when the Alaska Supreme Court ruled that its state constitution requires that witnesses who are compelled to testify be given the more protective transactional immunity from prosecution, rather than the use immunity or derivative immunity required by the federal constitution. *State v. Gonzalez*, 853 P.2d 526 (Alaska 1993). A defendant may assert the defense of immunity by a pretrial motion. Despite a grant of immunity, a witness may be prosecuted for making material false statements under oath. *United States v. Apfelbaum*, 445 U.S. 115, 100 S.Ct. 948, 63 L.Ed.2d 250 (1980) (see Chapter 13).

Other Forms of Immunity

Sometimes a prosecutor, with approval of the court, grants a witness **contractual immunity**. The purpose is to induce a suspect to testify against someone and thereby enable the prosecution to obtain a conviction not otherwise obtainable because of the constitutional protection against self-incrimination. This type of immunity is rarely granted if other available evidence will lead to a conviction. The authority to grant immunity in federal courts is vested in the U.S. Attorney with approval of the Attorney General or certain authorized assistants. 18 U.S.C.A. § 6003(b). At the state level, such authority is generally vested in the chief prosecuting officer (that is, the district or state attorney).

Under international law, a person who has diplomatic status and serves as part of a diplomatic mission, as well as members of the diplomat's staff and household, are immune from arrest and prosecution, thus enjoying **diplomatic immunity**. The expectation, of course, is that American diplomats and their dependents and staff members will enjoy like immunity in foreign nations. Diplomatic immunity attaches to the sovereign state, not to the individual diplomat. In instances of egregious misconduct, a foreign state may be asked to waive the diplomat's immunity. In 1997, Republic of Georgia envoy Gueorgui Makharadze was involved in a traffic accident in Washington, D.C., while driving while intoxicated. The accident resulted in the death of one person and injuries to four others. At the request of the U.S. government, Georgia withdrew Makharadze's diplomatic immunity. He pled guilty to involuntary manslaughter and aggravated assault and was sentenced to prison.

Another form of immunity is referred to as **legislative immunity** and is constitutionally based. Article I, Section 6 of the U.S. Constitution provides that members of Congress, in all cases except treason, felony, and breach of the peace, are privileged from arrest during attendance at and in going to and returning from legislative sessions. State constitutions generally include similar provisions for state lawmakers.

Double Jeopardy

The concept of forbidding retrial of a defendant who has been found not guilty developed from the common law. *Ex parte Lange*, 85 U.S. (18 Wall.) 163, 21 L.Ed. 872 (1873). The Fifth Amendment to the U.S. Constitution embodies this principle: "[N]or shall any person be subject for the same offence to be twice put in jeopardy of life or limb." The Double Jeopardy Clause was made applicable to the states through the Fourteenth Amendment in *Benton v. Maryland*, 395 U.S. 784, 89 S.Ct. 2056, 23 L.Ed.2d 707 (1969). Even before that, all states provided essentially the same protection through their constitutions or statutes, or through judicial decisions recognizing common-law principles.

In a 1957 Supreme Court decision, Justice Hugo L. Black expressed the rationale underlying the Double Jeopardy Clause:

> The underlying idea, one that is deeply ingrained in at least the Anglo-American system of jurisprudence, is that the State with all its resources and power should not be allowed to make repeated attempts to convict an individual for an alleged offense, thereby subjecting him to embarrassment, expense and ordeal and compelling him to live in a continuing state of anxiety and insecurity, as well as enhancing the possibility that even though innocent he may be found guilty. *Green v. United States*, 355 U.S. 184, 187-188, 78 S.Ct. 221, 223, 2 L.Ed.2d 199, 204 (1957).

The subject of **double jeopardy** is very complex, but certain principles seem clear. Jeopardy attaches once the jury is sworn in, *Crist v. Bretz*, 437 U.S. 28, 98 S.Ct. 2156, 57 L.Ed.2d 24 (1978), or when the first witness is sworn in to testify in a nonjury trial, *Serfass v. United States*, 420 U.S. 377, 95 S.Ct. 1055, 43 L.Ed.2d 265 (1975). The defense of double jeopardy may be asserted by pretrial motion.

The Double Jeopardy Clause forbids a second prosecution for the same offense after a defendant has been acquitted. *Ball v. United States*, 163 U.S. 662, 16 S.Ct. 1192, 41 L.Ed. 300 (1896). In recent years, this principle has been applied even after a conviction. *United States v. Wilson*, 420 U.S. 332, 95 S.Ct. 1013, 43 L.Ed.2d 232 (1975). But if a defendant appeals a conviction and prevails, it is not double jeopardy for the prosecution to retry the defendant, unless the appellate court rules that there was insufficient evidence to sustain the defendant's conviction. *Burks v. United States*, 437 U.S. 1, 98 S.Ct. 2141, 57 L.Ed.2d 1 (1978). Note the distinction between a conviction reversed by a higher court on the basis of **insufficient evidence** and a conviction that is vacated, with a new trial ordered, based on the **weight of the evidence**. In the latter case, a retrial of the defendant would not constitute double jeopardy. *Tibbs v. Florida*, 457 U.S. 31, 102 S.Ct. 2211, 72 L.Ed.2d 652 (1982). Nor is it double jeopardy to retry a defendant if the trial court, at the defendant's request, has declared a mistrial. *Oregon v. Kennedy*, 456 U.S. 667, 102 S.Ct. 2083, 72 L.Ed.2d 416 (1982). If, however, the government moves for a mistrial, the defendant objects, and the court grants the mistrial, the prosecution must establish a **manifest necessity** for the mistrial in order for a retrial to be permitted. An example of a manifest necessity might be a highly improper opening statement by the defendant's counsel. *Arizona v. Washington*, 434 U.S. 497, 98 S.Ct. 824, 54 L.Ed.2d 717 (1978).

Some offenses are crimes against both the federal and state governments. The policy, and in some instances state law, forbids a second prosecution once an offender has been prosecuted in a different jurisdiction. Because separate sovereigns are involved, under our federal system the Double Jeopardy Clause does not preclude prosecution by both the federal and state governments. *Bartkus v. Illinois*, 359 U.S. 121, 79 S.Ct. 676, 3 L.Ed.2d 684 (1959). Nevertheless, this principle does not allow

Double Jeopardy

CASE-IN-POINT

In a high-profile case in 1992, four Los Angeles police officers were tried by jury in a California state court on charges arising out of the beating of Rodney King, an African American motorist stopped by the police for traffic infractions. The event was videotaped by an onlooker and televised nationally. The jury's verdict of not guilty was followed by considerable outrage and large-scale rioting in Los Angeles. Despite the acquittal on state charges, the federal government brought new charges against the officers for violating King's civil rights. Their pleas that the new federal charges were barred by the Double Jeopardy Clause of the Fifth Amendment were rejected by the U.S. District Court, and in April 1993 two of the four officers were convicted after a jury trial. 833 F. Supp. 769. On appeal, the Ninth Circuit said that "there is no evidence that the federal prosecution was a 'sham' or a 'cover' for the state prosecution."

United States v. Koon, 34 F.3d 1416 (9th Cir. 1994).

two courts within a state to try an accused for the same offense. Therefore, a person who has been prosecuted in a city or county court cannot be tried again in any court in the state for the same offense. *Waller v. Florida*, 397 U.S. 387, 90 S.Ct. 1184, 25 L.Ed.2d 435 (1970).

In addition to protecting against a second prosecution for the same offense after conviction or acquittal, the Double Jeopardy Clause protects against multiple punishments for the same offense. *North Carolina v. Pearce*, 395 U.S. 711, 89 S.Ct. 2072, 23 L.Ed.2d 656 (1969). However, the Constitution does not define "same offense." In 1932 the Supreme Court said the following:

> The applicable rule is that, where the same act or transaction constitutes a violation of two distinct statutory provisions, the test to be applied to determine whether there are two offenses or only one is whether each provision requires proof of an additional fact which the other does not. *Blockburger v. United States*, 284 U.S. 299, 304, 52 S.Ct. 180, 182, 76 L.Ed. 306, 309 (1932).

The ***Blockburger* test** compares the elements of the crimes in question. It is a tool of interpretation and creates a presumption of legislative intent, but it is not designed to contravene such intent. Rather, the Supreme Court has said that the "legislative intent," if clear, determines the scope of what constitutes "same offenses." *Missouri v. Hunter*, 459 U.S. 359, 103 S.Ct. 673, 74 L.Ed.2d 535 (1983); *Albernaz v. United States*, 450 U.S. 333, 101 S.Ct. 1137, 67 LEd.2d 275 (1981). In 1980 the Supreme Court reviewed a case where the defendant was first convicted of failing to slow down to avoid an accident with his car. Later he was charged with manslaughter arising from the same incident. After reciting the "elements" test in *Blockburger*, the Court stated that

> if in the pending manslaughter prosecution Illinois relies on and proves a failure to slow to avoid an accident as the reckless act necessary to prove manslaughter, Vitale [the defendant] would have a substantial claim of double jeopardy under the Fifth and Fourteenth Amendments of the U.S. Constitution. *Illinois v. Vitale*, 447 U.S. 410, 420, 100 S.Ct. 2260, 2267, 65 L.Ed.2d 228, 238 (1980).

The *Blockburger* test examines the elements, not the facts. Since the Supreme Court's decision in *Illinois v. Vitale*, supra, not all courts have regarded *Blockburger* as the exclusive method of determining whether successive prosecutions violate the principle of double jeopardy. Indeed, some courts look also to the evidence to be presented to prove those crimes. For example, the Connecticut Supreme Court, citing *Vitale*, held that the prosecution of a defendant for operating a vehicle under the influence of intoxicants after being acquitted for manslaughter with a motor vehicle while intoxicated was barred by principle of double jeopardy. Even though the offenses were not the same under the *Blockburger* test, the evidence offered to prove a violation of the offense charged in the first prosecution was to be the sole evidence offered to prove an element of the offense charged in the second prosecution. Thus, the court held the second prosecution was barred by the principle of double jeopardy. *State v. Lonergan*, 566 A.2d 677 (Conn. 1989). Other courts continue to determine the issue of double jeopardy by applying the *Blockburger* test. See, for example, *Butler v. State*, 816 S.W.2d 124 (Tex. App. 1991).

In *Grady v. Corbin*, 495 U.S. 508, 110 S.Ct 2084, 109 L.Ed.2d 548 (1990), the Supreme Court, by a 5–4 vote, continued to follow the approach in *Vitale*. The Court said that "if to establish an essential element of an offense charged in that prosecution, the government will prove conduct that constitutes an offense for which the defendant has already been prosecuted," a second prosecution may not be undertaken. 495 U.S. at 510, 110 S.Ct. at 2087, 109 L.Ed.2d at 557. This became known as the **same evidence test** and barred a second prosecution based on the same conduct by the defendant that was at issue in the first prosecution. In June 1993, however, in *United States v. Dixon*, 509 U.S. 688, 113 S.Ct. 2849, 125 L.Ed.2d 556 (1993), by a 5–4 margin, the Court overruled *Grady v. Corbin*, replacing the same evidence test for double jeopardy analysis by a return to the **same elements test** from *Blockburger*, which bars punishment for offenses that have the same elements, or when one offense includes or is included in another offense. In *Dixon*, the Court also ruled that a criminal contempt conviction represents a "jeopardy" that triggers the bar against a second prosecution for the same offense. After the Supreme Court's decision in *United States v. Dixon*, the Connecticut Supreme Court revisited its decision in *State v. Lonergan*, 566 A.2d 677 (Conn. 1989) and adopted the *Blockburger* "same elements" approach. *State v. Alvarez*, 778 A.2d 938 (Conn. 2001).

In 1994 the U.S. Supreme Court invalidated a Montana tax on the possession of illegal drugs that was imposed on a party already convicted of possession of illegal drugs. The Court ruled that the added tax was punishment in violation of the Double Jeopardy Clause. *Dept. of Revenue of Montana v. Kurth Ranch*, 511 U.S. 767, 114 S.Ct. 1937, 128 L.Ed.2d 767 (1994). After a defendant won dismissal of DUI-related charges in Colorado on the basis that his driver's license had already been revoked because of the offense, defense attorneys began to assert a double jeopardy defense to DUI prosecutions. They argued that, on the basis of *Montana v. Kurth Ranch*, an administrative revocation of the accused's driver's license constituted "punishment" that barred a subsequent prosecution for DUI. In July 1996, the Colorado Supreme Court unanimously held that "imposition of criminal sanctions subsequent to an administrative driver's license revocation proceeding does not constitute the imposition of multiple punishments and does not violate the Double Jeopardy Clause." *Deutschendorf v. People*, 920 P.2d 53, 61 (Colo. 1996). The court's opinion appears to be consistent with what other courts have said on this issue. In *United States v. Reyes*, 87 F.3d 676 (5th Cir. 1996), the government imposed a three-day unpaid suspension of a civilian Air Force employee for operating a motor vehicle while intoxicated on an Air Force base. In that instance, the court held, the government was acting as an employer, not as a sovereign, and the suspension was not "punishment" under the Double Jeopardy Clause.

As we noted earlier, the dual sovereignty of the federal government and the states allow separate trials of a defendant for the same offense. In the past, this has not been a major problem because it has been governmental policy not to cause duplicate prosecutions. Some deviations from this policy have occurred in recent years, however.

Statutes of Limitation

A **statute of limitations** is a legislative enactment that places a time limit on the prosecution of a crime. Common law placed no time limits on prosecution. There is no federal constitutional basis to limit the time in which a prosecution can be initiated. Nonetheless, the federal government and almost all states have enacted laws that prescribe certain time limits for prosecution of most offenses, excluding murder. There are two primary public policy reasons for enacting statutes of limitations on the prosecution of crimes. First, it is generally accepted that a person should not be under threat of prosecution for too long a period. Second, after a prolonged period, proof is either unavailable or, if available, may not be credible.

Statutes of limitations seldom place time limits on prosecutions for murder and other very serious offenses. This was dramatized in 1994, when Byron de la Beckwith was convicted for the June 1963 murder of Medgar Evers. Evers was an official of the National Association for the Advancement of Colored People, and his death galvanized support for the enactment of civil rights laws in the 1960s. Two trials in 1964 ended in deadlocked juries. But after extended litigation and a lapse of more than thirty years since the victim's death, a Mississippi jury found Beckwith guilty of killing Evers. On December 22, 1997, the Mississippi Supreme Court affirmed Beckwith's conviction. *Beckwith v. State*, 707 So.2d 547 (Miss. 1997).

Under most statutes of limitations, the period for prosecution begins when a crime is committed rather than when it is discovered. The period ends when an arrest warrant is issued, an indictment is returned, or an information is filed. The period of limitations is interrupted while a perpetrator is a fugitive or conceals himself or herself from authorities. This cessation of the statute of limitations is often referred to as the **tolling** of the statutory period.

Federal statutes of limitations provide a five-year limitation on the prosecution of noncapital crimes. 18 U.S.C.A. § 3282 *et seq.* Although limitation periods vary among the states, the Ohio law appears representative:

> Except as otherwise provided in this section, a prosecution shall be barred unless it is commenced within the following periods after an offense is committed:
>
> (1) For a felony other than aggravated murder or murder, six years;
> (2) For a misdemeanor other than a minor misdemeanor, two years;
> (3) For a minor misdemeanor, six months. Page's Ohio Rev. Code Ann. § 2901.13 (A).

There is a conflict among the various jurisdictions as to whether a statute of limitations in a criminal action is an affirmative defense. An affirmative defense that is not pled is ordinarily deemed waived, but some courts have said that such a waiver must be knowing and voluntary. In *State v. Pearson*, 858 S.W.2d (Tenn. 1993), the Tennessee Supreme Court treated the statute of limitations as waivable by a defendant when it is about to run out, indicating that a defendant may wish to waive the protection of the statute. The court cited an instance where a defendant needs to gain time for plea bargaining and another instance where a defendant who is charged with a more serious offense that is not time barred might want to waive the statute of limitations on a lesser included offense. But, as the court pointed out, any waiver of the statute of limitations must be knowingly and voluntarily entered. Other courts follow the rule that the statute of limitations is jurisdictional and that if the state's information or indictment discloses that the prosecution is initiated beyond the period allowed by the applicable statute of limitations, the prosecution is barred. See, for example, *People v. Ware*, 39 P.3d 1277 (Colo. App. 2001).

But what if the defendant is prosecuted for an offense not barred by the statute of limitations but found guilty of a lesser offense that is time barred? In *State v. Leonard*, 543 S.E.2d 655 (W.Va. 2000), the West Virginia Supreme Court of Appeals barred such a prosecution. It noted that numerous courts have held that a defendant cannot be convicted of a lesser offense upon prosecution for a greater crime that includes the lesser offense when the prosecution is commenced after the statute of limitations has run out on the lesser offense.

Defenses Based on Improper Government Conduct

There are two defenses that are based on improper government conduct. The defense of entrapment aims to prevent the government from manufacturing crime. This defense is widely asserted in prosecution for narcotics violations, for these cases are frequently based on undercover police operations. The defense of selective prosecution is infrequently imposed and has achieved very limited success. Nevertheless, it is designed to prevent the government from singling out an individual for prosecution based on impermissible grounds.

Entrapment

Law enforcement officers may provide an opportunity for a predisposed person to commit a crime, but they are not permitted to "manufacture" crime by implanting criminal ideas into innocent minds. Therefore, a person who has been induced to commit an offense under these latter circumstances may plead the defense of **entrapment**. A defendant who claims to have committed an offense as a result of inducement by an undercover police officer or a confidential police informant often asserts the defense of entrapment. It is not available to a defendant who has been entrapped by a person not associated with the government or police. See *Henderson v. United States*, 237 F.2d 169 (5th Cir. 1956).

Entrapment was not a defense under the common law, and, strictly speaking, it is not based on the Constitution. Nevertheless, it has long been recognized in federal and state courts in the United States. In 1980 the Tennessee Supreme Court acknowledged that Tennessee was the only state in the Union that did not allow entrapment as a defense, and proceeded to remedy the situation by declaring, "From this day forward entrapment is a defense to a Tennessee criminal prosecution." *State v. Jones*, 598 S.W.2d 209, 212 (Tenn. 1980). In 1989 the Tennessee legislature codified the law on entrapment and required a defendant who pleads entrapment to so advise the prosecution. Tenn. Code Ann. § 39-11-505.

In a landmark case arising during Prohibition days, the U.S. Supreme Court held that a federal officer had entrapped a defendant by using improper inducements to cause him to buy illegal liquor for the officer. The Court observed that the evidence revealed that the defendant, Sorrells, had not been predisposed to commit a crime but had been induced by the government agent to do so. The Court opined that entrapment occurs when criminal conduct involved is "the product of the creative activity of [law enforcement officers]." *Sorrells v. United States*, 287 U.S. 435, 451, 53 S.Ct. 210, 216, 77 L.Ed. 413, 422 (1932).

In *Sorrells*, the majority of the justices viewed entrapment as an issue of whether the defendant's criminal intent originated in the mind of the officer, or whether the defendant was predisposed to commit the offense. This focus on the predisposition of the defendant has come to be known as the **subjective test of entrapment**. A minority of justices in *Sorrells* would have applied what is now known as the **objective test of entrapment**. Under this view, the court would simply determine whether the police methods were so improper that they likely induced or ensnared a person into committing a crime.

In the past, the majority of federal and state courts followed the subjective view. Thus, a person who pled entrapment was held to have admitted commission of the offense. See, for example, *United States v. Sedigh*, 658 F.2d 1010 (5th Cir. 1981); *State v. Amodei*, 563 P.2d 440 (Kan. 1977). A jury would then proceed to determine whether the defendant committed the crime because of a predisposition, or instead was improperly induced to do so by the police.

The subjective approach to entrapment has the disadvantage of not providing the police with any bright lines for enforcement. Moreover, in proving predisposition, the prosecutor often brings in evidence of a defendant's past conduct that may be otherwise inadmissible. This can prejudice the jury with respect to arriving at a verdict on the principal offense charged.

In *United States v. Dion*, 762 F.2d 674 (8th Cir. 1985), modified, 476 U.S. 734 (1986), the U.S. Court of Appeals for the Eighth Circuit provided the following detailed list of factors appropriate for distinguishing predisposed defendants from nonpredisposed defendants:

(1) whether the defendant readily responded to the inducement offered;
(2) the circumstances surrounding the illegal conduct;
(3) "the state of mind of a defendant before government agents make any suggestion that he shall commit a crime";
(4) whether the defendant was engaged in an existing course of conduct similar to the crime for which he is charged;
(5) whether the defendant had already formed the "design" to commit the crime for which he is charged;
(6) the defendant's reputation;
(7) the conduct of the defendant during the negotiations with the undercover agent;
(8) whether the defendant has refused to commit similar acts on other occasions;
(9) the nature of the crime charged; and
(10) "[t]he degree of coercion present in the instigation law officers have contributed to the transaction" relative to the "defendant's criminal background."

Although the traditional view of courts has been that a defendant who asserts entrapment as a defense admits the offense charged, there have been conflicting decisions in the federal courts between this view and the more modern view, which holds that a defendant may assert entrapment without being required to concede commission of the crime or any element thereof. The U.S. Supreme Court resolved the issue in *Mathews v. United States*, 485 U.S. 58, 108 St. 883, 99 L.Ed.2d 54 (1988). The Court ruled that a defendant who pleads entrapment does not necessarily admit to the crime charged or any element thereof. The Court's decision affects only the federal courts; state courts vary in their approach as to whether a defendant who pleads entrapment admits the crime charged, with their views sometimes being based on state laws providing for the defense of entrapment.

Where courts follow the objective view, the judge, not the jury, determines whether the police methods were so improper as to constitute entrapment. See, for example, *People v. D'Angelo*, 257 N.W.2d 655 (Mich. 1977). Some federal courts have simply said that where police conduct is outrageous, it becomes a question of law for the judge to determine whether governmental misconduct is so shocking as to be a violation of due process of law. See, for example, *United States v. Wylie*, 625 F.2d 1371 (9th Cir. 1980). In courts that strictly follow the objective view, the defendant's predisposition to commit an offense is irrelevant. The objective approach has the advantage of enabling the courts to scrutinize governmental action to ensure that outrageous methods are not employed in seeking to ferret out crime.

In 1993 the Wyoming Supreme Court declined to adopt the objective theory of entrapment. Nevertheless, it indicated that a defendant can rely on "outrageous government conduct" as a defense if the circumstances reveal police conduct that violates fundamental fairness and is shocking to the universal sense of justice mandated by the Due Process Clauses of the Fifth and Fourteenth Amendments. *Rivera v. State*, 846 P.2d 1 (Wyo. 1993).

Recent decisions indicate that the subjective and objective tests can coexist. Some state courts now first determine whether a defendant who pleads entrapment has been ensnared by outrageous police methods. If so, the judge dismisses the charges against the ensnared defendant. If not, the court then allows the defendant to attempt to establish the defense of entrapment by proving improper inducement. The prosecution usually counters with evidence showing the defendant's prior criminal activity and ready acquiescence in committing the crime charged. The court then instructs the jury to determine whether the defendant committed the crime because of his or her predisposition or through inducement by the police. At least two states have adopted this general approach. See *Cruz v. State*, 465 So.2d 516 (Fla. 1985); *State v. Talbot*, 364 A.2d 9 (N.J. 1976).

An excerpt from the Florida Supreme Court's decision in *Cruz v. State* is reproduced on the companion website.

Dissatisfied with the Florida Supreme Court's decision in *Cruz v. State*, supra, which provided for the trial court to first determine whether a defendant who pleads entrapment has been ensnared by outrageous police methods, the Florida legislature enacted a new subjective-model entrapment statute. West's Fla. Stat. 777.201. After passage of the statute, the Supreme Court of Florida held that, in enacting section 777.201, the legislature effectively eliminated the objective test in *Cruz*. Nevertheless, the court observed that the legislature cannot prohibit the judiciary from objectively reviewing the issue of entrapment to the extent that such a review involves the Due Process Clause of Article I, Section 9 of the Florida Constitution. *Munoz v. State*, 629 So.2d 90 (Fla. 1993).

Two principal reasons account for the increased assertion of the defense of entrapment in recent years. First, numerous violations of narcotics laws have been prosecuted on the basis of undercover police activity and evidence given by confidential police informants. Second, there has been increased attention to prosecuting corruption involving government officials.

One of the most highly publicized cases resulted from the 1980 Abscam operation, in which FBI agents posed as wealthy Arab businessmen and attempted to buy influence from members of Congress. Despite their claims of entrapment, several members of Congress were found guilty of offenses involving misuse of office. See, for example, *United States v. Jenrette*, 744 F.2d 817 (D.C. Cir. 1984).

In 1987 Keith Jacobson was indicted for violating the Child Protection Act of 1984, 18 U.S.C.A. § 2252(a)(2)(A), which criminalizes the knowing receipt through

A Promise of Sex—Entrapment as a Matter of Law

Law enforcement officers told a female that she might not be prosecuted for possession of cocaine if she would become a confidential informant. She agreed and met with the defendant, James Banks, a suspected drug dealer, on two nights. The meetings included "kissing and hugging," after which she told Banks that if he "could get her something [they] would get together for the weekend, fool around and party." The defendant obtained some cocaine for her, and as a result, he was arrested. The trial judge dismissed the charges because the uncontested facts established that the officers used a method with a substantial risk of persuading or inducing the defendant to commit a criminal offense.

The state appealed the dismissal. The appellate court affirmed: "When law enforcement agencies utilize confidential informants who use sex, or the express or implied promise thereof, to obtain contraband the defendant did not already possess, there is no way for the courts or anyone else to determine whether such inducement served only to uncover an existing propensity or created a new one. This violates the threshold objective test."

State v. Banks, 499 So.2d 894 (Fla. App. 1986).

the mails of a "visual depiction [that] involves the use of a minor engaging in sexually explicit conduct." At trial, Jacobson contended the government entrapped him into committing the crime. A jury found him guilty, and his conviction was affirmed by the court of appeals. In evaluating the evidence at Jacobson's trial, the U.S. Supreme Court found that when it was still legal to do so, Jacobson ordered some magazines containing photos of nude boys. After Congress enacted the Child Protection Act, making this illegal, two government agencies learned that Jacobson had ordered the magazines. The agencies sent mail to Jacobson through fictitious organizations to explore his willingness to break the law. He was literally bombarded with solicitations, which included communications decrying censorship and questioning the legitimacy and constitutionality of the government's efforts to restrict availability of sexually explicit materials. He finally responded to an undercover solicitation to order child pornography and was arrested after a controlled delivery of the explicit sexual materials.

After pointing out that for twenty-six months government agents had made Jacobson the target of repeated mailings, the Court held that the prosecution failed to produce evidence that Jacobson was predisposed to break the law before the government directed its efforts toward him. Adding that government agents may not implant a criminal design in an innocent person's mind and then induce commission of a crime, the Court reversed his conviction, observing that Congress had not intended for government officials to instigate crime by luring persons otherwise innocent to commit offenses. *Jacobson v. United States*, 503 U.S. 540, 112 S.Ct. 1535, 118 L.Ed.2d 174 (1992).

The Supreme Court's decision in *Jacobson v. U.S.* is excerpted on the companion website.

In 1994 the U.S. Court of Appeals for the Seventh Circuit rendered an *en banc* decision holding that when a defendant pleads entrapment, the government must prove that the defendant was not only "willing" to commit the offense charged but also that he or she was "ready" to commit the offense in the absence of official encouragement. *United States v. Hollingsworth*, 27 F.3d 1196 (7th Cir. 1994).

Because the Supreme Court's decision in *Jacobson v. United States* is not grounded on constitutional principles, it affects only federal law enforcement activities. Nonetheless, it signals that state enforcement authorities should not play on the weaknesses of innocent parties to beguile them into committing crimes.

CASE-IN-POINT

Rejecting the Defense of Selective Prosecution

In 1982 David Alan Wayte was indicted for willfully failing to register under the Military Selective Service Act. Wayte sought dismissal of the indictment on the ground of selective prosecution. He contended that he and the others being prosecuted had been singled out of an estimated 674,000 nonregistrants because they had voiced opposition to the Selective Service requirements. The district court dismissed the indictment on the ground that the government had failed to rebut Wayte's *prima facie* showing of selective prosecution. The case was eventually heard by the U.S. Supreme Court. The Court held that the government's passive enforcement policy, under which it prosecuted only those nonregistrants who reported themselves or were reported by others, did not violate the First or Fifth Amendments to the Constitution.

Wayte v. United States, 470 U.S. 598, 105 S.Ct. 1524, 84 L.Ed.2d 547 (1985).

Selective Prosecution

Selective enforcement of the criminal law is not itself a constitutional violation; therefore, without more, it does not constitute a defense. *Oyler v. Boles*, 368 U.S. 448, 82 S.Ct. 501, 7 L.Ed.2d 446 (1962). There are many cases rejecting the defense of **selective prosecution**. To prevail, a defendant must ordinarily demonstrate that other similarly situated persons have not been prosecuted for similar conduct and that the defendant's selection for prosecution was based on some impermissible ground such as race, religion, or the exercise of the First Amendment right of free speech. *United States v. Jennings*, 991 F.2d 725 (11th Cir.1993); *United States v. Arias*, 575 F.2d 253 (9th Cir. 1978).

In 1996 the Supreme Court reviewed a case where defendants indicted for federal narcotics violations filed a pretrial motion for the discovery of information that they contended would show that they were being selectively prosecuted because of their race. The Court held that the defendants failed to establish an entitlement to discovery based on their claim because they failed to produce any credible evidence that similarly situated defendants of other races could have been prosecuted but were not. *United States v. Armstrong*, 517 U.S. 456, 116 S.Ct. 1480, 134 L.Ed.2d 687 (1996).

In *United States v. Eagleboy*, 200 F.3d 1137 (8th Cir. 1999), the defendant, who was not a member of a federally recognized Indian tribe, was charged with possessing hawk parts in violation of the Migratory Bird Treaty Act (MBTA). Had the defendant been a member of a federally recognized Indian tribe, he would not have been charged with a violation of the MBTA. Pointing to this policy, the defendant moved to dismiss on the ground of selective prosecution. The U.S. Court of Appeals for the Eighth Circuit held that Eagleboy was not selectively prosecuted. The court said that the government's policy of not enforcing the act against recognized Indian tribes distinguished between persons on the basis of membership in a federally recognized Indian tribe, not on the basis of race.

Nontraditional Defenses

Although they are seldom successful, defendants sometimes employ novel and innovative defenses. We previously discussed the status of the battered-woman– and battered-child–syndrome defenses, which, though not traditional, can no longer be considered novel. In this section, we discuss some of the more interesting novel defenses. These include unusual religious practices, the victim's negligence, premenstrual syndrome (PMS), compulsive gambling, post-traumatic stress syndrome (PTSS), the junk food defense, television intoxication, and pornographic intoxication. In instances where a novel defense leads to an acquittal, appellate courts do not have an opportunity to evaluate the legal basis of the defense. This is because the prosecution is not permitted to appeal an acquittal.

Unusual Religious Beliefs and Practices

The courts have long rejected contentions by defendants that they have been commanded by God or the scriptures to commit illegal acts. See *Hotema v. United States*, 186 U.S. 413, 22 S.Ct. 895, 46 L.Ed. 1225 (1902). Moreover, laws prohibiting religious rites that endanger the lives, health, or safety of the participants or others are customarily upheld by the courts. This is illustrated by the decision of the Kentucky Court of Appeals in *Lawson v. Commonwealth*, 164 S.W.2d 972 (Ky. 1942). There, despite the defendants' contentions that their constitutional guarantees of freedom of religion were violated, the court upheld the constitutionality of a statute making it a misdemeanor for anyone to handle snakes or reptiles in connection with any religious service.

Courts have traditionally upheld the right of parents to raise their children by their own religious beliefs, ruling that the state's interest must yield to parental religious beliefs that preclude medical treatment, so long as the child's life is not immediately imperiled. See, for example, *In re Green*, 292 A.2d 387 (Pa. 1972). Nevertheless, the courts have held that where a child's life is imperiled, the parents have an affirmative duty to provide medical care that will protect the child's life. Thus, an appellate court upheld a conviction of parents for manslaughter when it found that a child's death was directly caused by the parents' failure to secure needed medical care. *Commonwealth v. Barnhart*, 497 A.2d 616 (Pa. Super. 1985). In about half of the states, child abuse and criminal neglect statutes permit parents to choose spiritual means or prayer as a response to illness without regard to a child's medical condition. In *State v. McKown*, 461 N.W.2d 720 (Minn. App. 1990), aff'd 475 N.W.2d 63 (1991), the court upheld the dismissal of manslaughter charges against a parent and stepparent who relied on spiritual means and failed to secure medical treatment for an eleven-year-old boy. The child died allegedly as a result of medical problems resulting from diabetes.

The need to furnish medical care to children poses a problem of balancing the parents' interests in bringing up their offspring in accordance with their religious beliefs against the interest of the state in the preservation of life. In January 1988, the press reported that the American Academy of Pediatrics urged the repeal of laws allowing parents to reject medical treatment for their children on religious grounds. The academy pointed out that about three-fourths of the states have laws that permit some rejection of medical care on religious or philosophical grounds. However, the academy noted, courts have frequently intervened to order certain treatments for minors.

Victim's Negligence

Federal and state courts hold that a victim's negligence, credulity, or wrongdoing is not a defense to a prosecution. *United States v. Kreimer*, 609 F.2d 126 (5th Cir. 1980); *State v. Lunz*, 273 N.W.2d 767 (Wis. 1979). Likewise, because a crime is an offense against society as well as against the victim, it follows that a victim's forgiveness or condoning does not relieve an actor of criminal responsibility.

Premenstrual Syndrome

Premenstrual syndrome (PMS) refers to certain physiological changes that occur in some women, usually in the days close to the onset of menstruation. This results from hormonal imbalance and can cause serious depression and irritability. In certain cases, medical treatment is required. Some argue that a woman so affected should be allowed to assert PMS as a defense to criminal conduct because some physicians say that PMS directly affects behavior. Nevertheless, PMS has not been accepted as a defense in the United States. In England, it has been recognized as a basis for mitigating punishment.

Compulsive Gambling

Evidence of compulsive gambling is generally not considered as a defense unless it rises to the level of insanity. For example, a defendant was convicted of entering a bank with intent to commit larceny and robbery. On appeal, he argued that the trial court erred in instructing the jury that "as a matter of law pathological gambling disorder is not a disease or defect within the meaning of the American Law Institute test for insanity." The U.S. Court of Appeals, which was still applying the former ALI standard, rejected his contention. *United States v. Gould*, 741 F.2d 45 (4th Cir. 1984).

Post-Traumatic Stress Syndrome

Post-traumatic stress syndrome (PTSS) commonly refers to the unique stresses suffered during combat, often manifesting in such symptoms as flashbacks, outbursts of anger, and blocked-out memories. After World War I, these conditions were usually referred to as "shell shock." Following World War II, the term "combat fatigue" was often used to describe such anxiety disorders. Present generations have heard these conditions described as "post-traumatic stress syndrome." Because of the bizarre type of warfare that service personnel endured in Vietnam, the unpopularity of the war, the availability of drugs, and the difficulties encountered in adjusting to civilian life, many veterans suffered severe psychological reactions. To a lesser extent, the stress of combat in Operation Desert Storm also caused delayed traumatic stress syndrome. Undoubtedly, the stress of combat operations in the present military operations in Afghanistan and Iraq can be expected to cause similar results.

Although not a legal defense in itself, in some instances PTSS may affect a defendant's understanding to the point of allowing a plea of insanity. More frequently, PTSS will be introduced as evidence bearing on a defendant's intent or offered at a sentencing hearing in an effort to mitigate punishment.

The "Junk Food" Defense

Dan White, a former city supervisor, shot and killed the mayor of San Francisco in 1978. Following this, he killed another supervisor, who was a leader of the local gay community. In defense to charges of first-degree murder, White's counsel sought to establish that his client was depressed by having gorged himself on junk food. White was convicted of manslaughter instead of murder, giving some credence to reports that the jury may have accepted White's defense. This was jury action, so it set no precedent to establish any such defense.

Television Intoxication

An adolescent boy was tried in Miami for the first-degree murder of an elderly woman. He attempted to establish insanity on the basis of psychiatric testimony concerning the effects of "involuntary subliminal television intoxication." The trial court rejected his claim. An appellate court, stating that the trial judge correctly limited the evidence to the requirements of the *M'Naghten* rule, found no difficulty in upholding the trial court's decision. *Zamora v. State*, 361 So.2d 776 (Fla. App. 1978).

Pornographic Intoxication

There is a lively academic debate over the effect of pornography on the psyche. Does it stimulate sexual violence? Some defendants have attempted to employ a "pornography intoxication defense," but with little success. For example, in *Schiro v. Clark*, 963 F.2d 962 (7th Cir. 1992), a federal appellate court held that acting under the influence of pornography could not be used to mitigate the defendant's death sentence for rape and murder.

Postpartum Depression

Postpartum depression refers to a group of symptoms a new mother may experience after giving birth. It involves severe depression, and in cases where it doesn't give rise to qualify for a defense of insanity, in cases involving infanticide it has been offered in an effort to mitigate punishment.

XYY Chromosome Abnormality

Growing evidence indicates that a person's genes influence behavior, and there has been speculation in media reports that people accused of violent crimes might find a medical basis to assert a "my genes made me do it" defense. While this is not recognized as a specific defense, there is some medical evidence indicating that the presence of an extra Y chromosome may lead to physical and mental problems that cause an affected person to act aggressively. Some defendants have used evidence of this abnormality as a basis for the insanity defense.

Multiple Personality Defense

One who asserts a multiple personality defense argues that he or she did not commit the offense alleged; rather, another personality of which the defendant has no memory and no control committed the crime. In October 2000, the press reported that a woman in Kansas City, Missouri, who pled not guilty by reason of insanity to several offenses, contended that her multiple personalities were responsible for the deaths of her two young sons in 1999. Her lawyers and expert witnesses said she had severe psychosis and an alternate personality named Sharon, who controlled her actions. Notwithstanding her claim, the defendant was found guilty of murder and a series of child abuse charges.

Black Rage and Urban Survival Defenses

Based on claims that have developed over the years in response to perceptions of social needs are the "black rage defense" and the "urban survival defense." These are usually offered with the hope that a defendant's punishment will be mitigated by the social conditions they expose.

In the black rage defense, some African American defendants charged with violent crime against a white person have sought to absolve or mitigate their conduct on the basis of years of oppression and racist hostility endured at the hands of white Americans. Proponents contend that as a result of racism, substandard education, inadequate employment opportunities, and substandard housing and medical care, African American defendants can justify retaliatory action against white citizens. Critics point out that if courts were to accept black rage as a legal defense, it could lead to the impossible task of assessing claims of discrimination by criminal defendants of a variety of ethnic, and even religious, backgrounds.

Similar to the black rage defense is the advocacy of an "urban survival syndrome" defense based upon a defendant's having lived under substandard environmental conditions in a deteriorated urban neighborhood plagued with drug dealers and acts of violence that often include threats of deadly force.

Conclusion

Despite the fact that the prosecution has met its burden of proving the elements of a crime, a defendant has the opportunity to not only dispute such proof but also to affirmatively assert defenses to the conduct charged. The traditional common-law defenses that allow a defendant to raise issues of lack of capacity, excuse, justification, and justifiable use of force have been augmented by constitutional and statutory defenses and defenses challenging improper government conduct. Concepts of criminal responsibility and criminal defenses will continue to evolve in response to our increased knowledge of human behavior and society's balance of the rights of the individual against society's legitimate demand for protection. Some nontraditional defenses could even become viable, given new social science and medical research.

Chapter Summary

- **LO1** Defendants who plead not guilty to a criminal charge may not only rely on their general denial; they may also offer any defense (sometimes called a negative defense) not required to be specifically pled. A defendant merely has the burden of producing evidence of a negative defense. A defense that must be specifically pled is classified as an affirmative defense—that is, one that does not simply negate an element of the crime but, rather, consists of new matter relied on as an excuse or justification for the defendant's otherwise illegal conduct.
- **LO2** English common law conclusively presumed that a child younger than seven could not commit a crime. This presumption was rebuttable for a child between seven and fourteen years old; children over fourteen were treated as adults. The defense of infancy still exists under modern American law, but instances of it are very rare. Today, most youthful offenders are dealt with in the juvenile justice system rather than in the adult criminal courts, but statutes commonly provide that juveniles charged with more serious offenses can be tried as adults.
- **LO3** The common law did not excuse those who became voluntarily intoxicated from criminal responsibility. Most American courts allow voluntary intoxication as a defense to specific-intent crimes but reject it for general-intent crimes. But the trend is to prohibit voluntary intoxication as a defense to any crime. Involuntary intoxication relieves criminality if a defendant no longer knows right from wrong.
- **LO4** All persons are presumed sane unless previously adjudicated insane. Even one adjudicated insane may be found guilty of a crime committed during a lucid interval. The insanity defense (*M'Naghten* rule) originated in England in 1843

and provides that insanity cannot be a defense unless "at the time of committing the act, the party accused as labouring under such a defect of reason, from disease of the mind, as not to know the nature and quality of the act he was doing; or, if he did know it, that he did not know what he was doing was wrong." It became the test for insanity in federal and state courts in the United States. As psychology and psychiatry developed new theories of mental capacity, some courts followed the ALI standard, which provides that persons are not responsible for criminal conduct if they lack substantial capacity either to appreciate the wrongfulness of their conduct or to conform their conduct to the requirements of the law. Most federal courts adopted the ALI standard, but after an assailant who shot President Reagan in 1981 was acquitted under the ALI standard, Congress enacted the Insanity Defense Reform Act of 1984. The new act essentially reestablished the *M'Naghten* rule in federal courts and made insanity an affirmative defense. Many state courts follow the *M'Naghten* standard; others follow more liberal tests. Some require the prosecution to refute claims of insanity; others classify insanity as an affirmative defense and require the defendant to prove insanity, usually by a preponderance of the evidence. Some states provide for verdicts of guilty but mentally ill. Others have abolished the defense of insanity altogether.

- **LO5** Federal and state courts generally follow the common law and hold that duress can be a defense only when it involves present threats that cause well-grounded apprehensions of death or serious injury; duress cannot excuse an intentional killing of an innocent person.

- **LO6** Early common law recognized that "a man may break the words of the law . . . through necessity." American courts hold that if there is a reasonable legal alternative to violating the law, the defense of necessity fails. In most cases, necessity has been unavailing to defendants espousing social and political causes. In some sexual offenses consent might be a defense, but this cannot apply in a prosecution for having sexual relations with a minor. Otherwise consent to criminal conduct is not a defense.

- **LO7** The maxim "ignorance of the law is no excuse" remains the generally accepted view. Nevertheless, where a mistaken view of the law (such as title to property) negates the specific-intent element of a crime, mistake of law can be a defense. Historically, American courts have held that a mistake of fact is not recognized as a defense to a general-intent crime unless the mistake is a reasonable one for a person to make under the circumstances. But even an unreasonable mistake may be asserted as a defense to a specific-intent crime. Recent court decisions indicate that a mistake of fact may be a defense if it negates the existence of the mental state essential to the crime charged. Mistake of fact is unavailing as a defense in strict liability crimes.

- **LO8** The defense of alibi does not deny that a crime was committed. Rather, the defendant denies the ability to have perpetrated such crime because of having been elsewhere at the time. Statutes or court rules commonly require that to assert alibi as a defense, a defendant must notify the prosecution in advance of trial and furnish the names of witnesses the defendant intends to use to support the alibi.

- **LO9** The defense of justifiable use of force applies to claims of self-defense in assaultive and homicidal offenses. At common law, a person attacked had a duty "to retreat to the wall" before using deadly force in self-defense. Most courts reject that doctrine and hold that a person attacked or threatened may use any force reasonably necessary to prevent harm as long as the person using such force is where he or she has a right to be and acts without fault and in reasonable fear or apprehension of death or great bodily harm. A minority of courts hold that a person who can safely retreat must do so before using deadly force. The law has traditionally applied an objective test for the use of deadly force, but today many courts apply a subjective standard of reasonableness to determine whether circumstances are sufficient to induce an honest and reasonable belief that force must be used. Generally, when a defendant raises an issue of self-defense, the prosecution must prove that the accused did not act in self-defense.

- **LO10** There is a developing trend that when a woman kills her batterer and pleads self-defense, expert testimony about battered woman syndrome (BWS) is admissible to explain how her experiences affected her perceptions of danger and honest belief in its imminence. There is a movement to allow a child who has been abused over an extended period to assert the battered child syndrome (BCS) in defense of charges for killing or injuring a parent.

- **LO11** Common law allowed the use of reasonable force to prevent the commission of a felony or to protect household members who were endangered. This principle was codified in many jurisdictions. The trend in American jurisdictions is to allow a person "to stand in the shoes of the victim" and to use such reasonable force as is necessary to defend anyone, irrespective of relationship, from harm. The common law "castle doctrine" permits the use of deadly force against an intruder into a dwelling, but does not justify using deadly force in taking a life to repel a mere trespass. The right to defend other property is more limited and, if someone is killed or injured as a result of a spring gun or similar mechanical device, the party who set it or caused it to be set will generally be held criminally responsible for any resulting death or injury. The trend is to expand the right of self-defense, and half of the states have enacted "stand your ground" laws providing that a person does not have a duty to retreat before using deadly force.

- **LO12** Today the majority of states, either by statute or judicial decision, provide that a person may not resist an arrest with force, even if the arrest is illegal. Most states have statutes or police regulations that specify the degree of force that police may use to apprehend violators. Police officers are usually permitted to use whatever force is reasonably necessary to effect an arrest and are not required to retreat from an aggressor. In 1985 the Supreme Court limited an officer's use of deadly force to situations where it is necessary to prevent the escape of a suspect who poses a significant threat of death or serious injury to the officer or others.

- **LO13** The Fifth Amendment to the Constitution provides that "no person . . . shall be compelled in any criminal case to be a witness against himself." It is applicable to the states through the Fourteenth Amendment. A witness compelled to give incriminating testimony receives use immunity. This means that the testimony given cannot be used against the witness. Some states grant transactional immunity to a witness who testifies under a grant of immunity. This protects a witness from prosecution for any activity mentioned in the witness's testimony. A witness who testifies under a grant of immunity may be prosecuted for making material false statements under oath. Contractual immunity is sometimes granted to a witness to enable the prosecutor to obtain a conviction not otherwise obtainable because of the constitutional protection against self-incrimination. Authority to grant immunity in federal courts is vested in the U.S. Attorney with approval of the Attorney General or certain authorized assistants. At the state level, such authority is generally vested in the chief prosecuting officer.

- **LO14.** Transactional immunity is a broader protection that protects a witness from prosecution for any activity mentioned in the witness's testimony. A person with diplomatic status, who serves as part of a diplomatic mission, and members of the diplomat's staff and household enjoy diplomatic immunity from arrest and prosecution. The U.S. Constitution provides that members of Congress, in all cases except treason, felony, and breach of the peace, are privileged from arrest during attendance at and in going to or from legislative sessions. State constitutions generally include similar provisions for state lawmakers.

- **LO15** The Fifth Amendment to the U.S. Constitution provides: "[N]or shall any person be subject for the same offence to be twice put in jeopardy of life or limb." It is applicable to the states through the Fourteenth Amendment. Jeopardy attaches once the jury is sworn in or when the first witness is sworn to testify in a nonjury trial. The Double Jeopardy Clause forbids a second prosecution for the same offense after a defendant has been acquitted. It recently has been applied to prevent a second prosecution after a conviction. But if a defendant prevails in an appeal, it is not double jeopardy to retry the defendant unless the appellate court rules that there was insufficient evidence to sustain the defendant's conviction. The Double Jeopardy Clause does not preclude a prosecution by both the federal and state governments, but the policy, and in some instances state law, forbids a second prosecution once an offender has been prosecuted in a different jurisdiction. Courts usually apply the *Blockburger* test, which bars punishment for offenses that have the same elements, or when one offense is included in another offense.

- **LO16** Common law placed no time limits on prosecution. There is no federal constitutional basis for limiting the time in which a prosecution can be initiated. A statute of limitations is a legislative enactment that places a time limit on the prosecution of a crime, and the federal government and almost all states have enacted laws that prescribe certain time limits for prosecution of offenses, excluding murder. The twin rationales are that a person should not be under threat of prosecution for too long a period, and that after a prolonged period, proof is either unavailable or may not be credible. Statutes of limitations seldom place time limits on prosecutions for murder and other very serious offenses.

- **LO17** Unknown at common law, entrapment consists of law enforcement inducing a person who is predisposed to commit a crime to commit that crime. It is a defense in all federal and state courts. It is designed to prevent the government from manufacturing crime and is widely asserted in drug cases based on testimony of confidential informants. Most courts follow the subjective test, which focuses on whether a defendant's predisposition caused the defendant to commit the crime charged. A minority of courts apply an objective test whereby the court simply determines whether outrageous police methods induced a person to commit a crime. If the court so finds, the judge dismisses the charges against the ensnared defendant.

- **LO18** The selective prosecution defense is designed to prevent the government from singling out an individual for prosecution based on impermissible grounds. To prevail, a defendant who pleads selective prosecution must demonstrate that the defendant's prosecution is based on race, religion, or the exercise of the First Amendment rights of free speech, and that other similarly situated persons have not been prosecuted for similar conduct.

- **LO19** Some defendants employ novel and innovative defenses. These include unusual religious practices, victim's negligence, premenstrual syndrome (PMS), compulsive gambling, post-traumatic stress syndrome (PTSS), the junk food defense, television and pornographic intoxication, and other novel situations. In isolated cases, reliance on one or more of these nontraditional offenses might result in a jury acquitting a defendant or a conviction for a lesser offense. In other instances reliance on one or more of these innovative theories might result in a lesser punishment.

Key Terms

criminal responsibility Refers to the set of doctrines under which individuals are held accountable for criminal conduct.

negative defense Any criminal defense not required to be specifically pled.

preponderance of the evidence Evidence that has greater weight than countervailing evidence.

affirmative defense Defense to a criminal charge where the defendant bears the burden of proof. Examples include automatism, intoxication, coercion, and duress.

infancy The condition of being below the age of legal majority.

intoxication Condition in which a person has impaired physical or mental capacities due to the ingestion of drugs or alcohol.

voluntary intoxication The state of becoming drunk or intoxicated of one's own free will.

involuntary intoxication Intoxication that is not the result of a person's intentional ingestion of an intoxicating substance. A person may become involuntarily intoxicated through the trickery or fraud of another person or through the inadvertent ingestion of medicine.

insanity A degree of mental illness that negates the legal capacity or responsibility of the affected person.

not guilty by reason of insanity A plea that admits criminal conduct but raises the insanity defense.

M'Naghten rule Under this rule, for a defendant to be found not guilty by reason of insanity, it must be clearly proved that, at the time of committing the act, the defendant was suffering such a defect of reason, from disease of the mind, as not to know the nature and quality of the act he was doing; or, if he did know it, that he did not know what he was doing was wrong.

irresistible impulse A test for insanity that allowed a person who knew an act was wrong but acted under an uncontrollable desire or duress of mental disease to be excused from a criminal act.

Durham test A test for determining insanity developed by the U.S. Court of Appeals for the District of Columbia Circuit in the case of *Durham v. United States* (1954). Under this test, a person is not criminally responsible for an unlawful act if it was the product of a mental disease or defect.

ALI Standard A test proposed by American Law Institute to determine if a defendant is legally insane. See also **substantial capacity test**.

substantial capacity test The doctrine that a person is not responsible for criminal conduct if at the time of such conduct, as a result of mental disease or defect, the person lacked substantial capacity either to appreciate the wrongfulness of his or her conduct or to conform his or her conduct to the requirements of the law.

right from wrong test See *M'Naghten* Rule.

insanity Defense Reform Act of 1984 An act of Congress that specifies that insanity is an affirmative defense to a prosecution under a federal statute and details the requirements for establishing such a defense.

clear and convincing evidence standard An evidentiary standard that is higher than the standard of "preponderance of the evidence" applied in civil cases but lower than the standard of "beyond a reasonable doubt" applied in criminal cases. For example, under the new federal standard for the affirmative defense of insanity, the defendant must establish the defense of insanity by "clear and convincing evidence."

beyond a reasonable doubt The standard of proof that is constitutionally required to be met before a defendant can be found guilty of a crime or before a juvenile can be adjudicated as a delinquent.

guilty but mentally ill A form of verdict that may be rendered in some states where the jury finds that the defendant's mental illness does not deprive the defendant of substantial capacity sufficient to satisfy the insanity test but warrants the defendant's treatment in addition to incarceration.

automatism The condition under which a person performs a set of actions during a state of unconsciousness.

alibi Defense to a criminal charge that places the defendant at some place other than the scene of the crime at the time the crime occurred.

duress The use of illegal confinement or threats of harm to coerce someone to do something he or she would not do otherwise.

battered woman syndrome A group of symptoms typically manifested by a woman who has suffered continued physical or mental abuse, usually from a male with whom she lives.

necessity A condition that compels or requires a certain course of action.

mistake of law An erroneous opinion of legal principles applied to a set of facts.

mistake of fact A defense asserting that a criminal defendant acted from an innocent misunderstanding of fact rather than from a criminal purpose.

justifiable use of force The necessary and reasonable use of force by a person in self-defense, defense of another, or defense of property.

deadly force The degree of force that may result in the death of the person against whom the force is applied.

nondeadly force Force that does not result in death.

self-defense The protection of one's person against an attack.

retreat rule The common-law requirement that a person being attacked "retreat to the wall" before using deadly force in self-defense.

objective test for the use of deadly force Under this test, the judge or jury places themselves in the shoes of a hypothetical reasonable and prudent person to determine whether a defendant's use of deadly force was permissible.

subjective standard of reasonableness A test used by courts to determine whether it was appropriate for a defendant to use deadly force in self-defense. Under this approach, the jury is asked to place itself in the shoes of the defendant.

battered child syndrome A group of symptoms typically manifested by a child who has suffered continued physical or mental abuse, often from a parent or person having custody of the child.

reasonable force The maximum degree of force that is necessary to accomplish a lawful purpose.

defense of others The defense asserted by one who claims the right to use reasonable force to prevent the commission of a felony against another person.

defense of habitation The right of a defendant charged with an offense to assert that he or she used reasonable force to protect his or her home or property.

castle doctrine An exception to the retreat rule allowing the use of deadly force by a person who is protecting his or her home and its inhabitants from attack, especially from a trespasser who intends to commit a felony or inflict serious bodily harm.

immunity Exemption from civil suit or prosecution. See also **use immunity** and **transactional immunity**.

use immunity A grant of immunity that forbids prosecutors from using immunized testimony as evidence in criminal prosecutions.

transactional immunity A grant of immunity applying to all offenses that a witness's testimony relates to.

contractual immunity A grant by a prosecutor with approval of a court that makes a witness immune from prosecution in exchange for the witness's testimony.

diplomatic immunity A privilege to be free from arrest and prosecution that is granted under international law to diplomats, their staff, and their household members.

legislative immunity Either of two special immunities given to members of Congress: (1) the exemption from arrest while attending a session of the body to which the member belongs, excluding an arrest for treason, breach of the peace or a felony; or (2) the exemption from arrest or questioning for any speech or debate entered into during a legislative session.

double jeopardy The condition of being tried twice for the same criminal offense.

insufficient evidence Evidence that falls short of establishing what is required by law, usually referring to evidence that does not legally establish an offense or a defense.

weight of the evidence The balance or preponderance of the evidence. Weight of the evidence is to be distinguished from "legal sufficiency of the evidence," which is the concern of an appellate court.

manifest necessity That which is clearly or obviously necessary or essential.

***Blockburger* test** A test applied by courts to determine if the charges against a defendant would constitute a violation of the constitutional prohibition against double jeopardy—that is, being tried twice for the same offense. The *Blockburger* test holds that it is not double jeopardy for a defendant to be tried for two offenses if each offense includes an element that the other offense does not.

same evidence test A test applicable to the Double Jeopardy Clause of the Fifth Amendment. If, to establish an essential element of an offense charged, the government will prove conduct that constitutes an offense for which the defendant has already been prosecuted, a second prosecution is barred.

same elements test Test that bars separate punishment for offenses that have the same elements or for one offense that includes or is included in another offense.

statute of limitations A law proscribing prosecutions for specific crimes after specified periods of time.

tolling Causing to cease. For example, one who conceals himself or herself from the authorities generally causes a tolling of the statutes of limitation on the prosecution of a crime.

entrapment The act of government agents inducing someone to commit a crime that the person would not otherwise be disposed to commit.

subjective test of entrapment Whether the defendant's criminal intent originated in the mind of the police officer or the defendant was predisposed to commit the offense.

objective test of entrapment Under this approach to determining whether police engaged in entrapment, a court inquires whether the police methods were so improper that they were likely to induce or ensnare a reasonable person into committing a crime.

selective prosecution Singling out defendants for prosecution on the basis of race, religion, or other impermissible classifications.

Questions for Thought and Discussion

1. In general, courts permit intoxication evidence only to the extent that it negates the *mens rea* of a specific-intent crime. Should evidence of voluntary intoxication be allowed for both general-intent and specific-intent crimes? Several states have recently enacted statutes making voluntary intoxication inadmissible as a defense to any crime. What position have the courts of your state taken on this issue?
2. What is the test for insanity in your state? Who bears the burden of proof once the defendant introduces some evidence of insanity? Do you think the test in your state adequately protects (a) the public and (b) the defendant's rights?
3. Should the courts recognize battered woman syndrome as a defense to assaultive and homicidal crimes by a woman living with a man who continually batters her? What position does your state take on this issue?
4. Explain the difference between the objective and subjective approaches to the defense of entrapment. Which approach is more just? Why?
5. Should the law require a person to retreat when attacked in his or her own home? Should the law make a distinction between co-occupant? Explain the justification for your view.
6. A few states have recently enacted statutes removing any duty to retreat if a person is attacked in a vehicle or other place where he or she has a right to be. Some allow a person attacked to presume the attacker intends to do bodily harm and allows the vehicle occupant to use any force necessary in defense, with no duty to retreat. Supporters often characterize them as "stand your ground" laws. Some opponents call them "shoot first" laws. Do you think such laws are justifiable?
7. Increasingly, states have enacted "anti-hazing" laws aimed particularly at the initiation procedures of certain fraternal organizations. Most make it a misdemeanor; a few make it a felony where serious injury results from hazing. Should these laws permit defendants accused of hazing to assert the victim's consent as a defense?
8. The Fifth Amendment to the U.S. Constitution requires the court to grant use immunity to a witness who is required to testify over a legitimately invoked right of self-incrimination. In some states, a witness who testifies under a grant of immunity is given transactional immunity, a broader protection than the federal constitution requires. Explain the difference between the two categories of immunity.

9. To what extent, if at all, do you think the courts should interfere with the right of a parent to opt for spiritual, as opposed to medical, healing for a child who suffers from a curable disease?

10. Can one make a credible argument that any one of the nontraditional defenses outlined in the chapter should be accepted as a defense to criminal conduct?

11. The majority of courts hold that ignorance or even a *bona fide* belief that a minor is of legal age does not constitute a defense to prosecution of such strict liability offenses as (a) voluntary sexual relations with a minor and (b) sale of intoxicating liquor to a minor. Do you think a state should adopt a statute that would excuse either or both of such offenses where the defendant made an inquiry as to a person's age and the person appeared to be of legal age?

12. The maxim "ignorance of the law is no excuse" is derived from an age when laws were much simpler than today's sophisticated legal codes. Assume you are working as a staff person for a state legislator who tells you she intends to introduce a bill to "clearly define when a person's 'mistake of the law' should be excused." She asks you to do some research and prepare a memorandum of points that such a bill should include to enable her to discuss her proposal with a legislative committee. What are some of the key points that you would recommend?

Problems for Discussion and Solution

1. Immediately following a catastrophic hurricane, Benjamin Saint entered several local stores that had suffered heavy damage and took food, water, and ice. He called himself a "proud looter" as he handed the items out to stranded persons who had taken refuge at a local school building. If prosecuted for looting, would Saint likely be able to establish the defense of necessity?

2. The state commenced prosecution of the defendant for grand theft within the statutory four-year period of limitations. The jury found the defendant not guilty of grand theft, but guilty of petit theft, a lesser included offense. The one-year statute of limitations for petit theft had run out before the prosecution commenced. Does the defendant have a viable issue to rise on appeal?

3. While taking his nightly walk, Charley Goodneighbor saw Joe Macho commit a battery on Charlene Lovely, a fourteen-year-old girl. Goodneighbor came to Lovely's defense and struck Macho so hard it fractured his skull. The police arrested both Macho and Goodneighbor. Goodneighbor explained to the police that he came to Lovely's aid to prevent her from being injured by Macho. What factors will the prosecutor probably consider in determining whether to file charges against Goodneighbor?

4. Nathan Ninja, who holds a black belt in karate, arrives at his home to find an intruder fleeing from the garage. Ninja pursues the intruder across the front yard and catches him in the street. An exchange of blows renders the intruder unconscious. A medical examination reveals substantial brain damage to the intruder as a result of the blows inflicted by Ninja. In a prosecution for aggravated battery, can Ninja successfully assert as a defense that his use of force was necessary to protect his habitation?

5. Sally Shopper drives a 1995 gray Honda Accord. She parks it in a shopping center lot while she shops. Two hours later, Shopper enters a car parked nearby that is almost identical to hers. As she drives away, the owner spots her and demands that a nearby police officer stop her. Just as the officer approaches her, Shopper realizes that she is in someone else's vehicle. Had she looked at the vehicle more

carefully, she would have observed that it had a license tag from a different state and some unique bumper stickers. On complaint of the owner, the officer arrests Shopper and charges her with theft. What is Shopper likely to assert in her defense?

6. A destitute homeless man steals food from a convenience market. When prosecuted for theft, he pleads the defense of necessity. The prosecutor urges the trial judge to strike the defense on the ground that the defendant could have qualified for assistance from local welfare organizations. Should the defendant be allowed to present his defense to the jury? Do you think he has a credible defense? Why or why not?

7. A defendant was found guilty of having forcible sexual intercourse with a fifteen-year-old female of previous chaste character. He is charged, convicted, and sentenced for violating two statutes: (a) common-law rape involving force and lack of consent and (b) statutory rape involving intercourse with a minor of previous chaste character. On appeal, the defendant contends that his sentence violates the Double Jeopardy Clause of the Fifth Amendment. What arguments will his counsel likely present to the appellate court? What should be the appellate court's decision?

8. The police suspect Mary Jane Hemphill of having sold marijuana at the Sibannac Bar. An undercover agent approaches her and asks her to go out with him. After a movie, the agent says that he would like to buy some marijuana for his close friend. At first, Hemphill makes no response. They make another date, and after a very pleasant evening together, the undercover agent pleads with Hemphill to help him find marijuana for his friend. She agrees, and the next day she delivers a quantity of the contraband to the agent, who gives her $200. As he concludes his purchase, the undercover agent arrests Hemphill and charges her with the sale of contraband. Hemphill's attorney pleads entrapment at her trial. Do you think her defense will be successful? Why or why not?

9. Boris Bottlemore has just finished celebrating his new job promotion by consuming ten double shots of bourbon in a bar near his home. He staggers from the bar to his home, which is one of twenty identical row houses on his block. In his inebriated state, Bottlemore mistakes his neighbor's home for his own. Finding the door unlocked, he enters and promptly raids the refrigerator. He then collapses on a couch in the living room and passes out. The next morning, Patty Purebred is shocked to find a stranger sleeping in her living room and her refrigerator standing open, with food strewn across the kitchen floor. She telephones the police, who arrive and take Bottlemore into custody, charging him with burglary. What defense or defenses are available to Bottlemore? What would you assess his chances before a jury to be?

APPENDIX **A**

Access to the Law through Legal Research

The Nature of Legal Research

Successful legal research requires a systematic method of finding the law applicable to a particular problem or set of facts. Before beginning research, it is helpful, if not essential, for the criminal justice professional or student to have a basic understanding of the law and the legal system.

After assembling the relevant facts and completing a preliminary analysis of the problem, the researcher must find the applicable constitutional and statutory materials and then search for authoritative interpretations of the law. Interpretations are usually found in appellate court decisions construing the particular constitutional provision or statute in analogous situations. These judicial decisions are referred to as cases in point. Legislative and judicial sources of the law are referred to as primary sources because they are authoritative.

A variety of other legal materials, called secondary sources, are available to the researcher. These consist of legal encyclopedias, textbooks by scholars and practitioners, law reviews published by law schools, and journals and periodicals published by various legal organizations. These secondary sources are extremely helpful to the researcher, especially to one unfamiliar with the law in a given area.

Getting Started in Legal Research

Once you become knowledgeable about the sources of the law and the process of its development by courts and you develop the skill of analyzing a problem, you can get started in legal research. Here is a suggestion that can help. If you attend a college at or near a law school, a law librarian might help you in the use of law books or electronic sources. Or you might get assistance from law students, as they usually take a course in legal research in their first year. If you are working from home, do not overlook the fact that in many communities, local governments, courthouses, and bar associations have established law libraries that are usually available to the public; some of these may even offer the free use of legal research databases and other electronic sources.

Legal research has changed rapidly due to the Internet, and more information is becoming available online every day. But before undertaking online research, it is essential that the legal researcher become knowledgeable about the books that are the traditional professional tools for legal research, when those books are the best sources to use, and when to go online instead.

Primary Legal Sources

Federal and state constitutions are often the beginning points in legal research in the criminal justice area because they provide the framework for our government and guarantee certain basic rights to the accused. As explained in this text, the rights of an accused are protected by several provisions of the federal constitution and the Bill of Rights. Most state constitutions afford criminal defendants similar protections. Thus, a person concerned about the legality of an arrest, search, or seizure would examine the relevant federal and state constitutional provisions and then seek to determine how the courts have construed the law in analogous situations.

Federal offenses are defined in statutes enacted by the U.S. Congress, and state offenses are defined in statutes enacted by state legislatures. Federal statutes (in sequence of their adoption) are published annually in the *United States Statutes at Large*. Most states have similar volumes, called session laws, which incorporate the laws enacted during a given session of the legislature. These federal and state laws are initially compiled in sequence of their adoption. Later they are merged into legal codes that systematically arrange the statutes by subject and provide an index. Of far greater assistance to the criminal justice researcher are commercially prepared versions of these codes that classify all federal and state laws of a general and permanent nature by subject and include reference materials and exhaustive indexes. These volumes are kept current by periodic supplements and revised volumes.

The *United States Code Annotated*

One popular compilation of the federal law widely used by lawyers, judges, and criminal justice professionals is the *United States Code Annotated*. The "U.S.C.A.," as it is known, is published by Thomson/West. The U.S.C.A. consists of fifty separate titles that conform to the text of the Official Code of the Laws of the United States. For instance, Title 18 is titled "Crimes and Criminal Procedure" and is of particular interest to the criminal justice researcher. Each section of statutory law in the U.S.C.A. is followed by a series of annotations consisting of court decisions interpreting the particular statute, along with historical notes, cross-references, and other editorial features. The U.S.C.A. also has a General Index, printed annually, that will guide the researcher to a particular title and section number by subject. If the researcher knows only the popular name of a federal statute, the corresponding U.S. Code title and section number can be found in the Popular Name Table. A sample page from the U.S.C.A. is included as Exhibit 1. A sample page from the Popular Name Table is included as Exhibit 2. The U.S.C.A. is kept up to date by the use of "pocket parts," annual updates with the latest laws and amendments, which are slipped into the back pockets of the individual volumes so that the researcher can easily find the latest versions of the laws.

Annotated State Codes

Most states have annotated statutes published by either the state or a private publisher. For example, West's *Annotated California Codes* follows the same general format as the U.S.C.A. A sample page is included as Exhibit 3. Annotated statutes are popular aids to legal research and can save the researcher valuable time in locating cases in point. They are especially effective tools for locating interpretations of criminal statutes.

CHAPTER 87—PRISONS

Sec.
1791.   Traffic in contraband articles.
1792.   Mutiny, riot, dangerous instrumentalities prohibited.

Cross References

Escape and rescue, see section 751 et seq. of this title.

§ 1791.   Traffic in contraband articles

Whoever, contrary to any rule or regulation promulgated by the Attorney General, introduces or attempts to introduce into or upon the grounds of any Federal penal or correctional institution or takes or attempts to take or send therefrom anything whatsoever, shall be imprisoned not more than ten years.

(June 25, 1948, c. 645, 62 Stat. 786.)

Historical and Revision Notes

Reviser's Note. Based on Title 18, U.S.C., 1940 ed., §§ 753j, 908 (May 14, 1930, c. 274, § 11, 46 Stat. 327; May 27, 1930, c. 339, § 8, 46 Stat. 390).

Section consolidates sections 753j and 908 of Title 18, U.S.C., 1940 ed. The section was broadened to include the taking or sending out of contraband from the institution. This was suggested by representatives of the Federal Bureau of Prisons and the Criminal Division of the Department of Justice. In other respects the section was rewritten without change of substance.

The words "narcotic", "drug", "weapon" and "contraband" were omitted, since the insertion of the words "contrary to any rule or regulation promulgated by the attorney general" preserves the intent of the original statutes.

Words "guilty of a felony" were deleted as unnecessary in view of definitive section 1 of this title. (See also reviser's note under section 550 of this title.)

Minor verbal changes also were made.

Cross References

Bureau of Prisons employees, power to arrest without warrant for violations of this section, see section 3050 of this title.

West's Federal Forms

Sentence and fine, see § 7531 et seq.

Code of Federal Regulations

Federal penal and correctional institutions, traffic in contraband articles, see 28 CFR 6.1.

Library References

Prisons ⚮17½.
C.J.S. Prisons § 22.

Notes of Decisions

Aiding and abetting 7	Articles prohibited 3
Admissibility of evidence 13	Assistance of counsel 11

585

EXHIBIT 1 *United States Code Annotated.* Source: Reprinted with permission from 18 U.S.C.A. § 1791. Copyright 1984 by West Publishing Co., 1-800-328-9352.

Crimes and Criminal Procedure—Continued
Oct. 28, 1992, Pub.L. 102–550, Title XIII, Subtitle A, § 1353, Title XV, Subtitle A, §§ 1504(c),
1512(a), (c), 1522(a), 1523(a), 1524, 1525(c)(1), 1526, 1527, 1528, 1530, 1531, 1533, 1534,
1536, Subtitle D, § 1543, Subtitle E, §§ 1552, 1553, 1554, 106 Stat. 3970, 4055, 4057,
4063, 4064, 4065, 4066, 4067, 4069, 4070, 4071 (Title 18, §§ 474, 474A, 504, 981, 982,
984, 986, 1510, 1905, 1956, 1957, 1960, 6001)
Oct. 28, 1992, Pub.L. 102–561, 106 Stat. 4233 (Title 18, § 2319)
Oct. 29, 1992, Pub.L. 102–572, Title I, § 103, Title VII, §§ 701, 703, 106 Stat. 4507, 4514, 4515
(Title 18, §§ 3143, 3154, 3401, 3603)

Criminal Appeals Act
Mar. 2, 1907, ch. 2564, 34 Stat. 1246 (See Title 18, § 3731)

Criminal Code
Mar. 4, 1909, ch. 321, 35 Stat. 1088 (See Title 18, chapters 1–15)
June 25, 1910, ch. 431, § 6, 36 Stat. 857 (See Title 18, §§ 1853, 1856)
Mar. 4, 1921, ch. 172, 41 Stat. 1444 (See Title 18, §§ 831–835)
Mar. 28, 1940, ch. 73, 54 Stat. 80 (See Title 18, § 1382)
Apr. 30, 1940, ch. 164, 54 Stat. 171 (See Title 18, § 1024)
June 6, 1940, ch. 241, 54 Stat. 234 (See Title 18, § 13)
June 11, 1940, ch. 323, 54 Stat. 304 (See Title 18, § 7)
Apr. 1, 1944, ch. 151, 58 Stat. 149 (See Title 18, § 491)
Sept. 27, 1944, ch. 425, 58 Stat. 752 (See Title 18, § 371)
June 8, 1945, ch. 178, 59 Stat. 234 (See Title 18, §§ 371, 1503, 1505)

Criminal Fine Enforcement Act of 1984
Pub.L. 98–596, Oct. 30, 1984, 98 Stat. 3134 (Title 18, §§ 1, 1 note, 3565, 3565 note, 3569, 3579,
3591 to 3599, 3611 note, 3621 to 3624, 3651, 3655, 4209, 4214; Title 18, F.R.Crim.Proc.
Rules 12.2, 12.2 note)

Criminal Fine Improvements Act of 1987
Pub.L. 100–185, Dec. 11, 1987, 101 Stat. 1279 (Title 18, §§ 1 note, 18, 19, 3013, 3559, 3571,
3572, 3573, 3611, 3611 note, 3612, 3663; Title 28, § 604)

Criminal Justice Act Revision of 1984
Pub.L. 98–473, Title II, § 1901, Oct. 12, 1984, 98 Stat. 2185 (Title 18, § 3006A)

Criminal Justice Act Revision of 1986
Pub.L. 99–651, Title I, Nov. 14, 1986, 100 Stat. 3642 (Title 18, § 3006A)

Criminal Justice Act of 1964
Pub. L. 88–455, Aug. 20, 1964, 78 Stat. 552 (Title 18, § 3006A)

Criminal Law and Procedure Technical Amendments Act of 1986
Pub.L. 99–646, Nov. 10, 1986, 100 Stat. 3592 (Title 18, §§ 1 note, 3, 17, 18, 113, 115, 201, 201
note, 203, 203 note, 209, 219, 351, 373, 513, 524, 666, 1028, 1029, 1111, 1153, 1201,
1366, 1512, 1515, 1791, 1791 note, 1793, 1961, 1963, 2031, 2032, 2113, 2232, 2241, 2241
notes, 2242, 2243, 2244, 2245, 2315, 2320, 3050, 3076, 3141, 3142, 3143, 3143 note, 3144,
3146, 3147, 3148, 3150a, 3156, 3156 note, 3185, 3522, 3551 note, 3552, 3552 note, 3553,
3553 notes, 3556, 3561, 3561 note, 3563, 3563 notes, 3579, 3579 notes, 3583, 3583 note,
3603, 3603 note, 3624, 3624 note, 3671, 3671 note, 3672, 3672 note, 3673, 3673 note,
3681, 3682, 3731, 3742, 4044, 4045, 4082, 4203, 4204, 4208, 4209, 4210, 4214, 4217,
5003, 5037, 5037 note; Title 18, F.R.Crim.Proc. Rules 12.2, 29, 29 note, 32, 32 note,
32.1, 32.1 note; Title 21, §§ 802, 812, 845a, 875, 878, 881; Title 28, §§ 546, 992, 993,
994, 1921, 1921 note; Title 42, §§ 257, 300w–3, 300w–4, 9511, 10601, 10603, 10604)
Pub.L. 100–185, § 4(c), Dec. 11, 1987, 101 Stat. 1279 (Title 18, § 18)
Pub.L. 100–690, Title VII, §§ 7012 to 7014, Nov. 18, 1988, 102 Stat. 4395 (Title 18, §§ 18,
1961, 4217)

Criminal Victims Protection Act of 1990
Pub.L. 101–581, Nov. 15, 1990, 104 Stat. 2865 (Title 11, §§ 101 note, 523, 523 note, 1328)
Pub.L. 101–647, Title XXXI, Nov. 29, 1990, 104 Stat. 4916 (Title 11, §§ 101 note, 523, 523
note, 1328)

Critical Agricultural Materials Act
Pub.L. 95–592, Nov. 4, 1978, 92 Stat. 2529 (Title 7, §§ 178, 178a to 178n, 1314f); Pub.L.
98–284, May 16, 1984, 98 Stat. 184 (Title 7, §§ 178, 178 note, 178a to 178i, 178k to
178n)
Pub.L. 99–198, Title XIV, § 1439, Dec. 23, 1985, 99 Stat. 1559 (Title 7, § 178c)
Pub.L. 101–624, Title XVI, § 1601(e), Nov. 28, 1990, 104 Stat. 3704 (Title 7, § 178n)

EXHIBIT 2 Popular Name Table (from U.S.C.A.). Source: Reprinted with permission from
U.S.C.A. Copyright 1992 by West Publishing Co., 1-800-328-9352.

Title 12 SEARCH WARRANTS § 1524

warrant. People v. Golden (1971) 97 Cal.Rptr. 476, 20 C.A.3d 211.

4. Affidavits

"Oral" procedure is permitted only as to affidavit in support of search and warrant itself must be in writing. Bowyer v. Superior Court of Santa Cruz County (1974) 111 Cal.Rptr. 628, 37 C.A.3d 151, rehearing denied 112 Cal.Rptr. 266, 37 C. A.3d 151.

For an affidavit based on informant's hearsay statement to be legally sufficient to support issuance of a search warrant, two requirements must be met: (1) affidavit must allege the informant's statement in language that is factual rather than conclusionary and must establish that informant spoke with personal knowledge of the matters contained in such statement, and (2) the affidavit must contain some underlying factual information from which magistrate issuing the warrant can reasonably conclude that informant was credible or his information reliable. People v. Hamilton (1969) 77 Cal.Rptr. 785, 454 P.2d 681, 71 C.2d 176.

5. Arrest

An arrest without a warrant may not be made on a belief, founded on information received from a third person, that a misdemeanor is being committed. Ware v. Dunn (1947) 183 P.2d 128, 80 C.A.2d 936.

Arrest under warrant issued by justice of peace directed to any sheriff "in the state," where proper sheriff did receive warrant and executed it, and person arrested was not prejudiced, and was not ground for complaint by person arrested, notwithstanding under statutes warrant should have been directed to any sheriff "in the county". Elliott v. Haskins (1937) 67 P.2d 698, 20 C.A.2d 591.

6. Unreasonable searches

Alleged action of city police on specified occasions in blocking off designated portions of city and stopping all persons and automobiles entering or leaving the blocked off area and searching them with-out first obtaining a search warrant and without having probable cause for believing the searched individuals to have violated some law or that automobiles were carrying contraband, would be unconstitutional as being "unreasonable searches and seizures". Wirin v. Horrall (1948) 193 P.2d 470, 85 C.A.2d 497.

7. Admissibility of evidence

Rule excluding in criminal prosecutions evidence obtained through unlawful searches and seizures by police and governmental officers does not apply to evidence obtained by a private person, not employed by nor associated with a governmental unit. People v. Johnson (1957) 315 P.2d 468, 153 C.A.2d 870.

Evidence obtained in violation of constitutional guarantees against unreasonable searches and seizures is inadmissible. People v. Cahan (1955) 282 P.2d 905, 44 C.2d 434, 50 A.L.R.2d 513.

In a prosecution for burglary in the second degree, the fact that articles claimed to have been taken were seized from the person of accused without warrant in violation of Const.Art. 1, § 19 (repealed; see, now, Const.Art. 1, § 13) did not render their introduction in evidence error, although the court overruled the motion of accused to have the articles returned to him. People v. Watson (1922) 206 P. 648, 57 C.A. 85.

8. Federal and state warrants distinguished

Although a California municipal court judge is a "judge of a court of record" and thus authorized to issue federal warrants, the search warrant in question was clearly issued under state, not federal, authority, where it was issued by a California municipal judge on a California form, on the application of a California narcotics agent, and where there was no attempt to comply with the requirements of Fed. Rules of Cr.Proc. rule 41, 18 U.S.C. A. U. S. v. Radlick (C.A.1978) 581 F.2d 225.

§ 1524. Issuance; grounds; special master

(a) A search warrant may be issued upon any of the following grounds:

(1) When the property was stolen or embezzled.

(2) When the property or things were used as the means of committing a felony.

(3) When the property or things are in the possession of any person with the intent to use it as a means of committing a public of-

519

EXHIBIT 3 *West's Annotated California Code.* Source: Reprinted with permission from *West's Annotated California Codes,* Vol. 51A, § 1524. Copyright 1982 by West Publishing Co., 1-800-328-9352.

The National Reporter System

Volumes containing appellate court decisions are referred to as reporters. The National Reporter System, by Thomson/West, includes decisions from the U.S. Supreme Court, the lower federal courts, and the state appellate courts. Reporters are available in bound volumes, on CD-ROM, and online through Westlaw.

Decisions of the U.S. Supreme Court are officially published in the *United States Reports* (abbreviated U.S.). Two private organizations also report these decisions in hardcover volumes. The *Supreme Court Reporter* (abbreviated S.Ct.) is published by Thomson/West, and *Lawyers Edition,* now in its second series (abbreviated L.Ed.2d), is published by West/Lawyers Cooperative. Although the three reporters have somewhat different editorial features, the opinions of the Supreme Court are reproduced identically in all three reporters.

References to judicial decisions found in the reporters are called citations. U.S. Supreme Court decisions are often cited to all three publications—for example, *Miranda v. Arizona,* 384 U.S. 436, 86 S.Ct. 1602, 16 L.Ed.2d 694 (1966). For each of these publications, the citation tells you exactly where the case is published. For example, "384 U.S. 436" means that the *Miranda* case is in volume 384 of the United States Reports on page 436. A sample page from West's *Supreme Court Reporter* is included as Exhibit 4.

Since 1889, the decisions of the U.S. courts of appeals have been published in *West's Federal Reporter,* now in its third series (abbreviated F.3d). Decisions of federal district (trial) courts are published in *West's Federal Supplement,* which is now in its second series (abbreviated F. Supp. 2d). A citation to a case in *Federal Reporter* will read, for example, *Newman v. United States,* 817 F.2d 635 (10th Cir. 1987). This refers to a 1987 case reported in volume 817, page 635 of the *Federal Reporter,* second series, decided by the United States Court of Appeals for the Tenth Circuit. A citation to *United States v. Klopfenstine,* 673 F. Supp. 356 (W.D. Mo. 1987), refers to a 1987 federal district court decision from the western district of Missouri, reported in volume 673, page 356 of the *Federal Supplement.*

Additional federal reporters publish the decisions from other federal courts (for example, bankruptcy and military appeals), but the federal reporters referred to earlier are those most frequently used by criminal justice professionals.

The Regional Reporters

The decisions of the highest state courts (usually but not always called supreme courts) and the decisions of other state appellate courts (usually referred to as intermediate appellate courts) are found in seven regional reporters, West's *California Reporter,* and the *New York Supplement.* Regional reporters, with their abbreviations in parentheses, include decisions from the following states:

- *Atlantic Reporter* (A. and A.2d): Maine, Vermont, New Hampshire, Connecticut, Rhode Island, Pennsylvania, New Jersey, Maryland, Delaware, and the District of Columbia
- *North Eastern Reporter* (N.E. and N.E.2d): Illinois, Indiana, Massachusetts, New York (court of last resort only—other New York appellate courts have their opinions in the New York Supplement), and Ohio
- *North Western Reporter* (N.W. and N.W.2d): North Dakota, South Dakota, Nebraska, Minnesota, Iowa, Michigan, and Wisconsin

384 U.S. 436

Ernesto A. MIRANDA, Petitioner,

v.

STATE OF ARIZONA.

Michael VIGNERA, Petitioner,

v.

STATE OF NEW YORK.

Carl Calvin WESTOVER, Petitioner,

v.

UNITED STATES.

STATE OF CALIFORNIA, Petitioner,

v.

Roy Allen STEWART.

Nos. 759–761, 584.

Argued Feb. 28, March 1 and 2, 1966.

Decided June 13, 1966.

Rehearing Denied No. 584
Oct. 10, 1966.

See 87 S.Ct. 11.

Criminal prosecutions. The Superior Court, Maricopa County, Arizona, rendered judgment, and the Supreme Court of Arizona, 98 Ariz. 18, 401 P.2d 721, affirmed. The Supreme Court, Kings County, New York, rendered judgment, and the Supreme Court, Appellate Division, Second Department, 21 A.D.2d 752, 252 N.Y.S.2d 19, affirmed, as did the Court of Appeals of the State of New York at 15 N.Y.2d 970, 259 N.Y.S.2d 857, 207 N.E.2d 527. The United States District Court for the Northern District of California, Northern Division, rendered judgment, and the United States Court of Appeals for the Ninth Circuit, 342 F.2d 684, affirmed. The Superior Court, Los Angeles County, California, rendered judgment and the Supreme Court of California, 62 Cal.2d 571, 43 Cal. Rptr. 201, 400 P.2d 97, reversed. In the first three cases, defendants obtained certiorari, and the State of California obtained certiorari in the fourth case. The Supreme Court, Mr. Chief Justice Warren, held that statements obtained from defendants during incommunicado interrogation in police-dominated atmosphere, without full warning of constitu-

tional rights, were inadmissible as having been obtained in violation of Fifth Amendment privilege against self-incrimination.

Judgments in first three cases reversed and judgment in fourth case affirmed.

Mr. Justice Harlan, Mr. Justice Stewart, and Mr. Justice White dissented; Mr. Justice Clark dissented in part.

1. Courts ⬥397½

Certiorari was granted in cases involving admissibility of defendants' statements to police to explore some facets of problems of applying privilege against self-incrimination to in-custody interrogation and to give concrete constitutional guidelines for law enforcement agencies and courts to follow.

2. Criminal Law ⬥393(1), 641.1

Constitutional rights to assistance of counsel and protection against self-incrimination were secured for ages to come and designed to approach immortality as nearly as human institutions can approach it. U.S.C.A.Const. Amends. 5, 6.

3. Criminal Law ⬥412.1(4)

Prosecution may not use statements, whether exculpatory or inculpatory, stemming from custodial interrogation of defendant unless it demonstrates use of procedural safeguards effective to secure privilege against self-incrimination. U.S.C.A.Const. Amend. 5.

4. Criminal Law ⬥412.1(4)

"Custodial interrogation", within rule limiting admissibility of statements stemming from such interrogation, means questioning initiated by law enforcement officers after person has been taken into custody or otherwise deprived of his freedom of action in any significant way. U.S.C.A.Const. Amend. 5.

> See publication Words and Phrases for other judicial constructions and definitions.

EXHIBIT 4 *Supreme Court Reporter.* Source: Reprinted with permission from 86 S.Ct. 1602. Copyright 1967 by West Publishing Co., 1-800-328-9352.

- *Pacific Reporter* (P., P.2d and P.3d): Washington, Oregon, California, Montana, Idaho, Nevada, Utah, Arizona, Wyoming, Colorado, New Mexico, Kansas, Oklahoma, Alaska, and Hawaii
- *Southern Reporter* (So., So.2d and So.3d): Florida, Alabama, Mississippi, and Louisiana
- *South Eastern Reporter* (S.E. and S.E.2d): Virginia, West Virginia, North Carolina, South Carolina, and Georgia
- *South Western Reporter* (S.W., S.W.2d and S.W.3d)): Texas, Missouri, Arkansas, Kentucky, and Tennessee

For many states (in addition to New York and California), West publishes separate volumes reporting the decisions as they appear in the regional reporters. *Pennsylvania Reporter* and *Texas Cases* are examples of this.

The following examples of citation forms appear in some of the regional reporters:

- *State v. Hogan,* 480 So.2d 288 (La. 1985). This refers to a 1985 decision of the Louisiana Supreme Court found in volume 480, page 288 of the *Southern Reporter,* second series.
- *State v. Nungesser,* 269 N.W.2d 449 (Iowa 1978). This refers to a 1978 decision of the Iowa Supreme Court found in volume 269, page 449 of the *North Western Reporter,* second series.
- *Henry v. State,* 567 S.W.2d 7 (Tex. Cr. App. 1978). This refers to a 1978 decision of the Texas Court of Criminal Appeals found in volume 567, page 7 of the *South Western Reporter,* second series.

A sample page from *Southern Reporter,* second series, is included as Exhibit 5.

Syllabi, Headnotes, and Key Numbers

The National Reporter System and the regional reporters contain not only the official text of each reported decision but also a brief summary of the decision, called the syllabus, and one or more topically indexed "headnotes." These headnotes briefly describe the principles of law expounded by the court and are indexed by a series of topic "key numbers." West assigns these key numbers to specific points of decisional law. For instance, decisions dealing with first-degree murder are classified under the topic "homicide" and assigned a key number for each particular aspect of that crime. Thus, a homicide case dealing with the intent requirement in first-degree murder may be classified as "Homicide 9—Intent and design to effect death." Using this key number system, a researcher can locate headnotes of various appellate decisions on this aspect of homicide and is, in turn, led to relevant decisional law.

In addition, each of these volumes contains a table of statutes construed in the cases reported in that volume, with reference to the American Bar Association's *Standards for Criminal Justice.*

United States Law Week
United States Law Week, published by the Bureau of National Affairs, Inc., Washington, D.C., presents a weekly survey of American law. *Law Week* includes all the latest decisions from the U.S. Supreme Court as well as significant current decisions from other federal and state courts.

imprisonment. It is indeed unlikely that the enactment of art. 893.1 was designed to punish more severely those who commit negligent homicide than perpetrators of second degree murder, manslaughter, aggravated battery, etc.

In summary, therefore, we find as regards defendant's second assignment of error that the art. 893.1 enhancement is not constitutionally infirm as cruel, unusual and excessive punishment; that the absence of art. 894.1 sentence articulation in this case was harmless, there existing in this record sufficient factors to support this penalty which is well within the statutory range; that the two year penalty imposed in this case under § 14:95.2 is illegal; that art. 893.1 is applicable to all felonies, including those specially enumerated in § 14:95.2 and that therefore the art. 893.1 enhancement in this case is valid.

Decree

Accordingly, defendant's conviction is affirmed; his sentence is reversed and the case remanded for resentencing in accordance with the views expressed herein and according to law.

CONVICTION AFFIRMED; SENTENCE REVERSED; CASE REMANDED.

DIXON, C.J., and DENNIS, J., concur.

WATSON, J., dissents as to requiring notice.

STATE of Louisiana

v.

Patrick HOGAN.

No. 84–K–1847.

Supreme Court of Louisiana.

Dec. 2, 1985.

Defendant was convicted in the First Judicial District Court, Parish of Caddo, Charles R. Lindsay, J., of aggravated battery, and he appealed. The Court of Appeal, 454 So.2d 1235, affirmed, and defendant's petition for writ of review was granted. The Supreme Court, Calogero, J., held that: (1) sentence enhancement by reason of use of a firearm in commission of a felony was not constitutionally infirm as cruel, unusual and excessive; (2) existence of some mitigating factors did not preclude enhancement; (3) imposition of an additional two-year penalty for use of a gun while attempting commission of a specified felony was impermissible when not preceded by an appropriate notice; and (4) enhancement was not invalid, however, since minimum sentence mandated by use of firearm was applicable to all felonies.

Conviction affirmed, sentence reversed, and case remanded.

Dennis, J., concurred.

Watson, J., dissented as to requiring notice.

1. Criminal Law ⟐1206.1(1), 1213.2(1)

General sentencing enhancement statute [LSA-R.S. 14:34, 14:95; LSA-C.Cr.P. art. 893.1] applicable when a firearm is used in commission of a felony, does not impose cruel, unusual, and excessive punishment and is not constitutionally infirm on its face or as applied. U.S.C.A. Const. Amend. 8.

2. Criminal Law ⟐1213.8(7)

Imposition of mandatory minimum sentence under enhancement statute [LSA-R.S. 14:34, 14:95; LSA-C.Cr.P. art. 893.1]

EXHIBIT 5 *Southern Reporter.* Source: Reprinted with permission from 480 So.2d 288. Copyright 1986 by West Publishing Co., 1-800-328-9352.

Criminal Law Reporter

Also published by the Bureau of National Affairs, Inc., the weekly *Criminal Law Reporter* reviews contemporary developments in the criminal law. It is an excellent source of commentaries on current state and federal court decisions in the criminal law area.

The Digests

West also publishes *Decennial Digests*, which topically index all the appellate court decisions from the state and federal courts. Digests are tools that enable the researcher to locate cases in point through topics and key numbers. By finding a particular topic and key number and looking it up in the pertinent digest, the researcher can locate other cases on the narrow point of law covered by that key number. The *Decennial Digests* are kept current by a set called the General Digests so that the researcher can always find the latest cases. The *Eleventh Decennial Digest, Part I*, covers cases from 1996 to 2001.

A series of federal digests contains key number headnotes for decisions of the federal courts. The current series published by West is *Federal Practice Digest 4th*. In addition, separate digests are published for some states as well as for the Atlantic, North Western, Pacific, and South Eastern reporters.

The index at the beginning of each topic identifies the various points of law by numerically arranged key numbers. In addition to the basic topic of criminal law, many topics in the field of criminal law are listed by specific crimes (such as homicide, forgery, and bribery). Procedural topics such as arrest and search and seizure are also included. The digests contain a descriptive word index and a table of cases sorted by name, listing the key numbers corresponding to the decisions. Thus, the researcher can find, by key number, reference topics that relate to the principles set out in the headnotes prepared for each judicial decision. A researcher who locates a topic and key number has access to all reported decisions on this point of law. A sample page from the *Texas Digest*, second series, is reprinted as Exhibit 6.

Shepard's Citations

Shepard's Citations is a series that provides the judicial history of cases by reference to the volume and page number of the cases in the particular reporters. Because the law is constantly changing and new laws and decisions come out all the time, it is essential that a researcher keep up to date and know if there are new cases or what might have happened to a case the researcher has found. By using the symbols explained in this work, the researcher can determine whether a particular decision has been affirmed, followed, distinguished, modified, or reversed by subsequent court decisions. Most attorneys "Shepardize" the cases they cite in their law briefs to support various principles of law. There is a separate set of *Shepard's Citations* for the U.S. Supreme Court reports, for the federal appellate and district courts, for each regional reporter, and for each state that has an official reporter. *Shepard's* can also be found on Lexis.

KeyCite

Another source that is used for updating a case history, and locating cases that refer to it, is KeyCite, available online as part of Westlaw. Like *Shepard's* (both print and computer versions), KeyCite gives the history of a case and subsequent cases that

For references to other topics, see Descriptive-Word Index

was observed in act of smoking a marihuana cigarette, for violation of narcotics laws, was legal. Code Cr.Proc.Tex.1925, arts. 212, 215; 26 U.S.C.A. §§ 2557(b) (1), 2593(a).

Rent v. U. S., 209 F.2d 893.

D.C.Tex. 1975. Arrest and subsequent detention of husband plaintiff by deputies without warrant was not unlawful where husband plaintiff appeared to be intoxicated in public place. 28 U.S.C.A. § 1343; 42 U.S.C.A. §§ 1983, 1985; U.S.C.A.Const. Amend. 4; Vernon's Ann.Tex.C.C.P. art. 14.01.

Lamb v. Cartwright, 393 F.Supp. 1081, affirmed 524 F.2d 238.

D.C.Tex. 1972. The "presence" of the officer, under Texas statute providing that a police officer may arrest an offender without a warrant for any offense committed in his "presence" or within his view, is satisfied if the violation occurs within reach of the officer's senses. Vernon's Ann.Tex.C.C.P. art. 14.01(b).

Taylor v. McDonald, 346 F.Supp. 390.

D.C.Tex. 1967. It is not the case that officer may arrest person committing felony in his presence irrespective of whose privacy officer must violate in order to place commission of felony in his presence.

Gonzales v. Beto, 266 F.Supp. 751, affirmed State of Tex. v. Gonzales, 388 F.2d 145.

Tex.Cr.App. 1981. Observation by police officer of the exchange of money between defendant and another person for tinfoil bindles coupled with officer's knowledge that heroin is normally packaged in tinfoil bindles was sufficient to provide probable cause to believe that an offense had been committed and, thus, defendant's warrantless arrest was valid under statute which allows peace officer to arrest an offender without a warrant "for any offense committed in his presence or within his view." Vernon's Ann.C.C.P. art. 14.01(b).

Boyd v. State, 621 S.W.2d 616.

Tex.Cr.App. 1981. Where defendant was observed in supermarket placing a steak and bottle of bath oil in her purse and observed leaving the store without paying for such items and was apprehended and placed in custody of city police officer who had been summoned by the manager, defendant's arrest was lawful. Vernon's Ann.C.C.P. art. 18.16.

Stewart v. State, 611 S.W.2d 434.

Tex.Cr.App. 1980. Peace officer need not determine whether material in question is in fact obscene in order to make a valid arrest for offense of commercially distributing obscene material; warrantless arrest is proper if there is probable cause to believe the publication commercially distributed in officer's pres-

ence or within his view was obscene. Vernon's Ann.C.C.P. art. 14.01(b); V.T.C.A., Penal Code § 43.21(1).

Carlock v. State, 609 S.W.2d 787.

Tex.Cr.App. 1980. Fact that defendants were in possession of a stolen gun several hours prior to their arrest was not a sufficient basis for the officers' conclusion that defendants were committing an offense within their presence so as to justify a warrantless arrest.

Green v. State, 594 S.W.2d 72.

Tex.Cr.App. 1979. Defendant had no reasonable expectation of privacy while sitting in a restaurant, so that, upon observing drug transaction in plain view from public vantage point outside the restaurant and recognizing it as offense, officers were authorized to make warrantless arrest. Vernon's Ann.C.C.P. art. 14.01.

Hamilton v. State, 590 S.W.2d 503.

Tex.Cr.App. 1979. Where defendants' vehicle was not stopped by any overt action on the part of off-duty police officers, who simply turned around and began to follow defendants' vehicle after spotting it traveling in the opposite direction and noting that defendants appeared to be smoking a marihuana cigarette, where it was only after defendants stopped at a traffic light that one officer was able to approach the vehicle and then noticed the odor of marihuana, and where it was at that point that the officer directed defendants to pull over to the side of the street and get out of their car, the arrest and subsequent search were reasonable under the circumstances. Vernon's Ann.C.C.P. art. 14.01(b).

Isam v. State, 582 S.W.2d 441.

Tex.Cr.App. 1979. Although detective did not view any of the reading matter of the magazine before making warrantless arrest of seller, the magazine's front and back covers, depicting an act of fellatio on a nude male and an act of cunnilingus on a nude female, gave the officer sufficient probable cause to reasonably believe that a violation of the obscenity statute had occurred in his presence and within his view justifying a warrantless arrest. V.T.C.A., Penal Code § 43.21(1); Vernon's Ann.C.C.P. art. 14.01(b).

Price v. State, 579 S.W.2d 492.

Tex.Cr.App. 1979. Though the scope of an investigation cannot exceed the purposes which justify initiating the investigation, if, while questioning a motorist regarding the operation of his vehicle, an officer sees evidence of a criminal violation in open view or in some other manner acquires probable cause with respect to a more serious charge, the officer may arrest for that offense and, incident thereto, conduct an additional search for physical evidence. Vernon's Ann.Civ.St. art.

see Vernon's Annotated Texas Statutes

EXHIBIT 6 *Texas Digest 2d.* Source: Reprinted with permission from West's *Texas Digest 2d,* Vol. 6, Page 155. Copyright 1982 by West Publishing Co., 1-800-328-9352.

have cited it. Among other useful features that KeyCite has is a ranking system for the later cases, which shows which cases have discussed or explained the original one in detail and which give a mere mention of the case. This is of great help to the researcher who might otherwise be faced with a long list of cases to read and no way to differentiate their value.

Secondary Sources

Legal authorities other than constitutions, statutes, ordinances, regulations, and court decisions are called secondary sources, yet they are essential tools in legal research. A basic necessity for any legal researcher's work is a good law dictionary. Several are published, and *Black's Law Dictionary* (9th ed.), published by Thomson/West, is one of the best known. *Black's* is available both in print and computer disk media.

Legal Encyclopedias

Beyond dictionaries, the most common secondary legal authorities are legal encyclopedias. These are arranged alphabetically by subject and are used much like any standard encyclopedia. There are two principal national encyclopedias of the law: *Corpus Juris Secundum* (C.J.S.), published by West, and *American Jurisprudence*, second edition (Am.Jur.2d), published by West /Lawyers Cooperative. A sample page from C.J.S. appears as Exhibit 7. Appellate courts frequently include citations to these encyclopedias, as well as to cases in the reporters, to document the rules and interpretations contained in their opinions. Each of these encyclopedias is an excellent set of reference books; one significant difference is that *Corpus Juris Secundum* cites more court decisions, whereas *American Jurisprudence 2d* limits footnote references to the leading cases pertinent to the principles of law in the text. *Corpus Juris Secundum* includes valuable cross-references to West topic key numbers and other secondary sources, including forms. *American Jurisprudence 2d* includes valuable footnote references to another of the company's publications, *American Law Reports,* now in its fifth series. These volumes (cited as A.L.R.) include annotations to the decisional law on selected topics. For example, a 1987 annotation from A.L.R. entitled "Snowmobile Operation as D.W.I. or D.U.I." appears in 56 A.L.R. 4th 1092. Both *Corpus Juris Secundum* and *American Jurisprudence 2d* are supplemented annually by cumulative pocket parts and are exceptionally well indexed. They serve as an excellent starting point for a researcher because they provide a general overview of topics. A general index for each is published annually, and researchers should use this first to find their specific subjects and section numbers.

For example, a person researching the defenses available to a defendant charged with forgery would find a good discussion of the law in this area in either of these encyclopedias. A citation to the text on defenses to forgery found in *Corpus Juris Secundum* would read as follows: 37 C.J.S. Forgery § 41; in *American Jurisprudence 2d* it would read like this: 36 Am.Jur.2d Forgery § 42. In addition to these major national encyclopedias, some states have encyclopedias for the jurisprudence of their state—for example, *Pennsylvania Law Encyclopedia* and *Texas Jurisprudence.* Like the volumes of *Corpus Juris Secundum* and *American Jurisprudence 2d,* most encyclopedias of state law are annually supplemented with cumulative pocket parts.

religious beliefs.[38] The burden falls on prison officials to prove that the food available to a religious inmate is consistent with his dietary laws and provides adequate nourishment.[39] Thus, a prisoner who strictly adheres to Jewish dietary laws may be entitled to prepare his own meals during the Passover holiday,[40] and Muslim inmates may be entitled to a diet that provides them with adequate nourishment without requiring them to eat pork.[41]

However, where Muslim inmates are able to practice their religion conscientiously and still receive a sufficiently nutritious diet, the prison is not obligated to provide them with a special diet.[42]

Prison authorities are not required to supply a prisoner with a special religious diet where the prisoner's beliefs are not religious in nature.[43]

§ 95. Religious Names

Although under some authorities prisoners lose the right to change their names for religious purposes, other authorities generally preclude a categorical refusal to accord legal recognition to religious names adopted by incarcerated persons.

Library References

Prisons ⬤4(14).

Although it has been held that a common-law name change, even for religious purposes, is among the rights that inmates lose as inconsistent with their status as prisoners,[44] it has also been held that a state's categorical refusal to accord legal recognition to religious names adopted by incarcerated persons is not reasonably and substantially justified by considerations of prison discipline and order.[45]

Thus, the inmates' free exercise of religion may be burdened by prison officials who continue for all purposes to use the names under which the inmates were committed,[46] and it may be unlawful for the state to refuse to deliver mail addressed to the prisoner under his legal religious name.[47]

On the other hand, inmates are not entitled to have prison officials use their new names for all purposes.[48] For example, correctional authorities generally do not have to reorganize institutional records to reflect prisoners' legally adopted religious names.[49]

E. COMMUNICATIONS AND VISITING RIGHTS AND RESTRICTIONS

§ 96. Communications in General

Prison inmates have a right to communicate with people living in free society, but this right is not unfettered and may be limited by prison officials in order to promote legitimate institutional interests.

Library References

Prisons ⬤4(5, 6).

Prison inmates have a constitutional right to communicate with people living in free society.[50] However, this right is not absolute, and is subject

---

38. U.S.—Prushinowski v. Hambrick, D.C.N.C., 570 F.Supp. 863.

39. U.S.—Prushinowski v. Hambrick, D.C.N.C., 570 F.Supp. 863.

40. U.S.—Schlesinger v. Carlson, D.C.Pa., 489 F.Supp. 612.

41. U.S.—Masjid Muhammad-D.C.C. v. Keve, D.C.Del., 479 F.Supp. 1311.

42. U.S.—Masjid Muhammad-D.C.C. v. Keve, D.C.Del., 479 F.Supp. 1311.

43. U.S.—Africa v. Commonwealth of Pennsylvania, C.A.Pa., 662 F.2d 1025, certiorari denied 102 S.Ct. 1756, 456 U.S. 908, 72 L.Ed.2d 165.

44. U.S.—Salahuddin v. Coughlin, D.C.N.Y., 591 F.Supp. 353.

45. U.S.—Barrett v. Commonwealth of Virginia, C.A.Va., 689 F.2d 498.

46. U.S.—Masjid Muhammad-D.C.C. v. Keve, D.C.Del., 479 F.Supp. 1311.

47. U.S.—Barrett v. Commonwealth of Virginia, C.A.Va., 689 F.2d 498.

Masjid Muhammad-D.C.C. v. Keve, D.C.Del., 479 F.Supp. 1311.

48. U.S.—Azeez v. Fairman, D.C.Ill., 604 F.Supp. 357—Masjid Muhammad-D.C.C. v. Keve, D.C.Del., 479 F.Supp. 1311.

49. U.S.—Barrett v. Commonwealth of Virginia, C.A.Va., 689 F.2d 498.

Azeez v. Fairman, D.C.Ill., 604 F.Supp. 357.

Failure to follow statutory mechanism

Inmates' constitutional rights were not violated by failure of prison officials to recognize their use of Muslim names in records of department of correctional services, where inmates had not followed statutory mechanism for name change.

U.S.—Salahuddin v. Coughlin, D.C.N.Y., 591 F.Supp. 353.

50. U.S.—Pell v. Procunier, Cal., 94 S.Ct. 2800, 417 U.S. 817, 41 L.Ed.2d 495.

Inmates of Allegheny County Jail v. Wecht, D.C.Pa., 565 F.Supp. 1278.

Friends and relatives

U.S.—Hutchings v. Corum, D.C.Mo., 501 F.Supp. 1276.

501

EXHIBIT 7 *Corpus Juris Secundum.* Source: Reprinted with permission from *Corpus Juris Secundum*, Vol. 72, Prisons § 96, p. 501. Copyright 1987 by West Publishing Co., 1-800-328-9352.

Textbooks

Textbooks and other treatises on legal subjects often read much like encyclopedias; however, most address specific subjects in greater depth. One of the better-known textbooks is LaFave and Scott, *Criminal Law*, published by Thomson/West.

Law Reviews

Most leading law schools publish law reviews that contain articles, commentaries, and notes by academics, judges, lawyers, and law students who exhaustively research topics. Law review articles can be excellent sources of in-depth analysis and background information on specific legal topics. A citation for a recent law review article in the criminal justice field, "Consequences of Refusing Consent to a Search and Seizure," 75 S. Cal. L. Rev. 901 (2002), refers to a scholarly article published in volume 75 at page 901 of the *Southern California Law Review*.

Professional Publications and Other Useful Secondary Sources

An example of a professional publication is the *Criminal Law Bulletin*, published bimonthly by Warren, Gorham & Lamont of Boston. It contains many valuable articles of contemporary interest. For instance, "Probable Cause and the Fourth Amendment" was published in the September 2003 issue. The American Bar Association and most state bar associations publish numerous professional articles in their journals and reports. Some of these present contemporary views on the administration of justice; often they talk more about how the law is actually applied, not just the theory behind it that law review articles sometimes focus on.

The *Index to Legal Periodicals*, published by H. W. Wilson Company of the Bronx, New York, indexes articles from leading legal publications by subject and author. Another index for legal articles is the *Current Law Index*, published by Gale/Cengage in cooperation with the American Association of Law Libraries. These valuable research tools are found in many law libraries and are kept current by periodic supplements. Many college and law school libraries also have these available online. Periodicals published by law schools, bar associations, and other professional organizations can be valuable both in doing research and in gaining a perspective on many contemporary problems in the criminal justice field. The federal government also publishes numerous studies of value to the criminal justice professional and student.

Words and Phrases, another West publication, consists of numerous volumes alphabetically arranged in dictionary form. Hundreds of thousands of legal terms are defined with citations to appellate court decisions. The volumes are kept current by annual pocket part supplements. A sample page from *Words and Phrases* is reprinted as Exhibit 8 .

Computerized Legal Research

Increasingly, legal research is being done electronically using computerized legal databases such as Westlaw. Westlaw operates from a central computer system at the West headquarters in St. Paul, Minnesota, and has databases for state and federal statutes, appellate decisions, attorney general opinions, and certain legal periodicals.

RESISTANCE

RESISTANCE—Cont'd

Where a contract for the purchase of defendant's stock in plaintiff corporation provided that defendant should not concern himself in the manufacture or sale of resistance or steel armature binding wire, sheet, or strip, such manufactures must be understood as some alloy of copper used in the manufacture of electric apparatus which does not conduct electricity as freely as pure copper, which is the best conductor, and hence is called "resistance, wire, sheet, or strip." Driver-Harris Wire Co. v. Driver, 62 A. 461, 463, 70 N.J.Eq. 34.

Breaking of glass bottles on roadway over which pneumatic-tired trucks, which were loaded with goods being removed from building by United States Marshal under writ of replevin, were required to pass, held criminal contempt of court, since "resistance" as used in contempt statute includes willful purpose and intent to prevent execution of process of court. Russell v. United States, C.C.A.Minn., 86 F.2d 389, 394, 109 A.L.R. 297.

RESIST HORSES, CATTLE AND LIVE STOCK

Under the statute which requires railroad companies to maintain fences sufficient to "resist horses, cattle and live stock," an instruction that a company was required to maintain one sufficient to "turn stock" was not improper; the quoted terms being synonmous. Deal v. St. Louis, I. M. & S. Ry. Co., 129 S.W. 50, 52, 144 Mo.App. 684.

Under Rev.St.1899, § 1105, Mo.St.Ann. § 4761, p. 2144, requiring a railroad company to construct and maintain fences sufficient to prevent stock getting on the track, an instruction in an action under such section for injuries to stock, which defined a lawful fence as one sufficient "to resist horses, cattle, swine, and like stock," was not erroneous for using the phrase "to resist"; such phrase not being as strong as the phrase "to prevent" in the statute. Hax v. Quincy, O. & K. C. R. Co., 100 S.W. 693, 695, 123 Mo.App. 172.

RESISTING AN OFFICER

To constitute the offense of "resisting an officer," under Act March 8, 1831, § 9, it is not necessary that the officer should be assaulted, beaten, or bruised. Woodworth v. State, 26 Ohio St. 196, 200.

RESISTING AN OFFICER—Cont'd

A justice of the peace being a conservator of the peace, under Const. art. 7, § 40, and being, under Crawford & Moses' Dig. § 2906, without authority to make an arrest himself, act of one in resisting an arrest by a justice does not constitute offense of "resisting an officer," in violation of section 2585 et seq. Herdison v. State, 265 S.W. 84, 86, 166 Ark. 33.

"Resist," as used in Code, § 4476, providing for the punishment of any person who shall knowingly and willfully obstruct, resist, or oppose any officer or other person duly authorized in serving or executing any lawful process, imports force. The words "obstruct," "resist," or "oppose" mean the same thing, and the word "oppose" would cover the meaning of the word "resist" or "obstruct." It does not mean to oppose or impede the process with which the officer is armed, or to defeat its execution, but that the officer himself shall be obstructed. Davis v. State, 76 Ga. 721, 722.

RESISTING AN OFFICER IN DISCHARGE OF HIS DUTY

Where police officers investigated defendant's premises to determine whether he was killing sheep or cattle in alleged violation of an ordinance and after failing to discover indications of such killing one of officers informed defendant that he was under arrest and attempted to put upon his hand a wrist chain and defendant resisted such action for three or four minutes and then submitted quietly, defendant's actions did not constitute "resisting an officer in discharge of his duty" since officers had no right to arrest defendant. City of Chicago v. Delich, 1st Dist. No. 20,686, 193 Ill.App. 72.

Where police officers investigated defendant's premises to determine whether he was killing sheep or cattle in alleged violation of an ordinance and after failing to discover indications of such killing one of officers informed defendant that he was under arrest and attempted to put upon his hand a wrist chain and defendant resisted such action for three or four minutes and then submitted quietly, action of wife who took some part in the altercation with the officers did not constitute "resisting an officer in discharge of his duty," since officers had no right to arrest defendant. City of Chicago v. Delich, 1st Dist., No. 20,687, 193 Ill. App. 74.

612

EXHIBIT 8 *Words and Phrases.* Source: Reprinted with permission from *Words and Phrases*, Vol. 37, p. 612. Copyright 1992 by West Publishing Co., 1-800-328-9352.

For example, the law review article referred to earlier, "Consequences of Refusing Consent to a Search and Seizure," 75 S. Cal. L. Rev. 901 (2002), is available on Westlaw in the ScALR database and can be quickly retrieved by typing the citation—75 S. Cal. L. Rev. 901—into the "find this document" box on the welcome page. Subscribers can access Westlaw through the Internet. Westlaw users enter queries into the system to begin research, using connectors recognized by the system. A properly formulated query pinpoints the legal issue to be researched and instructs Westlaw to retrieve all data relevant to the query.

Westlaw also has a searching method that uses natural language, which allows queries to be entered in plain English without special terms or connectors. The statutes, cases, and other research results found on Westlaw can be printed, downloaded, or e-mailed. One of the most useful features of Westlaw is the ability to check the history of cases using KeyCite. When the researcher needs to update a large number of cases, Westlaw can save a tremendous amount of time and substantially reduce the possibility of error.

Lexis/Nexis is an excellent competing system. As with Westlaw, researchers can use Lexis/Nexis to find cases and statutes, search for items either by forming queries or using natural language, and find cases by typing in their citations. Unlike Westlaw, which has KeyCite to check citation history, Lexis/Nexis has an electronic version of *Shepard's* to check cites. It is a bit easier to use and more up-to-date than the printed *Shepard's* volumes.

Legal Research Using the Internet

The phenomenal growth of the Internet makes it impossible to firmly state what legal sources or sites currently are available because new things are being added constantly. The federal and state governments are among those rapidly adding data to the Internet, and for that reason a person looking for government information, or statutes and codes, is likely to find it on the Internet. Among the best ways to search for legal information is to use a comprehensive legal site such as ALSO!—American Law Sources On-line (www.lawsource.com)—which has a detailed listing of law websites for each state and for federal sources. ALSO! provides links to official sites such as those of government agencies, courts, and codes as well as other helpful sites such as state bar associations and legal aid groups. Another major site is Findlaw (www.findlaw.com), which uses categories to neatly divide legal information so that a user can search for the appropriate category and then find the information available on that topic or issue. Among Findlaw's categories are state law (further divided into categories for each individual state) and international law (indeed, the Internet is currently the best source for locating law from other countries). Another excellent source for federal information is Thomas (thomas.loc.gov), the Library of Congress website, which contains pending bills, federal laws, and links to other federal sites.

Findlaw's Supreme Court category offers U.S. Supreme Court opinions dating back to 1893 in a searchable format. In addition, the Legal Information Institute (LII) at Cornell University (www.law.cornell.edu/supct/) offers downloadable Supreme Court opinions. The LII archive now contains all opinions of the Court issued since May 1990 as well as hundreds of the most important historical decisions of the Court. The Supreme Court itself now has its own website, useful for finding information about pending or recently decided cases, at www.supremecourtus.gov.

More and more lower courts, both at the federal and state levels, are putting up their own websites, and often very recently decided cases can be found on them.

ALSO! is a good place to begin in trying to locate these sites, as its listing for each state includes links to courts of that state. (The researcher may notice that many states have websites that cover all of their courts; for example, www.flcourts.org, the Florida courts website, has links to extensive information from all Florida appellate courts and many of the trial-level courts, too.) Findlaw also can help the researcher find the statutes, court decisions, and court rules of most states, almost all of which are now on the Internet. Regular search engines such as Google and Yahoo can be very helpful in locating court sites and other legal information. When using one of these search engines to locate a particular court decision, it is important to be very specific. One might try a docket number or an obscure or unique term that is found in the case.

Although the Internet is convenient and low in cost, there are limitations to consider in doing research there. The Internet is a solid source for finding up-to-date information, such as current state statutes and some recent court decisions; it is also a good source for finding factual material, such as statistics and background information. Because most legal research involves finding more than just the latest cases and laws, however, a researcher will usually need to use other print or computer resources in addition to the Internet. When that is the case, the researcher will need to fall back on traditional methods of research.

How to Research a Specific Point of Law

The following example demonstrates how a legal researcher might employ the research tools discussed earlier to find the law applicable to a given set of facts. Consider this hypothetical scenario:

> Mary Jones, a student at a Florida college, filed a complaint accusing Jay Grabbo of taking her purse while she was walking across campus on the afternoon of November 20, 2008. In her statement to the police, Jones was vague on whether Grabbo had used any force in taking the purse and whether she had offered any resistance. She stated that she had recently purchased the purse for $49 and that it contained $22 in cash plus a few loose coins and personal articles of little value. Further inquiry by the police revealed that Grabbo was unarmed.

A researcher who needs to gain a general background on the offense of robbery and how it differs from theft can profitably consult one of the legal encyclopedias mentioned earlier. Someone with a general knowledge of criminal offenses might still need to review the offense of robbery from the standpoint of state law. If so, *Florida Jurisprudence 2d* or some similar text should be consulted.

Given a general knowledge of the crimes of theft and robbery, a likely starting point would be the state statutes. In this instance, reference could be made to the official Florida Statutes. But from a research standpoint, it might be more productive to locate the statutes proscribing theft and robbery in the index to *West's Florida Statutes Annotated* and review the statutes and pertinent annotations in both the principal volume and the pocket part. The researcher would quickly find the offense of theft defined in section 812.014 and the offense of robbery defined in section 812.13.

Research of the statutory law would disclose that under Florida law, the theft of Jones's purse would be petit theft in the second degree if the total value was less than $100. West's Fla. Stat. Ann. § 812.014. This offense is a misdemeanor for which the maximum penalty is sixty days in jail and a $500 fine. West's Fla. Stat. Ann. § 775.082

and § 775.083. Unarmed robbery, on the other hand, is defined in West's Fla. Stat. Ann. § 812.13(1) as

> the taking of money or other property which may be the subject of larceny from the person or custody of another, with intent to either permanently or temporarily deprive the person or the owner of the money or other property, when in the course of the taking there is the use of force, violence, assault, or putting in fear.

If in the course of committing the robbery the offender carried no firearm, deadly weapon, or other weapon, then the robbery is a felony of the second degree, punishable by fifteen years' imprisonment and a maximum fine of $10,000 as provided in sections 775.082, 775.083, or 775.084 (The latter statute refers to sentences for habitual offenders.) Therefore, it becomes very important to determine whether Grabbo should be charged with petit theft or robbery.

The researcher would then proceed to references noted under the topics of "force" and "resistance" following the text of the robbery statute. The annotated statutes would identify pertinent Florida appellate decisions on these points. For example, the researcher would find a note to *Mims v. State,* 342 So.2d 116 (Fla. App. 1977), indicating that purse snatching is not robbery if no more force is used than is necessary to physically remove the property from a person who does not resist. If the victim does resist and that resistance is overcome by the force of the perpetrator, however, the crime of robbery is complete. Another reference points the researcher to *Goldsmith v. State,* 573 So.2d 445 (Fla. App. 1991), which held that the slight force used in snatching a $10 bill from a person's hand without touching the person was insufficient to constitute robbery and instead constituted petit theft. Additional decisions refer to these and related points of law. For example, *Robinson v. State,* 680 So.2d 481 (Fla. App. 1999), indicates that while a stealthful taking may be petit theft, the force required to take someone's purse can make the offense robbery.

A further check into *West's Florida Statutes Annotated* reveals that the legislature enacted a new statute called "Robbery by Sudden Snatching" effective October 1, 1999. The new statute has been indexed as section 812.131 and provides,

> (1) "Robbery by sudden snatching" means the taking of money or other property from the victim's person, with intent to permanently or temporarily deprive the victim or the owner of the money or other property, when, in the course of the taking, the victim was or became aware of the taking. In order to satisfy this definition, it is not necessary to show that:
>
> > (a) The offender used any amount of force beyond that effort necessary to obtain possession of the money or other property; or
> >
> > (b) There was any resistance offered by the victim to the offender or that there was injury to the victim's person.

The new offense is a third-degree felony, punishable by a maximum of five years' imprisonment and a fine of $5,000. West's Fla. Stat. Ann. § 775.082 and § 775.083.

Annotations to Fla. Stat. § 775.082 reveal that in *Brown v. State,* 848 So.2d 361 (Fla. App. 2003), the court reversed a defendant's conviction for robbery by sudden snatching where the victim herself was unaware of the snatching of her purse at the time that her purse was taken. The court noted that the offense requires that property be taken from the victim's actual, physical possession and that because the evidence at the defendant's trial revealed that the victim was unaware of the snatching until after it had been accomplished, the defendant should be acquitted of the charge of robbery by sudden snatching.

In *Walker v. State*, 933 So.2d 1236 (Fla. App. 2006), the appellate court agreed with *Brown v. State* and reversed a defendant's conviction because the State failed to prove beyond a reasonable doubt that the victim knew that her property was being taken during the course of the taking. Finally, on April 18, 2008, in *Walls v. State*, 977 So.2d 802 (Fla. App. 2008) the court of appeals found that because the state presented no testimony or other evidence indicating that the defendant took the purse by snatching it from the victim's person, the court reduced the defendant's conviction to petit theft.

After locating these and other pertinent references, the researcher should go to the *Southern Reporter 2d* and *3d* read the located cases. After concluding the search, the researcher should "Shepardize" or "KeyCite" the decisions to determine whether they have been subsequently commented on, distinguished, or even reversed.

In view of the newer statute and the recent appellate court interpretation, before arriving at a conclusion, the researcher will likely need additional information from the victim as to her awareness of Grabbo's taking her purse and what, if any, force was involved. If the research is undertaken for the prosecutor or the police, they can determine whether any further factual investigation is necessary. They can then decide the charge to place against Grabbo and the proof required to sustain that charge. On the other hand, if the research is undertaken for a defense attorney, once charges are placed against the accused the defense attorney can obtain more precise information from the victim's testimony through discovery procedures. That, along with the results of the legal research, would assist counsel in advising Grabbo, assuming he is charged with a crime, on how to plead and what defenses may be available.

The steps outlined here are basic and are designed to illustrate rudimentary principles of gaining access to the criminal law on a particular subject. As previously indicated, another method might involve using digests with the key number system of research. Moreover, there will often be issues of interest still undecided by courts in a particular state. If so, then research into the statutes and court decisions of other states may be undertaken. The methodology and level of research pursued will often depend on the researcher's objective, knowledge of the subject, and experience in conducting legal research.

Conclusion

Understanding how to gain access to the primary and secondary sources of the criminal law is tremendously important. The ability to assemble relevant facts, analyze a problem, and conduct a systematic search for applicable authoritative statements of constitutional, statutory, and decisional law is a skill to be acquired by both the criminal justice student and the working professional. Professionally trained lawyers, who must make the critical judgments concerning the prosecution and defense of criminal actions, increasingly assign basic legal research to paralegal and criminal justice staff personnel. The ability to access the law through traditional as well as computerized methods will assist the student and professional in becoming better acquainted with the dynamics of the criminal law. Moreover, the honing of such skill will enhance a person's ability to carry out specific research assignments and to support his or her recommendations with relevant legal authorities.

The Constitution of the United States of America

We the People of the United States, in Order to form a more perfect Union, establish Justice, insure domestic Tranquility, provide for the common defence, promote the general Welfare, and secure the Blessings of Liberty to ourselves and our Posterity, do ordain and establish this Constitution for the United States of America.

Article I

Section 1. All legislative Powers herein granted shall be vested in a Congress of the United States, which shall consist of a Senate and House of Representatives.

Section 2. (1) The House of Representatives shall be composed of Members chosen every second Year by the People of the several States, and the Electors in each State shall have the Qualifications requisite for Electors of the most numerous Branch of the State Legislature.

(2) No Person shall be a Representative who shall not have attained to the age of twenty-five Years, and been seven Years a Citizen of the United States, and who shall not, when elected, be an Inhabitant of that State in which he shall be chosen.

(3) Representatives and direct Taxes shall be apportioned among the several States which may be included within this Union, according to their respective Numbers, which shall be determined by adding to the whole Number of free Persons, including those bound to Service for a Term of Years, and excluding Indians not taxed, three fifths of all other Persons. The actual Enumeration shall be made within three Years after the first Meeting of the Congress of the United States, and within every subsequent Term of ten Years, in such Manner as they shall by Law direct. The Number of Representatives shall not exceed one for every thirty Thousand, but each State shall have at Least one Representative; and until such enumeration shall be made, the State of New Hampshire shall be entitled to chuse three, Massachusetts eight, Rhode Island and Providence Plantations one, Connecticut five, New York six, New Jersey four, Pennsylvania eight, Delaware one, Maryland six, Virginia ten, North Carolina five, South Carolina five, and Georgia three.

(4) When vacancies happen in the Representation from any State, the Executive Authority thereof shall issue Writs of Election to fill such Vacancies.

(5) The House of Representatives shall chuse their Speaker and other Officers; and shall have the sole Power of Impeachment.

Section 3. (1) The Senate of the United States shall be composed of two Senators from each State, chosen by the Legislature thereof, for six Years; and each Senator shall have one Vote.

(2) Immediately after they shall be assembled in Consequence of the first Election, they shall be divided as equally as may be into three Classes. The Seats of the Senators of the first Class shall be vacated at the Expiration of the second Year, of the second Class at the Expiration of the fourth Year, and of the third Class at the Expiration of the sixth Year, so that one third may be chosen every second Year; and if Vacancies happen by Resignation, or otherwise, during the Recess of the Legislature of any State, the Executive thereof may make temporary Appointments until the next Meeting of the Legislature, which shall then fill such Vacancies.

(3) No Person shall be a Senator who shall not have attained, to the Age of thirty Years, and been nine Years a Citizen of the United States, and who shall not, when elected, be an Inhabitant of that State for which he shall be chosen.

(4) The Vice President of the United States shall be President of the Senate, but shall have no Vote, unless they be equally divided.

(5) The Senate shall chuse their other Officers, and also a President pro tempore, in the Absence of the Vice President, or when he shall exercise the Office of the President of the United States.

(6) The Senate shall have the sole Power to try all Impeachments. When sitting for that Purpose, they shall be on Oath or Affirmation. When the President of the United States is tried, the Chief Justice shall preside: And no Person shall be convicted without the Concurrence of two thirds of the Members present.

(7) Judgment in Cases of Impeachment shall not extend further than to removal from Office, and disqualification to hold and enjoy any Office of honor, Trust or Profit under the United States: but the Party convicted shall nevertheless be liable and subject to Indictment, Trial, Judgment and Punishment, according to Law.

Section 4. (1) The Times, Places and Manner of holding Elections for Senators and Representatives, shall be prescribed in each State by the Legislature thereof; but the Congress may at any time by Law make or alter such Regulations, except as to the Places of chusing Senators.

(2) The Congress shall assemble at least once in every Year, and such Meeting shall be on the first Monday in December, unless they shall by Law appoint a different Day.

Section 5. (1) Each House shall be the Judge of the Elections, Returns and Qualifications of its own Members, and a Majority of each shall constitute a Quorum to do Business; but a smaller Number may adjourn from day to day, and may be authorized to compel the Attendance of absent Members, in such Manner, and under such Penalties as each House may provide.

(2) Each House may determine the Rules of its Proceedings, punish its Members for disorderly Behaviour, and, with the Concurrence of two thirds, expel a Member.

(3) Each House shall keep a Journal of its Proceedings, and from time to time publish the same, excepting such Parts as may in their Judgment require Secrecy; and the Yeas and Nays of the Members of either House on any question shall, at the Desire of one fifth of those Present, be entered on the Journal.

(4) Neither House, during the Session of Congress, shall, without the Consent of the other, adjourn for more than three days, nor to any other Place than that in which the two Houses shall be sitting.

Section 6. (1) The Senators and Representatives shall receive a Compensation for their Services, to be ascertained by Law, and paid out of the Treasury of the United States. They shall in all Cases, except Treason, Felony and Breach of the Peace, be privileged from Arrest during their Attendance at the Session of their respective Houses, and in going to and returning from the same; and for any Speech or Debate in either House, they shall not be questioned in any other Place.

(2) No Senator or Representative shall, during the Time for which he was elected, be appointed to any civil Office under the Authority of the United States, which shall have been created, or the Emoluments whereof shall have been increased during such time; and no Person holding any Office under the United States, shall be a Member of either House during his Continuance in Office.

Section 7. (1) All Bills for raising Revenue shall originate in the House of Representatives; but the Senate may propose or concur with Amendments as on other Bills.

(2) Every Bill which shall have passed the House of Representatives and the Senate, shall, before it become a Law, be presented to the President of the United States; If he approve he shall sign it, but if not he shall return it, with his Objections to that House in which it shall have originated, who shall enter the Objections at large on their Journal, and proceed to reconsider it. If after such Reconsideration two thirds of that House shall agree to pass the Bill, it shall be sent, together with the Objections, to the other House, by which it shall likewise be reconsidered, and if approved by two thirds of that House, it shall become a Law. But in all such Cases the Votes of both Houses shall be determined by Yeas and Nays, and the Names of the Persons voting for and against the Bill shall be entered on the Journal of each House respectively. If any Bill shall not be returned by the President within ten Days (Sunday excepted) after it shall have been presented to him, the Same shall be a Law, in like Manner as if he had signed it, unless the Congress by their Adjournment prevent its Return, in which Case it shall not be a Law.

(3) Every Order, Resolution, or Vote to which the Concurrence of the Senate and House of Representatives may be necessary (except on a question of Adjournment) shall be presented to the President of the United States; and before the Same shall take Effect, shall be approved by him, or being disapproved by him, shall be re-passed by two thirds of the Senate and House of Representatives, according to the Rules and Limitations prescribed in the Case of a Bill.

Section 8. (1) The Congress shall have Power To lay and collect Taxes, Duties, Imposts and Excises, to pay the Debts and provide for the common Defence and general Welfare of the United States; but all Duties, Imposts and Excises shall be uniform throughout the United States;

(2) To borrow Money on the credit of the United States;

(3) To regulate Commerce with foreign Nations, and among the several States, and with the Indian Tribes;

(4) To establish an uniform Rule of Naturalization, and uniform Laws on the subject of Bankruptcies throughout the United States;

(5) To coin Money, regulate the Value thereof, and of foreign Coin, and to fix the Standard of Weights and Measures;

(6) To provide for the Punishment of counterfeiting the Securities and current Coin of the United States;

(7) To establish Post Offices and post Roads;

(8) To promote the Progress of Science and useful Arts, by securing for limited Times to Authors and Inventors the exclusive Right to their respective Writings and Discoveries;

(9) To constitute Tribunals inferior to the supreme Court;

(10) To define and punish Piracies and Felonies committed on the high Seas, and Offenses against the Law of Nations;

(11) To declare War, grant Letters of Marque and Reprisal, and make Rules concerning Captures on Land and Water;

(12) To raise and support Armies, but no Appropriation of Money to that Use shall be for a longer Term than two Years;

(13) To provide and maintain a Navy;

(14) To make Rules for the Government and Regulation of the land and naval Forces;

(15) To provide for calling forth the Militia to execute the Laws of the Union, suppress Insurrections and repel Invasions;

(16) To provide for organizing, arming, and disciplining, the Militia, and for governing such Part of them as may be employed in the Service of the United States, reserving to the States respectively, the Appointment of the Officers, and the Authority of training the Militia according to the discipline prescribed by Congress;

(17) To exercise exclusive Legislation in all Cases whatsoever, over such District (not exceeding ten Miles square) as may, by Cession of particular States, and the Acceptance of Congress, become the Seat of the Government of the United States, and to exercise like Authority over all Places purchased by the Consent of the Legislature of the State in which the Same shall be, for the Erection of Forts, Magazines, Arsenals, dock-Yards, and other needful Buildings;—And

(18) To make all Laws which shall be necessary and proper for carrying into Execution the foregoing Powers, and all other Powers vested by this Constitution in the Government of the United States, or in any Department or Officer thereof.

Section 9. (1) The Migration or Importation of such Persons as any of the States now existing shall think proper to admit, shall not be prohibited by the Congress prior to the Year one thousand eight hundred and eight, but a Tax or Duty may be imposed on such Importation, not exceeding ten dollars for each Person.

(2) The Privilege of the Writ of Habeas Corpus shall not be suspended unless when in Cases of Rebellion or Invasion the public Safety may require it.

(3) No Bill of Attainder or expost facto Law shall be passed.

(4) No Capitation, or other direct, Tax shall be laid, unless in Proportion to the Census or Enumeration herein before directed to be taken.

(5) No Tax or Duty shall be laid on Articles exported from any State.

(6) No Preference shall be given by any Regulation of Commerce or Revenue to the Ports of one State over those of another; nor shall Vessels bound to, or from, one State, be obliged to enter, clear or pay Duties in another.

(7) No Money shall be drawn from the Treasury, but in Consequence of Appropriations made by Law; and a regular Statement and Account of the Receipts and Expenditures of all public Money shall be published from time to time.

(8) No Title of Nobility shall be granted by the United States: And no Person holding any Office of Profit or Trust under them, shall, without the Consent of the Congress, accept of any present, Emolument, Office, or Title, of any kind whatever, from any King, Prince or foreign State.

Section 10. (1) No State shall enter into any Treaty, Alliance, or Confederation; grant Letters of Marque and Reprisal; coin Money; emit Bills of Credit; make any Thing but gold and silver Coin a Tender in Payment of Debts; pass any Bill of Attainder, expost facto Law, or Law impairing the Obligation of Contracts, or grant any Title of Nobility.

(2) No State shall, without the Consent of Congress, lay any Imposts or Duties on Imports or Exports, except what may be absolutely necessary for executing its inspection Laws: and the net Produce of all Duties and Imposts, laid by any State on Imports or Exports, shall be for the Use of the Treasury of the United States; and all such Laws shall be subject to the Revision and Control of the Congress.

(3) No State shall, without the Consent of Congress, lay any Duty of Tonnage, keep Troops, or Ships of War in time of Peace, enter into any Agreement or Compact with another State, or with a foreign Power, or engage in War, unless actually invaded, or in such imminent Danger as will not admit of Delay.

Article II

Section 1. (1) The executive Power shall be vested in a President of the United States of America. He shall hold his Office during the Term of four Years, and, together with the Vice President, chosen for the same Term, be elected, as follows:

(2) Each State shall appoint, in such Manner as the Legislature thereof may direct, a Number of Electors, equal to the whole Number of Senators and Representatives to which the State may be entitled in the Congress: but no Senator or Representative, or Person holding an Office of Trust or Profit under the United States, shall be appointed an Elector.

The Electors shall meet in their respective States, and vote by Ballot for two Persons, of whom one at least shall not be an Inhabitant of the same State with themselves. And they shall make a List of all the Persons voted for, and of the Number of Votes for each; which List they shall sign and certify, and transmit sealed to the Seat of the Government of the United States, directed to the President of the Senate. The President of the Senate shall, in the presence of the Senate and House of Representatives, open all the Certificates, and the Votes shall then be counted. The Person having the greatest Number of Votes shall be the President, if such Number be a Majority of the whole Number of Electors appointed; and if there be more than one who have such Majority, and have an equal Number of Votes, then the House of Representatives shall immediately chuse by Ballot one of them for President; and if no Person have a Majority, then from the five highest on the List the said House shall in like Manner chuse the President. But in chusing the President, the Votes shall be taken by States, the Representation from each State having one Vote; a quorum for this Purpose shall consist of a Member or Members from two thirds of the States, and a Majority of all the States shall be necessary to a Choice. In every Case, after the Choice of the President, the Person having the greatest Number of Votes of the Electors shall be the Vice President. But if there should remain two or more who have equal Votes, the Senate shall chuse from them by Ballot the Vice President.

(3) The Congress may determine the Time of chusing the Electors, and the Day on which they shall give their Votes; which Day shall be the same throughout the United States.

(4) No Person except a natural born Citizen, or a Citizen of the United States, at the time of the Adoption of this Constitution, shall be eligible to the Office of President; neither shall any Person be eligible to that Office who shall not have attained to the Age of thirty five Years, and been fourteen Years a Resident within the United States.

(5) In Case of the Removal of the President from Office, or of his Death, Resignation, or Inability to discharge the Powers and Duties of the said Office, the Same shall devolve on the Vice President, and the Congress may by Law provide for the Case of Removal, Death, Resignation or Inability, both of the President and Vice President, declaring what Officer shall then act as President, and such Officer shall act accordingly, until the Disability be removed, or a President shall be elected.

(6) The President shall, at stated Times, receive for his Services, a Compensation, which shall neither be increased nor diminished during the Period for which he shall have been elected, and he shall not receive within that Period any other Emolument from the United States, or any of them.

(7) Before he enter on the Execution of his Office, he shall take the following Oath or Affirmation:—"I do solemnly swear (or affirm) that I will faithfully execute the Office of President of the United States, and will to the best of my Ability, preserve, protect and defend the Constitution of the United States."

Section 2. (1) The President shall be Commander in Chief of the Army and Navy of the United States, and of the Militia of the several States, when called into the actual Service of the United States; he may require the Opinion, in writing, of the principal Officer in each of the executive Departments, upon any Subject relating to the Duties of their respective Offices, and he shall have Power to grant Reprieves and Pardons for Offenses against the United States, except in Cases of Impeachment.

(2) He shall have Power, by and with the Advice and Consent of the Senate, to make Treaties, provided two thirds of the Senators present concur; and he shall nominate, and by and with the Advice and Consent of the Senate, shall appoint Ambassadors, other public Ministers and Consuls, Judges of the supreme Court, and all other Officers of the United States, whose Appointments are not herein otherwise provided for, and which shall be established by Law: but the Congress may by Law vest the Appointment of such inferior Officers, as they think proper, in the President alone, in the Courts of Law, or in the Heads of Departments.

(3) The President shall have Power to fill up all Vacancies that may happen during the Recess of the Senate, by granting Commissions which shall expire at the End of their next Session.

Section 3. He shall from time to time give to the Congress Information of the State of the Union, and recommend to their Consideration such Measures as he shall judge necessary and expedient; he may, on extraordinary Occasions, convene both Houses, or either of them, and in Case of Disagreement between them, with Respect to the Time of Adjournment, he may adjourn them to such Time as he shall think proper; he shall receive Ambassadors and other public Ministers; he shall take Care that the Laws be faithfully executed, and shall Commission all the Officers of the United States.

Section 4. The President, Vice President and all Civil Officers of the United States, shall be removed from Office on Impeachment for, and Conviction of, Treason, Bribery, or other high Crimes and Misdemeanors.

Article III

Section 1. The judicial Power of the United States, shall be vested in one supreme Court, and in such inferior Courts as the Congress may from time to time ordain and establish. The Judges, both of the supreme and inferior Courts, shall hold their Offices during good Behaviour, and shall, at stated Times, receive for their Services, a Compensation, which shall not be diminished during their Continuance in Office.

Section 2. (1) The judicial Power shall extend to all Cases, in Law and Equity, arising under this Constitution, the Laws of the United States, and Treaties made, or which shall be made, under their Authority;—to all Cases affecting Ambassadors, other public Ministers and Consuls;—to all Cases of admiralty and maritime Jurisdiction;—to Controversies to which the United States shall be a party;—to Controversies between two or more States;—between a State and Citizens of another State;—between Citizens of different States;—between Citizens of the same State claiming Lands under Grants of different States, and between a State, or the Citizens thereof, and foreign States, Citizens or Subjects.

(2) In all Cases affecting Ambassadors, other public Ministers and Consuls, and those in which a State shall be Party, the supreme Court shall have original Jurisdiction. In all the other Cases before mentioned, the supreme Court shall have appellate

Jurisdiction, both as to Law and Fact, with such Exceptions, and under such Regulations as the Congress shall make.

(3) The Trial of all Crimes, except in Cases of Impeachment, shall be by Jury; and such Trial shall be held in the State where the said Crimes shall have been committed; but when not committed within any State, the Trial shall be at such Place or Places as the Congress may by Law have directed.

Section 3. (1) Treason against the United States, shall consist only in levying War against them, or in adhering to their Enemies, giving them Aid and Comfort. No Person shall be convicted of Treason unless on the Testimony of two Witnesses to the same overt Act, or on Confession in open Court.

(2) The Congress shall have Power to declare the Punishment of Treason, but no Attainder of Treason shall work Corruption of Blood, or Forfeiture except during the Life of the Person attainted.

Article IV

Section 1. Full Faith and Credit shall be given in each State to the public Acts, Records, and judicial Proceedings of every other State. And the Congress may by general Laws prescribe the Manner in which such Acts, Records and Proceedings shall be proved, and the Effect thereof.

Section 2. (1) The Citizens of each State shall be entitled to all privileges and Immunities of Citizens in the several States.

(2) A Person charged in any State with Treason, Felony, or other Crime, who shall flee from Justice, and be found in another State, shall on Demand of the executive Authority of the State from which he fled, be delivered up, to be removed to the State having Jurisdiction of the Crime.

(3) No Person held to Service of Labour in one State, under the Laws thereof, escaping into another, shall, in Consequence of any Law or Regulation therein, be discharged from such Service or Labour, but shall be delivered up on Claim of the Party to whom such Service or Labour may be due.

Section 3. (1) New States may be admitted by the Congress into this Union; but no new State shall be formed or erected within the Jurisdiction of any other State; nor any State be formed by the Junction of two or more States, or Parts of States, without the Consent of the Legislatures of the States concerned as well as of the Congress.

(2) The Congress shall have power to dispose of and make all needful Rules and Regulations respecting the Territory or other Property belonging to the United States; and nothing in this Constitution shall be so construed as to Prejudice any Claims of the United States, or of any particular State.

Section 4. The United States shall guarantee to every State in this Union a Republican Form of Government, and shall protect each of them against Invasion; and on Application of the Legislature, or of the Executive (when the Legislature cannot be convened) against domestic Violence.

Article V

The Congress, whenever two thirds of both Houses shall deem it necessary, shall propose Amendments to this Constitution, or, on the Application of the Legislatures of two thirds of the several States, shall call a Convention for proposing Amendments, which, in either Case, shall be valid to all Intents and Purposes, as Part of this Constitution, when ratified by the Legislatures of three fourths of the several States, or by Conventions in three fourths thereof, as the one or the other Mode of Ratification may be proposed by the Congress; Provided that no Amendment which may be made prior to the Year One thousand eight hundred and eight shall in any Manner affect the first and fourth Clauses in the Ninth Section of the first Article; and that no State, without its Consent, shall be deprived of its equal Suffrage in the Senate.

Article VI

(1) All Debts contracted and Engagements entered into, before the Adoption of this Constitution, shall be as valid against the United States under this Constitution, as under the Confederation.

(2) This Constitution, and the Laws of the United States which shall be made in Pursuance thereof; and all Treaties made, or which shall be made, under the Authority of the United States, shall be the supreme Law of the Land; and the Judges in every State shall be bound thereby, any Thing in the Constitution or Laws of any State to the Contrary notwithstanding.

(3) The Senators and Representatives before mentioned, and the Members of the several State Legislatures, and all executive and judicial Officers, both of the United States and of the several States, shall be bound by Oath or Affirmation, to support this Constitution; but no religious Test shall ever be required as a Qualification to any Office or public Trust under the United States.

Article VII

The Ratification of the Conventions of nine States, shall be sufficient for the Establishment of this Constitution between the States so ratifying the Same.

Articles in Addition to, and Amendment of, the Constitution of the United States of America, Proposed by Congress, and Ratified by the Several States, Pursuant to the Fifth Article of the Original Constitution

Amendment I (1791)

Congress shall make no law respecting an establishment of religion, or prohibiting the free exercise thereof; or abridging the freedom of speech, or of the press; or the right of the people peaceably to assemble, and to petition the Government for a redress of grievances.

Amendment II (1791)

A well regulated Militia, being necessary to the security of a free state, the right of the people to keep and bear Arms, shall not be infringed.

Amendment III (1791)

No Soldier shall, in time of peace be quartered in any house, without the consent of the Owner, nor in time of war, but in a manner to be prescribed by law.

Amendment IV (1791)

The right of the people to be secure in their persons, houses, papers, and effects, against unreasonable searches and seizures, shall not be violated, and no Warrants shall issue, but upon probable cause, supported by Oath or affirmation, and particularly describing the place to be searched, and the persons or things to be seized.

Amendment V (1791)

No person shall be held to answer for a capital, or otherwise infamous crime, unless on a presentment or indictment of a Grand Jury, except in cases arising in the land or naval forces, or in the Militia, when in actual service in time of War or public danger; nor shall any person be subject for the same offence to be twice put in jeopardy of life or limb; nor shall be compelled in any criminal case to be a witness against himself, nor be deprived of life, liberty, or property, without due process of law; nor shall private property be taken for public use, without just compensation.

Amendment VI (1791)

In all criminal prosecutions, the accused shall enjoy the right to a speedy and public trial, by an impartial jury of the State and district wherein the crime shall have been committed, which district shall have been previously ascertained by law, and to be informed of the nature and cause of the accusation; to be confronted with the witnesses against him; to have compulsory process for obtaining witnesses in his favor, and to have the Assistance of Counsel for his defence.

Amendment VII (1791)

In Suits at common law, where the value in controversy shall exceed twenty dollars, the right of trial by jury shall be preserved, and no fact tried by a jury, shall be otherwise re-examined in any Court of the United States, than according to the rules of the common law.

Amendment VIII (1791)

Excessive bail shall not be required, nor excessive fines imposed, nor cruel and unusual punishments inflicted.

Amendment IX (1791)

The enumeration in the Constitution, of certain rights, shall not be construed to deny or disparage others retained by the people.

Amendment X (1791)

The powers not delegated to the United States by the Constitution, nor prohibited by it to the States, are reserved to the States respectively, or to the people.

Amendment XI (1798)

The Judicial power of the United States shall not be construed to extend to any suit in law or equity, commenced or prosecuted against one of the United States by Citizens of another State, or by Citizens or Subjects of any Foreign State.

Amendment XII (1804)

The Electors shall meet in their respective states and vote by ballot for President and Vice-President, one of whom, at least, shall not be an inhabitant of the same state with themselves; they shall name in their ballots the person voted for as President, and in distinct ballots the person voted for as Vice-President, and they shall make distinct lists of all persons voted for as President, and of all persons voted for as Vice-President, and of the number of votes for each, which lists they shall sign and certify, and transmit sealed to the seat of the government of the United States, directed to the President of the Senate;—The President of the Senate shall, in the presence of the Senate and House of Representatives, open all the certificates and the votes shall then be counted;—The person having the greatest number of votes for President, shall be the President, if such number be a majority of the whole number of Electors appointed; and if no person have such majority, then from the persons having the highest numbers not exceeding three on the list of those voted for as President, the House of Representatives shall choose immediately, by ballot, the President. But in choosing the President, the votes shall be taken by states, the representation from each state having one vote; a quorum for this purpose shall consist of a member or members from two-thirds of the states, and a majority of all the states shall be necessary to a choice. And if the House of Representatives shall not choose a President whenever the right of choice shall devolve upon them, before the fourth day of March next following, then the Vice-President shall act as President, as in the case of the death or other constitutional disability of the President—The person having the greatest number of votes as Vice-President, shall be the Vice-President, if such number be a majority of the whole number of Electors appointed, and if no person have a majority, then from the two highest numbers on the list, the Senate shall choose the Vice-President; A quorum for the purpose shall consist of two-thirds of the whole number of Senators, and a majority of the whole number shall be necessary to a choice. But no person constitutionally ineligible to the office of President shall be eligible to that of Vice-President of the United States.

Amendment XIII (1865)

Section 1. Neither slavery nor involuntary servitude, except as a punishment for crime whereof the party shall have been duly convicted, shall exist within the United States, or any place subject to their jurisdiction.
Section 2. Congress shall have power to enforce this article by appropriate legislation.

Amendment XIV (1868)

Section 1. All persons born or naturalized in the United States and subject to the jurisdiction thereof, are citizens of the United States and of the State wherein they reside. No State shall make or enforce any law which shall abridge the privileges or immunities of citizens of the United States; nor shall any State deprive any person of life, liberty, or property, without due process of law; nor deny to any person within its jurisdiction the equal protection of the laws.

Section 2. Representatives shall be apportioned among the several States according to their respective numbers, counting the whole number of persons in each State, excluding Indians not taxed. But when the right to vote at any election for the choice of electors for President and Vice-President of the United States, Representatives in Congress, the Executive and Judicial officers of a State, or the members of the Legislature thereof, is denied to any of the male inhabitants of such State, being twenty-one years of age, and citizens of the United States, or in any way abridged, except for participation in rebellion, or other crime, the basis of representation therein shall be reduced in the proportion which the number of such male citizens shall bear to the whole number of male citizens twenty-one years of age in such State.

Section 3. No person shall be a Senator or Representative in Congress, or elector of President and Vice-President, or hold any office, civil or military, under the United States, or under any State, who, having previously taken an oath, as a member of Congress, or as an officer of the United States, or as a member of any State legislature, or as an executive or judicial officer of any State, to support the Constitution of the United States, shall have engaged in insurrection or rebellion against the same, or given aid or comfort to the enemies thereof. But Congress may by a vote of two-thirds of each House, remove such disability.

Section 4. The validity of the public debt of the United States, authorized by law, including debts incurred for payment of pensions and bounties for services in suppressing insurrection or rebellion, shall not be questioned. But neither the United States nor any State shall assume or pay any debt or obligation incurred in aid of insurrection or rebellion against the United States, or any claim for the loss or emancipation of any slave; but all such debts, obligations and claims shall be held illegal and void.

Section 5. The Congress shall have power to enforce, by appropriate legislation, the provisions of this article.

Amendment XV (1870)

Section 1. The right of citizens of the United States to vote shall not be denied or abridged by the United States or by any State on account of race, color, or previous condition of servitude.

Section 2. The Congress shall have power to enforce this article by appropriate legislation.

Amendment XVI (1913)

The Congress shall have power to lay and collect taxes on incomes, from whatever source derived, without apportionment among the several States, and without regard to any census or enumeration.

Amendment XVII (1913)

The Senate of the United States shall be composed of two Senators from each State, elected by the people thereof, for six years; and each Senator shall have one vote. The electors in each State shall have the qualifications requisite for electors of the most numerous branch of the State legislatures.

When vacancies happen in the representation of any State in the Senate, the executive authority of such State shall issue writs of election to fill such vacancies: Provided, That the legislature of any State may empower the executive thereof to make temporary appointments until the people fill the vacancies by election as the legislature may direct.

This amendment shall not be so construed as to affect the election or term of any Senator chosen before it becomes valid as part of the Constitution.

Amendment XVIII (1919)

Section 1. After one year from the ratification of this article the manufacture, sale, or transportation of intoxicating liquors within, the importation thereof into, or the exportation thereof from the United States and all territory subject to the jurisdiction thereof for beverage purposes is hereby prohibited.

Section 2. The Congress and the several States shall have concurrent power to enforce this article by appropriate legislation.

Section 3. This article shall be inoperative unless it shall have been ratified as an amendment to the Constitution by the legislatures of the several States, as provided in the Constitution, within seven years from the date of the submission hereof to the States by the Congress.

Amendment XIX (1920)

The right of citizens of the United States to vote shall not be denied or abridged by the United States or by any State on account of sex.

Congress shall have power to enforce this article by appropriate legislation.

Amendment XX (1933)

Section 1. The terms of the President and Vice President shall end at noon on the 20th day of January, and the terms of Senators and Representatives at noon on the 3rd day of January, of the years in which such terms would have ended if this article had not been ratified; and the terms of their successors shall then begin.

Section 2. The Congress shall assemble at least once in every year, and such meeting shall begin at noon on the 3rd day of January, unless they shall by law appoint a different day.

Section 3. If, at the time fixed for the beginning of the term of the President, the President elect shall have died, the Vice President elect shall become President. If a President shall not have been chosen before the time fixed for the beginning of his term, or if the President elect shall have failed to qualify, then the Vice President elect shall act as President until a President shall have qualified; and the Congress may by law provide for the case wherein neither a President elect nor a Vice President elect shall have qualified, declaring who shall then act as President, or the manner in which one who is to act shall be selected, and such person shall act accordingly until a President or Vice President shall have qualified.

Section 4. The Congress may by law provide for the case of the death of any of the persons from whom the House of Representatives may choose a President whenever the right of choice shall have devolved upon them, and for the case of the death of any of the persons from whom the Senate may choose a Vice President whenever the right of choice shall have devolved upon them.

Section 5. Sections 1 and 2 shall take effect on the 15th day of October following the ratification of this article.

Section 6. This article shall be inoperative unless it shall have been ratified as an amendment to the Constitution by the legislatures of three-fourths of the several States within seven years from the date of its submission.

Amendment XXI (1933)

Section 1. The eighteenth article of amendment to the Constitution of the United States is hereby repealed.

Section 2. The transportation or importation into any State, Territory or possession of the United States for delivery or use therein of intoxicating liquors, in violation of the laws thereof, is hereby prohibited.

Section 3. This article shall be inoperative unless it shall have been ratified as an amendment to the Constitution by conventions in the several States, as provided in the Constitution, within seven years from the date of the submission hereof to the States by the Congress.

Amendment XXII (1951)

Section 1. No person shall be elected to the office of the President more than twice, and no person who has held the office of President, or acted as President, for more than two years of a term to which some other person was elected President shall be elected to the office of the President more than once. But this Article shall not apply to any person holding the office of President when this Article was proposed by the Congress, and shall not prevent any person who may be holding the office of President, or acting as President, during the term within which this Article becomes operative from holding the office of President or acting as President during the remainder of such term.

Section 2. This Article shall be inoperative unless it shall have been ratified as an amendment to the Constitution by the legislatures of three-fourths of the several States within seven years from the date of its submission to the States by the Congress.

Amendment XXIII (1961)

Section 1. The District constituting the seat of Government of the United States shall appoint in such manner as the Congress may direct:

A number of electors of President and Vice President equal to the whole number of Senators and Representatives in Congress to which the District would be entitled if it were a State, but in no event more than the least populous State; they shall be in addition to those appointed by the States, but they shall be considered, for the purposes of the election of President and Vice President, to be electors appointed by a State; and they shall meet in the District and perform such duties as provided by the twelfth article of amendment.

Section 2. The Congress shall have power to enforce this article by appropriate legislation.

Amendment XXIV (1964)

Section 1. The right of citizens of the United States to vote in any primary or other election for President or Vice President, for electors for President or Vice President, or for Senator or Representative in Congress, shall not be denied or abridged by the United States or any State by reason of failure to pay any poll tax or other tax.

Section 2. The Congress shall have power to enforce this article by appropriate legislation.

Amendment XXV (1967)

Section 1. In case of the removal of the President from office or of his death or resignation, the Vice President shall become President.

Section 2. Whenever there is a vacancy in the office of the Vice President, the President shall nominate a Vice President who shall take office upon confirmation by a majority vote of both Houses of Congress.

Section 3. Whenever the President transmits to the President pro tempore of the Senate and the Speaker of the House of Representatives his written declaration that he is unable to discharge the powers and duties of his office, and until he transmits to them a written declaration to the contrary, such powers and duties shall be discharged by the Vice President as Acting President.

Section 4. Whenever the Vice President and a majority of either the principal officers of the executive departments or of such other body as Congress may by law provide, transmit to the President pro tempore of the Senate and the Speaker of the House of Representatives their written declaration that the President is unable to discharge the powers and duties of his office, the Vice President shall immediately assume the powers and duties of the office as Acting President.

Thereafter, when the President transmits to the President pro tempore of the Senate and the Speaker of the House of Representatives his written declaration that no inability exists, he shall resume the powers and duties of his office unless the Vice President and a majority of either the principal officers of the executive department or of such other body as Congress may by law provide, transmit within four days to the President pro tempore of the Senate and the Speaker of the House of Representatives their written declaration that the President is unable to discharge the powers and duties of his office. Thereupon Congress shall decide the issue, assembling within forty-eight hours for that purpose if not in session. If the Congress, within twenty-one days after receipt of the latter written declaration, or, if Congress is not in session, within twenty-one days after Congress is required to assemble, determines by two-thirds vote of both Houses that the President is unable to discharge the powers and duties of his office, the Vice President shall continue to discharge the same as Acting President; otherwise, the President shall resume the powers and duties of his office.

Amendment XXVI (1971)

Section 1. The right of citizens of the United States, who are eighteen years of age or older, to vote shall not be denied or abridged by the United States or by any State on account of age.

Section 2. The Congress shall have power to enforce this article by appropriate legislation.

Amendment XXVII (1992)

No law, varying the compensation for the services of the Senators and Representatives, shall take effect, until an election of Representatives shall have intervened.

Glossary

abortion The intentional termination of a pregnancy.

abuse of the elderly Infliction of physical or mental harm on elderly persons.

access device fraud The crime of knowingly producing, using, or trafficking in counterfeit credit cards, personal identification numbers, access codes, account numbers, etc. with the intent to fraudulently obtain money, goods, or services.

access devices Cards, plates, codes, electronic serial numbers, mobile identification numbers, personal identification numbers, telecommunications services and equipment, instrument identifiers, and other means that can be used to obtain goods or services.

accessories after the fact Persons who, with knowledge that a crime has been committed, conceal or protect the offender.

accessories before the fact Persons who aid or assist others in commission of an offense.

accomplices Persons who voluntarily unite with others in commission of an offense.

act of omission The failure to perform an act required by law.

actual possession Possession of something, with the possessor having immediate control.

actus reus A "wrongful act" which, combined with other necessary elements of a crime, constitutes criminal liability.

administrative-type act A ministerial act performed by executive officers in carrying out a duty assigned by law.

adultery Voluntary sexual intercourse between a married person and someone other than that person's spouse.

affirmative defense Defense to a criminal charge where the defendant bears the burden of proof. Examples include automatism, intoxication, coercion, and duress.

aggravated assault An assault committed with a dangerous weapon or with intent to commit a felony.

aggravated battery A battery committed by use of an instrument designed to inflict great bodily harm on the victim.

aggravated robbery A robbery made worse by one or more aggravating factors, such as the perpetrator being armed with a dangerous weapon or actually inflicting harm on the victim.

aiding and abetting Assisting in or otherwise facilitating the commission of a crime.

ALI standard A test proposed by the American Law Institute to determine if a defendant is legally insane. See also **substantial capacity test**.

alibi Defense to a criminal charge that places the defendant at some place other than the scene of the crime at the time the crime occurred.

antismoking laws State statutes or local ordinances prohibiting or restricting smoking in all or specified public places.

Antiterrorism and Effective Death Penalty Act A federal statute designed to effectuate reforms in administration of the death penalty by curtailing successive petitions for habeas corpus by prisoners sentenced to death.

antitrust violations Violations of laws designed to protect the public from price-fixing, price discrimination, and monopolistic practices in trade and commerce.

appellate courts Judicial tribunals that review decisions from lower tribunals.

arraignment An appearance before a court of law for the purpose of pleading to a criminal charge.

arson The crime of intentionally burning someone else's house or building; now commonly extended to other property as well.

asportation The carrying away of something. In kidnapping, the carrying away of the victim; in larceny, the carrying away of the victim's property.

assault The attempt to inflict bodily injury upon another person.

assisted suicide The act of aiding or assisting a person to take his or her life. An offense in some jurisdictions.

attempt An intent to commit a crime, coupled with an act taken toward committing the offense.

attorney general The highest legal officer of a state or of the United States.

automatism The condition under which a person performs a set of actions during a state of unconsciousness.

bankruptcy fraud Dishonest or deceitful acts committed by one who seeks relief under laws designed to protect honest debtors from their creditors.

battered child syndrome A group of symptoms typically manifested by a child who has suffered continued physical or mental abuse, often from a parent or person having custody of the child.

battered woman syndrome A group of symptoms typically manifested by a woman who has suffered continued physical or mental abuse, usually from a male with whom she lives.

battery The unlawful use of force against another person that entails some injury or offensive touching.

beyond a reasonable doubt The standard of proof that is constitutionally required to be met before a defendant can be found guilty of a crime or before a juvenile can be adjudicated as a delinquent.

bid rigging Illegally manipulating the submission of bids to obtain a contract, usually from a public body.

bigamy The crime of being married to more than one person at the same time.

bill of attainder A legislative act imposing punishment without trial upon persons deemed guilty of treason or felonies. Bills of attainder are prohibited by the U.S. Constitution.

Bill of Rights A written enumeration of basic rights, usually part of a written constitution—for example, the first ten amendments to the U.S. Constitution.

blackmail The vernacular term for extortion.

Blackstone's Commentaries A massive treatise on the English common law published 1765–1769 by Sir William Blackstone, a professor at Oxford University.

Blockburger test A test applied by courts to determine if the charges against a defendant would constitute a violation of the constitutional prohibition against double jeopardy—that is, being tried twice for the same offense. The Blockburger test holds that it is not double jeopardy for a defendant to be tried for two offenses if each offense includes an element that the other offense does not.

bootlegging The crime of knowingly trafficking in counterfeit labels affixed or designed to be affixed to copies of musical recordings, computer programs, motion pictures, etc.

Brady Bill Legislation passed by Congress in 1993 requiring a five-day waiting period before the purchase of a handgun, during which time a background check of the buyer is conducted.

brain death The complete cessation of activity of the central nervous system.

breaches of contract Violations of provisions of legally enforceable agreements that give the damaged party the right to recourse in a court of law.

breaches of the peace Crimes that disturb the public tranquility and order; a generic term encompassing disorderly conduct, riot, etc.

breaking and entering Forceful, unlawful entry into a building or conveyance.

Breathalyzer A device that detects the amount of alcohol in a sample of a person's breath.

bribery The crime of offering, giving, requesting, soliciting, or receiving something of value to influence a decision of a public official.

burglary At common law, breaking and entering a dwelling of another during the nighttime with the intent to commit a felony therein. Modern statutes typically expand the offense beyond dwellings and eliminate the "nighttime" element.

canons of construction Rules governing the judicial interpretation of constitutions, statutes, and other written instruments.

carjacking Taking a motor vehicle from someone by force and violence or by intimidation.

carnal knowledge An antiquated term for sexual intercourse.

castle doctrine An exception to the retreat rule. Allows the use of deadly force by a person who is protecting his or her home and its inhabitants from attack, especially from a trespasser who intends to commit a felony or inflict serious bodily harm.

causation The linkage between cause and effect. X can be said to cause Y if X precedes Y and Y could not have occurred in the absence of X.

child abuse Actions that physically, mentally, or emotionally endanger the welfare of a child.

child pornography Material depicting persons under the age of legal majority in sexual poses or acts.

child snatching Action taken by one parent to deliberately retain or conceal a child from the other parent.

churning Making purchases and sales of securities in a client's account simply to generate commissions for the broker.

civil contempt Being held in contempt of court pending the performance of some court-ordered act.

civil disobedience Deliberate violation of a criminal law considered to be unjust or unconstitutional in order to dramatize one's objection to the law.

civil forfeiture Taking of property used in or obtained through unlawful activity pursuant to a civil proceeding in which the property itself is named as the defendant.

civil infractions Noncriminal violations of a law; often refers to minor traffic violations.

civil rights In general, this term refers to all the rights protected by the federal and state constitutions and statutes. The term is often used to denote the right to be free from unlawful discrimination.

Clean Air Act A federal statute designed to enhance the quality of the air by regulating, deterring, and penalizing polluters.

Clean Water Act A federal statute designed to enhance the quality of bodies of public water by regulating, deterring, and penalizing polluters.

clear and convincing evidence standard An evidentiary standard that is higher than the standard of "preponderance of the evidence" applied in civil cases but lower than the standard of "beyond a reasonable doubt" applied in criminal cases. For example, under the new federal standard for the affirmative defense of insanity, the defendant must establish the defense of insanity by "clear and convincing evidence."

clear and present danger doctrine In constitutional law, the doctrine that the First Amendment does not protect those forms of expression that pose a "clear and present danger" of bringing about some substantive evil that government has a right to prevent.

commercial bribery Offering, soliciting, or accepting a benefit or consideration in respect to a business or professional matter in violation of a person's duty of fidelity.

common-law rape Rape as it was defined by the English common law, i.e., sexual intercourse by a male with a female, other than his wife, by force and against the will of the female.

community policing Style of police work that stresses development of close ties between police officers and the communities they serve.

community service A sentence or condition of probation requiring that the criminal perform some specific service to the community for some specified period of time.

compelling government interest A government interest sufficiently strong that it overrides the fundamental rights of persons adversely affected by government action or policy.

compounding a crime The acceptance of money or something else of value in exchange for an agreement not to prosecute a person for committing a crime.

Comprehensive Environmental Response, Compensation, and Liability Act (CERCLA) Federal statute commonly known as the Superfund Law. Its purpose is to finance cleanup and provide for civil suits by citizens. The act also imposes reporting requirements for the collection and disposal of solid wastes. CERCLA imposes criminal penalties on those who act in a supervisory capacity and who are in a position to detect, prevent, or abate a release of hazardous substances.

computer fraud An offense consisting of obtaining property or services by false pretenses through use of a computer or computer network.

Computer Fraud and Abuse Act Federal law criminalizing fraud and related activity in connection with computers.

computer trespass An offense consisting of the unauthorized copying, alteration, or removal of computer data, programs, or software.

concealed weapon A weapon carried on or about a person in such a manner as to hide it from the ordinary sight of another person.

consent Voluntarily yielding to the will or desire of another person.

consideration, prize, and chance The legal elements that constitute gambling under most statutes that make it an offense to gamble.

conspiracy The inchoate offense of two or more persons agreeing or planning to commit a target crime.

constitutional right of privacy Implied constitutional right allowing individuals to be free of government interference in intimate activities, especially those involving sex and reproduction.

constitutional supremacy The doctrine that the U.S. Constitution is the supreme law of the land and that all actions and policies of government must be consistent with it.

constructive intent Criminal intent inferred by law as a result of circumstances surrounding a party's actions.

constructive possession Being in the position to control something, even if it is not actually in one's possession.

contemnor A person found to be in contempt of court.

contraband Any property that is inherently illegal to produce or possess.

contractual immunity A grant by a prosecutor with approval of a court that makes a witness immune from prosecution in exchange for the witness's testimony.

Controlled Substances Act A federal law listing controlled substances according to their potential for abuse. States have similar statutes.

controlled substances Drugs designated as contraband or regulated such that they can be dispensed only with a doctor's prescription.

copyright A form of legal protection provided to the authors of original literary, musical, artistic, and architectural works as well as videos and computer software and databases.

corporate defendants Corporations charged with criminal offenses.

corpus delicti "The body of the crime." The material thing upon which a crime has been committed.

corrections system The system of prisons, jails, and other penal and correctional institutions.

counterfeiting Making an imitation of something with the intent to deceive—for example, making imitations of U.S. coins and currency.

Court of Appeals for the Armed Forces The court (formerly known as the Court of Military Appeals), consisting of five civilian judges, which reviews sentences affecting a general or flag officer or imposing the death penalty and cases certified for review by the judge advocate general of a branch of service. May grant review of convictions and sentences on petitions by service members.

court-martial A military tribunal convened by a commander of a military unit to try a person subject to the Uniform Code of Military Justice who is accused of violating a provision of that code.

courts of general jurisdiction Courts that conduct trials in felony and major misdemeanor cases. Also refers to courts that have jurisdiction to hear civil as well as criminal cases.

courts of limited jurisdiction Courts that handle pretrial matters and conduct trials in minor misdemeanor cases.

crime syndicates Associations or groups of people that carry out organized crime activities.

criminal contempt Punishment imposed by a judge against a person who violates a court order or otherwise intentionally interferes with the administration of the court.

criminal forfeiture Government confiscation of private property obtained through or otherwise involved in criminal activity pursuant to a criminal conviction of the owner of said property.

criminal responsibility Refers to the set of doctrines under which individuals are held accountable for criminal conduct.

criminal trial A trial in a court of law to determine the guilt or innocence of a person charged with a crime.

cruel and unusual punishments Criminal penalties that shock the moral conscience of the community—for example, torture and other extreme forms of corporal punishment. Prohibited by the Eighth Amendment to the U.S. Constitution.

curfew ordinances Ordinances requiring people, typically minors, to be off the streets by a certain time of night.

cybercrimes Crimes committed using computers and/or the Internet.

cyberstalking Harassing and threatening a person through persistent online contact so that the person is placed in fear for his or her safety.

deadly force The degree of force that may result in the death of the person against whom the force is applied.

death penalty Capital punishment; a sentence to death for the commission of a crime.

decisional law Law declared by appellate courts in their written decisions and opinions.

decriminalization of routine traffic offenses The recent trend toward treating minor motor vehicle offenses—for example, speeding—as civil infractions, rather than crimes.

defense attorney A lawyer who represents defendants in criminal cases.

defense of habitation The right of a defendant charged with an offense to assert that he or she used reasonable force to protect his or her home or property.

defense of others The defense asserted by one who claims the right to use reasonable force to prevent the commission of a felony against another person.

Department of Justice (DOJ) The department within the executive branch of the federal government that is headed by the Attorney General and staffed by U.S. Attorneys.

depraved mind or heart A serious moral deficiency; a high level of malice often linked to second-degree murder.

diplomatic immunity A privilege to be free from arrest and prosecution that is granted under international law to diplomats, their staff, and their household members.

direct contempt An obstructive or insulting act committed by a person in the immediate presence of the court.

disorderly conduct Illegal behavior that disturbs the public peace or order.

disorderly intoxication An offense, consisting of misbehavior by a person who is drunk, that results in disturbing the public peace or safety.

doctor-assisted suicide The commission of suicide with the aid of a physician.

doctrine of overbreadth Doctrine enabling a person to make a facial challenge to a law on the ground that the law might be applied in the future against activities protected by the First Amendment.

doctrine of transferred intent Doctrine originating in common law under which an actor's criminal intent associated with an act against an intended victim is transferred to an unintended victim who suffers the consequences of the defendant's act.

double jeopardy The condition of being tried twice for the same criminal offense.

driving under the influence (DUI) The crime of driving under the influence of alcohol or drugs.

driving while intoxicated (DWI) The crime of driving while intoxicated by alcohol or drugs.

driving with an unlawful blood-alcohol level (DUBAL) The offense of operating a motor vehicle while one's blood-alcohol level is higher than allowed by law.

drug courier profiling Occurs when police employ a set of characteristics thought to typify people engaged in drug smuggling in order to identify such persons.

drug court A specialized court or division of a court designed to deal specifically with defendants charged with violating laws proscribing the possession and use of controlled substances. Drug courts emphasize rehabilitation of offenders.

drug paraphernalia Items closely associated with the use of illegal drugs.

drug-testing requirements Laws, regulations, or policies that require individuals to undergo chemical testing of their urine to determine whether they are free of illicit drugs.

Due Process Clause The clause of the Fifth Amendment to the U.S. Constitution that prohibits the federal government from depriving persons within its jurisdiction of life, liberty, or property without due process of law. A similar provision in the Fourteenth Amendment imposes the same prohibition on state governments.

due process of law Procedural and substantive rights of citizens against government actions that threaten the denial of life, liberty, or property.

duress The use of illegal confinement or threats of harm to coerce someone to do something he or she would not do otherwise.

***Durham* test** A test for determining insanity developed by the U.S. Court of Appeals for the District of Columbia Circuit in the case of *Durham v. United States* (1954). Under this test, a person is not criminally responsible for an unlawful act if it was the product of a mental disease or defect.

embezzlement The crime of using a position of trust or authority to transfer or convert the money or property of another to oneself.

***en banc* hearing** A hearing in an appellate court in which all or a substantial number of the judges assigned to that court participate.

Endangered Species Act Federal statute designed to conserve ecosystems by preserving wildlife, fish, and plants. The act imposes criminal penalties against any person who knowingly violates regulations issued under the act.

endangering the welfare of a child Knowingly acting in a manner likely to be injurious to the physical, mental, or moral welfare of a child.

English common law Body of decisional law based largely on custom, as declared by English judges after the Norman Conquest of 1066.

enterprise An individual, partnership, corporation, association, or other legal entity; a union or group of individuals that is not a legal entity.

entrapment The act of government agents inducing someone to commit a crime that the person would not otherwise be disposed to commit.

enumerated powers Powers explicitly granted to governments by their constitutions.

environmental crime A violation of a criminal provision of an environmental statute such as the Clean Water Act, the Refuse Act, or another such statute.

Environmental Protection Agency (EPA) Independent agency within the executive branch of the national government with principal responsibility for the enforcement of federal environmental laws, promulgation of environmental regulations, and administration of environmental programs.

equal protection of the laws Constitutional requirement, made explicit in the Fourteenth Amendment, that the government afford the same legal protection to all persons.

error correction function The function of appellate courts in reviewing routine appeals and correcting the errors of trial courts.

escape Unlawfully fleeing to avoid arrest or confinement.

espionage The crime of turning over state secrets to a foreign government.

***ex post facto* law** A retroactive law that criminalizes an action that was legal at the time it was performed or increases punishment for a criminal act after it was committed.

excessive noise Unnecessarily loud sounds that interfere with the public peace and endanger the public health and welfare; sounds emitted that exceed the levels permitted by law or ordinance.

excusable homicide A death caused by accident or misfortune.

extortion Also known as blackmail; the crime of obtaining money or property by threats of force or the inducement of fear.

factual impossibility That which is in fact impossible to achieve. Unlike legal impossibility, this is not a defense to a charge of attempt.

fair hearing A hearing in which both parties have a reasonable opportunity to be heard—to present evidence and make arguments to an impartial decision maker.

fair notice The requirement, stemming from due process, that government provide adequate notice to a person before it deprives that person of life, liberty, or property.

False Claims Act A federal statute that makes it unlawful for a person to knowingly present a false or fraudulent claim to the U.S. government.

false imprisonment Also known as false arrest; the tort or crime of unlawfully restraining a person.

false pretenses The crime of obtaining money or property through misrepresentation.

False Statements Act A federal statute making it a crime for a person to knowingly make a false and material statement to a U.S. government agency to obtain a government benefit or in connection with performing work for the government.

Federal Anti-Riot Act A federal law enacted in 1968 that made it a crime to travel or use interstate or foreign commerce facilities in connection with inciting, participating in, or aiding acts of violence.

Federal Bureau of Investigation (FBI) The primary federal agency charged with investigating violations of federal criminal laws.

Federal Gun Control Act This 1968 statute prohibits firearms dealers from transferring handguns to people who are younger than twenty-one, nonresidents of the dealer's state, or who are otherwise prohibited by state or local laws from purchasing or possessing firearms. It also forbids possession of a firearm by, and transfer of a firearm to, people in a number of categories, including convicted felons, users of controlled substances, those adjudicated as incompetent or committed to mental institutions, illegal aliens, those dishonorably discharged from the military, those who have renounced their citizenship, and fugitives from justice.

federalism The constitutional distribution of government power and responsibility between the national government and the states.

felonies Serious crimes for which a person may be imprisoned for more than one year.

felony murder A homicide committed during the course of committing another felony other than murder (for example, armed robbery). The felonious act substitutes for the malice aforethought ordinarily required in murder.

fetal viability That point in pregnancy at which the fetus is capable of prolonged life outside the mother's womb.

field sobriety test A test administered by police to people suspected of driving while intoxicated. Usually consists of requiring the suspect to demonstrate the ability to perform such physical acts as touching one's finger to one's nose or walking backward.

fighting words Utterances that are inherently likely to provoke a violent response from the individual or group to which they are directed.

First Amendment Article I of the Bill of Rights, which recognizes the freedoms of religion, speech, press, and assembly as well as the right to petition government for a redress of grievances.

first-degree murder The highest degree of unlawful homicide, usually defined as "an unlawful act committed with the premeditated intent to take the life of a human being."

Food, Drug, and Cosmetic Act (FDCA) Federal law that prohibits traffic in food, drugs, and cosmetics prepared or handled under unsanitary circumstances or under conditions that render them injurious to health.

force The element of compulsion in such crimes against persons as rape and robbery.

forcible rape Sexual intercourse by force and against the will of the victim.

forgery The crime of making a false written instrument or materially altering a written instrument with the intent to defraud.

fornication Sexual intercourse between unmarried persons; an offense at common law.

Fourteenth Amendment Amendment to the U.S. Constitution ratified after the Civil War in 1868. Prohibits states from denying due process and equal protection of law to persons within their jurisdictions and provides Congress legislative power to enforce these prohibitions.

freedom of expression The right of the individual to express thoughts and feelings through speech, writing, and other media of expression; protected by the First Amendment to the U.S. Constitution.

freedom of religion The First Amendment right to the free exercise of one's religion without undue interference by government.

fundamental rights Those constitutional rights that have been declared to be fundamental by the courts. Include First Amendment freedoms, the right to vote, and the right to privacy.

gambling Operating or playing a game for money in the expectation of gaining more than the amount played.

gender-neutral offense A crime that may be committed by members of either sex against members of either sex.

general intent The state of mind to do something prohibited by law without necessarily intending to accomplish the harm that results from the illegal act.

general-intent statutes Statutes defining crimes that require only general intent, as distinct from specific intent, on the part of the violator.

grand jury A group of citizens convened either to conduct an investigation or to determine whether there is sufficient evidence to warrant the prosecution of an accused.

grand theft Major form of larceny; theft of a sufficient value of property to make the crime a felony.

guilty but mentally ill A form of verdict that may be rendered in some states where the jury finds that the defendant's mental illness does not deprive the defendant of substantial capacity sufficient to satisfy the insanity test but warrants the defendant's treatment in addition to incarceration.

gun control laws Laws regulating the manufacture, importation, sale, distribution, possession, or use of firearms.

Gun-Free School Zones Act Federal statute making it a crime "for any individual knowingly to possess a firearm at a place that the individual knows, or has reasonable cause to believe, is a school zone." This law was declared unconstitutional by the U.S. Supreme Court in *United States v. Lopez* (1995).

Hale's Rule English common law doctrine credited to Sir Matthew Hale, Lord Chief Justice in the seventeenth century, holding that a husband could not be charged with the rape of his wife.

hard-core pornography Material that is extremely graphic in its depiction of sexual conduct.

hate crimes Crimes in which the victim is selected on the basis of race, ethnicity, religion, gender, or sexual orientation.

hate speech Offensive speech directed at members of racial, religious, sexual, or ethnic minorities.

hazing Intentional or reckless physical or mental harassment, abuse, or humiliation, often as part of an initiation.

heat of passion A violent and uncontrollable rage resulting from a provocation that would cause such a response by a reasonable person.

Hobbs Act A 1946 act of Congress authorizing criminal penalties for whoever in any way or degree obstructs, delays, or affects commerce or the movement of any article or commodity in commerce by robbery or extortion or attempts or conspires so to do, or commits or threatens physical violence to any person or property in furtherance of a plan or purpose to do anything in violation of the act.

home invasion A more heinous form of burglary, in which the perpetrator is armed with a dangerous weapon or persons are present in the home at the time of the break-in.

homicide The killing of a human being.

hostage taking The act in which the perpetrator of a robbery or some other crime forcibly detains innocent bystanders.

identity theft The crime of using someone else's personal information—such as their name, social security number, or credit card number—without their permission to commit fraud or other crimes.

immigration offenses Violations of criminal provisions of the Immigration and Nationality Act, a federal law that relates to immigration.

imminent lawless action Unlawful conduct that is about to take place and that is inevitable unless there is intervention by the authorities.

immunity Exemption from civil suit or prosecution. See also **use immunity** and **transactional immunity**.

implied consent statutes Laws providing that by accepting a license, a driver arrested for a traffic offense consents to urine, blood, and breath tests to determine blood-alcohol content.

implied exception An exclusion that can reasonably be inferred or assumed based on the purpose and intent of an ordinance, statute, or contract.

implied powers Powers not expressly granted to government by a constitution but fairly implied by the document.

impotency Lacking in power; in reference to a male, the inability to achieve an erection.

incarceration Imprisonment.

incest Sexual intercourse with a close blood relative or, in some cases, a person related by affinity.

inchoate offense An offense preparatory to committing another crime. Inchoate offenses include attempt, conspiracy, and solicitation.

inciting a riot The crime of instigating or provoking a riot.

indecent exposure The intentional exposure in public of private areas of a person's body.

independent counsel A special prosecutor appointed to investigate and, if warranted, prosecute official misconduct.

indictment A formal document handed down by a grand jury accusing one or more persons of the commission of a crime or crimes.

indigent defendants Persons accused of crimes who cannot afford to retain private legal counsel and are therefore entitled to be represented by a public defender or a court-appointed lawyer.

indirect contempt An act committed outside the presence of the court that insults the court or obstructs a judicial proceeding.

infancy The condition of being below the age of legal majority.

information A document filed by a prosecutor under oath charging one or more persons with commission of a crime.

insanity A degree of mental illness that negates the legal capacity or responsibility of the affected person.

insanity Defense Reform Act of 1984 An act of Congress that specifies that insanity is an affirmative defense to a prosecution under a federal statute and details the requirements for establishing such a defense.

insider trading Transactions in securities by a person who operates inside a corporation and, by using material nonpublic information, trades to his or her advantage without first disclosing that information to the public.

insufficient evidence Evidence that falls short of establishing what is required by law; usually refers to evidence that does not legally establish an offense or a defense.

intellectual property Products of the human intellect, such as inventions, plays, stories, films, music, and trade secrets.

intent to deprive The willful design to take goods or services from another without permission or authority of law.

intermediate appellate courts Judicial tribunals, consisting of three or more judges, that review decisions of trial courts but that are subordinate to the final appellate tribunals.

interstate commerce Economic activity between or among states or affecting more than one state.

intoxication Condition in which a person has impaired physical or mental capacities due to the ingestion of drugs or alcohol.

involuntary intoxication Intoxication that is not the result of a person's intentional ingestion of an intoxicating substance. A person may become involuntarily intoxicated through the trickery or fraud of another person or through the inadvertent ingestion of medicine.

involuntary manslaughter The unintentional killing of another person as the result of gross or wanton negligence.

irresistible impulse A test for insanity that allowed a person who knew an act was wrong but acted under an uncontrollable desire or duress or mental disease to be excused from a criminal act.

judicial review The power of courts of law to review governmental acts and declare them null and void if they find them to be unconstitutional.

jurisdiction The authority of a court to hear and decide certain categories of legal disputes. Jurisdiction relates to the authority of a court over the person, subject matter, and geographical area.

jury A group of citizens convened for the purpose of deciding factual questions relevant to a civil or criminal case.

justifiable homicide Killing another in self-defense or defense of others when there is serious danger of death or great bodily harm to self or others or when authorized by law.

justifiable use of force The necessary and reasonable use of force by a person in self-defense, defense of another, or defense of property.

juvenile court A judicial tribunal having jurisdiction over minors defined as juveniles who are alleged to be status offenders or to have committed acts of delinquency.

juvenile delinquency Actions of a juvenile in violation of the criminal law.

kidnapping for ransom The offense of unlawfully taking and confining a person until a specified payment is made to the offender.

kidnapping The forcible abduction and carrying away of a person against that person's will.

larceny A synonym for theft. At common law, larceny was defined as the unlawful taking of property with the intent of permanently depriving the owner of same.

lawmaking function One of the principal functions of an appellate court; often referred to as the law development function.

legal impossibility A defense allowed in some jurisdictions when, although the defendant intended to commit a crime, it was impossible to do so because the completed act was not a crime.

legislative immunity Either of two special immunities given to members of Congress: (1) the exemption from arrest while attending a session of the body to which the member belongs, excluding an arrest for treason, breach of the peace or a felony; or (2) the exemption from arrest or questioning for any speech or debate entered into during a legislative session.

legislative intent The purpose the legislature sought to achieve in enacting a particular provision of law.

legislature An elected lawmaking body such as the United States Congress or a state assembly.

lewd and lascivious conduct Indecent exposure of a person's private parts in public; indecent touching or fondling of a child.

littering The crime of disposing of garbage or other waste material along a public street or road, or in public parks, beaches, or waterways.

loan-sharking The practice of lending money at illegal rates of interest.

loitering Standing around idly; "hanging out."

lottery A drawing in which prizes are distributed to winners selected by lot from among those who have participated by paying consideration.

M'Naghten **rule** Under this rule, for a defendant to be found not guilty by reason of insanity, it must be clearly proved that, at the time of committing the act, the defendant was suffering such a defect of reason, from disease of the mind, as not to know the nature and quality of the act he was doing; or, if he did know it, that he did not know what he was doing was wrong.

mail fraud A scheme devised or intended to defraud or to obtain money or property by fraudulent means, or using or causing the use of the mails in furtherance of the fraudulent scheme.

mala in se "Evils in themselves." Refers to crimes such as murder, rape, arson, and robbery that are universally condemned.

mala prohibita "Prohibited evils." *Mala prohibita* offenses are those that are wrong primarily because the law declares them to be wrong, as distinct from *mala in se* offenses, which are deemed to be inherently evil.

malice aforethought The mental predetermination to commit an illegal act.

malicious mischief Synonym for vandalism; the willful destruction of the property of another person.

mandatory child restraint laws Laws requiring that children below a specified age be restrained by approved safety devices when riding in automobiles.

mandatory seat belt laws Laws requiring automobile drivers and passengers to wear seat belts.

manifest necessity That which is clearly or obviously necessary or essential.

manslaughter The crime of unlawfully killing another person without malice.

marital exception The traditional common-law principle that a husband could not be guilty of raping his wife.

mayhem At common law, the crime of injuring someone so as to render that person less able to fight.

Megan's Law Name applied to statutes that require convicted sex offenders, upon release from prison, to register with local law enforcement agencies. (The statute was named in memory of Megan Kanka, who died in 1994 at the hands of a released offender.)

mens rea "Guilty mind"; criminal intent.

Migratory Bird Act Federal law protecting certain species of migratory birds from hunting within the United States and its territories.

misdemeanors Minor offenses, usually punishable by fine or imprisonment for less than one year.

misprision of felony The crime of concealing a felony committed by another.

mistake of fact A defense asserting that a criminal defendant acted from an innocent misunderstanding of fact rather than from a criminal purpose.

mistake of law An erroneous opinion of how legal principles apply to a set of facts.

Model Penal Code (MPC) Published by the American Law Institute (ALI), the MPC consists of general provisions concerning criminal liability, sentences, defenses, and definitions of specific crimes. The MPC is not law; rather, it is designed to serve as a model code of criminal law for all states.

monetary fines Sums of money that offenders are required to pay as punishment for the commission of crimes.

money laundering The offense of disguising illegal income to make it appear legitimate.

motive A person's conscious reason for acting; what someone seeks to accomplish by engaging in particular conduct.

motor vehicle violations Minor crimes or infractions involving the operation of motor vehicles.

murder At common law, the unlawful killing of one person by another with malice aforethought (premeditation).

necessity A condition that compels or requires a certain course of action.

negative defense Any criminal defense not required to be specifically pled.

negligence standard The basic standard for liability in civil cases: the failure to exercise ordinary care or caution.

no bill Decision of a grand jury not to return an indictment.

noise ordinances Local laws restricting the making of excessive noise.

nolle prosequi A formal entry by a prosecutor who declines to proceed further in the prosecution of an offense; commonly called a *nol pros.*

nondeadly force Force that does not result in death.

not guilty by reason of insanity A plea that admits criminal conduct but raises the insanity defense.

nullen crimen, nulla poena, sine lege "There is no crime, there is no punishment, without law." Refers to the doctrine that one cannot be found guilty of a crime unless there is a violation of an existing provision of law defining the applicable criminal conduct.

numbers racket A common form of illegal gambling in which one places a bet on a number with the hope that it will correspond to a preselected number.

objective test for the use of deadly force Under this test, the judge or jury places themselves in the shoes of a hypothetical reasonable and prudent person to determine whether a defendant's use of deadly force was permissible.

objective test of entrapment Under this approach to determining whether police engaged in entrapment, a court inquires whether the police methods were so improper that they were likely to induce or ensnare a reasonable person into committing a crime.

obscenity Explicit sexual material that is patently offensive, appeals to a prurient or unnatural interest in sex, and lacks serious scientific, artistic, or literary content.

obstruction of justice The crime of impeding or preventing law enforcement or the administration of justice.

one-year-and-a-day rule A common-law rule that to convict a defendant of homicide, not more than a year and a day can intervene from the defendant's criminal act to the death of the victim.

order maintenance The police officer's function of keeping the peace, as distinct from enforcement of the law.

ordinance Laws enacted by local governing bodies such as city councils and county commissions.

Organized Crime Control Act of 1970 Federal law dealing with organized crime. Title IX of the act is entitled "Racketeer Influenced and Corrupt Organizations" and is commonly referred to by the acronym RICO.

organized crime Syndicates involved in racketeering and other criminal activities.

overt act A visible act by an individual.

panhandling Begging for money in public.

parens patriae "The parent of the country." Refers to the role of the state as the guardian of minors, mentally ill individuals, and other legally disabled persons.

Parental Kidnapping Prevention Act (PKPA) A federal act adopted in 1980 designed to prevent jurisdictional conflicts over child custody matters. The primary goal of the statute is to reduce any incentive for parental child snatching.

parole Conditional release from jail or prison of a person who has served part of his or her sentence.

partial-birth abortion A method of abortion in which the fetus is partially delivered before its life is terminated and it is removed from the mother's body.

patent A government grant of the right to exclude others from producing or using a discovery or invention for a certain period of time.

patently offensive That which is obviously offensive or disgusting.

pattern of racketeering To obtain a conviction under the federal RICO statute, the government must establish the defendant's involvement in a "pattern of racketeering" that requires proof of the occurrence of at least two predicate acts of racketeering within a period of ten years, excluding any period of imprisonment.

penitentiary Prison. Literally, a place for doing penance.

perjury by contradictory statements Commission of the offense of perjury by a witness who makes conflicting statements under oath.

perjury The crime of making a material false statement under oath.

petit jury A trial jury; usually composed of either six or twelve persons.

petit theft Minor form of larceny; theft of property of sufficiently small value that the offense is classified as a misdemeanor.

***Pinkerton* Rule** Rule enunciated by the Supreme Court in *Pinkerton v. United States* (1946) holding that a member of a conspiracy is liable for all offenses committed in furtherance of the conspiracy.

plain meaning rule The judicial doctrine holding that if the meaning of a text is plain, a court may not interpret it but must simply apply it as written.

plea bargaining Negotiations between a defendant and a prosecutor whereby the defendant agrees to plead guilty in exchange for some concession (such as a reduction in the number of charges brought).

poaching Taking of game illegally, either by hunting protected species, hunting out of season, hunting in areas in which hunting is prohibited, or violating restrictions as to the number or size of animals that may be taken.

point source Any discernible, confined, and discrete conveyance from which pollutants are or may be discharged.

police departments Agencies, established by municipalities and sometimes states, whose function is to enforce the criminal laws within their respective jurisdictions

police power The power of government to legislate to protect public health, safety, welfare, and morality.

polygamy The state or practice of having more than on spouse simultaneously.

possession of burglar's tools The knowing control of instruments, machines, or substances designed to enable one to forcefully break into buildings or vaults in order to carry out the intent to steal or destroy property.

possession The actual or constructive control or occupancy of real or personal property.

predicate acts Prior acts of racketeering used to demonstrate a pattern of racketeering in a RICO prosecution.

premeditation Deliberate decision or plan to commit a crime.

preparatory conduct Actions taken in preparation to commit a crime.

preponderance of the evidence Evidence that has greater weight than countervailing evidence.

presumption of innocence In a criminal prosecution, a person accused of a crime is presumed innocent until proven guilty beyond a reasonable doubt.

pretrial diversion A program in which a first-time offender is afforded the opportunity to avoid criminal prosecution by participating in some specified treatment, counseling, or community service.

price-fixing Sellers unlawfully entering into agreements as to the price of products or services.

principals Parties whose conduct involves direct participation in a crime.

principle of legality The principle that there can be no crime or punishment in the absence of law.

probation Conditional release of a convicted criminal in lieu of incarceration.

procedural criminal law The branch of the criminal law that deals with the processes by which crimes are investigated, prosecuted, and punished.

profanity Irreverence toward sacred things; foul language.

prosecutor A public official empowered to initiate criminal charges and conduct prosecutions.

prosecutor's information An accusatorial document filed under oath by a prosecutor charging a person with one or more violations of the criminal law; similar to an indictment issued by a grand jury.

prostitution The practice of selling sexual favors.

provocation Refers to conduct that prompts another person to react through criminal conduct.

proximate cause The cause that is nearest a given effect in a causal relationship.

prurient interest An excessive or unnatural interest in sex.

public defender An attorney responsible for defending indigent persons charged with crimes.

public drunkenness The offense of appearing in public while intoxicated.

public forum A public space generally acknowledged as appropriate for public assemblies or expressions of views.

Quiet Communities Act Federal law enacted in 1978 to protect the environment against noise pollution.

Racketeer Influenced and Corrupt Organizations (RICO) A federal law enacted in 1970 that imposes civil and criminal liability where two or more acts of racketeering show a pattern of criminal activity carried on by an enterprise. (Many states now have adopted RICO laws.)

racketeering A system of organized crime traditionally involving the extortion of money from businesses by intimidation, violence, or other illegal methods.

rape shield laws Statutes that protect the identity of a rape victim and/or prevent disclosure of a victim's sexual history.

rape trauma syndrome A recurring pattern of physical and emotional symptoms experienced by rape victims.

rational basis test The judicial requirement that legislation must be rationally related to a legitimate government objective in order to survive constitutional challenge.

reasonable doubt standard The standard of proof used by a judge or jury to determine whether criminal charges against a defendant have been proven. The term "beyond a reasonable doubt" is often defined as "moral certainty."

reasonable force The maximum degree of force that is necessary to accomplish a lawful purpose.

recantation The withdrawal or repudiation of previous statements. In some instances, a person who has lied under oath is permitted to recant to avoid being charged with perjury.

receiving stolen property Knowingly receiving possession and control of personal property belonging to another with the intent to permanently deprive the owner of possession of such property.

Refuse Act A section of the Rivers and Harbors Act that makes it unlawful to discharge refuse matter of any kind into any navigable water of the United States.

regulatory offenses Criminal offenses of statutory origin dealing with public health and the environment. The term is also used to denote noncriminal violations of regulations promulgated by government agencies in the executive branch.

resisting arrest The crime of obstructing or opposing a police officer making an arrest.

Resource Conservation and Recovery Act (RCRA) The major federal law dealing with the transportation, storage, and disposal of hazardous waste.

responsible corporate officer A person who holds a supervisory position in an organization, and may be subject to criminal liability for regulatory offenses committed by subordinates.

restitution The act of compensating someone for losses suffered.

retreat rule The common-law requirement that a person being attacked "retreat to the wall" before using deadly force in self-defense.

right from wrong test See *M'Naghten* Rule.

right of privacy Constitutional right to engage in intimate personal conduct or make fundamental life decisions without interference by the government.

right to die The asserted right to terminate one's own life under certain circumstances; also refers to termination of extraordinary means of life support.

right to keep and bear arms Right to possess certain weapons; protected against governmental infringement by the Second Amendment to the U.S. Constitution.

right to refuse medical treatment The right of a patient—or a patient's surrogate in some instances—to refuse to allow doctors to administer medical treatment.

riot A public disturbance involving acts of violence, usually by three or more persons.

Rivers and Harbors Act The first major environmental statute enacted by Congress. The Act authorizes the Army Corps of Engineers to regulate the use of the navigable waters of the United States.

robbery The crime of taking money or property from a person against that person's will by means of force or intimidation.

rout At common law, a disturbance of the peace that was similar to a riot but failed to carry out the intended purpose.

rule of law The idea that law, not the discretion of officials, should govern public affairs.

rules of evidence Legal rules governing the admissibility of evidence at trial.

rules of procedure Rules promulgated by courts of law under constitutional or statutory authority governing procedures for trials and other judicial proceedings.

rules of statutory interpretation Rules developed by courts to determine the meaning of legislative acts.

rules of the road Rules for the operation of motor vehicles on the public streets.

sabotage The crime of infiltrating and destroying a nation's war-making capabilities.

same elements test Test that bars separate punishment for offenses that have the same elements or for one offense that includes or is included in another offense.

same evidence test A test applicable to the Double Jeopardy Clause of the Fifth Amendment. If, to establish an essential element of an offense charged, the government will prove conduct that constitutes an offense for which the defendant has already been prosecuted, a second prosecution is barred.

scope of an agent's authority In white-collar crime cases, the scope of an agent's authority depends on whether the commission of the offense was authorized, requested, commanded, performed, or recklessly tolerated by the board of directors or by a high managerial agent acting on behalf of the corporation within the scope of his or her office or employment.

second-degree murder A killing perpetrated by any act imminently dangerous to another and evincing a depraved mind regardless of human life, although without any premeditated design to effect the death of any particular individual.

Securities and Exchange Act The 1934 act of Congress regulating the sale of securities in interstate commerce.

sedition The crime of advocating or working toward the violent overthrow of one's own government.

seduction The common-law crime of inducing a woman to have sexual intercourse outside of wedlock on the promise of marriage.

selective prosecution Singling out defendants for prosecution on the basis of race, religion, or other impermissible classifications.

self-defense The protection of one's person against an attack.

separation of powers Constitutional assignment of legislative, executive, and judicial powers to different branches of government.

session laws Collection of laws enacted during a particular legislative session.

sexual contact The intentional touching of the victim's intimate parts or the intentional touching of the clothing covering the immediate area of the victim's intimate parts, if that intentional touching can reasonably be construed as being for the purpose of sexual arousal or gratification.

sexual penetration Sexual intercourse, cunnilingus, fellatio, anal intercourse, or any other intrusion, however slight, of any part of a person's body or any object into the genital or anal openings of another person's body.

sheriff The chief law enforcement officer of a county.

Sherman Antitrust Act A federal statute prohibiting any contract, combination, or conspiracy in restraint of trade. The act is designed to protect and preserve a system of free and open competition. Its scope is broad and reaches individuals and entities in for-profit and nonprofit activities as well as local governments and educational institutions.

simple kidnapping The abduction of another person without a demand for ransom.

sodomy Oral or anal sex between persons or sex between a person and an animal. The latter act is commonly referred to as bestiality.

solicitation The inchoate offense of requesting or encouraging someone to engage in illegal conduct.

special agents Officers of the FBI with the power to make arrests and use force in the enforcement of federal law.

specific intent The mental purpose to accomplish a particular thing prohibited by law, such as the death of another person.

specific-intent statute A statute defining criminal conduct in which the offender must harbor a specific intent to accomplish a prohibited result.

speedy and public trial An open and public criminal trial held without unreasonable delay as required by the Sixth Amendment to the U.S. Constitution.

sports bribery Offering anything of value to a participant or official in an amateur or professional athletic contest to vary his or her performance.

spousal abuse Physical, emotional, or sexual abuse of one's husband or wife.

stalking Following or placing a person under surveillance and threatening that person with bodily harm, sexual assault, confinement, or restraint, or placing that person in reasonable fear of bodily harm, sexual assault, confinement, or restraint.

stare decisis The doctrine of deciding cases based on precedent.

state supreme court The highest appellate court of a state.

state's attorneys State prosecutors.

status offenses Noncriminal conduct on the part of juveniles that may subject them to the authority of a juvenile court.

status One's condition or situation.

statute A generally applicable law enacted by a legislature.

statute of limitations A law proscribing prosecutions for specific crimes after specified periods of time.

statutes Generally applicable laws enacted by a legislature.

statutory rape The strict liability offense of having sexual intercourse with a minor, irrespective of the minor's consent.

strict judicial scrutiny Judicial review of government action or policy in which the ordinary presumption of constitutionality is reversed.

strict liability Criminal responsibility based solely on the commission of a prohibited act.

strict liability offenses Offenses that do not require proof of the defendant's intent.

structuring Engaging in multiple smaller transactions to avoid currency reporting requirements.

subjective standard of reasonableness A test used by courts to determine whether it was appropriate for a defendant to use deadly force in self-defense. Under this approach, the jury is asked to place itself in the shoes of the defendant.

subjective test of entrapment Whether the defendant's criminal intent originated in the mind of the police officer or the defendant was predisposed to commit the offense.

subornation of perjury The crime of procuring someone to lie under oath.

substantial capacity test The doctrine that a person is not responsible for criminal conduct if at the time of such conduct, as a result of mental disease or defect, the person lacked substantial capacity either to appreciate the wrongfulness of his or her conduct or to conform his or her conduct to the requirements of the law.

substantial step A significant movement toward completion of an intended result.

substantive criminal law That branch of the criminal law that defines criminal offenses and defenses and specifies criminal punishments.

suicide The intentional taking of a person's own life.

sworn officers Law enforcement officers sworn to uphold the Constitution and laws of the United States and of their own states.

symbolic speech Expression by displaying symbols, making gestures, and so forth.

tangible property Property that has physical form, substance, and value in itself.

target crime A crime that is the object of an attempt, solicitation, or conspiracy.

tax fraud False or deceptive conduct performed with the intent of violating revenue laws, especially the Internal Revenue Code.

terrorism The crime of inflicting terror on a population through the indiscriminate killing of people and destruction of property, often with explosive devices.

theft of computer services Stealing software, data, computer access codes, computer time, or related services.

time, place, and manner regulations Government limitations on the time, place, and manner of expressive activities in the public forum.

tolling Causing to cease. For example, one who conceals himself or herself from the authorities generally causes a tolling of the statutes of limitation on the prosecution of a crime.

torts Noncriminal wrongs or injuries, other than breaches of contract, for which the remedy is a civil suit for damages.

Toxic Substances Control Act Federal statute authorizing the Environmental Protection Agency to prohibit the manufacture, distribution, or use of chemicals that present unreasonable risks to the environment and to regulate the disposal of such chemicals.

trade secret A formula, pattern, physical device, idea, process, compilation of information, or other information that provides a business with a competitive advantage.

trademark A distinctive word, phrase, or graphic symbol used to distinguish a commercial product.

trademark counterfeiting The offense of using a registered trademark to falsely market a product or service.

traffic court Court of limited jurisdiction whose main function is the adjudication of traffic offenses and other minor misdemeanors.

transactional immunity A grant of immunity applying to all offenses that a witness's testimony relates to.

treason The crime of making war against one's own government or giving aid and comfort to its enemies.

treatment programs Programs designed to rehabilitate offenders. The term is most commonly used in connection with alcohol or drug abuse rehabilitation.

trial courts Judicial tribunals usually presided over by one judge who conducts proceedings and trials in civil and criminal cases with or without a jury.

true bill An indictment handed down by a grand jury in a criminal case.

two-witness rule A requirement that to prove a defendant guilty of perjury, the prosecution must prove the falsity of the defendant's statements either by two witnesses or by one witness and corroborating documents or circumstances.

U.S. Code The comprehensive and systematic collection of federal laws currently in effect.

unconstitutional as applied Refers to a declaration by a court of law that a statute is invalid insofar as it is enforced in some particular context.

unconstitutional per se Refers to a law that is unconstitutional on its face, meaning that it is invalid under any given circumstances.

Uniform Child Custody Jurisdiction and Enforcement Act (UCCJEA) A law in force in all fifty states that generally continues jurisdiction for custody of children in the home or resident state of the child.

Uniform Code of Military Justice (UCMJ) A code of laws enacted by Congress that governs military service personnel and defines the procedural and evidentiary requirements in military law and the substantive criminal offenses and punishments.

United States Attorneys Lawyers appointed by the president with consent of the U.S. Senate to prosecute federal crimes in federal judicial districts.

United States Code Annotated (U.S.C.A.) An annotated version of the United States Code. The annotations include references to court decisions and other legal authorities.

United States Congress The national legislature of the United States, consisting of the Senate and the House of Representatives.

United States Courts of Appeals The twelve intermediate appellate courts of appeals in the federal system that sit in specified geographical areas of the United States and in which panels of appellate judges hear appeals in civil and criminal cases, primarily from the U.S. District Courts.

United States District Courts The principal trial courts in the federal system, which sit in ninety-four districts. Usually, one judge hears proceedings and trials in civil and criminal cases.

United States Marshals Law enforcement officers of the U.S. Department of Justice who are responsible for enforcing federal laws, enforcing federal court decisions, and effecting the transfer of federal prisoners.

United States Supreme Court The highest court in the United States, consisting of nine justices, that has jurisdiction to review, by appeal or writ of certiorari, the decisions of lower federal courts and many decisions of the highest courts of each state.

unlawful assembly A group of individuals, usually five or more, assembled to commit an unlawful act or to commit a lawful act in an unlawful manner.

USA PATRIOT Act Controversial act of Congress enacted in 2001 to strengthen the federal government's efforts to combat terrorism.

use immunity A grant of immunity that forbids prosecutors from using immunized testimony as evidence in criminal prosecutions.

uttering a forged instrument The crime of passing a false or worthless instrument, such as a check, with the intent to defraud or injure the recipient.

vagrancy The common-law offense of going about without any visible means of support.

vagueness doctrine Doctrine of constitutional law holding unconstitutional (as a violation of due process) legislation that fails to clearly inform the person of what is required or proscribed.

vandalism Synonym for malicious mischief; the willful destruction of the property of another person.

vehicular homicide Homicide resulting from the unlawful and negligent operation of a motor vehicle.

vice Immoral conduct such as prostitution, gambling, or the use of narcotics.

victim A person who is the object of a crime or tort.

void for vagueness Doctrine of constitutional law holding unconstitutional (as a violation of due process) legislation that fails to clearly inform the person of what is required or proscribed.

voluntary intoxication The state of becoming drunk or intoxicated of one's own free will.

voluntary manslaughter The intentional killing of a human without malice or premeditation and usually occurring during a sudden quarrel or in the heat of passion.

voyeurism The practice of seeking sexual gratification by observing the naked bodies or sexual acts of others, usually from a hidden vantage point.

weapons of mass destruction Weapons designed to kill large numbers of people and/or damage extensive areas. Includes nuclear, radiological, biological, and chemical weapons.

weapons offenses Violations of laws restricting or prohibiting the manufacture, sale, transfer, possession, or use of certain firearms.

weight of the evidence The balance or preponderance of the evidence. Weight of the evidence is to be distinguished from "legal sufficiency of the evidence," which is the concern of an appellate court.

well-regulated militia This phrase, from the Second Amendment to the U.S. Constitution, refers to a citizen army subject to government regulations. In the early history of the United States, the militia was the set of able-bodied men who could be pressed into military service by the governor of the state. The National Guard is its modern counterpart.

Wharton's Rule Named after Francis Wharton, a well-known commentator on criminal law, this rule holds that two people cannot conspire to commit a crime such as adultery, incest, or bigamy inasmuch as these offenses involve only two participants.

white-collar crimes Economic offenses characterized by deception or abuse of trust and often involving the use of computers or other modern technologies.

wire fraud A fraudulent scheme that uses interstate television, radio, or wire communications.

worthless check statutes Laws making it an offense to knowingly pass a worthless check.

writ of certiorari Order issued by an appellate court to grant discretionary review of a case decided by a lower court.

zero-tolerance law A statute that the enacting authority claims will be enforced zealously and without exception.

zoning Local laws regulating the use of land.

Case Index

Subject Index